Advanced PL/SQL Programming
The Definitive Reference

Boobal Gansean

DEDICATION

To the man, who always dreamt the dreams of the youngsters!

In memory of, "The Missile Man"

Dr. A. P. J. Abdul Kalam, Former President of India.

And, to my family.

Advanced PL/SQL Programming
The Definitive Reference

By Boobal Ganesan

Copyright © 2017 by Rampant TechPress. All rights reserved.

Printed in the United States of America.

Published by Rampant TechPress, Kittrell, North Carolina, USA

Oracle In Focus Series: Book #53

Series Editor: Donald K. Burleson

Editors: Dhanya Premkumar, PMP, Donald K. Burleson

Production Editors: Janet Burleson

Cover Design: Janet Burleson

Printing History:

July 2017 for First Edition

ISBN-13 978-0986119446

Table of Contents

Advanced PL/SQL Programming

Introduction to PL/SQL

In this chapter, we will discuss about the Oracle PL/SQL programming concepts from its origin to its present trend. The chapter outlines the benefits and characteristics of the PL/SQL language in the following sections.

1. An overview on the relational model by Codd.
2. Different types of blocks, their similarities and dissimilarities.
3. Control structures and its different types.
4. Different types of subprograms, their calling methods, characteristics and dependencies.

Relational Database Evolution

In 1970 Edgar Frank Codd, a data scientist working for IBM, published a paper under the name "A Relational Model of Data for Large Shared Data Banks". IBM accepted this fascinating theory and subsequently an interactive language named SEQUEL under the database SYSTEM R was developed in 1979 by them.

Codd in his paper not only introduced the relational model in particular, but the whole idea of data modelling. He stressed the importance of using the predicate logic ideas as a foundation for the database management and to deal with the data in the relational form, he suggested relational calculus and relational algebra as the base.

In his relational model theory, his primary focus was not so much on the relational model, but mostly on the data redundancy and consistency. Indeed, his introduction states that the relational "view" enjoys many advantages over the "graphical" model which was the preferred model that then.

His relational model proposal primarily consisted of the two sections described below.

Relational Model and Normal Form

In this section, the inadequacies of the existing non-inferential models and the concept of universal data sublanguage are discussed. The relational view of data provides the means of describing the data with its natural structure only without imposing any additional structure for the machine representation. This model also provides the overall idea of creating a superior data language which results in maximum independence between the programs and the machine representation.

Further advantages of the relational view are, that it forms a strong base for consistency, derivability and redundancy of the relations, whereas on the other hand, the graphical model spawned confusions on these terminologies.

Finally, the relational view clearly evaluates the scope and the logical limitations of the current system and also the merits of competing the representations of data within a single system.

Data Dependencies

The provision of data dictionary tables in the modern system represents the major advancements in the data independently. These tables help in changing the characteristics of data representation preserved in the databases. The three major kinds of data dependencies which are to be removed are ordering dependence, indexing dependence and access path dependence.

Ordering Dependence

There are multiple different ways of storing the elements of data in the databases.

- Some data are not concerned about ordering.
- Some data are concerned with a particular ordering.
- Some data are concerned in several ordering.

The graphical models normally permit application programs to assume that the order of representation of the data from the file is similar to the data stored order. These kind of systems which take advantage of the stored ordering are likely to fail if the ordering is replaced by a different one. These kind of ordering dependency can be avoided by solving significant implementation.

Indexing Dependence

In the context of formatted data, an index is usually thought to be a performance oriented component of a database and it tends to improve performance when an update or selection is performed and at the same time, loses performance when insertions or deletions are performed.

Different data systems take widely different approach towards indexing. Some data systems provide indexing on all attributes and other provides users with a choice of no indexing at all or indexing only on the primary keys. Application programs enjoying the advantage of these indexing chains must refer to them by their names. These programs tend to fail when the chains are later removed.

Access Path Dependence

Many of the data systems provide users with data of tree structured files or slightly more general network models of the data. If these trees or networks changes, the applications developed to work with these systems tend to become logically impaired.

A Relational View of Data

This section urges the users to interact with a relational model of the data consisting of a collection of time varying relationships than relations.

The term relation is used in its accepted mathematical sense. Given sets $A1$, $A2$, ..., An (not necessarily distinct), B is a relation on these n sets if it is a set of n-tuples, each of which has its first element from $A1$, its second element from $A2$, and so on. We shall refer to A as the jet domain of B. As defined above, B is said to have degree n. Relations of degree 1 are often called unary, degree 2 binary, degree 3 ternary, and degree n n-ary.

The totality of the data in a database may be considered as a collection of time varying relations. These relations are of varied degrees and as time progresses, each n-nary relations may result in the insertion of new n-tuples, deletion/ modification of any of its existing n-tuples.

Normal Form

A relation with simple domains can be stored in a two dimensional column arrays and non-simple domains can be represented using a complicated data structure. The procedure for eliminating the non-simple domains with the help of domain combination is called as normalization.

If the normalization as defined above is considered to be applicable, the un-normalized relations must satisfy the below conditions.

1. The graph of interrelationships of the non-simple domains is a collection of time.
2. There should be no primary key with a non-simple domain component.

Linguistic Aspects

The acceptance of the relational model permits the creation of a universal sub language based on a relational calculus. Such a language will provide immense power to all other proposed data languages and it will be a strong choice for embedding with varied host languages.

Expressible, Named and Stored Relations

The named set is the total collection of the relations that a data language can identify it by a simple name. Examples of named sets are declarations and identifiers.

The expressible set is a collection of all relations that can be identified by expressions in a community. Examples of expressible sets are "<" and "=".

Redundancy and Consistency

Operations on Relations

This section primarily concentrates on the manipulative part of the relational data model. The below operations are defined in this section.

1. If a permutation is applied to the columns of an n-nary relation, the resulting relation is said to be a permutation of the given relation.

2. If a certain number of columns are selected from a relation and then if the duplicated rows are removed from the resulting array, the final relational array is said to be a projection of the given relation.

3. The circumstances under which two relations having some domain in common can be combined together to form a relationship to preserve all the information in the given relation is said to be a join.

4. The two relations are composed only if there exists a join between them. If there are more than one join possible between the given two relations, it does not comply, for there is a possibility of more than one composition between them.

5. The relation A acting upon the relation B to generate a subset of B is through the operation restriction of B by A.

Redundancy

This section gives you a deep insight on the strong and weak redundancies.

1. A collection of relations is to be strongly redundant, if it holds at least one relation that contains a projection which is derivable from the other projections of relations from the collection.

2. A set of relations is said to be weakly redundant, if it has a relation that contains a projection which is not derivable from the other members in the collection, but is always a projection of some join of other projections of relations in that set.

Consistency

Considering a set of relations, the system should be provided with the information if there are any associated redundancies to this set, so that the set can enforce consistency. The set is said to be consistent only, if it conforms to the provided redundancies.

The Birth of Oracle as a Relational Database

Lawrence Joseph "Larry" Ellison, who was working for Ampex Corporation, after analyzing the Codd's theory saw a tremendous business potential in the relational database software and started a consultancy named Software Development Laboratories (SDL) along with two of his colleagues Bob Miner and Ed Oates. He then invented a relational database which he named it Oracle, as a tribute to his CIA funded database project (At Ampex Corporation) called as ORACLE (Oak Ridge Automatic Computing Logical Engine). Later he renamed his company to Oracle Corporation to closely align itself with its primary product.

Evolution of Oracle

This section explains the evolution of Oracle from its inception as a relational database and then out numbering its competitors for the past 3 decades as the world's most robust and flexible relational database.

Oracle version 2 (1979) was the very first commercial release and they named it as version 2 as they believed that any potential customer will be more hesitant to buy the very first version of any software. This version had the complete implementation of SQL but lacked reliability.

Oracle version 3 (1983) was completely rewritten in C language to support portability beyond the range of operating systems. This version of Oracle solved the reliability issue with the earlier release. Any SQL statement executed here would either be committed or rolled back.

Oracle version 4 (1984) improved the stability and read consistency. For example, the transaction performed between the accounts is not miscomputed when a query is being executed.

Oracle version 5.1 (1985) and 5.2 (1986) worked as a distributed database by introducing the first every service/ client relational database so that a client running on a machine in one location could access a server over a network. This version also supported distributed querying as one query could access data stored from more than one location.

Oracle version 6 (1988) introduced a new architecture on the availability of the database during a transaction. This version primarily changed the locking method from table level to row level, resulting in better system throughput when many users are accessing the database. This version also allowed hot backups, the process of taking a backup of the database while it is still in use.

Oracle version 7 (1992) solved the procedural limitation of the SQL by allowing the database users to create Programmable Logical Structured Query Language in short PL/SQL codes and thus making it an efficient programming language of all the fourth generation languages. This version allowed us to create Procedures, Functions and Triggers along with distributed transactions and security methods allowing programmers to create complex business rules.

Oracle version 8 (1997) was designed to work with Oracle's Network Computer and this version supported OLTP system, HTML and Java interface. Oracle version 8.1 (1998) supported parallel processing with Linux, which eliminated the highly costing downtime.

Oracle version 9i (2001) introduced the concept of Real Application Clustering and provided high availability in the Oracle database. This version allowed the database to integrate relational and multidimensional processing and introduced the concept of table compression, which reduced the disk size from 3 to 10 times and increased the performance when accessing the data.

Oracle version 10g (2003) introduced us to the grid technology for sharing the hardware resources against the data centers, thus lowering the infrastructure cost. By introducing Oracle 10g Express Edition, Oracle gave the entry level business corporations to make the most of the Oracle technology with no cost at all.

Oracle version 11g (2007) introduced some salient features like flashback data archive, virtual column, parallel back up of the same files, case sensitive passwords and wide range of performance and optimization enhancements making it a more stable release of all the time.

Oracle version 12c (2013) is out of Oracle's major innovation which supported multi-tenancy – an option which allows us to share common infrastructure like memory and background processes between multiple databases. These are called as "pluggable" databases which are plugged into a "container" or "master" database. The main advantage of this technology is to possibly allow n- number of databases to run on a single hardware with complete security and isolation between them.

PL/SQL Architecture

The PL/SQL is a case insensitive, robust procedural extension of the SQL. SQL allows its statements to be directly included in the PL/SQL blocks and still looks like a single language together as they are tightly coupled with each other as there are no APIs needed to bind them together unlike the other programming languages.

SQL has become the standard database language due to its flexibility, reliability and easy learning methodology. It uses common English words as commands like Create, Select, Insert, Delete, Drop and et cetera, so that the learner does not feel like learning an alien language.

The PL/SQL language supports high portability, security and as it is tightly coupled with SQL, there is no transformation needed between them in terms of data types as the data types in SQL are available in PL/SQL too. Column values with DATE, Varchar2, Number types are also available with the same names in PL/SQL language. This coupling reduces the development and learning time. There is a technique in PL/SQL called as Anchored variables which allow us to work with variables of a table's column's data type without the need of specifying it explicitly. Thus saving on the code maintenance when the column data type's size is changed or the data type by itself is changed to another data type.

The only loosely coupled SQL – PL/SQL action was the execution of data definition, data control, and session control statements like object creation, modification and session level parameter changes in PLSQL which was also solved with the help of the dynamic query processing technique. The dynamic query processing consists of two methods, Native Dynamic SQL and the DBMS_SQL package. The DBMS_SQL package is used when the number of columns needed for the dynamic processing is unknown. The syntax of the static statements has been known before the compilation, whereas the syntax of the dynamic statements is known only at the runtime as the important details like table name, column name and query formation are confirmed only at the runtime. Thus making PL/SQL to support both static and dynamic SQL makes it more flexible and versatile.

PL/SQL serves to encapsulate the SQL statements and the PL/SQL methods like control statements, conditional loops and object oriented programming helps in building complex business structure. If it isn't for PL/SQL, these individual statements will be processed one at a time by Oracle thus increasing the performance overhead and network trafficking.

With reference to the below PL/SQL architectural image fig. 1.1, a subprogram is invoked and flows through the PL/SQL engine as the primary process. The PL/SQL engine then separates the SQL statements and the PL/SQL statements and then passes it down to its respective executors.

SQL Engine

This engine parses, fetches and executes the SQL statements and returns the resultant or the exceptions occurred during the processing of the statement to the user's session or to the PL/SQL engine.

PL/SQL Engine

This engine allows the programmers to create, manage and execute the PL/SQL programs to interact with the database. PL/SQL engine can call SQL engine when there is an SQL code in it (Inserts, Updates, Deletes in a program unit) and the SQL engine can call the PL/SQL engine when there is a PL/SQL unit in it (Functions called through an SQL statement) which is a recursive feature. This process of switching between two engines based on the statement type is called as context switching. Frequent context switching results in performance overhead, which can be avoided using advanced PL/SQL methodologies like Bulk collect and FORALL.

External Programs

These are the non-database programs (like Java, C, PHP, et cetera) which are invoked through advanced interface methods in Oracle. Before the UTL_MAIL and UTL_SMTP utilities were created in Oracle, the only option to mail was through the other languages interaction by the PL/SQL engine.

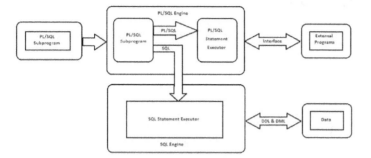

Fig.1.1. The PL/SQL Architecture

Features of PL/SQL

- Delivers high performance by executing SQL statements in bulk rather individually, thus avoiding call overhead.

- Creation of a complex business logic into a single program unit, thus promoting encapsulation and productivity.

- Integrates itself with SQL very tightly, thus reduces maintenance and complexity.

- Full portability – PL/SQL codes written in one operating system can be migrated successfully to another operating system running Oracle.

- Supports high security with the help of encryption and decryption logics which are available through the Oracle's inbuilt packages.

- Interaction with the other programming languages.

- Context switching overhead can be avoided using advanced PL/SQL concepts like bulk collect and FORALL.

- Performs Object oriented programming concepts like overloading.

PL/SQL Program Structure

A block is the basic unit of programming in PL/SQL which encapsulates a group of executable statements to accomplish a programmer's business need. A block is classified into the below two main types.

1. Anonymous block
2. Named block

PLSQL Block Structure

The structure of a PL/SQL block consists of the below four primary sections.

1. Header

This section is not available for an anonymous block, but only for the named blocks. This section holds information like the unit's type (whether it is a function or a procedure), unit's name, unit's owner name, list of parameters to be passed to the unit and the return type declaration (Only for functions).

2. Declaration

This is an optional section for both the anonymous blocks and the named blocks. In anonymous blocks, the keyword DECLARE indicates the starting of the declaration section and in the named blocks, the keyword IS or AS (both are synonymous and has no difference between each other) after the header section indicates the beginning of the declaration section. The declaration section's primary use if for declaring local variables and assigning default values to them, declaring cursors, types, subprograms like procedures and functions in the form of forward declaration.

3. Execution

This is a mandatory section for both the types of PL/SQL units and they require at least one executable statement in them to avoid compilation failure. This section allows us to process the business logic through variable assignment, data manipulation, loops, conditional statements, collections and etcetera. This section starts with the BEGIN keyword and ends with an END keyword.

4. Exception

This section helps in managing the exceptions raised by the statements in the execution section. This is also an optional section for both the PL/SQL unit types and helps the program unit from exiting abruptly during its execution by handling the runtime errors, also called as exceptions.

Anonymous Block

These are un-named blocks primarily used for calling a procedure or a function or to feed data into a database as a one-time activity. As they do not have a name, they cannot be called by any other block as it doesn't have a reference. These blocks cannot be

Advanced PL/SQL Programming

saved in a database for future use as they do not have a nameable header statement. Instead of that, they use a reserved keyword called as DECLARE which indicates the start of the program unit. These can also be nested inside another anonymous block, procedures and functions.

The below prototype defines the basic structure of an anonymous block.

```
DECLARE
 <Variable declaration>;
BEGIN
 <Executable statements>;
EXCEPTION
 <Exception handler>;
END;
/
```

Basic Anonymous Block

The following PL/SQL anonymous block functions as an addition program between two variables declared and assigned to default values in the declaration section.

> 🔔 Note: SERVEROUTPUT is an SQL*PLUS variable which has to be enabled to print the texts and variables passed as the input parameter to the DBMS_OUTPUT.PUT_LINE procedure.

```
1.   SET SERVEROUTPUT ON SIZE 200000
2.   DECLARE
3.   L_n_var1 number:=10;
4.   L_n_var2 number:=20;
5.   L_n_var3 number;
6.   BEGIN
7.   l_n_var3:=l_n_var1+l_n_var2;
8.   Dbms_output.put_line('The sum of the two variables is '||l_n_var3);
9.   END;
10. /
```

Result: The sum of the two variables is 30

Script Explanation

Line no.	Description
1	This environment variable opens up an output buffer of size limit of 200000.
2	Start of the declare section.
3,4	Two local variables l_n_var1 and l_n_var2 of the number data type is declared and assigned to 10 and 20 respectively.
5	The third local variable of the number data type is declared.

6	Start of the execution section of the block.
7	The variables l_n_var1 and l_n_var2 are summed up and the result is assigned to the third variable l_n_var3.
8	The local variable l_n_var3's value is printed using the DBMS_OUTPUT.PUT_LINE procedure.
9,10	End of the execution section of the block.

Anonymous Block with Exception Section

The following PL/SQL anonymous block tries to fetch an employee's first name based on the employee ID passed as a bind variable (Requests for the input at the run time). Here local variable declared for holding the employee's first name is an anchored variable, i.e., The data type is anchored from the Employees table's FIRST_NAME column, so that the data type changes or the precision changes on the specified column does not affect the program in any way.

```
1.  SET SERVEROUTPUT ON SIZE 200000
2.  DECLARE
3.  l_vc_first_name hr.employees.first_name%type;
4.  BEGIN
5.  SELECT first_name INTO l_vc_first_name FROM hr.employees WHERE
    employee_id=:id;
6.  dbms_output.put_line(q'(The employee's first name is
    )'||l_vc_first_name);
7.  EXCEPTION
8.  WHEN no_data_found THEN
9.  dbms_output.put_line('No such employee under the ID '||:id);
10. END;
11. /
```

Script Explanation

Line no.	Description
1	This environment variable opens up an output buffer of size limit of 200000
2	Start of the declare section of the block.
3	One anchored local variable l_vc_first_name with the data type as that of the Employees table's First_name column is created.
4	Start of the execution section of the block.
5	The first name of the employee for the input bind variable is assigned to the local variable l_vc_first_name.
6	The local variable l_vc_first_name is printed using dbms_output.put_line procedure. Here the quote literal is used to avoid the complication of handling a single quote inside the printable text.
7	Start of the exception section of the block.
8	The exception NO_DATA_FOUND is handled in the when clause to handle any exceptions raised when an invalid employee ID is passed to the bind variable.

Nested Anonymous Block

An anonymous block nested within another block is called as a child block or an enclosing block. The anonymous block that calls another block is called as the parent block or an enclosed block.

The main advantage of a nested block is that a scope for all the declared variables and the executable statements are created in such a way that the control of the program is improved.

The variables declared in the parent block has a public scope throughout the program and can be accessed inside the child block. The variables declared in the child block has a private scope for those variables and it will not be available anywhere outside the child block.

```
1.  SET SERVEROUTPUT ON SIZE 200000
2.  DECLARE
3.  l_n_emp_id hr.employees.employee_id%type;
4.  BEGIN
5.  SELECT employee_id
6.  INTO l_n_emp_id
7.  FROM hr.employees
8.  WHERE first_name=:first_name;
9.  dbms_output.put_line('The Employee ID for the Employee is
    '||l_n_emp_id);
10. DECLARE
11. l_vc_last_name hr.employees.last_name%type;
12. BEGIN
13. SELECT last_name
14. INTO l_vc_last_name
15. FROM hr.employees
16. WHERE employee_id=l_n_emp_id;
17. dbms_output.put_line(q'(The Employee's last name is
    )'||l_vc_last_name);
18. END;
19. EXCEPTION
20. WHEN no_data_found THEN
21. dbms_output.put_line('No such employee present for the first name -
    '||:first_name);
22. WHEN too_many_rows THEN
23. dbms_output.put_line('There are more than one employee with the first
    name - '||:first_name);
24. END;
25. /
```

Script Explanation

Line no.	Description
1	This environment variable opens up an output buffer of size limit of 200000.
2	Start of the declare section of the parent block.
3	An anchored local variable l_n_emp_Id data type as that of the Employees table's employee ID column is declared. Its scope is public.
4	Start of the execution section of the parent block.
5-8	The employee ID value from the employees table corresponding to the input bind variable for the first_name column is assigned to the local variable l_n_emp_id.
9	The local variable l_n_emp_id's value is printed using the dbms_output.put_line procedure.
10	Start of the declare section of the child block.
11	An anchored local variable l_vc_last_name with the data type as that of the Employees table's last_name column is declared. Its scope is private.
12	Start of the execution section of the child block.
13-16	The last name column valuefrom the employees table corresponding to the employee ID value from the local variable l_n_emp_id from the parent block is assigned to the local variable.
17	The local variable l_vc_last_name is printed using the dbms_output.put_line procedure. Here the quote literal is used to avoid the complication of handling a single quote inside the printable text.
18	End of the execution section of the child block.
19	Start of the exception section of the parent block.
20	The predefined exception NO_DATA_FOUND is handled in the when clause when there is no employee found for the first name provided as the input.
24	The input bind variable's first_name value is quoted as not found using the dbms_output.put_line procedure.
25	The exception TOO_MANY_ROWS is handled in this when clause.
26	The input bind variable's first_name value is quoted as it is found more than once using the dbms_output.put_line procedure.
27,28	End of the execution section of the parent block.

Control Structures

The control structures manage the flow of the program in a PL/SQL unit. The control structures are a simple yet powerful extension of the PLSQL language. It lets you process the data using the conditional, iterative, and sequential flow of control using IF-THEN-ELSE or CASE, FOR or WHILE or Simple LOOPs, GOTO statements respectively.

Conditional Structures

It is our need to always take turns in our code based on the circumstances. The conditional structure lets us deal with it in a simple way. That is, whether a sequence of code is to be executed or not is decided by the value from the condition. When the value is matched (or TRUE), a set of code is executed and when it is not, another set of code is executed. There are two types of conditional structures and they are IF and CASE statements.

IF Statement

IF statements are generally a programmable unit with a header and a footer. The header section starts the block with the IF keyword followed by series of conditional checks and the footer section ends the statement with the END IF keyword. There is a mandatory executable statement needed between each conditional check to make the unit free from compilation errors. The IF statement can be made multiple branching by adding optional n number of ELSIF statements followed by a series of conditional checks followed by an optional ELSE statement with no conditional checks.

Different Forms of IF Statements:

1. IF Statement.
2. IF THEN ELSE Statement.
3. IF THEN ELSIF Statement.

The conditional checks in the IF and ELSIF phrases can be of Relational (<, >, <=, >=, <> or !=), Boolean (TRUE, FALSE, NULL) or NULL (IS NULL, IS NOT NULL) comparisons and there can be multiple conditional checks in a single section separated by multiple conjoining operator (AND) or by include operator (OR).

Different Types of Conditional comparisons:

1. Null comparison
2. Boolean comparison
3. Relational comparison

 Note – Static variables or values cannot be compared to a column value from a select statement directly in the IF or ELSIF conditional check, instead the column value has to be assigned to a variable prior to the IF statement call and then the two variables can be compared in the IF statement.

The below prototype defines the basic structure of the IF statement.

```
IF <conditional check> then
<Executable statement>;
ELSIF <conditional check> then -- Optional check
<Executable statement>;
...
Else -- Optional check
<Executable statement>;
End if;
```

IF Statement with Null Comparison

In an Oracle database, Null value does not mean that the particular value is empty. It simply means Null or unknown. To compare a NULL value in an IF statement, relational operators will not result the desired output. Instead, IF <variable> is Null and IF <Variable> is not Null must be used for Null comparisons.

```
1.  SET SERVEROUTPUT ON SIZE 200000
2.  DECLARE
3.  l_n_var1 NUMBER:=:value;
4.  BEGIN
5.  IF l_n_var1 IS NULL THEN
6.  dbms_output.put_line('The value is Null');
7.  END IF;
8.  END;
9.  /
```

Script Explanation

Line no.	Description
1	This environment variable opens up an output buffer of size limit of 200000
2	Start of the declare section of the block.

3	A local variable l_n_var1 of the number data type is declared and assigned to a bind variable.
4	Start of the execution section of the block.
5	Start of the IF statement. The conditional statement section checks if the value of the variable is Null.
6	If the conditional check is a match, then the result is printed using the DBMS_OUTPUT.PUT_LINE procedure.
7	End of the IF statement.
8,9	End of the execution section of the block.

IF THEN ELSE Statement with Boolean Comparison

Boolean variables can hold True, False or Null values and they do not need any other variable for comparing themselves. Relational comparison of a Boolean variable with either true or false (IF<Boolean_variable>=True or IF<Boolean_variable>=False) will not result in the desired output as the only way to validate them is using IF <Boolean_variable> for true conditions and IF not <Boolean_variable> for false conditions. If the Boolean variable is not initialized, it holds Null and the above both conditions fail.

```
1.  SET SERVEROUTPUT ON SIZE 200000
2.  DECLARE
3.  l_b_var1 BOOLEAN:=:value;
4.  BEGIN
5.  IF l_b_var1 THEN
6.  dbms_output.put_line('The Boolean value is True');
7.  ELSE
8.  dbms_output.put_line('The Boolean value is Not True');
9.  END IF;
10. END;
11. /
```

Script Explanation

Line no.	Description
1	This environment variable opens up an output buffer of size limit of 200000
2	Start of the declare section of the block.
3	A local variable l_b_var1 of BOOLEAN data type is declared and assigned to the input bind variable.
4	Start of the execution section of the block.
5	Start of the IF statement. The conditional statement section checks if the value of the variable is True.
6	If the conditional check is a match, then the result is printed as the Boolean value is true using the DBMS_OUTPUT.PUT_LINE procedure.

7,8	If the above condition is not matched, the program control is passed on to the ELSE section and prints that the Boolean value is not true using the DBMS_OUTPUT.PUT_LINE procedure.
9	End of the IF statement.
10,11	End of the execution section of the block.

IF THEN ELSIF Statement with Relational Comparison

The below block takes the DB server's date as input and checks in which quarter the date falls in its year and prints the result by using the conditional checks and the relational operators. The function to_char(SYSDATE,'Q') gives the quarter on which the input date falls on.

```
1.  SET SERVEROUTPUT ON SIZE 200000
2.  DECLARE
3.  l_d_date DATE:=sysdate;
4.  BEGIN
5.  IF TO_CHAR(l_d_date,'Q')=1 THEN
6.  dbms_output.put_line('We are in the first quarter of this year');
7.  ELSif TO_CHAR(l_d_date,'Q')=2 THEN
8.  dbms_output.put_line('We are in the second quarter of this year');
9.  ELSif TO_CHAR(l_d_date,'Q')=3 THEN
10. dbms_output.put_line('We are in the third quarter of this year');
11. ELSE
12. dbms_output.put_line('We are in the fourth quarter of this year');
13. END IF;
14. END;
15. /
```

Script Explanation

Line no	Description
1	This environment variable opens up an output buffer of size limit of 200000
2	Start of the declare section of the block.
3	One local variable l_d_date of DATE data type is declared and assigned to the Oracle server's current date.
4	Start of the execution section of the block.
5	Start of the IF statement. The conditional check performs the equal to check on the quarter extracted from the local variable date and compares it to 1. If matched, then proceeds inside this section else the control is moved on to the next ELSIF section.
6	If the conditional check is a match, then the desired result is printed in using the DBMS_OUTPUT.PUT_LINE procedure.
7	If the above conditional check at line 5 does not match, the control shifts to this ELSIF conditional check of comparing the quarter extracted from the local

	variable date to that of 2. If matched, then proceeds to traverse this section else moves on to the next ELSIF section.
8	If the conditional check is a match, then the desired result is printed using the DBMS_OUTPUT.PUT_LINE procedure.
9	If the above conditional check at line7 does not match, the control shifts to this ELSIF conditional check of comparing the quarter extracted from the local variable date to that of 3. If matched, then proceeds to traverse this section else moves on to the default ELSE section.
10	If the conditional check is a match, then the desired result is printed using the DBMS_OUTPUT.PUT_LINE procedure.
11,12	If none of the above IF conditions are matched, the program control is passed on to the default ELSE section and it then prints the default result using the DBMS_OUTPUT.PUT_LINE procedure.
13	End of the IF statement.
14,15	End of the execution section of the block.

CASE Statement

The CASE statement is similar to an IF-THEN-ELSE statement, but helps in better readability than the latter. The CASE statement is also a block with a header and a footer. The header section starts the statement with the CASE keyword followed by a series of conditional checks and the footer section ends the statement with an END CASE keyword. There is a mandatory executable statement needed in each of the conditional check sections to make the unit free from compilation errors. The CASE statement has optional n number of WHEN-THEN with one or more conditional checks separating each other by the conjoining operator (AND) or by the include operator (OR), and an ELSE section for the default result output if none of the conditions are satisfied.

The conditional checks in the WHEN-THEN phrases can be of Relational (<, >, <=, >=, <> or !=), Boolean (TRUE, FALSE, NULL) or NULL (IS NULL, IS NOT NULL) comparisons just like IF statement.

 Note: Static variables or values cannot be compared to a column value from a select statement directly in the WHEN-THEN conditional check, instead the column value has to be assigned to a variable prior to the CASE statement and then the two variables can be compared.

There are two types of CASE statements available in PL/SQL and they are,

1. **Simple CASE**: A simple case takes a scalar variable as an expression and compares it with a list of scalar values.

2. **Searched CASE**: A searched case takes a Boolean variable as an expression and compares the Boolean state of the comparison made in the when clause. The default Boolean value is true if not mentioned.

The below prototype defines the basic structure of the simple CASE statement.

```
CASE <Scalar Variable>
WHEN <Scalar value1> then
<Executable statement>;
WHEN <Scalar value2> then
<Executable statement>;
...
ELSE
<Executable statement>;
END CASE;
```

Simple CASE Example

```
1.   SET SERVEROUTPUT ON SIZE 200000
2.   DECLARE
3.   l_n_var1 NUMBER:=:value;
4.   BEGIN
5.   CASE l_n_var1
6.   WHEN 1 THEN
7.   dbms_output.put_line('The value is 1');
8.   WHEN 2 THEN
9.   dbms_output.put_line('The value is 2');
10.  WHEN 3 THEN
11.  dbms_output.put_line('The value is 3');
12.  ELSE
13.  dbms_output.put_line('The value is not 1 or 2 or 3');
14.  END CASE;
15.  END;
16.  /
```

Script Explanation

Line no.	Description
1	This environment variable opens up an output buffer of size limit of 200000
2	Start of the declare section of the block.
3	A local variable l_n_var1 of the number data type is declared and assigned to the input bind variable.
4	Start of the execution section of the block.
5	The CASE statement begins with the scalar variable l_n_var1 as its expression.

6	The scalar variable's value is checked with the value 1 in the WHEN clause.
7	If this conditional check at line 6 is a match, then the desired result is printed using the DBMS_OUTPUT.PUT_LINE procedure.
8	If the above conditional check at line 6 does not match, the control shifts to this WHEN section checking the variable with the value 2.
9	If this conditional check at line 8 is a match, then the desired result is printed using the DBMS_OUTPUT.PUT_LINE procedure.
10	If the above conditional check at line 8 does not match, the control shifts to this WHEN section checking the variable with the value 3.
11	If this conditional check at line 10 is a match, then the desired result is printed using the DBMS_OUTPUT.PUT_LINE procedure.
12,13	If none of the above conditions are matched, the program's control is passed on to the ELSE section and prints the default result using the DBMS_OUTPUT.PUT_LINE procedure.
14	End of the CASE statement.
15,16	End of the execution section of the block.

The below prototype defines the basic structure of a simple CASE statement.

```
CASE <Boolean Variable>
WHEN <variable1> = <variable2> then
<Executable statement>;
WHEN <variable1>><variable2> then
<Executable statement>;
...
ELSE
<Executable statement>;
END CASE;
```

Searched CASE Example

```
1.   SET SERVEROUTPUT ON SIZE 200000
2.   DECLARE
3.   l_n_var1 NUMBER:=:value;
4.   BEGIN
5.   CASE true
6.   WHEN l_n_var1=1 THEN
7.   dbms_output.put_line('The value is 1');
8.   WHEN l_n_var1=2 THEN
9.   dbms_output.put_line('The value is 2');
10.  WHEN l_n_var1=3 THEN
11.  dbms_output.put_line('The value is 3');
12.  ELSE
13.  dbms_output.put_line('The value is not 1 or 2 or 3');
14.  END CASE;
15.  END;
16.  /
```

Script Explanation

Line no.	Description
1	This environment variable opens up an output buffer of size limit of 200000
2	Start of the declare section of the block.
3	A local variable l_n_var1 of the number data type is declared and assigned to the input bind variable.
4	Start of the execution section of the block.
5	The CASE statement begins with the Boolean value True as its expression.
6	The scalar variable's value is equated with the value 1 in the WHEN clause.
7	If this conditional check at line 6 is a match, then the desired result is printed using the DBMS_OUTPUT.PUT_LINE procedure.
8	If the above conditional check at line 6 does not match, the control shifts to this WHEN section equating the variable with the value 2.
9	If this conditional check at line 8 is a match, then the result is using the DBMS_OUTPUT.PUT_LINE procedure.
10	If the above conditional check at line 8 does not match, the control shifts to this WHEN section checking the variable with the value 3.
11	If this conditional check at line 10 is a match, then the result is using the DBMS_OUTPUT.PUT_LINE procedure.
12,13	If none of the above conditions are matched, the program control is passed on to the default ELSE section and prints the default result using the DBMS_OUTPUT.PUT_LINE procedure.
14	End of the CASE statement.
15,16	End of the execution section of the block.

Iterative structure

Iterative statements are blocks with one or more executable statements which repeats itself for a specific number of time based on one or more conditions specified. These iterative statements or loops automatically terminate itself once it matches with a valid exit condition or when their iteration cycle is completed. There are three types of loops and they are the simple or infinite loop, the WHILE loop and the FOR loop.

In most of the situation where we want to write a looping code, we can achieve it from any of the above types, but end up with an additional number of lines of code increasing the complexity and maintenance of the program. So it is always better to use the right type of loop for the right situation.

Simple Loop

This loop is also called as an infinite loop because of the reason that there is no automatic loop terminator present in its loop structure. The termination can be achieved with the help of manual placement of a valid exit condition inside the loop. This loop structure can have one or more executable statements placed between the LOOP-END LOOP keywords. On each iteration, these executable statements get executed and the control shifts to the top of the loop and gets ready for the next iteration.

If the counter variable used inside the loop is not initialized, this loop's termination check will fail, resulting in repetition of the loop infinitely. A conditional statement is needed as a precautionary method to check if the counter variable is initialized or not.

In this type of loop, both the loop index and the exit criteria are to be maintained by the programmer. Usually this loop structure is used for achieving complex solutions.

The below prototype defines the basic structure of the simple loop statement which exits at the beginning of the loop (Guard at the beginning of the loop).

```
LOOP
Exit when <exit condition>;
<Executable statements>;
<Incremental Counter>;
END LOOP;
```

Example for Guard at the Beginning of the Loop

An anonymous block with a simple loop is created with an exit condition of the counter value equated to 5 at the start of the loop and then the executable statements are executed in the sequential order in the below example. As the exit condition is placed at the beginning the loop, once the exit condition is met, the rest of the executable statements in that particular iteration are skipped thus the counter value of 5 is not printed in this program.

```
1.  SET SERVEROUTPUT ON SIZE 200000
2.  DECLARE
3.  l_n_counter NUMBER:=1;
4.  BEGIN
5.  IF l_n_counter IS NOT NULL THEN
6.  LOOP
7.  EXIT
8.  WHEN l_n_counter=5;
9.  dbms_output.put_line('Iterator: '||l_n_counter);
10. l_n_counter:=l_n_counter+1;
11. END LOOP;
12. End if;
13. END;
14. /
```

Result:

```
Iterator: 1
Iterator: 2
Iterator: 3
Iterator: 4
```

Script Explanation

Line no.	Description
1	This environment variable opens up an output buffer of size limit of 200000.
2	Start of the declare section of the block.
3	A local variable l_n_counter of the number data type is declared and assigned the value 1.
4	Start of the execution section of the block.
5	An IF condition is placed to check if the counter variable l_n_counter is initialized or not.
6	Start of the simple loop.
7,8	An exit condition is placed for terminating the loop when the counter variable reaches 5.
9	The counter variable l_n_counter is printed using the DBMS_OUTPUT.PUT_LINE procedure.
10	The counter variable l_n_counter is incremented by 1 for every iteration.
11	End of the simple loop.
12	End of the IF condition.
13,14	End of the execution section of the block.

The below prototype defines the basic structure of the simple loop statement which exit at the end of the loop (Guard at the end of the loop).

```
LOOP
<Incremental Counter>;
<Executable statements>;
Exit when <exit condition>;
END LOOP;
```

Example for Guard at the End of the Loop

This loop runs at least once before its termination as the EXIT condition is placed at the end after the all executable statements.

```
1.   SET SERVEROUTPUT ON SIZE 200000
2.   DECLARE
3.   l_n_counter NUMBER:=1;
4.   BEGIN
5.   IF l_n_counter IS NOT NULL THEN
6.   LOOP
7.   dbms_output.put_line('Iterator: '||l_n_counter);
```

```
8.  l_n_counter:=l_n_counter+1;
9.  EXIT
10. WHEN l_n_counter=5;
11. END LOOP;
12. End if;
13. END;
14. /
```

Result:

```
Iterator: 1
Iterator: 2
Iterator: 3
Iterator: 4
```

Script Explanation

Line no.	Description
1	This environment variable opens up an output buffer of size limit of 200000.
2	Start of the declare section of the block.
3	A local variable l_n_counter of the number data type is declared and assigned the value 1.
4	Start of the execution section of the block.
5	An IF condition is placed to check if the counter variable is initialized or not.
6	Start of the Simple loop.
7	The counter variable l_n_counter is printed using the DBMS_OUTPUT.PUT_LINE procedure.
8	The counter variable l_n_counter is incremented by 1 for every iteration.
9,10	An exit condition is placed for terminating the loop when the counter variable reaches 5.
11	End of the Simple loop.
12	End of the IF condition.
13,14	End of the execution section of the block.

FOR Loop

The FOR loop runs one or more executable statements placed within its loop structure while the loop index value is between the lower bound and the upper bound.

The below prototype defines the basic structure of the FOR loop.

```
For <loop_index> in [Reverse] <lower_bound> .. <upper_bound> loop
<Executable statements>;
End loop <loop_index>;
```

Note: Reverse keyword is optional in the FOR loop's structure. The <loop_index> placed after the END LOOP syntax is optional and it is meant for identifying a particular loop's end with ease.

The <lower_bound> value cannot be greater than the <upper_bound> value, else the loop will not run even once.

The <upper_bound> value cannot be lower than the <lower_bound> value, else the loop will not run even once.

 Note: If the <lower_bound> and the <upper_bound> values are equal, the FOR loop executes only once irrespective of its bound value.

While the reverse keyword is placed, the <loop_index> value starts at the <lower_bound> and increments itself by 1 for each iteration of the loop until it reaches the <upper_bound>.

While the reverse keyword is not placed, the <loop_index> value starts at the <upper_bound> and decrements itself by 1 for each iteration of the loop until it reaches the <lower_bound>.

Basic FOR Loop

The below script runs the loop for 5 times starting from the lower bound value 1 incrementing it by 1 until it reaches the upper bound value 5.

```
1.  BEGIN
2.  FOR loop_index IN 1..5
3.  LOOP
4.  dbms_output.put_line(loop_index);
5.  END LOOP loop_index;
6.  END;
7.  /
```

Result:

1
2
3
4
5

Script Explanation

Line no.	Description
1	Start of the execution section of the block.
2,3	Start of the FOR loop statement with lower bound value as 1 and upper bound value as 5.
4	The loop index value is printed using the DBMS_OUTPUT.PUT_LINE procedure.
5	End of the FOR loop.
6,7	End of the execution section of the block.

FOR Loop with the REVERSE Keyword

The below script runs the loop for 5 times starting from the upper bound value 5 decrementing itself by 1 until it reaches the lower bound value 1 as the reverse keyword is mentioned in its structure.

```
1.  BEGIN
2.  FOR loop_index IN reverse 1 .. 5
3.  LOOP
4.  dbms_output.put_line(loop_index);
5.  END LOOP loop_index;
6.  END;
7.  /
```

Result:

```
5
4
3
2
1
```

Script Explanation

Line no.	Description
1	Start of the execution section of the block.
2,3	The start of the FOR loop statement with the lower bound value as 1, upper bound value as 5 and reverse keyword placed.
4	The loop index value is printed using the DBMS_OUTPUT.PUT_LINE procedure.
5	End of the FOR loop.
6,7	End of the execution section of the block.

FOR Loop with Decimal Loop Index Value

The below FOR loop can have decimal values for its lower bound and upper bound values. These loop index values are rounded off to its nearest value and then the loop starts its execution process. In the below example, the lower bound value of 1.1 is rounded off to 1 and the upper bound value of 5.5 is rounded off to 6, thus the loop runs for 6 times starting from the rounded lower bound value of 1 through the rounded upper bound value of 6.

```
1.  BEGIN
2.  FOR loop_index IN 1.1 .. 5.5
3.  LOOP
4.  dbms_output.put_line(loop_index);
5.  END LOOP loop_index;
6.  END;
7.  /
```

Result:

```
1
2
3
4
5
6
```

Script Explanation

Line no.	Description
1	Start of the execution section of the block.
2,3	Start of the FOR loop statement with lower bound value as 1.1 and upper bound value as 5.5.
4	The loop index value is printed using the DBMS_OUTPUT.PUT_LINE procedure.
5	End of the FOR loop.
6,7	End of the execution section of the block.

FOR Loop with Non-Numeric Loop Index Value

The loop index is implicitly created with PLS_INTEGER data type and when the lower bound and the upper bound values of a FOR loop are of non-numeric literals, the loop's execution fails resulting in an exception. The below example immediately raises the predefined exception VALUE_ERROR when executed.

```
1.  BEGIN
2.  FOR loop_index IN 'A' .. 'D'
3.  LOOP
4.  dbms_output.put_line(loop_index);
5.  END LOOP loop_index;
6.  END;
7.  /
```

Error report:
ORA-06502: PL/SQL: numeric or value error: character to number conversion error

```
ORA-06512: at line 2
06502. 00000 -  "PL/SQL: numeric or value error%s"
```

Script Explanation

Line no.	Description
1	Start of the execution section of the block.
2,3	Start of the FOR loop statement with lower bound value as 'A' and upper bound value as 'D'.
4	The loop index value is printed using the DBMS_OUTPUT.PUT_LINE .procedure
5	End of the FOR loop.
6,7	End of the execution section of the block.

FOR Loop Index

The loop index value has its scope inside the FOR loop's structure only and when it is accessed outside its structure, the loop fails with the below compilation error.

```
1.  BEGIN
2.  FOR loop_index IN 1 .. 5
3.  LOOP
4.  dbms_output.put_line(loop_index);
5.  END LOOP loop_index;
6.  dbms_output.put_line(loop_index);
7.  END;
8.  /
```

```
Error report:
ORA-06550: line 6, column 24:
PLS-00201: identifier 'LOOP_INDEX' must be declared
ORA-06550: line 6, column 3:
PL/SQL: Statement ignored
06550. 00000 -  "line %s, column %s:\n%s"
*Cause:    Usually a PL/SQL compilation error.
```

Script Explanation

Line no.	Description
1	Start of the execution section of the block.
2,3	Start of the FOR loop statement with lower bound value as 1 and upper bound value as 5.
4	The loop index value is printed using the DBMS_OUTPUT.PUT_LINE procedure.
5	End of the FOR loop.
6	The loop index value is printed using the DBMS_OUTPUT.PUT_LINE procedure.
7,8	End of the execution section of the block.

The statements inside the loop can access the loop index's value, but it can never be assigned with any value. Once the loop's execution is completely done, the loop index's value is reset to Null. The below example fails with a compilation error when its loop index is used as an assignment target.

```
1.   BEGIN
2.   FOR loop_index IN 1 .. 5
3.   LOOP
4.   loop_index:=10;
5.   dbms_output.put_line(loop_index);
6.   END LOOP loop_index;
7.   END;
8.   /
```

Error report:
```
ORA-06550: line 4, column 5:
PLS-00363: expression 'LOOP_INDEX' cannot be used as an assignment target
ORA-06550: line 4, column 5:
PL/SQL: Statement ignored
06550. 00000 -  "line %s, column %s:\n%s"
*Cause:    Usually a PL/SQL compilation error.
```

Script Explanation

Line no.	Description
1	Start of the execution section of the block.
2,3	Start of the FOR loop statement with lower bound value as 1 and upper bound value as 5.
4	The loop index is assigned to the value 10.
5	The loop index value is printed using the DBMS_OUTPUT.PUT_LINE procedure.
6	End of the FOR loop.
7,8	End of the execution section of the block.

WHILE Loop

This loop repeats one or more executable statements placed in its structure based on the condition at the beginning of the loop. On each iteration, these executable statements get executed and the control shifts to the top of the loop, and then it checks the entry condition and if it is satisfied, the control gets ready for the next iteration else, the loop will be terminated and control passes on to the next section.

Note – If the entry condition is not satisfied when the control reaches the WHILE loop, the complete WHILE loop will be skipped from execution and then the control proceeds on to the next section and the loop will not be executed even once.

Unlike the simple loops, only the index value has to be managed by the programmer and the exit condition will be automatically taken care by the loop's entry condition.

In this loop type, if the counter variable or the entry condition variable is not initialized, the loop will not be executed even once as this is a "guard at the beginning of the loop" type thus an extra IF-END IF conditional check is not required for avoiding infinite loop execution.

The below prototype defines the basic structure of a WHILE loop.

```
WHILE <condition> loop
<Executable statements>;
End loop;
```

Here, the <condition> can be single or multiple separated by conjoining operator (AND) or include operator (OR) and can be of either Relational, Boolean or Null check.

Simple WHILE Loop

```
1.   DECLARE
2.   l_n_var1 NUMBER:=1;
3.   BEGIN
4.   WHILE l_n_var1<=5 loop
5.   dbms_output.put_line(l_n_var1);
6.   l_n_var1 :=l_n_var1+1;
7.   END LOOP;
8.   END;
9.   /
```

Result:
1
2
3
4
5

Script Explanation

Line no.	Description

1	Start of the declare section of the block.
2	The local variable l_n_var1 of the number data type is created and assigned to 1.
3	Start of the execution section of the block.
4	Start of the WHILE loop with the condition as l_n_var1<=5.
5	The local variable's value is printed using the DBMS_OUTPUT.PUT_LINE procedure.
6	The local variable l_n_var1 is incremented by 1 for each iteration.
7	End of the WHILE loop.
8,9	End of the execution section of the block.

EXIT and CONTINUE Statements

These statements cannot be used outside the loops and are meant for exiting a loop either unconditionally using Exit and Continue statements or conditionally using Exit-When and Continue-When statements.

EXIT Statement

The Exit statement exits the current iteration of the loop unconditionally and transfers the control to the end of the current loop.

```
EXIT;
```

In the below example, an Exit statement placed inside the FOR loop statement transfers the control unconditionally to the end of the current loop.

```
1.  BEGIN
2.  FOR loop_index IN 1..5
3.  LOOP
4.  dbms_output.put_line(loop_index);
5.  EXIT;
6.  END LOOP loop_index;
7.  dbms_output.put_line('Loop has been terminated');
8.  END;
9.  /
```

Result:
1
Loop has been terminated

Script Explanation

Line no.	Description
1	Start of the execution section of the block

2,3	Start of the FOR loop with the lower bound value as 1 and the upper bound value as 5.
4	The loop index's value is printed using the DBMS_OUTPUT.PUT_LINE procedure.
5	Exit statement is placed.
6	End of the FOR loop.
7	The loop's termination is indicated using the DBMS_OUTPUT.PUT_LINE procedure.
8,9	End of the execution section.

EXIT WHEN Statement

The Exit-When statement exits the current iteration of the loop once the condition in it's WHEN clause is satisfied, and transfers the control to the end of the current loop.

```
Exit when <condition>;
```

Whenever the control reaches the EXIT-WHEN statement inside the loop, its condition is evaluated. If the evaluated condition is satisfied, the control is transferred to the end of the current loop, if not, the statement does nothing and the loop stays alive and proceeds executing the statements present in its current iteration.

To prevent the loop from running infinitely, a statement inside the loop must make the condition to be true. In the below Simple loop example, a counter variable increments itself by 1 and the loop terminates once the counter variable reaches 5 by the EXIT-WHEN condition.

```
1.   DECLARE
2.   l_n_var1 NUMBER:=1;
3.   BEGIN
4.   LOOP
5.   dbms_output.put_line(l_n_var1);
6.   EXIT
7.   WHEN l_n_var1=5;
8.   l_n_var1   :=l_n_var1+1;
9.   END LOOP;
10. dbms_output.put_line('Loop has been terminated');
11. END;
12. /
```

Result:
```
1
2
3
4
5
Loop has been terminated
```

Script Explanation

Line no.	Description
1	Start of the declare section of the block.
2	The local variable l_n_var1 of the number data type is declared and defaulted to 1.
3	Start of the execution section of the block.
4	Start of the simple loop.
5	The local variable l_n_var1 is printed using the DBMS_OUTPUT.PUT_LINE procedure.
6,7	Exit when condition is placed in a condition of l_n_var1=5.
8	The local variable l_n_var1 is incremented by 1 for every iteration.
9	End of the simple loop.
10	The loop's termination is indicated using the DBMS_OUTPUT.PUT_LINE procedure.
11,12	End of the execution section of the block.

CONTINUE Statement

The Continue statement exits the current iteration of the loop unconditionally and then transfers the control to the next iteration of the current loop.

```
Continue;
```

In the below example, the Continue statement exits the current iteration of the FOR loop and transfers the control to the next iteration without executing the statement present after it.

```
1.  BEGIN
2.  FOR loop_index IN 1..5
3.  LOOP
4.  dbms_output.put_line(loop_index);
5.  dbms_output.put_line('Before the Continue statement');
6.  CONTINUE;
7.  dbms_output.put_line('After the Continue statement');
8.  END LOOP loop_index;
9.  dbms_output.put_line('Loop has been terminated');
10. END;
11. /
```

Result:
```
1
Before the Continue statement
2
Before the Continue statement
3
Before the Continue statement
4
Before the Continue statement
5
```

```
Before the Continue statement
Loop has been terminated
```

Script Explanation

Line no.	Description
1	Start of the execution section of the block.
2,3	Start of the FOR loop with the lower bound value as 1 and the upper bound value as 5.
4	The loop index's value is printed for every iteration using the DBMS_OUTPUT.PUT_LINE procedure.
5	The start of the continue statement is indicated using the DBMS_OUTPUT.PUT_LINE procedure.
6	The continue statement is placed.
7	The end of the continue statement is indicated using the DBMS_OUTPUT.PUT_LINE procedure.
8	End of the FOR loop.
9	The loop's termination is indicated using the DBMS_OUTPUT.PUT_LINE procedure.
10,11	End of the execution section.

CONTINUE WHEN Statement

The Continue-When statement exits the current iteration of the loop when the condition in it's WHEN clause is satisfied and then transfers the control to the next iteration of the current loop.

```
Continue when <condition>;
```

Whenever the control reaches the Continue-When statement during the loop iteration, it's WHEN condition is evaluated. If the evaluation is satisfied, the control is transferred to the next iteration of the current loop, if not satisfied, the statement does nothing and the loop stays alive and proceeds executing the statements present for the current iteration.

In the below example, the Continue-When statement exits the current iteration of the FOR loop once it's WHEN condition is satisfied, in this case when the loop index turns 3, the condition is satisfied and then transfers the control to the next iteration without executing the statement present after it.

```
1.  BEGIN
2.  FOR loop_index IN 1..5
3.  LOOP
4.  CONTINUE
```

Iterative structure **35**

```
5.   WHEN loop_index=3;
6.   dbms_output.put_line(loop_index);
7.   END LOOP loop_index;
8.   dbms_output.put_line('Loop has been terminated');
9.   END;
10.  /
```

Script Explanation

Line no.	Description
1	Start of the execution section of the block.
2,3	Start of the FOR loop with the lower bound value as 1 and the upper bound value as 5.
4,5	The continue statement is placed with the condition loop_index=3.
6	The loop index's value is printed for every iteration using the DBMS_OUTPUT.PUT_LINE procedure.
7	End of the FOR loop.
8	The loop's termination is indicated using the DBMS_OUTPUT.PUT_LINE procedure.
9,10	End of the execution section.

Sequential Control Structure

Unlike the other control statements, the sequential control statements GOTO and NULL are not crucial to the PL/SQL programming and these should be sparsely used to avoid code complexity and maintenance as it is hard to identify the code traverse direction.

GOTO Statement

The GOTO statement transfers the control to a label unconditionally. The label must be unique in its scope and must be preceded with at least one executable statement. If there are more than one label with the same name, the block fails with a compilation error.

Unnecessary use of the GOTO statement results in increasing the complexity and maintenance of the code.

```
GOTO <label_name>;
```

The GOTO statement must be followed by the label name (without the angle braces) and the label name used by the GOTO statement must be enclosed by two angle braces as like below.

```
<<label_name>>
```

 Note: The GOTO statement can traverse both forward and reverse in the code.

A simple GOTO Statement

In the below example, the GOTO statement is effectively used in identifying whether the input number is either odd or even.

```
1.   DECLARE
2.   l_n_var1   NUMBER:=:value;
3.   l_vc_var2 VARCHAR2(30);
4.   BEGIN
5.   IF mod(l_n_var1,2) =1 THEN
6.   l_vc_var2        :='The input number is Odd';
7.   GOTO print_output;
8.   END IF;
9.   l_vc_var2:='The input number is even';
10.  <<print_output>>
11.  dbms_output.put_line(l_vc_var2);
12.  END;
13.  /
```

Script Explanation

Line no.	Description
1	Start of the declare section of the block.
2	A local variable l_n_var1 is declared with the data type, number and is defaulted to a bind variable.
3	A local variable l_vc_var2 is declared with the data type varchar2 with a precision of 30.
4	Start of the execution section of the block.
5	An IF condition is placed to check the modulus of the local variable l_n_var1 by 2 is equal to 1.
6	The local variable l_vc_var2 is assigned as Odd.
7	A GOTO statement passing the control to the label print_output is placed.
8	End of the IF condition.
9	The local variable l_vc_var2 is assigned as Even.
10	The label print_output is placed.
11	The local variable l_vc_var2's value is printed using the DBMS_OUTPUT.PUT_LINE procedure.

GOTO Statement as a Loop

The GOTO statement can be used to form a loop by transferring the control from the end of the code to its start and terminating this artificial loop structure using an IF condition as shown below. Here the understandability of the loop is made complex by using the GOTO statement.

```
1.   DECLARE
2.   l_n_var1 NUMBER:=0;
3.   BEGIN
4.   <<artificial_loop>>
5.   l_n_var1:=l_n_var1+1;
6.   dbms_output.put_line(l_n_var1);
7.   IF l_n_var1!=10 THEN
8.   GOTO artificial_loop;
9.   END IF;
10.  END;
```

Result:
```
1
2
3
4
5
6
7
8
9
10
```

Script Explanation

Line no.	Description
1	Start of the declare section of the block.
2	A local variable l_n_var1 is declared with the data type, number and is defaulted to 0.
3	Start of the execution section of the block.
4	A label named artificial_loop is placed.
5	The local variable l_n_var1 is incremented to 1 for each call from the Goto statement to the label.
6	The local variable l_vc_var1's value is printed using the DBMS_OUTPUT.PUT_LINE procedure.
7	An IF condition is placed to check if the local variable l_n_var1 is not equal to 10 or not. If the condition is satisfied the control passes into the IF condition else, the control jumps the IF condition and passes on to the end of the execution block
8	A Goto statement with artificial_loop label is placed.
9	End of the IF statement.
10	End of the execution section of the block.

Restrictions with GOTO Statement

The GOTO statement imposes the following restrictions.

1. A GOTO statement cannot transfer the control into an IF statement, Case statement, Loop statement or a sub-block.

2. A GOTO statement cannot branch from one IF statement to another or from one Case statement's When clause to another.

3. A GOTO statement cannot transfer the control from an outer block into a sub-block jumping blocks in between them.

4. A GOTO statement cannot be used for ending a subprogram. To do this, either use a return statement or place the GOTO statement to branch to a place right before the end of the subprogram.

5. A GOTO statement cannot be used to branch from an exception handler back into the current block. However, a GOTO statement can branch from an exception handler to its enclosing block.

Null Statement

The Null statement is used only for passing the control to the next statement. This is referred to as no-op (no operation) in some languages.

```
Null;
```

Null statement in Anonymous block

In the below example, the Null statement avoids the compilation error as this block does not have any other executable statement than Null in it.

```
BEGIN
NULL;
END;
```

Named Block

These are named blocks that can take parameters and can be invoked at any point of time. These are mainly used for encapsulating a business logic and can be permanently stored in the database in the form of procedures and functions. Their header determines whether the unit is a procedure or a function and it can be accessed anytime in future when required as it is permanently stored in the database.

Advantages of Subprograms

1. **Performance:** Application makes a single call to the subprograms to run a block of statements which is better than running a bunch of SQL statements thus, avoiding call overhead between the application and the database.

2. **Security**: The subprograms are secure since the code resides in the database, thus, hiding the subprogram's internal implementation of the business logic. The application only calls the subprograms to execute them.

3. **Extensibility**: That is, it allows you to create our own code to suit our needs.

4. **Modularity**: That is, the subprograms act as a plug and play thus, helps in breaking a program into manageable, well defined logical modules.

5. **Reusability**: After the subprogram is validated, it can be confidently reused across multiple applications with no second thought.

6. **Maintainability**: If there is a bug or an enhancement, only the affected subprogram is impacted thus, code maintainability is simplified.

7. **Memory Allocation**: The subprograms take the advantage of the shared memory capabilities of an Oracle database. A single copy of the subprogram loaded into the memory can be used by multiple users for execution. Sharing the same code by many users reduces the memory requirements for multiple applications substantially.

Named Block Vs Anonymous Block

The subprograms are created and stored in the database as database objects. The subprograms are compiled once during its creation and can be run any number of times later without recompiling the unit. The status of the subprograms can be verified in the data dictionary tables available by default in the database.

In Contrast to the subprograms, the anonymous blocks once created, places its compiled code in the SGA, but it does not store the source code and the compiled version in the database, for rerunning the code beyond the current session. The anonymous block does not provide any parameter support.

Procedures

A procedure is the derived form of the anonymous block structure which can be identified by its own unique name. It is stored in the database as a database object and it has a header and a body section. The header section consists of the name of the procedure, the parameters for passing IN, OUT and INOUT parameters to a procedure. The body section consists of the declaration section, execution section and the exception section just like the anonymous blocks. These are called as standalone procedures when they are not defined within the context of any package.

The below prototype defines the syntax for creating a procedure.

```
Create [or Replace] Procedure <Procedure_name> [Parameters_list]
[AuthID Definer | Current_user]
Is|as
<Declaration_statements>;
Begin
<Executable_statements>;
Exception
[Exception_section]
End [Procedure_name];
```

> Note: IS and AS keywords are synonymous with each other and can be used alternatively. Generally, IS is used for the procedures in a package and AS is used for the standalone procedures for improving readability.

The below prototype defines the syntax for compiling or decompiling a procedure.

```
Alter procedure <procedure_name> compile | decompile;
```

The below prototype defines the syntax for dropping a procedure.

```
Drop procedure <procedure_name>;
```

OR Replace

The "OR Replace" clause recreates the procedure if it is already present in the database. This clause can be used for modifying the definition of the procedure without dropping, recreating and re-granting the necessary object privileges already granted earlier. The function based indexes depending on this procedure will be disabled.

Invoker Rights Clause

The invoker rights clause decides whether the procedure is to be executed with the privileges and in the schema of the owner of the procedure or with the privileges and in the schema of the user who executes it.

Authid Current_user

If Current_user syntax is specified in the Authid clause, the procedure gets executed with the privileges and in the schema of the user who runs the procedure. This procedure will then be created with invoker-rights.

The external names in the queries, DML operations and dynamic queries resolve in the name of the current user.

Authid definer

If definer syntax is specified in the Authid clause, the procedure gets executed with the privileges and in the schema of the user who owns the procedure. This procedure will then be created with definer-rights.

The external names in the queries, DML operations and dynamic queries resolve in the name of the schema where the procedure resides.

> Note: The Return statement is not mandatory for the procedures. But when used, it exits the procedure and skips the further execution.

A Simple Stand Alone Procedure

The below procedure when executed, creates a standalone procedure with the name proc_cube with one input parameter ip_n_var1 of the number data type and one output parameter op_n_var2 of number datatype.

The following procedure when called, returns the cube value of the input parameter.

```
1.  CREATE OR REPLACE
2.  PROCEDURE proc_cube(
3.  ip_n_var1 IN NUMBER,
4.  op_n_var2 OUT NUMBER)
5.  IS
6.  BEGIN
7.  op_n_var2:=ip_n_var1*ip_n_var1*ip_n_var1;
8.  END proc_cube;
```

```
9.  /
```

The below message is returned to the user once the procedure creation script is executed.

```
PROCEDURE PROC_CUBE compiled
```

Script Explanation

Line no.	Description
1,2	A procedure named proc_cube's header is placed with REPLACE keyword. Replace keyword allows the procedure to be recreated if it is already present in the database.
3,4	The procedure's parameters are declared. The input parameter is ip_n_var1 with number data type and the output parameter is op_n_var2 with number data type.
5	Start of the declare section of the procedure.
6	Start of the execution section of the procedure.
7	The output variable op_n_var2 is assigned with the cube of the input variable ip_n_var1 by multiplying the input variable thrice with itself.
8,9	End of the procedure.

Calling a Procedure

A procedure can be called either via SQL*Plus or by an anonymous block.

SQL*Plus Method

The below illustration shows the process of executing a procedure from SQL*Plus.

```
1.  SET serveroutput ON;
2.  VARIABLE l_n_var1 number;
3.  EXECUTE proc_cube(5,:l_n_var1);
4.  EXECUTE dbms_output.put_line(:l_n_var1);
5.  /
```

```
Result:
125
```

Script Explanation

Line no.	Description
1	This environment variable opens up an output buffer of size limit of 200000.
2	A variable l_n_var1 of the number data type is declared.
3	Execute command is used for executing the procedure proc_cube with the input parameter as 5 and the output parameter as a bind variable.

Named Block   **43**

| 4 | Execute command is used for printing the output bind variable l_n_var1's value using the dbms_output.put_line procedure. |
| 5 | End of the PL/SQL unit. |

Anonymous Block Method

The below illustration shows the process of calling a procedure from an anonymous block.

```
1.  DECLARE
2.  l_n_var1 NUMBER;
3.  BEGIN
4.  proc_cube(3,l_n_var1);
5.  dbms_output.put_line(l_n_var1);
6.  END;
7.  /
```

Result:
27

Script Explanation

Line no.	Description
1	Start of the declare section of the block.
2	A variable l_n_var1 of the number data typeis declared.
3	Start of the execution section of the block.
4	The procedure proc_cube is called with input parameter as 3 and the variable l_n_var1 is used as the output variable.
5	The local variable l_n_var1's value is printed using the DBMS_OUTPUT.PUT_LINE procedure.
6,7	End of the execution section of the block.

Declaring a Procedure in an Anonymous Block

The below approach explains how a procedure can be declared in an anonymous block without creating them permanently in the database. The declaration of the procedure should be always at the end of the declare section of an anonymous block, after all the necessary declarations of the anonymous block are declared else, the block will fail with a compilation error.

The below snippet declares a procedure with two input variables and one output variable all in number data types. When the two parameters of the procedure are passed with two numbers, the output variable returns the product of those.

These procedures cannot be viewed in the data dictionary tables as these are not permanently saved in the database.

```
1.  DECLARE
2.  l_n_var1 NUMBER;
3.  PROCEDURE proc_prod(
4.  ip_n_var1 IN NUMBER,
5.  ip_n_var2 IN NUMBER,
6.  op_n_var3 OUT NUMBER)
7.  IS
8.  BEGIN
9.  op_n_var3:=ip_n_var1*ip_n_var2;
10. END;
11. BEGIN
12. proc_prod(3,5,l_n_var1);
13. dbms_output.put_line(l_n_var1);
14. END;
15. /
```

Result:
27

Script Explanation

Line no.	Description
1	Start of the declare section of the block.
2	A variable l_n_var1 of the number data type is declared.
3	Start of the declaration of the procedure proc_prod in the block.
4,5,6	The input variables ip_n_var1, ip_n_var2 and the output variable op_n_var3 are declared with number data type.
7	Start of the declare section of the procedure.
8	Start of the execution section of the procedure.
9	The output variable is assigned to the product of the two input variables.
10	End of the execution section of the procedure.
11	Start of the execution section of the block.
12	The procedure proc_prod is called with the input variables 3, 5 and the local variable l_n_var1 is used for fetching the output variable's result.
13	The local variable l_n_var1's value is printed using the DBMS_OUTPUT.PUT_LINE procedure.
14,15	End of the execution section of the block.

Functions

A function, just like a procedure, is also a derived form of an anonymous block which can be identified by its own unique name. It is also stored in the database as a database object and it has a header and a body section. The header section consists of the name of the procedure, the parameters for passing IN, OUT and INOUT parameters to a procedure along with a mandatory return statement declaration. The body section consists of the declaration section, execution section and the exception section just like the anonymous blocks. In the body section, after all the executable statements are placed, a mandatory return statement has to be placed to make the code free from compilation error.

The below prototype defines the creation of a function.

```
Create [or replace] function <Function_name> [Parameters_list]
Return <data type>
[Authid Definer | Current_use]
[Deterministic | Parallel_enabled | Pipelined]
[Result_cache] [Relies_on <table_name>]
Is | as
<Declaration_statements>;
Begin
<Executable_statements>;
Return <Value> | <Variable>;
Exception
[Exception_section];
End [Function_name];
```

> 🔔 Note: IS and AS keywords are synonymous with each other and can be used alternatively. Generally, IS is used for the functions in a package and AS is used for the functions which are not placed in a package for improving readability.

The below prototype defines the syntax for compiling or decompiling a function.

```
Alter function <function_name> compile | decompile;
```

The below prototype defines the syntax for dropping a function.

```
Drop function <function_name>;
```

OR Replace

The "OR Replace" clause recreates the function if it is already present in the database. This clause can be used for modifying the definition of the function without dropping, recreating and re-granting the necessary object privileges already granted earlier. The function based indexes depending on this function will be disabled.

Invoker Rights Clause

The invoker rights clause decides whether this function is to be executed with the privileges and in the schema of the owner of the function or with the privileges and in the schema of the user who executes it.

Authid Current_user

If Current_user syntax is specified in the Authid clause, the function gets executed with the privileges and in the schema of the user who runs the function. This function will then be created with invoker-rights.

The external names in the queries, DML operations and dynamic queries resolve in the name of the current user.

Authid definer

If definer syntax is specified in the Authid clause, the function gets executed with the privileges and in the schema of the user who owns the function. This function will then be created with definer-rights.

The external names in the queries, DML operations and dynamic queries resolve in the name of the schema where the function resides.

Return Clause

Every function must return a value, thus a specific data type has to be mentioned during the function creation. The return clause's data type can be of any data type supported by PL/SQL.

Deterministic Clause

The deterministic clause indicates that the function always returns the same result whenever the function is called with the same input values as its arguments.

The function based indexes and the materialized views with FAST REFRESH or ENABLE QUERY REWRITE options mentioned.

When the deterministic clause is mentioned in the above context, the Oracle database will attempt to reuse the results whenever possible rather than re-executing the function. If this clause is mentioned in a function that uses package variables or that

---

access database in way affecting the return result, the expected results may not be returned if Oracle chooses not to re-execute the function again.

Parallel Enable Clause

Parallel_enable is an optimization hint which indicates that this function can be executed from a parallel query operation or from a parallel execution server.

Pipelined Clause

The pipelined clause instructs the Oracle database to return the results of a table function in an iterative manner.

A Simple Function

The below function when executed, creates a function with the name func_math with one input parameter ip_n_var1 of the number data type and the return type of varchar2.

The following function when called returns irrespective of the input parameter being odd or even.

```
1.   CREATE OR REPLACE
2.   FUNCTION func_math(
3.   ip_n_var1 IN NUMBER)
4.   RETURN VARCHAR2
5.   IS
6.   BEGIN
7.   RETURN (CASE mod(ip_n_var1,2) WHEN 0 THEN 'Even' ELSE 'Odd' END);
8.   END;
9.   /
```

The below message is returned to the user once the procedure creation script is executed.

```
FUNCTION FUNC_MATH compiled
```

Script Explanation

Line no.	Description

1,2	The function func_math's header is placed with REPLACE keyword. Replace keyword allows the procedure to be recreated if it is already present in the database.
3	The function's input parameter, ip_n_var1 is declared with number data type
4	The function's return type varchar2 is declared.
5	Start of the declare section of the procedure.
6	Start of the execution section of the procedure.
7	The return variable returns the result of the modulus of the input variable ip_n_var1 by 2. A case statement converts 0 to Even else Odd and assigns the value of the return statement.
8,9	End of the procedure.

Calling a Function

A function can be called either via a select statement or by an anonymous block.

Select Statement

The below illustration shows the process of executing a procedure from SQL*Plus.

```
Select func_math(5) from dual;
```

Result:
Odd

The DUAL table in Oracle is owned by the SYS user and has one column named DUMMY with the data type Varchar2(1) and one row with the value 'X'. This table was created by Charles Weiss when he was trying to duplicate rows while working with the internal views. SYS has created a public synonym over this table for other users to access this table. This table is primarily used for selecting pseudo columns such as sysdate, nextval, currval, rownum, rowid and for mathematical manipulations. In Oracle 10g, the performance implications of this table has been increased by using a FAST DUAL mechanism.

Restrictions of Calling a Function from a Select Statement

Unlike procedures, the functions can be called from a Select statement unless it violates the database purity rules. They are

1. A function called from a Select statement cannot contain any DML, TCL or DDL statements.
2. A function called from an Update or Delete statements cannot query (Select) or perform any transactions (DML) on the same table.
3. A function called from a Select statement cannot have any out parameters.

Anonymous Block Method

The below illustration shows the process of calling a function from an anonymous block.

```
1.  DECLARE
2.  l_vc_var1 VARCHAR2(10);
3.  BEGIN
4.  l_vc_var1:=func_math(5);
5.  dbms_output.put_line(l_vc_var1);
6.  END;
7.  /
```

Result:
Odd

Script Explanation

Line no.	Description
1	Start of the declare section of the block.
2	A variable l_vc_var1 of varchar2 data type with the precision 10 is declared.
3	Start of the execution section of the block.
4	The variable l_vc_var1 is assigned to the function func_math's call return value with the input 5.
5	The local variable l_vc_var1's value is printed using the DBMS_OUTPUT.PUT_LINE procedure.
6,7	End of the execution section of the block.

Declaring a Function in an Anonymous Block

The below approach explains how a function can be declared in an anonymous block without creating them permanently in the database. The declaration of the function should be always at the end of the declare section of an anonymous block after all the necessary declarations of the anonymous block are declared.

These functions cannot be viewed in the data dictionary tables as these are not permanently saved in the database.

```
1.  DECLARE
2.  l_n_var1  NUMBER;
3.  l_vc_var2 VARCHAR2(30);
4.  FUNCTION func_conv(
5.  ip_vc_var1 IN VARCHAR2,
6.  op_vc_var2 OUT VARCHAR2)
7.  RETURN NUMBER
8.  IS
9.  BEGIN
10. op_vc_var2:=upper(ip_vc_var1);
```

```
11. RETURN LENGTH(ip_vc_var1);
12. END;
13. BEGIN
14. l_n_var1:=func_conv('Hello World!',l_vc_var2);
15. dbms_output.put_line('The Length of the input is '||l_n_var1);
16. dbms_output.put_line('The input in upper case is '||l_vc_var2);
17. END;
18. /
```

Result:
The Length of the input is 12
The input in upper case is HELLO WORLD!

Script Explanation

Line no.	Description
1	Start of the declare section of the block.
2	The variable l_n_var1 of the number data type is declared.
3	The variable l_vc_var2 of varchar2 data type with precision 30 is declared.
4	Start of the declaration of the function func_conv.
5	The input parameter ip_vc_var1 of varchar2 data type is declared.
6	The output parameter op_vc_var2 of varchar2 data type is declared.
7	The return statement's data type is declared as the number.
8	Start of the declare section of the function.
9	Start of the execution section of the function.
10	The case of the input parameter ip_vc_var1 is converted to upper and assigned to the output parameter op_vc_var2.
11	The length of the input parameter ip_vc_var1 is calculated and returned using the RETURN statement.
12	End of the execution section of the function
13	Start of the execution section of the block.
14	The function func_conv is called with the text 'Hello World!' as its input parameter and the local variable l_vc_var2 is used as its output variable and the function is assigned to another local variable l_n_var1.
15	The local variable l_n_var1's value is printed using the DBMS_OUTPUT.PUT_LINE procedure.
16	The local variable l_vc_var2's value is printed using the DBMS_OUTPUT.PUT_LINE procedure.
17,18	End of the execution section of the block.

Differences between the Parameter Types in the Subprograms

S. No.	IN	OUT	INOUT
1	This is the default parameter mode.	These parameters have to be explicitly mentioned.	
2	This parameter is passed by reference.	These parameters are by default passed by value, but can be changed to pass by reference by using the NOCOPY hint.	
3	This parameter can have default values.	These parameters cannot have default values for them.	
4	This parameter accepts values from the calling environment and processes it inside the program.	This parameter returns a value from the program to the calling environment.	This parameter may accept a value from the calling environment or returns a value to the calling environment.

Actual and Formal Parameters

The subprogram's interaction with the programmers is using their parameters. There are two different types of parameters, and they are.

Actual Parameters

The parameters which are passed from the calling subprogram are called as actual parameters. In the below example, the variables used for calling the procedure are called as actual parameters and their scope exists outside the procedure too.

```
Declare
L_n_var1 number:=10;
L_n_var2 number:=10;
L_n_var3 number;
Begin
Proc_math(l_n_var1,l_n_var2,l_n_var3);
Dbms_output.put_line('The Result is '||l_n_var3);
End;
```

Formal Parameters

The parameters which are declared in the header section of a subprogram's parameter list are called as formal parameters. In the below example, the function func_emp returns the salary and department name of an employee when his ID, Name, Joining date is passed as the input parameters to the function. These parameters, which act as the placeholders for the actual parameters when the function is called are the formal parameters and their scope is only inside the subprogram and not outside.

```
CREATE OR REPLACE
  FUNCTION func_emp(
      emp_id          IN NUMBER,
      emp_name        IN VARCHAR2,
      emp_join_date IN DATE,
      emp_dept OUT VARCHAR2)
    RETURN NUMBER
  IS
  BEGIN
    ..
    RETURN emp_sal;
  END;
  /
```

Call Notation

There are multiple methods of associating the actual parameters with the formal parameters during a subprogram call. And they are,

Positional Notation

The process of associating the actual parameter implicitly by considering the position of the formal parameters in the subprogram's header is called as the positional notation. With the positional notation, the PL/SQL compiler associates the first actual parameter from the subprogram call with the first formal parameter of the subprogram, second actual parameter from the subprogram call with the second formal parameter of the subprogram and so on.

The function in the above example can be called using the positional notation as like below,

```
DECLARE
  l_vc_dept VARCHAR2(30);
  l_n_sal   NUMBER;
BEGIN
  l_n_sal:=func_emp(7815,'John','13-June-2011',l_vc_dept);
  dbms_output.put_line('The Employee''s dept is '||l_vc_dept);
  dbms_output.put_line('The Employee''s sal is '||l_n_sal);
END;
/
```

In the above example, the actual parameters 7815, 'John', '13-June-2011' and the variable l_vc_dept are in the exact order of their formal parameters declared in the function header.

Named Notation

The process of associating the actual parameter explicitly by the formal parameter's name in the subprogram's header is called as the positional notation. The combination symbol => is used for combining the formal and the actual parameters during the named notation call.

The prototype for the named notation call of a procedure is as below,

```
Procedure_name(formal_parameter1=>actual_parameter1,formal_parameter2=>actua
l_parameter2,..);
```

As the name of the formal parameters is provided explicitly, the PL/SQL compiler does not have to rely on the order of the parameters to make the association between the formal and the actual parameters.

The function in the above example can be called using the named notation as like below. Here the order of the parameters are shuffled but the function identifies the parameters using their named notation.

```
DECLARE
   l_vc_dept VARCHAR2(30);
   l_n_sal   NUMBER;
BEGIN

l_n_sal:=func_emp(emp_name=>'John',emp_id=>7815,emp_dept=>l_vc_dept,emp_join
_date=>'13-June-2011');
   dbms_output.put_line('The Employee''s dept is '||l_vc_dept);
   dbms_output.put_line('The Employee''s sal is '||l_n_sal);
END;
/
```

Mixed Notation

The process of using both the positional notation and the named notation together is called as mixed notation. The important rule to keep in mind while performing this type of notation is that the positional notations should be used before the usage of the named notation. If a parameter is populated using the named notation, all subsequent parameters must also be populated using the named notation.

The function in the above example can be called using the mixed notation as like below. In the below example, the first two parameters are populated using the positional notation and the rest parameters are populated using the named notation.

```
DECLARE
  l_vc_dept VARCHAR2(30);
  l_n_sal   NUMBER;
BEGIN
  l_n_sal:=func_emp(7815,'John',emp_join_date=>'13-June-
2011',emp_dept=>l_vc_dept);
  dbms_output.put_line('The Employee''s dept is '||l_vc_dept);
  dbms_output.put_line('The Employee''s sal is '||l_n_sal);
END;
/
```

The parameters using for the population can be skipped if it is not a mandatory one (by defaulting the parameter to some value during the subprogram creation).

Packages

The Packages are a schema object which groups logically related PL/SQL variables, types, procedures and functions as components in the libraries. Unlike the procedures and functions, the packages store the prototype of their public constructs in their specification section and their implementation is stored in their body section.

The specification declares the public constructs that can be referenced outside the package context. The specification section acts as an interface for the other applications.

The body can declare and define constructs which are accessible only within the package, and not outside of them unlike the specification section.

Benefits of using Packages

The packages help in creating a simple, clear and a secure code with the following features,

Performance

When a subprogram in a package is invoked, the entire package is loaded into the memory and will be available across all the users connected to the database. Subsequent calls to the same package does not need any disk I/O operation instead the package is accessed from the memory, thus plays a vital role in the memory management.

Privacy and Security

The packages shares the interface information in their specification section itself and hides the implementation details present in the body section. Thus, allowing changes to the implementation without affecting the application interface.

Encapsulation

The packages allow us to group logically related objects like types, variables, exceptions, cursors and subprograms as named PL/SQL modules. Thus, making the package easy to understand and making the interfaces simple and clear. This plays a vital role in the application development.

Maintenance

The changes in the subprogram of a package does not require any changes to its specification. Not even a compilation is required. As the maintenance of a package can be done module wise, the cost and complexity for the maintenance is very less.

Availability

The public variables and the cursors live throughout the session. They let us maintain data across a complete session without storing them permanently in the database.

Reusability

Object oriented concepts like overloading helps in reusing the subprograms thus, avoiding large code area.

Package Specification

The package specification (usually called as the spec) is the mandatory section of a package and a package cannot exist without its spec. The section is like a blueprint for the body section containing the declaration of variables, cursors, types, objects, and the prototypes of the functions and the procedures which are also called as the forward declaration. The implementation of the subprograms, once prototyped, must have their implementation only in the body section. The package specification cannot contain any executable section in them. The components declared in the specification are optional because it is possible to create the body section without any of these components except for procedures and functions which once declared must be implemented in the body.

The public constructs declared in the specification have their life throughout a session and they can be accessed outside the package by qualifying the construct by their package name. Variables declared in the specification section if also declared again in the body, the package compilation will fail stating that a variable has been declared more than once and this scenario should be avoided. When a package specification is compiled, the state of the package body will be decompiled.

> 🔔 Note: A variable declared as CONSTANT in the specification cannot be used as an assignment target anywhere in the package body.

The subprograms (Procedures and functions) in the specification section are merely a forward referencing prototype of their implementation in the body. These prototypes define the procedures and functions with their signatures and return types (for functions only) and create a namespace for them.

The below listing shows the declaration of a procedure in a package specification where its second parameter is made optional by defaulting it to Null.

```
Procedure proc_emp(emp_id number, emp_name varchar2 default null);
```

The below listing shows the declaration of a function in a package specification with its parameters and return type defined.

```
Function func_dept(dept_id number) return varchar2;
```

Package Body

The package body contains the implementation of the subprograms which were declared in the specification. The package body, optionally contains a BEGIN-END block which gets executed during the first time of package invocation. This is used for initializing the global variables. The local constructs in the package body are limited to the scope of the package only and cannot be accessed outside of them. When a package body is compiled, the state of the specification remains the same.

All the pragmas (compiler directives) are declared only in the specification section except for the pragma SERIALLY_REUSABLE which has to be declared both in the specification and in the body.

The below prototype defines the syntax for creating a package.

Specification

```
Create [or Replace] Package <Package_name>
Is
[Pragma_declaration];
[Public_constructs_declaration];
End [Package_name];
/
```

Body

```
Create [or Replace] Package body <Package_name>
Is
[Local_constructs_declaration];
[Local_constructs_definition];
[Public_constructs_definition];
[BEGIN-END Block];
End [Package_name];
/
```

The below prototype defines the syntax for compiling or decompiling a package.

```
Alter package <package_name> compile | decompile [specification | body];
```

The below prototype defines the syntax for dropping a package.

```
Alter package [body] <package_name>;
```

A Simple Package

In the below listing, the package pkg_emp has one procedure for inserting the employee details and one function for incrementing the employee's salary.

```
1.    CREATE OR REPLACE
2.    PACKAGE pkg_emp
3.    IS
4.    PROCEDURE proc_emp_insert(
5.    ip_emp_name     IN VARCHAR2,
6.    ip_emp_dob      IN DATE,
7.    ip_emp_job_desc IN VARCHAR2,
8.    ip_emp_sal      IN NUMBER,
9.    op_status OUT VARCHAR2);
10.   FUNCTION func_emp_updatesal(
11.   ip_emp_id    IN NUMBER,
12.   ip_raise_per IN NUMBER)
13.   RETURN VARCHAR2;
14.   END pkg_emp;
15.   /
16.   CREATE OR REPLACE
17.   PACKAGE body pkg_emp
18.   IS
19.   PROCEDURE proc_emp_insert(
```

```
20. ip_emp_name      IN VARCHAR2,
21. ip_emp_dob       IN DATE,
22. ip_emp_job_desc IN VARCHAR2,
23. ip_emp_sal       IN NUMBER,
24. op_status OUT VARCHAR2)
25. IS
26. BEGIN
27. INSERTINTO emp (empid,empname,empdob,empjob,empsal)
28. VALUES
29. (seq_emp_id.nextval,ip_emp_name,ip_emp_dob,ip_emp_job_desc,ip_emp_sa
    l);
30. COMMIT;
31. op_status:='The Employee '||ip_emp_name||' has been successfully
    registered in the database';
32. END proc_emp_insert;
33. FUNCTION func_emp_updatesal
34. (
35. ip_emp_id    IN NUMBER,
36. ip_raise_per IN NUMBER
37. )
38. RETURN VARCHAR2
39. IS
40. BEGIN
41. UPDATE emp
42. SET empsal =empsal+((empsal*ip_raise_per)/100)
43. WHERE empid=ip_emp_id;
44. COMMIT;
45. RETURN 'The raise for the Employee ID '||ip_emp_id||' has been
    successfully applied';
46. END func_emp_updatesal;
47. END pkg_emp;
48. /
```

After the above package creation script is executed, Oracle returns the success message as below,

```
PACKAGE PKG_EMP compiled
PACKAGE BODY PKG_EMP compiled
```

Script Explanation

Line No.	Description
1,2	Start of the header of the package pkg_emp's specification.
3	Start of the declaration section of the package specification.
4-9	The procedure proc_emp_insert is declared with the necessary parameters.
10-13	The function func_emp_updatesal is declared with the necessary parameters and return statement.
14,15	End of the package pkg_emp's specification.
16,17	Start of the header of the package pkg_emp's body.
18	Start of the declaration section of the package body.
19-24	Start of the procedure proc_emp_insert's implementation with necessary parameters same like that of its definition in the specification.

25	Start of the declaration section of the procedure proc_emp_insert.
26	Start of the execution section of the procedure proc_emp_insert.
27-29	An insert statement inserting the input parameters into the employee table along with a user defined sequence for the ID column.
30	The insert statement is committed.
31	The success message for the procedure completion is saved in the out parameter.
32	End of the execution section of the procedure.
33-37	Start of the function func_emp_updatesal's implementation with necessary parameters same like that of its definition in the specification.
38	The return statement's data type is declared as Varchar2.
39	Start of the declare section of the function.
40	Start of the execution section of the function.
41-44	The employee's salary is incremented based on the input parameters and is committed.
45	The success message for the function completion is returned using the return statement.
46	End of the execution section of the function.
47,48	End of the execution section of the package.

Procedure call

The procedure call can be made by qualifying the procedure name with the package's name in an anonymous block with appropriate parameter values as like below.

```
1.   DECLARE
2.   l_vc_status VARCHAR2(100);
3.   BEGIN
4.   pkg_emp.proc_emp_insert(ip_emp_name=>'John',ip_emp_dob=>'30-Sep-
     1989', ip_emp_job_desc=>'Oracle
     Developer',ip_emp_sal=>750000,op_status=>l_vc_status);
5.   dbms_output.put_line(l_vc_status);
6.   END;
7.   /
```

Result
The Employee John has been successfully registered in the database

Script Explanation

Line No.	Description
1	Start of the declare section of the block.
2	A local variable l_vc_status is declared with the data type varchar2 and precision 100.
3	Start of the execution section of the block.

4	The procedure proc_emp_insert is called by qualifying it with the package's name with appropriate parameters using the named notation
5	The local variable l_vc_status's value is printed using the DBMS_OUTPUT.PUT_LINE procedure.
6,7	End of the execution section of the block.

Function call

The function call can also be made by qualifying the function name with the package's name in an anonymous block with appropriate parameter values as like below.

```
1.   DECLARE
2.   l_vc_status VARCHAR2(100);
3.   BEGIN
4.   l_vc_status:=pkg_emp.func_emp_updatesal(ip_emp_id=>1,ip_raise_per=>2
     0);
5.   dbms_output.put_line(l_vc_status);
6.   END;
7.   /
```

> 🔔 Note – This function can also be called from a Select statement if there is no DML statement present in it. Yet this can be achieved by making the function's transaction into private by using the pragma AUTONOMOUS_TRANSACTION.

Script Explanation

Line No.	Description
1	Start of the declare section of the block.
2	A local variable l_vc_status is declared with the data type varchar2 and precision 100.
3	Start of the execution section of the block.
4	The function func_emp_updatesal is called by qualifying it with the package's name with appropriate parameters using the named notation and is assigned to the local variable l_vc_status.
5	The local variable l_vc_status's value is printed using the DBMS_OUTPUT.PUT_LINE procedure.
6,7	End of the execution section of the block.

Forward Referencing

The process of declaring a subprogram before its call to its implementation is called as forward referencing. The forward referencing can be done both in the specification and in the body.

In the below example, a package pkg_fwd_ref is created with the procedure proc1 declared in its specification and proc1, proc2 implemented in its body. The call to the procedure proc2 can be only made through the proc1 as it is a private construct. Here, the procedure Proc2 does not need a declaration as it is placed prior to its caller's (Proc1) implementation as the single-pass parsers reads the code from the top to the bottom.

```
1.  CREATE OR REPLACE
2.  PACKAGE pkg_fwd_ref
3.  IS
4.  PROCEDURE proc1(
5.  ip_caller1 VARCHAR2);
6.  END pkg_fwd_ref;
7.  /
8.  CREATE OR REPLACE
9.  PACKAGE body pkg_fwd_ref
10. IS
11. PROCEDURE proc2(
12. ip_caller2 VARCHAR2)
13. IS
14. BEGIN
15. dbms_output.put_line('Procedure Proc2 has been called by
    '||ip_caller2);
16. END Proc2;
17. PROCEDURE proc1(
18. ip_caller1 VARCHAR2)
19. IS
20. BEGIN
21. dbms_output.put_line('Procedure Proc1 has been called by
    '||ip_caller1);
22. proc2('Proc1');
23. END Proc1;
24. END pkg_fwd_ref;
25. /
```

Result:
Procedure Proc1 has been called by User
Procedure Proc2 has been called by Proc1

Script Explanation

Line No.	Description
1,2	Start of the header of the package pkg_fwd_ref's specification.
3	Start of the declare section of the package specification.
4,5	The procedure proc1 is declared with one input parameter.
6,7	End of the package pkg_fwd_ref's specification.

8,9	Start of the header of the package pkg_fwd_ref's body.
10	Start of the declare section of the package pkg_fwd_ref's body.
11,12	Start of the procedure proc2's implementation with one input parameter.
13	Start of the declare section of the procedure proc2.
14	Start of the execution section of the procedure proc2.
15	The procedure proc2's caller information is printed using the dbms_output.put_line procedure.
16	End of the execution section of the procedure proc2.
17,18	Start of the procedure proc1's implementation with one input parameter.
19	Start of the declare section of the procedure proc1.
20	Start of the execution section of the procedure proc1.
21	The procedure proc1's caller information is printed using the dbms_output.put_line procedure.
22	The procedure proc2 is called with the text 'Proc1' as its input parameter.
23	End of the execution section of the procedure proc1.
24	End of the package pkg_fwd_ref's body.

If the procedure Proc2 is placed below for the implementation of the procedure Proc1, the above package will fail as the declaration for the procedure Proc2 is not found. Thus, declaring the procedure Proc2 prior to the implementation of the procedure Proc1 can solve this issue as shown in the below example.

```
1.  Create or replace
2.  PACKAGE pkg_fwd_ref
3.  IS
4.  PROCEDURE proc1(
5.  ip_caller1 VARCHAR2);
6.  END;
7.  /
8.  Create or replace
9.  PACKAGE body pkg_fwd_ref
10. IS
11. procedure proc2(ip_caller2 varchar2);
12. PROCEDURE proc1(
13. ip_caller1 VARCHAR2)
14. IS
15. BEGIN
16. dbms_output.put_line('Procedure Proc1 has been called by
    '||ip_caller1);
17. proc2('Proc1');
18. END proc1;
19. PROCEDURE proc2(
20. ip_caller2 VARCHAR2)
21. IS
22. BEGIN
23. dbms_output.put_line('Procedure Proc2 has been called by
    '||ip_caller2);
24. END proc2;
25. END pkg_fwd_ref;
26. /
```

```
Result:
Procedure Proc1 has been called by User
Procedure Proc2 has been called by Proc1
```

Script Explanation

Line No.	Description
1,2	Start of the header of the package pkg_fwd_ref's specification.
3	Start of the declare section of the package specification.
4,5	The procedure proc1 is declared with one input parameter.
6,7	End of the package pkg_fwd_ref's specification.
8,9	Start of the header of the package pkg_fwd_ref's body.
10	Start of the declare section of the package pkg_fwd_ref's body.
11	The procedure proc2 is declared.
12,13	Start of the procedure proc1's implementation with one input parameter.
14	Start of the declare section of the procedure proc1.
15	Start of the execution section of the procedure proc1.
16	The procedure proc1s caller information is printed using the dbms_output.put_line procedure.
17	The procedure proc2 is called with the text 'Proc1' as its input parameter.
18	End of the execution section of the procedure proc1.
19,20	The start of the procedure proc2's implementation with one input parameter.
21	Start of the declare section of the procedure proc2.
22	Start of the execution section of the procedure proc2.
23	The procedure proc2's caller information is printed using the dbms_output.put_line procedure.
24	End of the execution section of the procedure proc2.
25	End of the package pkg_fwd_ref's body.

Overloading

The process of creating procedures or functions with the same name but with differences in its signature is called as Overloading. The overloading subprograms can have a difference in the number of formal parameters or difference in the data types of the formal parameters in its respective positions. A subprogram cannot be overloaded just by having a different formal parameter name. When two subprograms are created with same name, same number of parameters, and same data type for the formal parameters in its respective positions, but with a difference in the names of its formal parameters, the package will not raise any compilation errors but throws ambiguity error during its call. The subprogram overloading aids in code modularity and reduces the design complexity.

> 🔔 Note: The subprograms which are not part of a package cannot be overloaded.

In the below example, the package pkg_overloading contains two functions with two parameters differing by their data types and two procedures which differs by their number of parameters are created for explaining the overloading concepts.

```
1.   CREATE OR REPLACE
2.   PACKAGE pkg_overloading
3.   IS
4.   FUNCTION func(ip_var1 NUMBER, ip_var2 VARCHAR2)
5.   RETURN VARCHAR2;
6.   FUNCTION func(ip_var1 VARCHAR2, ip_var2 NUMBER)
7.   RETURN VARCHAR2;
8.   PROCEDURE PROC(ip_var1 NUMBER, ip_var2 NUMBER, op_var3 OUT VARCHAR2);
9.   PROCEDURE PROC(ip_var1 NUMBER, ip_var2 NUMBER, ip_var3 NUMBER, op_var4
     OUT VARCHAR2);
10.  END pkg_overloading;
11.  /
12.  CREATE OR REPLACE
13.  PACKAGE body pkg_overloading
14.  IS
15.  FUNCTION func(
16.  ip_var1 NUMBER,
17.  ip_var2 VARCHAR2)
18.  RETURN VARCHAR2
19.  IS
20.  l_vc_var1 VARCHAR2(200);
21.  BEGIN
22.  l_vc_var1:='The Function having its first parameter as Number data type
     and the second parameter as Varchar2 data type is called';
23.  RETURN l_vc_var1;
24.  END func;
25.  FUNCTION func(
26.  ip_var1 VARCHAR2,
27.  ip_var2 NUMBER)
28.  RETURN VARCHAR2
29.  IS
30.  l_vc_var1 VARCHAR2(200);
31.  BEGIN
32.  l_vc_var1:='The Function having its first parameter as Varchar2 data
     type and the second parameter as Number data type is called';
33.  RETURN l_vc_var1;
34.  END func;
35.  PROCEDURE PROC(
36.  ip_var1 NUMBER,
37.  ip_var2 NUMBER,
38.  op_var3 OUT VARCHAR2)
39.  IS
40.  BEGIN
41.  op_var3:='The Procedure with three parameters is called';
42.  END Proc;
43.  PROCEDURE PROC(
44.  ip_var1 NUMBER,
45.  ip_var2 NUMBER,
```

```
46. ip_var3 NUMBER,
47. op_var4 OUT VARCHAR2)
48. IS
49. BEGIN
50. op_var4:='The Procedure with four parameters is called';
51. END Proc;
52. END Pkg_overloading;
53. /
```

Script Explanation

Line No.	Description
1,2	Start of the header of the package pkg_overloading's specification.
3	Start of the declare section of the package specification.
4,5	A function Func with parameters ip_var1 of the number data type and ip_var2 of varchar2 data type and varchar2 as its return data type is declared.
6,7	A function Func with parameters ip_var1 of varchar2 data type and ip_var2 of the number data type and varchar2 as its return data type is declared.
8	A procedure Proc with two input parameters of number data type and one output parameter with varchar2 data type is declared.
9	A procedure Proc with three input parameters of number data type and one output parameter with varchar2 data type is declared.
10,11	End of the package's specification.
12,13	Start of the header of the package pkg_overloading's body.
14	Start of the declare section of the package
15-18	The start of the implementation of the function Func with parameters ip_var1 of the number data type and ip_var2 of varchar2 data type and varchar2 as its return data type.
19	Start of the declare section of the function.
20	A local variable l_vc_var1 with a data type of varchar2 and precision of 200 is declared.
21	Start of the execution section of the function.
22	The local variable l_vc_var1 is assigned with the function details.
23	The local variable l_vc_var1 is returned using the return statement.
24	End of the execution section of the function.
25-28	The start of the implementation of the function Func with parameters ip_var1 of varchar2 data type and ip_var2 of the number data type and varchar2 as its return data type.
29	Start of the declare section of the function.
30	A local variable l_vc_var1 with a data type of varchar2 and precision of 200 is declared.
31	Start of the execution section of the function.
32	The local variable l_vc_var1 is assigned with the function details.
33	The local variable l_vc_var1 is returned using the return statement.

34	End of the execution section of the function.
35-38	Start of the implementation of a procedure Proc with two input parameters with number data type and one output parameter with varchar2 data type.
39	Start of the declare section of the procedure.
40	Start of the execution section of the procedure.
41	The output variable op_var3 is assigned with the procedure details.
42	End of the execution section of the procedure.
43-47	Start of the implementation of a procedure Proc with three input parameters with number data type and one output parameter with varchar2 data type.
48	Start of the declare section of the procedure.
49	Start of the execution section of the procedure.
50	The output variable op_var4 is assigned with the procedure details.
51	End of the execution section of the procedure.
52,53	End of the package's body.

Function Overloading

The overloading of the functions in the above package can be analyzed in the below executions.

 Note: The change in only the return type of the function's header cannot be considered for overloading.

The below listing calls the function Func with its first actual parameter value as 1 and its second actual parameter value as 'Hi'. By this call, the function Func with the first parameter as a number data type and second parameter as varchar2 data type is called in this context.

```
DECLARE
  l_vc_var1 VARCHAR2(200);
BEGIN
  l_vc_var1:=pkg_overloading.func(1,'Hi');
  dbms_output.put_line(l_vc_var1);
END;
/
```

Result:
The Function having its first parameter as Number data type and the second parameter as Varchar2 date type is called.

The below listing calls the function Func with its first actual parameter value as 'Hi' and its second actual parameter value as 1. By this call, the function Func with first parameter as varchar2 data type and second parameter as a number data type is called in this context.

```
DECLARE
  l_vc_var1 VARCHAR2(200);
BEGIN
  l_vc_var1:=pkg_overloading.func('Hi',1);
  dbms_output.put_line(l_vc_var1);
END;
/
```

Result:
The Function having its first parameter as Varchar2 data type and the second
parameter as Number data type is called.

Procedure Overloading

The overloading of the procedures in the above package can be analyzed in the below
executions.
The below listing calls the procedure Proc with its first actual parameter value as 1,
second actual parameter value as 2 and its output parameter is assigned to the local
variable l_vc_var1. By this call, the procedure Proc with three parameters is called in
this context.

```
DECLARE
  l_vc_var1 VARCHAR2(200);
BEGIN
  pkg_overloading.proc(1,2,l_vc_var1);
  dbms_output.put_line(l_vc_var1);
END;
/
```

Result:
The Procedure with three parameters is called.

The below listing calls the procedure Proc with its first actual parameter value as 1,
second actual parameter value as 2, third actual parameter as 3 and its output parameter
is assigned to the local variable l_vc_var1. By this call, the procedure Proc with four
parameters is called in this context.

```
DECLARE
  l_vc_var1 VARCHAR2(200);
BEGIN
  pkg_overloading.proc(1,2,3,l_vc_var1);
  dbms_output.put_line(l_vc_var1);
END;
/
```

Result:
The Procedure with four parameters is called.

Object Management in the Database Catalog

The Oracle database allows numerous objects like tables, views, procedures, functions, packages, and much more to be created in its database. The easiest way to find, manage and validate any object and its associated dependencies is through the Oracle supplied data dictionary objects. These objects act as a repository for holding information about the database itself. The data dictionary objects are generally tables and views storing data like any other table and view in the database. These objects are stored in the system table space in its database.

The data dictionary tables stores the information about the entire database and they should be accessed only by Oracle as these are normalized and the data are encrypted.

The data dictionary views are created with information in an understandable format from the data dictionary tables. The users are advised to use these views rather than their underlying tables.

These objects are owned by the user SYS and no user should modify these objects in the SYS schema as any possible change in these objects could disrupt the normal functioning of the Oracle database.

The data dictionary views consist of sets of three views for each underlying base table with different scopes. They are

S. No.	Privilege	Scope
1	User	This view gives information on the objects only from the user's database.
2	All	This view gives information on the objects for whom the users have access to.
3	Dba	This view gives information on the objects in all the users. Generally used by the DBAs for the database maintenance.

1. The total list of available data dictionary objects can be found by querying the below select statement.

```
Select * from dict[ionary];
```

This query results into information with two columns, one containing the table/ view name and the other column containing its comments.

Table Name	Comments
USER_CONS_COLUMNS	Information about accessible columns in constraint definitions
ALL_CONS_COLUMNS	Information about accessible columns in constraint definitions
DBA_CONS_COLUMNS	Information about accessible columns in constraint definitions

2. The total list of available objects in the current schema can be retrieved by querying the below query.

```
SELECT object_name,
  object_type,
  created,
  last_ddl_time,
  status
FROM user_objects
WHERE object_name IN ('EMP','FUNC_MATH','PROC_CUBE');
```

OBJECT_NAME	OBJECT_TYPE	CREATED	LAST_DDL_TIME	STATUS
EMP	TABLE	05-04-16	05-04-16	VALID
FUNC_MATH	FUNCTION	04-04-16	04-04-16	VALID
PROC_CUBE	PROCEDURE	03-04-16	05-04-16	VALID

The information retrieved from the above query helps in understanding the type of the object we are dealing with, the date of creation of the object, the date in which the object is last modified and its status.

3. To find the total list of arguments for a particular subprogram, the below statement can be queried for the desired result.

```
SELECT object_name,
  argument_name,
  data_type,
  defaulted,
  in_out,
  data_length
FROM user_arguments
WHERE object_name IN ('FUNC_MATH','PROC_CUBE');
```

OBJECT_NAME	ARGUMENT_NAME	DATA_TYPE	DEFAULTED	IN_OUT	DATA_LENGTH
FUNC_MATH	IP_N_VAR1	NUMBER	N	IN	22
FUNC_MATH		VARCHAR2	N	OUT	
PROC_CUBE	OP_N_VAR2	NUMBER	N	OUT	22
PROC_CUBE	IP_N_VAR1	NUMBER	N	IN	22

The above query returns the total list of the arguments and its data type along with its precision the subprogram is held with other information like whether the argument is defaulted or not along with its mode. In the above result set table, for the function FUNC_MATH, one parameter with the data type varchar2 remains Null. The reason is this argument corresponds to the return statement. All the functions will have one argument with its name and its length Null in this data dictionary view.

4. The data dictionary view to list down the subprogram related features can be queried using the below select statement.

```
SELECT object_name,
  object_type,
  pipelined,
  parallel,
  interface,
  deterministic,
  authid
FROM user_procedures
WHERE object_name IN ('FUNC_MATH','PROC_CUBE');
```

OBJECT_NAME	OBJECT_TYPE	PIPELINED	PARALLEL	INTERFACE	DETERMINISTIC	AUTHID
FUNC_MATH	FUNCTION	NO	NO	NO	NO	DEFINER
PROC_CUBE	PROCEDURE	NO	NO	NO	NO	CURRENT_USER

The result set shows the attributes of the parameters in the form of flags. If the function's attributes like pipelining, deterministic and parallel execution are enabled, their flags turn YES in the data dictionary view. If the subprograms have any interfaces to external programs, the INTERFACE column flags them to the user. Finally, the authid of the subprogram is indicated in the AUTHID column.

5. The source code of the subprograms can be retrieved by querying this data dictionary view as shown below.

```
SELECT * FROM user_source WHERE name = 'PROC_CUBE';
```

NAME	TYPE	LINE	TEXT
PROC_CUBE	PROCEDURE	1	PROCEDURE proc_cube(
PROC_CUBE	PROCEDURE	2	ip_n_var1 IN NUMBER,
PROC_CUBE	PROCEDURE	3	op_n_var2 OUT NUMBER) AUTHID CURRENT_USER
PROC_CUBE	PROCEDURE	4	IS
PROC_CUBE	PROCEDURE	5	BEGIN
PROC_CUBE	PROCEDURE	6	op_n_var2:=ip_n_var1*ip_n_var1*ip_n_var1;
PROC_CUBE	PROCEDURE	7	END;

The result set shows the type of the object and its source code along with its line numbers from the data dictionary view.

6. The dependencies of a subprogram can be retrieved by querying the below data dictionary view query.

```
SELECT name,
   type,
   referenced_owner,
   referenced_name,
   referenced_type,
   dependency_type
FROM user_dependencies
WHERE name ='PKG_EMP';
```

NAME	TYPE	REFERENCED_OW NER	REFERNCED_NA ME	REFERENCED_TY PE	DEPDENCY_TY PE
PKG_EM P	PACKAG E BODY	HR	STANDARD	PACKAGE	HARD
PKG_EM P	PACKAG E	HR	STANDARD	PACKAGE	HARD
PKG_EM P	PACKAG E BODY	HR	PKG_EMP	PACKAGE	HARD
PKG_EM P	PACKAG E BODY	HR	SEQ_EMP_ID	SEQUENCE	HARD
PKG_EM P	PACKAG E BODY	HR	EMP	TABLE	HARD

The above result set shows the objects which are dependent to the inquired object/ subprogram and its dependency type, either hard dependency or soft dependency.

Summary

This chapter toured us to the history of the relational database, its evolution and also about the PL/SQL internal architecture. We have seen a detailed discussion on the basic structure of the PL/SQL anonymous block along with its various types in the next section. The later section helped us in getting a clear insight on the control structures and its different types with adequate number of examples. A clear understanding on the procedures, functions and packages along with their similarities, dissimilarities, data dictionary tables and dependent objects related information has been provided in the final section of the chapter.

In the next chapter, we will discuss on the exceptions concept and its part in PL/SQL programming with adequate number examples.

Errors and Warnings in PL/SQL

In this chapter, we will brieflydiscuss PL/SQL errors and warnings.

1. Different types of PL/SQL errors.

    a. Compilation errors and its characteristics with suitable examples.

    b. Run-time errors and its different types, functionalities with various examples.

2. DML error log table and its effectiveness in handling the bulk SQL errors along with their restrictions.

3. The different modifiers and qualifier types in the PL/SQL warnings with supporting examples.

PL/SQL Errors

The PL/SQL program unit starts its execution by transferring its control from the program header (in case of a subprogram, the CREATE statement will be its header and in case of an anonymous block, the DECLARE or the BEGIN section will be its header) through its BODY section until it reaches the final END statement executing all the appropriate statements present in them. The state in which a PL/SQL program fails to propagate through its intended flow of execution is called as an error.

There are two types of errors in Oracle PL/SQL. They are compilation errors and run time errors (also called as Exceptions) which are explained below in detail.

Compilation Errors

The PL/SQL subprogram units during its creation will be undergoing a process called as a compilation. During this compilation process, the compiler will actively check the PL/SQL program for any syntax or semantics failure. This process is called as parsing and it ensures that the subprogram meets the lexical usage rules of the programming language.

Syntax check: The syntax of the subprogram is verified in this process. This process checks for any misspelled keywords, statements, forgot to terminate a statement or any formats which are not supported by Oracle.

Semantic check: The validity of the objects to which the subprogram is dependent is verified in this process (Whether the tables, columns, subprograms referred are present, valid in status and available for the user). This is a data dictionary check.

If any of the above checks fails, the compilation of the unit fails with an appropriate compilation error.

Anonymous Block with a Compilation Error

The status of an anonymous block facing a compilation error cannot be checked unless it is executed each time as it cannot be permanently stored in the database.

The below example shows that an anonymous block is created for fetching the count of the total number of employees from the EMPLOYEE table. The EMPLOYEE table which is referenced in this block is present in the schema B but the block is executed from the schema A. As there are no necessary grants available for the schema B over the table from the schema A, the block will fail with the below error report.

```
1.  SET SERVEROUTPUT ON SIZE 200000;
2.  DECLARE
3.  l_n_emp_cnt NUMBER;
4.  BEGIN
5.  SELECT COUNT(employee_id) INTO l_n_emp_cnt FROM employees;
6.  dbms_output.put_line('The total employee count is '||l_n_emp_cnt);
7.  END;
8.  /
```

```
Error report:
ORA-06550: line 4, column 51:
PL/SQL: ORA-00942: table or view does not exist
ORA-06550: line 4, column 3:
PL/SQL: SQL Statement ignored
06550. 00000 -  "line %s, column %s:\n%s"
*Cause:    Usually a PL/SQL compilation error.
*Action:
```

Script Explanation:

Line No.	Description
1	This environment variable opens up an output buffer of size limit of 200000.
2	Start of the declare section of the block.
3	A local variable l_n_emp_cnt of the number data type is declared.
4	Start of the execution section of the block.
5	The total count of employees from the EMPLOYEES table is assigned into the local variable l_n_emp_cnt. This schema (B) does not have enough privileges over the table EMPLOYEES which is present in the schema A.
6	The local variable l_n_emp_cnt's value is printed using the DBMS_OUTPUT.PUT_LINE procedure.
7,8	End of the execution section of the block.

This compilation error can be rectified by granting the appropriate privilege to the target schema B from the source schema A for the specific table (In this case a SELECT grant is required) and then the block has to be modified by qualifying the EMPLOYEES table with the source schema's name as like below.

```
5.  SELECT COUNT(employee_id) INTO l_n_emp_cnt FROM A.employees;
```

Subprogram with a Compilation Error

Unlike the anonymous blocks, the status of a subprogram or any other objects can be verified in the database using the data dictionary tables and views once after the subprogram or the object is created and stored in the database.

In the below example, a function FUNC_LENGTH is created for returning the length of the string passed as its input. The declaration of the RETURN statement of this function is commented on the line number 4 which will make the program unit to fail during its compilation check.

```
1.   CREATE OR REPLACE
2.     FUNCTION func_length(
3.        ip_vc_var1 IN VARCHAR2)
4.       --Return number
5.     IS
6.        l_vc_var1 VARCHAR2(100);
7.     BEGIN
8.        l_vc_var1:=ip_vc_var1;
9.        RETURN LENGTH(l_vc_var1);
10.    END;
11.    /
```

```
FUNCTION FUNC_LENGTH compiled
Errors: check compiler log
```

Script Explanation:

Line No.	Description
1,2,3	A function func_length is created with one input parameter ip_vc_var1 of varchar2 data type is declared.
4	The return statement is declared and commented.
5	Start of the declaration section of the function.
6	A local variable l_vc_var1 of varchar2 data type with precision 100 is declared.
7	Start of the execution section of the block.
8	The input parameter ip_vc_var1's value is assigned to the local variable l_vc_var1.
9	The length of the local variable l_vc_var1 is returned using the return statement.
10,11	End of the execution section of the block.

> Note: When the RETURN statement [at line no. 9] is commented, the function will not face any compilation error thus making it VALID when it is created. During its call, the function fails with a default error message 'Function returned without value' which does not fall under the run-time error category too. This is an undefined error which is not documented.

Even though this function did not pass its compilation check, it is still created in the database with an INVALID status. This function and its status information can be verified by using the below data dictionary view query.

```
SELECT object_name,
  object_type,
  created,
  last_ddl_time,
  status
FROM user_objects
WHERE object_name='FUNC_LENGTH';
```

Query Result:

OBJECT_NAME	OBJECT_TYPE	CREATED	LAST_DDL_TIME	STATUS
FUNC_LENGTH	FUNCTION	14-04-16	15-04-16	INVALID

To fix this function, the commented return statement's declaration has to be uncommented and the function creation script has to be re-executed so that the existing copy of the function will be replaced with the new one making the function VALID.

Compilation Restriction against Dependent Subprograms

When a child subprogram which is referred by a parent subprogram is INVALID, the status of all the parent subprograms referring to this child either directly or indirectly will turn INVALID. Thus, whenever the subprogram with INVALID status has to be compiled to make it VALID after making the necessary changes to it, it has to follow the rule of compiling its immediate parent subprograms first followed by its root parents in its hierarchical order.

In the below example, the procedures PROC_EMP1 and PROC_EMP2 are created for the purpose of retrieving the highest paid employee in an office. The procedures PROC_EMP1 and PROC_EMP2 are created in the schemas B and C respectively, whereas the underlying table EMPLOYEES is available in the schema A. The necessary privilege for the table has been provided only to the schema B. The procedure PROC_EMP2 turns INVALID due to the unavailability of the necessary privilege to access this table. Thus, making its dependent procedure PROC_EMP1 also INVALID.

```
1.   CREATE OR REPLACE
2.   PROCEDURE proc_emp2(
3.   ip_n_emp_id NUMBER)
4.   IS
5.   l_vc_first_name employees.first_name%type;
6.   BEGIN
7.   SELECT first_name
8.   INTO l_vc_first_name
9.   FROM employees
10.  WHERE employee_id=ip_n_emp_id;
11.  dbms_output.put_line (l_vc_first_name||' is the highest paid
     employee!!');
12.  END;
13.  /
```

```
PROCEDURE PROC_EMP2 compiled
Errors: check compiler log
```

Script Explanation:

Line No.	Description
1,2,3	A procedure proc_emp2 is created with one input parameter ip_n_emp_id of the number data type is declared.
4	Start of the declaration section of the procedure.
5	One anchored local variable l_vc_first_name with the data type as that of the Employees table's First_name column is declared.

6	Start of the execution section of the block.
7-10	The first name column value from the EMPLOYEES table of the input employee ID from the procedure proc_emp1 is assigned to the local variable l_vc_first_name. This schema (C) does not have enough privileges on the EMPLOYEES table which is present in the schema A.
11	The local variable l_vc_first_name's value is printed using the dbms_output.put_line procedure.
12,13	End of the execution section of the block.

```
1.  CREATE OR REPLACE
2.  PROCEDURE proc_emp1
3.  IS
4.  l_n_emp_id A.employees.employee_id%type;
5.  BEGIN
6.  SELECT employee_id
7.  INTO l_n_emp_id
8.  FROM A.employees
9.  WHERE salary=
10. (SELECT MAX(salary) FROM A.employees
11. );
12. proc_emp2(l_n_emp_id);
13. END;
14. /
```

```
PROCEDURE PROC_EMP1 compiled
Errors: check compiler log
```

Script Explanation:

Line No.	Description
1,2	A procedure proc_emp1 is created.
3	Start of the declaration section of the procedure.
4	One anchored local variable l_n_emp_9d with the data type as that of the Employees table's employee_id column is declared.
5	Start of the execution section of the block.
6-11	The employee ID of the employee who is earning the maximum of salary out of all the employees in the EMPLOYEES table is assigned to the local variable l_n_emp_id. This schema (B) has the necessary privileges on the table EMPLOYEES which is present in the schema A.
12	The procedure proc_emp2 is called with the local variable l_n_emp_id passed as its input parameter.
13,14	End of the execution section of the block.

These procedure's status information can be verified by using the below data dictionary view query.

```
SELECT object_name,
```

```
  object_type,
  created,
  last_ddl_time,
  status
FROM user_objects
WHERE object_name IN ('PROC_EMP1','PROC_EMP2');
```

Query Result:

OBJECT_NAME	OBJECT_TYPE	CREATED	LAST_DDL_TIME	STATUS
PROC_EMP1	PROCEDURE	15-04-16	15-04-16	INVALID
PROC_EMP2	PROCEDURE	15-04-16	15-04-16	INVALID

Their appropriate error messages can be found in the below data dictionary view query under the ALL user's privilege for the specified objects as below.

```
SELECT owner,
  name,
  type,
  line,
  text
FROM ALL_ERRORS
WHERE name IN ('PROC_EMP1','PROC_EMP2');
```

Query Result:

OWNER	NAME	TYPE	LINE	TEXT
C	PROC_EMP2	PROCEDURE	4	PLS-00201: identifier 'EMPLOYEES.FIRST_NAME' must be declared
C	PROC_EMP2	PROCEDURE	4	PL/SQL: Item ignored
C	PROC_EMP2	PROCEDURE	8	PL/SQL: ORA-00942: table or view does not exist
C	PROC_EMP2	PROCEDURE	6	PL/SQL: SQL Statement ignored
C	PROC_EMP2	PROCEDURE	10	PLS-00320: the declaration of the type of this expression is incomplete or malformed
C	PROC_EMP2	PROCEDURE	10	PL/SQL: Statement ignored
B	PROC_EMP1	PROCEDURE	11	PLS-00905: object SYS.PROC_EMP2 is invalid
B	PROC_EMP1	PROCEDURE	11	PL/SQL: Statement ignored

Once the necessary table privileges are provided to the child procedure PROC_EMP2 (in this case, SELECT privilege), the status of the procedure can be changed to VALID by compiling this procedure using the procedure ALTER statement as like below,

---

```
ALTER PROCEDURE proc_emp2 compile;
```

The status of the parent procedure PROC_EMP1 remains INVALID, whereas its child procedure PROC_EMP2 turns VALID. The query result of the USER_OBJECTS data dictionary view after the above ALTER statement execution is shown below.

OBJECT_NAME	OBJECT_TYPE	CREATED	LAST_DDL_TIME	STATUS
PROC_EMP1	PROCEDURE	15-04-16	15-04-16	INVALID
PROC_EMP2	PROCEDURE	15-04-16	15-04-16	VALID

Now, the parent procedure PROC_EMP1's status can be made VALID by compiling it by executing the below ALTER statement

```
ALTER PROCEDURE proc_emp1 compile;
```

The query result of the USER_OBJECTS data dictionary view after the above ALTER statement execution shows that both the procedures are now in the VALID state as below.

OBJECT_NAME	OBJECT_TYPE	CREATED	LAST_DDL_TIME	STATUS
PROC_EMP1	PROCEDURE	15-04-16	15-04-16	VALID
PROC_EMP2	PROCEDURE	15-04-16	15-04-16	VALID

Lexical Errors

The lexical errors occur when any keywords are misspelled, forgotten or not present when mandatorily needed by the program.

In the below example, the variable l_c_var1 with the data type CHAR having a default precision of 1 byte is declared and assigned to a string with two characters. When this anonymous block is executed even though when there is an exception section, the program unit fails with a compilation error as the line number 3 is not logically acceptable by the compiler.

```
1.   SET SERVEROUTPUT ON SIZE 200000;
2.   DECLARE
3.   l_c_var1 CHAR:='AB';
4.   BEGIN
5.   dbms_output.put_line(l_c_var1);
6.   EXCEPTION
7.   WHEN OTHERS THEN
8.   dbms_output.put_line(SQLCODE||' '||sqlerrm);
9.   END;
10. /
```

```
Error report:
ORA-06502: PL/SQL: numeric or value error: character string buffer too small
ORA-06512: at line 2
06502. 00000 -  "PL/SQL: numeric or value error%s"
*Cause:
*Action:
```

Script Explanation:

Line No.	Description
1	This environment variable opens up an output buffer of size limit of 200000.
2	Start of the declaration section of the block.
3	A local variable l_c_var1 of char data type with default precision of 1 byte is declared and assigned with the text 'AB'.
4	Start of the execution section of the block.
5	The local variable l_c_var1's value is printed using the dbms_output.put_line procedure.
6	Start of the exception section of the block.
7	A when clause is defined with the OTHERS handler accepting all incoming errors.
8	The error code (SQLCODE) and the error message (SQLERRM) values are printed using the dbms_output.put_line procedure.
9,10	End of the execution section of the block.

But when the same variable is assigned to a bind variable (The value of the variable is assigned during the run time), the compiler does not fail the unit as there is a possibility of the program to pass, when the input bind value is of a single character and to fail when the input bind value is more than a single character and the benefit of the doubt is given to the programmer in this case by passing the compilation.

```
1.   SET SERVEROUTPUT ON SIZE 200000;
2.   DECLARE
3.   l_c_var1 CHAR:=:value;
4.   BEGIN
5.   dbms_output.put_line(l_c_var1);
6.   EXCEPTION
7.   WHEN OTHERS THEN
8.   dbms_output.put_line(SQLCODE||' '||sqlerrm);
9.   END;
10. /
```

Script Explanation:

Line No.	Description
1	This environment variable opens up an output buffer of size limit of 200000.
2	Start of the declaration section of the block.
3	A local variable l_c_var1 of char data type with a default precision of 1 byte is declared and assigned to a bind variable.
4	Start of the execution section of the block.
5	The local variable l_c_var1's value is printed using the dbms_output.put_line procedure.
6	Start of the exception section of the block.
7	A when clause is defined with the OTHERS handler accepting all incoming errors.
8	The error code (SQLCODE) and the error message (SQLERRM) values are printed using the dbms_output.put_line procedure.
9,10	End of the execution section of the block.

During the above anonymous block execution, the program compiles successfully and prompts the user for a run time value for the bind variable. When the bind variable is passed with two characters (For e.g., AB), the program unit fails with a run time error (also called as an Exception) with the block completion success message and the exception message as below.

```
anonymous block completed
-6502 ORA-06502: PL/SQL: numeric or value error: character string buffer too
small
```

Run-Time Errors

The errors which occur during the program's execution after the compilation check is performed are called as the run-time errors or the exceptions. These errors are mostly data related and can occur in all the sections of the block like, DECLARE (CREATE section in case of a subprogram), BEGIN-END and even in the EXCEPTION section. When an exception is encountered, the control of the program unit is transferred to the current block's exception handling section. Within the exception section, the WHEN clause evaluates the exception which has been raised with the exception defined in its clause. When it matches, the statements inside that particular WHEN clause are executed. If these statements encounter into an Exception, the program control will look for an exception section in the enclosing block and if there are no exception handling sections found during this exception occurrence, the program unit will be unconditionally terminated from its execution skipping the rest of the statements from the program unit with an appropriate error code and an error message describing the exception occurred.

The OTHERS handler in the last WHEN clause handles all types of exceptions when the exception occurred does not match with any of the exception handlers defined in the previously defined WHEN clauses in the current block.

The below prototype defines the basic structure of an Exception section.

```
DECLARE
BEGIN
  <Executable_statements>;
EXCEPTION
WHEN <Exception_name1> THEN
    <Executable_statements> | <Subprogram_call> | <Anonymous_block>;
WHEN <Exception_name2> THEN
    <Executable_statements> | <Subprogram_call> | <Anonymous_block>;
  ..
WHEN OTHERS THEN
  <Executable_statements> | <Subprogram_call> | <Anonymous_block>;
END;
/
```

> 🔔 Note: The OTHERS handler must be always mentioned at the last out of all the WHEN clauses as it could override the other handlers. Oracle by default fails the program during the compilation if this happens.

There are four categories of exceptions available in PL/SQL and they are

Predefined Unnamed Exceptions

These exceptions are the Oracle predefined errors which do not have any name associated to them. These types of exceptions have a predefined unique error code and an error message but without a name. These exceptions occur in a rare situation and that is why these are not named.

These exceptions can be handled using the below two methods,

1. By handling them using the OTHERS handler.

2. By associating a name to its error code explicitly using the PRAGMA compiler called as EXCEPTION_INIT.

Using the OTHERS handler

In the below example, the common un-named exception DEADLOCK (Error code - 60) is manually created and handled using the OTHERS handler. For this, a table named DEADLOCK_TEST is created in the schema A with two columns COL1 with number data type and COL2 with varchar2 data type with a precision of 100. Two rows with COL1 values as 1, 2 and COL2 as Null are inserted for the manipulation and is committed as like below.

```
1.  CREATE TABLE deadlock_test (col1 NUMBER, col2 VARCHAR2(100));
2.  INSERT INTO deadlock_test VALUES (1,NULL);
3.  INSERT INTO deadlock_test VALUES (2,NULL);
4.  COMMIT;
```

A deadlock can be experienced in the session 2 by executing the below scripts in the respective schemas mentioned below.

```
1.  --- Session 1
2.  UPDATE deadlock_test SET col2='Session 1' WHERE col1=1;
3.  --- Session 2
4.  UPDATE deadlock_test SET col2='Session 2' WHERE col1=2;
5.  SET SERVEROUTPUT ON SIZE 200000;
6.  BEGIN
7.  UPDATE deadlock_test SET col2='Session 2' WHERE col1=1;
8.  EXCEPTION
9.  WHEN OTHERS THEN
10. dbms_output.put_line('Error Code is '||SQLCODE);
11. dbms_output.put_line('Error Message is '||sqlerrm);
12. END;
13. /
14. --- Session 1
15. UPDATE deadlock_test SET col2='Session 1' WHERE col1=2;
```

```
Error Code is -60
Error Message is ORA-00060: deadlock detected while waiting for resource
```

Script Explanation:

Line No.	Description
1	Session 1 is opened up for the operation.
2	An update statement updating the COL2 column of the DEADLOCK_TEST table to 'SESSION 1' for the COL1 column value 1 is executed.
3	Session 2 is opened up for the operation.
4	An update statement updating the COL2 column of the DEADLOCK_TEST table to 'SESSION 2' for the COL1 column value 2 is executed.
5	This environment variable opens up an output buffer of size limit of 200000.
6	Start of the execution section of the block.
7	An update statement updating the COL2 column of the DEADLOCK_TEST table to 'SESSION 2' for the COL1 column value 1 is executed.
8	Start of the exception section of the block.
9	A when clause is defined with the OTHERS handler accepting all incoming errors.

10,11	The error code (SQLCODE) and the error message (SQLERRM) values are printed using the dbms_output.put_line procedure.
12,13	End of the execution section of the block.
14	An update statement updating the COL2 column of the DEADLOCK_TEST table to 'SESSION 1' for the COL1 column value 2 is executed.

The conflict between the session 1 and 2 is automatically detected by the Oracle server and is resolved by rolling back the anonymous block in the session 2 which was involving in the deadlock.

Using the PRAGMA Compiler

The un-named system exceptions can be assigned with a name explicitly by using the pragma compiler Exception_init. Exception_init will associate the Oracle predefined error code to a user defined name so that this name can be used in the WHEN clause of the exception section explicitly.

> 🔔 Note: The Pragma is a compiler directive, which manipulates the behavior of the program during the compile time rather at the run time.

The prototype of using the Pragma compiler Exception_init in an anonymous block is shown below,

```
DECLARE
  <User_defined_exception_name> EXCEPTION;
  Pragma exception_init(<User_defined_exception_name>,
<Predefined_error_code>);
BEGIN
  <Executable_statements>;
  ...
EXCEPTION
WHEN <User_defined_exception_name> THEN
    <Executable_statements> | <Subprogram_call> | <Anonymous_block>;
END;
/
```

The same example described above for the deadlock can be modified for explaining the Pragma compiler below (Only the anonymous block of the code has been modified and shown below. For testing purpose, kindly use the code from the above example, replacing this block),

---

PL/SQL Errors

85

```
5.  DECLARE
6.  deadlock_error EXCEPTION;
7.  pragma exception_init(deadlock_error,-60);
8.  BEGIN
9.  UPDATE deadlock_test SET col2='Session 2' WHERE col1=1;
10. EXCEPTION
11. WHEN deadlock_error THEN
12. dbms_output.put_line('Error Code is '||SQLCODE);
13. dbms_output.put_line('Error Message is '||sqlerrm);
14. END;
15. /
```

```
Error Code is -60
Error Message is ORA-00060: deadlock detected while waiting for resource
```

Script Explanation:

Line #	Description
5	Start of the declare section of the block.
6	A variable deadlock_error is declared of exception data type.
7	The pragma exception_init is declared with its first parameter as the local variable deadlock_error and the second variable as the dead lock's error code -60.
8	Start of the execution section of the block.
9	An update statement updating the COL2 column of the DEADLOCK_TEST table to 'SESSION 2' for the COL1 column value 1 is executed.
10	Start of the exception section of the block.
11	A when clause is defined by the user defined exception deadlock_error handler.
12,13	The error code (SQLCODE) and the error message (SQLERRM) values are printed using the dbms_output.put_line procedure.
14,15	End of the execution section of the block.

Predefined Named Exceptions

These are the named Oracle defined exceptions which are implicitly raised by the system when a program unit violates an RDBMS rule. The chances of these exception's occurrences are high and that is why these are named by the system. These exceptions are defined and declared in the STANDARD package in the SYS schema. Whenever an exception occurs in a program, the Oracle server checks and matches it from the list of exceptions in this package. As these exceptions come with a name, these can be explicitly handled in the WHEN clause of the exception section. Meanwhile, the OTHERS handler also does its job of handling these exceptions if they are not handled prior to them.

> Note: The predefined named exceptions can also be raised explicitly using the RAISE command.

A Simple Predefined Exception

In the below example, an integer is being divided by 0 which is mathematically undefined. Thus, the system raises a predefined error "ZERO_DIVIDE" with an error code and an appropriate error message.

```
DECLARE
  l_n_var1 NUMBER;
BEGIN
  l_n_var1:=1/0;
EXCEPTION
WHEN zero_divide THEN
  dbms_output.put_line(SQLCODE);
  dbms_output.put_line(sqlerrm);
END;
/
```

```
-1476
ORA-01476: divisor is equal to zero
```

Operator usage in Predefined Exception

When an action to be performed during an exception is common for more than one exception, the relational operator OR can be used to avoid writing an extra WHEN clause thus, increasing the code readability by reducing the scripting as below,

The EMPLOYEES table from the HR schema is taken from the below example,

```
1.  SET SERVEROUTPUT ON SIZE 200000
2.  DECLARE
3.  l_n_emp_id NUMBER;
4.  BEGIN
5.  SELECT employee_id
6.  INTO l_n_emp_id
7.  FROM hr.employees
8.  WHERE upper(first_name)=UPPER(:first_name);
9.  dbms_output.put_line('The employee ID of '||:first_name||' is
    '||l_n_emp_id);
10. EXCEPTION
11. WHEN no_data_found OR too_many_rows THEN
12. dbms_output.put_line(SQLCODE);
13. dbms_output.put_line(sqlerrm);
14. END;
15. /
```

1. When the bind value is Steven, the result is

```
-1422
ORA-01422: exact fetch returns more than requested number of rows
```

2. When the bind value is Alex, the result is

```
100
ORA-01403: no data found
```

3. When the bind value is Neena, the result is

```
The employee ID of Neena is 101
```

Script Explanation:

Line No.	Description
1	This environment variable opens up an output buffer of size limit of 200000.
2	Start of the declaration section of the block.
3	A local variable l_n_emp_id of the number data type is declared.
4	Start of the execution section of the block.
5-8	The employee ID of the employee from the EMPLOYEES table for the input bind variable of the first name is assigned to the local variable l_n_emp_id. Here the predefined function UPPER is used on the both sides of the WHERE condition to avoid case issues as a best practice.
9	The local variable l_n_emp_id's value is printed using the dbms_output.put_line procedure.
10	Start of the exception section of the block.
11	A when clause is defined with the NO_DATA_FOUND handler and the TOO_MANY_ROWS handler separated by the relational operator OR accepting both the errors.
12,13	The error code (SQLCODE) and the error message (SQLERRM) values are printed using the dbms_output.put_line procedure.
14,15	End of the execution section of the block.

Raising a Predefined Exception Explicitly

A Predefined error can be explicitly raised using the RAISE command. In the below example, the predefined exception NO_DATA_FOUND is explicitly raised and handled by using the RAISE command.

```
BEGIN
  raise no_data_found;
EXCEPTION
WHEN no_data_found THEN
  dbms_output.put_line(SQLCODE);
  dbms_output.put_line(sqlerrm);
END;
/
```

```
100
ORA-01403: no data found
```

User-defined Named Exceptions

Other than the predefined exceptions, Oracle allows us to explicitly define and declare exceptions based on our business rules and these are called as user defined exceptions. These exceptions have to be explicitly declared, raised and handled by the user in their program unit.

```
1.  SET SERVEROUTPUT ON SIZE 200000
2.  DECLARE
3.  L_vc_status VARCHAR2(30);
4.  odd_hours    EXCEPTION;
5.  BEGIN
6.  IF trim(TO_CHAR(sysdate,'HH24')) BETWEEN 18 AND 24 OR
    trim(TO_CHAR(sysdate,'HH24')) BETWEEN 0 AND 6 THEN
7.  raise odd_hours;
8.  ELSE
9.  pkg_library.proc_book_register(ip_vc_book_name=>'The Jungle Book',
    op_vc_status=>l_vc_status);
10. dbms_output.put_line(l_vc_status);
11. END IF;
12. EXCEPTION
13. WHEN odd_hours THEN
14. dbms_output.put_line('Please try again during the library hours!');
15. dbms_output.put_line('Error Code is '|| SQLCODE);
16. dbms_output.put_line('Error Message is '||sqlerrm);
17. END;
18. /
```

```
Please try again during the library hours!
Error Code is 1
Error Message is User-Defined Exception
```

Script Explanation:

Line No.	Description
1	This environment variable opens up an output buffer of size limit of 200000.
2	Start of the declaration section of the block.
3	A local variable l_vc_status of varchar2 data type with a precision value of 30 bytes is declared.
4	A local variable odd_hours of exception data type is declared.
5	Start of the execution section of the block.
6	Start of the IF condition checking whether the system date's time is between 12 AM to 6 AM or 6 PM to 12 PM.
7	If the IF condition on the line 6 is satisfied, the odd_hours exception is raised using the raise statement.
8	If the IF condition on the line 6 is not satisfied, the program control is transferred into this else section.
9	The library package is called with the first input parameter as a book's name and the second output parameter returning the status of the package's execution assigning it to the local variable l_vc_status.

10	The local variable l_vc_status is printed using the dbms_output.put_line procedure.
11	End of the IF condition.
12	Start of the exception section of the block.
13	A when clause with the predefined exception odd_hours exception handler is defined.
14	An error message requesting the users to try again during the library hours is printed using the dbms_output.put_line procedure.
15,16	The error code (SQLCODE) and the error message (SQLERRM) values are printed using the dbms_output.put_line procedure.
17,18	End of the execution section of the block.

In the above example, the program runs into a user defined exception when a person tries to register a book in the library during the odd hours. By default, the user defined exceptions are mapped to an error code of value 1 and an error message of "User-defined Exception" which is printed in the above script's result section.

The exception is raised explicitly by using the RAISE command and is handled in the WHEN clause of the exception section identified by its name.

Exception Overriding

When a predefined exception name is used as a user defined exception, the local declaration will override the global declaration in the STANDARD package and the predefined exception will not be handled unless it is qualified with its package name STANDARD. Re-declaration of the predefined exceptions should be avoided to reduce unnecessary confusions in the code.

In the below example, the anonymous block has used the predefined exception NO_DATA_FOUND as its user defined exception name and has handled it in the exception section. Also, there is another WHEN clause to handle the predefined NO_DATA_FOUND exception which is qualified with its package name STANDARD.

```
1.  SET SERVEROUTPUT ON SIZE 200000
2.  DECLARE
3.  l_n_count NUMBER;
4.  l_vc_first_name employees.first_name%type;
5.  no_data_found EXCEPTION;
6.  BEGIN
7.  SELECT COUNT(*) INTO l_n_count FROM employees;
8.  IF l_n_count =0 THEN
9.  raise no_data_found;
10. END IF;
11. SELECT first_name
12. INTO l_vc_first_name
13. FROM employees
14. WHERE employee_id=:employee_id;
```

```
15. dbms_output.put_line('Total number of employees is '||l_n_count);
16. dbms_output.put_line('The name of the employee with the ID
    '||:employee_id||' is '||l_vc_first_name);
17. EXCEPTION
18. WHEN no_data_found THEN
19. dbms_output.put_line('There are no employees in the table!!');
20. WHEN standard.no_data_found THEN
21. dbms_output.put_line('No such employee found for the ID
    '||:employee_id);
22. END;
23. /
```

Script Explanation:

Line No.	Description
1	This environment variable opens up an output buffer of size limit of 200000.
2	Start of the declaration section of the block.
3	A local variable l_n_count of the number data type is declared.
4	A local anchored variable l_vc_first_name of a data type as that of the first_name column from the EMPLOYEES table is declared.
5	A local variable no_data_found of exception data type is declared.
6	Start of the execution section of the block.
7	The count of total employees from the EMPLOYEES table is assigned to the local variable l_n_count.
8	Start of the IF condition checking whether the local variable l_n_count is 0 or not.
9	If the IF condition in line 8 is satisfied, the user defined exception no_data_found is raised using the raise statement.
10	End of the IF statement.
11-14	The first_name column's value from the EMPLOYEES table for the input bind variable of the employee ID is assigned to the local variable l_vc_first_name.
15	The local variable l_n_count's variable holding the total number of employees from the EMPLOYEES table is printed using the dbms_output.put_line procedure.
16	The local variable l_vc_first_name holding the first name of the employee for the employee_id bind variable is printed using the dbms_output.put_line procedure.
17	Start of the exception section of the block.
18	A when clause handling the user defined exception no_data_found is defined.
19	A default message stating that there are no employees in the EMPLOYEES table is printed using the dbms_output.put_line procedure.
20	A when clause handling the predefined exception no_data_found qualified by its package name STANDARD is defined.
21	A default message stating that there is no such employee present for the employee ID bind variable is printed using the dbms_output.put_line procedure.
22,23	End of the execution section of the block.

Re-raising an Exception

An exception can be re-raised either to pass the control of the exception to the enclosing block or to log the error into a table and then raise it to an application or to a user. To re-raise an exception, the command RAISE has to be placed in the exception section after the logging of the information is done.

> 🔔 Note: The exception name can be optionally placed after the RAISE command.

In the below example, the exception ZERO_DIVIDE is logged into a table right before it is re-raised to the user or to the application.

```
1.   SET SERVEROUTPUT ON SIZE 200000
2.   DECLARE
3.   l_n_var1 NUMBER;
4.   BEGIN
5.   L_n_var1:= 1/0;
6.   EXCEPTION
7.   WHEN zero_divide THEN
8.   INSERT INTO log_table VALUES (log_seq.nextval,SQLCODE ||'
     '||sqlerrm);
9.   raise;
10.  END;
11.  /
```

Script Explanation:

Line No.	Description
1	This environment variable opens up an output buffer of size limit of 200000.
2	Start of the declaration section of the block.
3	A local variable l_n_var1 of the number data type is declared.
4	Start of the execution section of the block.
5	The integer 1 is divided by the integer 0 and is assigned to the variable l_n_var1.
6	Start of the exception section of the block.
7	A when clause handling the predefined exception zero_divide is defined.
8	The error code (SQLCODE) and the error message (SQLERRM) values are logged into a table.
9	The exception raise is re-raised using the RAISE statement.
10,11	End of the exception section of the block.

User Defined Unnamed Exceptions

The built in procedure RAISE_APPLICATION_ERROR in the DBMS_STANDARD package can be used for displaying the user defined error message and the error number whose range must be between -20000 to -20999. The exception raised by this procedure cannot be handled explicitly with a name as it does not have one and must be handled only through the OTHERS handler. Whenever this exception occurs, all the uncommitted transactions in the current session will be rolled back to its previous state.

> 🔔 Note: The error code of the predefined exceptions cannot be used in this procedure.

The prototype for defining this exception is shown below,

```
RAISE_APPLICATION_ERROR(<Error_code>, <Error_message> [, True | False]);
```

The first parameter mandatorily accepts an error code between the range of -20000 to -20999. The second parameter accepts a user defined error message of 2048 kb of string at most. The third parameter is an optional one which accepts a Boolean value. When True is passed as the third parameter, this error is added to the top of the list of all other errors which has occurred in this program unit during the execution. By default, it is False.

```
1.   CREATE OR REPLACE TRIGGER trg_emp_detail_chk
2.   Before UPDATE ON employees
3.   DECLARE
4.   permission_denied EXCEPTION;
5.   BEGIN
6.   IF trim(TO_CHAR(sysdate,'Day')) IN ('Saturday', 'Sunday') THEN
7.   raise_application_error(-20000, 'You are not authorized to do any
     modification in the weekends!!');
8.   END IF;
9.   END;
10. /
```

Script Explanation:

Line No.	Description
1	A trigger trg_emp_detail_chk is created.
2	The trigger timing is declared as BEFORE UPDATE on the EMPLOYEES table.
3	Start of the declare section of the trigger.
4	A local variable permission_denied of exception data type is declared.
5	Start of the execution section of the trigger.

6	Start of the IF condition checking whether the day of the system time is either Saturday or Sunday or not.
7	The procedure raise_application_error is called with the first parameter value as -20000 and the second parameter with a default text stating that the user is not authorized to do any modification in the weekends.
8	End of the IF statement.
9,10	End of the exception section of the block.

In the above example, a trigger has been created in the schema A to stop any modification to the EMPLOYEES table's data during the weekend. This trigger fires the user defined error message when the below UPDATE statement is executed during the weekend.

```
UPDATE employees SET salary=salary+1000 WHERE employee_id=100;
```

```
Error report:
SQL Error: ORA-20000: You are not authorized to do any modification in the
weekends!!
ORA-06512: at "A.TRG_EMP_DETAILL_CHK", line 4
ORA-04088: error during execution of trigger 'A.TRG_EMP_DETAILL_CHK'
20000. 00000 -  "%s"
*Cause:     The stored procedure 'raise_application_error'
            was called which causes this error to be generated.
*Action:    Correct the problem as described in the error message or contact
            the application administrator or DBA for more information.
```

Raising User Defined Exception with RAISE_APPLICATION_ERROR Procedure

The user defined exception can be combined with the RAISE_APPLICATION_ERROR procedure to result into an exception with a user defined name, user defined error code and a user defined message.

In the below example, the employee, whose salary is more than 10000 will be facing an exception which is handled explicitly in the WHEN clause using the user defined exception name. The result of the exception when an appropriate employee ID is passed to the bind variable is printed below.

```
1.  SET SERVEROUTPUT ON SIZE 200000
2.  DECLARE
3.  l_n_salary NUMBER;
4.  sal_high   EXCEPTION;
5.  pragma exception_init(sal_high,-20001);
6.  BEGIN
7.  SELECT salary INTO l_n_salary FROM employees WHERE
    employee_id=:employee_id;
8.  IF l_n_salary>10000 THEN
9.  raise_application_error(-20001,'Salary is high');
```

```
10. END IF;
11. EXCEPTION
12. WHEN sal_high THEN
13. dbms_output.put_line(SQLCODE);
14. dbms_output.put_line(sqlerrm);
15. END;
16. /
```

Result

```
-20001
ORA-20001: Salary is high
```

Script Explanation:

Line No.	Description
1	This environment variable opens up an output buffer of size limit of 200000.
2	Start of the declaration section of the block.
3	A local variable l_n_salary of the number data type is declared.
4	A local variable sal_high of exception data type is declared.
5	The pragma exception_init with the first parameter as the user defined exception sal_high and the second parameter -20001 is declared.
6	Start of the execution section of the block.
7	The salary of the employee from the EMPLOYEES table for the employee_id bind variable is assigned to the local variable l_n_salary.
8	Start of the IF statement checking if the local variable l_n_salary is greater than 10000 or not.
9	The procedure raise_application_error is called with the first parameter value as -20001 and the second parameter with a default text stating that the employee's salary is high.
10	End of the IF statement
11	Start of the exception section of the block.
12	A when clause handling the predefined exception sal_high is defined.
13,14	The error code (SQLCODE) and the error message (SQLERRM) values are printed using the dbms_output.put_line procedure.
15,16	End of the execution section of the block.

Retrieving an Error Message using the Error Code

The error message of an error code can be retrieved by passing it to the SQLERRM procedure as like below.

The error code -1403 is passed as an input to the SQLERRM procedure resulting in the appropriate error message as shown below,

---

```
BEGIN
  dbms_output.put_line(sqlerrm(-1403));
END;
```

Result:
ORA-01403: no data found

Tracking the Propagation of the Exceptions in PL/SQL Code

To find the exact position where the exception has occurred is always a tough job for the programmers to identify. To rectify this issue, a procedure FORMAT_ERROR_BACKTRACE in the DBMS_UTILITY package has been introduced in the Oracle version 10g. This procedure back traces the exception by propagating through the nested programs to bring in the exact route of the exception propagation.

In the below example, the predefined exception NO_DATA_FOUND has been explicitly raised to capture the error code using both SQLCODE and the back trace procedures.

```
BEGIN
  raise no_data_found;
EXCEPTION
WHEN OTHERS THEN
  dbms_output.put_line('Backtrace =>
'||dbms_utility.format_error_backtrace);
  dbms_output.put_line('SQLCODE => '||SQLCODE);
END;
/
```

Result:

Backtrace => ORA-06512: at line 2
SQLCODE => 100

The above result shows that the back trace procedure has produced the line number along with the ORA error code, whereas the SQLCODE procedure provided us with much less information.

After the failure of the SQLERRM procedure to truncate the error message more than 512 characters lead us to the creation of FORMAT_ERROR_STACK procedure of the utility package which allows us to print up to 2000 characters without any truncation. This utility procedure is very much advantageous during the RAISE_APPLICATION_ERROR call with the third optional parameter is set to True which stacks up the error messages.

DML Error Log Table

DML error logging is one of the major innovations in the release 10g R2 to trap the error prone data into an error log table for future analysis. This logging process is very much effective during the bulk SQL operations. This is similar to the SAVE EXCEPTIONS in the FORALL construct in PL/SQL which is introduced in the release 9i.

To start with this logging process, an error log table has to be created either automatically by using the CREATE_ERROR_LOG procedure in the DBMS_ERRLOG package with necessary parameters in place or manually by using the traditional DDL method of creating tables.

The automatic method of creating the error log table creates five default columns prefixed with ORA_ERR and the rest of the columns are added from the source table which are to be logged. The procedure accepts the first mandatory parameter with the source table name within quotes and the optional second parameter with the target error table name. If the second parameter is not provided, by default a table is created with its name prefixed with ERR$_ followed by the first 25 characters of the source table name.

In the below example, an error log table with a user suggested name is created for the EMPLOYEES table.

```
BEGIN
dbms_errlog.create_error_log(dml_table_name=>'EMPLOYEES',
err_log_table_name=>'EMPLOYEES_ERR_TAB');
END;
/
```

The manual method of creating the error log table provides more control over the source columns which are to be added in the target table whereas the automatic method duplicates all the supported columns unconditionally. Other than the source columns which are chosen by the user in the manual method, there are 5 mandatory columns which are to be added to the target table in any order and those are shown below,

```
CREATE TABLE err$_log_table
   (
    ora_err_number$ NUMBER, -- This column stores the Oracle error number.

    ora_err_mesg$ VARCHAR2(2000), -- This column stores the Oracle error
message.

    ora_err_rowid$ rowid, -- This column stores the row ID of the affected
column in case of update and delete else it stays Null.
```

```
    ora_err_optyp$ VARCHAR2(2), -- This column stores the type of operation.
I for insert, U for update and D for delete.

    ora_err_tag$   VARCHAR2(2000) - This column stores the optional tag
value supplied in the logging clause.
  );
```

The next step after the error log table is created is the logging of the errors. The prototype of the logging clause is shown below,

```
LOG ERRORS [INTO <User_defined_target_table_name>] [Tag_statement] [reject
limit <INTEGER | UNLIMITED>];
```

- The INTO clause is not mandatory if the table is created automatically using the inbuilt procedure or if the name is of the format ERR$_||SUBSTR(SOURCE_TABLE_NAME, 1, 25).

- The TAG_STATEMENT is a simple text which the user passes optionally for better readability of the error.

- The REJECT LIMIT clause is technically not mandatory. If it is not mentioned, by default the reject limit is 0 which fails the SQL even if one error occurs, similar to the traditional SQL operation.

- The limit can be an integer or UNLIMITED. This parameter defines the limit of errors by which the SQL statement should fail. If specified UNLIMITED, the SQL script never fails allowing unlimited errors to be logged.

In the below example, there are 3 SELECT queries with employee information which are combined together using the UNION set operator. The first SELECT query fails due to NULL email column value and the third SELECT query fails due to NULL hire date column value as these columns are not null in the EMPLOYEES table. The second SELECT query is the only compatible record for insertion into the EMPLOYEES table.

```
INSERT INTO employees
SELECT 207 employee_id,
   'Bruce' first_name,
   'Wayne' last_name,
   NULL email,
   '515.123.7181' phone_number,
   '13-June-2011' hire_date,
   'SH_CLERK' job_id,
   15000 salary,
   NULL commission_pct,
```

```
  101 manager_id,
  110 department_id
FROM dual
UNION
SELECT 208 employee_id,
  'Tony' first_name,
  'Stark' last_name,
  'TSTARK' email,
  '650.507.9922' phone_number,
  '13-June-2011' hire_date,
  'MK_MAN' job_id,
  25000 salary,
  NULL commission_pct,
  100 manager_id,
  20 department_id
FROM dual
UNION
SELECT 209 employee_id,
  'Clark' first_name,
  'Kent' last_name,
  'CKENT' email,
  '650.507.9923' phone_number,
  NULL hire_date,
  'AD_ASST' job_id,
  10000 salary,
  NULL commission_pct,
  101 manager_id,
  10 department_id
FROM dual log errors
INTO employees_err_tab reject limit unlimited;
```

```
1 rows inserted.
```

After the above INSERT script is executed, the script output states that 1 record has been inserted and the other 2 records are logged in the error table.

By issuing the below SELECT on the error log table, the failed rows can be verified, fixed and re-inserted into the database.

```
SELECT ora_err_number$,
  ora_err_mesg$,
  ora_err_rowid$,
  ora_err_optyp$,
  ora_err_tag$,
  employee_id,
  first_name,
  last_name
FROM employees_err_tab;
```

Query Result:

ORA_ ERR_ NUMB ER$	ORA_ERR_ MESG$	ORA _ERR _RO WID$	ORA _ERR _OPT YP$	ORA _ERR _TAG $	EMPLOY EE_ID	FIRST_NAME	LAST_NAME

| 1400 | "ORA-01400: cannot insert NULL into ("A"."EMPLOYEES"."EMAIL") | I | 207 | Bruce | Wayne |
| 1400 | "ORA-01400: cannot insert NULL into ("SYS"."EMPLOYEES"."HIRE_DATE") | I | 209 | Clark | Kent |

Errors Handled by DML Error Logging Table

1. Constraint violations like NOT NULL, UNIQUE, CHECK and REFERENTIAL.

2. Too large column values.

3. Trigger execution failures.

4. Type conversion errors.

5. Partition mapping errors.

6. "Unable to get a stable set of rows" error in MERGE.

Restrictions on DML Error Logging Table

1. Errors and constraint violations from Long, LOB, Object, Nested table columns cannot be handled.

2. Deferred constraints cannot be handled.

3. The direct path insert, merge or an update raising a unique constraint or an index violation cannot be handled.

PL/SQL Warnings

From the version 10g, Oracle allows us to capture the warnings generated by the compiler during a subprogram's compilation. These warnings are not that serious to raise a compilation error, but may result in a run time error or a performance degradation. Examples of PL/SQL warnings are,

1. Unreachable code in a program unit.

2. Using deprecated functionality.

3. A reserved keyword used as a variable name.

The warnings can be enabled or disabled by setting the database initialization parameter PLSQL_WARNINGS either by issuing an ALTER statement or by using the dedicated DBMS_WARNING package.

The scope of the warnings can be determined by executing the ALTER statement for either the SYSTEM or the SESSION level. In the DBMS_WARNING package, the procedure ADD_WARNING_SETTING_CAT is used for enabling or disabling a warning and has its third parameter dedicated for defining its scope.

The prototype for the ALTER statement to enable/ disable the warning is shown below,

```
ALTER <SESSION | SYSTEM > SET PLSQL_WARNINGS='[ENABLE | DISABLE | ERROR]:
[ALL | SEVERE | INFORMATIONAL | PERFORMANCE | WARNING_NUMBER]';
```

The prototype for the procedure ADD_WARNING_SETTING_CAT to enable/ disable the warning is shown below,

```
DBMS_WARNING.ADD_WARNING_SETTING_CAT (warning_category IN VARCHAR2,
warning_value IN VARCHAR2, scope IN VARCHAR2);
```

Qualifier Values/ Warning Values

1. **Enable**: Enable a specific or a set of warnings.

2. **Disable**: Disable a specific or a set of warnings.

3. **Error**: Treat a specific or a set of warnings as errors.

Modifier Values/ Warning Category

1. **All**: The warning messages in all categories are applied to the qualifier.

2. **Severe**: The warning messages in the severe category are applied to the qualifier.

3. **Informational**: The warning messages in the informational category are applied to the qualifier.

4. **Performance**: The warning messages in the performance category are applied to the qualifier.

Scope

1. **Session**: The changes made to the database initialization parameter are valid only for the particular session.

2. **System**: The changes made to the database initialization parameter are valid throughout the system across all sessions.

To view the current warning settings, the below PL/SQL script can be executed,

```
Exec DBMS_OUTPUT.PUT_LINE (DBMS_WARNING.GET_WARNING_SETTING_STRING());
```

```
Result:
ENABLE:ALL
```

Enabling/ Disabling a Warning

1. To enable all warning messages.

• System Level

```
ALTER SYSTEM SET plsql_warnings = 'enable:all';
```

```
Exec DBMS_WARNING.ADD_WARNING_SETTING_CAT ('Severe', 'Enable', 'System');
```

2. To enable severe performance warnings.

• Session Level

```
ALTER SESSION SET plsql_warnings = 'Enable:Severe', 'Enable:Performance';
```

```
1.   Exec DBMS_WARNING.ADD_WARNING_SETTING_CAT ('Performance', 'Enable',
     'Session');

2.   Exec DBMS_WARNING.ADD_WARNING_SETTING_CAT ('Severe', 'Enable',
     'Session');
```

3.   To enable all warnings and treat the performance warnings as errors.

• System Level

```
ALTER SYSTEM SET plsql_warnings = 'Enable:all', 'Error:Performance';
```

```
1.   Exec DBMS_WARNING.ADD_WARNING_SETTING_CAT ('All', 'Enable', 'System');

2.   Exec DBMS_WARNING.ADD_WARNING_SETTING_CAT ('Performance', 'Error',
     'System');
```

4.   To enable the unreachable code warning using its warning code.

• Session Level

```
ALTER SESSION SET plsql_warnings = 'Enable:06002';
```

```
Exec DBMS_WARNING.ADD_WARNING_SETTING_CAT ('06002', 'Enable', 'Session');
```

Warning Code Range

The warning codes are prefixed with 'PLW-'.

1.   The severe code is in the range of 05000 to 05999.

2.   The informational code is in the range of 06000 to 06999.

3.   The performance code is in the range of 07000 to 07249.

In the below example (Consider all the warnings have been enabled for the current session), the reserved keyword NAME has been used as a variable name which raises the below informational warning.

```
1.   CREATE OR REPLACE
2.   PROCEDURE proc_warning_test1
3.   IS
4.   name VARCHAR2(100):='Abdul Kalam';
5.   BEGIN
6.   DBMS_OUTPUT.PUT_LINE(name);
7.   END;
8.   /
```

```
PROCEDURE PROC_WARNING_TEST1 compiled
Warning: PLW-06010: keyword "NAME" used as a defined name
```

Script Explanation:

Line No.	Description
1,2	The procedure proc_warning_test1 is created.
3	Start of the declaration section of the procedure.
4	A local variable name of varchar2 data type with a precision of 100 bytes is declared and assigned to the name 'Abdul Kalam'.
5	Start of the execution section of the block.
6	The local variable name's is printed using the dbms_output.put_line procedure.
7,8	End of the execution section of the block.

In the below example (Consider all the warnings have been enabled for the current session), an informational warning is raised as a part of the code is un-reachable.

```
1.   CREATE OR REPLACE
2.   PROCEDURE proc_warning_test2
3.   IS
4.   L_B_VAR1 CONSTANT BOOLEAN:= TRUE;
5.   BEGIN
6.   IF l_b_var1 THEN
7.   DBMS_OUTPUT.PUT_LINE('The Boolean value is True');
8.   ELSE
9.   DBMS_OUTPUT.PUT_LINE('The Boolean value is False');
10.  END IF;
11.  END;
12.  /
```

```
PROCEDURE PROC_WARNING_TEST2 compiled
Warning: PLW-06002: Unreachable Code
```

Script Explanation:

Line No.	Description
1,2	The procedure proc_warning_test2 is created.
3	Start of the declaration section of the procedure.
4	A local variable l_b_var1 of the Boolean data type is declared and assigned to the value TRUE.

5	Start of the execution section of the block.
6	Start of the IF statement checking whether the local variable l_b_var1 is true or not.
7	If the condition of the IF statement in the line 6 is satisfied, the default text stating that the Boolean value as True is printed using the dbms_output.put_line procedure.
8	If the IF condition in the line 6 is not satisfied, the default text stating that the Boolean value as False is printed using the dbms_output.put_line procedure.
9	End of the IF statement.
10	End of the execution statement of the block.

After the warnings have been enabled using the ALTER statement or using the inbuilt package, the procedure for which the warning has to be verified has to be compiled if it already exists in the database as like below,

```
Alter procedure Proc_warning_test1 compile;
```

Once, after the procedure is compiled, the warnings raised for this procedure can be verified in the ERRORS data dictionary view with the attribute value set to WARNING as like below,

```
SELECT NAME,
  TYPE,
  LINE,
  TEXT,
  ATTRIBUTE,
  MESSAGE_NUMBER
FROM user_errors
WHERE name='PROC_WARNING_TEST1'
And attribute='WARNING';
```

Query Result:

NAME	TYPE	LINE	TEXT	ATTRIBUTE	MESSAGE _NUMBER
PROC_ WARNIN G_TEST 1	PROCEDURE	3	PLW-06010: keyword "NAME" used as a defined name	WARNING	6010

Summary

In this chapter, we have toured through the compilation errors and the run time errors, analyzing their characteristics, types, similarities and dissimilarities with various examples. In the next section, we have understood the DML error log table and have learnt what they are capable of along with their restrictions in handling errors few types of situations with appropriate examples. The last section explained us about the PL/SQL warnings and their different qualifier types, modifier types and scope types. We have also learnt the multiple ways in which a warning can be enabled and disabled along with suitable examples.

In the next chapter, we will be learning about the different types of PL/SQL data types and understand their characteristics, range of operation with supporting examples.

Character Sets and Data Types in PL/SQL

In this chapter, we will discuss character sets and data types in detail.

4. Introduction to Unicode and supplementary characters.

5. Different types of Unicode encodings.

6. Unicode support in Oracle along with the various Unicode types used in Oracle over the time.

7. Different types of data types in PL/SQL and their purpose, difference and performance analysis in details.

Introduction to Unicode

Unicode is a universal encoded character set that allows us to store characters from multiple languages. Unicode groups all the characters, irrespective of the program, language or the platform and assigns a unique code value to them for processing.

Supplementary Characters

The initial version of Unicode used 16 bits for encoding each character. By using 2 bytes for the encode process, a total of 65,536 characters only could be represented. This was not sufficient to represent all the characters in the world. To overcome this limitation, the supplementary characters were defined by the Unicode standard. The supplementary characters are the characters in the Unicode character set outside of the Basic Multilingual Plane (BMP). The Basic Multilingual Plane (BMP) consists of the first 65,536 characters in the Unicode character set and the rest are used by the supplementary characters.

Unicode Encodings

There are more than one Unicode encoding implementation standards based on the ways in which the characters are represented by the binary codes. Converting between

---

these standards can be done using a simple algorithm based bit wise operation. The different encoding schemes are described below.

UTF-8 Encoding

UTF-8 is an 8-bit variable width encoding methodology which is a strict superset of the 7-bit ASCII implementation. This means that all the characters from the 7-bit ASCII implementation is available in UTF-8 with the same code values. One Unicode character in this encoding method can be of either 8-bit, 16-bit, 24-bit or 32-bit. This encoding method is vastly used on the UNIX platforms, HTML and most of the internet browsers. The main advantage of UTF-8 encoding is the ease of migration as it is the same as that of the 7-bit ASCII method.

UCS-2 Encoding

This is a 16-bit fixed width encoding method, where each character is 16-bit in size regardless of the language. UCS-2 can encode characters defined up to Unicode standard 3.0 only, so there is no possibility of adding any supplementary characters additionally. The main advantage of this encoding method is the faster processing of string as all characters are of the same size.

UTF-16 Encoding

UTF-16 is a 16-bit variable width encoding of Unicode. This is basically an extension of the UCS-2 method, providing support for supplementary character's addition which are defined in the Unicode 3.1.

One character can be of either 16-bit or 32-bit in this encoding and the supplementary characters are represented in 32-bit. The main advantage of this encoding method is the memory consumption, most of the Asian characters stored in this method is about 16-bit in size, whereas UTF-8 occupied a minimum of 24-bit for the same character storage.

Oracle Unicode Support

Unicode was accepted and implemented in Oracle starting from the version 7. From then on, there were many series of migrations in the encoding methods resulting in a character set with the support of most of the characters used in the world.

The Oracle naming convention for its character set is shown below.

```
<Language> <Bit size> <Encoding method>
```

The encoding methods used in Oracle are explained below.

AL24UTF-FSS

This was the first Unicode character set supported by Oracle in the version 7.2 as a database character set. This is an acronym for AL – All languages, 24- Bit size, UTF-FSS – encoding scheme. This followed the UTF-8 encoding methodology in the Unicode standard 1.1 which is unsupported in the Oracle version 9i. The migration of the existing AL24UTF-FSS is to upgrade to UTF8 prior to the version 9i migration.

UTF8

This was the UTF-8 encoded character set in the Oracle version 8 and 8i and it did not follow the Oracle naming convention for the Unicode characters. UTF8 followed the Unicode version of 2.1 between the versions 8.0 and 8.1.6, and was upgraded to the version of 3.0 during 8.1.7 and 9i. Even though the specific supplementary characters were not assigned in the version 3.0, their allocation were already done so that they don't corrupt the actual data inside the database when they are migrated to the version 3.1.

UTFE

This is the UTF8 database character set for the Extended Binary Coded Decimal Interchange Code (EBCDIC) platforms, which is an 8-bit character encoding mainly used on IBM mainframe and IBM midrange computer operating systems.

AL32UTF-8

This is the UTF-8 encoded character set introduced in the Oracle version 9i and continues till 12c as the database character set. This database character set supports the latest version of the Unicode standard with the support for the newly defined supplementary characters which are stored in 32-bit. The database character set supports CHAR, VARCHAR2, CLOB and LONG data types. This does not support the national character set.

AL16UTF-16

This is the UTF-16 encoded character set introduced in the Oracle version 9i and continues till 12c as the national character set. The national character determines the set of SQL data types such as NCHAR, NVARCHAR2 and NCLOB. This does not support the database character set.

Character Set Data Dictionary Objects

1. **NLS_SESSION_PARAMETERS** view shows the NLS parameters and their values for the particular session and it does not display any information on character set.

2. **NLS_INSTANCE_PARAMETERS** view shows the current NLS instance parameters that have been explicitly set and their parameter values.

3. **NLS_DATABASE_PARAMETERS** view shows the values of the NLS parameters of the database which are created during the database creation.

The Character Set Migration Prerequisites

The prototype for changing the database's character set is shown below,

```
Alter database [database_name] character set <New_character_set>;
```

> 🔔 Note: The character set can only be changed at the database level and not at the session level.

The character set migration can be performed using the CSALTER script which is present as an inbuilt utility in the database character set scanner and this can be used only if all the schema data are a subset of the new character set. The new character set is a superset of the current character set if all the characters in the database are present in the new character set with the same code point value.

Introduction to PL/SQL Data types

Data type acts as a place holder for the data and determines the limit, format and the range of the data we deal with. A data of a certain type cannot be placed in an unmatched data type, for e.g., A string data cannot be placed in a NUMBER data type. The figure Fig 3.1 depicts the relationship between the data and its data type.

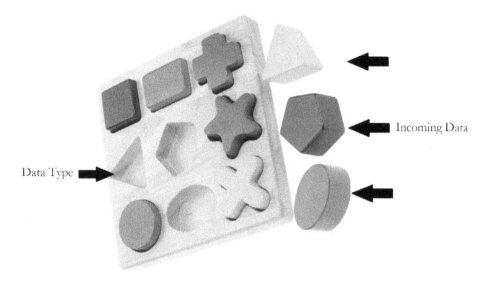

Data Type

Incoming Data

Fig 3.1. Relationship between Data and Data type

There are four different types of data types in PL/SQL and they are explained below,

PL/SQL Scalar Data Types

The scalar data type is a linear atomic type with no variable components in it and holds a single literal value.

A subtype on the other hand is a derived form of the base type with an optional constraint on it. These can be either constrained or unconstrained.

There are four predefined scalar data types as explained below.

PL/SQL Numeric Data Types

PL/SQL supports an increasing variety of numeric data types for the mathematical calculation purposes. The different numeric data types are described below.

Number

This is the super-type for all the numeric data types available in PL/SQL. This stores positive, negative, zero and floating point numbers. This is an internal data type used by the system, thus, it is slower than the other numeric types. As the number data type

---

is commonly available in other languages and as it is an internal type in Oracle, this is extremely portable at the cost of performance.

The prototype for the number data type is shown below,

```
Number [(precision [, scale])]
```

For an integer, the scale is zero, meaning that there is no decimal point value allowed and the precision ranges between 1 and 38, e.g.,

```
Number (5)
```

For a floating point number, the scale ranges between -84 and 127 with a default 0. E.g.,

```
Number (2,3)
```

Predefined Subtypes of Number Data Type

1. **Integer/ Int/ Smallint:** These are internal data types as like the Number data type, but with an extra constraint of scale value as 0. This is similar to Number (38,0). This type is much slower than the Number data type as it has an extra constraint imposed on it.

2. **Numeric/ Decimal/ Dec:** These are the same as Number data type, but with a fixed precision of 38 and a scale value of 0. This constraint can be changed by issuing a user defined precision and a scale of Number data type's range.

   E.g., Numeric = Number (38,0) and Numeric (29,3) = Number (29,3).

3. **Double Precision/ Float:** These are floating point number data type with a maximum of 126 digits (Rounded off to 38 digits).

   E.g., Double Precision = Float (126) and Float = Float (126).

4. **Real**: These are floating point number data type with a maximum of 63 digits (Rounded off to 18 digits).

   E.g., Real = Float (63).

PLS_INTEGER/ BINARY_INTEGER

After 10g, both PLS_INTEGER and BINARY_INTEGER shares the same characteristics and are synonymous to each other. These data types store data in a hardware arithmetic format and are much faster in performance and occupies less storage space compared to a number data type and its subtypes which uses the library arithmetic method of storage. As these follow the hardware format, these are less likely to be ported to other systems.

> 🔔 Note: Use PLS_INTEGER/ BINARY_INTEGER data types, while performing more calculations for better performance.

These data types have a range of -2,147,483,648 through +2,147,483,647. When a calculation involving these data types crosses their range during run time, they raise an overflow exception as like below.

```
DECLARE
  l_bi_var1 binary_integer:=2147483647;
BEGIN
  l_bi_var1:=l_bi_var1+1;
  dbms_output.put_line(l_bi_var1);
END;
/
```

```
Error report:
ORA-01426: numeric overflow
ORA-06512: at line 4
01426. 00000 -  "numeric overflow"
*Cause:    Evaluation of an value expression causes an overflow/underflow.
*Action:   Reduce the operands.
```

Predefined Subtypes of Number Data Type

> 🔔 Note: These data types raise a VALUE ERROR when it is assigned with values out of their range during the compile time and NUMERIC OVERFLOW when it is assigned with the values out of their range during the run time.

1. **Signtype:** It uses the values -1, 0, 1 and Null from the PLS_INTEGER datatype.

2. **Natural**: This type uses the non-negative values of the PLS_INTEGER range. i.e., 0 to +2,147,483,647 and Null.

3. **NaturalN**: This has the similar range as that of the Natural data type, but with an additional not null constraint imposed on it.

4. **Positive**: This type uses the non-negative, non-zero values of the PLS_INTEGER range. i.e., 1 to +2,147,483,647 and Null values.

5. **PositiveN**: This has the similar range as that of the Positive data type, but with an additional not null constraint imposed on it.

6. SIMPLE_INTEGER

This subtype was introduced in Oracle version 11g. This data type has the same range as that of the PLS_INTEGER data type, but with an additional NOT NULL constraint on it. SIMPLE_INTEGER also checks for the overflow when the value assigned to this data type is out of its range during the compile time but not during the run time.

This type tends to perform more than PLS_INTEGER when the PLSQL_CODE_TYPE is set to NATIVE as the computations are done directly through the hardware. When the PLSQL_CODE_TYPE is set to INTERPRETED, the performance gain is minimal.

The below example depicts the nature of the SIMPLE_INTEGER data type when an out of range value is assigned to it during the compile time raising a compilation error.

```
DECLARE
  l_si_var1 simple_integer:=2147483648;
BEGIN
  NULL;
END;
/
```

```
Error report:
ORA-01426: numeric overflow
ORA-06512: at line 2
01426. 00000 -  "numeric overflow"
*Cause:    Evaluation of an value expression causes an overflow/underflow.
*Action:   Reduce the operands.
```

In the below example, the SIMPLE_INTEGER data type is assigned with the positive extreme value in the range during the compile time and is summed up with a positive integer to produce an out of range value which does not throw any error, but results the sum value with a negative sign (l_si_var1+1 at line 4 is converted to -(l_si_var1+1)).

```
DECLARE
l_si_var1 simple_integer:=+2147483647;
BEGIN
l_si_var1:=l_si_var1+1;
dbms_output.put_line('The result of the sum is '||l_si_var1);
END;
/
```

Result:
The result of the sum is -2147483648

In the below example, the SIMPLE_INTEGER data type is assigned with the negative extreme value in the range during the compile time and is subtracted with an integer to produce an out of range value which does not throw any error, but results the value with a negative sign (l_si_var1-1 at line 4 is converted to abs(l_si_var1)-1).

```
DECLARE
l_si_var1 simple_integer:=-2147483648;
BEGIN
l_si_var1:=l_si_var1-1;
dbms_output.put_line('The result of the subtraction is '||l_si_var1);
END;
/
```

Result:
The result of the subtraction is 2147483647

BINARY_FLOAT and BINARY_DOUBLE

These data types are introduced in the Oracle version 10g and they use the machine arithmetic format unlike the Number data type. These do not accept any precision to it as they use binary precision and not decimal precision. BINARY_FLOAT is a 32-bit, single precision, IEEE-754 floating point format, whereas, BINARY_DOUBLE is a 64-bit, single precision, IEEE-754 floating point format.

 Note: Use these data types for calculations involving large numerical computations.

These support a greater range of numbers represented either larger or smaller and uses less memory space for storage compared to the Number data type. These do not raise any overflow or underflow errors, thus the use of these data types must be made under caution.

Predefined Subtypes of Number Data Type

1. **SIMPLE_FLOAT**: This is the subtype of BINARY_FLOAT data type with the same range as that of its super type, but with an additional NOT NULL constraint imposed upon it.

2. **SIMPLE_DOUBLE**: This is the subtype of BINARY_DOUBLE data type with the same range as that of its super type, but with an additional NOT NULL constraint imposed upon it.

These data types tend to produce better performance than their super types when the PLSQL_CODE_TYPE is set to NATIVE as the mathematical calculations are performed directly in the hardware. The performance improvement is less when the PLSQL_CODE_TYPE is set to INTERPRETED mode.

Performance Comparison between Numeric Data Type

The below code compares the multiple numeric data types and displays the time duration consumed by them individually for different PLSQL_CODE_TYPE parameters.

```
1.  SET serveroutput ON 20000
2.  DECLARE
3.  l_n_var1 NUMBER            := 0;
4.  l_i_var2 INTEGER           := 0;
5.  l_pi_var3 pls_integer      := 0;
6.  l_bi_var4 binary_integer   := 0;
7.  l_si_var5 simple_integer   := 0;
8.  l_n_loop_counter NUMBER    := 100000000;
9.  l_n_start_time    NUMBER;
10. BEGIN
11. /*Number data type*/
12. l_n_start_time := dbms_utility.get_time;
13. FOR loop_counter IN 1 .. l_n_loop_counter
14. LOOP
15. l_n_var1 := l_n_var1 + l_n_var1;
16. END LOOP;
17. dbms_output.put_line('Time duration taken by Number data type : ' ||
    (dbms_utility.get_time - l_n_start_time)/100 || ' seconds');
18. /*Integer data type*/
19. l_n_start_time := dbms_utility.get_time;
20. FOR loop_counter IN 1 .. l_n_loop_counter
21. LOOP
22. l_i_var2 := l_i_var2 + l_i_var2;
23. END LOOP;
24. dbms_output.put_line('Time duration taken by Integer data type : '
    || (dbms_utility.get_time - l_n_start_time)/100 || ' seconds');
25. /*PLS_INTEGER data type*/
26. l_n_start_time := dbms_utility.get_time;
27. FOR loop_counter IN 1 .. l_n_loop_counter
```

```
28. LOOP
29. l_pi_var3 := l_pi_var3 + l_pi_var3;
30. END LOOP;
31. dbms_output.put_line('Time duration taken by PLS_INTEGER data type :
    ' || (dbms_utility.get_time - l_n_start_time)/100 || ' seconds');
32. /*BINARY_INTEGER data type*/
33. l_n_start_time := dbms_utility.get_time;
34. FOR loop_counter IN 1 .. l_n_loop_counter
35. LOOP
36. l_bi_var4 := l_bi_var4 + l_bi_var4;
37. END LOOP;
38. dbms_output.put_line('Time duration taken by BINARY_INTEGER data
    type : ' || (dbms_utility.get_time - l_n_start_time)/100 || '
    seconds');
39. /*SIMPLE_INTEGER data type*/
40. l_n_start_time := dbms_utility.get_time;
41. FOR loop_counter IN 1 .. l_n_loop_counter
42. LOOP
43. l_si_var5 := l_si_var5 + l_si_var5;
44. END LOOP;
45. dbms_output.put_line('Time duration taken by SIMPLE_INTEGER data
    type : ' || (dbms_utility.get_time - l_n_start_time)/100 || '
    seconds');
46. END;
47. /
```

Result in INTERPRETED mode:
```
Time duration taken by Number data type : 11.2 seconds
Time duration taken by Integer data type : 15.89 seconds
Time duration taken by PLS_INTEGER data type : 7.05 seconds
Time duration taken by BINARY_INTEGER data type : 6.94 seconds
Time duration taken by SIMPLE_INTEGER data type : 6.81 seconds
```

Result in NATIVE mode:
```
Time duration taken by Number data type : 11 seconds
Time duration taken by Integer data type : 15.26 seconds
Time duration taken by PLS_INTEGER data type : 6.85 seconds
Time duration taken by BINARY_INTEGER data type : 6.88 seconds
Time duration taken by SIMPLE_INTEGER data type : 6.69 seconds
```

Script Explanation

Line No.	Description
1	This environment variable opens up an output buffer of size limit of 200000.
2	Start of the declaration section of the block.
3-7	Five variables of data type Number, Integer, PLS_INTEGER, BINARY_INTEGER, SIMPLE_INTEGER are created and defaulted to 0 respectively.
8	A local variable l_n_loop_counter of Number type for the loop counter value is declared and defaulted to 100000000.
9	A local variable l_n_start_time of Number type is declared for capturing the time in hsecs.
10	Start of the execution section of the block.
11	The performance validation of the Number data type starts.

Introduction to PL/SQL Data types

12	The time in hsecs from the utility function, dbms_utility.get_time is assigned to the variable l_n_start_time.
13,14	Start of the FOR loop with the range 1..100000000.
15	The variable l_n_var1 is summed up with itself and then assigned to itself over the loop counter range to check its performance.
16	End of the FOR loop.
17	The time taken by the variable of Number type is calculated by finding the difference between the current time in hsecs and the start time captured in the variable l_n_start_time and dividing it by 100 to find the result in seconds is printed using the procedure dbms_output.put_line.
18	The performance validation of the Integer data type starts.
19-24	Steps 12-17 is repeated for the Integer variable.
25	The performance validation of the PLS_INTEGER data type starts.
26-31	Steps 12-17 is repeated for the PLS_INTEGER variable.
32	The performance validation of the BINARY_INTEGER data type starts.
33-38	Steps 12-17 is repeated for the BINARY_INTEGER variable.
39	The performance validation of the SIMPLE_INTEGER data type starts.
40-45	Steps 12-17 is repeated for the SIMPLE_INTEGER variable.
46,47	End of the execution section of the block.

In the below snippet, the multiple real data types are compared and their time duration is individually calculated and displayed for different PLSQL_CODE_TYPE parameters.

```
1.  SET serveroutput ON 20000
2.  DECLARE
3.  l_n_var1 DECIMAL          := 0.1;
4.  l_f_var2 FLOAT            := 0.1;
5.  l_r_var3 REAL             := 0.1;
6.  l_bf_var4 binary_float   := 0.1;
7.  l_bd_var5 binary_double  := 0.1;
8.  l_n_loop_counter NUMBER := 100000000;
9.  l_n_start_time   NUMBER;
10. BEGIN
11. /*Decimal data type*/
12. l_n_start_time := dbms_utility.get_time;
13. FOR loop_counter IN 1 .. l_n_loop_counter
14. LOOP
15. l_n_var1 := l_n_var1 + l_n_var1;
16. END LOOP;
17. dbms_output.put_line('Time duration taken by Decimal data type : '
     || (dbms_utility.get_time - l_n_start_time)/100 || ' seconds');
18. /*Float data type*/
19. l_n_start_time := dbms_utility.get_time;
20. FOR loop_counter IN 1 .. l_n_loop_counter
21. LOOP
22. l_f_var2 := l_f_var2 + l_f_var2;
23. END LOOP;
```

```
24. dbms_output.put_line('Time duration taken by Float data type : ' ||
    (dbms_utility.get_time - l_n_start_time)/100 || ' seconds');
25. /*Real data type*/
26. l_n_start_time := dbms_utility.get_time;
27. FOR loop_counter IN 1 .. l_n_loop_counter
28. LOOP
29. l_r_var3 := l_r_var3 + l_r_var3;
30. END LOOP;
31. dbms_output.put_line('Time duration taken by Real data type : ' ||
    (dbms_utility.get_time - l_n_start_time)/100 || ' seconds');
32. /*BINARY_FLOAT data type*/
33. l_n_start_time := dbms_utility.get_time;
34. FOR loop_counter IN 1 .. l_n_loop_counter
35. LOOP
36. l_bf_var4 := l_bf_var4 + l_bf_var4;
37. END LOOP;
38. dbms_output.put_line('Time duration taken by BINARY_FLOAT data type
    : ' || (dbms_utility.get_time - l_n_start_time)/100 || ' seconds');
39. /*BINARY_DOUBLE data type*/
40. l_n_start_time := dbms_utility.get_time;
41. FOR loop_counter IN 1 .. l_n_loop_counter
42. LOOP
43. l_bd_var5 := l_bd_var5 + l_bd_var5;
44. END LOOP;
45. dbms_output.put_line('Time duration taken by BINARY_DOUBLE data type
    : ' || (dbms_utility.get_time - l_n_start_time)/100 || ' seconds');
46. END;
47. /
```

Result in INTERPRETED mode:
```
Time duration taken by Decimal data type : 15.21 seconds
Time duration taken by Float data type : 10.01 seconds
Time duration taken by Real data type : 10.14 seconds
Time duration taken by BINARY_FLOAT data type : 7.51 seconds
Time duration taken by BINARY_DOUBLE data type : 8.33 seconds
```

Result in NATIVE mode:
```
Time duration taken by Decimal data type : 15.2 seconds
Time duration taken by Float data type : 10 seconds
Time duration taken by Real data type : 9.98 seconds
Time duration taken by BINARY_FLOAT data type : 7.53 seconds
Time duration taken by BINARY_DOUBLE data type : 8.35 seconds
```

Script Explanation

Line No.	Description
1	This environment variable opens up an output buffer of size limit of 200000.
2	Start of the declaration section of the block.
3-7	Five variables of data type Decimal, Float, Real, Binary_float, Binary_double are created and defaulted to 0.1 respectively.
8	A local variable l_n_loop_counter of Number type for the loop counter value is declared and defaulted to 100000000.
9	A local variable l_n_start_time of Number type is declared for capturing the time in hsecs.

10	Start of the execution section of the block.
11	The performance validation of the Decimal data type starts.
12	The time in hsecs from the utility function, dbms_utility.get_time is assigned to the variable l_n_start_time.
13,14	Start of the FOR loop with the range 1..100000000.
15	The variable l_n_var1 is summed up with itself and then assigned to itself over the loop counter range to check its performance.
16	End of the FOR loop.
17	The time taken by the variable of Number type is calculated by finding the difference between the current time in hsecs and the start time captured in the variable l_n_start_time and dividing it by 100 to find the result in seconds is printed using the procedure dbms_output.put_line.
18	The performance validation of the Float data type starts.
19-24	Steps 12-17 is repeated for the Float variable.
25	The performance validation of the REAL data type starts.
26-31	Steps 12-17 is repeated for the REAL variable.
32	The performance validation of the BINARY_FLOAT data type starts.
33-38	Steps 12-17 is repeated for the BINARY_FLOAT variable.
39	The performance validation of the BINARY_DOUBLE data type starts.
40-45	Steps 12-17 is repeated for the BINARY_DOUBLE variable.
46,47	End of the execution section of the block.

User Defined Subtypes

From the Oracle version 7.1, the system allows us to create a special data type called as subtypes over the existing predefined or user defined data types. A subtype does not create a new data type rather a derived formed by the base type. A subtype may or may not constrain the values allowed by the base data type.

The prototype for declaring a subtype is shown below,

```
Subtype <Subtype_name> IS <Base_type> [RANGE <Start_value>..<End_value>]
[NOT NULL];
```

Constrained Subtype

A constrained subtype restricts the values normally allowed by its base type. In the below example, a subtype is created using the BINARY_INTEGER data type, but with the restriction on the values allowed by using the range keyword. When the variable is assigned with a value outside its range, the unit fails with a VALUE_ERROR as shown below.

Advanced PL/SQL Programming

```
1.  SET SERVEROUTPUT ON SIZE 200000;
2.  DECLARE
3.  subtype constrained_bi
4.  IS
5.  binary_integer range 1..10;
6.  l_cbi_var1 constrained_bi;
7.  BEGIN
8.  l_cbi_var1:=:value;
9.  dbms_output.put_line(l_cbi_var1);
10. END;
11. /
```

1. When the bind value is 10.

```
Result:
10
```

2. When the bind value is 11.

```
Error report:
ORA-06502: PL/SQL: numeric or value error
ORA-06512: at line 7
06502. 00000 -  "PL/SQL: numeric or value error%s"
*Cause:
*Action:
```

Script Explanation

Line No.	Description
1	This environment variable opens up an output buffer of size limit of 200000.
2	Start of the declare section of the block.
3,4,5	A subtype Constrained_bi is declared by Binary_integer type with a range of 1 to 10.
6	A local variable l_cbi_var1 is declared with Constrained_bi subtype.
7	Start of the execution section of the block.
8	The variable l_cbi_var1 is assigned with a bind value.
9	The variable l_cbi_var1 is printed using the procedure dbms_output.put_line.
10,11	End of the execution section of the block.

In the below example, a NOT NULL constraint is imposed on the number data type to make sure no null values are assigned to the variable.

```
1.  SET SERVEROUTPUT ON SIZE 200000;
2.  DECLARE
3.  subtype notnullnum IS NUMBER NOT NULL;
4.  l_nnn_var1 notnullnum:=:value;
5.  BEGIN
6.  dbms_output.put_line(l_nnn_var1);
7.  END;
8.  /
```

Introduction to PL/SQL Data types

1. When the bind value is 5.

```
Result:
5
```

2. When the bind value is Null.

```
Error report:
ORA-06502: PL/SQL: numeric or value error
ORA-06512: at line 3
06502. 00000 -  "PL/SQL: numeric or value error%s"
*Cause:
*Action:
```

Script Explanation

Line No.	Description
1	This environment variable opens up an output buffer of size limit of 200000.
2	Start of the declare section of the block.
3	A subtype NOTNULLNUM is declared of Number type with a NOT NULL constraint.
4	A local variable l_nnn_var1 is declared with NOTNULLNUM subtype and is assigned to a bind variable.
5	Start of the execution section of the block.
6	The variable l_nnn_var1 is printed using the procedure dbms_output.put_line.
7,8	End of the execution section of the block.

Unconstrained Subtype

Unconstrained subtypes on the other hand is a mere change of name for the base type to enhance the readability and flexibility in the applications.

In the below example, three data types created specifically for name, address and description with appropriate precision to improve readability and better usage of the data types.

```
1.  SET SERVEROUTPUT ON SIZE 200000;
2.  DECLARE
3.  subtype Name_dt IS    VARCHAR2(15);
4.  subtype address_dt IS VARCHAR2(100);
5.  subtype desc_dt IS    VARCHAR2(500);
6.  l_ndt_first_name name_dt;
7.  l_ndt_last_name name_dt;
8.  l_adt_address address_dt;
9.  l_ddt_description desc_dt;
10. BEGIN
11. l_ndt_first_name :='Randy';
```

```
12. l_ndt_last_name   :='Orton';
13. l_adt_address     :='Suite 512 - Park town, New Jersey - 5134, USA';
14. l_ddt_description:='Oracle PL/SQL developer with 5 years of experience
    in banking domain...';
15. END;
16. /
```

Script Explanation

Line No.	Description
1	This environment variable opens up an output buffer of size limit of 200000.
2	Start of the declare section of the block.
3	A subtype Name_dt is declared by Varchar2 data type with a precision of 15.
4	A subtype Address_dt is declared by Varchar2 data type with a precision of 100.
5	A subtype Desc_dt is declared by Varchar2 data type with a precision of 500.
6,7	The local variables l_ndt_first_name and l_ndt_last_name are declared with the subtype Name_dt.
8	The local variable l_adt_address is declared with the subtype Address_dt.
9	The local variable l_ddt_description is declared with the subtype desc_dt.
10	Start of the execution section of the block.
11,12	The local variables l_ndt_first_name and l_ndt_last_name are assigned with a random first name and last name.
13	The local variable l_adt_address is assigned to a random address.
14	The local variable l_ddt_description is assigned with a random description.
15,16	End of the execution section of the block.

PL/SQL Character Data Types

The variables assigned with character data types are also called as free-form variables which are capable of storing alphabets, numbers and special characters. There are different types of character data types serving multiple purposes and they are explained below.

Char

The Char data type is used for storing fixed length character strings. When this data type is declared, a maximum length for storing the characters has to be specified, which can range between 1 and 32,767. If there is no precision is defined in its declaration, the maximum length will be defaulted to 1. The precision of the data type can be either in characters or bytes depending on the NLS_LENGTH_SEMANTICS initialization parameter in the character set which is defined during the database creation. Either the precision is in characters or in bytes, the maximum range limit will be always 32,767.

The prototype for declaring the Char data type is shown below,

```
Char [Maximum_range [CHAR | BYTE]];
```

This datatype has a subtype CHARACTER which is currently synonymous with its base type.

When the characters assigned to the char variable are more than its defined maximum range, the unit fails with a VALUE_ERROR.

When the characters assigned to the char variable are less than its defined maximum range, the remaining range is right padded with empty spaces to fill them up to its maximum defined range.

In the below example, a variable with Char data type is assigned to a string of length 4 with no extra spaces to it. But when it is printed out from the assigned variable, it has extra 6 spaces assigned to it internally and its length is equal to its maximum length defined in the declaration.

```
DECLARE
  l_c_var1 CHAR(10):='Hello';
BEGIN
  dbms_output.put_line('The string is '''||l_c_var1||'''');
  dbms_output.put_line('The length of the string is '||LENGTH(l_c_var1));
END;
/
```

```
Result:
The string is 'Hello     '
The length of the string is 10
```

Varchar2

The Varchar2 data type is used for storing variable length character strings. It is exactly similar to Char except for the fact that it will not append any extra spaces to fill the left out area to meet its maximum defined range. Unlike Char, a mandatory maximum precision is required during its declaration. The range of Varchar2 data type is 1 to 32,767 similar to the Char type. When the characters assigned to this data type assigned variable is more than its defined maximum range, the unit fails with a VALUE_ERROR.

This data type has a subtype VARCHAR, which is currently synonymous with its base type. This data type is meant only for backward compatibility and is advised not to be used in the future as it is deprecated.

The prototype for declaring the Varchar2 data type is shown below,

```
Varchar2 <Maximum_range [CHAR | BYTE] >;
```

RAW

The Raw datatype is used for storing binary data, also called as raw data such as an image file. The Raw data type has a range of 1 to 32,767 and a mandatory precision definition is required during its declaration just like Varchar2 type. The only difference between these two types is that the system will not try to interpret or perform any character set conversion on the data stored in this format.

The prototype for declaring the RAW data type is shown below,

```
Raw <Maximum_range [CHAR | BYTE] >;
```

Long

The Long data type is used for storing variable length character strings like texts, images and short documents. It is a subtype of the Varchar2 data type with a range of 1 to 32,760.

> Note: The Long data type is currently made available only for backward compatibility to support the existing applications. In the future, kindly make use of a CLOB or NCLOB instead of this data type.

The prototype for declaring the Long data type is shown below,

```
Long [Maximum_range [CHAR | BYTE]];
```

Long RAW

The Long RAW data type is identical to the Long type except for the fact that the Oracle system will not try to interpret or perform any character set conversion on the data stored in this type.

The prototype for declaring the Long RAW data type is shown below,

```
Long Raw [Maximum_range [CHAR | BYTE]];
```

NLS Character Types

The 8-bit ASCII character set is not enough for representing characters from different languages as they require more than one byte to represent a single character. Oracle introduced National Language Support (NLS) for manipulating single byte or multiple byte data using the database character set and national language support respectively.

PL/SQL has two data types for handling NLS data and they are,

NChar

The NChar data type has the same properties of that of the Char type but supports foreign language characters. When the NLS character set is a fixed-width character set, then the maximum range indicates the length in characters and when the NLS character is a variable-width character set, then the maximum range indicates the length in bytes.

The data can be transferred from Char data type to NChar data type without any loss, but the vice versa could result in some data loss if the character set of Char data type does not have the characters which are present in the NChar type variable.

The prototype for declaring the NChar data type is shown below,

```
NChar [Maximum_range [CHAR | BYTE]];
```

NVarchar2

The NVarchar2 data type has the same properties of that of the Varchar2 type but supports foreign language characters. When the NLS character set is a fixed-width character set, then the maximum range indicates the length in characters and when the NLS character is a variable-width character set, then the maximum range indicates the length in bytes.

The data can be transferred from Varchar2 data type to NVarchar2 data type without any loss, but the vice versa could result in some data loss if the character set of Varchar2 data type does not have the characters which are present in the NVarchar2 type variable.

The prototype for declaring the NVarchar2 data type is shown below,

```
NVarchar2 <Maximum_range [CHAR | BYTE]>;
```

RowID and URowID

The physical storage location of a row can be identified with the help of the value of the pseudo column RowID present in its table. The RowID stores the address of the particular row from a table. The RowID data type stores only physical address, whereas the URowID (Universal RowID) data type can store physical, logical and foreign RowIDs.

 Note: RowID is available only for backward compatibility. In the future, please use URowID.

PL/SQL Boolean Data Type

The Boolean data type in PL/SQL allows us to store True, False and Null values which help us in processing the logical states of a program unit.

This data type is only available in PL/SQL and not in SQL, thus using Boolean values in an SQL statement has always been impossible until Oracle version 12cR1.

Boolean Enhancements in 12cR1

In the below example, a function has been created with an input variable of type Boolean returning a Varchar2 result describing the input parameter value in a string format.

```
1.   CREATE OR REPLACE
2.   FUNCTION func_boo(
3.   ip_b_var1 BOOLEAN)
4.   RETURN VARCHAR2
5.   IS
6.   BEGIN
7.   RETURN
8.   CASE
9.   WHEN ip_b_var1 THEN
10.  'True'
11.  WHEN NOT ip_b_var1 THEN
12.  'False'
13.  ELSE
14.  'Null'
15.  END;
16.  END;
17.  /
```

Script Explanation

Line No.	Description
1,2,3	The function func_boo is created with one input parameter ip_b_var1 of the Boolean data type.
4	The return type of the function is declared as Varchar2.
5	Start of the declaration section of the function.
6	Start of the execution section of the function.
7-15	The Return statement is placed for returning the text 'True' when the Boolean value True is passed as the input parameter, 'False' when the Boolean value False is passed as the input parameter or 'Null' when the Boolean value Null is passed as the input parameter to the function using a CASE statement.
16,17	End of the execution section of the function.

This function cannot be invoked through an SQL statement as the input parameter's data type is not supported by SQL. Thus the below method has been used until R12.1 version for these situations.

> Note: This function cannot be used in an SQL statement when its return type is a Boolean.

```
1.  SET SERVEROUTPUT ON SIZE 200000;
2.  DECLARE
3.  L_vc_var1 VARCHAR2(10);
4.  L_b_var2 BOOLEAN:=true;
5.  BEGIN
6.  L_vc_var1:=func_boo(l_b_var2);
7.  dbms_output.put_line(l_vc_var1);
8.  END;
9.  /
```

Result:
True

Script Explanation:

Line No.	Description
1	This environment variable opens up an output buffer of size limit of 200000.
2	Start of the declare section of the block.
3	A local variable l_vc_var1 of the Varchar2 data type is declared with a precision value 10.
4	A local variable l_b_var2 of the Boolean data type is declared and defaulted to True.

5	Start of the execution section of the block.
6	The function func_boo's return value for the input parameter as the local variable l_b_var2 is assigned to the local variable l_vc_var1.
7	The variable l_vc_var1 is printed using the procedure dbms_output.put_line.
8,9	End of the execution section of the block.

> 🔔 Note: This function cannot be used in the SQL statement if the Boolean value is directly used in the SQL statement rather than a variable assignment.

From R12.1 version, the above anonymous block can be rewritten as like below. This methodology is not possible prior to this release.

```
1.  SET SERVEROUTPUT ON SIZE 200000;
2.  DECLARE
3.  L_vc_var1 VARCHAR2(10);
4.  L_b_var2 BOOLEAN:=true;
5.  BEGIN
6.  SELECT func_boo(L_b_var2) INTO L_vc_var1 FROM dual;
7.  dbms_output.put_line(L_vc_var1);
8.  END;
9.  /
```

Result:
True

Script Explanation:

Line No.	Description
1	This environment variable opens up an output buffer of size limit of 200000.
2	Start of the declare section of the block.
3	A local variable l_vc_var1 of the Varchar2 data type is declared with a precision value 10.
4	A local variable l_b_var2 of the Boolean data type is declared and defaulted to True.
5	Start of the execution section of the block.
6	A select statement invoking the function func_boo's for the input parameter as the local variable l_b_var2 assigns its return value to the local variable l_vc_var1.
7	The variable l_vc_var1 is printed using the procedure dbms_output.put_line.
8,9	End of the execution section of the block.

In the below example, the above created function's result is checked in a decode statement to print out the description of its result. This scenario is not possible for the releases prior to 12cR1 version.

```
1.  SET SERVEROUTPUT ON SIZE 200000;
2.  DECLARE
3.  l_vc_var1 VARCHAR2(30);
4.  l_b_var2 BOOLEAN:=true;
5.  BEGIN
6.  SELECT DECODE(func_boo(l_b_var2), 'True', 'The value is True', 'False',
    'The value is False', 'The value is Null')
7.  INTO l_vc_var1
8.  FROM dual;
9.  dbms_output.put_line(l_vc_var1);
10. END;
11. /
```

Result:
The value is True

Script Explanation:

Line No.	Description
1	This environment variable opens up an output buffer of size limit of 200000.
2	Start of the declare section of the block.
3	A local variable l_vc_var1 of the Varchar2 data type is declared with a precision value 30.
4	A local variable l_b_var2 of the Boolean data type is declared and defaulted to True.
5	Start of the execution section of the block.
6	A select statement invoking the function func_boo's for the input parameter as the local variable l_b_var2 in a decode statement assigns the appropriate descriptive text for the return value and assigns it to the variable l_vc_var1.
7	The variable l_vc_var1 is printed using the procedure dbms_output.put_line.
8,9	End of the execution section of the block.

In the below example, the function created above is used in the WHERE condition to print the result of the function. This scenario of function usage is also not possible prior to 12cR1.

```
1.  SET SERVEROUTPUT ON SIZE 200000;
2.  DECLARE
3.  l_vc_var1 VARCHAR2(10);
4.  l_b_var2  BOOLEAN:=false;
5.  BEGIN
6.  SELECT CASE COUNT(*)
7.  WHEN 1
8.  THEN 'True'
9.  ELSE 'Not True'
10. END
11. INTO l_vc_var1
12. FROM dual
13. WHERE func_boo(l_b_var2)='True';
14. dbms_output.put_line(l_vc_var1);
15. END;
16. /
```

Result:
Not True

Script Explanation:

Line No.	Description
1	This environment variable opens up an output buffer of size limit of 200000.
2	Start of the declare section of the block.
3	A local variable l_vc_var1 of the Varchar2 data type is declared with a precision value 10.
4	A local variable l_b_var2 of the Boolean data type is declared and defaulted to False.
5	Start of the execution section of the block.
6-13	A select statement invoking the function func_boo's for the input parameter as the local variable l_b_var2 in its WHERE condition comparing it to the Boolean value True. If this condition matches, the select query assigns the variable l_vc_var1 with the text 'True' and if it does not match, the select query assigns the variable l_vc_var1 with the text 'Not True' based on the count function.
14	The variable l_vc_var1 is printed using the procedure dbms_output.put_line.
15,16	End of the execution section of the block.

PL/SQL Date and Timestamp Data Types

The Date and Timestamp data types are used for storing and manipulating the date and time values. These are quite complicated compared to the other data types as they require a special format for storage and processing.

Oracle allows us to perform arithmetic operations on the Date and the Timestamp data types between a Date/ Timestamp variable and an integer or between two Dates/ Timestamp variables.

Date

The Date data type can be used for storing fixed length date-time, which includes Date, Month, Year, Hours, Minutes and Seconds. The valid Date ranges between January 1, 4712 BC to December 31, 9999 AD. The Oracle server's date can be retrieved by querying the SYSDATE function. The date format is set by the NLS_DATE_FORMAT initialization parameter.

The default format of date in Oracle is **DD-MON-YY HH:MI:SS AM**

The prototype for declaring a Date data type is shown below,

```
Date;
```

Timestamp

The Timestamp data type is an extension of the Date data type with an additional Fraction for a precise date storage and retrieval. The Oracle server's Timestamp can be retrieved by querying the SYSTIMESTAMP function. The Timestamp format is set by the NLS_TIMESTAMP_FORMAT initialization parameter.

The default format of Timestamp in Oracle is **DD-MON-YY HH:MI:SS:FF9 AM**

The prototype for declaring a Timestamp data type is shown below,

```
Timestamp[Fraction_range];
```

Where, the Fraction_range ranges between 0 to 9 by default if it is not mentioned, it is 6. This determines the number of digits of the fraction field.

Timestamp with Time Zone

The Timestamp with Time Zone data type is the further extension of the Timestamp data type with a time zone displacement. Here, the time zone determines the difference between the local time and the universal time (UTC). The Timestamp format is set by the NLS_TIMESTAMP_TZ_FORMAT initialization parameter.

The default format of Timestamp with Time Zone in Oracle as below,

DD-MON-YY HH:MI:SS:FF9 AM TZH:TZM

The prototype for declaring a Timestamp with time zone data type is shown below,

```
Timestamp[Fraction_range] With Time Zone;
```

Where, the Fraction_range ranges between 0 to 9 by default if it is not mentioned, it is 6. This determines the number of digits of the fraction field.

Timestamp with Local Time Zone

In this data type, there will be no time zone mentioned in the result in contrast to its name. This data type when assigned to a Timestamp data with a different time zone, it will be normalized to the current time zone and stores the result. Its format is similar to that of the Timestamp data type.

The prototype for declaring a Timestamp with local time zone data type is shown below,

```
Timestamp[Fraction_range] With Local Time Zone;
```

Where, the Fraction_range ranges between 0 to 9 by default if it is not mentioned, it is 6. This determines the number of digits of the fraction field.

In the below example, the variable Timestamp with time zone is assigned to a Timestamp value with -5:00 time zone. When this variable is assigned to the variable with the data type Timestamp with Local Time Zone, the Timestamp value is adjusted to the current time zone (+5:30) and returned as result.

```
1.  SET SERVEROUTPUT ON SIZE 200000;
2.  DECLARE
3.  l_tl_var1 TIMESTAMP WITH LOCAL TIME ZONE;
4.  l_tt_var2 TIMESTAMP WITH TIME ZONE;
5.  BEGIN
6.  l_tt_var2:='30-Sep-89 04.32.12.20 PM -5:00';
```

```
7.   l_tl_var1:=l_tt_var2;
8.   dbms_output.put_line(l_tl_var1);
9.   END;
10.  /
```

Result:
01-OCT-89 03.02.12.200000 AM

Script Explanation:

Line No.	Description
1	This environment variable opens up an output buffer of size limit of 200000.
2	Start of the declare section of the block.
3	The local variable l_tl_var1 is declared with the data type Timestamp with local time zone.
4	The local variable l_tt_var2 is declared with the data type Timestamp with time zone.
5	Start of the execution section of the block.
6	The local variable l_tt_var2 is assigned with a Timestamp with time zone value.
7	The variable l_tt_var2 is assigned to the variable l_tl_var1.
8	The variable l_tl_var1 is printed using the procedure dbms_output.put_line.
9,10	End of the execution section of the block.

PL/SQL Interval Data Types

The Interval data types are used for storing and processing periods of time in the forms of Days, Hours, Minutes, Seconds and Fractions or Years and Months.

Interval Year to Month

This data type can be used for storing and manipulating intervals of years and months. The default format of Interval Year to Month data is **YYY-MM**.

The prototype for declaring an Interval Year to Month data type is shown below,

```
Interval Year[(Precision)] to Month;
```

The precision defines the number of digits in the Year. The range is 0 to 4 and the default is 2.

In the below example, the data type Interval Year to Month is processed under different scenarios.

```
1.   SET SERVEROUTPUT ON SIZE 200000;
2.   DECLARE
```

```
3.   l_iym_var1 interval YEAR(3) TO MONTH;
4.   BEGIN
5.   l_iym_var1:= interval '123-6' YEAR TO MONTH;
6.   dbms_output.put_line('Result 1: '||l_iym_var1);
7.   l_iym_var1:='123-6';
8.   dbms_output.put_line('Result 2: '||l_iym_var1);
9.   l_iym_var1:= interval '123' YEAR;
10.  dbms_output.put_line('Result 3: '||l_iym_var1);
11.  l_iym_var1:=interval '6' MONTH;
12.  dbms_output.put_line('Result 4: '||l_iym_var1);
13.  END;
14.  /
```

Result:
```
Result 1: +123-06
Result 2: +123-06
Result 3: +123-00
Result 4: +000-06
```

Script Explanation:

Line No.	Description
1	This environment variable opens up an output buffer of size limit of 200000.
2	Start of the declare section of the block.
3	The local variable l_iym_var1 is declared with the data type Interval Year(3) to Month.
4	Start of the execution section of the block.
5	The variable l_iym_var1 is assigned to year and month values of an interval year (3) to month value using explicit conversion.
6	The variable l_iym_var1 is printed using the procedure dbms_output.put_line.
7	The variable l_iym_var1 is assigned to year and month values of an interval year (3) to month value using implicit conversion.
8	The variable l_iym_var1 is printed using the procedure dbms_output.put_line.
9	The variable l_iym_var1 is assigned with only the year value of an interval year(3) to month value using explicit conversion.
10	The variable l_iym_var1 is printed using the procedure dbms_output.put_line.
11	The variable l_iym_var1 is assigned with only the month value of an interval year(3) to month value using explicit conversion.
12	The variable l_iym_var1 is printed using the procedure dbms_output.put_line.
13,14	End of the execution section of the block.

Interval Day to Second

This data type can be used for storing and manipulating intervals of Days, Hours, Minutes, Seconds and Fractions. The default format of the Interval Day to Second data is **DD HH:MI:SS.FF.**

The prototype for declaring an Interval Day to Second data type is shown below,

```
Interval Day[(Leading_precision)] to Second[(Fraction_precision)];
```

The Leading_precision defines the number of digits in the Day field and the Fraction_precision defines the number of digits in the Fraction field. The range is 0 to 9 and the default is 2 for the Day field and 6 for the Fraction field.

In the below example, the data type Interval Day to Second is processed under different scenarios.

```
1.   SET SERVEROUTPUT ON SIZE 200000;
2.   DECLARE
3.   l_ids_var1 interval DAY TO second;
4.   BEGIN
5.   l_ids_var1:= interval '12 12:12:12.12' DAY TO second;
6.   dbms_output.put_line('Result 1: '||l_ids_var1);
7.   l_ids_var1:= '12 12:12:12.12';
8.   dbms_output.put_line('Result 2: '||l_ids_var1);
9.   l_ids_var1:= interval '12' DAY;
10.  dbms_output.put_line('Result 3: '||l_ids_var1);
11.  l_ids_var1:= interval '12' Hour;
12.  dbms_output.put_line('Result 4: '||l_ids_var1);
13.  l_ids_var1:= interval '12' Minute;
14.  dbms_output.put_line('Result 5: '||l_ids_var1);
15.  l_ids_var1:= interval '12' Second;
16.  dbms_output.put_line('Result 6: '||l_ids_var1);
17.  END;
18.  /
```

```
Result:
Result 1: +12 12:12:12.120000
Result 2: +12 12:12:12.120000
Result 3: +12 00:00:00.000000
Result 4: +00 12:00:00.000000
Result 5: +00 00:12:00.000000
Result 6: +00 00:00:12.000000
```

Script Explanation:

Line No.	Description
1	This environment variable opens up an output buffer of size limit of 200000.
2	Start of the declare section of the block.

3	The local variable l_ids_var1 is declared with the data type Interval day to second.
4	Start of the execution section of the block.
5	The variable l_ids_var1 is assigned with day, hour, minute, second and fraction values of an interval day to second value using explicit conversion.
6	The variable l_ids_var1 is printed using the procedure dbms_output.put_line.
7	The variable l_ids_var1 is assigned with day, hour, minute, second and fraction values of an interval day to second value using implicit conversion.
8	The variable l_ids_var1 is printed using the procedure dbms_output.put_line.
9	The variable l_ids_var1 is assigned with only the day value of an interval day to second value using explicit conversion.
10	The variable l_ids_var1 is printed using the procedure dbms_output.put_line.
11	The variable l_ids_var1 is assigned to only the hour value of an interval day to second value using explicit conversion.
12	The variable l_ids_var1 is printed using the procedure dbms_output.put_line.
13	The variable l_ids_var1 is assigned to only the minute value of an interval day to second value using explicit conversion.
14	The variable l_ids_var1 is printed using the procedure dbms_output.put_line.
15	The variable l_ids_var1 is assigned to only the second value of an interval day to second value using explicit conversion.
16	The variable l_ids_var1 is printed using the procedure dbms_output.put_line.
17,18	End of the execution section of the block.

PLSQL LOB Data Types

The LOB data types are mainly used for storing and manipulating large blocks of structured data like large blocks of character strings or unstructured data such as, audio files, images, video files and large text documents. These data types preferred over Long types as these are frequently enhanced in each release to cope up with the business needs, whereas on the other hand, the Long types are hardly enhanced.

PL/SQL works on these data types through their LOB locators. The LOB locators are stored in an external file, either inside the row (inline) or outside the row (outline). These locators are stored in the columns in any of the LOB types with a unique identifier for the current transaction to restrict other sessions from accessing the corresponding LOB data.

This section gives you a brief insight on the different LOB data types, whereas, their implementation and manipulation methods are covered deeply in the chapter 15, *Manipulating Large Objects in PL/SQL.*

There are four different types of predefined LOB types and these are explained below,

CLOB and NCLOB

CLOB and NCLOB data types store large blocks of either fixed-width or variable-width character data in the database. These data types use character set based storage, thus, these data types cannot support multimedia files in them. The CLOB data type uses the database character set and the NCLOB data type supports national character set for storing foreign characters. The maximum size of these data types can be up to 128TB which is based on their database block's size.

The variables holding data in this format can be assigned to either CHAR/ NCHAR or VARCHAR2/ NVARCHAR2 when they do not cross over these data types maximum range.

The locators in CLOB and NCLOB data types points to a large block of character string data.

The prototype for declaring CLOB and NCLOB data types are shown below,

```
L_cl_var1 clob;
L_ncl_var2 nclob;
```

BLOB

The BLOB data type stores large blocks of unstructured data with no character set semantics like image files, audio clips and video files. The maximum size of this data type is 128TB which is dependent to the database block's size.

The locator stored in this data type directs to the large block of large unstructured binary object.

The prototype for declaring a BLOB data type is shown below,

```
L_bl_var1 blob;
```

BFILE

The BFILE data type store unstructured multimedia files just like BLOB but stores them out of the database and in the operating system. As the data are stored in the operating system, the maximum size of this data type depends on the hardware limit of the operating system. These files cannot be modified and can only be read.

The locator stored in this data type route to the data file which is stored outside the database in the operating system.

PL/SQL Composite Data Types

These data types, unlike the scalar types, have internal components representing multiple data types under a single composite type. These data types are used for meeting with the complex business requirements. These are explained in detail in the Chapter 6, *The PL/SQL Collections*.

PL/SQL Referential Data Types

These data types are used as a reference to point a private memory area for processing an SQL statement containing all necessary data for satisfying the business need. These can be achieved by using Cursors and Ref Cursors in PL/SQL which are explained in detail in the Chapter 7, *The Cursors and Ref-cursors in PL/SQL*.

Summary

In this chapter, we have toured through the introduction of Unicode technology along with its different encoding schemes. The next section explained us about the Oracle's Unicode support over the various times and the different types of character sets and their data dictionary objects in Oracle. The second part of the chapter explained us about the four different types of data types available in PL/SQL along with their similarities, dissimilarities, performance analysis, usages and their current enhancements in detail with suitable examples.

The next chapter will help us in learning the dynamic query processing techniques in PL/SQL with various supporting examples.

Dynamic Query Processing Techniques in PL/SQL

In this chapter, we will discuss PL/SQL dynamic query processing in detail,

8. Introduction to Dynamic SQL, its different types and its main use in programming.

9. Understanding the Native Dynamic SQL methodology with various real time examples and latest enhancements.

10. Dusting the attention less DBMS_SQL API and its associated subprograms with supporting suitable examples along with their special functionality that is dependent only to this API.

Introduction to Dynamic SQL

Dynamic SQL is a power-packed programming methodology that allows us to generate and execute SQL statements and PL/SQL blocks at run time. During the compile time, the dynamic SQL statements are considered as a mere character string and will not be validated against the objects in the database, providing a greater advantage to the programmers with the flexibility of re-arranging the program, based on the business requirements during the run time. The process of using the SQL statements that are not embedded in our source program and are constructed as strings which are parsed and executed at run time, is called as Dynamic SQL processing technique.

This method of programming is mainly useful when,

1. Writing unpredictable and ad-hoc programs.

2. When there is a need for the PL/SQL program units to process data definition language (DDL) statements and data control language (DCL) statements

3. When a part of an SQL statement or a PL/SQL block like table name, column name, number of parameters, and data type of the input and the output variables are not known during the compile time.

The below figure shows the basic idea of processing a dynamic query.

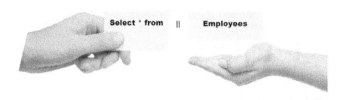

Fig.4.1 Dynamic Query Processing Technique Illustration

There are two methods in which any dynamic SQL can be processed. They are, Native Dynamic SQL language and DBMS_SQL API which are explained below,

Native Dynamic SQL (NDS)

Native dynamic SQL is a simple and an efficient tool, which was introduced in the Oracle version 9i as a replacement to the DBMS_SQL API. Even though NDS were created as a replacement for the DBMS_SQL API, it lacks to perform some functionality that is effectively done by the API which is covered in the DBMS_SQL section.

This method of programming is easy and concise to use, as we need fewer lines of code to construct dynamic SQL in NDS unlike the API. As this is a native method, the PL/SQL interpreter has a built in support making it more efficient than the DBMS_SQL API.

In NDS, the EXECUTE IMMEDIATE and OPEN FOR statements helps in parsing and executing the dynamic SQLs. This chapter actively explains the EXECUTE IMMEDIATE statement and the OPEN FOR statement is covered in the chapter 7, *The Cursors and Ref-cursors in PL/SQL.*

The prototype for declaring the EXECUTE IMMEDIATE statement is shown below,

```
EXECUTE IMMEDIATE <'Dynamic_string'>
[[BULK COLLECT] INTO <Define_variable[, Define_variable]...Record_variable>]
[USING [IN | OUT | IN OUT] Bind_argument
    [, [IN | OUT | IN OUT] Bind_argument] ...]
[RETURNING | RETURN [BULK COLLECT] INTO Bind_argument [, Bind_argument]
...];
```

- Dynamic_string can be either an SQL statement or a PL/SQL block with constructive objects embedded in them.

- Define_variable holds the result of the Dynamic_string's execution. For multi-row result, BULK COLLECT INTO clause is used. For more information on this clause, please refer the chapter 6, *The PL/SQL Collections.*

- Bind_argument in the USING clause works as the bind variable for the Dynamic_string with IN, OUT and IN OUT parameter modes. These bind arguments cannot be used for passing schema objects like table name and column name.

- Bind_argument in the RETURNING INTO/ RETURN INTO clause help in returning any column value(s) from the Dynamic_string's execution which are type compatible to each other. This clause works only for the INSERT, DELETE and UPDATE operations. For returning multi-row column values, BULK COLLECT INTO clause is used. For more information on this clause, please refer the chapter 6, *The PL/SQL Collections.*

All the bind variables are to be placed only in the USING clause and if not mentioned, the parameter mode is IN by default. For the DML statements with the RETURNING INTO clause, by default the parameter mode for the bind variable will be OUT.

Bind Variables

The bind variables play a vital role in the memory management and performance enhancement in dynamic SQL processing. When an SQL query is executed multiple times with different hard-coded values, it parses every single time based on the unique hard-coded values as like below,

```
1.  DELETE FROM employees WHERE employee_id=100;
2.  DELETE FROM employees WHERE employee_id=101;
3.  DELETE FROM employees WHERE employee_id=102;
```

By executing the V$SQL view with the appropriate columns, the parsing information related to the above statements can be gathered as like below,

```
SELECT sql_id,
  sql_text,
  first_load_time,
  hash_value,
  executions
FROM v$sql
WHERE sql_text LIKE 'DELETE FROM employees WHERE employee_id=%';
```

Script output:

SQL_ID	SQL_TEXT	FIRST_LOAD_TIME	HASH_VALUE	Executions

6mrtzn6s56nhq	DELETE FROM employees WHERE employee_id=100	2016-05-04/01:39:08	2958250518	1
04bukanmmv3yp	DELETE FROM employees WHERE employee_id=102	2016-05-04/01:40:14	658345941	1
7k3z2wxb8mx92	DELETE FROM employees WHERE employee_id=101	2016-05-04/01:40:12	1451881762	1

In the above result set, all three queries are parsed with different hash values.

However, when the query statement uses a bind variable instead of the hard-coded value, the query does not parse for the multiple values of the bind variable but only once irrespective of the number of executions.

```
DELETE FROM employees WHERE employee_id=:employee_id;
```

Now, the below V$SQL query results as,

```
SELECT sql_id,
   sql_text,
   first_load_time,
   hash_value,
   executions
FROM v$sql
WHERE sql_text LIKE 'DELETE FROM employees WHERE employee_id=%';
```

Script output:

SQL_ID	SQL_TEXT	FIRST_LOAD_TIME	HASH_VALUE	Executions
85cyrmn7 pjawc	DELETE FROM employees WHERE employee_id= :employee_id	2016-05-04/02:02:59	257469324	3

By examining the above result set, it shows that only one instance of the query is parsed irrespective of the number of times the statement is executed. The last column, EXECUTIONS shows the number of times this query is executed with different bind values. The reason behind this behavior is, the parsing of the query happens right before the bind value assignment thus, the query is common to multiple bind values. Failing to use the bind variables may fill up the shared pool space with a large number of identical queries resulting in bad performance and resource containment.

This bind variable lookup can also be achieved on a query without a bind variable by setting the database parameter CURSOR_SHARING to FORCE. The default value for this parameter is EXACT which does not replace the literal with a bind variable and each unique statement uses a unique plan for it. When this parameter is set to FORCE, it forces the statements that differ in some literals, but are otherwise identical, to share an implicit cursor.

> Note: The CURSOR_SHARING parameter value SIMILAR has been deprecated in the release R12.1 due to the fact that this setting causes a lot of implications on the number of child cursors created for a single parent.

The CURSOR_SHARING parameter can be set at the database level or at the session level by either using the keyword SYSTEM or SESSION in the below statement,

```
Alter session | system set CURSOR_SHARING=FORCE;
```

When this parameter is set to FORCE, the system will treat the queries which differs in some literal values similar to the query executed with a bind variable, thus reducing unwanted hard parsing and a large amount of shared pool garbage.

In the below anonymous block, the employee IDs 100 through 105 are deleted from the employees table by dynamically assigning the table name and the column name in the run time.

> Note: The bind values cannot be used for passing schema objects.

```
1.  SET SERVEROUTPUT ON 200000;
2.  DECLARE
3.  l_vc_table_name  VARCHAR2(30):='Employees';
4.  l_vc_column_name VARCHAR2(30):='Employee_id';
5.  BEGIN
6.  FOR i IN 100..105
7.  LOOP
8.  EXECUTE immediate 'delete from '||l_vc_table_name||' where
    '||l_vc_column_name||'='||i;
9.  END LOOP i;
10. Commit;
11. END;
```

Script Explanation

Line No.	Description
1	This environment variable opens up an output buffer of size limit of 200000.
2	Start of the declare section of the block.
3	The local variable l_vc_table_name is declared with VARCHAR2 data type with a precision of 30 characters and is defaulted to the text 'EMPLOYEES'.
4	The local variable l_vc_column_name is declared with VARCHAR2 data type with a precision of 30 characters and is defaulted to the text 'EMPLOYEE_ID'.
5	Start of the execution section of the block.
6,7	Start of the FOR loop with the range 100 to 105.
8	A dynamic DELETE statement is formed by using the table name and the column name from the local variables l_vc_table_name and l_vc_column_name respectively. This dynamically formed DELETE statement is then parsed and executed using the EXECUTE IMMEDIATE statement for the loop's range values assigned to its WHERE condition in an orderly fashion.
9	End of the FOR loop.
10	The DML operation performed in the step 8 is committed.
11,12	End of the execution section of the block.

Here, as stated in the above cases, the above anonymous block can be effectively modified by using the bind value as like below,

```
1.  SET SERVEROUTPUT ON 200000;
2.  DECLARE
3.  l_vc_table_name  VARCHAR2(30):='Employees';
4.  l_vc_column_name VARCHAR2(30):='Employee_id';
5.  BEGIN
6.  FOR i IN 100..105
7.  LOOP
8.  EXECUTE immediate 'delete from '||l_vc_table_name||' where
    '||l_vc_column_name||'=:i' using i;
9.  END LOOP i;
10. Commit;
11. END;
12. /
```

Script Explanation

Line No.	Description
1	This environment variable opens up an output buffer of size limit of 200000.
2	Start of the declare section of the block.
3	The local variable l_vc_table_name is declared with VARCHAR2 data type with a precision of 30 characters and is defaulted to the text 'EMPLOYEES'.

4	The local variable l_vc_column_name is declared with VARCHAR2 data type with a precision of 30 characters and is defaulted to the text 'EMPLOYEE_ID'.
5	Start of the execution section of the block.
6,7	Start of the FOR loop with the range 100 to 105.
8	A dynamic DELETE statement is formed by using the table name and the column name from the local variables l_vc_table_name and l_vc_column_name respectively. This dynamically formed DELETE statement is then parsed and executed using the EXECUTE IMMEDIATE statement with a placeholder in its WHERE condition which gets its value from the loop's range value in the form of a bind value.
9	End of the FOR loop.
10	The DML operation performed in the step 8 is committed.
11,12	End of the execution section of the block.

Placeholder Duplication

The placeholders in a dynamic SQL statement are associated with the bind variables in the USING clause by position and not by the name. So, if the same placeholder repeats itself in an SQL statement, the bind value must correspond to its each appearance in the USING clause.

> 🔔 Note: The dynamic SQL statements must not end with a statement terminator (semicolon).

For example, in the below example, the table TABLE_NAME has four columns with the first, third and the fourth column corresponding to the bind argument VAL1 and the second column corresponds to the bind argument VAL2. Here, the USING clause functions as like below.

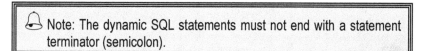

```
1.  SET SERVEROUTPUT ON 200000;
2.  BEGIN
3.  EXECUTE immediate 'insert into table_name values (:val1, :val2,
    :val1, :val1)' USING 'A', 'B', 'A', 'A';
4.  Commit;
5.  END;
6.  /
```

Script Explanation

Line No.	Description
1	This environment variable opens up an output buffer of size limit of 200000.
2	Start of the execution section of the block.

3	An INSERT statement is dynamically formed with four placeholders which gets their values from the four bind variables in the USING clause. This dynamically generated statement is then executed using the EXECUTE IMMEDIATE clause.
4	The DML operation performed in the step 3 is committed.
5,6	End of the execution section of the block.

However, in dynamic PL/SQL blocks, only the unique placeholders are associated with the bind variables in the USING clause by position. Thus, if a placeholder repeats multiple times in the PL/SQL block, all unique appearances correspond to a single bind variable in the USING clause.

> 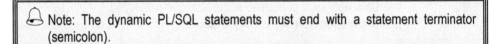 Note: The dynamic PL/SQL statements must end with a statement terminator (semicolon).

In the below example, the table TABLE_NAME with the first, third and the fourth column corresponding to the bind variable VAL1 and the second column corresponding to the bind variable VAL2 are associated in the USING clause based on the uniqueness of the placeholders by their position as below.

```
1.  SET SERVEROUTPUT ON 200000;
2.  BEGIN
3.  EXECUTE immediate 'BEGIN insert into table_name values (:val1,
    :val2, :val1, :val1); END;' USING 'A', 'B';
4.  Commit;
5.  END;
6.  /
```

Script Explanation

Line No.	Description
1	This environment variable opens up an output buffer of size limit of 200000.
2	Start of the execution section of the block.
3	An anonymous block with an INSERT statement is dynamically formed with four placeholders which gets their values from the 2 bind variables in the USING clause. This dynamically generated block is then executed using the EXECUTE IMMEDIATE clause.
4	The DML operation performed in the step 3 is committed.
5,6	End of the execution section of the block.

Passing Null as Bind Argument

When there is a need for us to pass Null value as a bind argument to a dynamic SQL statement or to a Dynamic PL/SQL block, like in the below example,

```
1.  SET SERVEROUTPUT ON 200000;
2.  DECLARE
3.  l_n_emp_id NUMBER:=100;
4.  BEGIN
5.  EXECUTE immediate 'Update Employees set commission_pct=:val1 where
    employee_id=:val2' USING NULL,l_n_emp_id;
6.  Commit;
7.  END;
8.  /
```

```
Error report:
ORA-06550: line 5, column 94:
PLS-00457: expressions have to be of SQL types
ORA-06550: line 5, column 2:
PL/SQL: Statement ignored
06550. 00000 -  "line %s, column %s:\n%s"
*Cause:    Usually a PL/SQL compilation error.
*Action:
```

Script Explanation

Line No.	Description
1	This environment variable opens up an output buffer of size limit of 200000.
2	Start of the declare section of the block.
3	A local variable l_n_emp_id is declared with NUMBER data type and defaulted to the integer 100.
4	Start of the execution section of the block.
5	An UPDATE statement is dynamically formed with one placeholder in the SET clause and another one in the WHERE condition which gets its values from the bind variables in the USING clause sequentially. The first placeholder has NULL value as its bind value and the second placeholder has the local variable l_n_emp_id as its bind value.
6	The DML operation performed in the step 5 is committed.
7,8	End of the execution section of the block.

The above listing fails with a compilation error because passing the literal Null is not allowed in the USING clause. However, the above script can be re-written effectively as like below to avoid this error.

```
1.  SET SERVEROUTPUT ON 200000;
2.  DECLARE
3.  l_n_emp_id NUMBER:=100;
4.  l_n_comm   NUMBER;
5.  BEGIN
```

```
6.   EXECUTE immediate 'Update Employees set commission_pct=:val1 where
     employee_id=:val2' USING l_n_comm, l_n_emp_id;
7.   Commit;
8.   END;
9.   /
```

anonymous block completed

Script Explanation

Line No.	Description
1	This environment variable opens up an output buffer of size limit of 200000.
2	Start of the declare section of the block.
3	A local variable l_n_emp_id is declared with NUMBER data type and defaulted to the integer 100.
4	A local variable l_n_comm is declared with NUMBER data type.
5	Start of the execution section of the block.
6	An UPDATE statement is dynamically formed with one placeholder in the SET clause and another one in the WHERE condition which gets its values from the bind variables in the USING clause sequentially. These two placeholders have the local variables l_n_comm and l_n_emp_id as their bind values respectively.
7	The DML operation performed in the step 6 is committed.
8,9	End of the execution section of the block.

The compilation error caused due to the literal Null passing in the USING clause is now rectified by replacing the literal with an un-initialized variable.

Dynamic DML Statement

 Note: The dynamic DML statement does not perform auto-commit when executed. To complete the transaction, the system waits for a COMMIT or a ROLLBACK like a standard DML statement.

The below listing serves to increment the salary of an employee with the provided increment value and returns the updated salary to the user. The local variables l_n_inc and l_n_emp_id in IN mode acts as inputs to the dynamic query and the RETURNING INTO clause returns the placeholder :val3 to the target local variable l_n_upd_sal in OUT mode which is then printed to the calling environment.

```
1.   SET SERVEROUTPUT ON 200000;
2.   DECLARE
```

```
3.   l_n_emp_id  NUMBER:=110;
4.   l_n_inc     NUMBER:=500;
5.   l_n_upd_sal NUMBER;
6.   l_vc_query  VARCHAR2(1000);
7.   BEGIN
8.   l_vc_query:='Update Employees set salary=salary+:val1 where
     employee_id=:val2 returning salary into :val3';
9.   EXECUTE immediate l_vc_query USING IN l_n_inc, IN l_n_emp_id
     RETURNING INTO l_n_upd_sal;
10.  Commit;
11.  dbms_output.put_line('The updated salary for the employee
     '||l_n_emp_id||' is '||l_n_upd_sal);
12.  END;
13.  /
```

Result:
The updated salary for the employee 110 is 8700

Script Explanation

Line No.	Description
1	This environment variable opens up an output buffer of size limit of 200000.
2	Start of the declare section of the block.
3	A local variable l_n_emp_id is declared with NUMBER data type and defaulted to the integer 110.
4	A local variable l_n_inc is declared with NUMBER data type and defaulted to the integer 500.
5	A local variable l_n_upd_sal is declared with NUMBER data type.
6	A local variable l_vc_query is declared with VARCHAR2 data type with a precision of 1000 characters.
7	Start of the execution section of the block.
8	An UPDATE statement on the EMPLOYEES table is dynamically formed for incrementing an employee's salary. This dynamic statement has its first placeholder in the SET clause, second placeholder in the WHERE condition and the third placeholder in the RETURNING INTO clause. This dynamically formed UPDATE statement is assigned to the local variable l_vc_query.
9	The dynamic query in the local variable l_vc_query is parsed and then executed in the EXECUTE IMMEDIATE clause. The first two placeholders gets their values from the local variables l_n_inc and l_n_emp_id bind variables with IN mode and the third placeholder is returned to l_n_upd_sal bind variable with OUT mode.
10	The DML operation performed in the step 9 is committed.
11	The updated salary of the employee is printed using the system procedure DBMS_OUTPUT.PUT_LINE.
12,13	End of the execution section of the block.

Dynamic DDL Statement

Whenever we want to create a standalone script for dropping any schema object, we have to make sure that we perform a check on the object's presence so that the DDL statement does not throw any 'object not found' type error.

 Note: The objects used in the dynamic statement will not be listed in the *_DEPENDENCIES data dictionary view.

In the below example, the script does a conditional check for the table's presence before it is dropped by using the FOR loop with the local table's list from the data dictionary view. If the corresponding table is present, the FOR loop passes the control to the dynamic DDL statement and executes it else, the statement is skipped from execution.

```
1.   SET SERVEROUTPUT ON 200000;
2.   DECLARE
3.   l_vc_table_name VARCHAR2(30):='PRODUCT';
4.   BEGIN
5.   FOR loop_counter IN
6.   (SELECT table_name FROM user_tables WHERE table_name=l_vc_table_name
7.   )
8.   LOOP
9.   EXECUTE immediate 'Drop table '||loop_counter.table_name||' cascade
     constraints' ;
10.  END LOOP loop_counter;
11.  END;
12.  /
```

Script Explanation

Line No.	Description
1	This environment variable opens up an output buffer of size limit of 200000.
2	Start of the declare section of the block.
3	A local variable l_vc_table_name is declared with VARCHAR2 data type with a precision of 30 characters and is defaulted to the text 'PRODUCT'.
4	Start of the execution section of the block.
5,6,8	Start of the Cursor FOR loop with the USER_TABLES data dictionary view having a WHERE condition equated to the local variable l_vc_table_name.
9	A DROP table statement is dynamically created with its table name from the table_name column from the FOR loop with CASCADE CONSTRAINTS clause added to it.
10	End of the FOR loop.
11,12	End of the execution section of the block.

Dynamic PL/SQL Block Handling Large String

Prior to the Oracle version 11g, the native dynamic SQL supported processing of strings up to 32k in length only and from this release, Oracle allows the usage of CLOB columns as an argument in NDS eradicating the length constraint of 32k.

In the below example, a CLOB variable is initially assigned to the alphabet 'A' for 32767 times using the RPAD function. This CLOB variable is then appended to itself using the DBMS_LOB.APPEND procedure resulting in doubling the content. This append process is performed for N number of times, resulting in a very huge sized CLOB variable. This variable is then inserted into the CLOB column of a table using the dynamic SQL processing technique.

In the below snippet, after multiple appends, the length of the CLOB variable inserted into the table is of 4 million characters in length.

```
1.   SET SERVEROUTPUT ON 200000;
2.   DECLARE
3.     l_cl_var1 CLOB:=rpad('A',32767,'A');
4.     l_n_length NUMBER;
5.     l_vc_table_name varchar2(30):='NDS_CLOB';
6.   BEGIN
7.     dbms_lob.append(l_cl_var1,l_cl_var1);
8.     dbms_output.put_line('The length of the manipulated LOB is
       '||dbms_lob.getlength(l_cl_var1));
9.     dbms_lob.append(l_cl_var1,l_cl_var1);
10.    dbms_output.put_line('The length of the manipulated LOB is
       '||dbms_lob.getlength(l_cl_var1));
11.    dbms_lob.append(l_cl_var1,l_cl_var1);
12.    dbms_output.put_line('The length of the manipulated LOB is
       '||dbms_lob.getlength(l_cl_var1));
13.    dbms_lob.append(l_cl_var1,l_cl_var1);
14.    dbms_output.put_line('The length of the manipulated LOB is
       '||dbms_lob.getlength(l_cl_var1));
15.    dbms_lob.append(l_cl_var1,l_cl_var1);
16.    dbms_output.put_line('The length of the manipulated LOB is
       '||dbms_lob.getlength(l_cl_var1));
17.    dbms_lob.append(l_cl_var1,l_cl_var1);
18.    dbms_output.put_line('The length of the manipulated LOB is
       '||dbms_lob.getlength(l_cl_var1));
19.    dbms_lob.append(l_cl_var1,l_cl_var1);
20.    dbms_output.put_line('The length of the manipulated LOB is
       '||dbms_lob.getlength(l_cl_var1));
21.    EXECUTE immediate 'insert into '||l_vc_table_name||' values
       (:clob_value)' USING l_cl_var1;
22.    Commit;
23.    SELECT dbms_lob.getlength(col1) INTO l_n_length FROM nds_clob;
24.    dbms_output.put_line('The length of the CLOB column is
       '||l_n_length);
25.  END;
26.  /
```

```
Result:
The length of the manipulated LOB is 65534
The length of the manipulated LOB is 131068
The length of the manipulated LOB is 262136
The length of the manipulated LOB is 524272
The length of the manipulated LOB is 1048544
The length of the manipulated LOB is 2097088
The length of the manipulated LOB is 4194176
The length of the CLOB column is 4194176
```

Script Explanation

Line No.	Description
1	This environment variable opens up an output buffer of size limit of 200000.
2	Start of the declare section of the block.
3	A local variable l_cl_var1 is declared with CLOB data type and defaulted to the text 'A' for 32,767 times.
4	A local variable l_n_length is declared with NUMBER data type.
5	A local variable l_vc_table_name is declared with VARCHAR2 data type with a precision of 30 characters and is defaulted to the text 'NDS_CLOB'.
6	Start of the execution section of the block.
7-20	The local variable l_cl_var1 is multiplied with itself for N number of times using the DBMS_LOB.APPEND procedure and the length of the variable is printed using the system procedure DBMS_OUTPUT.PUT_LINE.
21-22	An INSERT statement is dynamically generated with its table name from the local variable l_vc_table_name and a placeholder in its VALUES clause where it gets its value from the multiple times manipulated CLOB column l_cl_var1 in the USING clause and committed.
23	The length of the CLOB column value from the table NDS_CLOB is measured using the procedure DBMS_LOB.GETLENGTH function and is printed using DBMS_OUTPUT.PUT_LINE procedure.
24,25	End of the execution section of the block.

In the below listing, the text *null;* is appended to a CLOB variable until it reaches 30,000 characters in length using the RPAD function. This specific length of 30,000 is taken for consideration because the input text *null;* is about 5 characters in length and it is completely divisible by 30,000 such that there will be no character loss in the input text even after multiple appends.

The CLOB variable is then multiplied by itself for N number of times using the DBMS_LOB.APPEND procedure resulting in a CLOB variable of size 480,000 characters. This variable is then used as the body for creating a procedure using the EXECUTE IMMEDIATE method.

```
1.  SET SERVEROUTPUT ON 200000;
2.  DECLARE
3.  l_cl_var1 CLOB:=rpad('null;',30000,'null;');
4.  l_cl_var2 CLOB;
5.  l_n_length NUMBER;
6.  BEGIN
7.  dbms_lob.append(l_cl_var1,l_cl_var1);
8.  dbms_output.put_line('The length of the manipulated CLOB value is
    '||dbms_lob.getlength(l_cl_var1));
9.  dbms_lob.append(l_cl_var1,l_cl_var1);
10. dbms_output.put_line('The length of the manipulated CLOB value is
    '||dbms_lob.getlength(l_cl_var1));
11. dbms_lob.append(l_cl_var1,l_cl_var1);
12. dbms_output.put_line('The length of the manipulated CLOB value is
    '||dbms_lob.getlength(l_cl_var1));
13. dbms_lob.append(l_cl_var1,l_cl_var1);
14. dbms_output.put_line('The length of the manipulated CLOB value is
    '||dbms_lob.getlength(l_cl_var1));
15. l_cl_var2:='create or replace procedure proc_clob_test is begin
    '||l_cl_var1||' end;';
16. dbms_output.put_line('The length of the procedure is
    '||dbms_lob.getlength(l_cl_var2));
17. EXECUTE immediate l_cl_var2;
18. END;
19. /
```

Error report:
```
ORA-24344: success with compilation error
ORA-06512: at line 16
24344. 00000 -  "success with compilation error"
*Cause:    A sql/plsql compilation error occurred.
*Action:   Return OCI_SUCCESS_WITH_INFO along with the error code
```

Result:
```
The length of the manipulated CLOB value is 60000
The length of the manipulated CLOB value is 120000
The length of the manipulated CLOB value is 240000
The length of the manipulated CLOB value is 480000
The length of the procedure is 480057
```

Script Explanation

Line No.	Description
1	This environment variable opens up an output buffer of size limit of 200000.
2	Start of the declare section of the block.
3	A local variable l_cl_var1 is declared with CLOB data type and defaulted to the text 'null;' until the size of the variable reaches 30,000 in length.
4	A local variable l_cl_var1 is declared with CLOB data type.
5	A local variable l_n_length is declared with NUMBER data type.
6	Start of the execution section of the block.
7-14	The local variable l_cl_var1 is multiplied by itself for N number of times using the DBMS_LOB. APPEND procedure and the length of the variable is printed using the system procedure DBMS_OUTPUT. PUT_LINE.

15	A procedure proc_clob_test is dynamically created with the local CLOB variable l_vc_var1 as its body text. This procedure script is assigned to the local CLOB variable l_vc_var2.
16	The length of the CLOB variable l_vc_var2 is found by using the DBMS_LOB.GETLENGTH procedure and is printed using the system procedure DBMS_OUTPUT.PUT_LINE.
17	The local CLOB variable l_vc_var2 with the procedure creation script is parsed and executed using the EXECUTE IMMEDIATE statement.
18,19	End of the execution section of the block.

This procedure created with large body text throws a weird error message *ORA-24344: success with compilation error*. This error means that there is an internal unknown error produced during the procedure creation. The error is created because, the input text *null;* which is multiplied numerous times by itself is in a single row and the procedure is created with a large one row in its body that was unable to be processed by the system.

The compilation error raised during the procedure creation can be viewed from the data dictionary view USER_ERRORS as like below,

```
SELECT name, type, position, text, attribute FROM user_errors where
name='PROC_CLOB_TEST';
```

Script output:

NAME	TYPE	POSITION	TEXT	ATTRIBUTE
PROC_CLOB_TEST	PROCEDURE	21284	PLS-00801: internal error [*** ASSERT at file pdy7.c, line 7614; pdy7F102_Output_Line_Table - Lines_In_Segment = 96004; PROC_CLOB_TEST__SYS_P __92599[1, 480036]]	ERROR

The above result set is produced as a result of executing the ERRORS view shows that the errors created are in an unreadable format. When this procedure is then compiled later with proper formatting, frees itself from the compilation error that occurred earlier and is ready for functioning.

The below snippet and the result log shows that the procedure is executed successfully in less time, even though it has a very large body text.

```
Exec proc_clob_test;
```

```
Elapsed: 00:00:00.355
```

```
anonymous block completed
```

Advanced PL/SQL Programming

NDS Enhancements in 12c

Prior to the Oracle version 12c, it was impossible to process functions with Boolean inputs in SQL statements using NDS method. This is because the Boolean data type is unsupported by SQL and this limitation is leveraged in the release R12.1.

To explain this enhancement in detail, the function below is created with Boolean input parameter which returns the strings 'True', 'False' and 'Null' when the input Boolean value is True, False and Null respectively.

```
1.   CREATE OR REPLACE
2.   FUNCTION func_boo(
3.   ip_b_var1 BOOLEAN)
4.   RETURN VARCHAR2
5.   IS
6.   BEGIN
7.   RETURN
8.   CASE
9.   WHEN ip_b_var1 THEN
10.  'True'
11.  WHEN NOT ip_b_var1 THEN
12.  'False'
13.  ELSE
14.  'Null'
15.  END;
16.  END;
17.  /
```

Script Explanation

Line No.	Description
1-4	The function FUNC_BOO is created with one Boolean variable ip_b_var1 and with the RETURN data type as VARCHAR2
5	Start of the declare section of the function.
6	Start of the execution section of the function.
7-15	A CASE statement returning the string 'True', 'False' and 'Null' when the input Boolean parameter is True, False and Null respectively is returned using the RETURN statement.
16,17	End of the execution section of the function.

In the below example, the above function in an SQL statement is processed using the NDS method with its name dynamically appended to the statement at run time. Here the function in the SELECT statement accepts Boolean bind variable and results as below.

```
1.   SET SERVEROUTPUT ON 200000;
2.   DECLARE
3.   L_vc_var1      VARCHAR2(10);
4.   L_b_var2       BOOLEAN      :=true;
5.   l_vc_func_name VARCHAR2(30):='FUNC_BOO';
```

```
6.  BEGIN
7.  EXECUTE immediate 'SELECT '||l_vc_func_name||'(:L_b_var2)  FROM dual'
    INTO L_vc_var1 USING l_b_var2;
8.  dbms_output.put_line(L_vc_var1);
9.  END;
10. /
```

Result:

True

Script Explanation

Line No.	Description
1	This environment variable opens up an output buffer of size limit of 200000.
2	Start of the declare section of the block.
3	A local variable l_vc_var1 is declared with VARCHAR2 data type with a precision of 10 characters.
4	A local variable l_b_var2 is declared with BOOLEAN data type and defaults to the Boolean value True.
5	A local variable l_vc_func_name is declared with VARCHAR2 data type with a precision of 30 characters and is defaulted to the string 'FUNC_BOO'.
6	Start of the execution section of the block.
7	A SELECT statement with the function call is dynamically formed for the function FUNC_BOO having a placeholder as its input parameter which gets its value from the local variable l_b_var2 in the USING clause is dynamically formed and executed using the EXECUTE IMMEDIATE clause. The result of the function call is assigned to the local variable l_vc_var1.
8	The local variable l_vc_var1 is printed using the system procedure DBMS_OUTPUT.PUT_LINE
9,10	End of the execution section of the block.

In the below example, the above function with Boolean input parameter is executed dynamically where its name is appended to the SELECT statement at run time. The DECODE function in the SELECT statement modifies the return value from the function FUNC_BOO and returns it in a more readable format.

```
1.  SET SERVEROUTPUT ON 200000;
2.  DECLARE
3.  l_vc_var1       VARCHAR2(30);
4.  l_b_var2        BOOLEAN     :=true;
5.  l_vc_func_name VARCHAR2(30):='FUNC_BOO';
6.  BEGIN
7.  EXECUTE immediate 'SELECT DECODE('||l_vc_func_name||'(:l_b_var2),
    ''True'', ''The value is True'', ''False'', ''The value is False'',
    ''The value is Null'') FROM dual' INTO l_vc_var1 USING l_b_var2;
8.  dbms_output.put_line(l_vc_var1);
9.  END;
10. /
```

Result:

The value is True

Script Explanation

Line No.	Description
1	This environment variable opens up an output buffer of size limit of 200000.
2	Start of the declare section of the block.
3	A local variable l_vc_var1 is declared with VARCHAR2 data type with a precision of 30 characters.
4	A local variable l_b_var2 is declared with BOOLEAN data type and defaults to the Boolean value True.
5	A local variable l_vc_func_name is declared with VARCHAR2 data type with a precision of 30 characters and is defaulted to the string 'FUNC_BOO'.
6	Start of the execution section of the block.
7	A SELECT statement with a DECODE function on the function call is dynamically formed for the function FUNC_BOO having a placeholder as its input parameter which gets its value from the local variable l_b_var2 in the USING clause is dynamically formed and executed using the EXECUTE IMMEDIATE clause. Here the DECODE function converts the FUNC_BOO's return value in a more readable way and the result of the DECODE function is then assigned to the local variable l_vc_var1.
8	The local variable l_vc_var1 is printed using the system procedure DBMS_OUTPUT.PUT_LINE
9,10	End of the execution section of the block.

In the below example, the above function's result helps in satisfying the WHERE condition of the SELECT statement which was impossible prior to R12.1 as the function has its input parameter's data type as Boolean. The function's name is appended to the dynamic string at the run time and the input Boolean variable for the function is passed as a bind variable in the USING clause.

```
1.   SET SERVEROUTPUT ON 200000;
2.   DECLARE
3.   l_vc_var1       VARCHAR2(10);
4.   l_b_var2        BOOLEAN      :=false;
5.   l_vc_func_name VARCHAR2(30):='FUNC_BOO';
6.   BEGIN
7.   EXECUTE immediate 'SELECT
8.   CASE COUNT(*)
9.   WHEN 1
10.  THEN ''True''
11.  ELSE ''NOT True''
12.  END
13.  FROM dual
14.  WHERE '||l_vc_func_name||'(:l_b_var2)=''True''' INTO l_vc_var1 USING
     l_b_var2;
15.  dbms_output.put_line(l_vc_var1);
16.  END;
17.  /
```

```
Result:
Not True
```

Script Explanation

Line No.	Description
1	This environment variable opens up an output buffer of size limit of 200000.
2	Start of the declare section of the block.
3	A local variable l_vc_var1 is declared with VARCHAR2 data type with a precision of 10 characters.
4	A local variable l_b_var2 is declared with BOOLEAN data type and defaults to the Boolean value False.
5	A local variable l_vc_func_name is declared with VARCHAR2 data type with a precision of 30 characters and is defaulted to the string 'FUNC_BOO'.
6	Start of the execution section of the block.
7	A SELECT statement with a CASE statement returning the text 'True' when the count is 1 and 'Not True' when the count is not equal to 1 from a dual table with the function FUNC_BOO's call in the WHERE condition equating it's RETURN value to the text 'True'. Here the function FUNC_BOO has its input parameter as a placeholder and this placeholder gets its value from the local variable l_b_var2. This dynamically generated SELECT statement is then parsed and executed using the EXECUTE IMMEDIATE statement and its result is assigned to the local variable l_vc_var1.
8	The local variable l_vc_var1 is printed using the system procedure DBMS_OUTPUT.PUT_LINE
9,10	End of the execution section of the block.

Dynamic PL/SQL Block for Duplication Deletion across the Database

One of the main performance degrading factors in a de-normalized database is the duplication of the rows in a table. In most of the OLAP modeled databases, the input to the tables is often in file format and if the loading method is not monitored properly, there is a possibility of loading the same file over and over resulting in a humongous table with duplicated entries.

The below script helps in removing the duplicates from all the tables in a database using the native dynamic SQL processing technique with the help of the data dictionary views alongside. There is also a limitation on the data types of the columns to be used for the duplication removal as the base for this process would be an SQL duplication removal query that will be formed dynamically for each table with all its columns. The columns with data types LONG, CLOB, BLOB, BFILE, XML, OBJECTS cannot be used for duplication check as they cannot be used in an SQL statement effectively for comparison. This block does not fail when there is a Null value in a column as Null check is also performed for all the columns.

The duplication check can also be limited to a single table by passing the table's name in the WHERE condition of the USER_TABLES view.

```
1.  SET SERVEROUTPUT ON 200000;
2.  DECLARE
3.  l_vc_query1 VARCHAR2(32767);
4.  BEGIN
5.  FOR loop_table IN
6.  (SELECT table_name FROM user_tables
7.  )
8.  LOOP
9.  l_vc_query1:='Delete from '||loop_table.table_name||' t1 Where
    t1.rowid not in ( Select max(t2.rowid) from
    '||loop_table.table_name||' t2 Where 1=1 ';
10. FOR loop_column IN
11. (SELECT column_name,
12. data_type
13. FROM user_tab_cols
14. WHERE table_name=loop_table.table_name
15. AND (data_type LIKE 'INTERVAL%'
16. OR data_type LIKE 'TIMESTAMP%'
17. OR data_type  IN ('BINARY_DOUBLE', 'BINARY_FLOAT','CHAR', 'DATE',
    'FLOAT', 'NCHAR', 'NUMBER', 'NVARCHAR2', 'RAW', 'ROWID',
    'UROWID', 'VARCHAR2'))
18. AND column_id IS NOT NULL
19. )
20. LOOP
21. IF loop_column.data_type IN
    ('BINARY_DOUBLE','BINARY_FLOAT','CHAR','FLOAT','NCHAR','NUMBER','
    NVARCHAR2','VARCHAR2') THEN
22. l_vc_query1    :=l_vc_query1||' and
    nvl(t1.'||loop_column.column_name||',''0'') =
    nvl(t2.'||loop_column.column_name||',''0'')';
23. ELSIF loop_column.data_type ='RAW' THEN
24. l_vc_query1    :=l_vc_query1||' and
    nvl(t1.'||loop_column.column_name||',utl_raw.cast_to_raw(''hi''))
    =
    nvl(t2.'||loop_column.column_name||',utl_raw.cast_to_raw(''hi''))
    ';
25. ELSIF loop_column.data_type ='DATE' THEN
26. l_vc_query1    :=l_vc_query1||' and
    nvl(t1.'||loop_column.column_name||',to_date(''31-Dec-9999'')) =
    nvl(t2.'||loop_column.column_name||',to_date(''31-Dec-9999''))';
27. ELSIF loop_column.data_type LIKE 'TIMESTAMP%' THEN
28. l_vc_query1:=l_vc_query1||' and
    nvl(t1.'||loop_column.column_name||',to_timestamp(''31-Dec-
    9999'')) =
    nvl(t2.'||loop_column.column_name||',to_timestamp(''31-Dec-
    9999''))';
29. ELSIF loop_column.data_type LIKE 'INTERVAL DAY%' THEN
30. l_vc_query1:=l_vc_query1||' and
    nvl(t1.'||loop_column.column_name||',numtodsinterval(1,''second''
    )) =
    nvl(t2.'||loop_column.column_name||',numtodsinterval(1,''second''
    ))';
31. ELSIF loop_column.data_type LIKE 'INTERVAL YEAR%' THEN
```

```
32.  l_vc_query1:=l_vc_query1||' and
     nvl(t1.'||loop_column.column_name||',numtoyminterval(1,''year''))
     =
     nvl(t2.'||loop_column.column_name||',numtoyminterval(1,''year''))
     ';
33.  ELSIF loop_column.data_type IN ('ROWID','UROWID') THEN
34.  l_vc_query1 :=l_vc_query1||' and
     nvl(t1.'||loop_column.column_name||',t2.rowid) =
     nvl(t2.'||loop_column.column_name||',t2.rowid)';
35.  ELSE
36.  l_vc_query1:=l_vc_query1||' and t1.'||loop_column.column_name||'
     = '||loop_column.column_name;
37.  END IF;
38.  END LOOP loop_column;
39.  l_vc_query1:=l_vc_query1||')';
40.  EXECUTE immediate (l_vc_query1);
41.  IF sql%rowcount>0 THEN
42.  Dbms_output.put_line('Duplication is found for the table
     '||loop_table.table_name||' and deleted.');
43.  END IF;
44.  COMMIT;
45.  END LOOP loop_table;
46.  END;
47.  /
```

Script Explanation

Line No.	Description
1	This environment variable opens up an output buffer of size limit of 200000.
2	Start of the declare section of the block.
3	A local variable l_vc_var1 is declared with VARCHAR2 data type with a precision of 32,767 characters.
4	Start of the execution section of the block.
5-8	Start of the cursor FOR loop which selects all the table names from the USER_TABLES data dictionary view.
9	The local variable l_vc_var1 is assigned to the partial duplication deletion data as *'Delete from '||loop_table.table_name||' t1 Where t1.rowid not in (Select max(t2.rowid) from '|| loop_table.table_name||' t2 Where 1=1 '*. Here, the table names for the duplication deletion query formed is taken from the cursor FOR loop's column value.
10-20	Start of the cursor FOR loop which selects all the column names and their corresponding data types from the table which is selected from the cursor FOR loop started at the line number 5 from the USER_TAB_COLS data dictionary view. The columns selected with this cursor FOR loop are restricted based on their data types and the allowed data types are BINARY_DOUBLE, BINARY_FLOAT, CHAR, DATE, FLOAT, NCHAR, NUMBER, NVARCHAR2, RAW, ROWID, UROWID, VARCHAR2, TIMESTAMP and INTERVAL.

21	Start of the IF condition which allows the columns with the data types BINARY_DOUBLE, BINARY_FLOAT, CHAR, FLOAT, NCHAR, NUMBER, NVARCHAR2, VARCHAR2.
22	The local variable l_vc_query1 is appended with the text ' *and nvl(t1.'||loop_column.column_name||',"0") = nvl(t2.'|| loop_column.column_name||',"0")'* which forms the AND condition for the partially formed duplication deletion query which is created in the line number 9. Here the NVL function on the both sides of the column names has its second parameter as '0' which is compatible for the data types listed in the above step number 21.
23	If the data type of the column from the cursor FOR loop does not match with the list of data types mentioned in the line number 21, then the control of the program shifts to this ELSIF condition which checks for the data type RAW.
24	The local variable l_vc_query1 is appended with the text ' *and nvl(t1.'|| loop_column.column_name||',utl_raw.cast_to_raw("hi")) = nvl(t2.'|| loop_column.column_name||',utl_raw.cast_to_raw("hi"))'* which forms the AND condition of the partially formed duplication deletion query which is created in the line number 9. Here the NVL function on the both sides of the column names has its second parameter as *utl_raw.cast_to_raw('hi')* which is compatible for the data type listed in the above step number 23.
25	If the data type of the column from the cursor FOR loop does not match with the data type mentioned in the line number 23, then the control of the program shifts to this ELSIF condition which checks for the data type DATE.
26	The local variable l_vc_query1 is appended with the text ' *and nvl(t1.'|| loop_column.column_name||',to_date("31-Dec-9999")) = nvl(t2.'|| loop_column.column_name||',to_date("31-Dec-9999"))'* which forms the AND condition of the partially formed duplication deletion query which is created in the line number 9. Here the NVL function on the both sides of the column names has its second parameter as *to_date('31-Dec-9999')* which is compatible for the data type listed in the above step number 25.
27	If the data type of the column from the cursor FOR loop does not match with the data type mentioned in the line number 25, then the control of the program shifts to this ELSIF condition which checks for the data type TIMESTAMP.
28	The local variable l_vc_query1 is appended with the text ' *and nvl(t1.'|| loop_column.column_name||',to_timestamp("31-Dec-9999")) = nvl(t2.'|| loop_column.column_name||',to_timestamp("31-Dec-9999"))'* which forms the AND condition of the partially formed duplication deletion query which is created in the line number 9. Here the NVL function on the both sides of the column names has its second parameter as *to_timestamp('31-Dec-9999')* which is compatible for the data type listed in the above step number 27.

29	If the data type of the column from the cursor FOR loop does not match with the data type mentioned in the line number 27, then the control of the program shifts to this ELSIF condition which checks for the data type INTERVAL DAY TO SECOND.
30	The local variable l_vc_query1 is appended with the text *' and nvl(t1.'|| loop_column.column_name||',numtodsinterval(1,"second")) = nvl(t2.'|| loop_column.column_name||',numtodsinterval(1,"second"))'* which forms the AND condition of the partially formed duplication deletion query which is created in the line number 9. Here the NVL function on the both sides of the column names has its second parameter as *numtodsinterval(1,'second')* which is compatible for the data type listed in the above step number 29.
31	If the data type of the column from the cursor FOR loop does not match with the data type mentioned in the line number 29, then the control of the program shifts to this ELSIF condition which checks for the data type INTERVAL YEAR TO MONTH.
32	The local variable l_vc_query1 is appended with the text *' and nvl(t1.'|| loop_column.column_name||',numtoyminterval(1,"year")) = nvl(t2.'|| loop_column.column_name||',numtoyminterval(1,"year"))'* which forms the AND condition of the partially formed duplication deletion query which is created in the line number 9. Here the NVL function on the both sides of the column names has its second parameter as *numtoyminterval(1,'year')* which is compatible for the data type listed in the above step number 31.
33	If the data type of the column from the cursor FOR loop does not match with the data type mentioned in the line number 31, then the control of the program shifts to this ELSIF condition which checks for the data type ROWID or UROWID.
34	The local variable l_vc_query1 is appended with the text *' and nvl(t1.'|| loop_column.column_name||',t2.rowid) = nvl(t2.'|| loop_column.column_name||',t2.rowid)'* which forms the AND condition of the partially formed duplication deletion query which is created in the line number 9. Here the NVL function on the both sides of the column names has its second parameter as *t2.rowid* which is compatible for the data types listed in the above step number 31. Here *t2.rowid* is the pseudo column ROWID from the table with the alias name T2.
35	If the data type of the column from the cursor FOR loop does not match with any of the data types mentioned in the above steps, the control of the program shifts to this final ELSE condition.
36	The local variable l_vc_query1 is appended with the text *' and t1.'|| loop_column.column_name||' = '|| loop_column.column_name'* which forms the AND condition of the partially formed duplication deletion query which is created in the line number 9.
37	End of the IF condition.

38	End of the cursor FOR loop loop_column.
39	The local variable l_vc_query1 is appended with a close bracket ')' which dynamically completes the duplication deletion query.
40	The local variable is then parsed and executed using the EXECUTE IMMEDIATE statement.
41	Start of the IF condition which checks for the condition SQL%ROWCOUNT>0. SQL%ROWCOUNT is a cursor attribute which returns the number of rows affected by the last DML operation.
42	The table name with duplicate rows is printed using the system defined procedure DBMS_OUTPUT.PUT_LINE.
43	End of the IF statement.
44	The DML operation performed in the step 40 is committed.
45	End of the cursor FOR loop loop_table.
46,47	End of the execution section of the block.

DBMS_SQL API

This has been the first ever created innovative solution for building dynamic SQL statements and PL/SQL blocks in the Oracle version 7 prior to the native method which is the widely accepted method due to its less coding complexity and easy understandability unlike its predecessor.

This API was enhanced to support collections in the version 8i and has groomed itself through the successive releases up to 12c. Nevertheless, the focus of dynamic scripting has been shifted to NDS from its availability in the Oracle version 9i and the DBMS_SQL API is available only for backward compatibility.

DBMS_SQL API has one additional feature, which is still not available in the native method. The API supports managing the dynamic statements when the number of columns or the data types of the returned columns are unknown during the run time that cannot be done through NDS.

This API supports various procedures and functions for processing the dynamic statements that are explained below.

OPEN_CURSOR

The OPEN_CURSOR function in the DBMS_SQL package when executed, opens up a cursor and returns a unique cursor ID which lives through the session. This cursor ID will be used as a reference for processing the dynamic query. This function does not have any formal parameters.

The prototype of the OPEN_CURSOR function is shown below with its return type as Integer data type,

```
Create or replace function open_cursor
Return integer
Is …
```

The prototype for using the OPEN_CURSOR function is shown below.

```
Dbms_sql.open_cursor;
```

In the below example, a cursor is opened and its unique ID is assigned to an integer variable and printed.

```
1.   SET SERVEROUTPUT ON 200000;
2.   DECLARE
3.   l_i_cursor_id INTEGER;
4.   BEGIN
5.   l_i_cursor_id:=dbms_sql.open_cursor;
6.   dbms_output.put_line('The cursor ID is '||l_i_cursor_id);
7.   Dbms_sql.close_cursor(l_i_cursor_id);
8.   END;
9.   /
```

Result:
The cursor ID is 1221907173

Script Explanation

Line No.	Description
1	This environment variable opens up an output buffer of size limit of 200000.
2	Start of the declare section of the block.
3	A local variable l_i_cursor_id is declared with INTEGER data type.
4	Start of the execution section of the block.
5	The function DBMS_SQL.OPEN_CURSOR is executed and its return value is assigned to the local variable l_i_cursor_id.
6	The local variable l_i_cursor_id is printed using the system procedure DBMS_OUTPUT.PUT_LINE.
7	The cursor is closed using the procedure DBMS_SQL.CLOSE_CURSOR with its input parameter as the local variable l_i_cursor_id
8,9	End of the execution section of the block.

Security Checks on a Cursor

The inappropriate use of cursor usage can be protected either during the binding and executing process or for every DBMS_SQL subprogram call. The checks performed are,

- The CURRENT_USER must be the same on the calling subprogram and the most recent parse.

- The roles enabled on the calling subprogram must be a superset of the roles enabled on the most recent parse.

These checks are performed using the overloading function OPEN_CURSOR which takes a formal parameter defining the security level with the allowed values Null, 1 and 2.

The prototype for defining an overloaded OPEN_CURSOR function is as below,

```
DBMS_SQL.OPEN_CURSOR(<Security_level>);
```

- When the security level is 1 or Null, the security checks are made only during the binding and executing process.

- When the security level is 2, the security checks are always made.

PARSE

The parse procedure checks the syntax of the dynamic statement and parses it with the cursor ID generated using the OPEN_CURSOR function explained in the above section.

The prototype for using the PARSE procedure is shown below,

```
DBMS_SQL.PARSE(<Cursor_ID>, <Dynamic_string>, <Language_flag>);
```

- **Cursor_ID** is a unique identifier for the cursor which is mapped to the dynamic string for processing.

- **Dynamic_string** is a dynamic SQL statement or a PL/SQL block which is to be parsed and executed.

- **Language_flag** specifies the Oracle database version's behavior and is of three types.

  ➤ **DBMS_SQL.V6 or 0**: Specifies the behavior of the Oracle database version 6.

> ➤ **DBMS_SQL.Native or 1:** Specifies the normal behavior of the Oracle database in which the program is executed.

> ➤ **DBMS_SQL.V7 or 2:** Specifies the behavior of the Oracle database version 7.

> 🔔 Note: The DDL statements are executed when they are parsed and the function DBMS_SQL.EXECUTE need not be used on them.

In the below example, a table creation is performed during the parsing stage itself using the PARSE procedure with NATIVE as its language.

```
1.  SET SERVEROUTPUT ON 200000;
2.  DECLARE
3.  l_i_cursor_id INTEGER;
4.  BEGIN
5.  l_i_cursor_id:=dbms_sql.open_cursor;
6.  dbms_sql.parse(l_i_cursor_id, 'create table parse_test1(col number)',
    dbms_sql.native);
7.  Dbms_sql.close_cursor(l_i_cursor_id);
8.  END;
9.  /
```

Script Explanation

Line No.	Description
1	This environment variable opens up an output buffer of size limit of 200000.
2	Start of the declare section of the block.
3	A local variable l_i_cursor_id is declared with INTEGER data type.
4	Start of the execution section of the block.
5	The function DBMS_SQL.OPEN_CURSOR is executed and its return value is assigned to the local variable l_i_cursor_id.
6	The procedure DBMS_SQL. PARSE is executed with its first parameter as the local variable l_i_cursor_id, the second parameter to a dynamic table creation statement and its third parameter as the function DBMS_SQL. NATIVE.
7	The cursor is closed using the procedure DBMS_SQL.CLOSE_CURSOR with its input parameter as the local variable l_i_cursor_id
8,9	End of the execution section of the block.

Inappropriate Use of a Cursor

When an inappropriate cursor ID is used in the PARSE procedure, the access to the DBMS_SQL package will be denied for the complete session. In the below example, a random integer is used in the PARSE function replacing the integer value from the OPEN_CURSOR function results in to the below shown error report.

```
1.  SET SERVEROUTPUT ON 200000;
2.  DECLARE
3.  l_i_cursor_id INTEGER;
4.  BEGIN
5.  l_i_cursor_id:=dbms_sql.open_cursor;
6.  dbms_sql.parse(12345678,'create table parse_test2(col
    number)',dbms_sql.native);
7.  Dbms_sql.close_cursor(l_i_cursor_id);
8.  END;
9.  /
```

```
Error report:
ORA-29471: DBMS_SQL access denied
ORA-06512: at "SYS.DBMS_SQL", line 1120
ORA-06512: at line 5
```

Script Explanation

Line No.	Description
1	This environment variable opens up an output buffer of size limit of 200000.
2	Start of the declare section of the block.
3	A local variable l_i_cursor_id is declared with INTEGER data type.
4	Start of the execution section of the block.
5	The function DBMS_SQL.OPEN_CURSOR is executed and its return value is assigned to the local variable l_i_cursor_id.
6	The procedure DBMS_SQL. PARSE is executed with its first parameter as a random integer, the second parameter to a dynamic table creation statement and its third parameter as the function DBMS_SQL. NATIVE.
7	The cursor is closed using the procedure DBMS_SQL.CLOSE_CURSOR with its input parameter as the local variable l_i_cursor_id
8,9	End of the execution section of the block.

After receiving the above error report, any further calls to the DBMS_SQL package will be denied as shown in the below example even though there is no illegal cursor usage.

```
1.  SET SERVEROUTPUT ON 200000;
2.  DECLARE
3.  l_i_cursor_id INTEGER;
4.  BEGIN
5.  l_i_cursor_id:=dbms_sql.open_cursor;
6.  dbms_output.put_line(l_i_cursor_id);
7.  Dbms_sql.close_cursor(l_i_cursor_id);
8.  END;
9.  /
```

```
Error report:
```

```
ORA-29471: DBMS_SQL access denied
ORA-06512: at "SYS.DBMS_SQL", line 1084
ORA-06512: at line 4
```

Script Explanation

Line No.	Description
1	This environment variable opens up an output buffer of size limit of 200000.
2	Start of the declare section of the block.
3	A local variable l_i_cursor_id is declared with INTEGER data type.
4	Start of the execution section of the block.
5	The function DBMS_SQL.OPEN_CURSOR is executed and its return value is assigned to the local variable l_i_cursor_id.
6	The local variable l_i_cursor_id is printed using the system procedure DBMS_OUTPUT.PUT_LINE.
7	The cursor is closed using the procedure DBMS_SQL.CLOSE_CURSOR with its input parameter as the local variable l_i_cursor_id
8,9	End of the execution section of the block.

EXECUTE

The dynamically created SQL and PL/SQL statements are executed using the EXECUTE function from the DBMS_SQL package. This function accepts one input formal parameter accepting the cursor ID which is associated with the parsed SQL statements or PL/SQL units. This function returns an integer value stating the number of rows affected from the execution process.

In the below example, an anonymous block printing a default message is parsed and executed using the PARSE and EXECUTE subprograms respectively.

```
1.  SET SERVEROUTPUT ON 200000;
2.  DECLARE
3.  l_i_cursor_id INTEGER;
4.  l_n_rowcount  NUMBER;
5.  BEGIN
6.  l_i_cursor_id:=dbms_sql.open_cursor;
7.  dbms_sql.parse(l_i_cursor_id,'begin dbms_output.put_line(''Execute
    function test!!''); end;',dbms_sql.native);
8.  l_n_rowcount:=dbms_sql.execute(l_i_cursor_id);
9.  Dbms_sql.close_cursor(l_i_cursor_id);
10. END;
11. /
```

```
Result:
Execute function test!!
```

Script Explanation

Line No.	Description
1	This environment variable opens up an output buffer of size limit of 200000.

2	Start of the declare section of the block.
3	A local variable l_i_cursor_id is declared with INTEGER data type.
4	A local variable l_n_rowcount is declared with NUMBER data type.
5	Start of the execution section of the block.
6	The function DBMS_SQL.OPEN_CURSOR is executed and its return value is assigned to the local variable l_i_cursor_id.
7	The procedure DBMS_SQL. PARSE is executed with its first parameter as the local variable l_i_cursor_id, the second parameter with a dynamic anonymous block which prints a default string message using the system defined procedure DBMS_OUTPUT. PUT_LINE and its third parameter as the function DBMS_SQL. NATIVE.
8	The function DBMS_SQL.EXECUTE is executed with its input parameter as the local variable l_i_cursor_id and the RETURN value is assigned to the local variable l_n_rowcount.
9	The cursor is closed using the procedure DBMS_SQL.CLOSE_CURSOR with its input parameter as the local variable l_i_cursor_id
10,11	End of the execution section of the block.

BIND_VARIABLE

The bind variables supplied to a dynamic query performing any DML operation needs to use the BIND_VARIABLE procedure from the DBMS_SQL package. When this dynamic query is executed, the bind values supplied through this procedure will be used in the placeholders.

The prototype for defining the BIND_VARIABLE procedure is shown below,

```
BIND_VARIABLE(<Cursor_ID>, <Placeholder_name>, <Variable | Value>);
```

Here, the Placeholder_name is the bind column name from the dynamic query and the Variable or the Value will be its replacing bind variable.

> 🔔 Note: The colon in the place holder placed on the line number 8 in the below example is not mandatory.

In the below example, a table is created using the PARSE procedure and a row is inserted into this table with a bind variable using the BIND_VARIABLE procedure which is then executed using the EXECUTE function in the DBMS_SQL package.

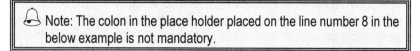

```
1.   SET SERVEROUTPUT ON 200000;
```

```
2.  DECLARE
3.  l_i_cursor_id INTEGER;
4.  l_n_rowcount   NUMBER;
5.  BEGIN
6.  l_i_cursor_id:=dbms_sql.open_cursor;
7.  dbms_sql.parse(l_i_cursor_id,'Create table bind_test1(col
    varchar2(30))',dbms_sql.native);
8.  dbms_sql.parse(l_i_cursor_id,'insert into bind_test1 values
    (:col)',dbms_sql.native);
9.  dbms_sql.bind_variable(l_i_cursor_id,':col','Oracle');
10. l_n_rowcount:=dbms_sql.execute(l_i_cursor_id);
11. dbms_output.put_line('The row count of the last executed DML
    statement is '||l_n_rowcount);
12. Dbms_sql.close_cursor(l_i_cursor_id);
13. END;
14. /
```

Result:
The row count of the last executed DML statement is 1

Script Explanation

Line No.	Description
1	This environment variable opens up an output buffer of size limit of 200000.
2	Start of the declare section of the block.
3	A local variable l_i_cursor_id is declared with INTEGER data type.
4	A local variable l_n_rowcount is declared with NUMBER data type.
5	Start of the execution section of the block.
6	The function DBMS_SQL.OPEN_CURSOR is executed and its return value is assigned to the local variable l_i_cursor_id.
7	The procedure DBMS_SQL. PARSE is executed with its first parameter as the local variable l_i_cursor_id, the second parameter with a dynamic create table statement and its third parameter as the function DBMS_SQL.NATIVE.
8	The procedure DBMS_SQL.PARSE is executed with its first parameter as the local variable l_i_cursor_id, the second parameter to a dynamic INSERT statement with a placeholder in the VALUES clause and its third parameter as the function DBMS_SQL.NATIVE.
9	The procedure DBMS_SQL.BIND_VARIABLE is executed with its first parameter as the local variable l_i_cursor_id, the second parameter as the placeholder name from the line number 8 and the third parameter as the string 'Oracle'.
10	The function DBMS_SQL.EXECUTE is executed with its input parameter as the local variable l_i_cursor_id and the RETURN value is assigned to the local variable l_n_rowcount.
11	The local variable l_n_rowcount is printed using the system defined procedure DBMS_OUTPUT.PUT_LINE.

| 12 | The cursor is closed using the procedure DBMS_SQL.CLOSE_CURSOR with its input parameter as the local variable l_i_cursor_id. |
| 13,14 | End of the execution section of the block. |

DEFINE_COLUMN

When the cursor is associated to a dynamic SQL statement, for each column in the statement, the DEFINE_COLUMN procedure has to be executed once to specify a variable. These columns in the dynamic SQL are identified using their relative positions starting from left to right as they appear in their statement. Thus the DEFINE_COLUMN procedure has its second parameter just to map the position of the column from the statement to the defined variable.

> 🔔 Note: The columns have to be defined before the query execution.

To define LONG columns, the procedure DEFINE_COLUMN_LONG has to be used instead.

The prototype for defining the DEFINE_COLUMN procedure is shown below,

```
DBMS_SQL.DEFINE_COLUMN(<Cursor_id>, <Relative_position>, <Defined_variable>
);
```

FETCH_ROWS

The FETCH_ROWS function acts as a flag which returns the integer value 1 for each row fetched from the cursor and 0 if no rows are fetched. This function when executed, returns the flag value of the current row in the cursor and moves the control on to the next row and returns the corresponding flag value during its next execution respectively.

The prototype for defining the FETCH_ROWS function is shown below,

```
DBMS_SQL.FETCH_ROWS(<Cursor_ID>);
```

In the below example, the first 3 rows from the EMPLOYEES table are parsed and executed. The cursor now holds 3 records from the EMPLOYEES table and when the FETCH_ROWS procedure is executed for 3 times, the value returned would be 1 and if it is executed for the 4th time, the function returns the value 0 as there is no 4th row available in the cursor.

```
1.  SET SERVEROUTPUT ON 200000;
2.  DECLARE
3.  l_i_cursor_id   INTEGER;
4.  l_n_rowcount    NUMBER;
5.  BEGIN
6.  l_i_cursor_id:=dbms_sql.open_cursor;
7.  dbms_sql.parse(l_i_cursor_id,'select first_name,last_name from
    employees where rownum<=3',dbms_sql.native);
8.  l_n_rowcount:=dbms_sql.execute(l_i_cursor_id);
9.  dbms_output.put_line('The FETCH_ROWS value before fetching the 1st row:
    '||dbms_sql.fetch_rows(l_i_cursor_id));
10. dbms_output.put_line('The FETCH_ROWS value before fetching the 2nd row:
    '||dbms_sql.fetch_rows(l_i_cursor_id));
11. dbms_output.put_line('The FETCH_ROWS value before fetching the 3rd row:
    '||dbms_sql.fetch_rows(l_i_cursor_id));
12. dbms_output.put_line('The FETCH_ROWS value before fetching the 4st row:
    '||dbms_sql.fetch_rows(l_i_cursor_id));
13. Dbms_sql.close_cursor(l_i_cursor_id);
14. END;
15. /
```

Result:
```
The FETCH_ROWS value before fetching the 1st row: 1
The FETCH_ROWS value before fetching the 2nd row: 1
The FETCH_ROWS value before fetching the 3rd row: 1
The FETCH_ROWS value before fetching the 4st row: 0
```

Script Explanation

Line No.	Description
1	This environment variable opens up an output buffer of size limit of 200000.
2	Start of the declare section of the block.
3	A local variable l_i_cursor_id is declared with INTEGER data type.
4	A local variable l_n_rowcount is declared with NUMBER data type.
5	Start of the execution section of the block.
6	The function DBMS_SQL.OPEN_CURSOR is executed and its return value is assigned to the local variable l_i_cursor_id.
7	The procedure DBMS_SQL.PARSE is executed with its first parameter as the local variable l_i_cursor_id, the second parameter to a dynamic SELECT query selecting the first name and the last name of the first 3 employees from the EMPLOYEES table and its third parameter as the function DBMS_SQL.NATIVE.
8	The function DBMS_SQL.EXECUTE is executed with its input parameter as the local variable l_i_cursor_id and the RETURN value is assigned to the local variable l_n_rowcount.
9-12	The function DBMS_SQL.FETCH_ROW is executed four times with its input parameter as the local variable l_i_cursor_id and returns the flag stating the confirmation on the rows retrieved.
13	The cursor is closed using the procedure DBMS_SQL.CLOSE_CURSOR with its input parameter as the local variable l_i_cursor_id.

14,15   End of the execution section of the block.

COLUMN_VALUE and VARIABLE_VALUE

The COLUMN_VALUE procedure determines the values of the columns retrieved by the FETCH_ROWS function. To fetch the LONG columns, COLUMN_VALUE_LONG procedure has to be used.

When there is an anonymous block with a subprogram call or a DML statement with a RETURN statement, VARIABLE_VALUE procedure has to be used.

The prototype for defining the COLUMN_VALUE and VARIABLE_VALUE procedures are shown below,

```
DBMS_SQL.COLUMN_VALUE(<Cursor_id>, <Relative_position>, <Defined_variable>);
```

```
DBMS_SQL.VARIABLE_VALUE(<Cursor_id>, <Placeholder_name>,
<Defined_variable>);
```

In the below example, a product is inserted into the PRODUCT table with all the columns passed as bind variable except for the primary key column which is generated as MAX(PRODUCT_ID) +1. This primary key column is returned to the program and is mapped to a defined variable using the VARIABLE_VALUE procedure as shown below,

```
1.  SET SERVEROUTPUT ON 200000;
2.  DECLARE
3.  l_i_cursor_id INTEGER;
4.  l_n_rowcount  NUMBER;
5.  l_vc_product_name product.product_name%type:='Solar Charger';
6.  l_d_product_launch_date product.product_launch_date%type:=DATE'1989-09-
    30';
7.  l_n_product_price product.product_price%type:=1000;
8.  l_n_pid NUMBER;
9.  BEGIN
10. l_i_cursor_id:=dbms_sql.open_cursor;
11. dbms_sql.parse(l_i_cursor_id,'insert into product values ((select
    max(product_id)+1 from product), :product_name, :product_launch_date,
    :product_price) returning product_id into :pid', dbms_sql.native);
12. dbms_sql.bind_variable(l_i_cursor_id, 'product_name',
    l_vc_product_name);
13. dbms_sql.bind_variable(l_i_cursor_id, 'product_launch_date',
    l_d_product_launch_date);
14. dbms_sql.bind_variable(l_i_cursor_id, 'product_price',
    l_n_product_price);
15. dbms_sql.bind_variable(l_i_cursor_id, ':pid', l_n_pid);
16. l_n_rowcount:=dbms_sql.execute(l_i_cursor_id);
17. dbms_sql.variable_value(l_i_cursor_id, ':pid', l_n_pid);
18. dbms_output.put_line('The Product ID is '||l_n_pid);
```

```
19. Dbms_sql.close_cursor(l_i_cursor_id);
20. END;
21. /
```

Result:
The Product ID is 100

Script Explanation

Line No.	Description
1	This environment variable opens up an output buffer of size limit of 200000.
2	Start of the declare section of the block.
3	A local variable l_i_cursor_id is declared with INTEGER data type.
4	A local variable l_n_rowcount is declared with NUMBER data type.
5	A local variable l_vc_product_name is declared with an anchor data type of the PRODUCT_NAME column from the PRODUCT table and is defaulted to the string 'Solar Charger'.
6	A local variable l_d_product_launch_date is declared with an anchor data type of the PRODUCT_LAUNCH_DATE column from the PRODUCT table and defaults to the date 30th of September, 1989 using the date literal.
7	A local variable l_n_product_price is declared with an anchor data type of the PRODUCT_PRICE column from the PRODUCT table and defaults to the integer 1000.
8	A local variable l_n_pid is declared with the data type NUMBER.
9	Start of the execution section of the block.
10	The function DBMS_SQL.OPEN_CURSOR is executed and its return value is assigned to the local variable l_i_cursor_id.
11	The procedure DBMS_SQL.PARSE is executed with its first parameter as the local variable l_i_cursor_id, the second parameter to a dynamic INSERT query which inserts data into the PRODUCT table with its first column data as the maximum of the product ID from the table, second, third and the fourth column values as placeholders :product_name, :product_launch_date, :product_price for the bind variables. This dynamic INSERT statement also returns the product ID column value into the placeholder :pid. The third parameter is assigned with the function DBMS_SQL.NATIVE.
12	The procedure DBMS_SQL.BIND_VARIABLE is executed for mapping the placeholders and the bind variables. Its first parameter has the local variable l_i_cursor_id, second parameter has the placeholder name :product_name and the third parameter have the local variable l_vc_product_name.
13	The procedure DBMS_SQL.BIND_VARIABLE is executed for mapping the placeholders and the bind variables. Its first parameter has the local variable l_i_cursor_id, second parameter has the placeholder name

	:product_launch_date and the third parameter has the local variable l_vc_product_launch_date.
14	The procedure DBMS_SQL.BIND_VARIABLE is executed for mapping the placeholders and the bind variables. Its first parameter has the local variable l_i_cursor_id, second parameter has the placeholder name :product_price and the third parameter have the local variable l_vc_product_price.
15	The procedure DBMS_SQL.BIND_VARIABLE is executed for mapping the placeholders and the bind variables. Its first parameter has the local variable l_i_cursor_id, second parameter have the placeholder name :pid and the third parameter has the local variable l_n_pid.
16	The function DBMS_SQL.EXECUTE is executed with its input parameter as the local variable l_i_cursor_id and the RETURN value is assigned to the local variable l_n_rowcount.
17	The procedure DBMS_SQL.VARIABLE_VALUE is executed, which assigns the out mode bind variable to a local variable. The procedure has its first parameter as the local variable l_i_cursor_id, the second parameter as the placeholder name :pid and the third parameter as the local variable l_n_pid.
18	The local variable l_n_pid is printed using the system defined procedure DBMS_OUTPUT.PUT_LINE.
19	The cursor is closed using the procedure DBMS_SQL.CLOSE_CURSOR with its input parameter as the local variable l_i_cursor_id.
20,21	End of the execution section of the block.

EXECUTE_AND_FETCH

The EXECUTE_AND_FETCH function executes the assigned cursor and fetches the rows. This function performs the job of both the EXECUTE function and the FETCH_ROWS function in a single call.

The prototype for defining the EXECUTE_AND_FETCH function is shown below,

```
DBMS_SQL.EXECUTE_AND_FETCH(<Cursor_id>);
```

In the below example, the first name and the last name of all the employees are parsed, defined and executed using the EXECUTE_AND_FETCH function. All the employee's information is printed using a SIMPLE LOOP formation with an exit condition of checking the return value of FETCH_ROWS function to be 0 or not. If the return value is 0, there are no more rows to be fetched and the loop is terminated. If the return value is 1, the current row from the cursor is printed.

```
1.  SET SERVEROUTPUT ON 200000;
2.  DECLARE
3.  l_i_cursor_id    INTEGER;
```

```
4.   l_n_rowcount    NUMBER;
5.   l_vc_first_name VARCHAR2(30);
6.   l_vc_last_name  VARCHAR2(30);
7.   BEGIN
8.   l_i_cursor_id:=dbms_sql.open_cursor;
9.   dbms_sql.parse(l_i_cursor_id,'select first_name,last_name from
     employees', dbms_sql.native);
10.  dbms_sql.define_column(l_i_cursor_id,1,l_vc_first_name,30);
11.  dbms_sql.define_column(l_i_cursor_id,2,l_vc_last_name,30);
12.  l_n_rowcount:=dbms_sql.execute_and_fetch(l_i_cursor_id);
13.  LOOP
14.  EXIT
15.  WHEN dbms_sql.fetch_rows(l_i_cursor_id)=0;
16.  dbms_sql.column_value(l_i_cursor_id,1,l_vc_first_name);
17.  dbms_sql.column_value(l_i_cursor_id,2,l_vc_last_name);
18.  dbms_output.put_line(l_vc_last_name||', '||l_vc_first_name);
19.  END LOOP;
20.  Dbms_sql.close_cursor(l_i_cursor_id);
21.  END;
22.  /
```

Result:
```
Lorentz, Diana
Greenberg, Nancy
Faviet, Daniel
Chen, John
...
...
```

Script Explanation

Line No.	Description
1	This environment variable opens up an output buffer of size limit of 200000.
2	Start of the declare section of the block.
3	A local variable l_i_cursor_id is declared with INTEGER data type.
4	A local variable l_n_rowcount is declared with NUMBER data type.
5	A local variable l_vc_first_name is declared with VARCHAR2 data type with a precision of 30 characters.
6	A local variable l_vc_last_name is declared with VARCHAR2 data type with a precision of 30 characters.
7	Start of the execution section of the block.
8	The function DBMS_SQL.OPEN_CURSOR is executed and its return value is assigned to the local variable l_i_cursor_id.
9	The procedure DBMS_SQL.PARSE is executed with its first parameter as the local variable l_i_cursor_id, the second parameter to a dynamic SELECT query selecting the first name and the last name from the EMLPOYEES table. The third parameter is assigned with the function DBMS_SQL.NATIVE.
10	The procedure DBMS_SQL.DEFINE_COLUMN is executed for defining the columns list from the dynamic SELECT query with respect to its relative

	position. The first parameter of this procedure has the local variable l_i_cursor_id, second parameter has the integer 1 and the third parameter has the local variable l_vc_first_name.
11	The procedure DBMS_SQL.DEFINE_COLUMN is executed for defining the columns list from the dynamic SELECT query with respect to its relative position. The first parameter of this procedure has the local variable l_i_cursor_id, second parameter has the integer 2 and the third parameter has the local variable l_vc_last_name.
12	The function DBMS_SQL.EXECUTE_AND_FETCH is executed with its input parameter as the local variable l_i_cursor_id and the RETURN value is assigned to the local variable l_n_rowcount.
13	Start of the SIMPLE loop.
14,15	An EXIT condition with a condition of DBMS_SQL.FETCH_ROWS(l_i_cursor_id)=0 is placed inside the SIMPLE loop.
16	The procedure DBMS_SQL.COLUMN_VALUE is executed, which assigns the out mode bind variable to a local variable. This procedure has its first parameter as the local variable l_i_cursor_id, second parameter has the integer 1 and the third parameter as the local variable l_vc_first_name.
17	The procedure DBMS_SQL.COLUMN_VALUE is executed, which assigns the out mode bind variable to a local variable. This procedure has its first parameter as the local variable l_i_cursor_id, second parameter has the integer 1 and the third parameter as the local variable l_vc_last_name.
18	The local variables l_vc_last_name and l_vc_first_name are concatenated together and printed using the system defined procedure DBMS_OUTPUT.PUT_LINE.
19	End of the SIMPLE loop.
20	The cursor is closed using the procedure DBMS_SQL.CLOSE_CURSOR with its input parameter as the local variable l_i_cursor_id.
21,22	End of the execution section of the block.

CLOSE_CURSOR

Closing the cursor at the end of the program helps in freeing the memory occupied by the cursor during the program and reduces the number of cursors alive during the session concurrently. A cursor can be closed by using the CLOSE_CURSOR procedure with the cursor ID as its formal parameter.

The prototype for defining a CLOSE_CURSOR procedure is shown below,

```
DBMS_SQL.CLOSE_CURSOR(<Cursor_ID>);
```

DBMS_SQL API: Method 4 Type Processing

The method 4 type is a scenario in which the program understands, parses, executes and fetches the dynamic statement without knowing its structure at the run time. This technique is not available in the native dynamic method and we depend solely on this API for performing any method 4 type scenario that is mostly uncommon and complex.

The package DBMS_SQL supports the Method-4 processing through two procedures, namely, DESCRIBE_COLUMNS and DESCRIBE_COLUMNS2. Initially the procedure DESCRIBE_COLUMNS was only present, which lacked supporting the column names with more than 32 characters leading to the development of DESCRIBE_COLUMNS2 procedure which allows column names up to 32,767 in length.

DESCRIBE_COLUMNS

The DESCRIBE_COLUMNS API describes the columns of the SELECT statement that is opened and parsed through a cursor. This procedure consists of one input parameter accepting the cursor ID that is active in the session and two output parameters producing the number of columns in the statement parsed by the cursor and their description respectively.

The syntax for this procedure is shown below,

```
PROCEDURE describe_columns(c IN INTEGER, col_cnt OUT INTEGER, desc_t OUT
desc_tab);
```

The third parameter has a nested table DESC_TAB as its data type which is created from the index by table DESC_REC which has its structure as below,

```
Type desc_rec
IS
  record
  (
    col_type binary_integer              := 0,
    col_max_len binary_integer           := 0,
    col_name VARCHAR2(32)                := '',
    col_name_len binary_integer          := 0,
    col_schema_name VARCHAR2(32)         := '',
    col_schema_name_len binary_integer   := 0,
    col_precision binary_integer         := 0,
    col_scale binary_integer             := 0,
    col_charsetid binary_integer         := 0,
    col_charsetform binary_integer       := 0,
    col_null_ok BOOLEAN                  := TRUE);
/
```

The above index by table structure has 11 columns that holds all possible information about the columns parsed through the cursor.

In the below listing, the EMPLOYEES table is parsed and then described using the DESCRIBE_COLUMNS procedure. All the necessary information corresponding to a column is retrieved from the nested table output parameter in the DECRIBE_COLUMNS procedure and is inserted into a test table that holds the column ID in its first column and the column description in its second column. The insertion is looped and the loop lives the range between 1 and the column count value returned by the DESCRIBE_COLUMNS procedure.

```
1.  SET SERVEROUTPUT ON 200000;
2.  DECLARE
3.  l_ntt_desc_tab dbms_sql.desc_tab;
4.  l_i_cursor_id INTEGER;
5.  l_i_col_cnt   INTEGER;
6.  l_vc_query    VARCHAR2(100):='select e.rowid,e.* from Employees e';
7.  BEGIN
8.  l_i_cursor_id:=dbms_sql.open_cursor;
9.  dbms_sql.parse(l_i_cursor_id, l_vc_query, dbms_sql.native);
10. dbms_sql.describe_columns(l_i_cursor_id, l_i_col_cnt, l_ntt_desc_tab);
11. FOR loop_dc IN 1..l_i_col_cnt
12. LOOP
13. INSERT INTO desc_col_test (col_id, col_desc) VALUES (loop_dc,
    'col_name:'||decode(l_ntt_desc_tab(loop_dc).col_name, Null, 'Null',
    l_ntt_desc_tab(loop_dc).col_name));
14. INSERT INTO desc_col_test (col_id, col_desc) VALUES (loop_dc,
    'col_type:'||decode(l_ntt_desc_tab(loop_dc).col_type, Null, 'Null',
    l_ntt_desc_tab(loop_dc).col_type));
15. INSERT INTO desc_col_test (col_id, col_desc) VALUES (loop_dc,
    'col_precision:'||decode(l_ntt_desc_tab(loop_dc).col_precision, Null,
    'Null', l_ntt_desc_tab(loop_dc).col_precision));
16. INSERT INTO desc_col_test (col_id, col_desc) VALUES (loop_dc,
    'col_max_len:'||decode(l_ntt_desc_tab(loop_dc).col_max_len, Null,
    'Null', l_ntt_desc_tab(loop_dc).col_max_len));
17. INSERT INTO desc_col_test (col_id, col_desc) VALUES (loop_dc,
    'col_name_len:'||decode(l_ntt_desc_tab(loop_dc).col_name_len, Null,
    'Null', l_ntt_desc_tab(loop_dc).col_name_len));
18. INSERT INTO desc_col_test (col_id, col_desc) VALUES (loop_dc,
    'col_schema_name:'||decode(l_ntt_desc_tab(loop_dc).col_schema_name,
    Null, 'Null', l_ntt_desc_tab(loop_dc).col_schema_name));
19. INSERT INTO desc_col_test (col_id, col_desc) VALUES (loop_dc,
    'col_schema_name_len:'||decode(l_ntt_desc_tab(loop_dc).col_schema_name_
    len, Null, 'Null', l_ntt_desc_tab(loop_dc).col_schema_name_len));
20. INSERT INTO desc_col_test (col_id, col_desc) VALUES (loop_dc,
    'col_scale:'||decode(l_ntt_desc_tab(loop_dc).col_scale, Null, 'Null',
    l_ntt_desc_tab(loop_dc).col_scale));
21. INSERT INTO desc_col_test (col_id, col_desc) VALUES (loop_dc,
    'col_charsetid:'||decode(l_ntt_desc_tab(loop_dc).col_charsetid, Null,
    'Null', l_ntt_desc_tab(loop_dc).col_charsetid));
22. INSERT INTO desc_col_test (col_id, col_desc) VALUES (loop_dc,
    'col_charsetform:'||decode(l_ntt_desc_tab(loop_dc).col_charsetform,
    Null, 'Null', l_ntt_desc_tab(loop_dc).col_charsetform));
```

```
23. IF l_ntt_desc_tab(loop_dc).col_null_ok THEN
24. INSERT INTO desc_col_test (col_id, col_desc) VALUES (loop_dc,
    'Nullable:Y');
25. ELSE
26. INSERT INTO desc_col_test (col_id, col_desc) VALUES (loop_dc,
    'Nullable:N');
27. END IF;
28. COMMIT;
29. END LOOP loop_dc;
30. END;
31. /
```

Script Explanation

Line No.	Description
1	This environment variable opens up an output buffer of size limit of 200000.
2	Start of the declare section of the block.
3	A local variable l_ntt_desc_tab is declared with dbms_sql.desc_tab nested table data type.
4	A local variable l_i_cursor_id is declared with INTEGER data type.
5	A local variable l_i_col_cnt is declared with INTEGER data type.
6	A local variable l_vc_query is declared with VARCHAR2 data type with a precision of 100 characters is defaulted to a dynamic SELECT query which selects the pseudo column and all other columns from the EMPLOYEES table.
7	Start of the execution section of the block.
8	The function DBMS_SQL.OPEN_CURSOR is executed and its return value is assigned to the local variable l_i_cursor_id.
9	The procedure DBMS_SQL.PARSE is executed with its first parameter as the local variable l_i_cursor_id, the second parameter as the local variable l_vc_query and the third parameter as the function DBMS_SQL.NATIVE.
10	The procedure DBMS_SQL.DESCRIBE_COLUMNS is executed with its input parameter as the local variable l_i_cursor_id and its first output parameter as the local variable l_i_col_cnt and the second output parameter as the local variable l_ntt_desc_tab.
11,12	Start of the FOR loop with its range between 1 and l_i_col_cnt.
13-27	An insert into the intermediate table DESC_COL_TEST with its first column value as the loop index value and its second column value as the different associative array parameters in the DESC_TAB nested table for each loop index value.
28	The INSERTs performed in the above step is committed.
29	End of the FOR loop.
30,31	End of the execution section of the loop.

After the necessary column information is inserted into the intermediate table, the data can be converted into a much more readable format by using the below SQL statement,

```
SELECT *
FROM
  (SELECT col_id,
    regexp_substr(col_desc,'[^:]+',1,1) col_desc_name,
    regexp_substr(col_desc,'[^:]+',1,2) col_desc_value
  FROM desc_col_test
  ) pivot (MAX(col_desc_value) FOR col_desc_name IN ('col_name' AS COL_NAME,
'col_type' AS COL_TYPE, 'col_precision' AS COL_PRECISION,
  'col_max_len' AS COL_MAX_LEN, 'col_name_len' AS COL_NAME_LEN,
  'col_schema_name' AS COL_SCHEMA_NAME, 'col_schema_name_len' AS
COL_SCHEMA_NAME_LEN,
  'col_scale' AS COL_SCALE, 'col_charsetid' AS COL_CHARSETID,
  'col_charsetform' AS COL_CHARSETFORM, 'Nullable' AS NULLABLE))
ORDER BY col_id;
```

Script Result:

COL_ID	COL_NAME	COL_TYPE	COL_PRECISION	COL_MAX_LEN	COL_NAME_LEN	COL_SCHEMA_NAME	COL_SCHEMA_NAME_LEN	COL_SCALE	COL_CHARSETID	COL_CHARSETFORM	NULLABLE
1	ROWID	11	0	16	5	Null	0	0	0	0	N
2	EMPLOYEE_ID	2	6	22	11	Null	0	0	0	0	Y
3	FIRST_NAME	1	0	20	10	Null	0	0	178	1	Y
4	LAST_NAME	1	0	25	9	Null	0	0	178	1	N
5	EMAIL	1	0	25	5	Null	0	0	178	1	N
6	PHONE_NUMBER	1	0	20	12	Null	0	0	178	1	Y
7	HIRE_DATE	12	0	7	9	Null	0	0	0	0	N
8	JOB_ID	1	0	10	6	Null	0	0	178	1	N
9	SALARY	2	8	22	6	Null	0	2	0	0	Y
10	COMMISSION_PCT	2	2	22	14	Null	0	2	0	0	Y
11	MANAGER_ID	2	6	22	10	Null	0	0	0	0	Y

| 12 | DEPAR TMENT _ID | 2 | 4 | 22 | 13 | Null | 0 | 0 | 0 | 0 | Y |

The above table data show the detailed information on the columns which are parsed through the cursor in a much readable format.

When a dynamic statement with its column more than 32 in length is used in the above block like the below query,

```
SELECT to_timestamp_tz('30-Sep-1989 04:32:00 PM +05:30','DD-MON-RR HH:MI:SS
AM TZH:TZM') at TIME ZONE 'UTC' FROM dual;
```

The block throws a run time error as shown below,

```
Error report:
ORA-06502: PL/SQL: numeric or value error: dbms_sql.describe_columns
overflow, col_name_len=90. Use describe_columns2
ORA-06512: at "SYS.DBMS_SQL", line 2070
ORA-06512: at line 9
06502. 00000 -  "PL/SQL: numeric or value error%s"
*Cause:
*Action:
```

The error states that the column name has exceeded its allowed length and it suggests us to use the DESCRIBE_COLUMNS2 API instead.

DESCRIBE_COLUMNS2

The DESCRIBE_COLUMNS2 API is identical to the DESCRIBE_COLUMNS API except for the increase in the length of the COL_NAME parameter which has been expanded to 32,767 from 32. Thus, this procedure is created as a replacement to its predecessor and the API DESCRIBE_COLUMNS is deprecated as a result.

The syntax for this procedure is shown below,

```
PROCEDURE describe_columns2(c IN INTEGER, col_cnt OUT INTEGER, desc_t OUT
desc_tab2);
```

The only difference between the structure of these two APIs is the data type of the second out parameter. The nested table DESC_TAB is changed to DESC_TAB2 along with the change in its underlying index by table as shown below.

```
Type desc_rec2
IS
  record
```

```
    (
      col_type binary_integer            := 0,
      col_max_len binary_integer         := 0,
      col_name VARCHAR2(32767)           := '',
      col_name_len binary_integer        := 0,
      col_schema_name VARCHAR2(32)       := '',
      col_schema_name_len binary_integer := 0,
      col_precision binary_integer       := 0,
      col_scale binary_integer           := 0,
      col_charsetid binary_integer       := 0,
      col_charsetform binary_integer     := 0,
      col_null_ok BOOLEAN                := TRUE);
```

The above index by table structure has 11 columns which are similar to DESC_REC index by table, but with the change in the precision of the COL_NAME attribute from 32 to 32,767.

In the below snippet, a dynamic statement having its column's length more than 32 is parsed and the column information is printed using the DESCRIBE_COLUMNS2 API as shown below,

```
1.  SET SERVEROUTPUT ON 200000;
2.  DECLARE
3.  l_ntt_desc_tab2 dbms_sql.desc_tab2;
4.  l_i_cursor_id INTEGER;
5.  l_i_col_cnt   INTEGER;
6.  l_vc_query    VARCHAR2(1000):=q'(SELECT to_timestamp_tz('30-Sep-1989
    04:32:00 PM +05:30', 'DD-MON-RR HH:MI:SS AM TZH:TZM') at TIME ZONE
    'UTC' FROM dual)';
7.  BEGIN
8.  l_i_cursor_id:=dbms_sql.open_cursor;
9.  dbms_sql.parse(l_i_cursor_id, l_vc_query, dbms_sql.native);
10. dbms_sql.describe_columns2(l_i_cursor_id, l_i_col_cnt,
    l_ntt_desc_tab2);
11. FOR loop_dc IN 1..l_i_col_cnt
12. LOOP
13. dbms_output.put_line('Column '||loop_dc||' is
    '||l_ntt_desc_tab2(loop_dc).col_name);
14. END LOOP loop_dc;
15. END;
16. /
```

Result:
Column 1 is TO_TIMESTAMP_TZ('30-SEP-198904:32:00PM+05:30','DD-MON-RRHH:MI:SSAMTZH:TZM')ATTIMEZONE'UTC'

Script Explanation

Line No.	Description
1	This environment variable opens up an output buffer of size limit of 200000.
2	Start of the declare section of the block.
3	A local variable l_ntt_desc_tab2 is declared with dbms_sql.desc_tab2 nested table data type.

4	A local variable l_i_cursor_id is declared with INTEGER data type.
5	A local variable l_i_col_cnt is declared with INTEGER data type.
6	A local variable l_vc_query is declared with VARCHAR2 data type with a precision of 100 characters is defaulted to a dynamic SELECT query which converts the timestamp from one time zone to another in a DUAL table.
7	Start of the execution section of the block.
8	The function DBMS_SQL.OPEN_CURSOR is executed and its return value is assigned to the local variable l_i_cursor_id.
9	The procedure DBMS_SQL.PARSE is executed with its first parameter as the local variable l_i_cursor_id, the second parameter as the local variable l_vc_query and the third parameter as the function DBMS_SQL.NATIVE.
10	The procedure DBMS_SQL.DESCRIBE_COLUMNS2 is executed with its input parameter as the local variable l_i_cursor_id and its first output parameter as the local variable l_i_col_cnt and the second output parameter as the local variable l_ntt_desc_tab2.
11,12	Start of the FOR loop with its range between 1 and l_i_col_cnt.
13	The column name which has a length of more than 32 characters is fetched from the nested table l_ntt_desc_tab2 for every loop index value.
14	End of the FOR loop.
15,16	End of the execution section of the block.

Summary

We started this chapter with an introduction to the dynamic SQL processing technique along with their different types. In the next section, we toured through the NDS method of dynamic statement processing along with their latest enhancements with numerous real time examples. We have also gained a better understanding of the DBMS_SQL API that is not commonly used compared to the native method along with their secret weapon, the Method 4 Type processing technique in the later section with appropriate examples.

In the next chapter, we will learn about the advanced SQL concepts like regular expressions and XML programming in Oracle.

Advanced SQL Concepts in Oracle

In this chapter, we will discuss the below topics in detail,

11. Introduction to Regular Expressions, POSIX standards and Perl influenced metacharacters along with different pattern matching modifiers.

12. Different types of Regular Expressions with various real time examples by implementing the different metacharacters with the regular expression condition and functions.

13. Understanding the origin of XML programming and Oracle's XML support.

14. Multiple types of XML function for generating and manipulating the XML data.

Introduction to Regular Expressions

Regular expressions are a powerful tool having a sequence of characters defining a search pattern to ease the string matching logic. A mathematician, Stephen Cole Kleene in 1956 through his mathematical notation, the *regular sets*, first formulated the concept of regular expressions. This theory became popular in text editor pattern matching and lexical analysis in compilers during the 1960's. Later, almost all programming languages adopted this theory and introduced the regular expression concepts in them.

The main advantage of the regular expressions is that they centralize the pattern matching logic inside the Oracle database, thus avoiding the intensive string processing of the middle-tier applications resulting in a solution that is more efficient.

There are two different types of characters through which regular expressions function. They are,

- **Metacharacters**: These are the operators that specify the type of search algorithm we specify for the pattern matching.

- **String Literals**: These are the texts on which the pattern matching is applied.

POSIX Extended Regular Expressions

POSIX or Portable Operating System Interface for uniX is a set of standards that defines some of the functionality supported by the UNIX operating system. The POSIX standard has three sets of standards. BRE for Basic, ERE for Extended and SRE for Simple Regular Expressions. Most modern regular expressions are extensions of the ERE, also the Oracle regular expression uses these standards only.

Oracle does not completely support the POSIX ERE standard. The POSIX standard states that it is illegal to back reference a character, which is not a metacharacter. Oracle supports this and simply ignores the backslash. For e.g., the string *b* is not a metacharacter, when it is placed prefixing with a backslash *b*, it is similar to the literal *b*. This means that all POSIX ERE standardized regular expressions can be used with Oracle, but not all the regular expressions, working with Oracle may be supported by fully POSIX ERE supported system.

Regular Expression Metacharacters in Oracle

Metacharacters are similar to the string literals, but with a special meaning which is used to identify the textual material of the given pattern and to process it using the regular expressions. The below topics defines the different operators in Oracle.

POSIX Metacharacters in Oracle

The below list of metacharacters supports the use of regular expressions passed to the SQL regular expression condition and functions. These metacharacters acknowledge to the POSIX standard.

POSIX Metacharacters List

Metacharacter	Description
*	Matches zero or more occurrences.
?	Matches zero or one occurrence.
+	Matches one or more occurrences.
|	Matches any one of the alternatives. This is similar to the OR operator.
.	Matches any character in the database character set except for Null and the new line character.
\	Any metacharacter followed by the backslash symbol is treated as a string literal to search for it. Using double backslash symbol (\\) treats the symbol backslash (\) as a string literal.
\n	This is the backreference expression where n is an integer between 1 and 9, matching the nth reference enclosed between the parenthesis preceding \n.

^	Matches the character in the beginning of the line in a string by default. In multiline mode, it matches the beginning of any line in the source string.
$	Matches the character at the end of the line in a string by default. In multiline mode, it matches the end of any line in the source string.
(...)	This is the grouping expression which treats the expression within the parenthesis as a group. This can be a character literal or an expression with operators.
[...]	This is the matching expression which specifies a list that matches any of the matches present in the list from the source string.
[^...]	This is the non-matching expression which specifies a list that does not match with any of the matches present in the list from the source string.
[. Element .]	This is the collating element operator in the POSIX standard. This operator lets us consider the multi-character collating element to be a single character. For e.g., the string *ch* comprises of two characters in English, whereas if the language Traditional Spanish is defined in the locale, it will be considered as a single character.
[[: Class :]]	Matches any character belonging to the specified character class. For e.g., the class [[:alpha:]] matches all the alphabets in the source string. The below table defines all the classes from the POSIX standard.

Class	Description
[[:alnum:]]	Matches all alphanumeric characters.
[[:alpha:]]	Matches all alphabetic characters.
[[:blank:]]	Matches all blank space characters.
[[:cntrl:]]	Matches all non-printing control characters.
[[:digit:]]	Matches all numeric digits.
[[:xdigit:]]	Matches all hexadecimal characters.
[[:punct:]]	Matches all punctuation characters.
[[:upper:]]	Matches all upper case alphabets.
[[:lower:]]	Matches all lower case alphabets.
[[:graph:]]	Matches all [[:punct:]], [[:upper:]], [[:lower:]], and [[:digit:]] characters.
[[:print:]]	Matches all printable characters.
[[:space:]]	Matches all space characters like carriage return, newline, form feed and vertical tab.
[a-z]	Matches all lower case alphabets. This is similar to [[:lower:]]. To match a set of lower case alphabets, specify a start and an end range. For e.g., [a-m] matches any lower case alphabet between the range *a* and *m* in the source string.
[A-Z]	Matches all upper case alphabets. This is similar to [[:upper:]]. To match a set of upper case alphabets, specify a start and an end range. For e.g., [A-D]

	matches any uppercase alphabet between the range A and D in the source string.
[0-9]	Matches all numeric digits. This is similar to [[:digits:]]. To match a set of digits, specify a start and an end range. For e.g., [0-5] matches the digits between the range 0 and 5 in the source string.
[A-Za-z0-9]	Matches all the alphanumeric characters. This is similar to [[:alnum:]]. The combination can be changed as per the requirement like [A-Z0-9], [a-mA-N], [0-7a-oA-H], etc.
[=Class=]	This is the character equivalence class matching all the characters of the same equivalence class in the current locale. For e.g., the expression [=n=] searches for all the characters in the same class like N and ñ from the source string El Niño in a Spanish locale.
{m}	Matches exactly m times.
{m,}	Matches at least m times.
{m, n}	Matches at least m times, but not more than n times.

Perl-Influenced Metacharacters in Oracle

Due to the popularity of the Perl language, Oracle database adopted some of its extensions even though they are not present in the POSIX standards. The below tabulation describes the Perl influenced metacharacters which are supported by Oracle database regular expression condition and functions.

Perl-Influenced Metacharacters List

Metacharacter	Description
\d	Matches a numeric character. The combination of POSIX and Perl-influenced metacharacter, for e.g., \d{2} matches exactly two numeric digits.
\D	Matches a non-numeric character.
\w	Matches a word character.
\W	Matches a non-word character.
\s	Matches a whitespace character. The combination of POSIX and Perl-influenced metacharacter, for e.g., \s{3} matches exactly three whitespace characters.
\S	Matches a non-whitespace character.
\A	Matches only at the beginning of the source string regardless of whether the search is a single line or multiline.
\Z	Matches only at the end of the source string regardless of whether the search is a single line or multiline.
*?	Matches the preceding pattern 0 or more times (non-greedy).

+?	Matches the preceding pattern 1 or more times (non-greedy).
??	Matches the preceding pattern element 0 or 1 time (non-greedy).
{n}?	Matches the preceding pattern element exactly n times (non-greedy).
{n,}?	Matches the preceding pattern element at least n times (non-greedy).
{n, m}?	Matches the preceding pattern element at least n but no more than m times (non-greedy).

Pattern Matching Modifiers

The Oracle database regular expression condition and functions use the match modifiers as below,

Match Modifier List

Modifier	Description
i	Specifies case insensitive search.
c	Specifies case sensitive search.
n	Allows the period (.) character to match the newline character. By default, the period (.) character does not match the newline character.
m	Specifies that the search is in multi-line mode. The metacharacters ^ and $ specify the start and end respectively, of any line in the source string rather only at the start and end of the source string.
x	Specifies that the white space characters are ignored during the search. By default, the white space characters are matched.

Oracle Regular Expression Elements

From the version 10gR1, Oracle allows us to use 3 different regular expression functions REGEXP_INSTR, REGEXP_SUBSTR, REGEXP_REPLACE and 1 regular expression condition REGEXP_LIKE in SQL and PL/SQL statements. These are similar to the functions INSTR, SUBSTR and REPLACE except that they allow us to specify the search pattern as a regular expression. An enhancement in the version 10gR2 included the support for PERL - style expressions. In the version 11gR1, Oracle introduced the 5th regular expression element, the REGEXP_COUNT function and added a new functionality of allowing users to use subexpressions in already existing functions REGEXP_INSTR and REGEXP_SUBSTR. These functions can be used on a bind variable, text literal or a column holding string data, such as CHAR, NCHAR, VARCHAR2, NVARCHAR2, CLOB and NCLOB columns.

Note: Regular expression condition and functions do not work with LONG columns.

The different regular expression elements in Oracle are explained below with suitable examples.

REGEXP_LIKE

The REGEXP_LIKE is a condition, unlike its peers, which are functions. This condition allows us to perform a regular expression matching using the POSIX notation in the WHERE and HAVING clauses of any SQL statement and as check constraints in tables. This clause produces a Boolean result which helps in limiting the number of rows returned by the SQL statement. This is an extension of the simple LIKE condition.

The prototype of the REGEXP_LIKE condition is shown below,

```
REGEXP_LIKE(<Source_string>, <Search_pattern>[, <Match_modifiers>]);
```

- **Source_string**: The string to be searched for.

- **Search_pattern**: The regular expression pattern that is to be searched for in the source string. This can be a combination of the POSIX and the Perl-influenced metacharacters mentioned in the earlier sections.

- **Match_modifiers**: This is an optional parameter. This parameter allows us to modify, the matching behavior of the function. The valid range of options is explained in the earlier section, *Pattern Matching Modifiers* section.

Basic Search

In the below example, the REGEXP_LIKE condition is used for searching simple texts *re* in the first name of all the employees. When the first name of an employee is found to have these two characters together in them, the condition returns TRUE, resulting in the selection of that employee's first name.

This search is similar to the normal LIKE condition search.

```
select first_name from employees where regexp_like (first_name,'re');
```

Result:
Karen
Kimberely
Irene
Karen
Trenna

Caret Search

In the below example, the search pattern has the Caret symbol prefixed to a combination of texts. The Caret symbol is a POSIX standard metacharacter, that forces the REGEXP_LIKE condition to search for the specific text combination at the start of the first name of all the employees and returns only the ones that complies with this condition.

```
select first_name from employees where regexp_like (first_name,'^Jo');
```

Result:
John
Joshua
John
John
Jonathon
Jose Manuel

Dollar Search

The below example, has a Dollar symbol placed at the end of a combination of texts. This Dollar symbol is also one of the POSIX standard metacharacter which forces the REGEXP_LIKE condition to search for the first name of all the employees with this specific text at its end and returns only of those who matches with them.

```
select first_name from employees where regexp_like (first_name,'an$');
```

Result:
Allan
Jean
Susan

Pipe Search

The Pipe symbol is one of the POSIX standard metacharacters that allows the REGEXP_LIKE condition to choose between two or more alternatives.

In the below example, the condition searches for the text combination *ni* or *ch* in the first name and returns them.

```
select first_name from employees where regexp_like (first_name,'ni|ch');
```

Result:
Daniel
Michael
Eleni
Danielle
Jennifer
Jennifer
Michael

The above same example is used again here, but this time with a case insensitive search. The third parameter in the below condition holds the match modifier *i* which enforces the case insensitive search rule on the condition. By default, without this parameter, the search would be a sensitive one.

The query returns two extra names *Charles* and *Christopher* from the above result due to the case insensitivity.

```
select first_name from employees where regexp_like (first_name,'ni|ch','i');
```
Result:
```
Daniel
Michael
Eleni
Christopher
Danielle
Charles
Jennifer
Jennifer
Michael
```

Here, the search performed is even more serious! The REGXP_LIKE condition searches for the first names which have a total of 6 characters where its second character can be either *e* or *i* and its fifth character can be either *r* or *l*. This kind of customized searches can be achieved with the help of the grouping expression which is denoted by the bracket symbol "( )" as shown below,

```
select first_name from employees where regexp_like (first_name,
'^G(e|i)ra(r|l)d$');
```
Result:
```
Gerald
Girard
```

Square Bracket Search

The square bracket search specifies a list of characters that searches for any match present in the list from the source string.

In the below snippet, the condition searches for the employees with the first name which has any of the alphabets *a*, *m* or *p* in them.

```
select first_name from employees where regexp_like (first_name,'[amp]');
```
Result:
```
Neena
Alexander
David
Valli
Diana
...
```

Here, the condition searches for the employees with their first name having any of the alphabets a, b, c or d in them.

```
select first_name from employees where regexp_like (first_name,'[abcd]');
```

Result:
Neena
Alexander
Bruce
David
Valli

...

The above same search can be rewritten using the alphabet range a-d as shown below.

```
select first_name from employees where regexp_like (first_name,'[a-d]');
```

Result:
Neena
Alexander
Bruce
David
Valli

...

The condition in the below listing looks for the first name of the employees which has two consecutive vowels in them. There are two square brackets in the search condition where the first one matches for the first vowel and the next bracket matches for another vowel character following the first one.

```
select first_name from employees where regexp_like (first_name,
'[aeiou][aeiou]');
```

Result:
Daniel
Jean
Diana
Douglas
Ismael

The below snippet has the condition which searches for the first names having any of the alphabets *b*, *d* or *h* which is followed by the character *a*.

```
select first_name from employees where regexp_like (first_name,'[bdh]a');
```

Result:
Adam
Shanta
Michael
Randall
Sundar

Period Search

The period character "." matches any character from the database character set except for the Newline character and Null.

The below listing shows that the condition searches for the first names having either *a*, *b*, *c* or *d*, followed by any character which is then followed by the character *h*.

```
select first_name from employees where regexp_like (first_name,'[a-d].h');
```

```
Result:
Sarath
Jonathon
```

In the below snippet, the condition searches for the first names which have either *a*, *b*, *c* or *d*, using the range search followed by any two characters which are then followed by the character *h*.

```
select first_name from employees where regexp_like (first_name,'[a-d]..h');
```

```
Result:
Matthew
Elizabeth
Martha
Sarah
```

Curly Bracket Search

The curly braces indicate the number of times a search must repeat itself immediately one after another in the condition.

The condition in the below query searches for the character *n* which is followed by another n as shown below,

```
select first_name from employees where regexp_like (first_name,'[n]{2}');
```

```
Result:
Trenna
Jennifer
Jennifer
Hermann
```

The below SQL searches for the first names having three consecutive vowels in them as shown below,

```
select first_name from employees where regexp_like (first_name, '[aeiou]
{3}');
```

```
Result:
Louise
```

Negated Search

This non-matching expression looks for a search that does not match with any of the matches in the source string.

The below statement, searches for all the characters other than the alphabets with case insensitivity. The result produces the name of the employee, which has a space in it as shown below.

```
select first_name from employees where regexp_like (first_name, '[^a-z]',
'i');
```

Result:
Jose Manuel

Email Validation Check

The email validation on the list of emails can be performed to check whether any of them violate the rules of email ID creation.

The below query statement selects the email IDs with the below rules,

1. The starting character must be an alphabet which is handled by the condition **^[A-Za-z]**.

2. The first part of the mail ID must contain only alphabets, numbers and periods which is handled by the condition **[A-Za-z0-9.]**.

3. The second part of the mail ID must be prefixed with an "at the rate of" (@) symbol and may contain only alphabets, numbers, hyphens and periods in them. This is handled by the condition **@[A-Za-z0-9.-]**.

4. The last and third part of the mail ID must be prefixed with a DOT followed by alphabets not less than 2 and no more than 4. This is handled by the condition **\.[A-Za-z]{2,4}$**. Here, **\.** Searches for the literal character DOT.

```
WITH t AS
  (SELECT 'brucewayne.1981@gmail.com' email FROM dual
  UNION ALL
  SELECT 'clark_kent@gmail.com' FROM dual
  UNION ALL
  SELECT '1Tonystark.1980@gmail.com' FROM dual
```

```
   UNION ALL
   SELECT 'peter@parker.1989@gmail.com' FROM dual
   )
SELECT *
FROM t
WHERE REGEXP_LIKE (EMAIL, '^[A-Za-z]+[A-Za-z0-9.]+@[A-Za-z0-9.-]+\.[A-Za-
z]{2,4}$');
```

Result:
brucewayne.1981@gmail.com

The email IDs which does not qualify can be printed out using the NOT operator
prefixed to the REGEXP_LIKE condition as shown below,

```
WITH t AS
   (SELECT 'brucewayne.1981@gmail.com' email FROM dual
   UNION ALL
   SELECT 'clark_kent@gmail.com' FROM dual
   UNION ALL
   SELECT '1Tonystark.1980@gmail.com' FROM dual
   UNION ALL
   SELECT 'peter@parker.1989@gmail.com' FROM dual
   )
SELECT *
FROM t
WHERE not REGEXP_LIKE (EMAIL,'^[A-Za-z]+[A-Za-z0-9.]+@[A-Za-z0-9.-]+\.[A-Za-
z]{2,4}$');
```

Result:
clark_kent@gmail.com
1Tonystark.1980@gmail.com
peter@parker.1989@gmail.com

REGEXP_COUNT

This function was introduced in the version 11g and it allows us to count the number
of times a pattern or a substring occurs in the source string. This is very different from
the plain COUNT function which is a column level function, whereas,
REGEXP_COUNT is a cell level function which operates on each cell individually.

The prototype of the REGEXP_COUNT function is shown below,

```
REGEXP_COUNT(<Source_string>, <Search_pattern>[, <Start_position>[,
<Match_modifiers>]])
```

- **Source_string**: The string to be searched for.

- **Search_pattern**: The regular expression pattern that is to be searched for in the
  source string. This can be a combination of the POSIX and the Perl-influenced
  metacharacters mentioned in the above section.

- **Start_position**: This is an optional parameter. This determines the position in the source string where the search starts. By default, it is 1, which is the starting position of the source string.

- **Match_modifiers**: This is an optional parameter. This parameter allows us to modify, the matching behavior of the function. The valid range of options is mentioned in the *Pattern Matching Modifiers* section explained above.

Text Count

The basic operation, which can be done using this function is to count for a character or a series of characters in the source string as shown below.

```
SELECT REGEXP_COUNT ('REGEXP_COUNT is a cell level function which operates
on each cell individually', 'cell', 1) regexp_count
FROM dual;
```

Result:
2

Digit Count

The below statement, searches for the number of numeric digits present in the source string using the Perl influenced metacharacter $\backslash d$.

```
SELECT REGEXP_COUNT ('REGEXP_COUNT is introduced in the Oracle version
11gR1', '\d', 1) regexp_count
FROM dual;
```

Result:
3

Vowels Count

The below shown listing counts for the total number of vowels in the source string with case sensitivity check turned ON by default (Based on the NLS_SORT parameter).

```
SELECT REGEXP_COUNT ('REGEXP_COUNT is a cell level function which operates
on each cell individually', '[aeiou]', 1) regexp_count
FROM dual;
```

Result:
22

The same snippet is used again for the vowel count, but this time with the case sensitivity turned OFF by setting the match modifier to *i* manually.

```
SELECT REGEXP_COUNT ('REGEXP_COUNT is a cell level function which operates
on each cell individually', '[aeiou]', 1, 'i') regexp_count
FROM dual;
```

Result:
26

Word Count

The total number of words in the source string can be found by using the below statement. The search pattern "[^]+" checks for characters other than the space character "[^]" followed by one or more non-space characters using the "+" operator.

```
SELECT REGEXP_COUNT ('REGEXP_COUNT is introduced in the Oracle version
11gR1', '[^ ]+',1) regexp_count
FROM dual;
```

Result:
8

Character count

The total number of characters in the source string can be found by using the below statement. The search pattern "(.)" searches for all possible characters in the source string.

```
SELECT REGEXP_COUNT ('REGEXP_COUNT is introduced in the Oracle version
11gR1', '(.)', 1) regexp_count
FROM dual;
```

Result:
54

DOT Count

The total number of DOT characters in the source string can be found using the below query statement. The search pattern "\." searches for the literal DOT in the source string. As DOT is a metacharacter, it is escaped using the escape operator backslash "\".

```
SELECT REGEXP_COUNT ('There.are.seven.dots.in.this.string.', '\.',1)
regexp_count
FROM dual;
```

Result:
7

REGEXP_INSTR

This function is an advanced extension of the already existing INSTR function, which returns the location of the expression pattern in the source string.

The prototype of the REGEXP_INSTR function is shown below,

```
REGEXP_INSTR(<Source_string>, <Search_pattern>[, <Start_position>[,
<Match_occurrence>[, <Return_option>[, <Match_modifier>]]]])
```

- **Source_string**: The string to be searched for.

- **Search_pattern**: The regular expression pattern that is to be searched for in the source string. This can be a combination of the POSIX and the Perl-influenced metacharacters mentioned in the above section.

- **Start_position**: This is an optional parameter. This determines the position in the source string where the search starts. By default, it is 1, which is the starting position of the source string.

- **Match_occurrence**: This is an optional parameter. This determines the appearance of the search pattern. By default, it is 1, which is the first appearance of the search pattern in the string.

- **Return_option**: This is an optional parameter. By default, it is 0.

  ➜ If 0, the position of the first occurrence is returned.

  ➜ If 1, the position of the character after the first occurrence is returned.

- **Match_modifiers**: This is an optional parameter. This parameter allows us to modify, the matching behavior of the function. The valid range of options is mentioned in the *Pattern Matching Modifiers* section explained above.

Text Position Search

The basic operation, which can be done using this function is to find the position of a character or a series of characters in the source string as shown below. The below statement returns the position of the first occurrence of the string INSTR in the source string with the return option as 0.

```
SELECT REGEXP_INSTR ('REGEXP_INSTR is an advanced extension of the INSTR
function', 'INSTR', 1, 1, 0, 'i') regexp_instr
FROM dual;
```

Result:
8

When the return option is changed to 1, the function returns the position of the character after INSTR, that is, the position of the space is returned in the below example,

```
SELECT REGEXP_INSTR ('REGEXP_INSTR is an advanced extension of the INSTR
function', 'INSTR', 1, 1, 1, 'i') regexp_instr
FROM dual;
```

Result:
13

Digit Position Search

The below statement, searches for the position of numeric digits present in the source string using the Perl influenced metacharacter \d. This function returns the position of the first digit in the source string, i.e., the position of the digit 1 is returned in the below example.

```
SELECT REGEXP_INSTR ('REGEXP_INSTR is introduced in the Oracle version 10g',
'\d', 1) regexp_instr
FROM dual;
```

Result:
50

Vowels Position Search

The below listing searches and returns the position of the first vowel in the source string with case sensitivity check turned OFF manually using the match modifier set to *i.*

```
SELECT REGEXP_INSTR ('REGEXP_INSTR is an advanced extension of the INSTR
function', '[aeiou]', 1, 1, 0, 'i') regexp_instr
FROM dual;
```

Result:
2

DOT Count

The position of the second occurring DOT character in the source string can be found using the below query statement. The search pattern "\." searches for the literal DOT in the source string. As DOT is a metacharacter, it is escaped using the escape operator backslash.

```
SELECT REGEXP_INSTR
('REGEXP_INSTR.is.an.advanced.extension.of.the.INSTR.function', '\.', 1, 2,
0, 'i') regexp_instr
FROM dual;
```

Result:
16

REGEXP_SUBSTR

The REGEXP_SUBSTR function is the advanced version of the classic SUBSTR function, allowing us to search for strings based on a regular expression pattern. This function returns a portion of the source string based on the search pattern but not its position. The substring returned by this function can be either of VARCHAR2 or CLOB data type in the same character set as that of the input source string.

The prototype of the REGEXP_SUBSTR function is shown below,

```
REGEXP_SUBSTR(<Source_string>, <Search_pattern>[, <Start_position>[,
<Match_occurrence>[, <Match_modifiers>]]])
```

- **Source_string**: The string to be searched for.

- **Search_pattern**: The regular expression pattern that is to be searched for in the source string. This can be a combination of the POSIX and the Perl-influenced metacharacters mentioned in the above section.

- **Start_position**: This is an optional parameter. This determines the position in the source string where the search starts. By default, it is 1, which is the starting position of the source string.

- **Match_occurrence**: This is an optional parameter. This determines the occurrence of the search pattern. By default, it is 1, which is the first appearance of the search pattern in the string.

- **Match_modifiers**: This is an optional parameter. This parameter allows us to modify, the matching behavior of the function. The valid range of options is mentioned in the *Pattern Matching Modifiers* section explained above.

The below shown example prints out the statement word by word for its corresponding match occurrence value.

```
SELECT regexp_substr('This is an interesting chapter','[[:alpha:]]+',1,1)
regexp_substr
FROM dual;
```

For the match occurrence value 1 (Fourth parameter),

```
Result:
This
```

Using the CONNECT BY LEVEL clause, all the words from the source string can be displayed for all possible the match occurrence values using the LEVEL keyword as the fourth parameter in the above query. The total number of match occurrences is found by counting the number of spaces in the input string and adding 1 to it using the REGEXP_COUNT function.

```
SELECT regexp_substr('This is an interesting chapter', '[[:alpha:]]+', 1,
level) regexp_substr
FROM dual
  CONNECT BY level<=regexp_count('This is an interesting chapter',' ')+1;
```

```
Result:
This
is
an
interesting
chapter
```

The below statement separates the string into multiple chunks by the separator ",", which is mentioned in the search pattern. The search pattern "[^ ,] +" negates the "," character and searches for the characters other than comma followed by a non-comma character in the source string.

```
SELECT regexp_substr('Apple,Orange,Mango,Grapes','[^,]+',1,1) regexp_substr
FROM dual;
```

For the match occurrence value 1 (Fourth parameter),

```
Result:
Apple
```

With the help of the CONNECT BY LEVEL clause, all the chunks of the source string can be displayed by using the LEVEL keyword as the match occurrence. Here, the CONNECT BY LEVEL clause generates the rows equal to the number of commas +1 in the source string.

```
SELECT regexp_substr('Apple,Orange,Mango,Grapes','[^,]+',1,level)
regexp_substr
FROM dual
  CONNECT BY level<=regexp_count('Apple,Orange,Mango,Grapes',',')+1;
```

Result:
```
Apple
Orange
Mango
Grapes
```

The below snippet takes out the website's name from a list of web pages. Here, the first part of the search pattern checks for a series of alphabets followed by a DOT character ([[:alpha:]]+\.) which searches and finds the match from the string as "www.". Then the rest of the search pattern ([a-zA-Z0-9._-]+) looks for a series of characters which can be an alphabet, number, DOT character, underscore and a hyphen. When a character other than listed in the previous statement is found, the search process is stopped. In this example, the domain names with their extension "domain-name.com", "domain_name.edu", "domain.name.org" are selected as the next character is a front slash (/).

```
WITH t AS
  (SELECT 'https://www.domain-name.com/page1.html' col FROM dual
  UNION ALL
  SELECT 'http://www.domain_name.edu/page_2.htm' FROM dual
  UNION ALL
  SELECT 'http://www.domain.name.org/page?3.htm' FROM dual
  )
SELECT regexp_substr(col,'[[:alpha:]]+\.[a-zA-Z0-9._-]+') FROM t;
```

Result:
```
www.domain-name.com
www.domain_name.edu
www.domain.name.org
```

In the below example, the source string has a Newline character "chr(10)" concatenated between the three names in the WITH clause. The search pattern (^[[:alpha:]]+) looks for the string starting with an alphabet until it finds another non-matching character (Non-alphabet), in this case, a Newline character.

This query is executed for three different match occurrences as shown below.

```
WITH t AS
   (SELECT 'Aamir'||chr(10)||'Ashok'||chr(10)||'Ashley' col FROM dual
   )
SELECT REGEXP_SUBSTR(col, '^[[:alpha:]]+',1,1)regexp_substr1,
   REGEXP_SUBSTR(col, '^[[:alpha:]]+',1,2)regexp_substr2,
   REGEXP_SUBSTR(col, '^[[:alpha:]]+',1,3)regexp_substr3
FROM t;
```

Result:
Aamir Null Null

However, when the match modifier is changed to multiline mode by using the literal *m* as the match modifier parameter, the same query considers the Newline character as a different line and assumes that these three names are in different lines and processes it.

When this query is executed for the same match occurrences as above,

```
WITH t AS
   (SELECT 'Aamir'||chr(10)||'Ashok'||chr(10)||'Ashley' col FROM dual
   )
SELECT REGEXP_SUBSTR(col, '^[[:alpha:]]+',1,1,'m')regexp_substr1,
   REGEXP_SUBSTR(col, '^[[:alpha:]]+',1,2,'m')regexp_substr2,
   REGEXP_SUBSTR(col, '^[[:alpha:]]+',1,3,'m')regexp_substr3
FROM t;
```

Result:
Aamir Ashok Ashley

REGEXP_REPLACE

This function is a successful extension of both the REPLACE and the TRANSLATE function. This function was introduced in the Oracle version 10g, which replaces a specific portion of the source string using a user customized regular expression based search pattern.

The prototype for the REGEXP_REPLACE function is shown below,

```
REGEXP_REPLACE(<Source_string>, <Search_pattern>[, <Replacement_string>[,
<Start_position>[, <Match_occurrence>[, <Match_modifiers>]]]])
```

- **Source_string**: The string to be searched for.

- **Search_pattern**: The regular expression pattern that is to be searched for in the source string. This can be a combination of the POSIX and the Perl-influenced metacharacters mentioned in the above section.

- **Replacement_string**: This is an optional parameter. The matched patterns will be replaced with the Replacement_string in the source string. If not mentioned, the replacement string will be Null.

- **Start_position**: This is an optional parameter. This determines the position in the source string where the search starts. By default, it is 1, which is the starting position of the source string.

- **Match_occurrence**: This is an optional parameter. This determines the occurrence of the search pattern. By default, it is 1, which is the first appearance of the search pattern in the string.

- **Match_modifiers**: This is an optional parameter. This parameter allows us to modify, the matching behavior of the function. The valid range of options is mentioned in the *Pattern Matching Modifiers* section explained above.

String Removal

The below statement has a mix of numbers, alphabets and punctuations in its source string. The first match pattern selects all the alphabets, the second match pattern selects all the digits and the third match pattern selects all the punctuations, removes them from the source string respectively, and prints the result.

```
WITH
  t AS
  ( SELECT'a0b1c2d3e4f5g6h7i8j9k!l@m#n$o%p^q&r*s(t)u_v+w-x=y[z]' col FROM
dual)
SELECT
  regexp_replace(col,'[[:alpha:]]') without_alphabets,
  regexp_replace(col,'[[:digit:]]') without_digits,
  regexp_replace(col,'[[:punct:]]') without_punctuations
FROM
  t;
```

Result:

WITHOUT_ALPHABETS
0123456789!@#$%^&*()_+-=[]

WITHOUT_DIGITS
abcdefghijk!l@m#n$o%p^q&r*s(t)u_v+w-x=y[z]

WITHOUT_PUNCTUATIONS
a0b1c2d3e4f5g6h7i8j9klmnopqrstuvwxyz

Symbol Removal

The below snippet removes all the special symbols from the source string and prints only the readable characters. This query is of much help while saving the emails and documents into the database by removing the unreadable special symbols as a data cleaning process.

```
select regexp_replace('Th∞is St●ring con♥tains ♫special sy■mbols','[^a-zA-Z
]') regexp_replace from dual;
```

Result:
```
This String contains special symbols
```

Space Removal

The below statement removes the spaces which are present more than once in the source string. This script plays a vital role in removing the unwanted spaces from a document or an email before storing them permanently in the database.

```
select regexp_replace('This    string   contains       more     than   one
spacing       between      the       words','( ){2,}',' ') regexp_replace
from dual;
```

Result:
```
This string contains more than one spacing between the words
```

Name Rearrange

The below listing re-arranges the last name and the first name from the source string in a user required format for reporting purposes.

```
select regexp_replace('Randy Orton','(.*) (.*)','\2, \1') regexp_replace
from dual;
```

Result:
```
Orton, Randy
```

Space Addition

The below SQL adds an extra space in between each character from the source string as shown below,

```
select regexp_replace('abcdefghijklmnopqrstuvwxyz','(.)','\1 ')
regexp_replace from dual;
```

Result:
```
a b c d e f g h i j k l m n o p q r s t u v w x y z
```

Security Measure

The below statement hides the middle portion of a number as a security measure. This process is done by the banking industry during the account-related communication by hiding the middle portion of the credit card, account number, phone number and by the email servers for OTP generation for user confirmation and security check.

```
select regexp_replace('91105434563452345623',
'(^[[:digit:]]{4})(.*)([[:digit:]]{4}$)', '\1**********\3') regexp_replace
from dual;
```

Result:
9110**********5623

Introduction to XML Programming

XML stands for eXtensible Markup Language, created in 1996 by Jon Bosak, Tim Bray and several others. The XML's predecessor was called as the Standard Generalized Markup Language (SGML) which was invented in the early 70s by Charles F. Goldfarb, Ed Mosher and Ray Lorie at the IBM laboratory. SGML despite its name, not a markup language, but a language which is used for specifying other markup languages. The SGML basically creates vocabularies which can be used for forming structural tags for the markup languages.

The SGML is a very much powerful, vast language, but was too complex and platform incompatible for the general use with lots of redundant features which were not used over 2 decades after its creation. Even though SGML created a big successful application, the HTML in the late 80s, it does not offer all the powerful features of SGML as it restricts us to use a finite set of operations to define a web page. The HTML is a powerful presentation application, but not human readable. This pullover created the XML language, which supports data exchange independent of platform and architecture. The first version of XML was XML 1.0 which was released on the market in February, 1998 and was immediately adopted by many programmers who always wanted a structural markup language but couldn't afford to handle the complexity of the SGML language.

Oracle Database XML Support

The Oracle database started supporting XML from the version 9iR2 by introducing a new data type called as XMLTYPE to facilitate native handling of XML data in the database. From then on, there was creation of numerous objects to support reliability, availability, scalability and security on the XML data processed in the database. The XML objects in Oracle operate on or returns XML data. The arguments used in these objects are not defined in the ANSI standard, but are defined as a part of the World Wide Web Consortium (W3C) standards. When an operation performed in any of the XML objects fails to satisfy the rules placed on the W3C standard, the program fails with an appropriate failure notice.

XPATH Expressions

XPath is a W3C standard expression set for navigating through the XML documents. XPath expression set considers the XML documents in a tree structure and provides us with the below constructs for branching between their nodes.

XPath Constructs List

XPath Expression	Description
/	Indicates the root of the tree and a path separator to identify the child node of any given node in an XPath expression.
//	Indicates the all the child nodes of the given node.
*	This is a wildcard character which is used for matching any child node.
[ ]	Indicates the predicate expressions using the binary operators such as AND, OR and NOT. Also denotes the index of a node element.

Generating XML Data Using Oracle Functions

XMLTYPE

This is a data type in Oracle that can be used for storing XML data in the database.

```
Create table xml_table(xml_data xmltype);
Insert into xml_table values ('<Employees><Name>Alex</Name><DOB>30-Sep-
1989</DOB><Job_ID>101</Job_ID><Sal>2000</Sal></Employees>');
Commit;
```

Result:
```
table XML_TABLE created.
1 rows inserted.
committed.
```

This can also be used as a construct for explicit conversion of string into XML as shown below,

```
SELECT xmltype('<Employees><Name>Alex</Name><DOB>30-Sep-
1989</DOB><Job_ID>101</Job_ID><Sal>2000</Sal></Employees>')
FROM dual;
```

```
Result:
<Employees>
  <Name>Alex</Name>
  <DOB>30-Sep-1989</DOB>
  <Job_ID>101</Job_ID>
  <Sal>2000</Sal>
</Employees>
```

When the XML tags are not properly handled during the explicit conversion, the statement fails with an *ORA-31011: XML parsing failed* error.

This construct can also be used for generating XML documents from the result of an SQL statement when joint forces with the ref cursor as shown in the below example. The GETCLOBVAL operator converts an XML type document into a CLOB data. For more details on ref cursors, please refer Chapter 7, *The Cursors and Ref-cursors in PL/SQL.*

```
DECLARE
  l_rc_var1 SYS_REFCURSOR;
  l_xt_var2 XMLTYPE;
BEGIN
  OPEN l_rc_var1 FOR SELECT first_name, last_name, email, phone_number,
hire_date, job_id, salary FROM employees WHERE employee_id IN (100,101);
  l_xt_var2 := XMLTYPE(l_rc_var1);
  dbms_output.put_line(l_xt_var2.getClobVal);
END;
/
```

```
Result:
<?xml version="1.0"?>
<ROWSET>
 <ROW>
  <FIRST_NAME>Steven</FIRST_NAME>
  <LAST_NAME>King</LAST_NAME>
  <EMAIL>SKING</EMAIL>
  <PHONE_NUMBER>515.123.4567</PHONE_NUMBER>
  <HIRE_DATE>17-JUN-03</HIRE_DATE>
  <JOB_ID>AD_PRES</JOB_ID>
  <SALARY>24000</SALARY>
 </ROW>
 <ROW>
  <FIRST_NAME>Neena</FIRST_NAME>
  <LAST_NAME>Kochhar</LAST_NAME>
  <EMAIL>NKOCHHAR</EMAIL>
  <PHONE_NUMBER>515.123.4568</PHONE_NUMBER>
  <HIRE_DATE>21-SEP-05</HIRE_DATE>
  <JOB_ID>AD_VP</JOB_ID>
  <SALARY>17000</SALARY>
 </ROW>
</ROWSET>
```

XMLELEMENT and XMLATTRIBUTES

XMLELEMENT function is used for constructing XML elements from the table data or a PL/SQL variable. This function accepts *n* number of parameters, out of which its first parameter constructs the name of the XML tag and the rest of its parameters constructs the content of the XML element as shown below,

The prototype of the XMLELEMENT function is shown below,

```
XMLELEMENT(<Element_Name>[,<Attribute_value1>[,<Attribute_value2>...]])
```

In the below example, the first name and the last name of the employees whose IDs mentioned in the WHERE condition of the SELECT statement are constructed as XML elements using this function.

```
SELECT xmlelement(Name,First_name,' ',last_name) XMLELEMENT
FROM employees
WHERE employee_id IN (100,101);
```

Result:
```
<NAME>Steven King</NAME>
<NAME>Neena Kochhar</NAME>
```

One XML element can be nested to a collection of XML elements and form a nested XML element as shown in the below snippet.

```
SELECT xmlelement(Name, First_name, ' ', last_name, xmlelement(phone,
phone_number), xmlelement(email, email)) XMLELEMENT
FROM employees
WHERE employee_id IN (100,101);
```

Result:
```
<NAME>Steven King<PHONE>515.123.4567</PHONE><EMAIL>SKING</EMAIL></NAME>
<NAME>Neena Kochhar<PHONE>515.123.4568</PHONE><EMAIL>NKOCHHAR</EMAIL></NAME>
```

The XMLATTRIBUTES function converts the column data or the PL/SQL variable into attributes of the parent element. This function must contain one or more attributes in a comma separated list and name of the attribute will be the column name or the variable name used in the comma separated list respectively.

The prototype of the XMLATTRIBUTES function is shown below,

```
XMLATTRIBUTES(<Attribute_Value1>[,<Attribute_Value2>...]])
```

In the below example, the employee's name is made an attribute using the XMLATTRIBUTE function, whilst the employee's personal information is made into multiple elements using the XMLELEMENT function.

```
SELECT xmlelement(Employee,xmlattributes(first_name
   ||' '
   ||last_name AS Name), xmlelement(phone,phone_number)
,xmlelement(email,email),xmlelement(sal,salary)) XMLATTRIBUTES
FROM employees
WHERE employee_id IN (100,101);
```

Result:
```
<EMPLOYEE NAME="Steven
King"><PHONE>515.123.4567</PHONE><EMAIL>SKING</EMAIL><SAL>24000</SAL></EMPLO
YEE>
<EMPLOYEE NAME="Neena
Kochhar"><PHONE>515.123.4568</PHONE><EMAIL>NKOCHHAR</EMAIL><SAL>17000</SAL><
/EMPLOYEE>
```

XMLFOREST

The XMLFOREST function accepts one or more parameters. This function converts all its argument parameters into XML data and then returns an XML fragment, which is the concatenation of these converted parameters. The tags take its name from the arguments passed.

The prototype of the XMLFOREST function is shown below,

```
XMLFOREST(<Attribute_value1>[,<Attribute_value2>...]])
```

In the below example, the personal information of the employees is formed into tags individually and are concatenated with each other as shown below,

```
SELECT xmlforest(First_name, last_name, phone_number, email) XMLFOREST
FROM employees
WHERE employee_id IN (100,101);
```

Result:
```
<FIRST_NAME>Steven</FIRST_NAME><LAST_NAME>King</LAST_NAME><PHONE_NUMBER>515.
123.4567</PHONE_NUMBER><EMAIL>SKING</EMAIL>
<FIRST_NAME>Neena</FIRST_NAME><LAST_NAME>Kochhar</LAST_NAME><PHONE_NUMBER>51
5.123.4568</PHONE_NUMBER><EMAIL>NKOCHHAR</EMAIL>
```

XMLAGG

The XMLAGG function takes a list of XML elements from one column and returns an aggregated XML document in a single cell.

The prototype of the XMLAGG function is shown below,

```
XMLAGG(<XML_ELEMENT> ORDER BY <VALUE>)
```

In the below listing, the XMLAGG function aggregates the XML element of the first name of two employees into a single cell XML data.

```
SELECT xmlagg(xmlforest(First_name) order by first_name) XMLAGG
FROM employees
WHERE employee_id IN (100,101);
```

Result:
<FIRST_NAME>Neena</FIRST_NAME><FIRST_NAME>Steven</FIRST_NAME>

But this result misses an enclosing parent tag to make it an XML document, which can be formed wrapping this query with the XMLELEMENT function as shown below,

```
SELECT xmlelement(Names,xmlagg(xmlforest(First_name) order by first_name))
XMLAGG
FROM employees
WHERE employee_id IN (100,101);
```

Result:
<NAMES><FIRST_NAME>Neena</FIRST_NAME><FIRST_NAME>Steven</FIRST_NAME></NAMES>

Prior to the creation of the LISTAGG function in the version 11gR2, XMLAGG was used for aggregating the column values. The below statement imitates the functioning of the LISTAGG function.

```
SELECT REPLACE(REPLACE(REPLACE(xmlagg(xmlforest(First_name)
ORDER BY
first_name),'</FIRST_NAME><FIRST_NAME>',','),'<FIRST_NAME>'),'</FIRST_NAME>'
) XMLAGG
FROM employees
WHERE employee_id IN (100,101);
```

Result:
Neena,Steven

XMLCONCAT

This function accepts zero or more XML elements in series as its parameters, concatenates them all into a single instance and returns the result of the concatenation.

The prototype of the XMLCONCAT function is shown below,

```
XMLCONCAT(<XML_Element1>,<XML_ELEMENT2>[,<XML_ELEMENT3>,...])
```

In the below SQL, the XML elements of the first name and the last name of the two employees are concatenated together using the XMLCONCAT function.

```
SELECT xmlconcat(xmlforest(First_name),xmlforest(last_name)) XMLCONCAT
FROM employees
WHERE employee_id IN (100,101);
```

Result:
```
<FIRST_NAME>Steven</FIRST_NAME><LAST_NAME>King</LAST_NAME>
<FIRST_NAME>Neena</FIRST_NAME><LAST_NAME>Kochhar</LAST_NAME>
```

This functionality can also be achieved with the help of the concatenation operator as shown in the below example. Here, the output produced is in Varchar2 data type, whereas the XMLCONCAT function results the output in XMLTYPE.

```
SELECT xmlforest(First_name)||xmlforest(last_name) XMLCONCAT
FROM employees
WHERE employee_id IN (100,101);
```

Result:
```
<FIRST_NAME>Steven</FIRST_NAME><LAST_NAME>King</LAST_NAME>
<FIRST_NAME>Neena</FIRST_NAME><LAST_NAME>Kochhar</LAST_NAME>
```

XMLCOMMENT

This function generates an XML comment using the input string passed as its parameter. The input string is converted to the form <!--*Input_string*--> which is the W3C standard for placing comments in an XML document.

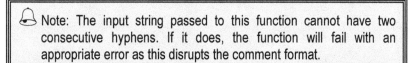
Note: The input string passed to this function cannot have two consecutive hyphens. If it does, the function will fail with an appropriate error as this disrupts the comment format.

When the input parameter is passed as Null, the function returns Null as its resultant.

```
SELECT xmlcomment('This is a comment line') xmlcomment FROM DUAL;
```

Result:
```
<!--This is a comment line-->
```

XMLCAST

This function was created in the version 11g and it casts the XML document or an XML element passed as its input parameter into a scalar data type of user's choice.

The prototype of the XMLCAST function is shown below,

```
XMLCAST(<XML_Document> | <XML_Element> as <Data_type>)
```

The below statement type casts the XML document's element value into a DATE type.

```
SELECT xmlcast(xmltype('<Date>2014-06-13</Date>') AS date) FROM dual;
```

```
Result:
13-JUN-14
```

XMLSEQUENCE

The XMLSEQUENCE function accepts an XML document or an XML element and returns a type of VARRAY with all the node's information.

The prototype of the XMLSEQUENCE function is shown below,

```
XMLSEQUENCE(<XML_Document> | <XML_Element>)
```

The below listing passes an XML document containing a video game's information to the XMLSEQUENCE function, which produces a VARRAY containing the XML document's content as shown below,

```
SELECT xmlsequence(xmltype('<Videogame>
<Type>Racing</Type>
<Name>NFS Most Wanted</Name>
<Version>2.0</Version>
<Size>5.5 GB</Size>
</Videogame>')) xmlsequence
FROM dual;
```

```
Result:
SYS.XMLSEQUENCETYPE(<Videogame>
<Type>Racing</Type>
<Name>NFS Most Wanted</Name>
<Version>2.0</Version>
<Size>5.5 GB</Size>
</Videogame>)
```

In the below example, the XMLSEQUENCE function's return type VARRAY is passed into a TABLE function which converts its nodes into multiple rows as shown below,

```
SELECT rownum,
  column_value
FROM TABLE(xmlsequence(extract(xmltype('<Videogame>
<Type>Racing</Type>
<Name>NFS Most Wanted</Name>
<Version>2.0</Version>
<Size>5.5 GB</Size>
</Videogame>'),'/Videogame/*')));
```

Result Set:

ROWNUM	COLUMN_VALUE
1	<Type>Racing</Type>
2	<Name>NFS Most Wanted</Name>
3	<Version>2.0</Version>
4	<Size>5.5 GB</Size>

DBMS_XMLGEN Package

This package converts the result of an SQL statement passed as inputs to its functions, into an XML document.

The GETXMLTYPE function converts the result of the input statement into an XMLTYPE data as shown below,

```
SELECT dbms_xmlgen.getxmltype('select first_name, last_name, phone_number,
email from employees where employee_id in (100,101)')
FROM dual;
```

Result:
```
<?xml version="1.0"?>
<ROWSET>
 <ROW>
  <FIRST_NAME>Steven</FIRST_NAME>
  <LAST_NAME>King</LAST_NAME>
  <PHONE_NUMBER>515.123.4567</PHONE_NUMBER>
  <EMAIL>SKING</EMAIL>
 </ROW>
 <ROW>
  <FIRST_NAME>Neena</FIRST_NAME>
  <LAST_NAME>Kochhar</LAST_NAME>
  <PHONE_NUMBER>515.123.4568</PHONE_NUMBER>
  <EMAIL>NKOCHHAR</EMAIL>
 </ROW>
</ROWSET>
```

The GETXML function converts the result of the input statement into an XML document of CLOB type as shown below,

```
SELECT dbms_xmlgen.getxml('select first_name, last_name, phone_number, email
from employees where employee_id in (100,101)')
FROM dual;
```

```
Result:
<ROWSET>
 <ROW>
  <FIRST_NAME>Steven</FIRST_NAME>
  <LAST_NAME>King</LAST_NAME>
  <PHONE_NUMBER>515.123.4567</PHONE_NUMBER>
  <EMAIL>SKING</EMAIL>
 </ROW>
 <ROW>
  <FIRST_NAME>Neena</FIRST_NAME>
  <LAST_NAME>Kochhar</LAST_NAME>
  <PHONE_NUMBER>515.123.4568</PHONE_NUMBER>
  <EMAIL>NKOCHHAR</EMAIL>
 </ROW>
</ROWSET>
```

Manipulating XML Data Using Oracle Functions

There are numerous functions in Oracle for manipulating the XML documents with an ease. For understanding them, we have created the below table which holds the details of a book available in a book store in an XML format as shown,

```
CREATE TABLE book_store (book_id NUMBER, book_author VARCHAR2(1000),
book_details_xml xmltype);

INSERT INTO library VALUES (1001,'John Wesley',
xmltype('<Rack1>
<Genre>Comics</Genre>
<Name>The Ironman</Name>
<Episode>4</Episode>
<Pages>25</Pages>
</Rack1>'));

Commit;
```

EXTRACTVALUE

This function accepts an XML document or an XML element and an XPath expression as its arguments and returns the scalar value of the expression's resultant node.

The prototype of the EXTRACTVALUE function is shown below,

```
EXTRACTVALUE(<XML_Document> | <XML_Element>, <XPath_Expression>)
```

The below SQL statement extracts the scalar value from the node /*Rack1*/*Name* as shown,

```
select extractvalue(book_details_xml, '/Rack1/Name')extractvalue from
book_store;
```

Result:
The Ironman

XMLTABLE

The XMLTABLE function returns the content of an XML document or an element in a relational table format.

The prototype for defining a XMLTABLE function is shown below,

```
SELECT * FROM <Table_name>, XMLTABLE(<Root_node> Passing
<Table_name.XML_Column_name> Columns <Child_node_name1> <Data_type> path
<Child_node1> <Child_node_name2> <Data_type> path <Child_node2> ... );
```

For understanding this function, the below demo table and data are created in the database.

```
CREATE TABLE Employee_details
  (Name VARCHAR2(30),Details xmltype
  );

INSERT INTO employee_details VALUES ('Yegappan Alagappan',
    '<Employee>
<DOB>1980-04-01</DOB>
<Designation>Technical Architect</Designation>
<Hire_date>2015-05-18</Hire_date>
<Job_ID>1011025</Job_ID>
<Salary>55000 $</Salary></Employee>'
  );

INSERT INTO employee_details VALUES ('Sivaramakrishnan',
    '<Employee>
<DOB>1988-08-16</DOB>
<Designation>Technical Lead</Designation>
<Hire_date>2016-05-18</Hire_date>
<Job_ID>1011024</Job_ID>
<Salary>35000 $</Salary></Employee>'
  );

INSERT INTO employee_details VALUES ('Thiyagu Thanthoni',
    '<Employee>
<DOB>1981-03-24</DOB>
<Designation>Vice President</Designation>
<Hire_date>2016-07-21</Hire_date>
<Job_ID>1011023</Job_ID>
<Salary>40000 $</Salary></Employee>'
```

```
  );

INSERT INTO employee_details VALUES ('Karthick Natarajan',
    '<Employee>
<DOB>1988-02-14</DOB>
<Designation>Senior Manager</Designation>
<Hire_date>2016-09-23</Hire_date>
<Job_ID>1011022</Job_ID>
<Salary>30000 $</Salary></Employee>'
  );

INSERT INTO employee_details VALUES ('Avinash Kamal',
    '<Employee>
<DOB>1988-07-27</DOB>
<Designation>Senior Software Engineer</Designation>
<Hire_date>2016-09-29</Hire_date>
<Job_ID>1011021</Job_ID>
<Salary>20000 $</Salary></Employee>'
  );

INSERT INTO employee_details VALUES ('Charles Jagan',
    '<Employee>
<DOB>1988-05-01</DOB>
<Designation>Analyst-I Application Programmer</Designation>
<Hire_date>2016-07-24</Hire_date>
<Job_ID>101101</Job_ID>
<Salary>10000 $</Salary></Employee>'
  );

Commit;
```

```
table EMPLOYEE_DETAILS created.
1 rows inserted.
1 rows inserted.
1 rows inserted.
1 rows inserted.
1 rows inserted.
committed.
```

When the XMLTYPE column of the EMPLOYEE_DETAILS table is passed as an input to the XMLTABLE function with appropriate paths, suitable data types and joined with its underlying table, the SQL returns a relation view of the XML document as shown below,

```
SELECT employee_details.name,
  emp.*
FROM employee_details, xmltable('/Employee' passing employee_details.details
columns
DOB DATE path '/Employee/DOB',
Designation VARCHAR2(100) path '/Employee/Designation',
Hire_date DATE path '/Employee/Hire_date',
Job_ID NUMBER path '/Employee/Job_ID',
Salary VARCHAR2(10) path '/Employee/Salary') Emp
ORDER BY employee_details.name ASC;
```

Result Set:

NAME	DOB	DESIGNATION	HIRE_DATE	JOB_ID	SALARY
Avinash Kamal	27-JUL-88	Senior Software Engineer	29-SEP-16	1011021	20000 $
Charles Jagan	01-MAY-88	Analyst-I Application Programmer	24-JUL-16	101101	10000 $
Karthick Natarajan	14-FEB-88	Senior Manager	23-SEP-16	1011022	30000 $
Sivaramakrishnan	16-AUG-88	Technical Lead	18-MAY-16	1011024	35000 $
Thiyagu Thanthoni	24-MAR-81	Vice President	21-JUL-16	1011023	40000 $
Yegappan Alagappan	01-APR-80	Technical Architect	18-MAY-15	1011025	55000 $

AppendChildXML

This function appends a user supplied XML tag onto the target XML document or an XML element in the path provided as the XPath expression.

The prototype for defining an AppendChildXML function is shown below,

```
AppendChildXML(<XML_Document> | <XML_Element>, <XPath_Expression>,
<Child_XML>)
```

The cost tag is added to the XML document for the book ID *1001* using the AppendChildXML function as shown below,

```
UPDATE book_store
SET book_details_xml= appendchildxml(book_details_xml, '/Rack1',
'<Cost>10$</Cost>') WHERE book_id=1001;
```

1 rows updated.

The addition of this child XML tag to the parent XML document can be verified by using the EXTRACTVALUE function as shown below,

```
select extractvalue(book_details_xml,'/Rack1/Cost') from book_store;
```

Result:
10$

When a duplicate child node is inserted into a single parent as shown below,

```
UPDATE book_store
SET book_details_xml=appendchildxml(book_details_xml,'/Rack1','<Cost>9$ for
membership holders</Cost>')
WHERE book_id      =1001;
```

1 rows updated.

The values of the duplicate child nodes can be retrieved by using the square brackets with the appropriate indicator on the child node name as shown below,

```
select extractvalue(book_details_xml,'/Rack1/Cost[1]') from book_store;
```

Result:
10$

```
select extractvalue(book_details_xml,'/Rack1/Cost[2]') from book_store;
```

Result:
9$ for membership holders

DELETEXML

This function deletes a user supplied XML tag from the target XML document or an XML element, which matches the path provided as the XPath expression.

The prototype for defining an DELETEXML function is shown below,

```
DELETEXML(<XML_Document> | <XML_Element>, <XPath_Expression>)
```

The SQL deletes the Cost tag from the parent XML document as shown below,

```
UPDATE book_store
SET book_details_xml=deletexml(book_details_xml,'/Rack1/Cost')
WHERE book_id        =1001;
```

1 rows updated.

After the *Cost* tag is deleted from the parent XML document, the EXTRACTVALUE function returns Null for that tag as it is not available anymore as shown below.

```
select extractvalue(book_details_xml,'/Rack1/Cost') from book_store;
```

Result:
Null

UPDATEXML

This function updates the scalar value of the XML tag in an XML document or an XML Element, which passed as an argument by the user.

The prototype for defining the UPDATEXML function is shown below,

```
UPDATEXML(<XML_Document> | <XML_Element>, <XPath_Expression>,
<Scalar_value>)
```

The *Pages* tag from the parent document is updated to 30 from 25 using this function as shown below,

```
UPDATE book_store
SET book_details_xml=updatexml(book_details_xml,'/Rack1/Pages/text()',30)
WHERE book_id       =1001;
```

After the update is performed, the changes can be verified by using the EXTRACTVALUE function as shown below,

```
select extractvalue(book_details_xml,'/Rack1/Pages') from book_store;
```

Result:
30

EXISTSNODE

The EXISTSNODE is a condition, unlike the others, which can be used in the WHERE condition of an SQL statement. This condition determines whether the traversal of the XML document or an XML element results in an available node or not.

This condition produces the literal 1 if the traversing node is found and 0 if it is not found.

The prototype for defining an EXISTSNODE condition is shown below,

```
EXISTSNODE(<XML_Document> | <XML_Element>, <XPath_Expression>)
```

The below SQL results in the scalar value of the node *Genre* only if it is present in the parent XML, else it returns no rows. This logic is handled by the EXISTSNODE condition as shown below,

```
SELECT extractvalue(book_details_xml,'/Rack1/Genre')
FROM book_store
WHERE existsnode(book_details_xml,'/Rack1/Genre')=1;
```

Result:
Comics

Summary

In this chapter, we have toured through the introduction of the regular expression origin and have understood the support of the POSIX standard and Perl-influenced metacharacters in Oracle. In the next section, we have learnt the different regular expression functions and conditions with sufficient real time examples. The second part of this chapter started with an introduction to the XML programming and its origination. The latter section explained us about the Oracle database's XML and its expression support. In the final section of the second part of this chapter, we have seen the different XML functions for creating and manipulating the XML documents and elements in detail with appropriate examples.

In the next chapter, we will be learning about the different types of Collections, Collection methods and their 12c enhancements.

The PL/SQL Types

This chapter gives you a high insight on all available PL/SQL types in Oracle with numerous examples, facts, and tips.

15. Introduction to the Object-Oriented Programming and its early stages of development and fame.

16. Introduction to the Object types along with their different methods and R12.1 enhancement.

17. Introduction to the Record types and their R12.1 enhancement.

18. Introduction to the different Collection types, characteristics, SET operators and collection methods.

19. Introduction to dropping a type and its dependent objects permanently from the database.

Introduction to Object Oriented Programming

The concept of Object Oriented Programming (OOP) acquired its acceptance in most of the programming languages because of its skill of reducing the cost and time for building complex applications by breaking them down into multiple logical entities when it is properly implemented. OOP is a programming model based on objects, which stores their data in the form of fields and their implementation in the form of procedures and functions, often known as methods.

The basic idea of Object Oriented Programming concepts was originated first in the SIMULA language, which was used for creating simulations in the 1960s. Alan Kay, who was at the University of Utah at that time, had a vision of a personal computer with graphics oriented applications using the SIMULA language. He then sold his idea to Xerox PARC and started working there with a team only to create the first personal computer, the Dynabook. The Dynabook was powered by a simulation and graphics oriented programming language called as Smalltalk, which is still available in the market but not widely used. The popularity of Object Oriented Programming gained its momentum in the late 70s. In the early 80s, Bjorn Stroustrup incorporated OOP into the C language resulting into C++, which was the first Object Oriented Programming language to be used widely for commercial purpose.

Introduction to Object Types

Similar to the PL/SQL packages in Oracle, an object type has a specification section, which acts as an interface to our applications by declaring attributes along with methods for manipulating the data. The object body implements the Object type by defining the methods declared in them just like a package body implementing its specification.

The object type acts as an interface to our applications by advertising the list of functions it supports but hides its implementation inside of them so that the client applications are not bound to any changes in the details of the object type by the programmer. The process of hiding the implementation logic of an object type is called as Abstraction. To replace the existing business rules in an object, we just have to replace the object body with a new one without affecting the client application calls as the structure of the object remains unchanged.

The instances of an Oracle object type are classified into Persistent and Transient based on their lifespan.

1. **Persistent Objects**: These types of objects are stored in the Oracle database permanently. The lifetime of this type of object can exceed the application accessing it unless it is explicitly removed from the database. The two types of persistent objects are,

    1.1 **Standalone Instances**: These are the referenced objects which are stored in the rows of an object table with a unique object identifier. These are called as referential objects, because of the fact that the references of these instances can be retrieved by a calling application.

    1.2 **Embedded Instances**: These are the non-referential objects and are not stored in the object table rows but embedded within the object structures. These instances do not have object identifiers unlike the standalone instances and cannot be referenced by the calling programs.

2. **Transient Objects**: By the name, the transient objects are temporary objects which are created and destroyed any time during an application, whose lifespan does not exceed that of the application. These cannot be converted into persistent objects as these are meant only for storing temporary values for computational purposes.

The object types can be used as,

1. Data type for a column in an Oracle table.

2. Data type for an object instance during its declaration in the PL/SQL program units.

3. Attributes of another object or a collection type.

4. Formal parameters in the procedure and function signature.

5. The return type for a function.

The section below describes the creation and the implementation of the object type specification and body respectively.

Object Type Specification

The objects in PL/SQL, similar to the packages in Oracle having variables and subprograms, has attributes and methods (can be either a function or a procedure) for storing and manipulating the input data transiently. In contrast to the PL/SQL packages, here we have some special types of methods like *Constructor*, *Static*, *Member*, *Map*, and *Order* each serving its own functionality. The parameter list for the Member and Static methods follows the same rules as that of the subprograms in the PL/SQL packages. All the attributes declared in the object specification can be accessed only after they are fully constructed through an object instance, unlike how the variables declared in a package works.

> ⌓ Note: Only a function may be a Map, Order or Constructor method.

The declaration of the elements in an object type specification must follow a specific ordering of Attributes first, followed by Constructor functions, a Member or Static methods, Map or Order functions in any order. If this rule is violated, the object type spec fails during its compilation with an error indicating that the declaration of the function is either incomplete or malformed.

The prototype for defining an object type specification is shown below,

```
CREATE [OR REPLACE] type <Object_name> [AUTHID [DEFINER | CURRENT_USER]]
IS | AS
   OBJECT
```

```
  (
     [<Instance_variable_name> <SQL_data_type | PLSQL_data_type |
Object_type>],
     [Constructor
   FUNCTION <Object_name> [<Parameter_list>]
     RETURN SELF
   AS
     RESULT],
     [[Member | Static]
   PROCEDURE <Procedure_name> [<Parameter_list>]],
     [[Member | Static]
   FUNCTION               <Function_name> [<Parameter_list>]
     RETURN               <SQL_data_type | PLSQL_data_type | Object_type>],
     [Map Member FUNCTION  <Function_name> [<Parameter_list>]
     RETURN               <Scalar_data_type>],
     [ORDER Member FUNCTION <Function_name> [<Parameter_list>]
     RETURN               <Integer_data_type>]) [NOT] [INSTANTIABLE] [NOT]
[FINAL];
```

> 🔔 Note: An object type may have only 1 MAP or 1 ORDER function.

- **Constructor Methods**: A Constructor method is a function which determines how the instances of the object types are built. The keyword SELF denotes the instance of the object currently invoking the method.

- **Member Methods**: These methods can be either a procedure or a function which is used for accessing an object instance's data. These are non-comparable methods unless we prefix with the methods MAP or ORDER which turns them into comparable methods. The MAP and ORDER methods can have only scalar and integer data types respectively.

- **Static Methods**: These methods can be either a procedure or a function similar to a Member method, but are independent of the current instance of the object type. This method does not have access to the SELF parameter.

- **Instantiable**: An instance of the object has to be created to use any object. If this keyword is prefixed with an NOT during the object creation, the object cannot be instantiated. The NOT Instantiable keyword says Oracle not to create any constructor function for the object.

   In the below example, an object OBJ_INST is created with one attribute having Number as its data type, where it is defined as NOT Instantiable and NOT Final.

```
CREATE OR REPLACE type obj_inst
IS
```

```
Object
(
   obj_n_var1 NUMBER) NOT Instantiable NOT Final;
/
```

When this object is initialized as shown in the below anonymous block, the unit fails with a compilation error stating that this object cannot be initialized as it is defined as NOT Instantiable.

> 🔔 Note: An object defined as NOT Instantiable must be defined as NOT Final too and not otherwise.

```
DECLARE
  l_obj_inst1 obj_inst:=obj_inst(20);
BEGIN
   NULL;
END;
/
```

```
Error report:
ORA-06550: line 2, column 25:
PLS-00713: attempting to instantiate a type that is NOT INSTANTIABLE
ORA-06550: line 2, column 15:
PL/SQL: Item ignored
06550. 00000 -  "line %s, column %s:\n%s"
*Cause:    Usually a PL/SQL compilation error.
```

- **Final:** To inherit an object, the object has to be inheritable. If an object is defined with the FINAL keyword, it means that no subtypes can be derived from the object. If this keyword is prefixed with an NOT, any subtype can override this object and its methods.

The below listing creates the specification section of the object OBJ_CALC which is created to function as a calculator.

```
CREATE OR REPLACE type obj_calc
IS
  Object
  (
    obj_n_var1 NUMBER,
    obj_n_var2 NUMBER,
    constructor
  FUNCTION obj_calc(
      self IN OUT obj_calc)
    RETURN SELF
  AS
    result,
    member FUNCTION addition(
```

```
    self IN obj_calc)
RETURN NUMBER,
member FUNCTION subtraction(
    self IN obj_calc)
RETURN NUMBER,
member FUNCTION multiplication(
    self IN obj_calc)
RETURN NUMBER,
member FUNCTION division(
    self IN obj_calc)
RETURN NUMBER,
member PROCEDURE PRINT(
    self IN OUT obj_calc)) Instantiable NOT final;
/
```

A method can only be accessed when an object's instance is in place. For a method to use the attributes of an object, a self-implied parameter, SELF, is available by default in all methods except the ones which are defined as a STATIC in nature. By default, the SELF parameter is in IN mode for the member functions and in IN OUT mode for the member procedures and the constructor functions.

Thus, the above object type specification creation script is the same as the below one,

```
CREATE OR REPLACE type obj_calc
IS
  Object
  (
    obj_n_var1 NUMBER,
    obj_n_var2 NUMBER,
    constructor
  FUNCTION obj_calc
    RETURN SELF
  AS
    result,
    member FUNCTION addition
    RETURN NUMBER,
    member FUNCTION subtraction
    RETURN NUMBER,
    member FUNCTION multiplication
    RETURN NUMBER,
    member FUNCTION division
    RETURN NUMBER,
    member PROCEDURE PRINT) Instantiable NOT final;
/
```

This object has one Constructor function, whose name matches with the object name and five member methods. The first four member functions are created for performing the calculation process and the last member procedure is used for printing the result of the calculation performed. The member methods are accessible only when an instance of the object is created. This object is defined as *Instantiable*, meaning that the object is capable of creating an object instance at any point in time and *Not Final*, meaning that the object is capable of acting as a super type.

Object Type Body

All the elements declared in the object type specification must be implemented in the object type body similar to the PL/SQL packages. But, unlike the PL/SQL packages, the object type body does not allow us to define any private subprograms or forward declarations, i.e., defining a method in the object type body and declaring it before its internal call is not allowed in the object type body's definition section. Also, the object type body allows us to declare functions and procedures in the declaration section similar to the PL/SQL packages. The only difference between the PL/SQL packages and the object types is that the latter must have the attributes and methods in its body, which are declared in its specification and nothing less or more. Methods can also be overloaded provided the fact that they follow the rules of overloading similar to the subprogram overloading in the PL/SQL packages.

As we have seen in the above paragraph, there is almost no difference in the implementation and working of the PL/SQL packages and the object types. All the functionalities that are coded in an object can obviously be replicated in a package. The script written in an object is related to OOPS model with methods and constructors that pertain to object itself, and the code in packages might totally be independent of any type of object in the database. Few pros of the objects over the packages are,

1. When we want to return an object result set, the packages and the object types work similarly, but when using the packages, we are in need of creating two objects (Package and Object type), but in the case of object types, they encapsulate the complete business logic into a single entity within themselves. Thus, the code maintenance and encapsulation is found to be better in the object types than using the packages.

2. When an SQL needs to sort an object type either explicitly by using the ORDER BY clause or implicitly by using the GROUP BY, UNION, DISTINCT clauses, the special comparison functions MAP and ORDER come in handy, which are available only in the object types and not in the packages.

The prototype for defining the object type body is shown below,

```
CREATE [OR REPLACE] OBJECT TYPE <Object_name> [AUTHID [DEFINER |
CURRENT_USER]]
IS | AS
  [CONSTRUCTOR FUNCTION <Object_name> [<Parameter_list>]
  RETURN SELF
AS
  RESULT
IS | AS
BEGIN
      <Executable_statements>;
```

```
    RETURN;
END <Object_name>];
[[MEMBER | STATIC] PROCEDURE <Procedure_name> [<Parameter_list>]
IS | AS
BEGIN
        <Execution_statements>;
END <Procedure_name>];
[[MEMBER | STATIC] FUNCTION <Function_name> [<Parameter_list>]
  RETURN <SQL_data_type | PLSQL_data_type | Object_type>
IS
BEGIN
        <Execution_statements>;
  RETURN <SQL_data_type | PLSQL_data_type | Object_type>;
END [Function_name]];
[MAP MEMBER FUNCTION <Function_name>[<Parameter_list>]
  RETURN <Scalar_data_type>
IS
BEGIN
        <Execution_statements>;
  RETURN <Scalar_data_type>;
END [Function_name]];
[ORDER MEMBER FUNCTION <Function_name> [<Parameter_list>]
  RETURN <Integer_data_type>;
IS
BEGIN
        <Execution_statements>;
  RETURN <Integer_data_type>;
END [<Function_name>]];
END [<Object_name>];
/
```

Note: An object type may have only 1 MAP or 1 ORDER function.

In the below listing, the object type body of the specification which is declared in the above section is defined. This object performs some basic calculation operation on the two attributes declared in the object specification and prints them.

```
CREATE OR REPLACE type body obj_calc
IS
  Constructor FUNCTION obj_calc RETURN self AS result
IS
BEGIN
  RETURN;
END;
member FUNCTION addition RETURN NUMBER
IS
  l_obj_calc1 obj_calc:=obj_calc(obj_n_var1,obj_n_var2);
BEGIN
  RETURN l_obj_calc1.obj_n_var1+l_obj_calc1.obj_n_var2;
END;
member FUNCTION subtraction RETURN NUMBER
IS
  l_obj_calc2 obj_calc:=obj_calc(obj_n_var1,obj_n_var2);
BEGIN
```

```
      RETURN l_obj_calc2.obj_n_var1-l_obj_calc2.obj_n_var2;
END;
member FUNCTION multiplication RETURN NUMBER
IS
   l_obj_calc3 obj_calc:=obj_calc(obj_n_var1,obj_n_var2);
BEGIN
   RETURN l_obj_calc3.obj_n_var1*l_obj_calc3.obj_n_var2;
END;
member FUNCTION division RETURN NUMBER
IS
   l_obj_calc4 obj_calc:=obj_calc(obj_n_var1,obj_n_var2);
BEGIN
   RETURN l_obj_calc4.obj_n_var1/l_obj_calc4.obj_n_var2;
END;
member PROCEDURE PRINT IS
   l_obj_calc5 obj_calc:=obj_calc(obj_n_var1,obj_n_var2);
BEGIN
   dbms_output.put_line('Addition of the two numbers is '||
l_obj_calc5.addition);
   dbms_output.put_line('Subtraction of the two numbers is '||
   l_obj_calc5.subtraction);
   dbms_output.put_line('Multiplication of the two numbers is '||
   l_obj_calc5.multiplication);
   dbms_output.put_line('Division of the two numbers is '||
l_obj_calc5.division);
END;
END;
/
```

This object can be kick-started by initializing it with two integer values and executing the *print* member procedure as shown below,

```
DECLARE
   l_obj_calc_var1 obj_calc:=obj_calc(8,4);
BEGIN
   l_obj_calc_var1.print;
END;
/
```

Result:

```
Addition of the two numbers is 12
Subtraction of the two numbers is 4
Multiplication of the two numbers is 32
Division of the two numbers is 2
```

Constructor Overriding

The Constructor methods are basically functions which determine the way in which the object instances are constructed, thus the name. The name of the Constructor function must be mandatorily matched with the object name. There can be more than one Constructor functions implemented, but their signatures must follow the subprogram overloading rule. If there are two similar Constructor functions declared, the object fails with a compilation error stating that there is a conflict between the Constructor functions created.

The primary action of these functions is that they return a new instance of the object which can either be defined by the system or user. The keyword SELF is used for accessing the object instances' parameter of the currently invoking method.

 Note: The RETURN statement in a Constructor function cannot include an expression as the function returns the copy of the instantiated object.

The object types by default have a system defined Constructor function with the default IN OUT parameter, SELF. Whenever an object's initialization has to be made user defined rather than plain initializing, a user defined constructor has to be created with a user-defined object instance value as shown in the below snippet. Here, the system-defined constructor is overridden by the user defined constructor with a user-defined initialization value.

```
CREATE OR REPLACE TYPE obj_cons
IS
  OBJECT
  (
    obj_var1 VARCHAR2(100),
    CONSTRUCTOR FUNCTION obj_cons RETURN SELF AS RESULT,
    CONSTRUCTOR FUNCTION obj_cons(obj_var1 VARCHAR2) RETURN SELF AS
    RESULT) INSTANTIABLE NOT FINAL;
  /
CREATE OR REPLACE TYPE BODY obj_cons
IS
  CONSTRUCTOR FUNCTION obj_cons RETURN SELF AS RESULT
IS
BEGIN
  Self.obj_var1:= 'Defaulted Initialization Value';
  RETURN;
END obj_cons;
CONSTRUCTOR FUNCTION obj_cons(obj_var1 VARCHAR2) RETURN SELF AS
  RESULT
IS
BEGIN
  self.obj_var1 := obj_var1;
  RETURN;
END obj_cons;
END;
/
```

In the below example, the system defined Constructor function calls the user defined Constructor function internally, hiding all the complexity of creating an object's instance.

```
DECLARE
   l_obj_cons_var1 obj_cons:=obj_cons();
BEGIN
   dbms_output.put_line(l_obj_cons_var1.obj_var1);
END;
/
```

Result:

```
Defaulted Initialization Value
```

In the below anonymous block, the user defined constructor is overridden by the constructor with the formal parameters. Here, a user-defined initialization value is passed in the arguments in the declaration section which overrides the default constructor value shown in the above listing.

```
DECLARE
   l_obj_cons_var1 obj_cons:=obj_cons('Overriding Constructor!');
BEGIN
   dbms_output.put_line(l_obj_cons_var1.obj_var1);
END;
/
```

Result:

```
Overriding Constructor!
```

Static Methods

The static methods are similar to the conventional PL/SQL subprograms which are invoked independently of instances of an object. The static methods can make use of its parent object, but are limited to work with only the instances which are created by them and not by the other methods in the object.

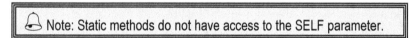 Note: Static methods do not have access to the SELF parameter.

In the below listing, an object is created with two attributes, one static function with one formal parameter returning an object instance and a member procedure acting as a printer. Here, the static function returns an instance of its parent object, meaning that it has to create an instance first before returning it to the calling program. Unlike calling the other method types by prefixing their instance name with the dot notation to the method name as *instance_name.method_name()*, the static methods are prefixed with the object name as they do not have access to the object's current instance as *object_name.method_name()*.

```
CREATE OR REPLACE type obj_static
IS
  object
  (
    obj_emp_id    NUMBER,
    obj_emp_name VARCHAR2(100),
    static FUNCTION func_static(ip_emp_id VARCHAR2)RETURN obj_static,
    member PROCEDURE PRINT(ip_var1 VARCHAR2));
  /
CREATE OR REPLACE type body obj_static
IS
  Static FUNCTION func_static(ip_emp_id VARCHAR2) RETURN obj_static
IS
  l_obj_var1 obj_static;
BEGIN
  SELECT
    obj_static(employee_id,last_name
    ||', '
    ||first_name)
  INTO
    l_obj_var1
  FROM
    employees
  WHERE
    employee_id=ip_emp_id;
  RETURN l_obj_var1;
END;
member PROCEDURE PRINT (ip_var1 VARCHAR2)
IS
BEGIN
  IF ip_var1='USER PROVIDED VALUE' THEN
    dbms_output.put_line('The Employee name provided for the ID '||
    self.obj_emp_id||' is '||self.obj_emp_name);
  elsif ip_var1='DATABASE VALUE' THEN
    dbms_output.put_line('The Employee name from the database for the ID '||
    self.obj_emp_id||' is '||self.obj_emp_name);
  END IF;
END;
END;
/
```

In the below example, the declaration section initializes the first object variable with user defined values using the constructor function and the second variable gets instantiated by calling the static function FUNC_STATIC. Both the variables are then in the scope of the PRINT procedure in its body, thus the procedure is called in the execution section of the unit with appropriate input values mentioning whether the Employee name is either user provided or taken from the database.

```
DECLARE
  l_obj_var1 obj_static:=obj_static(100,'Hunold, Alexander');
  l_obj_var2 obj_static:=obj_static.func_static(100);
BEGIN
  l_obj_var1.print('USER PROVIDED VALUE');
  l_obj_var2.print('DATABASE VALUE');
END;
/
```

Result:
```
The Employee name provided for the ID 100 is Hunold, Alexander
The Employee name from the database for the ID 100 is King, Steven
```

Comparison Methods

Comparison between the scalar variables can be easily achieved as they have a predefined order and a format for their data storage. But, comparing an object type having multiple attributes of various data types may not be done as easily like the scalar variables, as these do not have a defined axis for comparison. For achieving this purpose, Oracle has provided us with the MAP and the ORDER methods for comparing the object instances.

MAP Member Functions

The MAP member functions are used for performing comparisons between a single attribute of an object instance to a single attribute of another object instance. The MAP functions do not accept any formal parameters and must return a scalar data type, either CHAR, VARCHAR2, NUMBER or DATE, which can be easily compared by the system. The MAP member functions are used for validating object instances with a single attribute.

> Tips: The MAP functions cannot be implemented on Static functions, but Member functions only.

```
CREATE OR REPLACE TYPE obj_map
IS
  OBJECT
  (
    obj_var1 NUMBER,
    MEMBER PROCEDURE print,
    MAP MEMBER FUNCTION func_map RETURN NUMBER);
  /
CREATE OR REPLACE TYPE body obj_map
IS
  MEMBER PROCEDURE print
IS
BEGIN
  dbms_output.put_line(self.obj_var1);
END;
MAP MEMBER FUNCTION func_map RETURN NUMBER
IS
BEGIN
  RETURN obj_var1;
END;
END;
/
```

In the above snippet, an object is created with an attribute of the number data type, a member procedure for printing the attribute value of the current instance and an MAP member function returning the attribute of the current instance.

The attribute value for multiple instances can be compared with the help of the below anonymous block which has two instances of the object OBJ_MAP, which accepts bind values as their initialization parameter. In the execution section, the attribute values of the two instances of the objects are printed using the *print* procedure from the object. The IF condition merely checks for the equality between the two object instances, which internally calls the MAP member function and compares the result of the two instance's MAP member function's return value, which is the attribute value of the two instances ideally. The result of the comparison between the two object instance's attributes is printed appropriately using the PUT_LINE procedure.

```
DECLARE
  l_obj_map1 obj_map:=obj_map(:l_obj_map1);
  l_obj_map2 obj_map:=obj_map(:l_obj_map2);
BEGIN
  l_obj_map1.print;
  l_obj_map2.print;
  IF l_obj_map1=l_obj_map2 THEN
    dbms_output.put_line('The two instances are equal!!');
  ELSE
    dbms_output.put_line('The two instances are not equal!!');
  END IF;
END;
/
```

Result:
1. When l_obj_map1= 10 and l_obj_map2= 20 then,
10
20
The two instances are not equal!!
2. When l_obj_map1= 30 and l_obj_map2= 30 then,
30
30
The two instances are equal!!

ORDER Member Function

Unlike the MAP member function, the ORDER member function allows us to compare every attribute from an object instance with an another object instance. An ORDER function has a single actual parameter with the object's instance as its data type and compares the input instance with the current instance of the object attribute by attribute. The ORDER method must return a Number data type and the values are restricted between -1, 0, 1 and Null.

In the below listing, an object OBJ_ORDER is created with three attributes and an ORDER member function having an input parameter of current object type and its return data type is Number. The object type body contains the definition of the ORDER member function which compares all three attributes of the object instance passed as input to the ORDER function with that of the current instance.

```
CREATE OR REPLACE TYPE obj_order
IS
  OBJECT
  (
    obj_var1 VARCHAR2(100),
    obj_var2 VARCHAR2(100),
    obj_var3 VARCHAR2(100),
    ORDER MEMBER FUNCTION func_order(ip_obj_order obj_order) RETURN NUMBER)
  /
CREATE OR REPLACE TYPE body obj_order
IS
  ORDER MEMBER FUNCTION func_order(ip_obj_order obj_order) RETURN NUMBER
IS
BEGIN
  IF ip_obj_order.obj_var1=self.obj_var1 AND
     ip_obj_order.obj_var2=self.obj_var2 AND
     ip_obj_order.obj_var3=self.obj_var3 THEN
     RETURN 1;
  ELSIF ip_obj_order.obj_var1<>self.obj_var1 AND
        ip_obj_order.obj_var2<>self.obj_var2 AND
        ip_obj_order.obj_var3<>self.obj_var3 THEN
        RETURN 0;
  ELSIF ip_obj_order.obj_var1<>self.obj_var1 OR
        ip_obj_order.obj_var2<>self.obj_var2 OR
        ip_obj_order.obj_var3<>self.obj_var3 THEN
        RETURN -1;
  END IF;
END;
END;
/
```

The ORDER function can be tested by using the below anonymous block, where two instances of the object OBJ_ORDER are created and initialized to the bind variables for all the three attributes. The execution section of the unit uses the return value of the ORDER function called by first object's instance with the second object's instance as its parameter in the CASE statement and compares them with each other. The appropriate result of the comparison is then printed using the PUT_LINE procedure.

```
DECLARE
  l_vc_var1 VARCHAR2(100);
  l_obj_order1 obj_order:=obj_order(:l_obj_order11, :l_obj_order12,
```

```
     :l_obj_order13);
   l_obj_order2 obj_order:=obj_order(:l_obj_order21, :l_obj_order22,
   :l_obj_order23);
BEGIN
   CASE l_obj_order1.func_order(l_obj_order2)
   WHEN 1 THEN
      l_vc_var1:='All three attributes of the two instances match with each
other!';
   WHEN 0 THEN
      l_vc_var1:='All three attributes of the two instances do not match with
each other!!';
   WHEN -1 THEN
      l_vc_var1:='Some attributes matches and some attributes do not match
between the two instances!!!';
   END CASE;
   dbms_output.put_line(l_vc_var1);
END;
/
```

Results:

1. When l_obj_order11=1, l_obj_order12=2, l_obj_order13=3 and
    l_obj_order21=1, l_obj_order22=2, l_obj_order23=3 then

All three attributes of the two instances match with each other!

2. When l_obj_order11=10, l_obj_order12=20, l_obj_order13=30 and
    l_obj_order21=40, l_obj_order22=50, l_obj_order23=60 then

All three attributes of the two instances do not match with each other!!

3. When l_obj_order11=15, l_obj_order12=22, l_obj_order13=48 and
    l_obj_order21=17, l_obj_order22=22, l_obj_order23=56 then

Some attributes matches and some attributes do not match between the two
instances!!!

Inheritance

The objects are naturally extensible, meaning that the attributes and methods of one
object can be made available to one or more objects. This property is called as
inheritance. The object which inherits the behavior of other objects is called as a
Subtype and the object which is being inherited is called as the Supertype. When an
instance is created for the subtype, the instance inherits the behavior of both the
supertype and the subtype. A subtype cannot inherit the properties of two supertypes
when there is no relationship between them, similar to how a human child cannot have
more than one father or one mother. But the subtype created on a supertype can inherit
the properties of that supertype and all its parent supertypes if present.

A method in a supertype is by default overridden when the subtype provides a method
with the same name and type, similar to its supertype. This default behavior can be
changed by using the generalized invocation as shown below,

Consider a method *print* is available in both the supertype and its subtype,

- *(Instance_name as supertype).print* invocation will call the *print* method from the supertype.

- *(Instance_name as subtype).print* invocation will call the *print* method from the subtype.

In the below snippet, a supertype OBJ_SUPERTYPE is created with two attributes, one map member function comparing the employee ID and a member function for returning the name of the employee for a particular ID. This supertype is defined as NOT Final, thus this object can be inherited by any other types.

```
CREATE OR REPLACE type obj_supertype
IS
  object
  (
    obj_emp_id   VARCHAR2(30),
    obj_emp_name VARCHAR2(30),
    map member FUNCTION func_super_map RETURN NUMBER,
    member FUNCTION func_super_print RETURN VARCHAR2) NOT final;
  /
CREATE OR REPLACE type body obj_supertype
IS
  map member FUNCTION func_super_map
  RETURN NUMBER
IS
BEGIN
  RETURN obj_emp_id;
END;
member FUNCTION func_super_print
  RETURN VARCHAR2
IS
BEGIN
  RETURN 'The Employee details for the ID '||obj_emp_id||' is Name: '||
  obj_emp_name;
END;
END;
/
```

In the below listing, an instance for the object type OBJ_SUPERTYPE is created with user-defined initialization values in the declaration section. The execution section of the block makes a call to the member function and its return value is printed using the PUT_LINE procedure.

```
DECLARE
  l_obj_supertype obj_supertype:=obj_supertype(857, 'Thomas King');
BEGIN
  dbms_output.put_line(l_obj_supertype.func_super_print);
END;
/
```

Result:

The Employee details for the ID 857 is Name: Thomas King

A subtype has been created under the above supertype with two new attributes pertaining to it along with a member function having the same name as that of the super type's member function. In the body section, the member function calls the supertype's member function by prefixing the function name with the generalized invocation parameter, *Self AS obj_supertype*, and concatenating its return value with its own attribute's values. The obtained result set acts as the return value for the member function.

> Note: The keyword OVERRIDING is used in the subtype methods to override the supertype's methods. The methods overriding each other much match in their names, parameters and return types (in the case of functions) exactly.

```
CREATE OR REPLACE type obj_subtype under obj_supertype (
obj_emp_job VARCHAR2(30),
obj_emp_sal NUMBER,
overriding member FUNCTION func_super_print
  RETURN VARCHAR2);
/
CREATE OR REPLACE type body obj_subtype
AS
  overriding member FUNCTION func_super_print
  RETURN VARCHAR2
IS
BEGIN
  RETURN (self AS obj_supertype).func_super_print||', Job ID:
'||obj_emp_job||', Salary: '|| obj_emp_sal||'$';
END;
END;
/
```

The below anonymous block creates an instance of the subtype and initializes it with the user defined values. Here, the first two attributes in the constructor function initialization are overridden from the supertype and the next two attributes are its own. In the execution section, the first PUT_LINE procedure calls the member function from the supertype using the generalized invocation parameter, *(l_obj_subtype AS obj_supertype).func_super_print* and the second PUT_LINE procedure makes its call to the member function from the subtype using the generalized invocation parameter, *(l_obj_subtype AS obj_subtype).func_super_print*, both the invocations are performed on the subtype's instance variable l_obj_subtype.

```
DECLARE
  l_obj_subtype obj_subtype:=obj_subtype(857, 'Thomas King', 'Assistant
Manager', 3500);
BEGIN
  dbms_output.put_line((l_obj_subtype AS obj_supertype).func_super_print);
  dbms_output.put_line((l_obj_subtype AS obj_subtype).func_super_print);
END;
/
```

Result:

```
The Employee details for the ID 857 is Name: Thomas King
The Employee details for the ID 857 is Name: Thomas King, Job ID: Assistant
Manager, Salary: 3500$
```

In the below snippet, the subtype is initialized with the four attributes of user-defined values.

The execution section makes its first PUT_LINE procedure to call the member function of the supertype with the subtype's instance variable as its argument, returning the RETURN value of the supertype's member function. As the supertype has only access to the first two attributes of the subtype, the first PUT_LINE procedure returns only the values of the first two attributes from the initialization variable.

The second PUT_LINE procedure makes the call to the supertype's member function similar to its previous statement, but this time, a general invocation parameter, *(l_obj_subtype AS obj_subtype)* is passed as its argument, returning the complete initialization variable values. Here, the supertype's member function has overridden the subtype's member function, which is an uncommon behavior.

```
DECLARE
  l_obj_subtype obj_subtype:=obj_subtype(857, 'Thomas King', 'Assistant
Manager', 3500);
BEGIN
  dbms_output.put_line(obj_supertype.func_super_print(l_obj_subtype));
  dbms_output.put_line(obj_supertype.func_super_print((l_obj_subtype AS
obj_subtype)));
END;
/
```

Result:

```
The Employee details for the ID 857 is Name: Thomas King
The Employee details for the ID 857 is Name: Thomas King, Job ID: Assistant
Manager, Salary: 3500$
```

Restrictions in inheriting a Supertype:

1. When an object is created as Final, which is the default when not explicitly mentioned, means that no subtypes can be derived from it. NOT Final means that subtypes can be derived.

2. When a method is created as Final, means that subtypes cannot override it by providing their own implementation. NOT Final, which is the default if not explicitly mentioned, means that the supertype method can be overridden.

3. The attributes in the supertype cannot be overridden, meaning that the same name cannot be used for the attributes in the supertype and the subtype.

4. Only one MAP or one ORDER function may be implemented in a type hierarchy of supertypes and subtypes.

5. In a type hierarchy, if the supertype does not specify a MAP or an ORDER function, neither can its subtypes.

6. Only the MAP function can be overridden and not the ORDER function.

7. A static method and a member method in a subtype may not redefine a member method and a static method in the supertype respectively.

8. If an overridden method has default values for any of its parameters, then the overriding method must provide the same default values for the same parameters.

Subprograms using Object Types

The procedures and functions in PL/SQL can make use of the object types as IN, OUT and INOUT arguments for their parameters and RETURN values (in the case of functions).

In the below listing, an object type specification, OBJ_EMP is created with multiple attributes corresponding to an employee.

```
CREATE OR REPLACE type obj_emp
IS
  object
  (
    first_name    VARCHAR2(30),
    last_name     VARCHAR2(30),
    email         VARCHAR2(30),
    phone_number  VARCHAR2(30),
```

```
   job_id      VARCHAR2(30),
   hire_date   DATE);
 /
```

A function FUNC_OBJ is created with one input parameter for passing the employee ID and the object OBJ_EMP is made as the RETURN value's data type. The function body fetches the employee information for the input employee ID and assigns it to the object instance L_OBJ and The object instance is passed as the RETURN statement's argument as shown below.

> 🔔 Note: When the object gets its data through an INTO statement, the columns in the SELECT statement must be passed as input to the Constructor function (in this case OBJ_EMP) and the Constructor function's RETURN value is assigned to the object instance.

```
CREATE OR REPLACE FUNCTION func_obj(ip_emp_id NUMBER) RETURN obj_emp
  IS
    l_obj obj_emp;
  BEGIN
    SELECT obj_emp(first_name, last_name, email, phone_number, job_id,
hire_date) INTO l_obj
    FROM employees WHERE employee_id=ip_emp_id;
    RETURN l_obj;
  END;
  /
```

This function can be put to use by passing an available employee ID to its argument with a DOT operator followed by the object's attributes as shown below. Even when an unavailable employee ID is passed, the function does not fail with an NO_DATA_FOUND exception but assigns NULL value to the object.

```
SELECT
  func_obj(100).first_name first_name,
  func_obj(100).last_name last_name,
  func_obj(100).email email,
  func_obj(100).phone_number phone_number,
  func_obj(100).job_id job_id,
  func_obj(100).hire_date hire_date
FROM
  dual;
```

Result:

FIRST_NAME	LAST_NAME	EMAIL	PHONE_NUMBER	JOB_ID	HIRE_DATE
Steven	King	SKING	515.123.4567	AD_PRES	17-JUN-03

The above function can be made into a functional with clause from R12.1 onwards as shown below to return the same result set as above.

```
WITH
  FUNCTION func_obj(ip_emp_id NUMBER) RETURN obj_emp
IS
 l_obj obj_emp;
BEGIN
  SELECT
    obj_emp(first_name, last_name, email, phone_number, job_id, hire_date)
  INTO l_obj
  FROM
    employees
  WHERE
    employee_id=ip_emp_id;
  RETURN l_obj;
END;
SELECT
  func_obj(100).first_name first_name,
  func_obj(100).last_name last_name,
  func_obj(100).email email,
  func_obj(100).phone_number phone_number,
  func_obj(100).job_id job_id,
  func_obj(100).hire_date hire_date
FROM
  dual;
/
```

Object Type Enhancement in 12c

The ACCESSIBLE BY clause was introduced in R12.1, which can be added to packages, procedures, functions and types as an added security measure to restrict the database objects which are referencing them. The database objects which are allowed to access the secured PL/SQL units are called as a white list.

> 🔔 Note: The methods created in the object types do not support the ACCESSIBLE BY clause.

The prototype for managing the white list using the *Accessible by* clause is shown below,

```
ACCESSIBLE BY ([Object_type] <Object_name1>, [Object_type] <Object_name2>,
[Object_type] <Object_name3>, ...)
```

In the below listing, an object type TYPE_OBJ_WL is created with one attribute L_EMP_ID and a member function OBJ_FUNC_WL, which returns the name of the employee for the attribute's instance value. Here, the object type has the *accessible by* clause, which manages the white list containing the database objects list which is privileged to access this object type. The function FUNC_WL is added to the white list in the object type specification section.

```
CREATE OR REPLACE type type_obj_wl accessible BY (
FUNCTION func_wl)
IS
  object
  (
    l_emp_id VARCHAR2(50),
    member FUNCTION obj_func_wl
    RETURN VARCHAR2);
  /
CREATE OR REPLACE type body type_obj_wl
IS
  member FUNCTION obj_func_wl
  RETURN VARCHAR2
IS
  l_vc_name VARCHAR2(100);
BEGIN
  SELECT
    last_name
    ||', '
    ||first_name
  INTO
    l_vc_name
  FROM
    employees
  WHERE
    employee_id=self.l_emp_id;
  RETURN l_vc_name;
END;
END;
/
```

When this object is used in an anonymous block as shown below, the unit fails with a compilation error stating that the access to the object is prohibited.

```
DECLARE
  l_obj_wl type_obj_wl:=type_obj_wl(110);
BEGIN
  dbms_output.put_line(l_obj_wl.obj_func_wl);
END;
/
```

Error report –

```
ORA-06550: line 2, column 12:
PLS-00904: insufficient privilege to access object TYPE_OBJ_WL
```

In the below example, the function FUNC_WL (from the white list) is created and compiled, which uses the object type TYPE_OBJ_WL's member function and returns its result to the calling environment.

```
CREATE OR REPLACE FUNCTION func_wl(
    ip_emp_id NUMBER)
  RETURN VARCHAR2
IS
  l_obj_wl type_obj_wl:=type_obj_wl(ip_emp_id);
BEGIN
  RETURN l_obj_wl.obj_func_wl;
END;
/
```

The function can be called by executing it in a select statement with an appropriate employee ID as like below,

```
SELECT func_wl(110) FROM dual;
```

Result:

Chen, John

When the function with the same name as in the white list is locally declared in an anonymous block, the call to secure object still fails with the insufficient privilege error as shown below,

```
DECLARE
  l_vc_name VARCHAR2(50);
  FUNCTION func_wl(ip_emp_id NUMBER)
    RETURN VAR      CHAR2
  IS
    l_obj_wl type_obj_wl:=type_obj_wl(ip_emp_id);
  BEGIN
    RETURN l_obj_wl.obj_func_wl;
  END;
BEGIN
  SELECT func_wl(110) INTO l_vc_name FROM dual;
END;
/
```

Error report -

```
ORA-06550: line 6, column 14:
PLS-00904: insufficient privilege to access object TYPE_OBJ_WL
```

When the R12.1's *functional with* clause has the same name similar to the function from the white list, the select query still fails with the same error.

```
WITH
  FUNCTION func_wl(ip_emp_id NUMBER)
    RETURN VARCHAR2
  IS
    l_obj_wl type_obj_wl:=type_obj_wl(ip_emp_id);
  BEGIN
    RETURN l_obj_wl.obj_func_wl;
```

```
   END;
SELECT func_wl (110) FROM dual;
/
```

Error report -

```
ORA-06553: PLS-320: the declaration of the type of this expression is
incomplete or malformed
ORA-06552: PL/SQL: Item ignored
ORA-06553: PLS-904: insufficient privilege to access object TYPE_OBJ_WL
06553. 00000 -  "PLS-%s: %s"
*Cause:
*Action:
```

Thus, all our experiments show that only the database defined objects can be made secure and can be added to the white list.

Introduction to Record Types

The record types are composite data types, which are capable of storing the data composing of one row with one or more attributes similar to an object. The record type is a transient object, meaning that it cannot be created in the database, but can only be dynamically created in the declaration section and destroyed at the end of the PL/SQL unit instance's lifetime. As these cannot be permanently created in the database, they cannot be used as the data types for the database table columns, unlike the objects. There is no body section for the record types as in the object types, thus the benefits of methods cannot be enjoyed in this type.

The prototype for defining a user-defined record type is shown below,

```
Type <Type_name>
IS
  RECORD
  (
    <Attribute1> <Scalar_datatype | Composite_datatype> [NOT NULL :=
<Default_value>],
    <Attribute2> <Scalar_datatype | Composite_datatype> [NOT NULL :=
<Default_value>],
    ...);
```

The prototype for defining a record type based on a table's structure is shown below,

```
<Table_name>%rowtype;
```

The prototype for defining a record type based on a view's structure is shown below,

```
<View_name>%rowtype;
```

The prototype for defining a record type based on a cursor's structure is shown below,

```
<Cursor_name>%rowtype;
```

User Based Record Types

The user-defined record types allows us to create any number of attributes to the record type of our choice. The attributes optionally allow us to add an NOT NULL constraint on any attribute, but the default value has to be assigned in their declaration itself and not at the instance declaration as defined in the prototype.

In the below listing, a record type is created for holding information related to a car and is displayed using the PUT_LINE procedure as shown below,

```
DECLARE
type type_rec
IS
  record
  (
    car_id     NUMBER,
    car_make   VARCHAR2(100),
    car_model  VARCHAR2(100));
  l_rec_car_det1 type_rec;
  l_rec_car_det2 type_rec;
BEGIN
  l_rec_car_det1.car_id    :=1;
  l_rec_car_det1.car_make :='Audi';
  l_rec_car_det1.car_model:='R8';
  dbms_output.put_line('Record 1 values Car
ID=>'||l_rec_car_det1.car_id||
  ', Car make=>'||l_rec_car_det1.car_make||', Car model=>'||
  l_rec_car_det1.car_model);
  l_rec_car_det2             :=l_rec_car_det1;
  l_rec_car_det2.car_id    :=NULL;
  l_rec_car_det2.car_make :=NULL;
  l_rec_car_det2.car_model:=NULL;
  l_rec_car_det1            :=NULL;
END;
/
```

Result:

```
Record 1 values Car ID=>1, Car make=>Audi, Car model=>R8
```

Table Based Record Types

The anchor-based types enable us to create the record types under tables, views and cursors. The *%ROWTYPE* attribute allows us to create a record type of the underlying object without requiring us to manually enter all of their attributes explicitly.

In the below PL/SQL unit, a function FUNC_REC is dynamically created in the declaration section where its return type is a RECORD. The function returns the employee information for the input employee ID and that record is being used in the execution section of the block in the archival process as shown below,

```
DECLARE
   l_rt_emp employees%rowtype;
   FUNCTION func_rec(
      ip_emp_id NUMBER)
   RETURN employees%rowtype
   IS
   BEGIN
      SELECT
         *
      INTO
         l_rt_emp
      FROM
         employees
      WHERE
         employee_id=ip_emp_id;
      RETURN l_rt_emp;
   END;
BEGIN
   l_rt_emp:=func_rec(101);
   INSERT
   INTO
      employees_archive VALUES l_rt_emp;
   COMMIT;
END;
/
```

In the below example, a procedure PROC_REC is dynamically created in the declaration section having the record type of the employees table as its input parameter. This procedure then updates the employee's archival table with the input record type for a particular employee. The execution section of the block assigns an employee information into the employee record type instance and updates the last name to a user defined value. This manipulated record type is then passed as input to the dynamically created procedure to perform its process of updating the employee's archival data.

> 🔔 Note: When an update statement is executed using a record type in its SET clause, no other extra column will be allowed to update similar to the traditional update statements.

```
DECLARE
   l_rt_emp employees%rowtype;
PROCEDURE proc_rec(
   ip_rt_emp employees%rowtype)
```

```
  IS
  BEGIN
    UPDATE
      employees_archive
    SET
      row=ip_rt_emp
    WHERE
      employee_id=ip_rt_emp.employee_id;
    COMMIT;
  END;
  BEGIN
    SELECT
      *
    INTO
      l_rt_emp
    FROM
      employees
    WHERE
      employee_id       =101;
    l_rt_emp.last_name:='Williams';
    proc_rec(l_rt_emp);
  END;
  /
```

Record Type Enhancements in 12c

Prior to 12c, Oracle supported only SQL data types for binding the input and output type variables in the dynamic queries. On and after 12c, Oracle allows us to bind record type variables for IN and OUT type bind variables as shown below,

Here, the procedure PROC_REC is created which returns a record of the EMPLOYEES table type through its OUT parameter for the employee ID passed as its input.

```
CREATE OR REPLACE PROCEDURE proc_rec(
    ip_emp_id NUMBER,
    op_result OUT employees%rowtype)
IS
BEGIN
  SELECT * INTO op_result
  FROM
    employees
  WHERE
    employee_id=ip_emp_id;
END;
/
```

In the below anonymous block, the procedure PROC_REC is dynamically executed using the input and output bind variables L_N_EMP_ID and L_REC_EMP respectively. The result from the record set can be then accessed using the traditional DOT operator as shown below.

```
DECLARE
  l_n_emp_id NUMBER:=105;
  l_rec_emp employees%rowtype;
```

```
BEGIN
    EXECUTE immediate 'BEGIN proc_rec(:l_n_emp_id,:l_rec_emp); END;'
    USING IN l_n_emp_id, OUT l_rec_emp;
    DBMS_OUTPUT.PUT_LINE('Employee ID: ' || l_rec_emp.employee_id);
    DBMS_OUTPUT.PUT_LINE('First Name: ' || l_rec_emp.first_name);
    DBMS_OUTPUT.PUT_LINE('Last Name: ' || l_rec_emp.last_name);
    DBMS_OUTPUT.PUT_LINE('Email ID: ' || l_rec_emp.email);
    DBMS_OUTPUT.PUT_LINE('Phone Number: ' || l_rec_emp.phone_number);
    DBMS_OUTPUT.PUT_LINE('Hire Date: ' || l_rec_emp.hire_date);
    DBMS_OUTPUT.PUT_LINE('Job ID: ' || l_rec_emp.job_id);
    DBMS_OUTPUT.PUT_LINE('Salary: ' || l_rec_emp.salary);
    DBMS_OUTPUT.PUT_LINE('Commission : ' || l_rec_emp.commission_pct);
    DBMS_OUTPUT.PUT_LINE('Manager ID: ' || l_rec_emp.manager_id);
    DBMS_OUTPUT.PUT_LINE('Department ID ID: ' || l_rec_emp.department_id);
END;
/
```

Result:

```
Employee ID: 105
First Name: David
Last Name: Austin
Email ID: DAUSTIN
Phone Number: 590.423.4569
Hire Date: 25-JUN-05
Job ID: IT_PROG
Salary: 4800
Manager ID: 103
Department ID: 60
```

Introduction to Collection Types

The collections are homogeneous powerful single dimensional structures which are capable of managing large sets of ordered values belonging to the same type, where each element can be identified individually by their index value. The data processed by the collection are session specific and are stored in the user global area (UGA), which is stored in the SGA when using a shared server connection and in PGA when using a dedicated connection. There are three different collection types as Nested table, VARRAY and Associative array, which can be categorized based on multiple terminologies as described below.

Persistent and Transient

The collections are segregated into two types, Persistent, and Transient, based on their lifetime in the database. The persistent collection types can store their instances permanently in the database. Nested tables and VARRAYs fall under this category as these are capable of acting as the data types of columns in a database table. The non-persistent or transient collection types are not stored in the database permanently and have their lifetime limited to the duration of the PL/SQL unit. Associative arrays,

Nested tables, and VARRAYs fall under this category when they are declared dynamically in the declaration section of a PL/SQL unit, subprogram or a package.

Bounded and Unbounded

The collections are categorized into two types, Bounded, and Unbounded, based on the limit of the number of elements they can accommodate. The bounded collection types have a predefined limit on the number of elements to be accommodated. VARRAY is a bounded type, where its upper bound value has to be determined during their declaration. Nested table and Associative array fall under the unbounded category, where they do not have a limit on the number of elements they can accommodate them.

Numeric Index and String Index

The collection types are divided into two types, Numeric index type and String index type, based on the data type of the index value they use for their element storage. The numeric index based collection types allow us to define only integers as the index values of the elements. Nested table and VARRAY types follow numeric indexing, where they prohibit us in using any other type of index value for their list. The index value starts from 1 by default for these collection types. The string index type based collection types allow us to define characters as their element's index value. An associative array is a string index based collection type and it provides us with a flexibility of having either integer or string as its index type. This type also allows us to use negative integers for subscripts.

Sparse and Dense

The collections are split into two types, Sparse, and Dense, based on the element availability. The spare collections allow undefined or sequentialless elements, i.e., there can be gaps between the first and the last element in the collection. Nested table and Associative array are examples of the sparse collection, where they do not mind their elements getting deleted or removed from the sequence unless they are defined with an NOT NULL constraint. The dense collections must define all their elements with a value, at least Null unless it is defined with an NOT NULL constraint. They do not allow any gaps in their list and raise an error when we try to delete an element from their list. VARRAY is a dense collection type, and they do not allow us to make a gap in their element list.

The PL/SQL collection types do not support multidimensional structure with SQL data types. We can, however, build multidimensional collection structures using records, objects or other collection types as their element's data type.

Choosing a Collection Type

Choosing the right collection type for our application might be challenging as there could be multiple acceptable choices in a situation. The below section guarantees in providing a high insight of the advantages of one collection type over the other, which will help us in making up our mind to some extent.

When to choose an Associative array?

1. When we want to cache a small key-pair valued table in the memory for temporary lookup purpose.

2. When we need flexibility in our subscripts. This type allows string, negative integers, and non-sequential integers to be used as subscripts for the collection elements.

3. When we want to pass the collection to and from the database server using Oracle Call Interface (OCI) or the Oracle precompiler.

When to choose a Nested table?

1. When we want to store a large amount of persistent data in a table's column.

2. When we must not worry about the subscript going out of sequence due to updates and deletes performed over the collection elements.

3. When we do not know the maximum number of elements to be stored in a collection during its declaration.

When to choose a VARRAY?

1. When we want to store a small amount of persistent data in a table's column.

2. When we are more concerned about the number of elements stored in the collection.

3. When we want to preserve the order in which the elements are inserted into the collection.

Associative Arrays

The Associative arrays were the first ever collection type to be created in Oracle in its 7th version by the name, PL/SQL tables. Ironically, they have never been behaving anything like a traditional heap table back then. From the Oracle version 8, they were given a new name as Index-by tables, meaning that these are tables with index values. In this version, Oracle also introduced two new types, Nested table, and VARRAYs, grouping them all under a single section called as the Collections. With the release 9iR2, Oracle changed the name of the index by tables into associative arrays, as they were more like an array in structure and also allowed them to be indexed by either PLS_INTEGER, BINARY_INTEGER or VARCHAR2 data types. By allowing us to index by string, the associative arrays are far more flexible than the other two types with more real-time use in our applications.

These are sparsely populated, meaning that the index value does not have to be sequential, but needs to be unique. This type supports any integer to be its index value i.e., positive, negative, zero and even accepts mathematical expressions. As already discussed, the associative arrays are not capable of acting as data types for the table columns in the database, unlike the nested tables or VARRAYS. Thus, these can only be transient in nature.

Since 9i, there were not much of a change in the behavior of the associative arrays until 12c. The SQL support for the associative arrays is made available from the release R12.1 and higher by allowing the associative arrays to be accessed through the TABLE function and as bind variables during dynamic processing.

The prototype for defining an associative array is shown below,

```
TYPE <Type_name>
IS
  TABLE OF <Scalar_datatype | Composite_datatype> [NOT NULL] INDEX BY
  <PLS_INTEGER | BINARY_INTEGER | VARCHAR2(<Precision_value>) |
  STRING (<Precision_value>) | LONG>;
```

Precision_value: Between the range of 1 to 32,767.

The associative arrays do not require an initialization before element insertion as they do not own a constructor. Thus, there is no need for space allocation prior to assigning the values using the collection API *extend*.

In the below listing, an associative array is declared with VARCHAR2(50) as its element's data type and PLS_INTEGER as its index data type. The execution section of the block assigns the elements to some random index values and it is looped for the final display.

```
DECLARE
type type_aa
IS
  TABLE OF VARCHAR2(50) INDEX BY pls_integer;
  l_aa_var1 type_aa;
BEGIN
  l_aa_var1(-5):='APPEND';
  l_aa_var1(-3):='BIND';
  l_aa_var1(0) :='CONSTRUCT';
  l_aa_var1(3) :='DYNAMIC';
  l_aa_var1(5) :='EXTEND';
  FOR loop_aa IN l_aa_var1.first..l_aa_var1.last
  LOOP
    dbms_output.put_line(l_aa_var1(loop_aa));
  END LOOP loop_aa;
END;
/
```

Error report -

```
ORA-01403: no data found
ORA-06512: at line 14
01403. 00000 -  "no data found"
*Cause:    No data was found from the objects.
```

The FOR loop's index range is defined between L_AA_VAR1.FIRST, which is the least index value of the elements list [-5] and L_AA_VAR1.LAST, which is the greatest index value of the elements list [5]. Thus, the loop runs itself for the index values [-5], [-4], [-3], [-2], [-1], [0], [1], [2], [3], [4], [5]. As we have not assigned any elements for the indexes [-4], [-2], [-1], [1], [2], [4], the above block fails with the NO_DATA_FOUND error right at the index [-4] it.

To avoid this scenario, the collection API method *exists* is used in the FOR loop to avoid the exception and proceeds the elements for the next loop's index value as shown below,

```
DECLARE
type type_aa
IS
  TABLE OF VARCHAR2(50) INDEX BY pls_integer;
  l_aa_var1 type_aa;
BEGIN
  l_aa_var1(-5):='APPEND';
  l_aa_var1(-3):='BIND';
  l_aa_var1(0) :='CONSTRUCT';
  l_aa_var1(3) :='DYNAMIC';
  l_aa_var1(5) :='EXTEND';
  FOR loop_aa IN l_aa_var1.first..l_aa_var1.last
  LOOP
```

```
      IF l_aa_var1.exists(loop_aa) THEN
        dbms_output.put_line('Index value: '||loop_aa||'. Element value: '||
        l_aa_var1(loop_aa));
      END IF;
  END LOOP loop_aa;
END;
/
```

Result:

```
Index value: -5. Element value: APPEND
Index value: -3. Element value: BIND
Index value: 0. Element value: CONSTRUCT
Index value: 3. Element value: DYNAMIC
Index value: 5. Element value: EXTEND
```

In the below snippet, the index value is an arithmetic calculation, where its element can be accessed from a different arithmetic calculation providing that their resultant is equal. The different ways of fetching the element for the index [30] is shown in the below example.

```
DECLARE
type type_aa
IS
   TABLE OF VARCHAR2(50) INDEX BY pls_integer;
   l_aa_var1 type_aa;
BEGIN
   l_aa_var1(10+20):='ASSOCIATIVE ARRAY';
   dbms_output.put_line('The element value: '||l_aa_var1(10+20));
   dbms_output.put_line('The element value: '||l_aa_var1(20+10));
   dbms_output.put_line('The element value: '||l_aa_var1(30));
   dbms_output.put_line('The element value: '||l_aa_var1(50-20));
   dbms_output.put_line('The element value: '||l_aa_var1(60/2));
END;
/
```

Result:

```
The element value: ASSOCIATIVE ARRAY
The element value: ASSOCIATIVE ARRAY
The element value: ASSOCIATIVE ARRAY
The element value: ASSOCIATIVE ARRAY
The element value: ASSOCIATIVE ARRAY
```

In the below script, the associative array's element data type is declared as PLS_INTEGER and its index data type is defined as VARCHAR2(50). This array is used for saving the test scores of individual students from the STUDENTS table with their name as index value and their score value as the element. A cursor FOR loop is constructed with the STUDENTS table to display the scores of each student. The *exists* method is used here to take out the students, whose results are not available and handle them separately.

```
DECLARE
type type_aa
IS
  TABLE OF pls_integer INDEX BY VARCHAR2(50);
  l_aa_test_scores type_aa;
BEGIN
  l_aa_test_scores('Adam')     :=59;
  l_aa_test_scores('Samantha'):=70;
  l_aa_test_scores('Patrick') :=45;
  l_aa_test_scores('Manickam'):=75;
  l_aa_test_scores('Johnson') :=90;
  FOR loop_aa IN
  (
    SELECT
      stud_name
    FROM
      students
  )
  LOOP
    IF l_aa_test_scores.exists(loop_aa.stud_name) THEN
      dbms_output.put_line('Student name: '||loop_aa.stud_name||', Score:
'||l_aa_test_scores(loop_aa.stud_name));
    ELSE
      dbms_output.put_line('Student name: '||loop_aa.stud_name||
      ', Score: Not Available');
    END IF;
  END LOOP loop_aa;
END;
/
```

Result:

```
Student name: Adam, Score: 59
Student name: Felicia, Score: Not Available
Student name: Gerald, Score: Not Available
Student name: Johnson, Score: 75
Student name: Manickam, Score: 75
Student name: Nathen, Score: Not Available
Student name: Patrick, Score: 45
Student name: Samantha, Score: 70
```

Associative Array Enhancement in 12c

From the Oracle version 12c and above, the option for using the associative array in
the TABLE function and as a bind variable in the dynamic query has been enabled. The
below sections shows the detailed explanation of their enhancements.

Associative Array with the TABLE Function

Prior to 12c, Oracle allowed us to use the TABLE function only for the nested tables
and VARRAYs that are created in the database. From 12c and above, all the collection
types can enjoy the use of TABLE function even if they are locally declared with certain
limitations.

An associative array must be declared in a package separately and not in the same PL/SQL unit for it to use the TABLE function. In the below example, the package PKG_AA is created with an associative array having a record as its element's data type and PLS_INTEGER as its index's data type. This package also sports a function with the above said associative array as its return type. This function returns the employee ID and the name of the first 10 employees as shown below.

```
CREATE OR REPLACE PACKAGE pkg_aa
IS
type type_rec
IS
  record
  (
    Employee_id    NUMBER,
    Employee_name VARCHAR2(30));
type type_aa
IS
  TABLE OF type_rec INDEX BY pls_integer;
  FUNCTION func_aa RETURN type_aa;
END;
/
CREATE OR REPLACE PACKAGE body pkg_aa
IS
  FUNCTION func_aa
    RETURN type_aa
  IS
    l_aa_var1 pkg_aa.type_aa;
  BEGIN
    FOR loop_aa IN
    (
      SELECT rownum rn, employee_id, last_name||', '||first_name
employee_name
      FROM employees
      FETCH FIRST 10 rows only
    )
    LOOP
      l_aa_var1(loop_aa.rn).employee_id   :=loop_aa.employee_id;
      l_aa_var1(loop_aa.rn).employee_name:=loop_aa.employee_name;
    END LOOP loop_aa;
    RETURN l_aa_var1;
  END func_aa;
END pkg_aa;
/
```

The below anonymous block creates an instance of the associative array from the package PKG_AA and it is assigned to the function FUNC_AA's return value, which is then mimicked to a classic heap table using the TABLE function in an FOR loop for it to display the employee details as shown.

```
DECLARE
  l_aa_var1 pkg_aa.type_aa;
BEGIN
  l_aa_var1:=pkg_aa.func_aa;
  FOR loop_aa IN
  (
    SELECT
      *
    FROM
      TABLE(l_aa_var1)
  )
  LOOP
    dbms_output.put_line('Employee ID: '||loop_aa.employee_id||
    ', Employee Name: '||loop_aa.employee_name);
  END LOOP loop_aa;
END;
/
```

Result:

```
Employee ID: 100, Employee Name: King, Steven
Employee ID: 101, Employee Name: Williams, Neena
Employee ID: 102, Employee Name: De Haan, Lex
Employee ID: 103, Employee Name: Hunold, Alexander
Employee ID: 104, Employee Name: Ernst, Bruce
Employee ID: 105, Employee Name: Austin, David
Employee ID: 106, Employee Name: Pataballa, Valli
Employee ID: 107, Employee Name: Lorentz, Diana
Employee ID: 108, Employee Name: Greenberg, Nancy
Employee ID: 109, Employee Name: Faviet, Daniel
```

Associative Array as Bind Variable

Prior to 12c, Oracle prohibited associative arrays from acting as bind variables in the dynamic queries. From 12c and later releases, associative arrays can be used as bind variables of IN and OUT types.

For this scenario, the package PKG_AA is created with an associative array of type VARCHAR2(500) for the elements and PLS_INTEGER for its indexes. This package also has a procedure PROC_AA, which has the package declared the associative array as its OUT parameter. This procedure calculates the experience for a list of employees and assigns it to the OUT parameter as shown below,

```
CREATE OR REPLACE PACKAGE pkg_aa
IS
```

```
type type_aa
IS
  TABLE OF VARCHAR2(500) INDEX BY pls_integer;
  PROCEDURE proc_aa(op_aa_var1 OUT type_aa);
END;
/
CREATE OR REPLACE PACKAGE body pkg_aa
IS
  PROCEDURE proc_aa(op_aa_var1 OUT type_aa)
  IS
  BEGIN
    FOR loop_aa IN
    (
      SELECT
        rownum rn,
        last_name
        ||', '
        ||first_name employee_name,
        hire_date
      FROM
        employees
      FETCH
        FIRST 9 percent rows only
    )
    LOOP
      op_aa_var1(loop_aa.rn):='Total experience of '||loop_aa.employee_name
||' is '||REPLACE(ltrim(numtoyminterval(ROUND(sysdate-loop_aa.hire_date)/
      30,'Month'),'+0'),'-',' Years and ')||' Months';
    END LOOP loop_aa;
  END proc_aa;
END pkg_aa;
/
```

The below anonymous block depicts usage of the associative array as an OUT bound variable. The OUT parameter of the procedure *PKG_AA.PROC_AA* is bounded to the local variable L_AA_VAR1, which is then mimicked to a traditional heap table using the TABLE function and printed using the cursor FOR loop as shown below,

```
DECLARE
  l_aa_var1 pkg_aa.type_aa;
BEGIN
  EXECUTE immediate 'BEGIN pkg_aa.proc_aa(:l_aa_var1); END;' USING OUT
  l_aa_var1;
  FOR loop_aa IN
  (
    SELECT
      *
    FROM
      TABLE(l_aa_var1)
  )
  LOOP
    dbms_output.put_line(loop_aa.column_value);
  END LOOP loop_aa;
END;
/
```

Result:

```
Total experience of King, Steven is 13 Years and 02 Months
Total experience of Williams, Neena is 10 Years and 11 Months
Total experience of De Haan, Lex is 15 Years and 08 Months
Total experience of Hunold, Alexander is 10 Years and 07 Months
Total experience of Ernst, Bruce is 9 Years and 03 Months
Total experience of Austin, David is 11 Years and 02 Months
Total experience of Pataballa, Valli is 10 Years and 06 Months
Total experience of Lorentz, Diana is 9 Years and 06 Months
Total experience of Greenberg, Nancy is 14 Years and 00 Months
Total experience of Faviet, Daniel is 14 Years and 00 Months
```

Nested Table Type

The Nested table types are an extension to the associative arrays. The main advantages of the nested table types over the associative arrays are that the former can be used as data types for the database table columns and it can also be created permanently in the database for future use, unlike the latter as the associative array's lifespan is dependent on the lifespan of its underlying PL/SQL unit. Also like the associative arrays, the index value of the nested tables cannot be of string type, but only numeric which starts with 1 and not 0.

There is no upper bound limit to the nested table type, thus it can hold any number of elements to it. When a nested table type is created over a record type or an object type, it acts as a perfect replacement for the traditional heap tables.

The nested table can be created over a scalar data type like a number, varchar2, date or composite data types like records, objects and another nested table itself. When we try to create a type over the same type, we may face the mutually recursive type error as shown below,

```
CREATE OR REPLACE type type_ntt
IS
  TABLE OF type_ntt;
```

Error Report:

PLS-00318: type "TYPE_NTT" is malformed because it is a non-REF mutually recursive type

The prototype for declaring a nested table type temporarily in a PL/SQL unit is shown below,

```
TYPE <Type_name>
IS
  TABLE OF <Scalar_datatype | Composite_datatype>;
```

The prototype for creating a nested table type permanently in the database is shown below,

```
CREATE OR REPLACE TYPE <Type_name>
IS
  TABLE OF <Scalar_datatype | Composite_datatype>;
```

In the below code listing, the nested table type TYPE_NTT is declared locally in the block with VARCHAR2(50) as its element's data type. An instance variable is created for the nested table and it is initialized through the constructor function. To assign an element, the instance variable is first allocated with the necessary space by using the *extend* method. This method without any arguments allocates one element space and with a numeric argument, say *n*, allocates *n* element spaces.

If we forget to initialize the collection, the PL/SQL unit fails with an *ORA-06531: Reference to uninitialized collection* error and if the required space is not allocated before the element assignment, the PL/SQL unit fails with an *ORA-06533: Subscript beyond count* error.

```
DECLARE
type type_ntt
IS
  TABLE OF VARCHAR2(50);
  l_ntt_var1 type_ntt:=type_ntt();
BEGIN
  l_ntt_var1.extend;
  l_ntt_var1(1):='Advanced ';
  l_ntt_var1.extend(5);
  l_ntt_var1(2):='PL/SQL';
  l_ntt_var1(3):=' - ';
  l_ntt_var1(4):='The ';
  l_ntt_var1(5):='Definitive ';
  l_ntt_var1(6):='Reference';
  FOR loop_ntt IN 1..l_ntt_var1.count
  LOOP
    dbms_output.put(l_ntt_var1(loop_ntt));
  END LOOP loop_ntt;
  DBMS_OUTPUT.NEW_LINE;
END;
/
```

Result:
```
Advanced PL/SQL - The Definitive Reference
```

In the next scenario, an object type OBJ_EMP is created by employee ID, name and salary as below.

```
CREATE OR REPLACE type obj_emp
IS
  object
  (
```

```
      employee_id   NUMBER,
      employee_name VARCHAR2(100),
      salary        NUMBER);
  /
```

Then, the nested table TYPE_NTT is declared with the above object as its element type and the information of the first 5 employees is assigned to the nested table type's instance using the BULK COLLECT clause. Note that the object constructor function must be used for the columns in the select clause for the underlying element type is an object type. The elements of the nested table are then printed using an FOR loop as shown in the below code.

Comparing the below block with our previous example, we have not performed the initialization and the space allocation for the elements as these tasks are taken care by the BULK COLLECT clause by itself. During a bulk collect fetch, Oracle says the SQL engine to collect multiple records at a single stretch and load them into a collection, thus avoiding multiple contexts-switching between the SQL and the PL/SQL engines unnecessarily, which results in better performance.

```
DECLARE
type type_ntt
IS
  TABLE OF obj_emp;
  l_ntt_var1 type_ntt;
BEGIN
  SELECT
    obj_emp(employee_id,last_name
    ||', '
    ||first_name,salary) bulk collect
  INTO
    l_ntt_var1
  FROM
    employees
  FETCH
    FIRST 5 rows only;
  FOR loop_ntt IN l_ntt_var1.first..l_ntt_var1.last
  LOOP
    dbms_output.put_line('Emp ID: '||l_ntt_var1(loop_ntt).employee_id||
    ', Emp Name: '||l_ntt_var1(loop_ntt).employee_name||', Emp Salary: '||
    l_ntt_var1(loop_ntt).salary);
  END LOOP loop_ntt;
END;
/
```

Result:

```
Emp ID: 100, Emp Name: King, Steven, Emp Salary: 24000
Emp ID: 101, Emp Name: Williams, Neena, Emp Salary: 17000
Emp ID: 102, Emp Name: De Haan, Lex, Emp Salary: 17000
Emp ID: 103, Emp Name: Hunold, Alexander, Emp Salary: 9000
Emp ID: 104, Emp Name: Ernst, Bruce, Emp Salary: 6000
```

In the below example, the nested type TYPE_NTT is declared with its element type as Number and gets itself assigned with a list of employee IDs and prints them. Then, the element of the index [2] is deleted from the nested type using the *delete* method with the index value as its argument. After the element deletion, the remaining employee IDs from the type undergoes the salary increment process of 10% using the FORALL clause.

In a traditional FOR loop, the loop process is handled by the PL/SQL engine and the DML operations inside the loop is processed by the SQL engine, thus there is a heavy context switching between the two engines when the loop is holding a hand full of records for the operation. The FORALL clause is used for bulk binding a DML statement to make its execution faster than the traditional FOR loop by avoiding the context switching and its consequences.

Either FOR loop or FORALL clause, the counting starts from the lower bound value to the upper bound value and when an intermediate index value is not present, the PL/SQL unit fails with an NO_DATA_FOUND error as shown in the below snippet.

```
DECLARE
type type_ntt
IS
   TABLE OF NUMBER;
   l_ntt_var1 type_ntt;
BEGIN
   SELECT
      employee_id bulk collect
   INTO
      l_ntt_var1
   FROM
      employees
   FETCH
      FIRST 5 rows only;
   FOR loop_ntt IN l_ntt_var1.first..l_ntt_var1.last
   LOOP
      dbms_output.put_line('Element Index: '||loop_ntt||', Emp ID:
'||l_ntt_var1(
      loop_ntt));
   END LOOP loop_ntt;
   l_ntt_var1.delete(2);
   FORALL loop_ntt IN l_ntt_var1.first..l_ntt_var1.last
   UPDATE
      employees
   SET
      salary=salary+(salary*(10/100))
   WHERE
      employee_id=l_ntt_var1(loop_ntt);
END;
/
```

Partial Result:

```
Element Index: 1, Emp ID: 100
Element Index: 2, Emp ID: 101
Element Index: 3, Emp ID: 102
Element Index: 4, Emp ID: 103
Element Index: 5, Emp ID: 104
```

Error report -

```
ORA-22160: element at index [2] does not exist
ORA-06512: at line 16
22160. 00000 -  "element at index [%s] does not exist"
*Cause:    Collection element at the given index does not exist.
*Action:   Specify the index of an element which exists.
```

Thus, to avoid this scenario, Oracle has introduced the *in indices of* clause, which can be used only in a FORALL statement. This clause only works on the available indexes from the type and doesn't do a blind count like the traditional lower bound to upper bound counting.

The below block avoids the NO_DATA_FOUND exception by using the *in indices of* clause and prints out the number of rows affected by the update statement.

```
1.   DECLARE
2.   type type_ntt
3.   IS
4.     TABLE OF NUMBER;
5.     l_ntt_var1 type_ntt;
6.   BEGIN
7.     SELECT
8.       employee_id bulk collect
9.     INTO
10.      l_ntt_var1
11.    FROM
12.      employees
13.    FETCH
14.      FIRST 5 rows only;
15.    FOR loop_ntt IN l_ntt_var1.first..l_ntt_var1.last
16.    LOOP
17.      dbms_output.put_line('Element Index: '||loop_ntt||', Emp ID:
       '||l_ntt_var1(
18.        loop_ntt));
19.    END LOOP loop_ntt;
20.    l_ntt_var1.delete(2);
21.    dbms_output.put_line('Element index [2] has been deleted');
22.    FORALL loop_ntt IN indices OF l_ntt_var1
23.    UPDATE
24.      employees
25.    SET
26.      salary=salary+(salary*(10/100))
27.    WHERE
28.      employee_id=l_ntt_var1(loop_ntt);
29.    dbms_output.put_line('The total rows updated is
       '||sql%rowcount);
30. END;
31. /
```

Result:

```
Element Index: 1, Emp ID: 100
Element Index: 2, Emp ID: 101
Element Index: 3, Emp ID: 102
Element Index: 4, Emp ID: 103
Element Index: 5, Emp ID: 104
Element index [2] has been deleted
The total rows updated is 4
```

The *in indices of* syntax also allows us to provide a range of index values to be processed by an additional *between* clause as shown below,

```
22. FORALL loop_ntt IN indices OF l_ntt_var1 between 1 and 3
```

The *between* clause limits the index values, that are to be processed by the DML statement inside the FORALL clause. Thus, after replacing the FORALL clause in our example with the above-modified statement, the indexes [1] and [3] will only be processed by the FORALL clause as the index [2] has already been deleted in the line number 20. Thus, the result produced by the above block after the inclusion of the *between* clause is shown below,

Result:

```
Element Index: 1, Emp ID: 100
Element Index: 2, Emp ID: 101
Element Index: 3, Emp ID: 102
Element Index: 4, Emp ID: 103
Element Index: 5, Emp ID: 104
Element index [2] has been deleted
The total rows updated is 2
```

In the below example, the nested table type TYPE_NTT has been created and not declared like our previous scenarios. This nested table is created with the object type OBJ_NTT as its element's data type, which has the employee ID and the salary attributes.

```
CREATE OR REPLACE type obj_ntt
IS
   object
   (
     employee_id NUMBER,
     salary      NUMBER);
   /
CREATE OR REPLACE type type_ntt
IS
   TABLE OF obj_ntt;
   /
```

In the below anonymous block, an instance of the nested table type TYPE_NTT is created, which then takes the employee IDs and the incremented salary for the employees who has joined prior to the year 2002. The employees' salary before the increment is printed using the cursor FOR loop. In this cursor FOR loop, the type instance L_NTT_VAR1 mimics the traditional heap table with the help of the TABLE function.

> 🔔 Note: Prior to the release of 12c, the TABLE function works only on the nested table type and VARRAY type, that are created in the database and not declared.

The incremented salary from the nested table type is then merged into the original EMPLOYEES table while acting as a heap table and then the incremented salary of the employees is displayed as shown in the below example.

```
DECLARE
  l_ntt_var1 type_ntt;
BEGIN
  SELECT
    obj_ntt(employee_id,salary+(salary*(20/100))) bulk collect
  INTO
    l_ntt_var1
  FROM
    employees
  WHERE
    hire_date<'01-Jan-2002';
  FOR loop_ntt IN
  (
    SELECT
      e1.employee_id,
      e2.salary
    FROM
      TABLE(l_ntt_var1)e1,
      employees e2
    WHERE
      e1.employee_id=e2.employee_id
  )
  LOOP
    dbms_output.put_line('Salary of the employee ID
'||loop_ntt.employee_id||
    ' before the increment is '||loop_ntt.salary);
  END LOOP loop_ntt;
  MERGE INTO employees e1 USING TABLE(l_ntt_var1)e2 ON
  (
    e1.employee_id=e2.employee_id
  )
WHEN matched THEN
  UPDATE
  SET
```

```
    e1.salary=e2.salary;
  FOR loop_ntt IN
  (
    SELECT
      e1.employee_id,
      e2.salary
    FROM
      TABLE(l_ntt_var1)e1,
      employees e2
    WHERE
      e1.employee_id=e2.employee_id
  )
  LOOP
    dbms_output.put_line('Salary of the employee ID
'||loop_ntt.employee_id||
    ' after the increment is '||loop_ntt.salary);
  END LOOP loop_ntt;
END;
/
```

Result:

```
Salary of the employee ID 102 before the increment is 35841.17
Salary of the employee ID 102 after the increment is 43009.4
```

Nested Table Type Enhancement in 12c

From Oracle version 12c, the nested table types are enhanced to support the TABLE function even though if they are declared as transient objects. Yet they have a restriction that they have to be declared in a package specification and not in a subprogram or an anonymous block to use the TABLE function.

In the below code listing, the package PKG_NTT is created with a procedure and a nested table type with a record of two attributes as its element type. The procedure creates an instance for the nested table type and assigns up to five index values for the attributes. The instance variable is then processed in a cursor FOR loop with the help of the TABLE function mimicking the traditional heap table and then prints the attributes of the nested table type by using the PUT_LINE procedure as shown below.

```
CREATE OR REPLACE PACKAGE pkg_ntt
IS
type type_rec
IS
  record
  (
    movie_id   NUMBER,
    movie_name VARCHAR2(30));
type type_ntt
IS
  TABLE OF type_rec;
  procedure proc_ntt;
```

```
END;
/
CREATE OR REPLACE PACKAGE body pkg_ntt
IS
  PROCEDURE proc_ntt
  IS
    l_ntt_var1 type_ntt:=type_ntt();
  BEGIN
    l_ntt_var1.extend(5);
    l_ntt_var1(1).movie_id   :=1001;
    l_ntt_var1(1).movie_name:='Fight Club';
    l_ntt_var1(2).movie_id   :=1002;
    l_ntt_var1(2).movie_name:='The Prestige';
    l_ntt_var1(3).movie_id   :=1003;
    l_ntt_var1(3).movie_name:='The Butterfly Effect';
    l_ntt_var1(4).movie_id   :=1004;
    l_ntt_var1(4).movie_name:='Life is Beautiful';
    l_ntt_var1(5).movie_id   :=1005;
    l_ntt_var1(5).movie_name:='Swordfish';
    FOR loop_ntt IN
    (SELECT * FROM TABLE(l_ntt_var1))
    LOOP
      dbms_output.put_line('Movie ID: '||loop_ntt.movie_id||', Movie Name:
'||loop_ntt.movie_name);
    END LOOP loop_ntt;
  END proc_ntt;
END pkg_ntt;
/
```

The procedure PROC_NTT is then executed using the below statement to print out the movie ID and name.

```
Exec pkg_ntt.proc_ntt;
```

Result:

```
Movie ID: 1001, Movie Name: Fight Club
Movie ID: 1002, Movie Name: The Prestige
Movie ID: 1003, Movie Name: The Butterfly Effect
Movie ID: 1004, Movie Name: Life is Beautiful
Movie ID: 1005, Movie Name: Swordfish
```

VARRAY Type

The keyword VARRAY is expanded as VARYING ARRAY, which also acts as a replacement keyword for it in the type structure creation. This type was introduced in Oracle 8 for storing a fixed-size sequential collection of elements of the same type. The VARRAY type is densely populated, meaning that it cannot have any gaps between its elements unlike the associative array or the nested table type. It is also bounded, meaning that there is a predefined upper limit on the number of elements stored in this type. The upper bound value once defined during the type definition cannot be modified throughout its lifespan.

This type is similar to the arrays in the other programming languages like C and Java, but the index value in Oracle starts with 1 for this type and not 0, unlike the other languages. When we try to assign an element to the 0th index value, we can expect to get the *ORA-06532: Subscript outside of limit* exception.

The VARRAYs are mainly used in an environment where the number of elements to be stored/processed are already known and its size is very stable. Similar to the nested table types, the VARRAYs can also be created over a scalar data type like a number, varchar2, date or composite data types like records, objects, and another nested table or VARRAY type.

The prototype for declaring a VARRAY type transiently in a PL/SQL unit is shown below,

```
TYPE <Type_name>
IS
   [VARRAY | VARYING ARRAY] (<Bound_limit>) OF <Scalar_datatype |
Composite_datatype>;
```

The prototype for creating a VARRAY type persistently in the database is shown below,

```
CREATE OR REPLACE TYPE <Type_name>
IS
   [VARRAY | VARYING ARRAY] (<Bound_limit>) OF <Scalar_datatype |
Composite_datatype>;
```

In the below example, a VARRAY type is declared with its upper bound as 5 but when we try to allocate space for 6 elements using the *extend* method, we get an *ORA-06532: Subscript outside of limit* exception as shown below,

```
DECLARE
type type_varray IS varray(5) OF NUMBER;
l_vt_var1 type_varray:=type_varray();
BEGIN
   l_vt_var1.extend(6);
END;
/
```

Error report -

```
ORA-06532: Subscript outside of limit
ORA-06512: at line 5
06532. 00000 -  "Subscript outside of limit"
*Cause:    A subscript was greater than the limit of a varray
           or non-positive for a varray or nested table.
*Action:   Check the program logic and increase the varray limit
           if necessary.
```

In the above error report, the action tag suggests us not to allocate more than the upper limit or to increase the upper bound limit of the VARRAY to resolve this issue.

The below block describes the basic functioning of the VARRAY type having an upper bound limit of 5 with a record type of two attributes as its element type. The first 5 employee IDs and names are bulk fetched into the VARRAY's instance and are looped successfully for the display.

```
DECLARE
type type_rec
IS
  record
  (
    employee_id   NUMBER,
    employee_name VARCHAR2(100));
type type_varray IS varray(5) OF type_rec;
l_vt_var1 type_varray;
BEGIN
  SELECT
    employee_id,
    last_name
    ||', '
    ||first_name AS employee_name bulk collect
  INTO
    l_vt_var1
  FROM
    employees
  FETCH
    FIRST 5 rows only;
  FOR loop_vt IN l_vt_var1.first..l_vt_var1.last
  LOOP
    dbms_output.put_line(l_vt_var1(loop_vt).employee_id||': '||l_vt_var1(
    loop_vt).employee_name);
  END LOOP loop_vt;
END;
/
```

Result:

```
100: King, Steven
101: Williams, Neena
102: De Haan, Lex
103: Hunold, Alexander
104: Ernst, Bruce
```

In the below listing, a VARRAY type with 3 as its upper bound of VARCHAR2(1) as its element type is declared and assigned with A, B, C as its index values respectively. When the *delete* method is used for deleting the first element of the VARRAY type, the unit fails with a *PLS-00306: wrong number or types of arguments in call to 'DELETE'* exception.

```
DECLARE
type type_varray IS varray(3) OF VARCHAR2(1);
l_vt_var1 type_varray:=type_varray();
BEGIN
```

```
   l_vt_var1.extend(3);
   l_vt_var1(1):='A';
   l_vt_var1(2):='B';
   l_vt_var1(3):='C';
   l_vt_var1.delete(1);
END;
/
```

Error report –

```
ORA-06550: line 9, column 3:
PLS-00306: wrong number or types of arguments in call to 'DELETE'
ORA-06550: line 9, column 3:
PL/SQL: Statement ignored
```

When the same block is executed again, but this time with no parameters for the *delete* method, the unit is successfully completed. The *delete* method without any parameters deletes all the available elements in a VARRAY type. Thus, VARRAY type allows us to delete all the elements at once, but not individually.

```
DECLARE
type type_varray IS varray(3) OF VARCHAR2(1);
l_vt_var1 type_varray:=type_varray();
BEGIN
   l_vt_var1.extend(3);
   l_vt_var1(1):='A';
   l_vt_var1(2):='B';
   l_vt_var1(3):='C';
   l_vt_var1.delete;
END;
/
```

```
PL/SQL procedure successfully completed.
```

Similar to the *in indices of* clause, we have the *in values of* clause, which allows the values of one collection type to be used as the index pointers of another collection type. In the below example, nested table type of PLS_INTEGER datatype is declared and a VARRAY type of VARCHAR2 data type with an upper bound of 10 is declared.

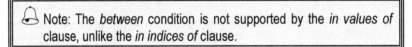

> 🔔 Note: The *between* condition is not supported by the *in values of* clause, unlike the *in indices of* clause.

The nested table type holds the below three element values,

Index Value	Element Value
1	5
2	6
3	7

The VARRAY type holds the below 10 element values,

Index Value	Element Value
1	A
2	B
3	C
4	D
5	E
6	F
7	G
8	H
9	I
10	J

In our below snippet, the nested table type is used in the *in values of* clause. Thus, the element values of the nested table type 5, 6, and 7 acts as the index values of the VARRAY type and processes the alphabets E, F, and G in the DML statement.

```
DECLARE
type type_ntt
IS
   TABLE OF pls_integer;
type type_vt IS varray(10) OF VARCHAR2(1);
l_ntt_var1 type_ntt:=type_ntt();
l_vt_var2 type_vt   :=type_vt();
BEGIN
   l_ntt_var1.extend(3);
   l_ntt_var1(1):=5;
   l_ntt_var1(2):=6;
   l_ntt_var1(3):=7;
   l_vt_var2.extend(10);
   l_vt_var2(1)  :='A';
   l_vt_var2(2)  :='B';
   l_vt_var2(3)  :='C';
   l_vt_var2(4)  :='D';
   l_vt_var2(5)  :='E';
   l_vt_var2(6)  :='F';
   l_vt_var2(7)  :='G';
   l_vt_var2(8)  :='H';
   l_vt_var2(9)  :='I';
   l_vt_var2(10):='J';
   FORALL loop_value IN VALUES OF l_ntt_var1
   INSERT INTO tbl_varray VALUES (l_vt_var2(loop_value));
END;
/
```

When we query the table TBL_VARRAY, it produces the below results.

Result:

```
E
F
G
```

In the below scripting, a VARRAY type is created over an object type having two attributes and has an upper bound value of 6.

```
CREATE OR REPLACE type type_obj
IS
  object
  (
    l_obj_var1 CHAR,
    l_obj_var2 VARCHAR2(50));
  /
CREATE OR REPLACE type type_vt IS varray(6) OF type_obj;
/
```

The below anonymous block creates an instance of the persistent VARRAY type TYPE_VT and is assigned with six element values. The VARRAY is then transformed into a virtual heap table with the help of the TABLE function. The VARRAY type elements are then displayed using a cursor FOR loop where the VARRAY type is mimicked as a traditional heap table with the help of the TABLE function as shown below,

```
DECLARE
  l_vt_var1 type_vt;
BEGIN
  l_vt_var1:=type_vt(type_obj('A', 'Attributes'),
                     type_obj('B', 'Bind Variables'),
                     type_obj('C', 'Context Switching'),
                     type_obj('D', 'Data Type'),
                     type_obj('E', 'Execute Immediate'),
                     type_obj('F', 'Forward Declaration'));
  FOR loop_vt IN
  (
    SELECT
      *
    FROM
      TABLE(l_vt_var1)
  )
  LOOP
    dbms_output.put_line(loop_vt.l_obj_var1||' for '||loop_vt.l_obj_var2);
  END LOOP loop_vt;
END;
/
```

Result:

```
A for Attributes
```

```
B for Bind Variables
C for Context Switching
D for Data Type
E for Execute Immediate
F for Forward Declaration
```

We normally use the implicit cursor attribute SQL%ROWCOUNT to find the number of rows affected during the previous DML operation. But, when dealing with a bulk operation, this attribute may not be of much help as we need the number of rows affected for each index value. The SQL%BULK_ROWCOUNT attribute serves this process by providing granular information about the number of rows affected during each iteration of the FORALL DML operation.

A VARRAY type with its upper bound as 6 is created over an object type with two attributes pertaining to the employee's identifier, and salary is created in the below snippet as shown below.

```
CREATE OR REPLACE type type_obj
IS
  object
  (
    employee_id NUMBER,
    salary      NUMBER);
  /
CREATE OR REPLACE type type_vt IS varray(6) OF type_obj;
/
```

In the below block of code, an instance of the above-created VARRAY type is created and is assigned with 6 employees ID and salary information. This list is then taken for a 10% increment using the FORALL statement, provided that the ID and the salary match for an employee. After the increment is performed, the SQL%ROWCOUNT attribute is then looped for the VARRAY type's index values to show the number of rows updated for the index values individually.

```
DECLARE
  l_vt_var1 type_vt:=type_vt();
BEGIN
  l_vt_var1.extend(6);
  l_vt_var1(1):=type_obj(101,20400);
  l_vt_var1(2):=type_obj(105,5760);
  l_vt_var1(3):=type_obj(109,10900);
  l_vt_var1(4):=type_obj(110,9840);
  l_vt_var1(5):=type_obj(112,8500);
  l_vt_var1(6):=type_obj(113,8280);
  FORALL loop_vt IN indices OF l_vt_var1
  UPDATE
    employees
  SET
    salary=l_vt_var1(loop_vt).salary+(l_vt_var1(loop_vt).salary*10)/100
  WHERE
    employee_id=l_vt_var1(loop_vt).employee_id
```

Introduction to Collection Types

```
   AND salary   =l_vt_var1(loop_vt).salary;
   FOR loop_vt IN l_vt_var1.first..l_vt_var1.last
   LOOP
      dbms_output.put_line('Index ['||loop_vt||'] has updated '||
      sql%bulk_rowcount(loop_vt)||' row(s).');
   END LOOP loop_vt;
END;
/
```

Result:

```
Index [1] has updated 1 row(s)
Index [2] has updated 1 row(s)
Index [3] has updated 0 row(s)
Index [4] has updated 1 row(s)
Index [5] has updated 0 row(s)
Index [6] has updated 1 row(s)
```

VARRAY Type Enhancement in 12c

The restriction of using the TABLE function only on the persistent VARRAY types has been revoked from and after the Oracle version 12c. The TABLE function can be used on the transient VARRAY types with a restriction of having them declared in the package specification and not elsewhere.

In the below code snippet, the package PKG_VT is created with a VARRAY type of a record data type with two attributes. The upper bound value of the VARRAY type is defined as 6. The package also sports a procedure PROC_VT for explaining the TABLE function used over the transient VARRAY type. The procedure creates an instance of the VARRAY type and allocates the spaces for the 6 elements. The instance variable is then assigned with some random car related element values. The TABLE function works perfectly on this transient VARRAY type and gives it a traditional heap table look inside the cursor FOR loop and prints the stored element values as shown in the below code.

```
CREATE OR REPLACE PACKAGE pkg_vt
IS
type type_rec
IS
  record
  (
    car_brand VARCHAR2(50),
    car_model VARCHAR2(50));
type type_vt IS varray(6) OF type_rec;
PROCEDURE proc_vt;
END;
/
CREATE OR REPLACE PACKAGE body pkg_vt
IS
  PROCEDURE proc_vt
  IS
```

```
    l_vt_var1 type_vt:=type_vt();
  BEGIN
  l_vt_var1.extend(6);
    l_vt_var1(1).car_brand:='Aston Martin';
    l_vt_var1(1).car_model:='One-77';
    l_vt_var1(2).car_brand:='Audi';
    l_vt_var1(2).car_model:='R8';
    l_vt_var1(3).car_brand:='Bugatti';
    l_vt_var1(3).car_model:='Veyron';
    l_vt_var1(4).car_brand:='Chevrolet';
    l_vt_var1(4).car_model:='Camaro';
    l_vt_var1(5).car_brand:='Jaguar';
    l_vt_var1(5).car_model:='XJ220';
    l_vt_var1(6).car_brand:='Tesla';
    l_vt_var1(6).car_model:='Model X';
    for loop_vt in (select * from table(l_vt_var1))loop
    dbms_output.put_line('Car Brand: '||loop_vt.car_brand||', Car Model:
'||loop_vt.car_model);
    end loop loop_vt;
  END;
END;
/
```

The procedure PROC_VT is then executed using the below statement, printing out the stored element values.

```
EXEC pkg_vt.proc_vt;
```

Result:

```
Car Brand: Aston Martin, Car Model: One-77
Car Brand: Audi, Car Model: R8
Car Brand: Bugatti, Car Model: Veyron
Car Brand: Chevrolet, Car Model: Camaro
Car Brand: Jaguar, Car Model: XJ220
Car Brand: Tesla, Car Model: Model X
```

Exceptions in Collections

The bulk binding feature was introduced in Oracle version 8i as the FORALL statement, which is used for the batch processing of large DML statements without the need of switching between the SQL and the PL/SQL engine for every single row. Even though the performance was increased using this feature, there is also a downside to it. When a single row from the DML operation fails, the FORALL statement fails entirely. To address this issue, Oracle has introduced the SAVE EXCEPTIONS clause. This clause instructs the system to skip the error prone rows and to process the rest perfectly fine rows rather failing the entire statement.

When the SAVE EXCEPTIONS clause is added to the FORALL statement, all the errors spotted during the batch processing are saved in the cursor

---

SQL%BULK_EXCEPTIONS, which stores a collection of records with two attributes as shown below.

- **ERROR_INDEX**: The index value of the collection element which failed during the DML operation is stored in this attribute.

- **ERROR_CODE**: The appropriate error code for the exception raised corresponding to the error index is stored in this attribute.

The exceptions raised during a FORALL DML operation can be captured by using the Oracle error code ORA-24381, when the SAVE EXCEPTIONS clause is used. During this time, the rest of the program code will not be continued and the control directly gets into the exception section once after the FORALL clause completes its operation successfully.

To portray the exceptions in bulk binding, an object type TYPE_OBJ is created with 6 attributes pertaining to an employee's information is created as shown below,

```
CREATE OR REPLACE type type_obj
IS
  object
  (
    emp_id          VARCHAR2(50),
    emp_first_name  VARCHAR2(50),
    emp_last_name   VARCHAR2(50),
    emp_email       VARCHAR2(50),
    emp_hire_date   VARCHAR2(50),
    emp_job_id      VARCHAR2(50));
  /
```

The below code depicts the complete functionality of the SAVE EXCEPTIONS clause in a FORALL statement. The code begins by assigning a name to the error code ORA-24381, which is the Oracle assigned error code for the bulk binding exceptions. The nested table type TYPE_NTT is created over the object type to store more than one employee information in a collective way. An instance of the nested table type is then created and assigned with 7 employees information. Here, the employee details for the index value [3] has a Null job ID, [5] has an invalid hire date and [6] has a Null last name, which all results into exceptions when they are inserted into the EMPLOYEES table having these validations.

When the employee information stored in the nested table is bulk inserted into the EMPLOYEES table with the SAVE EXCEPTIONS clause, the DML operation successfully completes where the error-prone data are formally collected into the system defined collection type BULK_EXCEPTIONS as shown in the below example.

The failed records can then be collected for analysis from the exception block by iterating the error prone records using the BULK_EXCEPTIONS.COUNT attribute. The index value and the error code of the failed records can be retrieved through the BULK_EXCEPTIONS.ERROR_INDEX and BULK_EXCEPTIONS.ERROR_CODE attributes as mentioned earlier. The corresponding error message for the error code can be retrieved by negating the error code and passing it to the SQLERRM function as its only formal parameter.

```
DECLARE
  bulk_error EXCEPTION;
  pragma exception_init(bulk_error, -24381);
type type_ntt
IS
  TABLE OF type_obj;
  l_ntt_var1 type_ntt:=type_ntt();
BEGIN
  l_ntt_var1.extend(7);
  l_ntt_var1(1):= type_obj('207', 'Marie', 'John', 'MJOHN1', '10-April-
2005', 'AD_PRES');
  l_ntt_var1(2):= type_obj('208', 'Abdul', 'Kalam', 'AKALAM2',
  '05-September-1995', 'IT_PROG');
  l_ntt_var1(3):= type_obj('209A', 'Rahul', 'Dravid', 'RDRAVID6',
  '02-August-2001', '');
  l_ntt_var1(4):= type_obj('210', 'Mike', 'Thompson', 'MTHOMS3',
  '29-December-1999', 'AD_VP');
  l_ntt_var1(5):= type_obj('211', 'Paul', 'Livingston', 'PLVNGS8',
  '22B-June-2008', 'FI_MGR');
  l_ntt_var1(6):= type_obj('212', 'King', '', 'KRAM8', '10-October-2005',
  'PU_CLERK');
  l_ntt_var1(7):= type_obj('213', 'Daniel', 'Morrison', 'DMORR4',
  '07-February-2011', 'SA_REP');
  FORALL loop_ntt IN indices OF l_ntt_var1 SAVE exceptions
  INSERT
  INTO
    employees
    (
      employee_id,
      first_name,
      last_name,
      email,
      hire_date,
      job_id
    )
    VALUES
    (
      l_ntt_var1(loop_ntt).emp_id,
      l_ntt_var1(loop_ntt).emp_first_name,
      l_ntt_var1(loop_ntt).emp_last_name,
      l_ntt_var1(loop_ntt).emp_email,
      l_ntt_var1(loop_ntt).emp_hire_date,
      l_ntt_var1(loop_ntt).emp_job_id
    );
  dbms_output.put_line('This message is printed only if there is no
exception raised in the FORALL statement!');
EXCEPTION
WHEN bulk_error THEN
```

```
   dbms_output.put_line('Total number of inserted rows: '||sql%rowcount);
   dbms_output.put_line('Total number of rejected rows: '||
   sql%bulk_exceptions.count);
   FOR loop_error IN 1..sql%bulk_exceptions.count
   LOOP
      dbms_output.put_line
      ('Error Index: '||sql%bulk_exceptions(loop_error).error_index||
       '. Error Code: '||sql%bulk_exceptions(loop_error).error_code||
       '. Error Message: '||sqlerrm(-
   sql%bulk_exceptions(loop_error).error_code));
   END LOOP loop_error;
END;
/
```

Result:

```
Total number of inserted rows: 4
Total number of rejected rows: 3
Error Index: 3. Error Code: 1722. Error Message: ORA-01722: invalid number
Error Index: 5. Error Code: 1861. Error Message: ORA-01861: literal does not
match format string
Error Index: 6. Error Code: 1400. Error Message: ORA-01400: cannot insert
NULL into ()
```

The error report shows us the number of successfully inserted records, the number of failed records and then lists all the failed records with supporting reasons for their failure.

Collection SET Operators

The collection set operators are introduced in the Oracle version 10g for processing one or more collection types to return an operated result set. Prior to 10g, we had to go through the trouble of traversing the collection types for every index value to compare them with another collection type, which has been liberated right now using the set operators for collections.

The different set operators available for the collection types are explained below,

SET

The *set* operator removes the duplicate elements of the collection type and thereby creates a new set of unique element values. This operator is similar to the *distinct* or *unique* keyword, which we often use to remove the duplicate rows in a SELECT statement. This operator also works as a comparison operator to check whether the collection type has any duplicates or not.

The prototype for defining the *set* operator is shown below,

```
SET (<Collection_type_name>)
```

The prototype for defining the *set* comparison operator is shown below,

```
<Collection_type_name> is [NOT] a SET
```

In the below example, a nested table type is created and assigned to duplicate elements, which is looped for display after removing their duplication using the *set* operator.

```
DECLARE
type type_ntt
IS
   TABLE OF NUMBER;
   l_ntt_var1 type_ntt:=type_ntt(1,2,2,3,4,4,4,5,5,6);
BEGIN
   l_ntt_var1:=SET(l_ntt_var1);
   FOR loop_ntt IN 1..l_ntt_var1.count
   LOOP
      dbms_output.put(l_ntt_var1(loop_ntt));
   END LOOP loop_ntt;
   dbms_output.new_line();
END;
/
```

Result:

```
1 2 3 4 5 6
```

In the below example, a nested table type is created and assigned to duplicate elements. The IF conditional check is performed on the nested table type using the *is a set* and *is not a set* operators to display whether the collection type has any duplicates or not. In this case, the control enters the ELSIF condition and prints that the collection type has duplicate elements in it.

```
DECLARE
type type_ntt
IS
   TABLE OF NUMBER;
   l_ntt_var1 type_ntt:=type_ntt(1,2,2,3,4,4,4,5,5,6);
BEGIN
   IF l_ntt_var1 IS a SET THEN
      dbms_output.put_line('This nested table type has no duplicates!');
   elsif l_ntt_var1 IS NOT a SET THEN
      dbms_output.put_line('This nested table type has duplicates!!');
   END IF;
END;
/
```

Result:

```
This nested table type has duplicates!!
```

Cardinality

The *cardinality* function prints the total number of elements in a nested table type while it does not work on VARRAY and associative array types. The main advantage of this function over the *count* method is that this function returns *null* when an uninitialized nested table type is passed as an argument to it.

The prototype for defining the *cardinality* function is shown below,

```
Cardinality(<Nested_table_type>)
```

In the below example, a nested table type is created with 10 elements assigned to it which are duplicates. This type is first counted using the *cardinality* function to print the total element count, including duplicates and then the *set* operator is used inside the *cardinality* function to print the total count of unique elements in the list followed by the usage of *cardinality* function returning a *null* over an uninitialized nested table type.

> ☖ Note: The *Count(Distinct<Column_name>)* in SQL is similar to *Cardinality(Set(Nested_table_type))* in PL/SQL collections.

```
DECLARE
type type_ntt
IS
  TABLE OF NUMBER;
  l_ntt_var1 type_ntt:=type_ntt(1,2,2,3,4,4,4,5,5,6);
  l_ntt_var2 type_ntt;
BEGIN
  dbms_output.put_line('The total count of the elements in L_NTT_VAR1 type
is '||cardinality(l_ntt_var1));
  dbms_output.put_line('The total count of the distinct elements in
L_NTT_VAR1 type is '||cardinality(SET(l_ntt_var1)));
  dbms_output.put_line('The total count of the elements in L_NTT_VAR2 type
is '||nvl(to_char(cardinality(l_ntt_var2)),'Null'));
END;
/
```

Result:

```
The total count of the elements in L_NTT_VAR1 type is 10
The total count of the distinct elements in L_NTT_VAR1 type is 6
The total count of the elements in L_NTT_VAR2 type is Null
```

Empty

This operator checks whether the nested table type is empty or not, sadly it does not work on the other two collection types.

The prototype for defining an *empty* set operator is shown below,

```
<Nested_table_type> is [NOT] Empty
```

In the example below, there are two instances of a nested table type are created. One instance is loaded and the other one is initialized to null. When we run the *empty* set operator, we are able to identify the empty and non-empty instances successfully.

> Note: If the nested table type is not initialized, this operator does not work.

```
DECLARE
type type_ntt
IS
  TABLE OF NUMBER;
  l_ntt_var1 type_ntt:=type_ntt(1,2,2,3,4,4,4,5,5,6);
  l_ntt_var2 type_ntt:=type_ntt();
BEGIN
  IF l_ntt_var1 IS NOT empty THEN
    dbms_output.put_line('The collection L_NTT_VAR1 is not empty');
  END IF;
  IF l_ntt_var2 IS empty THEN
    dbms_output.put_line('The collection L_NTT_VAR2 is empty');
  END IF;
END;
/
```

Result:

```
The collection L_NTT_VAR1 is not empty
The collection L_NTT_VAR2 is empty
```

Member of

The *member of* operator checks if the scalar literal or a bind value in the left operand is an element in the nested table type in the right operand and returns a Boolean result. The right operand can only be a nested table type and not a VARRAY or an associative array. The thumb rule is that the data type of the scalar variable must match with the data type of the elements in the nested table type.

The prototype for defining the *member of* operator is shown below,

```
<Scalar_variable> MEMBER OF <Nested_table_type>
```

In the below example, the functional with clause has one actual parameter of VARCHAR2 data type and returns the same. The clause has a nested table type declared with VARCHAR2 as its base element type and assigns a series of alphabets to it, which is then checked with the input bind value using the *member of* operator. When we run this query with a scalar value, we can identify whether the value is a member of the nested table type or not.

```
WITH
  FUNCTION func_member_of(ip_vc_var1 IN VARCHAR2) RETURN VARCHAR2
  IS
  type type_ntt IS TABLE OF VARCHAR2(1);
  l_ntt_var2 type_ntt :=type_ntt('A','B','C','D');
BEGIN
  IF ip_vc_var1 member OF l_ntt_var2 THEN
    RETURN 'The input is a member of the collection type';
  ELSE
    RETURN 'The input is not a member of the collection type';
  END IF;
END;
SELECT func_member_of(:ip_vc_var1) FROM dual;
/
```

Result:

1. When the bind value is B, the result is

The input is a member of the collection type

2. When the bind value is E, the result is

The input is a member of the collection type

Submultiset

The *submultiset* operator is similar to the *member of* operator except for the fact that it operates on two nested table types unlike the latter. The *submultiset* operator checks whether the left operand nested table type is a subset of the right operand nested table type by comparing them both and returns a Boolean value as a result. This operator can be only performed on two nested table type instances created by the same type and not on two different nested table types, even if they are identical. This operator does not work on VARRAYs and associative arrays.

The prototype for defining a *submultiset* operator is shown below,

```
<Nested_table_type1> submultiset of <Nested_table_type2>
```

The prototype for defining a negated *submultiset* operator is shown below,

```
NOT <Nested_table_type1> submultiset of <Nested_table_type2>
```

In the below example, there are 5 instances created over a single nested table type with varchar2(1) as its element type. The first instance holds the characters A, B, C and D which acts as the right operand in our program for the other four instances.

- The second instance holds the characters A and B, which when operated with the first instance, returns the result as a subset.

- The third instance holds the characters D and E, which when operated with the first instance, states as not a subset. This is because, even though the first element D is present in the first instance's elements list, the second element E is not found and thus it is returned as not a subset for the first instance.

- The fourth instance is just initialized and does not hold any values to it. When this instance is operated with the first instance, the operator returns the result that it is a subset.

- The first instance is just created and not even initialized in this context. When this instance is operated with the first instance, the operator says that it is not a subset.

```
DECLARE
type type_ntt
IS
  TABLE OF VARCHAR2(1);
  l_ntt_var1 type_ntt :=type_ntt('A','B','C','D');
  l_ntt_var2 type_ntt :=type_ntt('A','B');
  l_ntt_var3 type_ntt :=type_ntt('D','E');
  l_ntt_var4 type_ntt :=type_ntt();
  l_ntt_var5 type_ntt;
BEGIN
  IF l_ntt_var2 submultiset OF l_ntt_var1 THEN
    dbms_output.put_line('The type L_NTT_VAR2 is a submultiset of the type
L_NTT_VAR1');
  ELSE
    dbms_output.put_line('The type L_NTT_VAR2 is not a submultiset of the
type L_NTT_VAR1');
  END IF;
  IF not l_ntt_var3 submultiset OF l_ntt_var1 THEN
    dbms_output.put_line('The type L_NTT_VAR3 is not a submultiset of the
type L_NTT_VAR1');
  ELSE
    dbms_output.put_line('The type L_NTT_VAR3 is a submultiset of the type
L_NTT_VAR1');
  END IF;
  IF l_ntt_var4 submultiset OF l_ntt_var1 THEN
```

```
      dbms_output.put_line('The type L_NTT_VAR4 is a submultiset of the type
L_NTT_VAR1');
   ELSE
      dbms_output.put_line('The type L_NTT_VAR4 is not a submultiset of the
type L_NTT_VAR1');
   END IF;
   IF l_ntt_var5 submultiset OF l_ntt_var1 THEN
      dbms_output.put_line('The type L_NTT_VAR5 is a submultiset of the type
L_NTT_VAR1');
   ELSE
      dbms_output.put_line('The type L_NTT_VAR5 is not a submultiset of the
type L_NTT_VAR1');
   END IF;
END;
/
```

Result:

```
The type L_NTT_VAR2 is a submultiset of the type L_NTT_VAR1
The type L_NTT_VAR3 is not a submultiset of the type L_NTT_VAR1
The type L_NTT_VAR4 is a submultiset of the type L_NTT_VAR1
The type L_NTT_VAR5 is not a submultiset of the type L_NTT_VAR1
```

Multiset

The *multiset* operators are a bunch in number, which combines two or more collection types of the same type and returns a collection result of the same type that is appropriate to the operator used. These perform a similar operation to that of the SQL set operators, where the former works only on the collection types and the latter on the SQL SELECT statements.

Multiset operators with their SQL equivalents

Collection SET Operator	Equivalent SQL SET Operator
Multiset Union	Union all
Multiset Union all	Union all
Multiset Union Distinct	Union
Multiset Intersect	NA
Multiset Intersect Distinct	Intersect
Multiset Except	NA
Multiset Except Distinct	Minus

The below nested table type is created as a persistent object for explaining the different multiset operators.

```
CREATE OR REPLACE type type_ntt
IS
  TABLE OF VARCHAR2(1);
/
```

Multiset Union [All]

The *multiset union* operator evaluates two collection instances and returns a single instance, which contains all the elements from the input two instances. If there are any duplicate elements found, they are returned as such. This operator is identical to the *multiset union all* operator. This operator is equivalent to the *union all* operator in SQL.

In the below example, two instances of a single nested type are created. The first instance is assigned to A, B, C and D characters and the second instance is assigned to A and B characters. When they are operated, they just append the elements of the second nested table type instance of the first one.

```
WITH
   FUNCTION func_set RETURN type_ntt
IS
  l_ntt_var1 type_ntt :=type_ntt('A', 'B', 'C', 'D');
  l_ntt_var2 type_ntt :=type_ntt('A', 'B');
BEGIN
   RETURN l_ntt_var1 multiset UNION l_ntt_var2;
END;
SELECT * FROM TABLE(func_set);
/
```

Result:

```
A
B
C
D
A
B
```

Multiset Union Distinct

This operator works similar to the *multiset union* operator along with the duplication elements removal. This operator is equivalent to the *union* operator in SQL. The *distinct* keyword used in this operator cannot be replaced with its synonymous keyword *unique*.

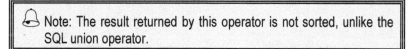 Note: The result returned by this operator is not sorted, unlike the SQL union operator.

In the below example, the functional with clause has two instances with a list of values assigned to them. The TABLE function in the select statement returns the total list of elements from the two instances removing the duplication without sorting them.

```
WITH
    FUNCTION func_set RETURN type_ntt
IS
  l_ntt_var1 type_ntt :=type_ntt('E', 'B', 'C', 'D');
  l_ntt_var2 type_ntt :=type_ntt('A', 'B');
BEGIN
    RETURN l_ntt_var1 multiset UNION Distinct l_ntt_var2;
END;
SELECT * FROM TABLE(func_set);
/
```

Result:

```
E
B
C
D
A
```

Multiset Intersect

The *multiset intersect* operator evaluates two collection instances of the same type and returns the common elements in them without any duplication removal. This operator does not have an equivalent SQL set operator.

In the below listing, the two instances of the nested table type are created and assigned to a list of values to them. The TABLE function returns the common duplicated unsorted elements from two instances.

```
WITH
    FUNCTION func_set RETURN type_ntt
IS
  l_ntt_var1 type_ntt :=type_ntt('A', 'A', 'C', 'D');
  l_ntt_var2 type_ntt :=type_ntt('A', 'A', 'B');
BEGIN
    RETURN l_ntt_var1 multiset intersect l_ntt_var2;
END;
SELECT * FROM TABLE(func_set);
/
```

Result:

```
A
A
```

Multiset Intersect Distinct

This operator works similar to the *multiset intersect* operator explained in the above section with additional duplicate element removal. In the below example, the operator works on the two instances loaded with a list of values with each other and return common unique unsorted element values using the TABLE function. Usually, the equivalent SQL set operator sorts their results, unlike this collection operator. The *distinct* keyword used in this operator cannot be replaced with its synonymous keyword *unique*.

```
WITH
   FUNCTION func_set RETURN type_ntt
IS
 l_ntt_var1 type_ntt :=type_ntt('B', 'B', 'A', 'A');
 l_ntt_var2 type_ntt :=type_ntt('A', 'A', 'C', 'C', 'B', 'B');
BEGIN
   RETURN l_ntt_var1 multiset intersect distinct l_ntt_var2;
END;
SELECT * FROM TABLE(func_set);
/
```

Result:

```
B
A
```

Multiset Except

The *multiset except* operator evaluates two similar collection instances and returns the remaining elements from the first instance after removing any matching elements from the second instance as its resultant. This operator does not have an SQL equivalent.

In the below example, the two instances with a list of elements are operated on the *multiset except* operator and returns the uncommon elements from the first instance without performing any duplication removal or sorting.

```
WITH
   FUNCTION func_set RETURN type_ntt
IS
 l_ntt_var1 type_ntt :=type_ntt('C', 'C', 'B', 'A', 'D');
 l_ntt_var2 type_ntt :=type_ntt('D', 'A');
BEGIN
   RETURN l_ntt_var1 multiset except l_ntt_var2;
END;
SELECT * FROM TABLE(func_set);
/
```

Result:

```
C
C
B
```

Introduction to Collection Types

Multiset Except Distinct

This operator works similar to the *multiset except* operator but performs an additional duplication removal operation to the result. This operator still does not sort its resultant, unlike its SQL equivalent. The *distinct* keyword used in this operator cannot be replaced with its synonymous keyword *unique*.

In the below example, the two instances with a list of elements are operated on this operator to return the uncommon elements list from the first instance with duplication check and no sorting.

```
WITH
   FUNCTION func_set RETURN type_ntt
IS
  l_ntt_var1 type_ntt :=type_ntt('C','C', 'B', 'A', 'D');
  l_ntt_var2 type_ntt :=type_ntt('D', 'A');
BEGIN
   RETURN l_ntt_var1 multiset except distinct l_ntt_var2;
END;
SELECT * FROM TABLE(func_set);
/
```

Result:

```
C
B
```

Collection Methods

The collection methods are the built-in functions and procedures that let us obtain information, modify, and traverse through a list of collection elements in an instance. These methods are created to simplify the access to the collection instance and its elements. These methods can be put to use by using the dot notation as shown below,

```
<Collection_instance>.<Collection_method>
```

The different collection methods available for our purpose are explained below.

Extend

The *extend* method allocates the space for one or more elements in a nested table type or a VARRAY type for storing the elements. These are actually procedures and are three in number with zero, one and two actual parameters, which serves in overloading.

- Extend(): Allocates one element space.

- Extend(n): Allocates *n* element space(s). This method fails when we cross the upper bound value in the VARRAY types.

- Extend(n, i): The first parameter *n* represents the number of element spaces to be allocated and the second parameter *i* represent the index value of the element that has to be copied to the newly allocated spaces.

In the below snippet, a nested table type is extended with no parameters, thus allocating one element space to the collection instance and a random integer is assigned to it. Then, the instance is extended again with 3 as its formal parameter literal, thus allocating three *null* spaces in the collection list. Finally, the nested table type instance extends to 3 as its first parameter and 1 as its second parameter, meaning that we have instructed the system to allocate 3 empty spaces to the collection list and copy the element value for the index [1] into these empty spaces. The total elements in the nested table type are then iterated for display as shown below.

```
DECLARE
type type_ntt
IS
  TABLE OF NUMBER;
  l_ntt_var1 type_ntt:=type_ntt();
BEGIN
  l_ntt_var1.extend();
  l_ntt_var1(1):=857;
  l_ntt_var1.extend(3);
  l_ntt_var1.extend(3,1);
  FOR loop_ntt IN 1..l_ntt_var1.count
  LOOP
     dbms_output.put_line('Index value ['||loop_ntt||']: Element value -
'||nvl(to_char(l_ntt_var1(loop_ntt)),'Null'));
  END LOOP loop_ntt;
END;
/
```

Result:
```
Index value [1]: Element value - 857
Index value [2]: Element value - Null
Index value [3]: Element value - Null
Index value [4]: Element value - Null
Index value [5]: Element value - 857
Index value [6]: Element value - 857
Index value [7]: Element value - 857
```

Exists

The *exists* method is actually a function returning the Boolean value *true* when the index value passed as its parameter has either a *null* or a *not null* element value and returns a *false* when the index value does not exist. The index value can be either a number or a string (in the case of an associative array with a string subscript).

In the below example, an associative array is verified to see if the input index exists or not.

```
DECLARE
type type_aa
IS
   TABLE OF NUMBER INDEX BY VARCHAR2(10);
   l_aa_var1 type_aa;
BEGIN
   l_aa_var1('A'):=100;
   l_aa_var1(10) :=null;
   IF l_aa_var1.exists('A') THEN
     dbms_output.put_line('The element at the index [A] exists!');
   ELSE
     dbms_output.put_line('The element at the index [A] does not exist!!');
   END IF;
   IF l_aa_var1.exists(10) THEN
     dbms_output.put_line('The element at the index [10] exists!');
   ELSE
     dbms_output.put_line('The element at the index [10] does not exist!!');
   END IF;
   IF l_aa_var1.exists(12) THEN
     dbms_output.put_line('The element at the index [12] exists!');
   ELSE
     dbms_output.put_line('The element at the index [12] does not exist!!');
   END IF;
END;
/
```

Result:

```
The element at the index [A] exists!
The element at the index [10] exists!
The element at the index [12] does not exist!!
```

Count

The *count* method is actually a function returning the total number of elements in a collection instance, which can be either null or not null. When the nested table type or VARRAY type is not initialized, this function fails with an *ORA-06531: Reference to uninitialized collection* error.

In the below PL/SQL unit, two instances of a nested table type with a number as its base data type is created and initialized. The first instance is assigned with 6 elements using the constructor method and the second instance is allocated with 20 element spaces using the *extend* method. The total number of elements available in these instances can be verified when the *count* method is used on them as shown below,

```
DECLARE
```

```
type type_ntt
IS
   TABLE OF NUMBER;
   l_ntt_var1 type_ntt:=type_ntt();
   l_ntt_var2 type_ntt:=type_ntt();
BEGIN
   l_ntt_var1:=type_ntt(1,2,3,4,5,6);
   l_ntt_var2.extend(20);
   dbms_output.put_line('The total elements count of the type instance
L_NTT_VAR1 is '||l_ntt_var1.count);
   dbms_output.put_line('The total elements count of the type instance
L_NTT_VAR2 is '||l_ntt_var2.count);
END;
/
```

Result:

```
The total elements count of the type instance L_NTT_VAR1 is 6
The total elements count of the type instance L_NTT_VAR2 is 20
```

Delete

The *delete* method is actually a procedure, which serves the purpose of deleting the element value and deallocating the space for the input index value. There are three *delete* procedures with zero, one and two input parameters serving its own purpose.

- Delete(): All the index elements from a collection instance are removed and their spaces are deallocated.

- Delete(n): The index value [n] from a collection instance is removed and its space is deallocated. The VARRAY type is dense in nature and when we delete a single element of their array using this method, the operation fails with an appropriate error.

- Delete(n, m): The index values from [n] through [m] from a collection instance is removed and their spaces are deallocated. The VARRAY type is dense in nature and when we delete a single element of their array using this method, the operation fails with an appropriate error.

In the below program, a nested table type with a number as its base type is declared and assigned with 10 elements. This type initially deletes the first element, then the elements from 2 through 5 followed by deleting all the rest elements, meanwhile displaying their counts at each level of deletion as shown below.

```
DECLARE
type type_ntt
IS
   TABLE OF NUMBER;
```

```
  l_ntt_var1 type_ntt:=type_ntt(1,2,3,4,5,6,7,8,9,10);
BEGIN
  dbms_output.put_line('The count before deleting the elements:
'||l_ntt_var1.count);
  l_ntt_var1.delete(1);
  dbms_output.put_line('The count after deleting the first element:
'||l_ntt_var1.count);
  l_ntt_var1.delete(2,5);
  dbms_output.put_line('The count after deleting the elements second through
five: '||l_ntt_var1.count);
  l_ntt_var1.delete;
  dbms_output.put_line('The count after deleting all the elements:
'||l_ntt_var1.count);
END;
/
```

Result:

```
The count before deleting the elements: 10
The count after deleting the first element: 9
The count after deleting the elements second through five: 5
The count after deleting all the elements: 0
```

Limit

The *limit* method is actually a function returning the highest possible subscript value of a collection instance. This function makes sense only when used with a VARRAY type by returning the upper bound value defined during its declaration and if used on a nested table type or an associative array, the function always returns a *null*.

In the below code snippet, a VARRAY type of 10 maximum elements is declared with Number as its base type. Even though this type is assigned to 5 elements, the *limit* returns the maximum possible subscript value as shown below.

```
DECLARE
type type_vt IS varray(10) OF NUMBER;
l_vt_var1 type_vt:=type_vt(1,2,3,4,5);
BEGIN
  dbms_output.put_line('The upper bound value of the VARRAY type L_VT_VAR1
is '||l_vt_var1.limit);
END;
/
```

Result:

```
The upper bound value of the VARRAY type L_VT_VAR1 is 10
```

First and Last

The *first* and *last* methods are actually functions that return the lowest and the highest subscript values for a collection instance. The index values can be either integer, in the case of nested table types and VARRAY types or string, in the case of associative arrays. If the collection type is empty, the *first* and *last* methods always return *null*.

In the below example, an associative array with string as its index is declared and assigned with few alphabets and their equivalent ASCII values. The first and the last index values of this associative array is then displayed using the *first* and *last* methods as shown below.

```
DECLARE
type type_aa
IS
   TABLE OF NUMBER INDEX BY VARCHAR2(1);
   l_aa_var1 type_aa;
BEGIN
   l_aa_var1('A'):=65;
   l_aa_var1('B'):=66;
   l_aa_var1('C'):=67;
   l_aa_var1('D'):=68;
   l_aa_var1('E'):=69;
   dbms_output.put_line('The first and last index value of the nested table
type L_AA_VAR1 is '||l_aa_var1.first||' and '||l_aa_var1.last);
END;
/
```

Result:

The first and last index value of the nested table type L_AA_VAR1 is A and E

Next and Prior

The *next* and *prior* methods are actually functions that returns the next and the previous collection subscript values for the input index passed as its parameter. If there is no next index available for the input index passed, the *next* method returns a null value. If there is no previous index available for the input index passed, the *prior* method returns a *null* value. In the case of a nested table or a VARRAY type, these functions return a PLS_INTEGER value and for the associative arrays, they return either a PLS_INTEGER, VARCHAR2 or a LONG value.

In the below example, an associative array with Number as its elements type and varchar2(1) index type is declared. This type is assigned with the ASCII values of the alphabets, which forms the corresponding index value. Looping a string indexed type is quite impossible without using the *next* and the *prior* methods as shown below. The smallest index value of the associative array is assigned to a scalar variable which is then looped using the *next* method to print all the available element values which are sparse and has string index value.

```
DECLARE
  l_vc_index VARCHAR2(1);
type type_aa
IS
  TABLE OF NUMBER INDEX BY VARCHAR2(1);
  l_aa_var1 type_aa;
BEGIN
  l_aa_var1('A')    :=65;
  l_aa_var1('B')    :=66;
  l_aa_var1('C')    :=67;
  l_aa_var1('D')    :=68;
  l_aa_var1('E')    :=69;
  l_vc_index        :=l_aa_var1.first;
  WHILE l_vc_index IS NOT NULL
  LOOP
    dbms_output.put_line(l_aa_var1(l_vc_index));
    l_vc_index:=l_aa_var1.next(l_vc_index);
  END LOOP;
END;
/
```

Result:

```
65
66
67
68
69
```

The above same example is used below but uses the *prior* method to loop the element values in a descending order.

```
DECLARE
  l_vc_index VARCHAR2(1);
type type_aa
IS
  TABLE OF NUMBER INDEX BY VARCHAR2(1);
  l_aa_var1 type_aa;
BEGIN
  l_aa_var1('A')    :=65;
  l_aa_var1('B')    :=66;
  l_aa_var1('C')    :=67;
  l_aa_var1('D')    :=68;
  l_aa_var1('E')    :=69;
  l_vc_index        :=l_aa_var1.last;
  WHILE l_vc_index IS NOT NULL
  LOOP
    dbms_output.put_line(l_aa_var1(l_vc_index));
    l_vc_index:=l_aa_var1.prior(l_vc_index);
  END LOOP;
END;
/
```

Result:

```
69
68
67
66
65
```

Trim

The *trim* method is actually a procedure, which trims the elements and deallocates their space from a collection instance starting from its highest index value. This procedure is actually an overloaded procedure with zero and one input parameters.

- Trim(): This method deallocates the space of the highest index value from a collection instance. When we try to trim a collection instance having no elements, we may encounter an error.

- Trim(n): This method deallocates the nth element spaces from the end of the collection in a collection instance. When we input parameter value passed to this method is greater than the result of the *count* method, we may encounter an error.

In the below block of code, a series of alphabets are assigned to the nested table type L_NTT_VAR1 as elements. The elements of the type are trimmed using the overloaded *trim* procedures and the total available elements in the nested table are displayed after each procedure execution as shown below.

```
DECLARE
type type_ntt
IS
  TABLE OF VARCHAR2(1);
  l_ntt_var1 type_ntt:=type_ntt('A', 'B', 'C', 'D', 'E', 'F', 'G', 'H', 'I',
  'J', 'K');
BEGIN
  dbms_output.put('Collection elements before trimming : ');
  FOR loop_ntt IN l_ntt_var1.first..l_ntt_var1.last
  LOOP
    dbms_output.put(l_ntt_var1(loop_ntt)||' ');
  END LOOP loop_ntt;
  dbms_output.new_line;
  l_ntt_var1.trim();
  dbms_output.put( 'Collection elements after trimming the last element: ');
  FOR loop_ntt IN l_ntt_var1.first..l_ntt_var1.last
  LOOP
    dbms_output.put(l_ntt_var1(loop_ntt)||' ');
  END LOOP loop_ntt;
  dbms_output.new_line;
  l_ntt_var1.trim(5);
```

```
   dbms_output.put ( 'Collection elements after trimming the last 5 elements:
')
   ;
   FOR loop_ntt IN l_ntt_var1.first..l_ntt_var1.last
   LOOP
      dbms_output.put (l_ntt_var1 (loop_ntt) ||' ');
   END LOOP loop_ntt;
   dbms_output.new_line;
END;
/
```

Result:

```
Collection elements before trimming: A B C D E F G H I J K
Collection elements after trimming the last element: A B C D E F G H I J
Collection elements after trimming the last 5 elements: A B C D E
```

Dropping a PL/SQL Type

The types created in a database can be removed permanently if they are no longer needed.

The prototype for dropping the type specification is shown below,

```
DROP TYPE <Type_name> [Validate | Force];
```

- **Validate**: This parameter makes a request to the database to perform a check on the type's dependencies. If any found, the drop operation fails with an appropriate error message. This is the default parameter.

- **Force**: This parameter forces the database to drop the type even though it has any dependencies. If there any types, objects or database tables dependent on the type to be dropped, they will be marked as useless permanently and cannot be put to use anymore. Thus, this option has to be used with utmost care as the drop operation once performed cannot be rolled back. This option is of good use when the type to be dropped is a subtype and its parent type has a dependency with a database table.

The prototype for dropping the type body is shown below,

```
DROP TYPE BODY <Type_name>;
```

In the below scenario, a nested table type TYPE_NTT, which does not have any dependency is dropped with an ease as shown below.

```
DROP TYPE TYPE_NTT VALIDATE;
```

But when a type has dependencies, dropping them is one tough job to undertake!

Consider the below example, where an object type TYPE_OBJ is created with one attribute of Number data type.

```
CREATE OR REPLACE type type_obj
IS
  object
  (
    l_obj_var1 NUMBER);
  /
```

A table TBL_OBJ is created with two columns, one with the object type TYPE_OBJ as its data type and another one as Number. Two rows are inserted into the table and committed.

```
CREATE TABLE tbl_obj (col1 type_obj, col2 number);

INSERT INTO tbl_obj VALUES (type_obj(10), 100);
INSERT INTO tbl_obj VALUES (type_obj(20), 200);
COMMIT;
```

When we try to drop this object type with the *validate* option, the script fails with a dependency check error as shown below,

```
DROP TYPE TYPE_OBJ VALIDATE;
```

```
Error report -

SQL Error: ORA-02303: cannot drop or replace a type with type or table
dependents
02303. 00000 -  "cannot drop or replace a type with type or table
dependents"
*Cause:    An attempt was made to drop or replace a type that has
           type or table dependents.
*Action:   For DROP TYPE, drop all type(s) and table(s) depending on the
           type and then retry the operation, or use the FORCE option.
           For CREATE TYPE, drop all type(s) and table(s) depending on the
           type and then retry the operation, or drop all table(s) depending
           on the type and retry with the FORCE option.
```

The action tag in the above error report suggests us to drop all the dependencies and then drop this object type or to drop this object type with a *force* option.

Dropping a PL/SQL Type

When we try to drop this object type with the *force* option as below, the object gets dropped permanently from the database and also drops all of its dependent objects.

```
DROP TYPE TYPE_OBJ FORCE;
```
Type TYPE_OBJ dropped.

In our case, the table TBL_OBJ with the object type dependent column COL1 has been dropped off along with its data. When we query the table, the query returns data from the column COL2 as shown below.

```
SELECT * FROM TBL_OBJ;
```

Query Result:

COL2
100
200

When we repeat the same scenario again, but this time the table TBL_OBJ has only one column with the object type OBJ_TYPE as its data type and gets data inserted to it as shown below,

```
CREATE TABLE tbl_obj(col1 type_obj);

INSERT INTO tbl_obj VALUES (type_obj(10));
INSERT INTO tbl_obj VALUES (type_obj(20));
COMMIT;
```

When we drop the object TYPE_OBJ with the *force* option, the column COL1 is now not dropped as it is the only column of the table. But the column does not have a data type to it when we query the data dictionary views as shown below,

```
SELECT
   table_name,
   column_name,
   data_type
FROM
   user_tab_columns
WHERE
   table_name='TBL_OBJ';
```

Query Result:

TABLE_NAME	COLUMN_NAME	DATA_TYPE
TBL_OBJ	COL1	NULL

When we try to query the table TBL_OBJ, we get the below error as its only column is inconsistent not having a data type associated with it.

```
SELECT * FROM TBL_OBJ;
```

Error Report:

```
ORA-04063: table "HR.TBL_OBJ" has errors
04063. 00000 -  "%s has errors"
*Cause:    Attempt to execute a stored procedure or use a view that has
           errors.  For stored procedures, the problem could be syntax
errors
           or references to other, non-existent procedures.  For views,
           the problem could be a reference in the view's defining query to
           a non-existent table.
           Can also be a table which has references to non-existent or
           inaccessible types.
*Action:   Fix the errors and/or create referenced objects as necessary.
```

The inconsistency is also found between the data dictionary views for this scenario as when we query the USER_TABLES view, the status of the table is shown as *valid*, but when we query the USER_OBJECTS view, the status for the table is *invalid* as shown below,

```
SELECT
  ut.table_name,
  ut.status user_tables_status,
  uo.status user_objects_status
FROM
  USER_TABLES ut,
  USER_OBJECTS uo
WHERE
  ut.table_name    =uo.object_name
AND ut.table_name ='TBL_OBJ';
```

Query Result:

TABLE_NAME	USER_TABLES_STATUS	USER_OBJECTS_STATUS
TBL_OBJ	VALID	INVALID

The table TBL_OBJ is now of no use as the error occurred on this table is permanent. This table cannot be put to use anymore and can only be dropped. Thus, when we perform a drop type operation with the *force* option, we might face some fatal database error if it is not handled properly.

Summary

We started this chapter by understanding the origination of the Object Oriented Programming concepts, its early development stages and its mass acceptance from the technologists. We then toured through the Object type specification and body with sufficient examples followed by analyzing their different methods. The next section taught us all about the Record types and their use in PL/SQL along with their R12.1 enhancement. The latter section gave us a high insight on the different Collection types, their SET operators and collection methods with appropriate supporting examples. The final section taught us the inconsistencies created in Oracle when we drop the PL/SQL types which are designed carelessly.

In this chapter, we have learned about all available PL/SQL types except Ref cursors, which are explained in detail in the next chapter along with the Cursors and their latest enhancements.

Cursors and Ref-Cursors in PL/SQL

This chapter gives us a detailed explanation of all available cursor types in Oracle with numerous examples, facts, and tips through the below topics,

20. Introduction to the cursor fundamentals, its execution cycle, and attributes.

21. Implicit cursors and their different types.

22. Explicit cursors, their different types, and the parameterized cursors.

23. Reference cursors and their different types.

24. Cursor Expressions as nested cursors and arguments.

25. TO_REFCURSOR and TO_CURSOR_NUMBER APIs in the DBMS_SQL package.

26. Implicit result sets in R12.1 explaining the RETURN_RESULT and GET_NEXT_RESULT APIs in the DBMS_SQL package.

27. Restrictions in the reference cursors.

Introduction to Cursor Fundamentals

The Oracle server allocates a chunk of private temporary workspace in the SGA called the context area for processing every single SQL statement encountered inside a PL/SQL block. This memory area holds the SQL query, its parsing information and the result set returned by the SQL query. The result set can then be processed either row by row or in bulk. As the context area is managed internally by the Oracle server, we do not have any control over it. The cursor can hold *n* number of rows, but can process only one row at a time. The record set held by the cursor is called as the active set.

> 🔔 Note: Cursors do not have a physical size as they are mere pointers to the memory area where the query results are stored.

The cursors are classified as implicit cursors and explicit cursors based on how manageable they are by the programmers.

The implicit cursors are created and managed by the Oracle server internally without the programmer intervention, whereas, on the other hand, the programmers are completely responsible for managing the complete execution cycle of the explicit cursors.

Cursor Execution Cycle

The cursor execution cycle is common for both the implicit and the explicit cursors, where it involves the stages which describe the processing of an SQL statement that is associated with the cursor. The execution cycle for the implicit cursors are taken care by the Oracle server itself, but in the case of explicit cursors, the programmers are fully responsible for implementing and controlling its execution cycle.

The execution cycle is mainly divided into three different stages and for the proper use of a cursor, all these steps must be followed in their mentioned sequential order.

OPEN

At this stage, the cursor is initialized and allocated with a portion of the private memory of the server process in the Process Global Area associated with the session for processing the SQL statement. During this stage, the cursor points to the allocated context area. This stage internally follows the below stages in the below-mentioned sequence.

PARSE: This is the primary step for processing the cursor associated SQL statement by undergoing the syntax and semantic checking. The syntax check verifies for any misspelled keywords. The semantic check mainly verifies for the object permission and for its validity. After this step, the binding process takes place, which is mentioned in the below step.

BIND: This step replaces all the bind variables present in the SQL statement with their actual value and gets it ready for the execution. If the bind value passed is not valid, no check is performed during the binding process, but a runtime error is thrown during the program execution.

EXECUTE: This phase executes the resulting SQL query from the above step, fetches the corresponding data from the database and loads them up in the pre-allocated context area. This process additionally sets up the record pointer to the first row of the query's result set.

FETCH

This stage pulls the data from the query result set stored in the context area in the above step. The cursor pointer is incremented by one row and points the next row in the result set sequence for every single row fetch. This stage also fetches rows in bulk using the BULK COLLECT clause and the number of rows to be fetched can be limited using the LIMIT clause. Once the cursor pointer reaches the last row of the result set, the pointer halts, and any further fetch statement returns only the last row from the result set.

CLOSE

This stage destroys the cursor's life in the current session and flushes out the context area. After the context area is freed up, this memory is then released back to the PGA and is readily available for future use. Beware of closing all the available explicit cursors after their usage, as the memory occupied by them may not be released back until the lifespan of their underlying program if this stage is not properly handled.

Cursor Attributes

The cursors internally store all useful information about the execution of the SQL statement that is associated with it and it can be retrieved with the help of the cursor attributes. The different available cursor attributes are *ROWCOUNT, ISOPEN, FOUND, NOTFOUND, BULK_ROWCOUNT,* and *BULK_EXCEPTIONS*. These attributes must be prefixed with their corresponding cursor name in case if it is an explicit cursor or must be prefixed with the text *SQL* if it is an implicit cursor, both the cases the cursor name and the attribute must be separated by the percentage "%" symbol.

ROWCOUNT

This attribute returns the number of rows fetched by the SQL statement associated with the cursor. Initially, before fetching any row set from the cursor, this attribute returns 0 and increments itself against the cursor pointer in the result set for every fetch operation. Once all the rows are fetched from the result set in the context area, this attribute returns the total count of the result set.

> Note: In the case of an explicit cursor, if the cursor is not open when this attribute is executed, the program fails with an *ORA-01001: invalid cursor* exception.

During an implicit cursor, this attribute returns the number of rows affected by the prior SQL statement only if there is no *commit* or *rollback* placed between the SQL statement and this attribute in a PL/SQL unit. If a *commit* or a *rollback* statement is placed in between them, this attribute will be reset to return 0.

ISOPEN

This attribute returns the Boolean value of *True* if the explicit cursor is already opened and returns a *False* if not. This attribute is used in the programs to avoid any errors occurred by operating a cursor without opening it in prior. This attribute always returns a *False* when used on an implicit cursor. This is the only attribute that operates outside the cursor execution cycle.

FOUND

This attribute returns the Boolean value of *True* if the cursor pointer points to a valid row from the recordset in the context area and returns a *False* if not. This attribute returns a *False* if there is no fetch operation initiated after opening an explicit cursor or when we try to fetch the cursor after reaching the last row of the record set.

> Note: In the case of an explicit cursor, if the cursor is not open when this attribute is executed, the program fails with an *ORA-01001: invalid cursor* exception.

In the case of implicit cursors, this attribute returns *True* if the prior SQL statement returns at least one row and if there is no *commit* or *rollback* placed between the SQL statement and this attribute in a PL/SQL unit. If a *commit* or a *rollback* statement is placed in between them, this attribute will be reset to return *False*.

NOTFOUND

This attribute is the opposite of the *FOUND* attribute discussed above. In an IF statement,

1. *If Not Cursor_name%FOUND* is similar to *If Cursor_name%NOTFOUND*.

2. *If Cursor_name%FOUND* is similar to *If Not Cursor_name%NOTFOUND*.

This attribute returns the Boolean value of *False* if the cursor pointer points to a valid row set and returns a *True* if not. This attribute returns a *False* if there is no fetch operation initiated after opening an explicit cursor and returns a *True* when we try to fetch the cursor after reaching the last row of the record set.

> 🔔 Note: In the case of an explicit cursor, if the cursor is not open when this attribute is executed, the program fails with an *ORA-01001: invalid cursor* exception.

In the case of implicit cursors, this attribute returns *False* if the prior SQL statement returns at least one row and if there is no *commit* or *rollback* placed between the SQL statement and this attribute in a PL/SQL unit. If a *commit* or a *rollback* statement is placed in between them, this attribute will be reset to return *True*.

BULK_ROWCOUNT & BULK_EXCEPTIONS

These attributes are only available for implicit cursors that are used in bulk processing when using a FORALL statement. These are explained in detail in the chapter no.6, *The PL/SQL Types*.

Implicit Cursors

The implicit cursors are automatically created and destroyed by the Oracle server whenever we execute an SQL statement inside a PL/SQL block. The Oracle server by default opens, fetches, processes, and closes the implicit cursor automatically without the need of a programmer intervention and that is why the implicit cursors are much faster compared to the explicit cursors, thus resulting in a simple and elegant code. The implicit cursors are further drilled down into two types based on the number of rows they process as shown below,

Single Row Implicit Cursors

This type of implicit cursors process at most one row by a SELECT INTO clause with one or more columns assigning them to individual static variables or to a collective record type variable. If the SQL encounters more than one row while processing, the block fails with an *ORA-01422: exact fetch returns more than requested number of rows* error at run time.

In the below example, the first name and the last name of an employee are assigned to two scalar variables using an INTO clause. The number of records resulted from this query is limited to one by using the WHERE condition. Thus, the number of rows processed by this implicit cursor can be found by using the attribute *rowcount* as shown in the block below.

```
DECLARE
   l_vc_first_name employees.first_name%type;
   l_vc_last_name employees.last_name%type;
BEGIN
   SELECT first_name, last_name
   INTO l_vc_first_name, l_vc_last_name
   FROM employees
   WHERE employee_id=120;
   dbms_output.put_line('Number of rows processed: '||sql%rowcount);
END;
/
```

Result:

Number of rows processed: 1

In the case of multiple column fetches, the traditional one to one assignment would be really expensive and tedious to maintain. This can be avoided by using an object type or a record type as shown in the below block of code. Here, the complete information of an employee is assigned to a record type anchor variable of the EMPLOYEES table type. The number of rows processed by this implicit cursor can be fetched using the *rowcount* attribute.

```
DECLARE
   l_rt_emp employees%rowtype;
BEGIN
   SELECT *
   INTO l_rt_emp
   FROM employees
   WHERE employee_id=120;
   dbms_output.put_line('Number of rows processed: '||sql%rowcount);
END;
/
```

Result:

Number of rows processed: 1

Multiple Row Implicit Cursors

In this type of implicit cursors, there is no restriction on the number of rows returned by the underlying SQL statement. These types of cursors can be created either by executing a DML statement, by using a BULK COLLECT clause or by using a cursor FOR loop embedded with a query.

In the below block, a DELETE statement creates a multi-row cursor implicitly and the number of rows affected by this statement can be found by using the *rowcount* cursor attribute.

 Note: If there is either a *commit* or a *rollback* statement placed right after the DML, the cursor attribute *rowcount* would reset to 0.

```
BEGIN
  DELETE FROM employees WHERE salary>=20000;
  dbms_output.put_line('Number of rows processed: '||sql%rowcount);
END;
/
```

Result:

Number of rows processed: 3

In the below code snippet, the BULK COLLECT clause allows us to process more than one row by creating an implicit cursor internally. The number of rows processed by this cursor can be found by fetching the *rowcount* attribute.

```
DECLARE
type type_ntt
IS
  TABLE OF employees%rowtype;
  l_ntt_emp type_ntt;
BEGIN
  SELECT * bulk collect INTO l_ntt_emp
  FROM
    employees
  WHERE
    hire_date>'01-Jan-2006';
  dbms_output.put_line('Number of rows processed: '||sql%rowcount);
END;
/
```

Result:

Number of rows processed: 56

Implicit Cursor FOR Loop

An implicit cursor FOR loop has a SELECT statement querying a table or a view instead of lower bound and upper bound values in the case of the traditional FOR loops. The cursor index of the FOR loop acts as a pointer to the result set processed by the associated SELECT statement in the private memory area known as the context area in the PGA. The cursor index points to each row and the period operator link the cursor index and the column alias in the SELECT statement for processing every row-column data for every loop spin.

The prototype for defining an implicit cursor FOR loop is shown below,

```
FOR <Loop_index> IN (<Select_statement>)
LOOP
<Executable_statements>;
END LOOP [<Loop_index>];
```

In the below listing, an implicit cursor FOR loop with a SELECT statement is processed for a set of employees. Here, the OPEN stage is started internally once the program control reaches the FOR loop, the FETCH operation is performed inside the loop and the CLOSE stage is performed once the program control exits the loop. Here, the loop's index name LOOP_EMP acts as the implicit cursor's name for fetching the record set of the cursor associated SELECT statement.

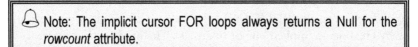

Note: The implicit cursor FOR loops always returns a Null for the *rowcount* attribute.

There is no need for an exit statement in any of the FOR loop types as it is internally handled by the cursor index. When the cursor index reads no more rows, the loop exits automatically.

```
BEGIN
  FOR loop_emp IN
  (SELECT *
    FROM
      employees
    WHERE salary>15000)
  LOOP
    dbms_output.put_line('Number of rows processed:
'||nvl(to_char(sql%rowcount),'Null'));
  END LOOP loop_emp;
END;
/
```

Result:

```
Number of rows processed: Null
Number of rows processed: Null
Number of rows processed: Null
Number of rows processed: Null
```

In the below snippet, an INTO clause is used in the SELECT query used in the implicit cursor FOR loop. When this block is executed, the cursor variable returns the required value, but the variable in the INTO clause remains *null*.

This is an inconsistent situation where the Oracle documentation has stated that an INTO clause is not allowed inside an implicit cursor FOR loop, but we are able to use one yet with no purpose.

Oracle documentation in 12c about the SELECT statement in the implicit cursor FOR loops,

🖫 **https://docs.oracle.com/database/121/LNPLS/cursor_for_loop_statement. htm#LNPLS1143**

SQL SELECT statement (not PL/SQL SELECT INTO statement).
For select_statement, PL/SQL declares, opens, fetches from, and closes an implicit cursor. However, because select_statement is not an independent statement, the implicit cursor is internal—you cannot reference it with the name SQL.

```
DECLARE
  l_vc_name VARCHAR2(100);
BEGIN
  FOR loop_emp IN
  (
    SELECT last_name ||', '||first_name name
    INTO l_vc_name
    FROM employees
    WHERE employee_id=123
  )
  LOOP
    dbms_output.put_line('Cursor Result: '||loop_emp.name);
    dbms_output.put_line('INTO clause Result: '||NVL(l_vc_name,'Null'));
  END LOOP loop_emp;
END;
/
```

Result:

```
Cursor Result: Vollman, Shanta
INTO clause Result: Null
```

Explicit Cursors

The explicit cursors are completely programmer driven, unlike the implicit cursors. These cursors must be declared with a SELECT statement in the declaration section of a PL/SQL unit prior to using them with a valid cursor name. The naming convention for the cursor name is similar to any variable name in PL/SQL. This cursor name acts as the pointer variable in the record set of the SELECT statement from the context area, where it increments itself to the next available row for each fetch operation performed.

> 🔔 Note: The explicit cursors can accommodate only SELECT statements and not DML statements.

Once the cursors are declared, they behave like an empty pointer. The actual cursor execution cycle begins only in the execution section of the program unit. When the cursor is opened, they get themselves a portion of the SGA for them to store their processed SELECT statement's information and the cursor points to the first row of the record set processed from the SELECT statement. The fetch process assigns the data pointed by the cursor pointer to a variable and increments the cursor pointer to the next row in the recordset if present. The close section then empties the context area and releases it.

> 🔔 Note: The cursors cannot be stored permanently in the database and they live only during the program's scope.

The prototype for declaring a cursor is shown below,

```
CURSOR <Cursor_name> [(<Parameter_name1> <Scalar_datatype |
Composite_datatype> DEFAULT <Default_value>, <Parameter_name2>
<Scalar_datatype | Composite_datatype> DEFAULT <Default_value>)]
return <record_type>
IS
  <Select_statement>;
```

The prototype for opening a cursor is shown below,

```
Open <Cursor_name>;
```

The prototype for fetching a cursor is shown below,

```
Fetch <Cursor_name> [Bulk Collect] Into <Scalar_variable |
Composite_variable> LIMIT <Limit_range>;
```

The prototype for closing a cursor is shown below,

```
Close <Cursor_name>;
```

In the below PL/SQL unit, a cursor CUR is declared with a SELECT query that returns the name of the employees whose salaries are greater than $15000. In the execution section of the block, the cursor is first opened using the *open* command. An IF statement which allows the program control to enter only if the cursor is opened prior to processing it using the cursor attribute *isopen* is used for avoiding any such errors. Inside the IF statement, a simple loop iterates the cursor for the total number of record sets it holds in its context area and fetches the employee name into a local variable for printing using the PUT_LINE procedure. The exit condition for this simple loop is defined by the cursor attribute *notfound* as shown. At last, the total number of records processed by the cursor is displayed using the cursor attribute *rowcount*. Finally, this block displays the names of the employees whose salary are greater than $15000.

```
DECLARE
  l_vc_name VARCHAR2(100);
  CURSOR cur
  IS
    SELECT last_name ||', ' ||first_name
    FROM employees
    WHERE salary>15000;
BEGIN
  OPEN cur;
  IF cur%isopen THEN
    LOOP
      FETCH cur INTO l_vc_name;
      EXIT
    WHEN cur%notfound;
      dbms_output.put_line(l_vc_name);
    END LOOP;
    dbms_output.put_line('The total rows processed by the cursor is
'||cur%rowcount);
  END IF;
  close cur;
END;
/
```

Result:

```
Hunold, Alexander
Russell, John
Partners, Karen
Hartstein, Michael
The total rows processed by the cursor is 4
```

When there are no records returned by the SELECT query that is associated with a cursor, there will be no error thrown and we may need to manually determine if there are any records available or not by using the cursor attributes as shown below.

The above program is tweaked with an additional IF condition to check if the cursor points to any rows or not before fetching it by using the *found* attribute.

```
DECLARE
  l_vc_name VARCHAR2(100);
  CURSOR cur
  IS
    SELECT last_name ||', ' ||first_name
    FROM employees
    WHERE salary>20000;
BEGIN
  OPEN cur;
  IF cur%isopen THEN
  if cur%found then
    LOOP
      FETCH cur INTO l_vc_name;
      EXIT
    WHEN cur%notfound;
      dbms_output.put_line(l_vc_name);
    END LOOP;
    dbms_output.put_line('The total rows processed by the cursor is
'||cur%rowcount);
    else
    dbms_output.put_line('No employees found!!');
    end if;
  END IF;
  close cur;
END;
/
```

Result:

No employees found!!

In the below example, the current salary of the employees from the transaction table is updated with its archival table, where the archival table takes care of the report generation purposes. The fetch stage of the explicit cursor processes more than one row using the BULK COLLECT INTO clause and the number of rows processed is limited using the LIMIT clause, where these rows are processed using the FORALL clause and then gets committed.

> Note: Simple SQL statements are preferred over PL/SQL scripts when bulk processing unless the business logic requires us to go only for PL/SQL.

```
DECLARE
  l_n_employee_id NUMBER;
  l_n_salary      NUMBER;
  CURSOR cur
  IS
    SELECT employee_id, salary FROM employees;
type type_rec
IS
  record
  (
    employee_id NUMBER,
    salary      NUMBER);
type type_ntt
IS
  TABLE OF type_rec;
  l_ntt_var1 type_ntt;
BEGIN
  OPEN cur;
  IF cur%isopen THEN
    LOOP
      FETCH
        cur bulk collect
      INTO
        l_ntt_var1 limit 1000;
      EXIT
    WHEN cur%notfound;
      forall loop_index IN indices OF l_ntt_var1
      UPDATE
        employees_archive
      SET
        salary=l_ntt_var1(loop_index).salary
      WHERE
        employee_id=l_ntt_var1(loop_index).employee_id;
      commit;
    END LOOP;
  END IF;
  CLOSE cur;
END;
/
```

PL/SQL procedure successfully completed.

FOR UPDATE and WHERE CURRENT OF Clause

The SELECT statement associated with the cursor does not have any locks on the rows it returns, allowing any session to perform any operation on those rows during the cursor operation.

When we want to issue a lock over the record set returned by the cursor associated SELECT query, we can opt for the FOR UPDATE clause, which automatically places an exclusive row-level lock on all the rows retrieved, forbidding any other session from performing a DML operation on them until we perform a *commit* or a *rollback* to release the lock.

This clause can also be extended to lock only the intended table in the SELECT query containing more than one table in joins using the FOR UPDATE OF clause. This clause becomes meaningless if we use a single table SELECT clause as the minimum lock is a row level in Oracle.

Oracle has provided us with the WHERE CURRENT OF clause for both DELETE and UPDATE statements inside a cursor's range to make changes to the last fetched row(s) from the cursor with an ease. When we want to update or delete the cursor fetched row(s) from the database, we don't have to form a UPDATE or a DELETE statement with a primary key mapping in its WHERE clause, instead, the WHERE CURRENT OF clause comes in handy.

In the below code listing, the employees joined before the year 2000 are archived and during the cursor process, no other session is permitted to make any changes to those employees using the FOR UPDATE clause. The employee deletion from the transaction table is performed using the WHERE CURRENT OF clause as shown below.

```
DECLARE
   l_rt_emp employees%rowtype;
   CURSOR cur
   IS
     SELECT
        *
     FROM
        employees
     WHERE
        TO_CHAR(hire_date,'RRRR')<'2000' FOR UPDATE;
BEGIN
   OPEN cur;
   LOOP
      FETCH cur INTO l_rt_emp;
      EXIT
   WHEN cur%notfound;
      INSERT
      INTO
        employees_archive VALUES l_rt_emp;
      DELETE
      FROM
        employees
      WHERE
        CURRENT OF cur;
   END LOOP;
   Commit;
   CLOSE cur;
END;
/
```

Once we open a cursor having a FOR UPDATE clause, all the rows returned by the SELECT statement are locked for our changes until a *commit* or a *rollback* is placed to release the lock. After a TCL operation is performed, the cursor pointer gets reset and the cursor will be no longer accessible, thus results in an error when fetched further as shown below. Thus, any TCL operation on the cursor record set has to be done only after fetching all the rows from the cursor context area using a loop process similar to the above listing example.

```
DECLARE
  l_rt_emp employees%rowtype;
  CURSOR cur
  IS
    SELECT
      *
    FROM
      employees
    WHERE
      TO_CHAR(hire_date,'RRRR')<'2000' FOR UPDATE;
BEGIN
  OPEN cur;
  COMMIT;
  FETCH cur INTO l_rt_emp;
END;
/
```

```
Error report -

ORA-01002: fetch out of sequence
ORA-06512: at line 14
01002. 00000 -  "fetch out of sequence"
```

The row limiting clause introduced in the Oracle version 12c, *Fetch First .. Rows Only* does not seem to work with the FOR UPDATE clause. When the *Fetch* clause is used with a cursor having a FOR UPDATE clause, the PL/SQL unit fails when we try to open the cursor with an *ORA-02014: cannot select FOR UPDATE from view with DISTINCT, GROUP BY, etc.* error. The error description shows that the internal mechanism for the *Fetch* clause uses either a *DISTINCT or a GROUP BY* clause which is not permitted alongside the FOR UPDATE clause. In this scenario, the cursor result set can be limited using the traditional *rownum* pseudo column. This scenario is portrayed in the below listing.

```
DECLARE
  CURSOR cur
  IS
    SELECT
      *
    FROM
      employees
  FETCH
    FIRST 10 rows only FOR UPDATE;
BEGIN
  OPEN cur;
END;
/
```

```
Error report -
ORA-02014: cannot select FOR UPDATE from view with DISTINCT, GROUP BY, etc.
ORA-06512: at line 4
ORA-06512: at line 11
02014. 00000 -  "cannot select FOR UPDATE from view with DISTINCT, GROUP BY,
etc."
```

When we associate a SELECT statement with more than one table joined together to a cursor with a FOR UPDATE clause, we end up locking all the tables in the FROM clause of the SELECT statement, where we just need to lock a single table for our purpose. The FOR UPDATE OF clause helps us in locking up the intended table rather all available tables. In the below example, the cursor CUR is associated with a SELECT statement having the tables EMPLOYEES and DEPARTMENTS joined in its FROM clause. The FOR UPDATE OF E.EMPLOYEE_ID clause in the below snippet locks up only rows of the EMPLOYEES table, thus making the DEPARTMENTS table available for modification to the other session users.

```
DECLARE
  CURSOR cur
  IS
    SELECT
      *
    FROM
      employees e,
      departments d
    WHERE
      e.department_id=d.department_id FOR UPDATE OF e.employee_id;
BEGIN
  OPEN cur;
END;
/
```

The WHERE CURRENT OF clause internally operates on the ROWID pseudo column of the rows returned by the cursor, thus we cannot use this clause on the cursor associated SELECT statement having more than one table joined.

In the below code listing, the salary for the employees from the IT department is given a raise of 10%. For this, the cursor CUR is associated with a SELECT statement joining the EMPLOYEES and the DEPARTMENTS tables with a FOR UPDATE OF clause on the employee ID. When we try to update the salary column of the EMPLOYEES table using the WHERE CURRENT OF clause, the block fails with an *ORA-01410: invalid ROWID* error as there is no way to specify the *rowid* as there are two tables.

```
DECLARE
  l_n_sal employees.salary%type;
  CURSOR cur
  IS
    SELECT
      e.salary
    FROM
      employees e,
      departments d
    WHERE
      e.department_id    =d.department_id
    AND d.department_name='IT' FOR UPDATE OF e.employee_id;
BEGIN
  OPEN cur;
  LOOP
    FETCH cur INTO l_n_sal;
    UPDATE
      employees
    SET
      salary=l_n_sal*1.10
    WHERE
      CURRENT OF cur;
    EXIT
  WHEN cur%notfound;
  END LOOP;
  Commit;
END;
/
```

Error report -

```
ORA-01410: invalid ROWID
ORA-06512: at line 20
01410. 00000 -   "invalid ROWID"
```

This scenario can be manhandled by fetching the *rowid* of the intended table in the cursor associated SELECT statement and using it in the WHERE clause of the DELETE or the UPDATE statement instead of the WHERE CURRENT OF clause as shown in the below listing.

```
DECLARE
  l_n_sal employees.salary%type;
  l_r_rowid rowid;
  CURSOR cur
  IS
    SELECT
      e.rowid,e.salary
    FROM
      employees e,
      departments d
    WHERE
      e.department_id    =d.department_id
    AND d.department_name='IT' FOR UPDATE OF e.employee_id;
BEGIN
  OPEN cur;
  LOOP
```

```
    FETCH
      cur
    INTO
      l_r_rowid,
      l_n_sal;
    UPDATE
      employees
    SET
      salary=l_n_sal*1.10
    WHERE
      rowid=l_r_rowid;
    EXIT
  WHEN cur%notfound;
  END LOOP;
END;
/
```

PL/SQL procedure successfully completed.

Explicit Cursor FOR Loop

The explicit cursor FOR loop is similar to an implicit one, except for the SELECT statement in its context is replaced by an explicit cursor, which is declared in the declaration section. Even though when an explicit cursor is associated with a FOR loop, the cursor execution cycle is internally handled by the FOR loop itself and not explicitly by the programmers. Similar to the implicit ones, the loop index acts as a pointer to the result set processed by the cursor associated SELECT statement and the period operator acts as a link between the loop index and the column alias of the cursor associated SELECT statement for processing each row's column data for every loop spin.

The prototype for defining an explicit cursor FOR loop is shown below,

```
FOR <Loop_index> IN (<Cursor_name>)
LOOP
<Executable_statements>;
END LOOP [<Loop_index>];
```

In the below script, an explicit cursor is declared with a SELECT statement, which returns all the employees who are earning more than $15000 and is processed in a FOR loop. Unlike the implicit cursor FOR loops, the *rowcount* attribute always returns a NOT NULL integer for determining the number of rows processed by the FOR loop as shown below,

```
DECLARE
  CURSOR cur
  IS
    SELECT
      *
```

```
    FROM
       employees
    WHERE
       salary>15000;
BEGIN
  FOR loop_emp IN cur
  LOOP
    dbms_output.put_line('Number of rows processed:
'||NVL(TO_CHAR(cur%rowcount),'Null'));
  END LOOP loop_emp;
END;
/
```

Results:

```
Number of rows processed: 1
Number of rows processed: 2
Number of rows processed: 3
Number of rows processed: 4
```

In the below snippet, an INTO clause is used in the SELECT query associated with the cursor. When this block is executed, the cursor variable returns the required value, but the variable in the INTO clause always remains *null* as shown below. Thus, only SQL SELECT statements must be used as the cursor associated statements and not others.

```
DECLARE
  l_vc_name VARCHAR2(100);
  CURSOR cur
  IS
    SELECT
      last_name
      ||', '
      ||first_name name
    INTO
      l_vc_name
    FROM
      employees
    WHERE
      employee_id=123;
BEGIN
  FOR loop_emp IN cur
  LOOP
    dbms_output.put_line('Cursor Result: '||loop_emp.name);
    dbms_output.put_line('INTO clause Result: '||NVL(l_vc_name,'Null'));
  END LOOP loop_emp;
END;
/
```

Results:

```
Cursor Result: Vollman, Shanta
INTO clause Result: Null
```

Parameterized Cursors

The parameterized cursors are the further extension to the explicit cursors having IN type parameters for limiting the number of rows processed by the cursor associated SELECT statement while opening them. These are similar to the way a procedure is passed with parameters in PL/SQL except that the parameter can be only of IN mode. The two types of parameterized cursors are.

Weak Parameterized Cursors

These types of cursors do not have any return type and are generally used in procedures, functions and anonymous blocks which are not encapsulated within a package.

In the below script, a cursor is created over the EMPLOYEES table with an input parameter, which is placed in the SELECT statement's WHERE condition. When the cursor is opened with an employee ID as its parameter value, it acts as a row limiter and returns only the row set corresponding to that employee ID, which is then fetched and processed, instead of processing all the employees as shown below.

```
DECLARE
  l_rt_emp employees%rowtype;
  CURSOR cur(ip_n_emp_id NUMBER)
  IS
    SELECT
      *
    FROM
      employees
    WHERE
      employee_id=ip_n_emp_id;
BEGIN
  OPEN cur(:ip_n_emp_id);
  FETCH
    cur
  INTO
    l_rt_emp;
  dbms_output.put_line(l_rt_emp.last_name||', '||l_rt_emp.first_name);
  CLOSE cur;
END;
/
```

In the below code snippet, a nested table of NUMBER type is created permanently in the database.

```
CREATE OR REPLACE type type_ntt
IS
  TABLE OF NUMBER;
  /
```

This nested type then acts as the data type of the cursor input parameter and the list of employee IDs passed as its input limits the number of rows returned by the SELECT statement during the cursor OPEN operation as shown in the below code listing. Basically, all the rows from the SELECT statement are taken into the context area initially and the input parameter just limits out a certain number row during the OPEN operation, which is then fetched and processed.

```
DECLARE
  l_rt_emp employees%rowtype;
  l_ntt_var1 type_ntt;
  CURSOR cur(ip_ntt_emp_id type_ntt)
  IS
    SELECT
      *
    FROM
      employees
    WHERE
      employee_id IN
      (
        SELECT
          *
        FROM
          TABLE(ip_ntt_emp_id)
      );
BEGIN
  l_ntt_var1:=type_ntt(200,201,202,203);
  OPEN cur(l_ntt_var1);
  LOOP
    FETCH
      cur
    INTO
      l_rt_emp;
    EXIT
  WHEN cur%notfound;
    dbms_output.put_line('Employee ID: '||l_rt_emp.employee_id||
    ' - Employee Name: '||l_rt_emp.last_name||', '||l_rt_emp.first_name);
  END LOOP;
  CLOSE cur;
END;
/
```

Results:

```
Employee ID: 200 - Employee Name: Whalen, Jennifer
Employee ID: 201 - Employee Name: Hartstein, Michael
Employee ID: 202 - Employee Name: Fay, Pat
Employee ID: 203 - Employee Name: Mavris, Susan
```

Strong Parameterized Cursors

These cursors have a return type and are primarily used in procedures, functions and anonymous blocks which are encapsulated within a package. The return type serves no other purpose than letting its calling environment know its structure from its package specification while hiding its business complexities and rules in its body.

The below nested table type is created with one VARCHAR2(50) data typed column.

```
CREATE OR REPLACE type type_ntt
IS
   TABLE OF VARCHAR2(50);
   /
```

The below package specification shows the parameterized cursor, its return type and the procedure header information that is sufficient for a calling environment to call them.

```
CREATE OR REPLACE PACKAGE pkg_param_cur
IS
   CURSOR cur(ip_ntt_first_name type_ntt)
     RETURN employees%rowtype;
     PROCEDURE proc_param_cur(
        ip_ntt_emp_name type_ntt);
   END;
   /
```

The body section of the cursor and the procedure are implemented in the below package body listing, where the list of first names of the employees passed as input to the procedure is used for limiting the record sets processed by the cursor associated SELECT statement when the cursor is opened with the procedure's input parameter as its own. The recordset opened by the cursor is then fetched and processed using a simple loop as shown in the below example.

```
CREATE OR REPLACE PACKAGE BODY pkg_param_cur
IS
   CURSOR cur(ip_ntt_first_name type_ntt)
     RETURN employees%rowtype
   IS
     SELECT
        *
     FROM
        employees
     WHERE
        EXISTS
        (
          SELECT
             1
          FROM
             TABLE(ip_ntt_first_name)
          WHERE
             column_value=first_name
        )
        order by first_name;
   PROCEDURE proc_param_cur(
```

Advanced PL/SQL Programming

```
         ip_ntt_emp_name type_ntt)
  IS
    l_rt_emp employees%rowtype;
  BEGIN
    OPEN cur(ip_ntt_emp_name);
    LOOP
      FETCH cur INTO l_rt_emp;
      EXIT
    WHEN cur%notfound;
      dbms_output.put_line('Employee ID: '||l_rt_emp.employee_id||
      '. Employee Name: '||l_rt_emp.last_name||', '||l_rt_emp.first_name);
    END LOOP;
  END;
END;
/
```

The procedure can be called by passing a list of employee first names as shown below,

```
EXEC pkg_param_cur.proc_param_cur(type_ntt('Alexander', 'Janette',
'Michael', 'Sundar', 'William'));
```

Results:

```
Employee ID: 103. Employee Name: Hunold, Alexander
Employee ID: 115. Employee Name: Khoo, Alexander
Employee ID: 156. Employee Name: King, Janette
Employee ID: 201. Employee Name: Hartstein, Michael
Employee ID: 134. Employee Name: Rogers, Michael
Employee ID: 166. Employee Name: Ande, Sundar
Employee ID: 206. Employee Name: Gietz, William
Employee ID: 171. Employee Name: Smith, William
```

Reference Cursors

The reference cursors in PL/SQL were introduced in the version 7 with minimal functionality, which has undergone some serious enhancements till the latest release R12.1, making it the most preferred mode for transferring result sets between Oracle server and its external client side applications.

The reference cursors are one of the PL/SQL data types, which can point to any number of SELECT statements at run time, unlike the explicit cursors, which are stuck to a single SELECT statement throughout its lifetime in a PL/SQL unit. The Ref-Cursors does not pass the entire result set in a huge sack, rather it just hands over the reference of that cursor to the calling program, thus making it more performance friendly. These can also be dynamic, meaning that they can process dynamic SQL statements, whilst the explicit cursors are static in nature. The primary advantage of the reference cursors over the static cursors is that they can be passed as IN, OUT and INOUT parameters between the different subroutines (also as return types for the functions) and the external calling environments. We can also handle all the cursor attributes in Ref-Cursors just how the static explicit cursors do it. These indigenous characteristics of the reference cursor make them more popular and flexible over the static cursors.

> 🔔 Note: The result set returned by the Ref-Cursors are read-only in nature, and they cannot be modified.

These PL/SQL types when returns a result set to the client, encounters an additional database round-trip as the actual data is never returned to the client program until they open the reference cursor and requests for them.

The dynamic cursors cannot be created permanently in the database, but can only be declared in the declaration section of anonymous blocks, subroutines or packages as *REF CURSOR* types. Initially, when they are declared, they are not associated with any memory space, but can be associated with any number of context areas during run time.

The prototype for defining a Ref-Cursor is shown below,

```
TYPE <TYPE_NAME> is REF CURSOR [RETURN <RECORD_TYPE>];
```

There are two types of Ref-Cursors based on whether they have a return type or not. They are,

Strong Reference Cursors

When a Ref-Cursor is defined with a return type, it is called as a strongly typed static Ref-Cursor. The return type of this static Ref-Cursor is usually the record structure of a table, view, nested table type, VARRAY type, or a user-defined record type, thus restricting it to return a single structure making it more specific and less prone to errors as the compiler can determine whether the record type structure of the Ref-Cursor's return statement matches with its SELECT statement or with its FETCH INTO structure before its execution itself.

A user defined Ref-Cursor can be used as a parameter for the subprograms only if it is declared in a package specification as shown below. The below package specification declares a strong Ref-Cursor returning the record type of the EMPLOYEES table's structure.

```
CREATE OR REPLACE PACKAGE pkg_refcur
IS
type type_refcur
IS
  ref
  CURSOR
    RETURN employees%rowtype;
  END;
  /
```

The below procedure acts as a server-side program with the Ref-Cursor declared in the above package spec defining its OUT parameter. The procedure returns the record set for the employees belonging to a particular department ID, that is passed as the procedure's input using the OPEN FOR statement.

```
CREATE OR REPLACE PROCEDURE proc_refcur(
    ip_dept_id NUMBER,
    op_rc_emp OUT pkg_refcur.type_refcur)
IS
BEGIN
  OPEN op_rc_emp FOR SELECT * FROM employees WHERE department_id=ip_dept_id;
END;
/
```

The below program acts as a client end program, where it makes a call to the server side program and gets the record set pertaining to the input department ID. As we are aware of the return type of the Ref-Cursor as it is a strongly defined type, we have created a user-defined record type for acting as the FETCH INTO variable. The Ref-Cursor declared in this program's scope is never opened as when it is assigned to the same Ref-Cursor's variable in the OUT parameter, the information of the cursor variable from the server program is copied into this variable, thus making it its alias. This variable is then looped for processing the returned result set as shown in the below listing.

```
DECLARE
  l_rc_var1 pkg_refcur.type_refcur;
  l_rt_var2 employees%rowtype;
BEGIN
  proc_refcur(90, l_rc_var1);
  LOOP
    FETCH
      l_rc_var1
    INTO
      l_rt_var2;
    EXIT
WHEN l_rc_var1%notfound;
    dbms_output.put_line('Emp ID: '||l_rt_var2.employee_id||' Emp Name: '||
    l_rt_var2.last_name||', '||l_rt_var2.first_name||' Emp Salary: '||
    l_rt_var2.salary);
END LOOP;
CLOSE l_rc_var1;
END;
/
```

Result:

```
Emp ID: 100 Emp Name: King, Steven Emp Salary: 24000
Emp ID: 101 Emp Name: Williams, Neena Emp Salary: 17000
Emp ID: 102 Emp Name: De Haan, Lex Emp Salary: 17000
```

The above program can also use a collection type for transferring the record set instead of a Ref-Cursor, but the main advantage of Ref-Cursor over the collection types is that the former does not pass any data, but the pointers locating the record sets in the database, where the latter duplicates the data and transfers it.

The cursor opened in the server program is closed by the client program in the above example. This scenario can be explained using a simple example shown below. Two cursor variables were created over a single Ref-Cursor type declared in the package specification. The variable L_RC_VAR1 is opened for a SELECT statement and the variable L_RC_VAR2 is closed. When we try to fetch from the variable L_RC_VAR1, which was initially opened, we face the *ORA-01001: invalid cursor* error. This scenario also works if the two variables are from two different programs of a single session, meaning that any number of variables created over a single Ref-Cursor behaves like an alias over each other. Thus, the cursor opened in a server program cannot be closed by itself and has to be done by the client program using the cursor variable created over the same cursor type, freeing up the space allocated by the cursor in the server program.

```
DECLARE
  l_rc_var1 pkg_refcur.type_refcur;
  l_rc_var2 pkg_refcur.type_refcur;
  l_rt_emp employees%rowtype;
BEGIN
  OPEN l_rc_var1 FOR SELECT * FROM employees;
  CLOSE l_rc_var2;
  FETCH l_rc_var1 INTO l_rt_emp;
END;
/
```

```
Error report -

ORA-01001: invalid cursor
ORA-06512: at line 7
01001. 00000 -  "invalid cursor"
```

Weak Reference Cursors

When a Ref-Cursor is defined without a return type, it is called as a weakly typed dynamic Ref-Cursor. There is no dependency on its return structure, thus making it open to all SELECT statements independent of its structure. Due to this reason, the compiler will not be able to determine whether the Ref-Cursor's SELECT statement matches with its FETCH INTO variable until its run time. Thus, the compatibility between the cursor variable and the variable it is fetched into must be carefully chosen.

The SYS_REFCURSOR cursor variable is an Oracle-defined weak Ref-Cursor type, which is pre-declared in the STANDARD package. We are free to use this Ref-Cursor type as parameters for our sub-routines and return type for the functions without needing to create them in a package specification, as it is already done by Oracle for us. As SYS_REFCURSOR is a weakly typed Ref-Cursor, it assumes any record structure as its return type during its run time. When we open a cursor variable created with the SYS_REFCURSOR type, a reference is created in the SGA, which can be then passed to another program or client environment as a cursor variable.

In the below code listing, the function FUNC_REFCUR has the Oracle defined weakly typed SYS_REFCURSOR as its return type for returning the result set of the EMPLOYEES table for a particular department, which is passed as its input parameter.

```
CREATE OR REPLACE FUNCTION func_refcur(
    ip_dept_id NUMBER)
  RETURN sys_refcursor
IS
  l_rc_var1 sys_refcursor;
BEGIN
  OPEN l_rc_var1 FOR SELECT * FROM employees WHERE department_id=ip_dept_id;
  RETURN l_rc_var1;
END;
/
```

When the function executed with a valid department ID as its input parameter, returns an active result set that can be used by the external client programs for further processing.

```
SELECT func_refcur(50) FROM dual;
```

After the external client programs fetch all the rows from the returned cursor, they must close the cursor to avoid having a lot many open cursors resulting in the *ORA-01000: maximum open cursors exceeded* exception. The total number of cursors opened and maximum open cursors allowed for a session can be found from the below SQL, which is derived from the data dictionary tables.

```
SELECT
  MAX(sess.value) AS current_open_cursors,
  param.value     AS max_open_cursors_allowed
FROM
  v$sesstat sess,
  v$statname stat,
  v$parameter param
WHERE
  sess.statistic# = stat.statistic#
AND stat.name   = 'opened cursors current'
AND param.name  = 'open_cursors'
GROUP BY
  param.value;
```

Query Result:

CURRENT_OPEN_CURSORS	MAX_OPEN_CURSORS_ALLOWED
20	300

The *ORA-01000: maximum open cursors exceeded* exception occurs when the *current_open_cursors* count exceeds the *max_open_cursors_allowed* in the above query. The maximum allowed open cursor can be tweaked as per user requirement using the below ALTER statement,

```
ALTER system SET open_cursors = 1000;
```

Setting up a maximum value for the OPEN_CURSORS parameter simply allocates a fixed number of array slots, but does not initialize any memory spaces. Even though setting this parameter to a maximum value does not likely take a toll on the memory, we must always mind ourselves not to increase it to a wild number.

In the below example, the function FUNC_REFCUR returns the result set to the table that is sent as its input parameter. Thus, the user can request for any table's result set at any time by just passing its name as the input parameter to this function.

```
CREATE OR REPLACE FUNCTION func_refcur(
    ip_vc_table_name VARCHAR2)
   RETURN sys_refcursor
IS
   l_rc_var1 sys_refcursor;
BEGIN
   OPEN l_rc_var1 FOR 'select * from '||ip_vc_table_name;
   RETURN l_rc_var1;
END;
/
```

The below statement has a bind variable, which accepts a table name and returns its result set when executed.

```
SELECT func_refcur(:hi) FROM dual;
```

A Ref-Cursor can shift its pointer from one SQL to another at run time, unlike the explicit cursors, which makes the former the preferred one over the latter. In the below snippet, an SYS_REFCURSOR variable is declared in the declaration section, which is then opened and fetched from the first row of the EMPLOYEES table returning two column values. Right after printing the fetched result set, this cursor variable again opens and fetches for the first row of the DEPARTMENTS table, returning two column values and printing them as shown below.

```
DECLARE
  l_rc_var1 sys_refcursor;
  l_n_var1  NUMBER;
  l_vc_var2 VARCHAR2(50);
BEGIN
  OPEN l_rc_var1 FOR SELECT employee_id,last_name||', '||first_name FROM
  employees
  FETCH
    FIRST 1 row only;
  FETCH
    l_rc_var1
  INTO
    l_n_var1,
    l_vc_var2;
  dbms_output.put_line(l_n_var1||' '||l_vc_var2);
  OPEN l_rc_var1 FOR SELECT department_id,
  department_name FROM departments
  FETCH
    FIRST 1 row only;
  FETCH
    l_rc_var1
  INTO
    l_n_var1,
    l_vc_var2;
  dbms_output.put_line(l_n_var1||' '||l_vc_var2);
  CLOSE l_rc_var1;
END;
/
```

Result:

```
100 King, Steven
10 Administration
```

Oracle's 12c enhancement, the functional WITH clause fails when we try to open it
statically either through an explicit cursor or through a Ref-Cursor. The below PL/SQL
unit fails while trying to open the weak Ref-Cursor for a functional WITH clause with
an *ORA-00905: missing keyword* error as shown below.

```
DECLARE
  l_rc_var1 sys_refcursor;
BEGIN
  OPEN l_rc_var1 FOR
WITH
  FUNCTION func RETURN sys.odcinumberlist IS l_ntt_var1 sys.odcinumberlist;
BEGIN
  SELECT
    level bulk collect
  INTO
    l_ntt_var1
  FROM
    dual
    CONNECT BY level<10;
  RETURN l_ntt_var1;
END;
SELECT
  *
FROM
  TABLE(func);
END;
/
```

```
Error report -

ORA-06550: line 6, column 12:
PL/SQL: ORA-00905: missing keyword
ORA-06550: line 5, column 1:
PL/SQL: SQL Statement ignored
06550. 00000 -  "line %s, column %s:\n%s"
*Cause:    Usually a PL/SQL compilation error.
*Action:
```

However, when the functional WITH clause is opened dynamically either using a strong or a weak Ref-Cursor, the program unit compiles and runs as expected. In the below listing, the functional WITH clause returning 10 rows of sequence numbers is opened dynamically and loop-fetched to print them horizontally using the PUT and the NEW_LINE procedures as shown below.

```
DECLARE
  l_rc_var1 sys_refcursor;
  l_n_var2 NUMBER;
BEGIN
  OPEN l_rc_var1 FOR
  'WITH
  FUNCTION func RETURN sys.odcinumberlist IS l_ntt_var1 sys.odcinumberlist;
BEGIN
  SELECT
    level bulk collect
  INTO
    l_ntt_var1
  FROM
    dual
    CONNECT BY level<=10;
  RETURN l_ntt_var1;
END;
SELECT
  *
FROM
  TABLE(func)';
  LOOP
    FETCH
      l_rc_var1
    INTO
      l_n_var2;
    EXIT
  WHEN l_rc_var1%notfound;
    dbms_output.put(l_n_var2||' ');
  END LOOP;
 dbms_output.new_line;
END;
/
```

Result:

```
1 2 3 4 5 6 7 8 9 10
```

Cursor Expression as Nested Cursors

A cursor can be nested into an SQL statement using the CURSOR expression. The CURSOR expressions are made available in PL/SQL from the Oracle version 9i and are majorly used for returning a complex parent-child data in the form of cursors in a single query.

The below SQL statement converts the EMPLOYEES table into a cursor and nests it to each corresponding department that the employees fall on.

```
SELECT
    d.department_id,
    d.department_name,
    CURSOR
    (
      SELECT
        employee_id,
        last_name
        ||','
        ||first_name
      FROM
        employees e
      WHERE
        e.department_id=d.department_id
    ) EMP_CUR
  FROM
    departments d;
```

The internal structure of how the above SQL data resides is shown in the below table.

DEPARTMENT_ID	DEPARTMENT_NAME	EMP_CUR
10	Administration	The Ref-Cursor result of the employee ID(s): 200.
20	Marketing	The Ref-Cursor result of the employee ID(s): 201, 202.
30	Purchasing	The Ref-Cursor result of the employee ID(s): 114, 115, 116, 117, 118, 119.
...	...	...
...	...	...

In the below anonymous block, the SQL query nesting the EMPLOYEES result set with the DEPARTMENTS table using the CURSOR expression is used in an explicit cursor. This cursor is then looped for fetching all the department IDs, names, and its associated employee information in the form of Ref-Cursors. This Ref-Cursor result set is then fetched again using a nested loop, printing both the employee and their corresponding department information using the PUT_LINE procedure as shown in the below example.

```
DECLARE
  l_n_dept_id    NUMBER;
  l_vc_dept_name VARCHAR2(30);
  l_rc_emp sys_refcursor;
type type_rec
IS
  record
  (
    employee_id    NUMBER,
    employee_name VARCHAR2(100));
  l_rt_emp type_rec;
  CURSOR cur
  IS
    SELECT
      d.department_id,
      d.department_name,
      CURSOR
      (
        SELECT
          employee_id,
          last_name
          ||', '
          ||first_name
        FROM
          employees e
        WHERE
          e.department_id=d.department_id
      )
  FROM
    departments d;
BEGIN
  OPEN cur;
  LOOP
    FETCH cur INTO l_n_dept_id, l_vc_dept_name, l_rc_emp;
    EXIT
  WHEN cur%notfound;
    LOOP
      FETCH l_rc_emp INTO l_rt_emp;
      EXIT
    WHEN l_rc_emp%notfound;
      dbms_output.put_line('Emp ID- '||l_rt_emp.employee_id||'; Emp Name-
'||l_rt_emp.employee_name||'; Dept ID- '||l_n_dept_id||'; Dept Name- '||
      l_vc_dept_name);
    END LOOP;
  END LOOP;
  CLOSE cur;
END;
/
```

Result:

```
Emp ID- 200; Emp Name- Whalen, Jennifer; Dept ID- 10; Dept Name-
Administration
Emp ID- 201; Emp Name- Hartstein, Michael; Dept ID- 20; Dept Name- Marketing
Emp ID- 202; Emp Name- Fay, Pat; Dept ID- 20; Dept Name- Marketing
...
```

...

...

Cursor Expression as Arguments

The below example shows us how the Ref-Cursors can be used as an input parameter for sub-routines. An object type TYPE_OBJ with EMPLOYEE table's structure is created as shown below.

```
CREATE OR REPLACE type type_obj
IS
  object
  (
    EMPLOYEE_ID     NUMBER(6,0),
    FIRST_NAME      VARCHAR2(20),
    LAST_NAME       VARCHAR2(25),
    EMAIL           VARCHAR2(25),
    PHONE_NUMBER    VARCHAR2(20),
    HIRE_DATE       DATE,
    JOB_ID          VARCHAR2(10),
    SALARY          NUMBER(8,2),
    COMMISSION_PCT  NUMBER(2,2),
    MANAGER_ID      NUMBER(6,0),
    DEPARTMENT_ID   NUMBER(4,0));
/
```

A nested table type TYPE_NTT is created over the object type TYPE_OBJ using the below script.

```
CREATE OR REPLACE type type_ntt
IS
  TABLE OF type_obj;
/
```

In the below example, the function FUNC_REFCUR accepts a Ref-Cursor input and returns a nested table type of EMPLOYEE table structure. The function's body fetches all the records from the Ref-Cursor's result set and assigns it to the record type L_RT_EMP of EMPLOYEE table structure, which is in turn assigned to the nested table type.

```
CREATE OR REPLACE FUNCTION func_refcur(
    ip_rc_emp pkg_refcur.type_refcur)
  RETURN type_ntt
IS
  l_rt_emp employees%rowtype;
  l_ntt_emp type_ntt      :=type_ntt();
  l_pi_counter pls_integer:=0;
BEGIN
  LOOP
    l_pi_counter:=l_pi_counter+1;
```

```
    FETCH
      ip_rc_emp
    INTO
      l_rt_emp;
    EXIT
  WHEN ip_rc_emp%notfound;
    l_ntt_emp.extend;
    l_ntt_emp(l_pi_counter):=type_obj(l_rt_emp.EMPLOYEE_ID,
l_rt_emp.FIRST_NAME, l_rt_emp.LAST_NAME, l_rt_emp.EMAIL,
l_rt_emp.PHONE_NUMBER, l_rt_emp.HIRE_DATE, l_rt_emp.JOB_ID, l_rt_emp.SALARY,
l_rt_emp.COMMISSION_PCT,l_rt_emp.MANAGER_ID, l_rt_emp.DEPARTMENT_ID);
  END LOOP;
RETURN l_ntt_emp;
END;
/
```

In the below SQL, the function is enclosed within the TABLE expression, which
converts the nested table type result into a table like structure. This function accepts an
SQL statement enclosed within the CURSOR expression as its input parameter, which
converts an SQL into a nested cursor that can be passed as Ref-Cursor argument to a
function. The enclosed SQL statement is on the EMPLOYEES table for the
department ID 60 and the function return the result set in a table-like structure for the
Ref-Cursor input as shown below.

```
SELECT * FROM TABLE(func_refcur(CURSOR(SELECT * FROM employees WHERE
department_id=60)));
```

Script Output:

EMPLOYEE_ID	FIRST_NAME	LAST_NAME	EMAIL	PHONE_NUMBER	HIRE_DATE	JOB_ID	SALARY	COMMISSION_PCT	MANAGER_ID	DEPARTMENT_ID
103	Alexander	Hunold	AHUNOLD	590.423.4567	03-JAN-06	IT_PROG	9000		102	60
104	Bruce	Ernst	BERNST	590.423.4568	21-MAY-07	IT_PROG	6000		103	60
105	David	Austin	DAUSTIN	590.423.4569	25-JUN-05	IT_PROG	4800		103	60
106	Valli	Pataballa	VPATABAL	590.423.4560	05-FEB-06	IT_PROG	4800		103	60
107	Diana	Lorentz	DLORENTZ	590.423.5567	07-FEB-07	IT_PROG	4200		103	60

TO_REFCURSOR

This function was added to the DBMS_SQL package in the Oracle release version 11 for converting a DBMS_SQL cursor ID into a weakly typed Ref-Cursor variable.

The structure of the TO_REFCURSOR function defined in the DBMS_SQL package is shown below,

```
DBMS_SQL.TO_REFCURSOR (ip_i_cursor_id IN INTEGER)
RETURN SYS_REFCURSOR;
```

Before we try to convert a DBMS_SQL cursor ID into a Ref-Cursor, it must be opened, parsed and executed. Otherwise, we might end up getting an error during its conversion.

 Note: Once we have the DBMS_SQL cursor ID converted into a Ref-Cursor, the DBMS_SQL cursor ID will be no longer of any use and we can access the cursor result set only from the resultant Ref-Cursor variable.

This function comes in handy when we know the structure of the cursor result set that is being processed, but we are unaware of the number or the types of bind variables which are used in the SQL statement. The DBMS_SQL package is used until we process the bind variables and then the control of the cursor is moved to the Ref-Cursor, from where the fetching and processing of the result set takes place.

In the below example, The DBMS_SQL package is used for parsing, binding a dynamic SQL statement with a pre-known return structure and then executing it. Once the cursor is executed, it is converted into a weakly typed Ref-Cursor for further fetching and processing.

```
DECLARE
  l_n_cursor_id NUMBER;
  l_n_bind_value number:=90;
  l_rc_var1 SYS_REFCURSOR;
  l_n_rowcount NUMBER;
  l_rt_emp EMPLOYEES%ROWTYPE;
BEGIN
  l_n_cursor_id := DBMS_SQL.open_cursor;
  DBMS_SQL.parse(l_n_cursor_id, 'SELECT * FROM EMPLOYEES WHERE
DEPARTMENT_ID=:DEPARTMENT_ID', DBMS_SQL.NATIVE);
  dbms_sql.bind_variable(l_n_cursor_id,':DEPARTMENT_ID',l_n_bind_value);
  l_n_rowcount := DBMS_SQL.EXECUTE(l_n_cursor_id);
  l_rc_var1    := DBMS_SQL.to_refcursor(l_n_cursor_id);
  LOOP
    FETCH
```

```
        l_rc_var1
    INTO
        l_rt_emp;
    EXIT
    WHEN l_rc_var1%notfound;
        dbms_output.put_line('Emp ID: '||l_rt_emp.employee_id||' Emp Name: '||
        l_rt_emp.last_name||', '||l_rt_emp.first_name);
    END LOOP;
    CLOSE l_rc_var1;
END;
/
```

Result:

```
Emp ID: 100 Emp Name: King, Steven
Emp ID: 101 Emp Name: Kochhar, Neena
Emp ID: 102 Emp Name: De Haan, Lex
```

TO_CURSOR_NUMBER

This function was added to the DBMS_SQL package in the Oracle release version 11 for converting either a strong or a weakly typed Ref-Cursor variable into an SQL cursor number, that can be processed by the DBMS_SQL package.

The structure of the TO_CURSOR_NUMBER function defined in the DBMS_SQL package is shown below,

```
DBMS_SQL.TO_CURSOR_NUMBER (ip_rc_var1 IN OUT SYS_REFCURSOR)
RETURN INTEGER;
```

This function is useful when we have a Ref-Cursor variable with an unknown return structure (A weakly typed Ref-Cursor). In the below example, a Ref-Cursor variable for which the names of the columns of their result set are known, but not their order or types, is converted into a DBMS_SQL cursor number using the TO_CURSOR_NUMBER function. The DESCRIBE_COLUMNS procedure then helps in defining the random appearing columns to their appropriate variables. After all the columns are defined, they are fetched and assigned to their appropriate variables for each row found from the cursor result set. Finally, the assigned variables are printed using the PUT_LINE procedure as shown in the below snippet.

```
DECLARE
    l_rc_var1 SYS_REFCURSOR;
    l_n_cursor_id       NUMBER;
    l_n_rowcount        NUMBER;
    l_n_column_count NUMBER;
    l_vc_first_name    VARCHAR2(30);
    l_vc_last_name     VARCHAR2(30);
```

```
  l_vc_employee_id VARCHAR2(30);
  l_ntt_desc_tab dbms_sql.desc_tab;
BEGIN
  OPEN l_rc_var1 FOR
  'SELECT EMPLOYEE_ID, FIRST_NAME, LAST_NAME FROM EMPLOYEES WHERE
EMPLOYEE_ID in (190, 191, 192, 193, 194)';
  l_n_cursor_id:= DBMS_SQL.to_cursor_number(l_rc_var1);
  dbms_sql.describe_columns(l_n_cursor_id,l_n_column_count,l_ntt_desc_tab);
  FOR loop_col IN 1..l_n_column_count
  LOOP
    dbms_sql.define_column(l_n_cursor_id,loop_col,
    CASE l_ntt_desc_tab(loop_col).col_name
    WHEN 'EMPLOYEE_ID' THEN
      l_vc_employee_id
    WHEN 'FIRST_NAME' THEN
      l_vc_first_name
    WHEN 'LAST_NAME' THEN
      l_vc_last_name
    END,50);
  END LOOP loop_col;
  LOOP
    l_n_rowcount:=dbms_sql.fetch_rows(l_n_cursor_id);
    EXIT
  WHEN l_n_rowcount=0;
    FOR loop_col IN 1..l_n_column_count
    LOOP
      CASE l_ntt_desc_tab(loop_col).col_name
      WHEN 'EMPLOYEE_ID' THEN
        dbms_sql.column_value(l_n_cursor_id,loop_col,l_vc_employee_id);
      WHEN 'FIRST_NAME' THEN
        dbms_sql.column_value(l_n_cursor_id,loop_col,l_vc_first_name);
      WHEN 'LAST_NAME' THEN
        dbms_sql.column_value(l_n_cursor_id,loop_col,l_vc_last_name);
      END CASE;
    END LOOP loop_col;
    dbms_output.put_line('Emp ID: '||l_vc_employee_id||' Emp Name: '||
    l_vc_last_name||', '||l_vc_first_name);
  END LOOP;
END;
/
```

Result:

```
Emp ID: 190 Emp Name: Gates, Timothy
Emp ID: 191 Emp Name: Perkins, Randall
Emp ID: 192 Emp Name: Bell, Sarah
Emp ID: 193 Emp Name: Everett, Britney
Emp ID: 194 Emp Name: McCain, Samuel
```

Implicit Result Sets in 12c

The implicit result sets are introduced in the Oracle version 12c to support the bare-bone SELECT statements to pass back their result sets to the client environments without the need of using either an INTO clause, a BULK COLLECT INTO clause, a FETCH clause, a cursor FOR loop or a Ref-Cursor for this purpose.

Prior to the Oracle release 12c, we are required to define *n* number of Ref-Cursors as OUT parameters to return *n* number of result sets. The implicit result set approach is adopted by many other databases that they can have procedures returning multiple kinds of results that are decided during their run time. When we plan for a migration between a non-Oracle and an Oracle database, this difference might end up making us do some vigorous changes to our and client procedures. The introduction of implicit result sets in Oracle eases the data migration between the applications supporting Oracle and non-Oracle databases without the need of changing our or client procedures.

This can be achieved by two newly introduced procedures in the DBMS_SQL package. They are RETURN_RESULT (For returning Ref-Cursor or DBMS_SQL cursor) and GET_NEXT_RESULT (For processing the implicit result sets in PL/SQL), which are explained below.

RETURN_RESULT

This procedure allows us to pass the Ref-Cursors or the DBMS_SQL cursor numbers implicitly rather than wanting us to define them explicitly as OUT parameters. There are two overloading procedures, one accepting a Ref-Cursor input and the other one accepting a DBMS_SQL cursor number input.

The structure of the RETURN_RESULT procedure accepting a Ref-Cursor as its input is shown below,

```
PROCEDURE RETURN_RESULT (
    IP_RC_VAR1 IN OUT SYS_REFCURSOR,
    OP_B_VAR2 IN BOOLEAN DEFAULT TRUE);
```

In the below example, a Ref-Cursor is opened for an SQL statement, which is then passed as input to the RETURN_RESULT procedure for implicitly returning the result set without needing any OUT parameters. There is actually no limit on the number of implicit result sets returned by a procedure, thus the same Ref-Cursor variable is opened again for another SQL statement, which also returns its result set implicitly using the same API.

```
CREATE OR REPLACE PROCEDURE proc_return_result
IS
  l_rc_var1 SYS_REFCURSOR;
BEGIN
  OPEN l_rc_var1 FOR SELECT employee_id, last_name||' '||first_name
  employee_name, email FROM employees;
  DBMS_SQL.RETURN_RESULT(l_rc_var1);
  OPEN l_rc_var1 FOR SELECT department_id, department_name FROM departments;
  DBMS_SQL.RETURN_RESULT(l_rc_var1);
```

```
END;
/
```

The structure of the RETURN_RESULT procedure accepting a DBMS_SQL cursor number input is shown below,

```
PROCEDURE RETURN_RESULT (
    IP_I_VAR1 IN OUT INTEGER,
    OP_B_VAR2 IN BOOLEAN DEFAULT TRUE);
```

In the below listing, the first SQL statement is opened, parsed and then executed using the DBMS_SQL APIs, which then implicitly returns its result set using the RETURN_RESULT procedure. The second SQL statement then returns its result set implicitly in the similar to the first SQL.

```
CREATE OR REPLACE PROCEDURE proc_return_result
IS
  l_n_rowcount  NUMBER;
  l_n_cursor_id NUMBER:=DBMS_SQL.open_cursor;
BEGIN
  DBMS_SQL.parse(l_n_cursor_id, 'SELECT employee_id, last_name||''
''||first_name employee_name, email FROM employees', DBMS_SQL.NATIVE);
  l_n_rowcount := DBMS_SQL.EXECUTE(l_n_cursor_id);
  DBMS_SQL.RETURN_RESULT(l_n_cursor_id);
  DBMS_SQL.parse(l_n_cursor_id, 'SELECT department_id, department_name FROM
departments', DBMS_SQL.NATIVE);
  l_n_rowcount := DBMS_SQL.EXECUTE(l_n_cursor_id);
  DBMS_SQL.RETURN_RESULT(l_n_cursor_id);
END;
/
```

Note that this procedure has neither input nor output parameters. When this procedure is executed, they implicitly return the result sets of their SQL statements in their corresponding order as shown below.

> 🔔 Note: The implicit result sets returned does not rely on the server output/ DBMS_OUTPUT package.

```
BEGIN
  proc_return_result;
END;
/
```

Result:

ResultSet #1

```
EMPLOYEE_ID EMPLOYEE_NAME     EMAIL
----------- ----------------  --------
100         King Steven       SKING
101         Kochhar Neena     NKOCHHAR
102         De Haan Lex       LDEHAAN
103         Hunold Alexander  AHUNOLD
...
...
...

107 rows selected

ResultSet #2

DEPARTMENT_ID DEPARTMENT_NAME
------------- ---------------
10            Administration
20            Marketing
30            Purchasing
40            Human Resources
50            Shipping
...
...
...

27 rows selected

PL/SQL procedure successfully completed.
```

GET_NEXT_RESULT

The result sets generated by the RETURN_RESULT API is meant to be processed by a client programming language, like C or Java, but they can also be processed in PL/SQL by using the GET_NEXT_RESULT procedure in the DBMS_SQL package.

There are two overloaded GET_NEXT_RESULT APIs in the DBM_SQL package. The first one returns a DBMS_SQL cursor number and the other returns a Ref-Cursor, for processing the returned result sets.

In the below anonymous block, the first overloaded procedure GET_NEXT_RESULT, returning a DBMS_SQL cursor number is used for processing the result set when we only know their column names but not their order or data type. Firstly, the cursor is opened, parsed and executed for the procedure returning implicit result sets. As we are unsure about the number of implicit result sets returned by the procedure, we loop the GET_NEXT_RESULT API until we fetch all the result sets' DBMS_SQL cursor number. Considering we are aware of the result set's column names but not their order or type, the DESCRIBE_COLUMNS API from the DBMS_SQL package helps us in defining (DEFINE_COLUMN API), fetching (FETCH_ROWS) and assigning (COLUMN_VALUE API) the result set columns to their appropriate variables, which is then printed using the PUT_LINE procedure as shown below.

```
DECLARE
  l_pi_cursor PLS_INTEGER;
  l_n_cursor_id NUMBER;
  l_n_rowcount PLS_INTEGER;
  l_pi_return PLS_INTEGER;
  l_n_column_count PLS_INTEGER;
  l_ntt_desc_tab DBMS_SQL.desc_tab;
  l_n_count              NUMBER:=0;
  l_vc_employee_name    VARCHAR2(30);
  l_vc_email            VARCHAR2(30);
  l_vc_employee_id      VARCHAR2(30);
  l_vc_department_id    VARCHAR2(30);
  l_vc_department_name VARCHAR2(30);
BEGIN
  l_pi_cursor := DBMS_SQL.open_cursor(TRUE);
  DBMS_SQL.parse(l_pi_cursor, 'BEGIN proc_return_result; END;',
DBMS_SQL.native);
  l_pi_return := DBMS_SQL.execute(l_pi_cursor);
  LOOP
    l_n_count:=l_n_count+1;
    BEGIN
      DBMS_SQL.get_next_result(l_pi_cursor, l_n_cursor_id);
    EXCEPTION
    WHEN NO_DATA_FOUND THEN
      EXIT;
    END;
    dbms_output.put_line('Result set #'||l_n_count);
    dbms_output.put_line('-------------');
dbms_sql.describe_columns(l_n_cursor_id,l_n_column_count,l_ntt_desc_tab);
    FOR loop_col IN 1..l_n_column_count
    LOOP
      dbms_sql.define_column(l_n_cursor_id,loop_col,
      CASE l_ntt_desc_tab(loop_col).col_name
      WHEN 'EMPLOYEE_ID' THEN
        l_vc_employee_id
      WHEN 'EMPLOYEE_NAME' THEN
        l_vc_employee_name
      WHEN 'EMAIL' THEN
        l_vc_email
      WHEN 'DEPARTMENT_ID' THEN
        l_vc_department_id
      WHEN 'DEPARTMENT_NAME' THEN
        l_vc_department_name
      END,50);
    END LOOP loop_col;
    LOOP
      l_n_rowcount:=dbms_sql.fetch_rows(l_n_cursor_id);
      EXIT
    WHEN l_n_rowcount=0;
      FOR loop_col IN 1..l_n_column_count
      LOOP
        CASE l_ntt_desc_tab(loop_col).col_name
        WHEN 'EMPLOYEE_ID' THEN
          dbms_sql.column_value(l_n_cursor_id,loop_col,l_vc_employee_id);
        WHEN 'EMPLOYEE_NAME' THEN
          dbms_sql.column_value(l_n_cursor_id,loop_col,l_vc_employee_name);
        WHEN 'EMAIL' THEN
          dbms_sql.column_value(l_n_cursor_id,loop_col,l_vc_email);
        WHEN 'DEPARTMENT_ID' THEN
```

```
        dbms_sql.column_value(l_n_cursor_id,loop_col,l_vc_department_id);
      WHEN 'DEPARTMENT_NAME' THEN
        dbms_sql.column_value(l_n_cursor_id,loop_col,l_vc_department_name);
      END CASE;
    END LOOP loop_col;
    dbms_output.put_line(trim(both ',' from
(l_vc_employee_id||','||l_vc_employee_name||','
      || l_vc_email||','||l_vc_department_id||','||l_vc_department_name)));
      l_vc_employee_id      :=NULL;
      l_vc_employee_name    :=NULL;
      l_vc_email            :=NULL;
      l_vc_department_id    :=NULL;
      l_vc_department_name:=NULL;
    END LOOP;
  END LOOP;
END;
/
```

In the below anonymous block, the second overloaded procedure GET_NEXT_RESULT, returning a Ref-Cursor variable is used for processing the result set when we are very well aware of the structure of each result set returned. Firstly, the cursor is opened, parsed and executed for the procedure that returns the implicit result sets. As we are not sure about the number of implicit result sets returned by the procedure, we loop the GET_NEXT_RESULT API until we fetch all the result sets' Ref-Cursor variable. This Ref-Cursor variable is fetched into a record type of its appropriate structure for every result set and then printed for display using the PUT_LINE procedure as shown below.

```
DECLARE
  l_pi_cursor PLS_INTEGER;
  l_rc_var1 SYS_REFCURSOR;
  l_return PLS_INTEGER;
  l_n_count NUMBER:=0;
type type_emp_rec
IS
  record
  (
    employee_id   VARCHAR2(30),
    employee_name VARCHAR2(30),
    email         VARCHAR2(30));
  l_rt_emp type_emp_rec;
type type_dept_rec
IS
  record
  (
    department_id   VARCHAR2(30),
    department_name VARCHAR2(30));
  l_rt_dept type_dept_rec;
BEGIN
  l_pi_cursor := DBMS_SQL.open_cursor(TRUE);
  DBMS_SQL.parse(l_pi_cursor, 'BEGIN proc_return_result; END;',
DBMS_SQL.native);
  l_return := DBMS_SQL.execute(l_pi_cursor);
  LOOP
```

```
      l_n_count:=l_n_count+1;
      BEGIN
        DBMS_SQL.get_next_result(l_pi_cursor, l_rc_var1);
      EXCEPTION
      WHEN NO_DATA_FOUND THEN
        EXIT;
      END;
      dbms_output.put_line('Result set #'||l_n_count);
      dbms_output.put_line('-------------');
      IF l_n_count=1 THEN
        LOOP
          FETCH
            l_rc_var1
          INTO
            l_rt_emp;
          EXIT
        WHEN l_rc_var1%notfound;
dbms_output.put_line(l_rt_emp.employee_id||','||l_rt_emp.employee_name
          ||','||l_rt_emp.email);
        END LOOP;
      elsif l_n_count=2 THEN
        LOOP
          FETCH
            l_rc_var1
          INTO
            l_rt_dept;
          EXIT
        WHEN l_rc_var1%notfound;
          dbms_output.put_line(l_rt_dept.department_id||','||
          l_rt_dept.department_name);
        END LOOP;
      ELSE
        dbms_output.put_line('Unknown Result set!!');
      END IF;
    END LOOP;
END;
/
```

Result:

```
Result set #1
-------------
100,King Steven,SKING
101,Kochhar Neena,NKOCHHAR
102,De Haan Lex,LDEHAAN
103,Hunold Alexander,AHUNOLD
...
...
...

Result set #2
-------------
10,Administration
20,Marketing
30,Purchasing
40,Human Resources
50,Shipping
...
...
...
```

Restrictions in the Reference Cursors

1. A Ref-Cursor variable cannot be declared in a package specification as a global entity. Instead, a Ref-Cursor type can be declared in a package specification and can be accessed globally.

2. The Ref-Cursor variables cannot be shared across servers using remote procedure calls.

3. The SELECT statement associated to a Ref-Cursor in an OPEN FOR statement cannot contain the FOR UPDATE clause.

4. The Ref-Cursor variables do not support any operator testing, i.e., arithmetic or comparison operators cannot be used for these variables.

5. The Ref-Cursor variables cannot be made as a column or attribute data type for tables, views, nested table types, associative array types, and VARRAYs. These variables enjoy its life until it closes, either explicitly by the programmers or implicitly when the session terminates.

6. They cannot be assigned with a *null*.

Summary

We have started our chapter by understanding the cursor fundamentals, their execution cycle, and attributes. In the next section, we learned the implicit cursors and their different types based on the number of rows they process along with the implicit cursor FOR loop. The next section taught us about the explicit cursors, their different types and how they can be parameterized. The final section explained us about the reference cursors, their types in detail. This section continued to explain us about the cursor expressions used as nested cursors and as arguments with sufficient examples, followed by the 11g introduced APIs for converting the cursor control between the Ref-Cursor and the DBMS_SQL cursor number and vice versa. The next portion of the section explained us in detail about the implicit result sets which are made available in Oracle release 12c for implicitly returning the result sets. The final section ended by showing us the restrictions in the reference cursors in Oracle.

The next chapter will teach us about the different cryptographic techniques available in Oracle for encrypting and decrypting the data.

Advanced Security Methods in PL/SQL

In this chapter, we are going to learn about the advanced security methods available in Oracle with lot many examples and facts so that we can be sure of what we need to do when we are in need of securing our precious data. This chapter consists of the below topics in detail.

28. Introduction to the Oracle Advanced Security Options like Transparent Data Encryption and Data Redaction with sufficient examples.

29. Introduction to Oracle Virtual Private Database (OVPD) and Fine-Grained Access Control Protocol for imposing row level security on the database tables and views.

30. Introduction to Cryptography in Oracle using the DBMS_CRYPTO package, its components, and its comparison with its predecessor, the DBMS_OBFUSCATION_TOOLKIT package.

31. Managing security using the definer's and invoker's rights for protecting the access rights of the database objects, along with their 12c enhancements.

Introduction to Oracle Advanced Security

To comply with the privacy regulations of data security, the Oracle Advanced Security has provided the below two features,

1. **Transparent Data Encryption** is used for encrypting the personal information such as Personal Account Numbers, Social Security Numbers, Credit Card Numbers, while at rest.

2. **Data Redaction** is used for masking the sensitive personal application data on the fly before leaving the database having them unaltered in the storage.

Introduction to Transparent Data Encryption

Transparent Data Encryption was introduced in the Oracle database version 10g R2 as a "data-at-rest" protection technique for encrypting sensitive data within the data files to prevent access to it outside the database. Oracle uses authentication, authorization and auditing mechanisms to secure its data inside the database, but not at the disk level, which is stored in the operating system. Oracle's Advanced Security Transparent Data Encryption (TDE) stops the attackers from circumventing the database and accessing sensitive information from the data files in the database layer at the Operating System level. However, at the same time these data are transparently decrypted and made available to the authorized applications and database users.

The TDE can encrypt individual database table columns or complete database tablespaces. TDE column and tablespace encryption use 2-tiered key-based architecture to transparently encrypt and decrypt the sensitive table columns and tablespaces respectively. The master encryption key is stored in an external security module, which can be either an Oracle software keystore (Software Security Module) or a hardware keystore (Hardware Security Module). Keystore is called as database wallet prior to the Oracle 12c release. This master encryption key (keystore) encrypts and decrypts the TDE table key or the tablespace key, which in turn encrypts and decrypts the database column or tablespace data respectively. The TDE is one of a kind in encrypting the entire storage of volumes by,

1. Protecting against many by-pass attacks.

2. It does not require any application changes as the application users can directly access the decrypted data.

3. Providing full key lifecycle management and switches to a new master key with no downtime by a simple key management technique.

4. Integrating with complementary technologies such as Oracle Multitenant, Oracle Advanced Compression, and Oracle Recovery Manager.

Transparent Data Encryption Components

There are two components of TDE. They are,

Transparent Data Encryption (TDE) Column Encryption

Transparent Data Encryption (TDE) column encryption can be used for encrypting a specific column data in the database tables that are confidential, such as credit card numbers, social security numbers (SSN) and personal account numbers (PAN). This approach is useful when,

1. The database tables are large in size.

2. The columns holding the sensitive information are pre-known.

Oracle Enterprise Manager Sensitive Data Discovery searches for sensitive data and finds them quickly, which can be then used for encryption. These encrypted columns remain encrypted even if the storage drives are amputated by the unauthorized professionals.

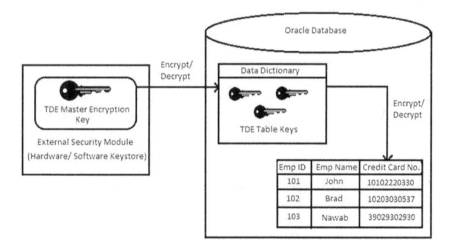

Fig 8.1. TDE Column Encryption

In the above figure, the TDE master encryption key is stored outside the database in an external security module, which is accessible only to authorized professionals and the TDE table keys are stored in the data dictionary encrypted by the master encryption key, which is then responsible for encrypting and decrypting the column data. One table key is uniquely created for a table containing one or more encrypted column. The master encryption key stored in the external security module uses an Oracle keystore, which was called as a wallet in the previous releases.

> Note: The table key is also called as a column key. This key is used for encrypting one or more columns in a database table, which is then stored in the Oracle data dictionary, encrypted with the master encryption key.

Transparent Data Encryption (TDE) Tablespace Encryption

Transparent Data Encryption (TDE) Tablespace encryption can be used for encrypting an entire tablespace. When we encrypt a tablespace, all of its objects are encrypted automatically. This method is useful when,

1.   When we want to protect an entire table and not just a few columns.

2.   When we have a lot of columns with sensitive data.

When we encrypt a tablespace, all of its data, like the undo logs and the redo logs are also protected. As the encryption occurs in bulk to all the objects in the tablespace, the performance is found to be enhanced through caching.

> Note: TDE Tablespace Encryption method does not encrypt data that are stored outside the database. For e.g., If we create a table with a BFILE column in an encrypted tablespace, this column may not be encrypted as the original content is stored in a directory outside the database.

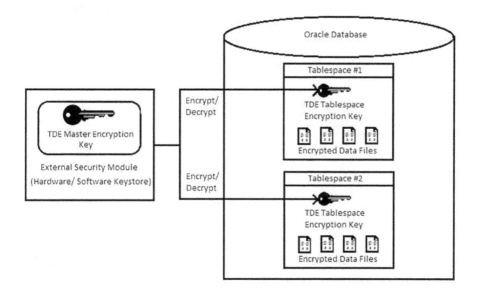

Fig 8.2. TDE Tablespace Encryption

In the above figure, the TDE master encryption key is stored outside the database in an external security module, whereas the TDE tablespace encryption key is stored in the header of the tablespace, that is encrypted with the master encryption key.

TDE tablespace encryption allows index range scans on the columns in its encrypted tablespace, which is not possible through TDE column encryption.

Managing Keystore and Encryption Keys

A software keystore acts similar to a container for storing the TDE master encryption keys. Below are the steps for managing the keystore and the encryption keys.

Step 1: Keystore Location Setup

Prior to creating a keystore, we must create its parent directory and configure it in the SQLNET.ORA as shown below,

```
ENCRYPTION_WALLET_LOCATION=
 (SOURCE=
  (METHOD=FILE)
   (METHOD_DATA=
    (DIRECTORY=OS_PATH_TO_KEYSTORE)))
```

If the directory is not configured in the SQLNET.ORA file, then the Oracle database looks for a keystore at the default location, which is *C:\ORACLE_HOME\<Database_name>\ADMIN\ORACLE\WALLET*.

> Note: In a multitenant environment, the keystore location is set for the entire multitenant container database (CDB), not for individual pluggable databases (PDBs).

The keystore location and its status can be verified by querying the V$ENCRYPTION_WALLET view.

- The WRL_PARAMETER column gives you the location.

- The STATUS column gives you the status of the keystore (NOT_AVAILABLE in case if there is no keystore available).

The following example shows how to configure a keystore location in SQLNET.ORA for a regular database system.

```
ENCRYPTION_WALLET_LOCATION=
 (SOURCE=
  (METHOD=FILE)
   (METHOD_DATA=
    (DIRECTORY=C:\ORACLE_HOME\<Database_name>\ADMIN\ORACLE\WALLET)))
```

Step 2: Software Keystore Creation

Once the keystore location is configured, we need to create a keystore to store the TDE master encryption keys. In a multi-tenant database environment, the keystore must be created in the ROOT container, which is shared by all the associated pluggable databases and by itself.

> Note: A keystore can be created by a database user, who has ADMINISTER KEY MANAGEMENT or an SYSKM privilege.

There are three types of software keystores. They are,

Password-Based Keystore

A password-based keystore requires a user password for protecting the master keys stored in the keystore.

The prototype for creating a keystore is shown below,

```
ADMINISTER KEY MANAGEMENT CREATE KEYSTORE '<Keystore_location>' IDENTIFIED
BY <Keystore_password>;
```

- **Keystore_location** is the path to the password-based keystore directory for which we want to create the keystore.

- **Keystore_password** is the password for the keystore.

For example, the below script helps us to create a keystore in the *C:\app\BoobalGanesan\admin\oracle\wallet* directory,

```
ADMINISTER KEY MANAGEMENT CREATE KEYSTORE
'C:\app\BoobalGanesan\admin\oracle\wallet' IDENTIFIED BY oracle;
```

After creating the keystore, the *ewallet.p12* file appears in the keystore location.

[Local] Auto-Login Keystore

As an alternative to the password-based keystores, we have the *auto-login* or *local auto-login* keystores, that we can use for avoiding opening the keystores manually every time. The auto-login software keystore can be opened from different computers from the parent computer, where the keystore was originally created, but the local auto-login software keystore can be opened only from the computer on which it was created.

The prototype for creating a keystore is shown below,

```
ADMINISTER KEY MANAGEMENT CREATE [LOCAL] AUTO_LOGIN KEYSTORE FROM KEYSTORE
'<Keystore_location>' IDENTIFIED BY <Keystore_password>;
```

- **LOCAL** restricts us to create local auto-login software keystore. Omitting this clause will make the keystore available for other computers.

- **Keystore_location** is the path to the password-based keystore directory for which we want to create the keystore.

- **Keystore_password** is the password for the keystore.

For example, to create an auto-login software keystore in the
C:\app\BoobalGanesan\admin\oracle\wallet directory,

```
ADMINISTER KEY MANAGEMENT CREATE AUTO_LOGIN KEYSTORE FROM KEYSTORE
'\C:\app\BoobalGanesan\admin\oracle\wallet' IDENTIFIED BY oracle;
```

After executing the above statement, the *cwallet.sso* file appears in the keystore

> Note: The software wallet file *ewallet.p12* must not be removed after creating the auto-login keystore as it is required for regenerating the TDE master encryption key in the future.

location.

Step 3: Open the Software Keystore

We must manually open the password-based software keystore before creating or accessing any TDE master encryption key in the keystore. But, the auto-login and the local auto-login keystores need not be manually opened as they will be automatically opened when an encryption operation must access the key. If needed, these keystores can be explicitly closed. The status of whether a keystore is opened or not can be checked by querying the STATUS column of the V$ENCRYPTION_WALLET data dictionary view.

The prototype for opening a keystore is shown below,

```
ADMINISTER KEY MANAGEMENT SET KEYSTORE OPEN IDENTIFIED BY
<Keystore_password> [Container = All | Current];
```

- **Keystore_password** is the password of the keystore.

- **Container** is used for the multi-tenant database.

  → **All** is used for setting the keystore in all of the pluggable databases in this container database.

  → **Current** is used for setting the keystore only in the current PDB.

For example, the below statement opens the keystore created in the *Step-2*.

```
ADMINISTER KEY MANAGEMENT SET KEYSTORE OPEN IDENTIFIED BY oracle;
```

Note: The status column of the V$ENCRYPTION_WALLET view reminds us with an OPEN_NO_MASTER_KEY status as we have not created a TDE master encryption key yet.

Step 4: Set the TDE Master Encryption Key

Once the keystore is open, we can set up a TDE master encryption key inside of it. This key is automatically generated by the Oracle database and we don't get to choose it. This key is primarily used for protecting the TDE table and the tablespace encryption keys. In a multitenant database, we need to create the TDE master encryption key for both the container and its associated pluggable databases.

The prototype for setting up the TDE master encryption key is shown below,

```
ADMINISTER KEY MANAGEMENT SET KEY [USING TAG 'Tag'] IDENTIFIED BY
<Keystore_password> [WITH BACKUP [USING 'Backup_identifier']] [CONTAINER =
ALL | CURRENT];
```

- **Tag** is the associated attributes that are defined by us.

- **Keystore_password** is the password of the keystore.

- **With Backup** option is used for creating a backup for the keystore. The optional **Using** clause is used for adding additional comments for the backup.

- **Container** is used for the multi-tenant database.

  → **All** is used for setting the keystore in all of the pluggable databases in this container database.

  → **Current** is used for setting the keystore only in the current PDB.

The command below is used for creating a TDE master encryption key while taking a backup of the keystore.

```
ADMINISTER KEY MANAGEMENT SET KEY IDENTIFIED BY oracle WITH BACKUP;
```

 Note: Once the TDE master encryption key is created, the status column of the V$ENCRYPTION_WALLET view changes from OPEN_NO_MASTER_KEY to OPEN.

Step 5: Encrypting Data

After completing the above keystore configuration steps, we can encrypt our data either in individual table columns or in entire tablespaces.

By default, TDE encrypts the data using the AES 192bit encryption algorithm technique. The TDE also allows us to choose the encryption algorithm of our choice from the below list.

Supported Encryption Algorithms

Algorithm	Parameter Name
Triple DES (Data Encryption Standard) (168 bits)	3DES168
AES (Advanced Encryption Standard) (128 bits)	AES128
AES (192 bits) (Default)	AES198
AES (256 bits)	AES256

Encrypting Column Data

TDE encryption can be performed over a set of datatypes and the size of the column to be encrypted must not exceed the maximum size defined below.

- BINARY_DOUBLE
- BINARY_FLOAT
- CHAR (Maximum Size: 1932 bytes)
- DATE
- INTERVAL DAY TO SECOND
- INTERVAL YEAR TO MONTH
- NCHAR (Maximum Size: 966 bytes)
- NUMBER
- NVARCHAR2 (Maximum Size: 16,315 bytes)
- RAW (Maximum Size: 32,699 bytes)
- TIMESTAMP (Includes TIMESTAMP WITH LOCAL TIME ZONE and TIMESTAMP WITH TIME ZONE)
- VARCHAR2 (Maximum Size: 32,699 bytes)

To create database tables with encrypted columns, we must use the ENCRYPT clause in its column definition in the CREATE TABLE statement as shown in the below example.

```
CREATE
  TABLE customer
  (
    cust_id      NUMBER,
    cust_name    VARCHAR2(100),
    cust_email   VARCHAR2(50) encrypt,
    cust_phone   NUMBER encrypt,
    cust_address VARCHAR2(3000) encrypt
  );
```

The TDE by default adds SALT (adding extra characters) to the column before its encryption. Adding SALT makes it tough for the stealers who use brute force method. We can also choose whether or not to SALT our column data before encrypting it irrespective of whether or not other encrypted columns use SALT.

We can also choose any other encrypting algorithm from the available list and define it through the USING clause as shown below,

```
CREATE
  TABLE customer
  (
    cust_id      NUMBER,
    cust_name    VARCHAR2(100),
    cust_email   VARCHAR2(50) encrypt no salt,
    cust_phone   NUMBER encrypt,
    cust_address VARCHAR2(3000) encrypt USING 'AES256'
  );
```

> 🔔 Note: All the encrypted columns in a table must use the same encryption algorithm. If we try to use different encryption algorithms for multiple columns in the same table, we may encounter ORA-28340: a different encryption algorithm has been chosen for the table exception.

The ALTER TABLE command can be used for encrypting columns in an existing table by either adding an encrypted column or by encrypting an already existing column.

To add an encrypted column to an existing table in the database,

```
ALTER TABLE customer ADD (cust_ssn VARCHAR2(11) ENCRYPT USING 'AES256' salt);
```

To encrypt an existing column in a table in the database,

```
ALTER TABLE customer MODIFY (cust_name encrypt);
```

To decrypt an existing column in a table in the database,

```
ALTER TABLE customer MODIFY (cust_name decrypt);
```

To add SALT to an encrypted column in a table in the database,

```
ALTER TABLE customer MODIFY (cust_email encrypt salt);
```

To remove SALT from an encrypted column in a table in the database,

```
ALTER TABLE customer MODIFY (cust_email encrypt no salt);
```

To change the encrypted key for the table containing one or more encrypted column,

```
ALTER TABLE customer rekey;
```

To change the encryption algorithm for the table containing one or more encrypted column,

```
ALTER TABLE customer rekey USING '3DES168';
```

The TDE also adds a Message Authentication Code (MAC) to the data for integrity checking. The default integrity algorithm is SHA-1.

```
ALTER TABLE customer rekey USING '3DES168' 'SHA-1';
```

We can also use the parameter NOMAC for bypassing the integrity check, thus saving up to 20bytes of disk space per encrypted value.

```
ALTER TABLE customer rekey USING '3DES168' 'NOMAC';
```

> Note: If the encrypted column is being indexed, it must be specified without SALT. If not, we may encounter `ORA-28338: cannot encrypt indexed column(s) with salt` exception.

Encrypting Tablespace Data

We can encrypt a tablespace only during its creation. Unlike encrypting an existing column data, an already existing tablespace cannot be encrypted, however, we can import data into an encrypted tablespace by using the Oracle data pump.

The TDE tablespace encryption encrypts or decrypts the data during the read and write operations, thus they do not have any datatype or index type restrictions placed upon them.

> 🔔 Note: We cannot encrypt a TDE tablespace with NO SALT option.

To create an encrypted tablespace,

```
CREATE TABLESPACE encrypt_12c datafile
  'C:\app\BoobalGanesan\product\12.1.0\dbhome_1\dbs\encrypt.dbf' size 1M
  encryption USING 'AES256' DEFAULT STORAGE (ENCRYPT);
```

Where the ENCRYPTION USING clause specifies the encryption algorithm, which we can choose from the range of available algorithm discussed earlier. If this clause is omitted, the default algorithm AES128 will be used for encryption.

The DATAFILE location stores the encrypted data of the objects in this tablespace.

TDE Data Dictionary Objects

*_ENCRYPTED_COLUMNS

This view displays information about the encrypted columns in the tables as shown below,

OWNER	TABLE_NAME	COLUMN_NAME	ENCRYPTION_ALG	SALT	INTEGRITY_ALG
C##	CUSTOMER	CUST_EMAIL	3 Key Triple DES 168 bits key	NO	NOMAC
C##	CUSTOMER	CUST_PHONE	3 Key Triple DES 168 bits key	YES	NOMAC
C##	CUSTOMER	CUST_ADDRESS	3 Key Triple DES 168 bits key	YES	NOMAC
C##	CUSTOMER	CUST_SSN	3 Key Triple DES 168 bits key	YES	NOMAC

USER_TABLESPACES

This view displays the information about the available tablespaces where one of its columns, ENCRYPTED, describes whether or not the tablespace is encrypted. If it is NO, the tablespace is not encrypted and if it is YES, then the tablespace is encrypted.

V$ENCRYPTED_TABLESPACES

This view displays the information about the encrypted tablespaces.

V$ENCRYPTION_KEYS

This view displays the information about the TDE master encryption keys.

V$ENCRYPTION_WALLET

This view displays the information about the keystore location and its status for TDE.

Introduction to Data Redaction

The Oracle advanced security data redaction was introduced in the Oracle version 12c, (and back-ported to 11.2.0.4), to support the "on-the-go" redaction of private information in a database query result prior to its display so that the original data is not available for the unauthorized users. The redaction is highly transparent to the database because there is no alteration of the original data in its storage but only disguised just before its display. While the data is being redacted, Oracle database maintains the unaltered data and preserves its referential integrities.

We can specify the application users who should see the redacted data through the SYS_CONTEXT function and we can also redact the column data based on the database parameter of the current database or the application user.

Performance wise, data redaction has proven high performance as the expressions are evaluated only once per execution, thus avoiding per row performance impact.

Security wise, data redaction avoids any means of data leak by preventing all possible policy bypasses. For example, when we try to copy the redacted column data into another table or into an un-redacted column, we may encounter the *ORA-28081: Insufficient privileges - the command references a redacted object* exception. This behavior can also be overridden with the EXEMPT REDACTION POLICY system privilege.

These characteristics of Oracle data redaction make it well suited for a range of applications in reporting, monitoring and analytical data processing.

Oracle Redaction Policies

To redact a column data, we must choose a redaction policy. These policies define what type of, how, and when the redaction must take place. The redaction policy methods can fully redact, partially redact or randomly redact the column data. We can also define a policy only for testing them without any data redaction.

The redaction policy also supports a policy expression which either displays the original data or the redacted data to different application users based on the expression's result (Either True or False). For security reasons, the functions and operator used in the policy expression may contain only SYS_CONTEXT and few other sessions based system-defined functions. User defined functions are not allowed as of R12.1.

> Note: We must need the EXECUTE privilege on the DBMS_REDACT package for creating redaction policies.

Procedures list on the DBMS_REDACT package

Procedure Name	Purpose
DBMS_REDACT.ADD_POLICY	Adds a redaction policy to a table or a view.
DBMS_REDACT.ALTER_POLICY	Modifies a redaction policy. E.g., adding new columns to the policy group.
DBMS_REDACT.UPDATE_FULL_REDACTION_VALUES	Updates the full redaction value for a given data type globally. Database restart is required to after using this procedure.
DBMS_REDACT.ENABLE_POLICY	Enables a redaction policy.
DBMS_REDACT.DISABLE_POLICY	Disables a redaction policy.
DBMS_REDACT.DROP_POLICY	Drops a redaction policy.

DBMS_REDACT.ADD_POLICY

This procedure is used for creating a data redaction policy.

The prototype for defining the ADD_POLICY procedure is shown below,

```
DBMS_REDACT.ADD_POLICY (
  object_schema              IN VARCHAR2 := NULL,
  object_name                IN VARCHAR2 := NULL,
  policy_name                IN VARCHAR2,
  policy_description         IN VARCHAR2 := NULL,
  column_name                IN VARCHAR2 := NULL,
  column_description         IN VARCHAR2 := NULL,
  function_type              IN BINARY_INTEGER := DBMS_REDACT.FULL,
  function_parameters        IN VARCHAR2 := NULL,
  expression                 IN VARCHAR2,
  enable                     IN BOOLEAN := TRUE,
  regexp_pattern             IN VARCHAR2 := NULL,
  regexp_replace_string      IN VARCHAR2 := NULL,
  regexp_position            IN BINARY_INTEGER :=1,
  regexp_occurrence          IN BINARY_INTEGER :=0,
  regexp_match_parameter     IN VARCHAR2 := NULL);
```

- **Object_schema** specifies the schema of the object which undergoes the redaction policy. By default, Oracle uses the current user's name.

- **Object_name** specifies the name of the table or the view, that undergoes the redaction policy.

- **Policy_name** specifies the user-defined unique policy name for creating the policy.

- **Policy_description** specifies the user-defined comment for the policy.

- **Column_name** specifies the name of the column that has to be redacted.

  → Only one column can be allowed for redaction during the policy creation. If we want to redact more than one column, we must make use of the ALTER_POLICY procedure after creating the policy.

  → Only one policy can be defined on one table/ view.

  → If the column name is omitted, the policy will be created with no columns which can be later used upon one or more columns using the ALTER_POLICY procedure.

  → We cannot define a policy on a virtual column.

  → We cannot define a policy on a column that is a part of the Virtual Private Database policy function.

- **Column_description** specifies the user-defined comment on the column that is being redacted.

- **Function_type** specifies the function method that sets the type of redaction. By default, it is DBMS_REDACT.FULL.

- **Function_parameters** specifies how the redaction must appear in the partial redaction function type.

- **Expression** specifies a relational expression to determine whether or not to redact the column data. Redaction takes place only if this expression results into True.

- **Enable** specifies whether or not to enable the policy during its creation. After the policy is created, we can enable or disable it using the ENABLE_POLICY and DISABLE_POLICY procedures respectively.

  → **True:** Enables the policy after its creation.

  → **False:** Disables the policy after its creation.

- `Regexp_pattern, Regexp_replace_string, Regexp_position, Regexp_position, Regexp_occurrence, Regexp_match_parameter` allows us to use regular expressions to redact the data either fully or partially.

Redaction Methods

The data redaction can be performed by using any of the below methods that suit our business need.

Full Redaction Policy

This method redacts the entire contents of the column data based on its datatype. This is the default method when the *function_type* parameter is omitted during the policy creation.

By default,

1. The column data with *character data types* are redacted to a *single space*.

---

2. The column data with *number data types* are redacted to a *zero*.

3. The column data with *date-time data types* are redacted to the *01-January-2001*.

To set the *function_type* parameter to full redaction, we must enter its value as DBMS_REDACT.FULL during the policy creation or ignore it.

In the below script, a policy REDACT_EMPLOYEE_DATA is created over the EMAIL column in the EMPLOYEES table in the schema C## with its *function_type* as DBMS_REDACT.FULL. Thus the entire EMAIL column gets redacted to a single space, which is the default redaction value for a string column. As this policy is to be applied for every user, the expression "1=1" is used so that it always returns the boolean TRUE.

```
BEGIN
  DBMS_REDACT.ADD_POLICY(
    object_schema    => 'C##',
    object_name      => 'EMPLOYEES',
    column_name      => 'EMAIL',
    policy_name      => 'REDACT_EMPLOYEE_DATA',
    function_type    => DBMS_REDACT.FULL,
    expression       => '1=1');
END;
/
```

After the policy creation, when we query the EMPLOYEES table, we may see the EMAIL column being redacted to a single space value as shown below,

```
SELECT employee_id, first_name, last_name, email, phone_number, salary
FROM
  employees
FETCH
  FIRST 5 rows only;
```

Query Result:

EMPLOYEE_ID	FIRST_NAME	LAST_NAME	EMAIL	PHONE_NUMBER	SALARY
100	Steven	King		515.123.4567	24000
101	Neena	Kochhar		515.123.4568	17000
102	Lex	De Haan		515.123.4569	17000
103	Alexander	Hunold		590.423.4567	9000
104	Bruce	Ernst		590.423.4568	6000

When we try to query the EMPLOYEES table having a single space in its EMAIL column, no luck! We get no rows.

```
SELECT employee_id, first_name, last_name, email, phone_number, salary
FROM
  employees
where email=' ';
```

Result:

```
no rows selected
```

When we query the EMPLOYEES table with an actual EMAIL value, we get the exact record set pertaining to the EMAIL as shown below,

```
SELECT employee_id, first_name, last_name, email, phone_number, salary
FROM
  employees
where email='SKING';
```

Query Result:

EMPLOYEE_I D	FIRST_NAM E	LAST_NAM E	EMAI L	PHONE_NUMBE R	SALAR Y
100	Steven	King		515.123.4567	24000

Thus, as already discussed, the data is redacted only during the display time and not during parsing or fetching.

UPDATE_FULL_REDACTION_VALUES

The default value of the redacted column based on its datatype can be verified by querying the below table, which is common for all the policies in the entire database.

```
SELECT
  number_value,
  date_value,
  varchar_value
FROM
  REDACTION_VALUES_FOR_TYPE_FULL;
```

Query Result:

NUMBER_VALUE	DATE_VALUE	VARCHAR_VALUE
0	01-JAN-2001	(Single space)

To change this default value, we must login with a SYSDBA privilege and execute the below procedure with a user defined default value as shown below,

```
EXEC DBMS_REDACT.UPDATE_FULL_REDACTION_VALUES (number_val=>7,
date_val=>to_date('10-Feb-2001'), varchar_val=>'R');
```

Note: After we have made our changes through the above procedure execution, we must *restart* our database instance to make the changes reflect throughout the entire database.

ALTER_POLICY

To alter a data redaction policy that is available in the database, we must use the ALTER_POLICY procedure.

The prototype for altering a data redaction policy is shown below,

```
DBMS_REDACT.ALTER_POLICY (
    object_schema          IN VARCHAR2 := NULL,
    object_name            IN VARCHAR2 := NULL,
    policy_name            IN VARCHAR2,
    action                 IN BINARY_INTEGER := DBMS_REDACT.ADD_COLUMN,
    column_name            IN VARCHAR2 := NULL,
    function_type          IN BINARY_INTEGER := DBMS_REDACT.FULL,
    function_parameters    IN VARCHAR2 := NULL,
    expression             IN VARCHAR2 := NULL,
    regexp_pattern         IN VARCHAR2 := NULL,
    regexp_replace_string  IN VARCHAR2 := NULL,
    regexp_position        IN BINARY_INTEGER := NULL,
    regexp_occurrence      IN BINARY_INTEGER := NULL,
    regexp_match_parameter IN VARCHAR2 := NULL,
    policy_description     IN VARCHAR2 := NULL,
    column_description     IN VARCHAR2 := NULL);
```

- **Action** specifies the alteration action to be performed over the existing data redaction policy. We can choose from one of the actions shown below,

  → **DBMS_REDACT.MODIFY_COLUMN** is used when we want to change the *column_name* parameter value.

  → **DBMS_REDACT.ADD_COLUMN** is used when we want to add another column for redaction along with the existing columns. This is the default parameter value if not mentioned explicitly.

  → **DBMS_REDACT.DROP_COLUMN** is used when we want to remove a column from the redaction policy list.

  → **DBMS_REDACT.MODIFY_EXPRESSION** is used when we want to modify the expression used in the policy.

Advanced PL/SQL Programming

→ **DBMS_REDACT.SET_POLICY_DESCRIPTION** is used when we want to modify the description of the policy.

→ **DBMS_REDACT.SET_COLUMN_DESCRIPTION** is used when we want to modify the description of the column, which is mentioned in the *column_name* parameter value.

In the below code listing, we have added the column SALARY to the policy REDACT_EMPLOYEE_DATA by using the DBMS_REDACT.ADD_COLUMN action parameter value.

```
BEGIN
 DBMS_REDACT.ALTER_POLICY(
    object_schema         => 'C##',
    object_name           => 'EMPLOYEES',
    policy_name           => 'REDACT_EMPLOYEE_DATA',
    action                => DBMS_REDACT.ADD_COLUMN,
    column_name           => 'SALARY',
    function_type         => DBMS_REDACT.FULL);
END;
/
```

When we query the EMPLOYEE table again, we can see that the SALARY column is redacted to our new default value 7 as shown below.

```
SELECT employee_id, first_name, last_name, email, phone_number, salary
FROM
  employees
FETCH
  FIRST 5 rows only;
```

Query Result:

EMPLOYEE_ID	FIRST_NAME	LAST_NAME	EMAIL	PHONE_NUMBER	SALARY
100	Steven	King		515.123.4567	7
101	Neena	Kochhar		515.123.4568	7
102	Lex	De Haan		515.123.4569	7
103	Alexander	Hunold		590.423.4567	7
104	Bruce	Ernst		590.423.4568	7

Partial Redaction Policy

The partial redaction policy method allows us to create policies that redact specific parts of the column data using the value DBMS_REDACT.PARTIAL for the *function_type* parameter. This type of redaction makes it very obvious to the people who look at them that these data are masked. For example, the credit card numbers, SSNs, and the account numbers are usually partially redacted to display only their last 4 digits and the rest of the digits are replaced with an asterisk (*) in our bank statements for safety purpose.

Fixed-Length Character Datatypes

Oracle data redaction has provided us with a set of predefined formats to configure policies when we are certain about the character length of our data.

Predefined Partial Fixed Character Formats

Format	Description
DBMS_REDACT. REDACT_US_SSN_F5	Redacts the first 5 characters of the column data holding the SSN when the column is a VARCHAR2 data type.
DBMS_REDACT. REDACT_US_SSN_L4	Redacts the first 5 characters of the column data holding the SSN when the column is a VARCHAR2 data type.
DBMS_REDACT. REDACT_US_SSN_ENTIRE	Redacts all the characters of the column data holding the SSN when the column is a VARCHAR2 data type.
DBMS_REDACT. REDACT_NUM_US_SSN_F5	Redacts the first 5 characters of the column data holding the SSN when the column is a NUMBER data type.
DBMS_REDACT. REDACT_NUM_US_SSN_L4	Redacts the last 5 characters of the column data holding the SSN when the column is a NUMBER data type.
DBMS_REDACT. REDACT_NUM_US_SSN_ENTIRE	Redacts all the characters of the column data holding the SSN when the column is a NUMBER data type.
DBMS_REDACT. REDACT_ZIP_CODE	Redacts the 5-digit postal code when the column is a VARCHAR2 data type.
DBMS_REDACT. REDACT_NUM_ZIP_CODE	Redacts the 5-digit postal code when the column is a NUMBER data type.
DBMS_REDACT. REDACT_DATE_MILLENNIUM	Redacts all dates to 01-JAN-2000.
DBMS_REDACT. REDACT_DATE_EPOCH	Redacts all dates to 01-JAN-1970.
DBMS_REDACT. REDACT_CCN16_F12	Redacts the first 12 digits of a 16 digit credit card number when the column is a VARCHAR2 data type.

In the below example, a data redaction policy is created over the column CCN containing the credit card information in the CUSTOMER table with its function parameter as DBMS_REDACT.REDACT_CCN16_F12 for masking the first 12 characters of the credit card numbers.

```
BEGIN
 DBMS_REDACT.ADD_POLICY(
    object_schema      => 'C##',
    object_name        => 'CUSTOMER',
    column_name        => 'CCN',
    policy_name        => 'REDACT_CUSTOMER_CCN',
    function_type      => DBMS_REDACT.PARTIAL,
    function_parameters => DBMS_REDACT.REDACT_CCN16_F12,
    expression         => '1=1');
END;
/
```

When we query the credit card numbers from the CUSTOMER table after creating the above data redaction policy, we get our redacted credit card numbers as shown below,

```
SELECT unredacted, ccn FROM customer;
```

Script Result:

UNREDACTED	CCN
5277-3563-2458-7562	****-****-****-7562
9543-3457-2473-7456	****-****-****-7456
7337-8333-7833-5277	****-****-****-5277
9535-3579-1345-3512	****-****-****-3512

Variable-Length Character Datatypes

We can redact the column information of character data types with the help of some special settings. When we enter the *function_type* parameter value as DBMS_REDACT.PARTIAL, the *function_parameters* parameter takes up to 5 comma separated values which are described below,

1. **Input Format:** This value defines how the input data is formatted. We must use the character *V* for every character from the input string that can be redacted and the character *F* for every character from the input string that can be considered as a separator (Hyphens, spaces, etc.).

2. **Output Format:** This value defines how the output data needs to be formatted. We must use the character *V* for every character from the input string that can be redacted and replace the character *F* from the input format with either a hyphen or any other separator.

3. **Mask Format:** This value defines a single character that is to be used for redaction. For example, X or * can be used as a masking character.

4. **Starting Position:** This value specifies the start position of the V character for redaction.

5. **Ending Position:** This value specifies the end position of the V character for redaction.

In the below code snippet, the phone number column from the CUSTOMER table is partially redacted using this special setting method. The phone numbers of *+1(234)567-8901* format are converted into *+1(***)***-8901* format by applying the appropriate *function_parameters* parameter value.

Also, the *expression* parameter is written in such a way that the redaction happens only for the users whose IP address is not equal to 127.0.0.1 using the SYS_CONTEXT function.

```
BEGIN
 DBMS_REDACT.ADD_POLICY(
    object_schema        => 'C##',
    object_name          => 'CUSTOMER',
    column_name          => 'CUST_PHONE',
    policy_name          => 'REDACT_CUSTOMER_PHONE',
    function_type        => DBMS_REDACT.PARTIAL,
    function_parameters  => 'VVFVVVFVVVFVVVV,VV(VVV)VVV-VVVV,*,3,8',
    expression => q'(sys_context('USERENV','IP_ADDRESS')!='127.0.0.1')');
END;
/
```

When we try to query the phone number column data of the CUSTOMER table after creating the above policy, it results as,

```
SELECT unredacted, cust_phone FROM customer;
```

Script Result:

UNREDACTED	CUST_PHONE
+1(643)833-3283	+1(***)***-3283
+1(414)843-7342	+1(***)***-7342
+1(252)735-2583	+1(***)***-2583
+1(542)743-7257	+1(***)***-7257

Number Datatypes

This type of redaction is useful when the data column is of NUMBER type and not any other. When we enter the *function_type* parameter value as DBMS_REDACT.PARTIAL, the *function_parameters* parameter takes up to 3 comma separated values which are described below,

1. **Mask Format:** This value defines a single digit between 0 to 9 that is to be used for redaction.

2. **Starting Position:** This value specifies the start position for redaction.

3. **Ending Position:** This value specifies the end position for redaction.

In the below example, the account number column of the CUSTOMER table is redacted with the digit 1 from the position 3 to 8 for all the OS users other than CHANDLER MURIEL BING using the SYS_CONTEXT function.

```
BEGIN
 DBMS_REDACT.ADD_POLICY(
   object_schema       => 'C##',
   object_name         => 'CUSTOMER',
   column_name         => 'CUST_ACC_NUM',
   policy_name         => 'REDACT_CUSTOMER_ACC_NUM',
   function_type       => DBMS_REDACT.PARTIAL,
   function_parameters => '1,3,8',
   expression   => q'(sys_context('USERENV','OS_USER')!='Chandler Muriel
Bing')');
END;
/
```

When we query the account number column from the CUSTOMER table in a non-matching OS user system after creating the above policy, the result set produced will be redacted as shown below.

```
SELECT unredacted, cust_acc_num FROM customer;
```

Script Result:

UNREDACTED	CUST_ACC_NUM
98305830673	98111111673
74059830476	74111111476
96385667598	96111111598
96358674498	96111111498

Date-Time Datatypes

This type of redaction is useful when the data column is of DATE type and not any other. When we enter the *function_type* parameter value as DBMS_REDACT.PARTIAL, the *function_parameters* parameter takes a single value with special settings in the below-described order.

1. m (lowercase): Redacts the month value.
    - To redact, append 1-12 after the character m (lowercase). For e.g., m4 will redact the month as APRIL.
    - To omit redaction, we must use M (uppercase).

2. d (lowercase): Redacts the date value.
    - To redact, append 1-31 to the character d (lowercase). For e.g., d5 will redact the date as 05. If we try to redact it to a higher date greater than

the last day of a month, the redacted value will be the last day of the month.

- To omit redaction, we must use D (uppercase).

3. y (lowercase): Redacts the year value.
   - To redact, append 1-9999 to the character y (lowercase). For e.g., y2016 will redact the year to 2016.
   - To omit redaction, we must use Y (uppercase).

4. h (lowercase): Redacts the hour value.
   - To redact, append 0-23 to the character h (lowercase). For e.g., h20 will redact the hour to 20.
   - To omit redaction, we must use H (uppercase).

5. m (lowercase): Redacts the minute value.
   - To redact, append 0-59 to the character m (lowercase). For e.g., m50 will redact the minute as 50.
   - To omit redaction, we must use M (uppercase).

> Note: The character m is used for redacting both the MONTH and the MINUTE values. We must identify them through their order to avoid confusion.

6. s (lowercase): Redacts the second value.
   - To redact, append 0-59 to the character s (lowercase). For e.g., s40 will redact the second to 40.
   - To omit redaction, we must use S (uppercase).

In the below code listing, the month value defaults to JAN and the year value is defaulted to 2016 for the *date of birth* column from the CUSTOMER table using the *function_parameters* parameter value.

```
BEGIN
 DBMS_REDACT.ADD_POLICY(
   object_schema      => 'C##',
   object_name        => 'CUSTOMER',
   column_name        => 'CUST_DOB',
   policy_name        => 'REDACT_CUST_DOB',
   function_type      => DBMS_REDACT.PARTIAL,
   function_parameters => 'm01Dy2016HMS',
   expression         => '1=1');
END;
/
```

When we query the *date of birth* column from the CUSTOMER table after creating the above policy, we get to see the redacted date as below,

```
SELECT unredacted, cust_dob FROM customer;
```

Script Result:

UNREDACTED	CUST_DOB
30-SEP-1989	30-JAN-2016
27-MAY-1962	27-JAN-2016
28-NOV-1974	28-JAN-2016
18-SEP-1991	18-JAN-2016

Regular Expression Based Redaction Policy

We can use the regular expression based redaction technique to mask a column data based on a pattern match when the *function_type* parameter is set to DBMS_REDACT.REGEXP. After setting the *function_type* parameter, we have to make use of the below parameters to build our regular expression based pattern matching.

- **REGEXP_PATTERN** parameter is used for defining the search pattern for matching the data.

- **REGEXP_REPLACE_STRING** parameter is used for replacing the strings that are matched by the REGEXP_PATTERN parameter.

- **REGEXP_POSITION** parameter specifies the starting position for the string search and replacement. This parameter accepts a positive integer indicating the *column_name* parameter's character position. The default is 1 or RE_BEGINNING format, meaning that the search starts from the first character of the column data.

- **REGEXP_OCCURRENCE** parameter defines at which occurrence the search and replace must occur. This parameter accepts all positive numbers to indicate the replace option.

  ➜ If we specify 0 or RE_ALL as its value, then all the occurrences of the match get replaced.

  ➜ If we specify 1 or RE_FIRST as its value, then the first occurrence of the match gets replaced.

→ If we specify any positive integer, say *n*, then the *n*th occurrence of the match gets replaced.

- **REGEXP_MATCH_PARAMETER** parameter allows us to change the default matching behavior. For e.g., to make the matching case insensitive, we must use the character *i* or the format RE_MATCH_CASE_INSENSITIVE.

We can use the below formats in place of the values for the REGEXP_PATTERN and REGEXP_REPLACE_STRING parameters in the DBMS_REDACT.ADD_POLICY procedure.

REGEXP_PATTERN & REGXP_REPLACE_STRING Default Formats

Format	Description
DBMS_REDACT. RE_PATTERN_ANY_DIGIT	Searches for any digit. Below are the supported REGEXP_REPLACE_STRING default formats.

FORMAT	DESCRIPTION
DBMS_REDACT. RE_REDACT_WITH_SINGLE_X	Replaces the data with a single X character for each actual data character.
DBMS_REDACT. RE_REDACT_WITH_SINGLE_1	Replaces the data with a single 1 digit for each actual character.

Format	Description
DBMS_REDACT. RE_PATTERN_CC_L6_T4	Searches for the digits in the credit card number having 6 leading and 4 trailing digits. Below are the supported REGEXP_REPLACE_STRING default formats.

FORMAT	DESCRIPTION
DBMS_REDACT. RE_REDACT_CC_MIDDLE_DIGITS	Replaces the middle digits in a credit card number.

Format	Description
DBMS_REDACT. RE_PATTERN_US_PHONE	Searches for any US telephone number format. Below are the supported REGEXP_REPLACE_STRING default formats.

FORMAT	DESCRIPTION
DBMS_REDACT. RE_REDACT_PHONE_L7	Replaces the last 7 digits of a US telephone number.

Format	Description
DBMS_REDACT. RE_PATTERN_EMAIL_ADDRESS	Searches for any email address. Below are the supported REGEXP_REPLACE_STRING default formats.

FORMAT	DESCRIPTION
DBMS_REDACT. RE_REDACT_EMAIL_NAME	Replaces the email name.

FORMAT	DESCRIPTION
DBMS_REDACT.RE_REDACT_EMAIL_DOMAIN	Replaces the email domain name.
DBMS_REDACT.RE_PATTERN_IP_ADDRESS	Searches for any IP address. Below are the supported REGEXP_REPLACE_STRING default formats.

FORMAT	DESCRIPTION
DBMS_REDACT.RE_REDACT_IP_L3	Replaces the last 3 digits of the IP address.

In the below code listing, we have created a policy for redacting the email name from a list of email addresses using the default parameter values as shown below,

- REGEXP_PATTERN parameter value as DBMS_REDACT.RE_PATTERN_EMAIL_ADDRESS.

- REGEXP_REPLACE_STRING parameter value as DBMS_REDACT.RE_REDACT_EMAIL_NAME.

- REGEXP_POSITION parameter value as DBMS_REDACT.RE_BEGINNING.

- REGXP_OCCURRENCE parameter value as DBMS_REDACT.RE_FIRST.

- REGEXP_MATCH_PARAMETER parameter value as DBMS_REDACT.RE_MATCH_CASE_INSENSITIVE.

```
BEGIN
 DBMS_REDACT.ADD_POLICY(
    object_schema          => 'C##',
    object_name            => 'CUSTOMER',
    column_name            => 'CUSTOMER_EMAIL',
    policy_name            => 'REDACT_CUSTOMER_EMAIL',
    function_type          => DBMS_REDACT.REGEXP,
    expression             => '1=1',
    regexp_pattern         => DBMS_REDACT.RE_PATTERN_EMAIL_ADDRESS,
    regexp_replace_string  => DBMS_REDACT.RE_REDACT_EMAIL_NAME,
    regexp_position        => DBMS_REDACT.RE_BEGINNING,
    regexp_occurrence      => DBMS_REDACT.RE_FIRST,
    regexp_match_parameter => DBMS_REDACT.RE_MATCH_CASE_INSENSITIVE);
END;
/
```

When we query the CUSTOMER table, we can see the name of the email address column being redacted to the default character *x* as shown below,

```
SELECT unredacted, customer_email FROM customer;
```

Script Result:

UNREDACTED	CUSTOMER_EMAIL
dennis_ritchie@yahoo.com	xxxx@yahoo.com
steve_jobs@gmail.com	xxxx@gmail.com
bill_gates@gmail.com	xxxx@gmail.com
larry_ellison@yahoo.com	xxxx@yahoo.com

In the case of customized regular expression redaction policy, we can enter our own regular expression match pattern, replace string, position value, occurrence value, and the match parameter values instead of the default parameter formats. In our below example, the account number column of 11 characters each, for a set of customers has been redacted by replacing the first 7 characters with the user defined string x. Here, the parameter values used are,

- REGEXP_PATTERN parameter value as '(\d\d\d\d)(\d\d\d)(\d\d\d\d)'.

- REGEXP_REPLACE_STRING parameter value as 'XXXXXX\3'.

- REGEXP_POSITION parameter value as 1.

- REGEXP_OCCURRENCE parameter value as 0.

- REGEXP_MATCH_PARAMETER parameter value as 'i'.

```
BEGIN
 DBMS_REDACT.ADD_POLICY(
    object_schema          => 'C##',
    object_name            => 'CUSTOMER',
    column_name            => 'CUST_ACC_NUM',
    policy_name            => 'REDACT_CUST_ACC_NUM',
    function_type          => DBMS_REDACT.REGEXP,
    expression             => '1=1',
    regexp_pattern         => '(\d\d\d\d)(\d\d\d)(\d\d\d\d)',
    regexp_replace_string  => 'XXXXXX\3',
    regexp_position        => 1,
    regexp_occurrence      => 0,
    regexp_match_parameter => 'i');
END;
/
```

When we query the account number field from the CUSTOMER table, we can see that the column has been redacted with 4 x characters in the place of first 7 characters.

```
SELECT unredacted, cust_acc_num FROM customer;
```

Script Result:

UNREDACTED	CUST_ACC_NUM
98237959239	XXXX9239
87395873094	XXXX3094
53069840568	XXXX0568
83859034854	XXXX4854

Random Redaction Policy

The random redaction policy redacts the entire value of a column by replacing it with a random value dynamically when we set the *function_type* parameter to DBMS_REDACT.RANDOM format. The redacted value dynamically changes every time we query the column data.

This type of redaction policy is suitable for hiding the redaction performed over a column data. For e.g., in the case of NUMBER and DATE type columns, it is difficult to differentiate between the original data and the redacted value.

In the below example, the date of birth field of the CUSTOMER table has been redacted to random display as shown below,

```
BEGIN
 DBMS_REDACT.ADD_POLICY(
   object_schema   => 'C##',
   object_name     => 'CUSTOMER',
   column_name     => 'CUST_DOB',
   policy_name     => 'REDACT_CUST_DOB',
   function_type   => DBMS_REDACT.RANDOM,
   expression      => '1=1');
END;
/
```

When we query the CUSTOMER table after creating the above policy, we can see the CUST_DOB have some random dates instead of the real data.

```
SELECT unredacted, cust_dob FROM customer;
```

Script Result 1:

UNREDACTED	CUST_DOB
30-SEP-1989	24-JUL-2000
27-MAY-1962	19-MAR-1925
28-NOV-1974	10-MAR-1967
18-SEP-1991	20-JUN-2010

When we re-query the CUSTOMER table, we can find some other random date as its redacted value.

Script Result 2:

UNREDACTED	CUST_DOB
30-SEP-1989	05-MAR-2008
27-MAY-1962	19-DEC-1944
28-NOV-1974	28-NOV-1983
18-SEP-1991	19-JAN-2011

No Redaction Policy

We can create a no-redaction policy with a view on a base table having a redaction policy applied over it. Thus, the view displays the original data whilst the table displaying the redacted value. This is mainly useful when we want to test the internal operation of our redaction policies. The no-redaction policy can be created when the *function_type* parameter is set to DBMS_REDACT.NONE format.

Consider the CUSTOMER table with the CUST_ACC_NUM and UNREDACTED column, both holding the account numbers of the customers. A view, namely VW_CUSTOMER has been created over the CUSTOMER table. Thus, when we create a random policy over the CUSTOMER table's CUST_ACC_NUM column as shown below,

```
BEGIN
 DBMS_REDACT.ADD_POLICY(
   object_schema    => 'C##',
   object_name      => 'CUSTOMER',
   column_name      => 'CUST_ACC_NUM',
   policy_name      => 'REDACT_CUST_ACC_NUM',
   function_type    => DBMS_REDACT.RANDOM,
   expression       => '1=1');
END;
/
```

The CUST_ACC_NUM column data from both the CUSTOMER table and the VW_CUSTOMER view are redacted as shown,

```
SELECT * FROM customer;
```

Script Result:

UNREDACTED	CUST_ACC_NUM
98237959239	72138399767
87395873094	49199813843
53069840568	17804846503
83859034854	56265914458

```
SELECT * FROM vw_customer;
```

Script Result:

UNREDACTED	CUST_ACC_NUM
98237959239	89415130236
87395873094	9864300578
53069840568	26743021800
83859034854	56707121006

To avoid the redacted data in the view, we must create a no-redaction policy over the view's CUST_ACC_NUM column as shown below,

```
BEGIN
 DBMS_REDACT.ADD_POLICY(
   object_schema    => 'C##',
   object_name      => 'VW_CUSTOMER',
   column_name      => 'CUST_ACC_NUM',
   policy_name      => 'REDACT_VW_CUST_ACC_NUM',
   function_type    => DBMS_REDACT.NONE,
   expression       => '1=1');
END;
/
```

Thus, when we query the view VW_CUSTOMER after creating the no-redaction policy, we can see that the data from the view is un-redacted but the table still showing the redacted values.

```
SELECT * FROM vw_customer;
```

Script Result:

UNREDACTED	CUST_ACC_NUM
98237959239	98237959239
87395873094	87395873094
53069840568	53069840568
83859034854	83859034854

DBMS_REDACT.DISABLE_POLICY

We can disable a redaction policy using this procedure. However, as long as the policy still exists in the database (either disabled or enabled), we may not be able to create another redaction policy on a table's column without dropping the existing one.

The prototype for disabling a policy is shown below,

```
DBMS_REDACT.DISABLE_POLICY (
   object_schema        IN VARCHAR2 DEFAULT NULL,
   object_name          IN VARCHAR2,
   policy_name          IN VARCHAR2);
```

In the below example, a redaction policy created over the CUSTOMER table is disabled by executing the below statement.

```
EXEC DBMS_REDACT.DISABLE_POLICY (object_schema=>'C##',
object_name=>'CUSTOMER', policy_name=>'REDACT_CUST_ACC_NUM');
```

DBMS_REDACT.ENABLE_POLICY

We can enable a redaction policy using this procedure. During the redaction policy creation, the system by default enables the policy.

The prototype for enabling a policy is shown below,

```
DBMS_REDACT.ENABLE_POLICY (
   object_schema        IN VARCHAR2 DEFAULT NULL,
   object_name          IN VARCHAR2,
   policy_name          IN VARCHAR2);
```

In the below example, a redaction policy created over the CUSTOMER table is enabled by executing the below statement.

```
EXEC DBMS_REDACT.ENABLE_POLICY (object_schema=>'C##',
object_name=>'CUSTOMER', policy_name=>'REDACT_CUST_ACC_NUM');
```

DBMS_REDACT.DROP_POLICY

An already existing redaction policy can be dropped by using this procedure. A redaction policy can be dropped even though it is enabled or disabled.

The prototype for dropping a policy is shown below,

```
DBMS_REDACT.DROP_POLICY (
   object_schema        IN VARCHAR2 DEFAULT NULL,
   object_name          IN VARCHAR2,
   policy_name          IN VARCHAR2);
```

In the below example, a redaction policy created over the CUSTOMER table is dropped by executing the below statement.

```
EXEC DBMS_REDACT.DROP_POLICY (object_schema=>'C##', object_name=>'CUSTOMER',
policy_name=>'REDACT_CUST_ACC_NUM');
```

Oracle Redaction Policy Data Dictionary Views

Oracle has provided the below three views that provide information about the redaction policies.

REDACTION_COLUMNS

This view provides us with all the information about the redacted column, including their function type, parameter, description of the policy, and their regular expression patterns as shown below.

```
SELECT
  object_owner,
  object_name,
  column_name,
  function_type,
  function_parameters,
  regexp_pattern,
  column_description
FROM
  REDACTION_COLUMNS;
```

Script Result:

OBJECT _OWNER	OBJECT _NAME	COLUMN _NAME	FUNCTIO N_TYPE	FUNCTION_P ARMETERS	REGEXP_ PATTERN	COLUMN_D ESCRIPTOIN
C##	VW_CU STOME R	CUST_A CC_NUM	NO REDACTI ON			Contains customer's account number.
C##	CUSTO MER	CUST_D OB	PARTIAL REDACTI ON	m1d1y2000		Contains customer's date of birth.
C##	EMPLOY EES	PHONE_ NUMBER	FULL REDACTI ON			Contains employee's phone number.
C##	EMPLOY EES	EMAIL	FULL REDACTI ON			Contains employee's email address.
C##	EMPLOY EES	SALARY	FULL REDACTI ON			Contains employee's salary.
C##	VW_CU STOME R	CUST_A CC_NUM	NO REDACTI ON			Contains customer's credit card number.

REDACTION_POLICIES

This view describes all the redaction policies created in the database. It provides information about the object's owner, name, policy name, expression used, status of the policy, and its description as shown below,

```
SELECT * FROM redaction_policies;
```

Script Result:

OBJECT_O WNER	OBJECT_N AME	POLICY_NAME	EXPRES SION	ENAB LE	POLICY_DESC RIPTION
C##	EMPLOYE ES	REDACT_EMP_EMAIL	1=1	YES	Redacts employee's email name.
C##	VW_CUST OMER	REDACT_VW_CUST_ ACC_NUM	1=1	YES	Redacts customer's account number.
C##	CUSTOME R	REDACT_CUST_SSN	1=1	YES	Partially redacts 1st 5 digits in SS numbers

REDACTION_VALUES_FOR_TYPE_FULL

This view describes the current default value for the data redaction policies of full redaction type for all the supported data types.

```
SELECT
  number_value,
  date_value,
  varchar_value
FROM
  REDACTION_VALUES_FOR_TYPE_FULL;
```

Script Result:

NUMBER_VALUE	DATE_VALUE	VARCHAR_VALUE
1	1-JAN-2001	(SINGLE SPACE)

Oracle Virtual Private Database (VPD) and Fine-Grained Access Control (FGAC) to Control Data Access

The Virtual Private Database (VPD) concept was first introduced in the Oracle version 8i and is one of the most common security features in the Oracle database evolution, serving as an interface between the PL/SQL functions and the database tables. The

PL/SQL functions compute a WHERE condition predicate that is appended to the SQL statements which are executed on a database transparently, restricting the access to the rows and the columns within the queried table.

This feature is also called as Fine-Grained Access Control (FGAC) and has a remarkable difference between the data redaction process, which is discussed in the earlier section. While the data redaction concentrates only on the column level data security, the VPD can secure both row level and column level data.

The VPD creates a virtual private look of the database table to the users who are restricted to access only the portion of the data from the table that are authorized for them. Since a dynamic WHERE condition is appended to the SQL statements which are secured under the VPD implementation, the structure of the original SQL is modified by a change in its access path, which seems to appear in the explain plan. Thus, utmost care has to be taken while designing the predicate clause in a such a way that it does not take a big toll on the performance of the SQL statement being executed.

Advantages of VPD over Access Controls

Implementing VPD security policy to our database objects has the below advantages rather creating access controls all over our application.

1. **Simplicity:** We can implement the VPD policy to a table, view, or synonym only once, rather repeating the implementation to all the database objects in our application.

2. **Security:** By implementing the VPD policy, the security is placed on the objects at the database level and not at the object level. Thus, accidental modification of the data using ad-hoc tools is prohibited when the VPD is in place.

3. **Flexibility:** The security policies can be created on a database column of a table or a view and can be applied to SELECT, INSERT, UPDATE, DELETE, and INDEX statements based on it. We can also have individual policies placed upon the above types of statements.

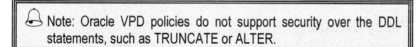
Note: Oracle VPD policies do not support security over the DDL statements, such as TRUNCATE or ALTER.

Virtual Private Database Policy Components

To implement the VPD security in the Oracle database, we must first create a function to create a dynamic predicate clause and then a policy to combine this function and the objects we need to secure.

Function Definition and Implementation Rules

The first step in enforcing the security over the database object is to create a function (Procedures are not supported) defining the WHERE condition predicate that we want to implement.

The function created must satisfy the below behavior,

- It must have two input parameters. One for the schema name and the other one for the object name with VARCHAR2 datatypes in their respective order mentioned. Even though these parameters are not needed by the function, those parameter values are supplied by the DBMS_RLS package during the policy creation.

- It must have a VARCHAR2 return type, that returns the restriction condition to be placed in the WHERE predicate of a query.

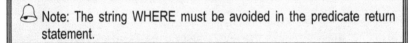
Note: The string WHERE must be avoided in the predicate return statement.

- The WHERE clause predicate can either be simplistic (with a simple arithmetic operated predicate) or be complex (with a predicate containing an application context), but it should be a valid syntax.

- The function body cannot select or transform the table on which the policy is about to be created.

The VPD Policy Creation

After creating the function that defines the WHERE clause predicate, we must associate this function with the database object by creating a VPD policy.

We can create the policy using the procedures offered by the DBMS_RLS package (RLS stands for Row Level Security). During the policy creation, we can also configure the fine-grained access control, that is, the types of SQL statements and the columns the policy protects. The policy starts functioning once we try to access data from this database object.

The Procedures offered by the DBMS_RLS package for handling Individual Policies

Procedure Name	Description
ADD_POLICY	Creates/ Adds a policy to a database table, view, or a synonym.
ENABLE_POLICY	Enables/ Disables an existing policy.
ALTER_POLICY	Alters an existing policy to associate or disassociate its attributes.
REFRESH_POLICY	Re-parses all the cached statements associated with a policy.
DROP_POLICY	Drops an existing policy.

Procedures offered by the DBMS_RLS package for handling Grouped Policies

Procedure Name	Description
CREATE_POLICY_GROUP	Creates a policy group.
ALTER_POLICY_GROUP	Alters the group policy to associate or disassociate its attributes.
DELETE_POLICY_GROUP	Drops an existing policy group.
ADD_GROUPED_POLICY	Adds a policy to the specified policy group.
ENABLE_GROUPED_POLICY	Enables a policy within a group.
REFRESH_GROUPED_POLICY	Re-parses all the cached statements associated with a refreshed policy.
DISABLE_GROUPED_POLICY	Disables a policy within a group.
DROP_GROUPED_POLICY	Drops a policy from a group.

Procedures offered by the DBMS_RLS package for handling Application Contexts

Procedure Name	Description
ADD_POLICY_CONTEXT	Adds the context for the active application.
DROP_POLICY_CONTEXT	Drops the context for the application.

Oracle VPD Policy Types

There are totally 5 policy types provided by the Oracle Virtual Private Database to satisfy our needs such as for using them in the hosting environments.

Policy Type	Description	Usage Situation
Dynamic (Default)	This is the default type of policy type if the POLICY_TYPE parameter is omitted. The policy function is executed each and every time a VPD protected query is executed.	For example, in applications that use the time for restricting users to access the table data.
Static	The policy function is executed only once and is shared in the SGA for every other session to use.	This is useful when the predicate clause is common for all the queries executed on a VPD protected table. This results in better performance as the policy function is executed only once.
Shared_static	It is similar to the Static policy type, but this type can be shared among multiple schema objects.	This type is useful when we can re-use the same predicate to multiple schema objects. This is highly used in data warehousing environments.
Context_sensitive	The policy function is executed only when the associated application context attribute changes starting from R12.1. Prior to this release, the policy function is executed every time any attribute of any context is changed.	This policy type is used when we want to enforce more than predicate for different users or groups.
Shared_context_sensitivity	The predicate is shared in the UGA when an SQL statement is parsed, which then can be shared among different objects in a database.	This is mainly used in a data warehousing environment where we want to share a single predicate with multiple database objects.

Fine-grained Access Control Implementation Rules

We can create Oracle VPD policies for SELECT, INSERT, UPDATE, DELETE, and INDEX statements. To specify an SQL statement type for the policy, we must use the *statement_types* parameter in the ADD_POLICY procedure. If we want to specify more than one type of SQL statement, we must separate them with a comma enclosed with a single quotation. When we omit this parameter, by default Oracle specifies all the SQL statement types except INDEX.

 Note: The Database users, who were granted the EXEMPT ACCESS POLICY privilege, either directly or through a database role, are exempted from Oracle VPD enforcements.

We must consider the below rules before setting up the *statement_types* parameter.

- When our application uses the MERGE statement, we must make sure that we set the *statement_types* parameter to INSERT, UPDATE, and DELETE or omit this parameter to set these statement types by default.

- When the users have their *statement_types* parameter set to INDEX, they have the privilege to see the data from all rows, even if the other statement types are not set.

A Simple Oracle VPD Policy Creation

Before creating an Oracle VPD policy, let us examine the plan for the EMPLOYEES table.

```
EXPLAIN PLAN FOR SELECT * FROM employees;
```

The EXPLAIN PLAN FOR statement parses and records the formatted plan in the plan table that has been generated by Oracle for executing the query.

```
SELECT * FROM TABLE(DBMS_XPLAN.DISPLAY);
```

The *display* function allows us to display the execution plan that is stored recently in the plan table.

Script Result:

PLAN_TABLE_OUTPUT

Plan hash value: 1445457117

```
--------------------------------------------------------------------------
| Id | Operation          | Name      | Rows | Bytes | Cost (%CPU)| Time     |
--------------------------------------------------------------------------
|  0 | SELECT STATEMENT   |           |  107 | 7383 |  2  (0)    | 00:00:01 |
|  1 | TABLE ACCESS FULL  | EMPLOYEES |  107 | 7383 |  2  (0)    | 00:00:01 |
--------------------------------------------------------------------------
```

In the above plan, we can see that all 107 rows of the EMPLOYEES table are returned from the query execution with a full table access.

The first step in creating an Oracle VPD is to create the policy function in a common user (In our case, say *admin_user*). Consider that all the employees have a database user created in their name (First_name||'_'||Last_name) for their purpose. For e.g., *Alexander_Hunold* is a username for a schema used by the employee- Alexander Hunold. Thus, the below function is created returning the department ID of the database user who calls it as its predicate statement. If the user accessing the EMPLOYEES table is not a valid employee, by default the predicate is returned as *DEPARTMENT_ID is null,* thus no employee details are displayed to them.

Note that even though the function does not need the schema name and the table name in its body functionality, we must create it with two input parameters of VARCHAR2 type as the VPD policy call expects the function like so.

```
CREATE OR REPLACE FUNCTION func_emp_vpd(
    ip_vc_schema_name IN VARCHAR2,
    ip_vc_table_name  IN VARCHAR2 )
  RETURN VARCHAR2
IS
  l_vc_return VARCHAR2(100);
BEGIN
  SELECT MAX('DEPARTMENT_ID = '||department_id)
  INTO
    l_vc_return
  FROM
    employees
  WHERE
    upper(first_name||'_'||last_name)=upper(USER);
  RETURN NVL(l_vc_return,'DEPARTMENT_ID is null');
END;
/
```

The Oracle VPD policy can be created using the ADD_POLICY procedure from the DBMS_RLS package. It requires the below parameters to be set for its creation,

- **OBJECT_SCHEMA** parameter is for setting the schema of the object on which the policy is to be applied. In this case, a common user who administers the VPD object, ADMIN_USER is set for this parameter.

- **OBJECT_NAME** parameter is for setting the object name on which the policy is to be applied. In this case, the table EMPLOYEES is set for this parameter.

- **POLICY_NAME** parameter is for setting the user defined unique policy name for its creation and unique identification. In this case, the user-defined name POLICY_EMP is set for this parameter.

- **FUNCTION_SCHEMA** parameter is for setting the schema name of the policy function created in the above section. In this case, a common user who administers the policy function, ADMIN_USER is set for this parameter.

- **POLICY_FUNCTION** parameter is for setting the policy function created in the above section. In this case, the policy function FUNC_EMP_VPD is set for this parameter.

- **STATEMENT_TYPES** parameter is for setting the fine-grained access control statement types. In this case, SELECT, INSERT, UPDATE, and DELETE statement types are set for this parameter. These statement types will be taken into consideration by default if we omit this parameter during the policy creation.

```
BEGIN
  DBMS_RLS.ADD_POLICY (
    object_schema    => 'admin_user',
    object_name      => 'employees',
    policy_name      => 'policy_emp',
    function_schema  => 'admin_user',
    policy_function  => 'func_emp_vpd',
    statement_types  => 'select, insert, update, delete'
  );
END;
/
```

After creating the policy, the VPD goes into effect immediately. When we try to query the EMPLOYEES table, we get the results pertaining to the department that the querying database user is associated with.

For example,

1. When we try to select the table data from the database user *steven_king*, we can see that the employees table returning all the employees corresponding to the employee *King, Steven*'s department ID (i.e., 90).

2. When we try to select the table data from the database user *nancy_greenberg*, we can see that the employees table returning all the employees corresponding to the employee *Nancy_Greenberg*'s department ID (i.e., 100).

Transparent Data Encryption Components

The below statement for retrieving the explain plan for the EMPLOYEES table is executed in the database user *david_austin*, whose department ID is 60.

```
EXPLAIN PLAN FOR SELECT * FROM employees;
```

The *display* function is then executed for displaying the stored plan details as shown below,

```
SELECT * FROM TABLE(DBMS_XPLAN.DISPLAY);
```

Script Result:

PLAN_TABLE_OUTPUT

Plan hash value: 223546141

Id	Operation	Name	Rows	Bytes	Cost (%CPU)	Time
0	SELECT STATEMENT		10	690	2 (0)	00:00:01
1	TABLE ACCESS BY INDEX ROWID	EMPLOYEES	10	690	2 (0)	00:00:01
* 2	INDEX RANGE SCAN	IDX_DEPTNO	10		1 (0)	00:00:01

Predicate Information (identified by operation id):
----

   2 - access("DEPARTMENT_ID"=60)

In the above plan, the policy function's predicate information is available as a result of a VPD process to filter the data returned. In addition, Oracle optimizer also uses an *index range scan* on the predicate clause containing the index IDX_DEPTNO for increasing the performance of the query's execution.

Column Level Oracle Virtual Private Database Policy

We can create a column-level Oracle VPD policy by setting up the SEC_RELEVANT_COLS parameter of the ADD_POLICY procedure in the

---

DBMS_RLS package. Here, the security is applied only when the security relevant columns are accessed.

After creating the policy function for the Oracle VPD process (We can use the above-created policy function in this case), we must create the below policy with the parameter SEC_RELEVANT_COLS set to the columns EMAIL, PHONE_NUMBER, and SALARY from the EMPLOYEES table in a comma separated manner enclosed within single quotes.

```
BEGIN
  DBMS_RLS.ADD_POLICY (
    object_schema     => 'admin_user',
    object_name       => 'employees',
    policy_name       => 'policy_emp_column_level',
    function_schema   => 'admin_user',
    policy_function   => 'func_emp_vpd',
    statement_types   => 'select, insert, update, delete',
    sec_relevant_cols => 'email, phone_number, salary'
  );
END;
/
```

When we query the EMPLOYEE table from the user *Shelley_Higgins* who is an employee in the department ID 110 as below,

```
SELECT employee_id, first_name, last_name, email, phone_number, salary,
department_id
FROM
  employees;
```

The only rows that are displayed are the ones which the user has the privileges to access all columns in a row. Thus, we will be able to find all the employees belonging to the department ID 110 as shown below.

Script Result:

EMPLOYEE_ID	FIRST_NAME	LAST_NAME	EMAIL	PHONE_NUMBER	SALARY	DEPARTMENT_ID
205	Shelley	Higgins	SHIGGINS	515.123.8080	12008	110
206	William	Gietz	WGIETZ	515.123.8181	8300	110

But when we query the EMPLOYEE table omitting the security relevant columns from the selection list in any user as below,

```
SELECT employee_id, first_name, last_name, department_id
FROM
  employees;
```

We will be able to find all the rows in all the departments from the EMPLOYEE table without any security policy applied to them as below,

Script Result:

EMPLOYEE_ID	FIRST_NAME	LAST_NAME	DEPARTMENT_ID
200	Jennifer	Whalen	10
201	Michael	Hartstein	20
202	Pat	Fay	20
114	Den	Raphaely	30
...	...	...	...
...	...	...	...
...	...	...	...

Column Masking in Oracle Virtual Private Database Policy

In the column level security, the VPD policy restricts the number of rows returned when our query references a sensitive column. But with the column masking functionality, we can display all the rows, including the security sensitive columns. However, the values of the sensitive columns are available only for the authorized predicate clause matching condition and the rest of the non-matching column values display *null*.

To enable this behavior, we must set the SEC_RELEVANT_COLS_OPT parameter to DBMS_RLS.ALL_ROWS format during the policy creation using the ADD_POLICY procedure from the DBMS_RLS package as shown below.

```
BEGIN
  DBMS_RLS.ADD_POLICY (
    object_schema      => 'admin_user',
    object_name        => 'employees',
    policy_name        => 'policy_emp_column_level',
    function_schema    => 'admin_user',
    policy_function    => 'func_emp_vpd',
    statement_types    => 'select, insert, update, delete',
    sec_relevant_cols  => 'email, phone_number, salary',
    sec_relevant_cols_opt => dbms_rls.all_rows
  );
END;
/
```

When we query the EMPLOYEE table from the user *pat_fay* who is an employee in the department ID 20 as below,

```
SELECT employee_id, first_name, last_name, email, phone_number, salary,
department_id
FROM
  employees;
```

Script Result:

EMPLOYEE_ID	FIRST_NAME	LAST_NAME	EMAIL	PHONE_NUMBER	SALARY	DEPARTMENT_ID
200	Jennifer	Whalen	(null)	(null)	(null)	10
201	Michael	Hartstein	MHARTSTE	515.123.5555	13000	20
202	Pat	Fay	PFAY	603.123.6666	6000	20
114	Den	Raphaely	(null)	(null)	(null)	30
115	Alexander	Khoo	(null)	(null)	(null)	30
116	Shelli	Baida	(null)	(null)	(null)	30
117	Sigal	Tobias	(null)	(null)	(null)	30
…	…	…	…	…	…	…
…	…	…	…	…	…	…
…	…	…	…	…	…	…

The column masking technique returned all the rows requested by the user *pat_fay* belonging to the department ID 20 but made the sensitive columns EMAIL, PHONE_NUMBER, and SALARY *null* for the employees belonging to other departments.

Oracle VPD Policy Creation using an Application Context

Application contexts are introduced in Oracle version 8i to support VPD policies to set the WHERE clause predicate when querying the policy protected tables. Later in 9i, the global application contexts were introduced to support shared-session applications.

The application contexts are session variables which hold information about the database and the session in the form of key-value pairs that are identified by labels called as *namespaces*.

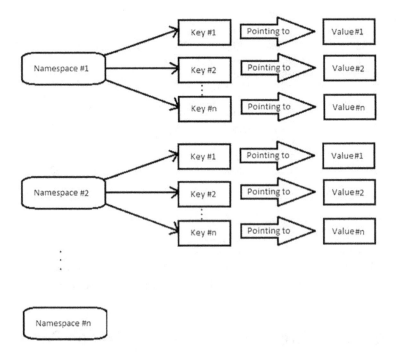

Fig. 8.3 Application Context Internal Architecture

The above figure depicts the relationship between namespaces (also called as the application contexts), keys and their respective values. We can create *n* number of namespaces which in turn can have more than one key which points to their respective values. There is no relationship between the application contexts, keys or values except for the ones inside their branch.

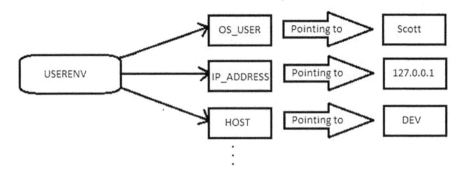

Fig. 8.4 System Defined Application Context

In the above example, the system-defined context USERENV is portrayed along with a few of its keys and their values.

Oracle stores these application context values in a secure data cache that is available either in the User Global Area (In the case of local contexts) or in the Shared Global Area (In the case of global contexts). Thus, these values are available throughout the session when they are set once. As the application contexts are stored in the cache, the performance of our applications increases. The application context values can be retrieved through the system defined function SYS_CONTEXT. This function accepts two parameters. They are the context name (namespace) and its input parameter (key).

 Note: The function doesn't validate the context name or its input parameter. If they are not available, the function simply returns *null* as its value. However, if we tend to use the context USERENV, supplying a wrong input parameter may result in *ORA-02003: invalid USERENV parameter* exception.

There are totally three general types of application contexts available in the Oracle database and they are,

- **Local Application Contexts:** These contexts are available only in the creator's session and these are stored in the UGA part of the memory.

- **Global Application Contexts:** These contexts can be accessed by all session users. Thus, these are stored in the SGA part of the memory.

- **Client-Session Based Application Contexts:** This context uses OCI (Oracle Call Interface) functions on the client side to set the context parameters to perform the necessary security check for restricting the user access. This type of context is also stored in the SGA memory.

Components for Creating an Application Context

In our case, we must create the global application contexts for implementing them with the Oracle VPD policies. We must use the below components to create and use the global application context.

- We must create an application context using the CREATE CONTEXT syntax. We have to make sure that the ACCESSED GLOBALLY clause is used during

---

its creation such that the context can be accessed globally across all the session instances.

- We must create a trusted procedure to set the attribute and the value for the context. During the context creation in the above step, the validity and permission of this procedure are not tested by the system. The system trusts that this procedure exists with valid permissions and then creates the context, thus these procedures are coined as trusted.

- After the trusted procedure is created, we must run it once, preferably during the user login such that the context values are set way before the user starts to access the database tables. We can do this by creating a database startup trigger to execute the trusted procedure automatically during a database startup.

Creating the Globally Accessible Context

The prototype for creating a context is shown below,

```
CREATE OR REPLACE CONTEXT <Context_name> USING
[Schema_name].[Trusted_procedure_name]
[[Initialized [Externally | Globally]] | [Accessed Globally]];
```

- **Context_name** is the user-defined unique name for identifying the context created.

- **Trusted_procedure_name** is the name of the trusted procedure that sets or resets the context attributes under the context name. For design flexibility, the validity and the existence of this procedure are not verified during the context creation.

- **Initialized** clause allows other entities to initialize this context.

  → **Externally** clause indicates that this context can be initialized using an OCI to establish a session.

  → **Globally** clause indicates that this context can be initialized from the LDAP directory when a global user connects to the database.

- **Accessed Globally** clause indicates that the application contexts set in this namespace are accessible by multiple sessions.

The context CONTEXT_VPD is created upon the trusted procedure PROC_VPD, which is yet to be created. This context is available for all the users connected to this database because of the ACCESSED GLOBALLY clause.

```
CREATE OR REPLACE CONTEXT context_vpd USING proc_vpd ACCESSED GLOBALLY;
```

Creating the Trusted Procedure

After the global context is created, we must create the trusted procedure. This procedure must contain a call to the DBMS_SESSION.SET_CONTEXT procedure sporting three input parameters for setting the context attributes and its values. The first parameter accepts the name of the context created in the above setup, the second parameter accepts a user-defined attribute name, and the third parameter accepts a value for the attribute created. The context set by this procedure will be reset once the session is terminated, thus we don't have to strain ourselves to reset them.

In the below code snippet, four attributes and their respective values are set in the CONTEXT_VPD application context. Here, the attributes are the database user IDs and their values are the department IDs for which the corresponding database user has access to.

```
CREATE OR REPLACE PROCEDURE proc_vpd
IS
BEGIN
  dbms_session.set_context('CONTEXT_VPD', 'USER1', 10);
  dbms_session.set_context('CONTEXT_VPD', 'USER2', 20);
  dbms_session.set_context('CONTEXT_VPD', 'USER3', 30);
  dbms_session.set_context('CONTEXT_VPD', 'USER4', 40);
END;
/
```

When we try to execute the system provided function SYS_CONTEXT in this context and attribute,

```
SELECT sys_context('CONTEXT_VPD','USER1') FROM dual;
```

Result:

(null)

It results *null* as we have not yet set by executing the trusted procedure at least once.

```
EXEC proc_vpd;
```

Thus, when we re-query the SYS_CONTEXT function after setting the attributes and the values by executing the trusted procedure,

```
SELECT sys_context('CONTEXT_VPD','USER1') FROM dual;
```

Result:

10

We can see that the values corresponding to the input attribute of the particular context are displayed.

Creating the Database Startup Trigger

In the below listing, a database startup trigger named TRG_VPD has created which fires as soon as the database is started. This trigger's body contains the trusted procedure call, which sets the context attributes and the values for the entire user session.

 Note: If there is an error in the database trigger or in the trusted procedure, it may be impossible to start the database. In that case, we must disable the database trigger until the issue is fixed.

```
CREATE OR REPLACE TRIGGER trg_vpd AFTER STARTUP ON DATABASE
  BEGIN
    proc_vpd;
  END;
  /
```

Components for Creating a VPD

After creating the necessary application contexts, we must create the policy function with a dynamic predicate clause and the VPD policy for merging this function and the objects we intend to secure.

Creating the Policy Function

A policy function with two input VARCHAR2 parameters defining the secure object's WHERE predicate is created below. Here, the database username is passed as the attribute parameter value to the SYS_CONTEXT function and its resulting department ID is returned as the WHERE clause predicate. When the SYS_CONTEXT function returns a *null* value, the *Department_id is null* predicate is returned by default. Thus, this policy function returns different department IDs for different users for which they have access to.

> 🔔 Note: The application context namespace and the attribute name are case-insensitive when passed as input parameters to the SYS_CONTEXT function.

```
CREATE OR REPLACE FUNCTION func_emp_vpd(
    ip_vc_schema_name IN VARCHAR2,
    ip_vc_table_name  IN VARCHAR2 )
 RETURN VARCHAR2
IS
  l_n_dept_id NUMBER;
BEGIN
  SELECT
    sys_context('CONTEXT_VPD',user)
  INTO
    l_n_dept_id
  FROM
    dual;
  RETURN
  CASE
  WHEN l_n_dept_id IS NOT NULL THEN
    'Department_id = '||l_n_dept_id
  ELSE
    'Department_id is null'
  END;
END;
/
```

Creating the VPD Policy

After creating the policy function, VPD policy can be created using the ADD_POLICY procedure from the DBMS_RLS package as shown below.

```
BEGIN
  DBMS_RLS.ADD_POLICY (
    object_schema     => 'admin_user',
    object_name       => 'employees',
    policy_name       => 'policy_emp',
    function_schema   => 'admin_user',
    policy_function   => 'func_emp_vpd',
    statement_types   => 'select, insert, update, delete'
  );
END;
/
```

Once the policy is created, when we try to access the EMPLOYEES table from the database user USER1 we tend to find all the employees belonging to the department ID- 10.

```
SELECT count(*) FROM employees;
```

Result:

1

Thus, when we try to access the EMPLOYEES table from the database user USER2, USER3, USER4, we tend to find all the employees belonging to the department IDs-20, 30, 40 respectively.

Oracle VPD Data Dictionary Views

View Name	View Comments
*_POLICIES	Describes all the Oracle VPD security policies for objects.
*_POLICY_ATTRIBUTES	Describes all the application context namespaces, attributes, and the VPD policy associations
*_POLICY_CONTEXTS	Describes all the application contexts defined for the database objects.
*_POLICY_GROUPS	Describes all the Oracle VPD policy groups defined for the database objects.
*_SEC_RELEVANT_COLS	Describes the security relevant columns of the security policies for the database objects.

VPD Gotchas!

- We should not use the FOR-UPDATE clause when querying VPD protected tables as the query might sometimes fail if they are too complex in nature.

- We must rewrite our outer joins and ANSI operations in our SQLs as some views may not merge and some indexes may not be used. This problem is a known optimization limitation.

- When we use flashback queries on a VPD protected object, then the current policies are applied to the old data, which may not result what we have expected.

- We cannot apply VPD policies to the objects owned by the SYS user.

- When we are exporting data using a direct path export operation, Oracle VPD policies are not enforced as the Oracle database reads data directly from the disk and not from the database where the policies are in effect.

Introduction to Cryptography

Oracle has provided the DBMS_CRYPTO package for data encryption starting from the version 10gR1 as an attempt to replace its predecessor, the DBMS_OBFUSCATION_TOOLKIT package. This package acts as a PL/SQL interface to encrypt and decrypt the data that are stored in the database tables. This package supports much industry-standardized encryption and hashing algorithm like DES, AES, MD5, etc. Advanced Encryption Standard or AES has been approved by the National Institutes of Standards and Technology (NIST) to replace the Data Encryption Standard (DES) algorithm.

The DBMS_OBFUSCATION_TOOLKIT package is still available in the Oracle version 12c, although Oracle recommends us to start using the DBMS_CRYPTO as the predecessor's capabilities are limited compared to this new package.

The below tabular column describes the differences between the two cryptographic packages in Oracle.

S. No.	Description	CRYPTO	OBFUSCATION TOOLKIT
1.	Cryptographic algorithms	This procedure supports the DES encryption methods along with the newer encryption algorithm, AES. They are DES, 3DES, AES, RC4, 3DES_2KEY.	This procedure supports only DES encryption methods, which is not widely used by many organizations. They are DES and 3DES.
2.	Ciphering methods.	This procedure supports both stream and block ciphering.	This procedure supports only block ciphering, thus limiting its usage across all types of data.
	1) Block ciphering process performs encryption on blocks of data.		
	2) Stream ciphering encrypts data in any form.		
3.	Hash algorithms – Modern secure	This procedure supports MD4 (Message Digest), MD5, SHA-1 (Secure	This procedure supports only MD5 (Message digest) hash algorithm and no

	algorithms for data integrity.	Hash Algorithm), SHA-2 (SHA-256, SHA-384, SHA-512).	modern, secure algorithms like SHA-1, SHA-2, etc.
4.	Keyed hash (MAC) algorithms – Message Authentication Code allows a hashed value of the message to be transmitted so that it is compared at the receiving end to check for the message integrity using a key.	This procedure supports HMAC_MD5, HMAC_SH1, HMAC_SH256, HMAC_SH384, HMAC_SH512 algorithms.	This procedure does not support any MAC creation.
5.	LOB support	This procedure supports LOB data types in their native format.	This procedure can support LOB data types only when they are converted to RAW format. Thus, resulting in code complexity in applications.
6.	Padding – Extra data have to be padded to make its length a multiple when we want to encrypt it using block ciphers.	This procedure supports PAD_PKCS5 (Public Key Cryptographic Standard -5), PAD_ZERO, PAD_NONE types.	This procedure needs to pad explicitly which is not considered as a secure method.

The DBMS_CRYPTO package replaces the DBMS_OBFUSCATION_TOOLKIT package by providing support for a range of new secure algorithms with easy usage. The algorithms 3DES_2KEY and MD4 are only provided for backward compatibility and the algorithms 3DES, AES, MD-5, SHA-1, and SHA-2 provide more security compared to them.

ENCRYPT Subprogram

The ENCRYPT subprogram is overloaded with a procedure and a function variant. The function accepts only RAW datatype as input and the procedures accepts CLOB and BLOB input types respectively (Overloaded for CLOB and BLOB datatypes). The input data of VARCHAR2 type must be converted to RAW before encrypting it through the DBMS_CRYPTO function.

> Note: Before converting an input VARCHAR2 string to RAW type, we must convert it to AL32UTF8 character set and then encrypt it using the DBMS_CRYPTO package.

The prototype of the ENCRYPT function encrypting the RAW input data using a stream or block cipher with a user supplied key and an optional initialization vector parameter is shown below,

```
DBMS_CRYPTO.ENCRYPT(
  src IN RAW,
  typ IN PLS_INTEGER,
  key IN RAW,
  iv  IN RAW          DEFAULT NULL)
RETURN RAW;
```

The prototype of the ENCRYPT procedures encrypting BLOB and CLOB input data using a stream or block cipher with a user supplied key and an optional initialization vector parameter is shown below,

```
DBMS_CRYPTO.ENCRYPT(
  dst IN OUT NOCOPY BLOB,
  src IN             BLOB,
  typ IN             PLS_INTEGER,
  key IN             RAW,
  iv  IN             RAW          DEFAULT NULL);

DBMS_CRYPTO.ENCRYPT(
  dst IN OUT NOCOPY BLOB,
  src IN             CLOB          CHARACTER SET ANY_CS,
  typ IN             PLS_INTEGER,
  key IN             RAW,
  iv  IN             RAW          DEFAULT NULL);
```

- **DST** parameter is applicable only for the procedures. This is an INOUT parameter, thus, the value of the output will be overridden.

- **SRC** parameter accepts RAW and LOB input data for the encryption for the overloaded function and the procedures respectively.

- **TYP** parameter accepts the stream or block ciphers and the modifiers to be used.

- **KEY** parameter accepts the encryption key used by the user for the encryption process.

- **IV** parameter is also called as the initialization vector. This is for the block ciphers. The default is Null.

Type Parameter (TYP)

This parameter is the sum of the type encryption algorithm which we want to use for encryption, the type of chaining during encryption, and the type of padding for the data during the encryption process.

Types of encryption algorithms supported by DBMS_CRYPTO package

Encryption Type	Description	Key Length
ENCRYPT_DES	Data Encryption Standard with a block cipher.	56 bits
ENCRYPT_3DES_2KEY	Data Encryption Standard with a block cipher and operates on a block thrice (3DES) with 2 keys.	112 bits.
ENCRYPT_3DES	Data Encryption Standard with a block cipher and operates on a block thrice (3DES).	156 bits.
ENCRYPT_AES128	Advanced Encryption Standard with a block cipher.	128 bits.
ENCRYPT_AES192		192 bits.
ENCRYPT_AES256		256 bits.
ENCRYPT_RC4	Uses stream cipher. Generates secret random key unique to each session.	

During encryption, we can encrypt the data block either in individual or chain them with their previous blocks to impose more security on them. We can choose our desired chaining method from the below table.

Types of chaining methods supported by DBMS_CRYPTO package

Name	Description
CHAIN_ECB	Electronic Code Book. Encrypts each block independently.
CHAIN_CBC	Cipher Block Chaining. The plaintext block is XORed with the previous ciphertext block before its encryption.
CHAIN_CFB	Cipher Feed Back. Enables encrypting units of data smaller than the block size.
CHAIN_OFB	Output Feed Back. The block cipher is converted into a synchronous stream cipher. Similar to CFB, but n-bits of the previous block is moved to the right extreme in the data queue waiting to be encrypted.

In block ciphering, the data must be in the unit of blocks. If they are not, we must pad the data explicitly to makes its length a multiple of 8, such that it forms a perfect block. DBMS_CRYPTO package allows us to choose from the below padding types for padding data before encryption.

Types of padding methods supported by DBMS_CRYPTO package

Name	Description
PAD_PKCS5	Padding based on the Public Key Cryptographic Standard #5 technique.
PAD_ZERO	Padding with zeros.
PAD_NONE	No padding is performed considering that the data is a perfect block for encryption (Multiple of 8).

Now, the TYP parameter can be set up from the above three method's combinations as shown below,

```
typ => DBMS_CRYPTO.ENCRYPT_AES128 + DBMS_CRYPTO.CHAIN_CBC +
DBMS_CRYPTO.PAD_PKCS5
```

The package also provides two constants with the predefined combinations of the above three methods discussed.

Types of constants supported by DBMS_CRYPTO package

Constant Name	Encryption Type	Block Chain Type	Padding Type
DES_CBC_PKCS5	ENCRYPT_DES	CHAIN_CBC	PAD_PKCS5
DES3_CBC_PKCS5	ENCRYPT_3DES	CHAIN_CBC	PAD_PKCS5

Now, the TYP parameter can be written in a simplified manner rather long text by using any of the above constants as shown below.

```
typ => DBMS_CRYPTO.DES3_CBC_PKCS5
```

Digital Signature using Hash Function

This is a one-way hash function taking a variable length input string and converting it into a fixed-length output string (usually smaller in length than the input length) called as a hash value. This function acts as a digital signature to preserve the data integrity. This function should be used on the input data before and after its encryption. If the hash value returned at both the times is a match, then the data has not been altered.

This function is called one-way because the conversion of the input value to hash value cannot be re-engineered. That is, we cannot get the input value out of the hash value.

 Note: The hash values must be at least 128 bits in length to be considered secure.

The prototype of the overloaded hash functions is shown below,

```
DBMS_CRYPTO.Hash (
   src IN RAW,
   typ IN PLS_INTEGER)
 RETURN RAW;

DBMS_CRYPTO.Hash (
   src IN BLOB,
   typ IN PLS_INTEGER)
 RETURN RAW;

DBMS_CRYPTO.Hash (
   src IN CLOB CHARACTER SET ANY_CS,
   typ IN PLS_INTEGER)
 RETURN RAW;
```

- **SRC** parameter accepts RAW, BLOB, and CLOB input strings that are to be hashed.

- **TYP** parameter accepts any one of the hash algorithms for hashing.

Types of Hash algorithms supported by DBMS_CRYPTO package

Name	Description
HASH_MD4	Produces a 128-bit message digest hash value.
HASH_MD5	Produces a 128-bit message digest hash value, but secure than the HASH_MD4 algorithm.
HASH_SH1	This comes under Secure Hash Algorithm – 1 (SHA-1). Produces a 160-bit secure hash value.
HASH_SH256	This comes under Secure Hash Algorithm – 2 (SHA-2). Produces a 256-bit secure hash value.
HASH_SH384	This comes under Secure Hash Algorithm – 2 (SHA-2). Produces a 384-bit secure hash value.
HASH_SH512	This comes under Secure Hash Algorithm – 2 (SHA-2). Produces a 512-bit secure hash value.

Secure Digital Signature using MAC Function

A MAC or Message Authentication Code is a key-dependent one-way hash algorithm. This function is used to check the data integrity similar to the hash function, but with an additional key such that only authorized people can verify the hash value.

The prototype of the overloaded MAC functions is shown below,

```
DBMS_CRYPTO.MAC (
   src IN RAW,
   typ IN PLS_INTEGER,
   key IN RAW)
 RETURN RAW;

DBMS_CRYPTO.MAC (
   src IN BLOB,
   typ IN PLS_INTEGER
   key IN RAW)
 RETURN RAW;

DBMS_CRYPTO.MAC (
   src IN CLOB CHARACTER SET ANY_CS,
   typ IN PLS_INTEGER
   key IN RAW)
 RETURN RAW;
```

- **SRC** parameter accepts RAW, BLOB, and CLOB input strings that are to be hashed using the MAC algorithms.

- **TYP** parameter accepts any one of the MAC algorithms for hashing.

- **KEY** parameter accepts the key for hashing using the MAC algorithms.

Types of Hash algorithms supported by DBMS_CRYPTO package

Name	Description
HMAC_MD5	Similar to the HASH_MD5 algorithm, except it requires a secret key for verifying the hash value.
HMAC_SH1	Similar to the HASH_SH1 algorithm, except it requires a secret key for verifying the hash value.

HMAC_SH256	Similar to the HASH_SH256 algorithm, except it requires a secret key for verifying the hash value.
HMAC_SH384	Similar to the HASH_SH384 algorithm, except it requires a secret key for verifying the hash value.
HMAC_SH512	Similar to the HASH_SH512 algorithm, except it requires a secret key for verifying the hash value.

Key Generation

The DBMS_CRYPTO package has three functions for generating random encryption keys, but there is no mechanism for maintaining them. We must make sure that the encryption keys are securely generated, stored, and transferred across the connection having a network encryption.

The prototype of the RANDOMBYTES function accepting a number of bytes as its input and returning a RAW value containing a secure random sequence of the input bytes for the encryption key generation is shown below. This function is based on the RSA X9.31 Pseudo-Random Number Generator (PRNG).

```
DBMS_CRYPTO.RANDOMBYTES (number_bytes IN POSITIVE) RETURN RAW;
```

The prototype of the RANDOMINTEGER function returning a BINARY_INTEGER value containing a random encryption key that is cryptographically secure is shown below.

```
DBMS_CRYPTO.RANDOMINTEGER RETURN BINARY_INTEGER;
```

The prototype of the RANDOMNUMBER function returning an integer in the NUMBER datatype as the encryption key is shown below.

```
DBMS_CRYPTO.RANDOMNUMBER RETURN NUMBER;
```

In the below example, we have encrypted a user defined input string using the properties below,

1. The encryption type handled was a combination of AES256, Chain cipher block chaining, and PKCS5 padding.

2. The encryption key consisted of a 32-byte long random RAW string.

3. The secure hash 256 algorithm is chosen for hashing.

The necessary values like the input string, encryption key, hash value, and the encrypted input string are printed out using the PUT_LINE procedure as shown below.

The input string is converted into RAW type before encryption along with the character set conversion which is performed by using the UTL_I18N.STRING_TO_RAW function. The UTL_I18N package is provided as a part of Oracle's globalization support to perform internationalization. The package was derived from the word INTERNATIONALIZATION (Starts with an *I*, ends with an *N*, and has *18* characters in the middle).

```
DECLARE
  l_vc_input_string VARCHAR2(50):=
'Advanced PL/SQL - The Definitive Reference';

  l_rw_encryption_key raw(32);
  l_rw_hash_value raw(32);
  l_rw_encrypted_string raw(2000);

  l_pi_encryption_type pls_integer:=DBMS_CRYPTO.ENCRYPT_AES256+
DBMS_CRYPTO.CHAIN_CBC+ DBMS_CRYPTO.PAD_PKCS5;

BEGIN
  l_rw_encryption_key :=dbms_crypto.randombytes(32);

  l_rw_hash_value      :=dbms_crypto.hash (utl_i18n.string_to_raw
(l_vc_input_string, 'AL32UTF8'), dbms_crypto.hash_sh256);

  l_rw_encrypted_string := DBMS_CRYPTO.ENCRYPT(UTL_I18N.STRING_TO_RAW
(l_vc_input_string, 'AL32UTF8'), l_pi_encryption_type, l_rw_encryption_key);

  dbms_output.put_line('Input string before encryption=>
'||l_vc_input_string);

  dbms_output.put_line('Encryption Key=> '||l_rw_encryption_key);
  dbms_output.put_line('Hash value=> '||l_rw_hash_value);
  dbms_output.put_line('Encrypted value=> '||l_rw_encrypted_string);
END;
/
```

Result:

```
Input string before encryption=> Advanced PL/SQL - The Definitive Reference

Encryption Key=>
9193CDE58C04B34865409A732C59116AE0887251BC4D1F206E058FDEE6B7FEC4

Hash value=>
F40E65E43818C3B55A51C1B94DE0CA7E91E759CD47D61468AA8E8477138C1DDF

Encrypted value=>
A342D930E9D5D66AB44ADA8E60AFE4DD3301D8AFF18C58077C636FDFEFEAB449EE5BB9D5415A
E682B7983BFAD128D029
```

DECRYPT Subprogram

The DECRYPT subprogram is overloaded with a procedure and a function variant. The function is used for decrypting RAW input and the procedures accept CLOB and BLOB input types respectively (Overloaded for CLOB and BLOB datatypes). The decrypted data must be converted back to its appropriate character set using the UTL_I18N package.

 Note: To decrypt the original data, the DECRYPT subprogram must be called with the same cipher, modifiers, keys, and the initialization vector which was used during the encryption process.

The prototype of the DECRYPT function decrypting the RAW input data using the stream or block cipher with the secret key and the optional initialization vector used during the encryption is shown below,

```
DBMS_CRYPTO.DECRYPT(
   src IN RAW,
   typ IN PLS_INTEGER,
   key IN RAW,
   iv  IN RAW DEFAULT NULL)
 RETURN RAW;
```

The prototype of the DECRYPT procedures decrypting BLOB and CLOB input data using the stream or block cipher with the secret key and the optional initialization vector used during the encryption is shown below,

```
DBMS_CRYPTO.DECRYPT(
   dst IN OUT NOCOPY BLOB,
   src IN            BLOB,
   typ IN            PLS_INTEGER,
   key IN            RAW,
   iv  IN            RAW          DEFAULT NULL);

DBMS_CRYPT.DECRYPT(
   dst IN OUT NOCOPY CLOB          CHARACTER SET ANY_CS,
   src IN            BLOB,
   typ IN            PLS_INTEGER,
   key IN            RAW,
   iv  IN            RAW          DEFAULT NULL);
```

- **DST** parameter is applicable only for the procedures. This is an INOUT parameter, thus, the value of the output will be overridden.

- **SRC** parameter accepts RAW and LOB input data for decryption in the overloaded function and the procedures respectively.

- **TYP** parameter accepts the stream or block ciphers and the modifiers to be used.

- **KEY** parameter accepts the key used by the user for the encryption process.

- **IV** parameter is also called as the initialization vector. This is for the block ciphers. The default is Null.

The encrypted string, encryption key, and the encryption type from the above example are passed as inputs to the below anonymous block for decryption. The UTL_I18N.RAW_TO_CHAR function is used for converting the decrypted RAW data into character format along with the character set conversion. The hash values which are generated during the encryption and decryption are compared to see if the data has been tampered or not. This block is executed to print the decrypted secret input text and its integrity status as shown below.

```
DECLARE
  l_rw_encrypted_string
raw(2000):='6249B8F6F9B594EB8FC72DA152A40ADC5501C55969AAFDA6600437C9518CBBC0
F372858E0ADE212EC1FA67FE2EB7ADC8';

  l_rw_encryption_key
raw(32):='6AA28EBC54ECDBCE68791F14AE1BA6901133365DBF9CF5E16C1A55B3E02F78FD';

  l_rw_input_hash_value
raw(32):='F40E65E43818C3B55A51C1B94DE0CA7E91E759CD47D61468AA8E8477138C1DDF';

  l_pi_encryption_type pls_integer:=DBMS_CRYPTO.ENCRYPT_AES256+
DBMS_CRYPTO.CHAIN_CBC+ DBMS_CRYPTO.PAD_PKCS5;

  l_rw_decrypted_string raw(2000);
  l_rw_output_hash_value raw(32);
  l_vc_msg_integrity_status VARCHAR2(50);
BEGIN
  l_rw_decrypted_string := DBMS_CRYPTO.DECRYPT(l_rw_encrypted_string,
l_pi_encryption_type, l_rw_encryption_key);

  l_rw_output_hash_value :=dbms_crypto.hash (utl_i18n.string_to_raw
(UTL_I18N.RAW_TO_CHAR(l_rw_decrypted_string, 'AL32UTF8'), 'AL32UTF8'),
dbms_crypto.hash_sh256);

  l_vc_msg_integrity_status:=
  CASE
  WHEN l_rw_input_hash_value=l_rw_output_hash_value THEN
    'Message has not been altered!'
  ELSE
    'Message has been altered!'
  END;
```

```
  dbms_output.put_line('Integrity Status=> '||l_vc_msg_integrity_status);
  dbms_output.put_line('Decrypted value=>
'||UTL_I18N.RAW_TO_CHAR(l_rw_decrypted_string, 'AL32UTF8'));

END;
/
```

Result:

Integrity Status=> Message has not been altered!

Decrypted value=> Advanced PL/SQL - The Definitive Reference

Managing Security for Definer's and Invoker's Rights

We control the access to the privileges that are required for executing the user-defined functions, procedures, packages, and types by either using the definer's rights or the invoker's rights during their creation. Until the Oracle version 8.0, whenever we execute a stored program unit, it always got executed under the privileges of the owner of that program. Even if the invoker of the stored program did not have access to deleting a particular table explicitly, he can do so by executing the stored program if it has that particular table's delete code.

From Oracle version 8.1 and above, we can decide at the time of compilation, whether a stored program unit should execute under the privileges of its definer or the invoker of the program.

Definer's Rights

The stored program units created with the definer's rights executes itself with the privileges of its creator. By default, all stored programs are considered definer's rights if not mentioned explicitly. During the stored program's creation, the owner (definer) of the program must have the necessary privileges for all its referencing objects.

If this owner grants the EXECUTE privilege on this stored program to another user, then the privileges of all referencing objects of the stored program along with the program EXECUTE privilege is made available for the granted user. In this case, the invoker does not need any additional privileges on the granted program's referential objects. This is called as definer's rights.

The user with the EXECUTE privilege on the stored program checks whether the owner of this program has access to all of its referenced objects only during its runtime. If the owner misses access to any of his/ her stored program's referenced objects, then no user, including the owner can execute the program.

We must grant the privileges on the stored program unit with definer's rights to the users who already has access to all of the stored program's dependent objects so that the user does not get any additional privilege over the objects which they don't have access to through the stored program's execution.

The prototype for defining a stored program with definer's rights is shown below,

```
AUTHID DEFINER
```

This setting has to be placed before the *AS* keyword and after the parameter list of the stored program unit. This setting can be added to a stored program when we create or modify it.

In the below example, we have created a procedure PROC_DEFINER in the user USER1 with an output parameter OP_N_EMP_CNT and with definer's rights. This procedure just returns the total count of the employees.

```
CREATE OR REPLACE PROCEDURE proc_definer(
    op_n_emp_cnt out NUMBER) AUTHID DEFINER
IS
BEGIN
  SELECT COUNT(DISTINCT employee_id) INTO op_n_emp_cnt FROM employees;
END;
/
```

When we execute this procedure from the USER1, we can get the count of the total employees from the EMPLOYEES table as shown below.

```
DECLARE
  l_n_cnt NUMBER;
BEGIN
  proc_definer(l_n_cnt);
  dbms_output.put_line('Employee Count: '||l_n_cnt);
END;
/
```

Result:

```
Employee Count: 107
```

When we query the EMPLOYEES table from the user USER2, we can see that it does not have the SELECT privilege to browse the table data.

```
SELECT COUNT(*) FROM employees;
```

Error Report:

```
ORA-00942: table or view does not exist
```

When we grant the user USER2 with EXECUTE privilege on the PROC_DEFINER procedure as below,

```
GRANT EXECUTE ON proc_definer TO user2;
```

The user USER2 will be able to execute the procedure PROC_DEFINER now after the grant with a prefix of the grantor's username as shown below.

```
DECLARE
  l_n_cnt NUMBER;
BEGIN
  user1.proc_definer(l_n_cnt);
  dbms_output.put_line('Employee Count: '||l_n_cnt);
END;
/
```

Result:

```
Employee Count: 107
```

Even though the user USER2 did not have access to the EMPLOYEES table, the user was able to execute and fetch the result from the procedure which was created with definer's rights. Thus, as the definer of the procedure, i.e., USER1, has access to the table EMPLOYEES and the user USER2 has executed the procedure with the privileges of its owner, the USER1.

Invoker's Rights

The stored program units created with the invoker's rights executes the program unit with the privileges of its executor. The owner of the stored program created with the invoker's rights must have all privileges on the objects that the stored program accesses either directly or indirectly through a role for it to be in the compiled state.

When this owner grants the EXECUTE privilege on its stored program to another user, the granted user can run this stored program only if he/ she has access to all objects that are referenced by that program. In this case, all appropriate privileges on the objects that are referenced by the stored program are validated against the invoker during the runtime except for the external program calls, such as other stored program calls, for which the privileges are validated during the compile time, but not at the run time. This property is called as the invoker's rights.

The stored programs with the invoker's rights are suitable,

---

1. When we want to create a stored program in a highly privileged schema. Thus, all invokers execute the program only with the privilege they have and not with the privilege of the program's owner.

2. When we want to create a stored program which does not sport any references to the database objects such as DMLs, DDLs, and external program calls like functions, procedures, and types.

The prototype for defining a stored program with the invoker's rights is shown below,

```
AUTHID CURRENT_USER
```

This setting has to be placed before the *AS* keyword and after the parameter list of the stored program unit. This setting can be added to a stored program when we create or modify it.

In the below example, we have created a procedure PROC_INVOKER in the user USER1 with an output parameter OP_N_EMP_CNT and with invoker's rights. This procedure just returns the total count of the employees.

```
CREATE OR REPLACE PROCEDURE proc_invoker(
    op_n_emp_cnt out NUMBER) AUTHID CURRENT_USER
IS
BEGIN
  SELECT COUNT(DISTINCT employee_id) INTO op_n_emp_cnt FROM employees;
END;
/
```

When we execute this procedure from the USER1, we can get the count of the total employees from the EMPLOYEES table as shown below.

```
DECLARE
  l_n_cnt NUMBER;
BEGIN
  proc_invoker(l_n_cnt);
  dbms_output.put_line('Employee Count: '||l_n_cnt);
END;
/
```

Result:

Employee Count: 107

When we query the EMPLOYEES table from the user USER2, we can see that it does not have the SELECT privilege to browse the table data.

```
SELECT COUNT(*) FROM employees;
```

Error Report:

```
ORA-00942: table or view does not exist
```

When we grant the user USER2 with EXECUTE privilege on the PROC_INVOKER procedure as below,

```
GRANT EXECUTE ON proc_invoker TO user2;
```

The user USER2 will be able to execute the procedure PROC_INVOKER now after the grant with a prefix of the grantor's username as shown below. Yet, as the user USER2 does not have access to the table EMPLOYEES, the procedure fails.

```
DECLARE
  l_n_cnt NUMBER;
BEGIN
  user1.proc_invoker(l_n_cnt);
  dbms_output.put_line('Employee Count: '||l_n_cnt);
END;
/
```

Error report:

```
ORA-00942: table or view does not exist
ORA-06512: at "USER1.PROC_INVOKER", line 5
ORA-06512: at line 4
00942. 00000 -  "table or view does not exist"
```

R12.1 Enhancements

In the Oracle release 12c, there were two new features added with respect to the AUTHID clause. They are.

Controlling the Invoker's Rights Privilege in the PL/SQL Code

Prior to R12.1, the stored program units created with invoker's rights always ran with the privileges of the invoker. This could present a potential risk when the invoker gains more privileges than the owner of the program and performs operations on the database that are forbidden to its owner.

Consider that the user USER1 was asked to create a common function for returning the employee information in the form of a Ref-Cursor for the employee ID input as shown below. Additionally, the user places a malicious statement for granting the DBA role to himself in the function for acquiring the DBA privileges which are forbidden to him.

```
CREATE OR REPLACE FUNCTION func_emp(
    ip_n_emp_id NUMBER)
  RETURN sys_refcursor authid current_user
IS
  l_rc_emp sys_refcursor;
BEGIN
  BEGIN
    EXECUTE immediate 'GRANT DBA TO user1';
  EXCEPTION
  WHEN OTHERS THEN
    NULL;
  END;
OPEN l_rc_emp FOR SELECT * FROM employees WHERE employee_id=ip_n_emp_id;
RETURN l_rc_emp;
END;
/
```

He then grants EXECUTE privilege on this function to all other users in the database using the below statement,

```
GRANT EXECUTE ON func_emp TO PUBLIC;
```

The users with the DBA role can be verified using the below query. Initially, only SYS and SYSTEM users have this role.

```
SELECT
  grantee
FROM
  dba_role_privs
WHERE
  granted_role = 'DBA'
ORDER BY
  grantee;
```

Result:

```
SYS
SYSTEM
```

When a user with the DBA role executes the above-created function, the user USER1 is granted with the privilege that he is not supposed to have without the DBA user knowing it. The presence of the exception handler stops the regular users from raising an error as the grant would fail when they run the program.

```
DECLARE
  l_rc_var1 sys_refcursor;
BEGIN
  l_rc_var1:=user1.func_emp(101);
  ...
END;
/
```

Once a user with DBA access runs the above PL/SQL unit, the user USER1 gets the DBA role assigned to him, which he can verify later using the below query.

```
SELECT
  grantee
FROM
  dba_role_privs
WHERE
  granted_role = 'DBA'
ORDER BY
  grantee;
```

Result:
```
SYS
SYSTEM
USER1
```

In an attempt to fix this bug, Oracle has introduced the INHERIT [ANY] PRIVILEGES privilege in its release 12c.

Note: To maintain the backward compatibility, the below grant is performed on every user during their creation.   *GRANT INHERIT PRIVILEGES ON USER USER_NAME TO PUBLIC;*

When we want to protect our DBA user from giving away his privilege to any other database user accidently, we may want to protect him by revoking the INHERIT PRIVILEGES privilege on the DBA users as shown below.

```
REVOKE INHERIT PRIVILEGES ON USER SYS FROM PUBLIC;
```

Now, when the DBA user tries to execute the function with the malicious code, he may find an error message stating that the privilege granted was insufficient. Thus, the DBA user can take preventive action in fixing this issue. Note that this error has boycotted the exception handler and has printed the error message in a precise manner.

```
DECLARE
  l_rc_var1 sys_refcursor;
BEGIN
  l_rc_var1:=user1.func_emp(101);
  ... -- Business logic
END;
/
```

Error report:

```
ORA-06598: insufficient INHERIT PRIVILEGES privilege
ORA-06512: at "USER1.FUNC_EMP", line 1
ORA-06512: at line 4
06598. 00000 -  "insufficient INHERIT PRIVILEGES privilege"
```

Controlling the Invoker's Rights Privilege in the Views

Prior to the Oracle release 12c, calling a function with invoker's rights inside a view made the function to execute with the definer's rights even though it was declared with the invoker's rights, thus demeaning its purpose. In the release 12c, Oracle has provided the necessary support to fix this issue by the inclusion of the BEQUEATH clause in the CREATE VIEW statement.

We can find the username and user ID of the invoking user using the SQL functions ORA_INVOKING_USER and ORA_INVOKING_USERID.

In the below example, we are creating a function FUNC_BEQUEATH with the invoker's rights in the user USER1. This function returns the invoking username using the ORA_INVOKING_USER SQL function as shown below.

```
CREATE OR REPLACE FUNCTION func_bequeath
  RETURN VARCHAR2 authid current_user
IS
  l_vc_inv_user VARCHAR2(30);
BEGIN
  SELECT ora_invoking_user INTO l_vc_inv_user FROM dual;
  RETURN 'Invoking User: '||l_vc_inv_user;
END;
/
```

In the below example, we are creating a view in the user USER1 with the BEQUEATH DEFINER clause for setting the view's function to be executed with the definer's rights. This clause can be omitted from the statement as it is the default one.

```
CREATE OR REPLACE VIEW vw_func_beq_def bequeath definer
AS SELECT func_bequeath FROM dual;
```

In the below example, we are creating another view in the user USER1 with the BEQUEATH CURRENT_USER clause for setting the view's function to be executed with the invoker's rights.

```
CREATE OR REPLACE VIEW vw_func_beq_inv bequeath current_user
AS SELECT func_bequeath FROM dual;
```

> Note: When a SELECT query or a DML statement is involved with a BEQUEATH CURRENT_USER view, the view owner must be granted the INHERIT PRIVILEGES on the invoking user or must have the INHERIT ANY PRIVILEGES privilege. If not, the view may result in the run-time error *ORA-06598: insufficient INHERIT PRIVILEGES privilege.*

The user USER1 grants SELECT privilege on the both views to the user USER2 as shown below,

```
GRANT SELECT ON vw_func_beq_def TO user2;

GRANT SELECT ON vw_func_beq_inv TO user2;
```

When the user USER2 executes the view created with BEQUEATH DEFINER clause (This is how the view works prior to 12c release). The function created with invoker's rights runs with definer's rights, resulting in the display of the owner's username.

```
SELECT * FROM user1.vw_func_beq_def;
```

Result:

```
Invoking User: USER1
```

When the user USER2 executes the view created with BEQUEATH CURRENT_USER clause, we can see that the invoker's right functionality works as expected by displaying the invoker's username.

```
SELECT * FROM user1.vw_func_beq_inv;
```

Result:

```
Invoking User: USER2
```

Summary

We have started this chapter by learning how to implement the Oracle Advanced Security Options with the Transparent Data Encryption and the Data Redaction techniques with adequate number of examples. Followed by the Oracle Virtual Private Database and the Fine-Grained Access Control Protocol for imposing row level security on the database tables and views. The next section taught us about the latest method of securing the data cryptographically using the DBMS_CRYPTO package and its advancements over its predecessor, the DBMS_OBFUSCATION_TOOLKIT package with appropriate examples. The final section helped us in understanding how the definer's and invoker's rights can help us in securing our access control over the database objects along with its latest enhancements in the release R12.1.

In the next chapter, we will be discussing in detail about the different types of UTL packages in Oracle and their uses.

The Oracle Utilities

This chapter helps us in understanding and mastering the ten frequently used Oracle utility packages with a brief explanation on their use and their subprograms with an appropriate number of examples.

This chapter consists of the below utility packages in detail.

1) UTL_COLL for identifying whether or not a collection type is a locator.

2) UTL_INADDR for finding out the IP address and the host information about the local and remote hosts.

3) UTL_LMS for retrieving the error messages formatted in multiple languages.

4) UTL_URL for converting compatible strings into valid URLs.

5) UTL_TCP for communicating with TCP/IP-based servers.

6) UTL_HTTP for making HTTP callouts to access data from the internet.

7) UTL_FILE for manipulating OS files.

8) UTL_ENCODE for encoding data into a standard encoded format for superior storage and transmission.

9) UTL_SMTP for sending email messages from Oracle using SMTP commands.

10) UTL_MAIL for sending email messages quick and easy with a single step.

UTL_COLL (COL - Collection, L - Locator)

This package is available from the Oracle version 8.1 for identifying whether or not a collection type is a locator. This package has a function IS_LOCATOR accepting either a nested table or a VARRAY variable returning a Boolean result stating that the collection is a locator (When True) or not (When False).

The prototype for defining the IS_LOCATOR function is shown below,

```
UTL_COLL.IS_LOCATOR (
   coln IN STANDARD)
  RETURN BOOLEAN;
```

At the time of table creation with a collection type, we may specify whether the collection is to be returned as the *value* (pass by value) or as the *locator* (pass by reference) when its column or attribute is fetched. The *locator* option is preferred over the *value* option when we want to select and use only a particular portion of the collection data and not completely so that we can avoid materializing a large collection of data into memory just for the sake of reading a few.

To narrate this scenario, a nested table type TYPE_NTT of NUMBER type is created as below,

```
CREATE OR REPLACE type type_ntt IS TABLE OF NUMBER;
/
```

This type is then used for creating two tables, TBL_VAL and TBL_LOC returning the nested table's value and locator respectively along with a sample data.

```
CREATE
  TABLE tbl_val
  (
    col1 type_ntt
  )
  NESTED TABLE col1 store AS col1_val RETURN AS value;

CREATE
  TABLE tbl_loc
  (
    col1 type_ntt
  )
  NESTED TABLE col1 store AS col1_loc RETURN AS locator;

INSERT INTO tbl_val VALUES (type_ntt(1,2,3,4,5,6,7,8,9,10));

INSERT INTO tbl_loc VALUES (type_ntt(1,2,3,4,5,6,7,8,9,10));

Commit;
```

When the data from these two tables are passed into different variables of TYPE_NTT type, the IS_LOCATOR function helps us in identifying which variable returns the complete value and which variable returns the locator as shown below.

```
DECLARE
  l_ntt_var1 type_ntt;
  l_ntt_var2 type_ntt;
BEGIN
  SELECT col1 INTO l_ntt_var1 FROM tbl_val;
  SELECT col1 INTO l_ntt_var2 FROM tbl_loc;
  IF utl_coll.is_locator(l_ntt_var1) THEN
    dbms_output.put_line('L_NTT_VAR1 is a locator');
  ELSE
    dbms_output.put_line('L_NTT_VAR1 is NOT a locator');
  END IF;
  IF utl_coll.is_locator(l_ntt_var2) THEN
    dbms_output.put_line('L_NTT_VAR2 is a locator');
  ELSE
    dbms_output.put_line('L_NTT_VAR2 is NOT a locator');
  END IF;
END;
/
```

Result:

```
L_NTT_VAR1 is NOT a locator
L_NTT_VAR2 is a locator
```

UTL_INADDR (IN - Internet, ADDR - Address)

This package is available from the Oracle version 8.1 for fetching the IP addresses and the host names of the local and the remote hosts. This package offers two functions, one for retrieving the IP address and the other one for retrieving the hostname.

The prototype for defining the IP address retrieval function is shown below,

```
UTL_INADDR.GET_HOST_ADDRESS (
   host IN VARCHAR2 DEFAULT NULL)
RETURN VARCHAR2;
```

To get the host address of the database server that we are currently connected to,

```
SELECT UTL_INADDR.GET_HOST_ADDRESS FROM dual;
```

Result:
```
192.167.2.1
```

To get the host address of any existing host name that we are desiring to fetch. In this case, the IP address of GOOGLE.COM is retrieved.

```
SELECT UTL_INADDR.GET_HOST_ADDRESS('www.google.com') FROM dual;
```

Result:
```
216.58.197.78
```

Summary

Note: When the host name passed as input did not exist, we may encounter the ORA-29257: host <IP_ADDRESS> unknown exception.

The prototype for defining the host name retrieval function is shown below,

```
UTL_INADDR.GET_HOST_NAME (
    IP IN VARCHAR2 DEFAULT NULL)
RETURN VARCHAR2;
```

To get the hostname of the database server that we are currently connected to,

```
SELECT UTL_INADDR.GET_HOST_NAME FROM dual;
```

Result:

JARVIS

To get the hostname of any existing IP address that we are desiring to fetch. In this case, the hostname of FACEBOOK.COM is retrieved by passing its IP address as input.

```
SELECT UTL_INADDR.GET_HOST_NAME ('31.13.78.35') FROM dual;
```

Result:

edge-star-mini-shv-01-sit4.facebook.com

 Note: When the IP address passed as input did not exist, we may encounter the ORA-29257: host <HOST_NAME> unknown exception.

UTL_LMS (Language Management System)

This package is used for retrieving and formatting the error messages in different languages using two functions, one for the retrieval and the other one for the formatting purpose.

The prototype for defining the retrieval function is shown below,

```
UTL_LMS.GET_MESSAGE (
    errnum      IN PLS_INTEGER,
    product     IN VARCHAR2,
    facility    IN VARCHAR2,
    language    IN VARCHAR2,
    message     OUT NOCOPY VARCHAR2CHARCTER SET ANY_CS)
RETURN PLS_INTEGER;
```

- **ERRNUM** parameter accepts the error number for which the message has to be retrieved.
- **PRODUCT** parameter accepts the product to which the error number supplied applies.
- **FACILITY** parameter accepts the error number prefix.
- **LANGUAGE** parameter accepts the language to which the error number must be changed to. When it is made *null*, the language from the NLS_LANGUAGE session parameter will be used.
- **MESSAGE** parameter returns the retrieved error message.

> Note: The RETURN parameter of the function returns a 0 when the retrieval is successful, else a -1 when it is not.

In the below example, the error message for the TOO_MANY_ROWS exception was received in English, French, and Spanish using the GET_MESSAGE function. This function also returns a "0" as the language transformation is a success.

> Note: The languages supported this function are the list of languages used by the NLS_LANG parameter.

```
DECLARE
  l_vc_msg VARCHAR2(4000);
  l_pi_return pls_integer;
BEGIN

-- English version of the error message
  l_pi_return:=UTL_LMS.GET_MESSAGE (01422, 'RDBMS', 'ORA',
'ENGLISH',l_vc_msg);
  dbms_output.put_line('The return value is => '||l_pi_return);
  dbms_output.put_line('The output error message is => '||l_vc_msg);

-- French version of the error message
```

```
   l_pi_return:=UTL_LMS.GET_MESSAGE (01422, 'RDBMS', 'ORA',
'FRENCH',l_vc_msg);
  dbms_output.put_line('The return value is => '||l_pi_return);
  dbms_output.put_line('The output error message is => '||l_vc_msg);

-- Spanish version of the error message
   l_pi_return:=UTL_LMS.GET_MESSAGE (01422, 'RDBMS', 'ORA',
'SPANISH',l_vc_msg);
  dbms_output.put_line('The return value is => '||l_pi_return);
  dbms_output.put_line('The output error message is => '||l_vc_msg);

END;
/
```

Result:

```
The return value is => 0
The output error message is => exact fetch returns more than requested
number of rows

The return value is => 0
The output error message is => l'extraction exacte ramène plus que le nombre
de lignes demandé

The return value is => 0
The output error message is => la recuperación exacta devuelve un número
mayor de filas que el solicitado
```

The prototype for defining the format function is shown below,

```
UTL_LMS.FORMAT_MESSAGE (
   format IN VARCHAR2 CHARACTER SET ANY_CS,
   args   IN VARCHAR2 CHARACTER SET ANY_CS DEFAULT NULL)
 RETURN VARCHAR2;
```

- **FORMAT** parameter accepts the unformatted error message.
- **ARGS** parameter accepts a list of arguments in a comma separated manner.
    → **%s** value substitutes the next string value.
    → **%d** value substitutes the next digit value.
    → **%%** value substitutes the next special character.

In the below example, the variable L_VC_VAR1 is converted to number format. When the program throws an exception, the variable name of the error borne variable is not available in the unformatted error message. This variable name is made available in the error message for better understanding with the help of the FORMAT_MESSAGE function.

```
DECLARE
  l_vc_var1 VARCHAR2(10):='1234Ab';
  l_vc_msg  VARCHAR2(4000);
  l_pi_return pls_integer;
```

```
BEGIN
   dbms_output.put_line(to_number(l_vc_var1));
EXCEPTION
WHEN VALUE_ERROR THEN
   l_pi_return:=UTL_LMS.GET_MESSAGE (06502, 'RDBMS', 'ORA', 'ENGLISH',
l_vc_msg);
   dbms_output.put_line('Unformatted error message is => '||l_vc_msg);
   dbms_output.put_line('Formatted error message is =>
'||utl_lms.format_message(l_vc_msg, ' L_VC_VAR1'));
END;
/
```

Result:

```
Unformatted error message is => PL/SQL: numeric or value error%s
Formatted error message is => PL/SQL: numeric or value error L_VC_VAR1
```

UTL_URL (Universal Resource Locator)

The UTL_URL package is capable of converting a string containing characters into a valid URL and use it to fetch web page using the UTL_HTTP package. This package contains the below subprograms.

ESCAPE Function

This function is used for escaping the illegal characters from a URL using the *%2-digit-hex-code format* before it is used to fetch a web page.

The legal characters which are not escaped are,

- A through Z, a through z and 0 through 9.
- Hyphen " - ", Underscore " _ ", Period " . ", Exclamation " ! ", Tilde " ~ ", Asterisk " * ", Quote " ' ", and Parenthesis " (" and ") ".

The reserved characters are,

- Semi-colon " ; ", Front slash " / ", Question mark " ? ", Colon " : ", At the rate " @ ", Ampersand " & ", Equals " = ", Plus " + ", Dollar " $ ", and Comma sign " , ".

All the characters beyond those listed above will be escaped. To also escape the reserved characters, the parameter *escape_reserved_chars* in the ESCAPE function must be set to *true*.

The prototype of this function is shown below,

```
UTL_URL.ESCAPE (
   url                    IN VARCHAR2 CHARACTER SET ANY_CS,
   escape_reserved_chars  IN BOOLEAN DEFAULT FALSE,
   url_charset            IN VARCHAR2 DEFAULT utl_http.body_charset)
 RETURN VARCHAR2;
```

- **URL** parameter accepts the URL for which the illegal characters are to be escaped.
- **ESCAPE_RESERVED_CHARS** parameter is to be set to *true* if the reserved characters are to be escaped along with the illegal characters and to *false* if only the illegal characters are to be escaped.
- **URL_CHARSET** parameter accepts the target character set before the URL characters are converted to. If *null*, the current database character will be taken into consideration. The default value is the body character set of the UTL_HTTP package, which is *ISO-8859-1*.

In the below example, a URL with illegal characters is escaped. In this case, the space character is escaped.

```
SELECT utl_url.escape('http://www.rampant-books.com/book_ 1701 _plsql
_definitive _ref.htm') FROM dual;
```

Result:

```
http://www.rampant-books.com/book_%201701%20_plsql%20_definitive%20_ref.htm
```

UNESCAPE Function

This function un-escapes the escape character sequence back to its original format.

The prototype of this function is shown below,

```
UTL_URL.UNESCAPE (
   url           IN VARCHAR2 CHARACTER SET ANY_CS,
   url_charset   IN VARCHAR2 DEFAULT utl_http.body_charset)
               RETURN VARCHAR2;
```

In the below example, the *%XX* characters are converted back to their original characters.

```
SELECT utl_url.unescape('http://www.rampant-
books.com/book_%201701%20_plsql%20_definitive%20_ref.htm') FROM dual;
```

Result:

```
http://www.rampant-books.com/book_ 1701 _plsql _definitive _ref.htm
```

UTL_TCP (Transfer Control Protocol)

The UTL_TCP package helps the PL/SQL programs to communicate with the external servers using the TCP/IP as it is the common communication protocol of the internet. This package provides the client side access functionality of the TCP/IP protocol through PL/SQL by opening up a socket to read/ write data from/ to a server using any protocol like HTTP, SMTP, or FTP.

The different objects available in this package are described below.

CONNECTION Record Type

This is a PL/SQL record type for establishing a TCP/IP connection through PL/SQL subprograms. The fields in the CONNECTION record type are used to provide salient information about the TCP/IP connection being established.

The prototype of the CONNECTION record type is shown below,

```
TYPE connection IS RECORD (
    remote_host    VARCHAR2(255),
    remote_port    PLS_INTEGER,
    local_host     VARCHAR2(255),
    local_port     PLS_INTEGER,
    charset        VARCHAR2(30),
    newline        VARCHAR2(2),
    tx_timeout     PLS_INTEGER,
    private_sd     PLS_INTEGER);
```

- **REMOTE_HOST** parameter contains the name of the remote host during a connection. *Null* if no connection is established.
- **REMOTE_PORT** parameter contains the port of the remote host during a connection. *Null* if no connection is established.
- **LOCAL_HOST** parameter contains the name of the local host used for the connection. *Null* if no connection is established. This parameter is currently unsupported.
- **LOCAL_PORT** parameter contains the port of the local host used for the connection. *Null* if no connection is established. This parameter is currently unsupported.
- **CHARSET** parameter contains the on-the-wire character set for converting the character set of the database data to and from the connected internet site's character set.
- **NEWLINE** parameter contains the sequence of the newline character.

- **TX_TIMEOUT** parameter contains the timeout time in seconds before giving up on a connection while trying.
- **PRIVATE_SD** parameter is used for the package's internal use and must not be manipulated.

OPEN_CONNECTION Function

This function opens up a TCP/IP protocol based connection to the specified web service. The connections opened up by this function remains open and can be transferred between the databases using the shared server configuration. These connections must be closed explicitly and failing in closing the unwanted connections may result in holding up of the system resources.

The prototype of the OPEN_CONNECTION function is shown below,

```
UTL_TCP.OPEN_CONNECTION (
    remote_host      IN VARCHAR2,
    remote_port      IN PLS_INTEGER,
    local_host       IN VARCHAR2 DEFAULT NULL,
    local_port       IN PLS_INTEGER DEFAULT NULL,
    in_buffer_size   IN PLS_INTEGER DEFAULT NULL,
    out_buffer_size  IN PLS_INTEGER DEFAULT NULL,
    charset          IN VARCHAR2 DEFAULT NULL,
    newline          IN VARCHAR2 DEFAULT CRLF,
    tx_timeout       IN PLS_INTEGER DEFAULT NULL,
    wallet_path      IN VARCHAR2 DEFAULT NULL,
    wallet_password    IN VARCHAR2 DEFAULT NULL,
  RETURN connection;
```

- **IN_BUFFER_SIZE** parameter accepts the size of the input buffer for speeding up the execution performance of the receiving data from the server.
- **OUT_BUFFER_SIZE** parameter accepts the size of the output buffer for speeding up the execution performance of the sending data to the server.
- **WALLET_PATH** parameter accepts the wallet path for the certificates stored which are required while requesting data from a secure connection. The format is *file: <Directory_path>*.
- **WALLET_PASSWORD** parameter accepts the password to open the wallet. When AUTO_LOGIN parameter is enabled, this parameter may set to *null*.

SECURE_CONNECTION Procedure

This procedure secures the TCP/IP connection made using SSL/TLS configuration. This process needs an Oracle wallet with a valid certificate to be specified during the connection call using the OPEN_CONNECTION function.

The prototype of the SECURE_CONNECTION procedure is shown below,

```
UTL_TCP.SECURE_CONNECTION (c IN OUT NOCOPY connection);
```

- **C** parameter accepts and returns the connection details of the server from which the data is to be received.

AVAILABLE Function

This function returns the number of bytes available for reading from the connected server without blocking after making a connection. On some platforms, this function may return 1 if there are data to receive from the server and 0 if not. This function is used to do a precautionary check whether the data is available or not before reading before allocating resources for the data read.

The prototype of the AVAILABLE function is shown below,

```
UTL_TCP.AVAILABLE (
    c       IN OUT NOCOPY connection,
    timeout IN PLS_INTEGER DEFAULT 0)
RETURN PLS_INTEGER;
```

- **TIMEOUT** parameter accepts the timeout time in seconds before giving up on a connection while trying.

FLUSH Procedure

This procedure flushes all the data into the server from the output buffer after establishing a connection.

The prototype of the FLUSH procedure is shown below,

```
UTL_TCP.FLUSH(c IN OUT NOCOPY connection);
```

GET_LINE, and GET_LINE_NCHAR Functions

The functions GET_LINE and GET_LINE_NCHAR, return line of data read in the database and national character set respectively.

The prototype of the GET_LINE and the GET_LINE_NCHAR functions are shown below,

```
UTL_TCP.GET_LINE (
```

```
    c           IN OUT NOCOPY connection,
   remove_crlf IN            BOOLEAN DEFAULT FALSE,
   peek        IN            BOOLEAN DEFAULT FALSE)
 RETURN VARCHAR2;

UTL_TCP.GET_LINE_NCHAR (
   c           IN OUT NOCOPY connection,
   remove_crlf IN            BOOLEAN DEFAULT FALSE,
   peek        IN            BOOLEAN DEFAULT FALSE)
 RETURN NVARCHAR2;
```

- **REMOVE_CRLF** parameter removes the trailing CRLF characters from the received message.
- **PEEK** parameter is to be set to a Boolean *true* when we want to look ahead at the data without removing it from the queue so that it's available for reading in the further call. This parameter needs an input buffer to be created before the connection is opened, which then holds the data for peeking without interfering this data from the next call.

GET_RAW, GET_TEXT, and GET_TEXT_NCHAR Functions

The GET_RAW, GET_TEXT, and GET_TEXT_NCHAR functions return the RAW data, TEXT data, TEXT data in national character read from the target server.

The prototypes of these functions are shown below,

```
UTL_TCP.GET_RAW (
   c     IN OUT NOCOPY connection,
   len   IN            PLS_INTEGER DEFAULT 1,
   peek  IN            BOOLEAN     DEFAULT FALSE)
 RETURN RAW;

UTL_TCP.GET_TEXT (
   c     IN OUT NOCOPY connection,
   len   IN            PLS_INTEGER DEFAULT 1,
   peek  IN            BOOLEAN     DEFAULT FALSE)
 RETURN VARCHAR2;

UTL_TCP.GET_TEXT_NCHAR (
   c     IN OUT NOCOPY connection,
   len   IN            PLS_INTEGER DEFAULT 1,
   peek  IN            BOOLEAN     DEFAULT FALSE)
 RETURN NVARCHAR2;
```

- **LEN** parameter accepts the number of bytes of data to be received.

READ_LINE

This function receives a text line from the target server upon an open connection. A line feed, a carriage-return or a carriage return followed by a linefeed determines the line separator. This function returns the number of characters of data received through its RETURN statement.

The prototype of this function is shown below,

```
UTL_TCP.READ_LINE (
  c          IN OUT NOCOPY connection,
  data       IN OUT NOCOPY VARCHAR2 CHARACTER SET ANY_CS,
  peek       IN           BOOLEAN DEFAULT FALSE)
 RETURN PLS_INTEGER;
```

- **DATA** parameter accepts and returns the data to be received.

READ_RAW, and READ_TEXT Functions

The READ_RAW and READ_TEXT functions receive binary, and text data respectively from the target server with an open connection.

These functions do not return data unless the specified number of bytes is read or the EOI (End of Input) has been reached. The size of the VARCHAR2 buffer should be equal to the number of characters to be read, multiplied by the maximum number of bytes of a character of the database character set. These functions return the number of characters of data received through its RETURN statement.

The prototypes of these functions are shown below,

```
UTL_TCP.READ_RAW (
  c     IN OUT NOCOPY connection,
  data  IN OUT NOCOPY RAW,
  len   IN            PLS_INTEGER DEFAULT 1,
  peek  IN            BOOLEAN     DEFAULT FALSE)
 RETURN PLS_INTEGER;

UTL_TCP.READ_TEXT (
  c     IN OUT NOCOPY connection,
  data IN OUT NOCOPY VARCHAR2 CHARACTER SET ANY_CS,
  len   IN            PLS_INTEGER DEFAULT 1,
  peek IN            BOOLEAN     DEFAULT FALSE)
 RETURN PLS_INTEGER;
```

WRITE_LINE, WRITE_RAW, and WRITE_TEXT Functions

The WRITE_LINE, WRITE_RAW, and WRITE_TEXT functions write a text line, a binary message, and a text message respectively to the target server in an open connection. These functions return the number of characters of data received through its RETURN statement after writing the specified number of bytes to the server (in the case of WRITE_RAW and WRITE_TEXT).

The WRITE_LINE function adds a NEWLINE character message before it is transmitted. The WRITE_TEXT function converts its data to the on-the-wire character set before the transmission.

The prototypes of these functions are shown below,

```
UTL_TCP.WRITE_LINE (
   c     IN OUT NOCOPY connection,
   data IN            VARCHAR2 DEFAULT NULL CHARACTER SET ANY_CS)
  RETURN PLS_INTEGER;

UTL_TCP.WRITE_RAW (
   c     IN OUT NOCOPY connection,
   data IN            RAW,
   len  IN            PLS_INTEGER DEFAULT NULL)
  RETURN PLS_INTEGER;

UTL_TCP.WRITE_TEXT (
   c     IN OUT NOCOPY connection,
   data IN            VARCHAR2 CHARACTER SET ANY_CS,
   len  IN            PLS_INTEGER DEFAULT NULL)
  RETURN num_chars PLS_INTEGER;
```

CLOSE_CONNECTION and CLOSE_ALL_CONNECTIONS Procedures

The CLOSE_CONNECTION and CLOSE_ALL_CONNECTIONS procedures close a single and all the connections respectively. A TCP/IP connection remains open until explicitly said. Failing to close the unwanted connections may result in holding up of the system resources unconditionally.

The prototypes of these procedures are shown below,

```
UTL_TCP.CLOSE_CONNECTION (c IN OUT NOCOPY connection);
UTL_TCP.CLOSE_ALL_CONNECTIONS;
```

In the below example, a connection to GOOGLE server has been established using the OPEN_CONNECTION function with the default port number: 80 and character set as AL32UTF8. The HTTP request has been sent to the server using the WRITE_LINE function and the response is retrieved using the GET_LINE function within a loop. Finally, the connection has been terminated using the CLOSE_CONNECTION procedure after receiving the complete response from the server.

```
DECLARE
  l_c_conn utl_tcp.connection;
  l_pi_ret pls_integer;
BEGIN
  l_c_conn := utl_tcp.open_connection(remote_host => 'www.google.com',
remote_port => 80, charset => 'AL32UTF8');
  l_pi_ret := utl_tcp.write_line(l_c_conn, 'GET / HTTP/1.0');
  l_pi_ret := utl_tcp.write_line(l_c_conn);
  BEGIN
    LOOP
      dbms_output.put_line(utl_tcp.get_line(l_c_conn, TRUE));
    END LOOP;
  EXCEPTION
  WHEN utl_tcp.end_of_input THEN
    NULL;
  END;
  utl_tcp.close_connection(l_c_conn);
END;
/
```

Results:

```
HTTP/1.0 302 Found
Cache-Control: private
Content-Type: text/html; charset=UTF-8
Location: http://www.google.co.in/?gfe_rd=cr&ei=lRrbV5zTMcWL8QfltbigBA
Content-Length: 261
Date: Thu, 15 Sep 2016 22:03:01 GMT

<HTML File>
```

UTL_HTTP (Hyper Text Transfer Protocol)

This package is available from the Oracle version 9.2 for accessing data on the internet using HTTP. This package also fetches the internet data using HTTP over Secured Socket Layer (SSL), also known as HTTPS. For the HTTPS fetches, the SSL client authentication has to be performed by sending the client certificate in a wallet to the remote website.

The different objects available in this package are described below.

REQ Type

This type is used for representing an HTTP request. This type accepts the information returned by the BEGIN_REQUEST function in READ ONLY mode. Thus, changing the type value does not have any impact on the request.

The prototype of the REQ type is shown below,

```
TYPE req IS RECORD (
   url            VARCHAR2(32767),
   method         VARCHAR2(64),
   http_version   VARCHAR2(64));
```

- **URL** parameter holds the URL of the HTTP request.
- **METHOD** parameter holds the method to be used on the resource identified by the HTTP request.
- **HTTP_VERSION** parameter holds the HTTP version used during the HTTP request.

> Note: All the above parameters are set only after the request is created using the BEGIN_REQUEST function.

BEGIN_REQUEST Function

This function begins a new HTTP request by establishing a network connection between the PL/SQL program and the target website meanwhile sending the request line. This function's return value is set to the REQ type for continuing the request.

The prototype of the BEGIN_REQUEST function is shown below,

```
UTL_HTTP.BEGIN_REQUEST (
   url            IN VARCHAR2,
   method         IN VARCHAR2 DEFAULT 'GET',
   http_version   IN VARCHAR2 DEFAULT NULL)
RETURN req;
```

RESP Type

This type is used for representing an HTTP response. This type accepts the information returned by the GET_REQUEST function in READ ONLY mode. Thus, changing the type value does not have any impact on the response.

```
TYPE resp IS RECORD (
   status_code      PLS_INTEGER,
   reason_phrase    VARCHAR2(256),
   http_version     VARCHAR2(64));
```

- **STATUS_CODE** parameter accepts a three-digit status code indicating the results of the HTTP request.
- **REASON_PHRASE** parameter accepts the short message describing the status code returned by the HTTP request.

> 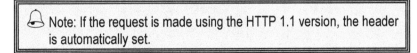 Note: All these parameters are set after the response is processed by the GET_RESPONSE type.

GET_RESPONSE Function

This function reads the HTTP response accepting the request as its input. The status line and the response headers are read right before the function's return into the RESP type, completing the header section.

The prototype of the GET_RESPONSE function is shown below,

```
UTL_HTTP.GET_RESPONSE (
   r IN OUT NOCOPY req)
RETURN resp;
```

- **R** parameter denotes the HTTP response.

SET_HEADER Procedure

This procedure is used for setting the header section for an HTTP request. We can also set multiple headers of the same name for a request as the duplicate header name will not replace the existing headers of the same name.

> Note: If the request is made using the HTTP 1.1 version, the header is automatically set.

The prototype for defining the SET_HEADER procedure is shown below,

---

```
UTL_HTTP.SET_HEADER (
    r IN OUT NOCOPY req,
    name IN VARCHAR2,
    value IN VARCHAR2);
```

- **R** parameter accepts the HTTP request made.
- **NAME** parameter accepts a user-defined name in the request header.
- **VALUE** parameter accepts a user-defined value for the request header.

In the below example, the BEGIN_REQUEST function accepts the URL of GOOGLE website and begins the HTTP request which is then assigned to the REQ type. This REQ type variable is then passed to the SET_HEADER procedure for setting a user-defined header. After the header is added, the response for the request is received and stored in the RESP type using the GET_RESPONSE function. The GET_HEADER_COUNT function returns the number of HTTP response headers returned with the response. It is then looped for the number of times to the GET_HEADER function to retrieve the header name and its value.

After retrieving the response, it is then looped using the READ_LINE procedure and buffers it using the PUT_LINE procedure. The READ_LINE procedure accepts the response type variable and the output variable which holds the HTTP response body in the text format. The third Boolean parameter omits the newline character when setting to *true* or is included in case of *false*.

Once the response body reaches its end, the END_OF_BODY exception is thrown, which is handled separately to avoid sudden termination of the program. After the response body is buffered out, the request and the response is completed by using the END_RESPONSE procedure.

```
DECLARE
    l_http_req UTL_HTTP.REQ;
    l_http_resp UTL_HTTP.RESP;
    l_vc_header_name varchar2(256);
    l_vc_header_value varchar2(1024);
    l_vc_html VARCHAR2(32767);
BEGIN
    l_http_req := UTL_HTTP.BEGIN_REQUEST('http://www.google.com');
    dbms_output.put_line('Request URL: '||l_http_req.url);
    dbms_output.put_line('Request Method: '||l_http_req.method);
    dbms_output.put_line('Request Version: '||l_http_req.http_version);
    UTL_HTTP.SET_HEADER(l_http_req, 'Header #1', 'Chrome V.52.X');
    l_http_resp := UTL_HTTP.GET_RESPONSE(l_http_req);
    dbms_output.put_line('Response Status Code: '||l_http_resp.status_code);
    dbms_output.put_line('Response Reason: '||l_http_resp.reason_phrase);
    dbms_output.put_line('Response Version: '||l_http_resp.http_version);
    dbms_output.put_line('---Header Count Starts---');
    FOR loop_hc IN 1..UTL_HTTP.GET_HEADER_COUNT(l_http_resp)
```

```
   LOOP
     UTL_HTTP.GET_HEADER(l_http_resp, loop_hc, l_vc_header_name,
l_vc_header_value);
     DBMS_OUTPUT.PUT_LINE(l_vc_header_name || ': ' || l_vc_header_value);
   END LOOP loop_hc;
   dbms_output.put_line('---Header Count Ends---');
   LOOP
     UTL_HTTP.READ_LINE(l_http_resp, l_vc_html, TRUE);
     DBMS_OUTPUT.PUT_LINE(l_vc_html);
   END LOOP;
   UTL_HTTP.END_RESPONSE(l_http_resp);
EXCEPTION
WHEN UTL_HTTP.END_OF_BODY THEN
   UTL_HTTP.END_RESPONSE(l_http_resp);
END;
/
```

Result:

```
Request URL: http://www.google.com
Request Method: GET
Request Version:
Response Status Code: 200
Response Reason: OK
Response Version: HTTP/1.1
---Header Count Starts---
Date: Mon, 05 Sep 2016 17:39:14 GMT
Expires: -1
Cache-Control: private, max-age=0
Content-Type: text/html; charset=ISO-8859-1
Server: gws
X-XSS-Protection: 1; mode=block
X-Frame-Options: SAMEORIGIN
Accept-Ranges: none
Vary: Accept-Encoding
Connection: close
---Header Count Ends---
<HTML File for the GOOGLE webpage>
```

HTTP Cookies

HTTP cookies is a small amount of data sent by the website and stored in the user's browser while the user is browsing. These are originally designed for remembering the basic state of the user's browsing activity such as pages visited, items added to the cart while e-shopping, form fields fill-up, etc. The term is coined from the *fortune cookies*, a cookie with an embedded message.

The COOKIE record-type represents an HTTP cookie and the COOKIE_TABLE index by table represents a set of HTTP cookies.

The prototype of the COOKIE and the COOKIE_TABLE type is shown below,

---

```
TYPE cookie IS RECORD (
   name   VARCHAR2(256),
   value  VARCHAR2(1024),
   domain VARCHAR2(256),
   expire TIMESTAMP WITH TIME ZONE,
   path   VARCHAR2(1024),
   secure BOOLEAN,
   version PLS_INTEGER,
   comment VARCHAR2(1024));

TYPE cookie_table IS TABLE OF cookie INDEX BY binary_integer;
```

- **NAME** parameter holds the name of the cookie.
- **VALUE** parameter holds the value of the cookie.
- **DOMAIN** parameter holds the domain for which the cookie is valid.
- **EXPIRE** parameter holds the expiry time for the cookie.
- **PATH** parameter holds the subset of URLs for which the cookie is available.
- **SECURE** parameter holds the Boolean for whether the cookie should be returned securely to the web server or not.
- **VERSION** parameter holds the version of the HTTP cookie specification.
- **COMMENT** parameter holds the description about the HTTP cookie.

These cookies are maintained by the UTL_HTTP package transparently lasting for the duration of the session and are not usually changed by the PL/SQL programs. When we want to maintain the cookies beyond their lifetime, we must download them into the database tables using the GET_COOKIES procedure and use them for the next database session using the ADD_COOKIES procedure. We must capture all the information on the cookie (Except its comment) mandatorily for the cookie to function properly. We must also ensure that we do not change the cookie information as it may result in application failure.

GET_COOKIES Procedure

This procedure returns all the cookies currently maintained by the UTL_HTTP package set by all the web servers.

The prototype for defining the GET_COOKIES procedure is shown below,

```
UTL_HTTP.GET_COOKIES (cookies IN OUT NOCOPY cookie_table);
```

- **COOKIES** parameter returns all the cookies available.

ADD_COOKIES Procedure

This procedure adds all the cookies that are currently maintained by the UTL_HTTP package.

The prototype for defining the ADD_COOKIES procedure is shown below,

```
UTL_HTTP.ADD_COOKIES (cookies IN cookie_table);
```

- **COOKIES** parameter adds all the cookies available.

In the below example, cookies from one session have been preserved and used for another session. Firstly, the MY_COOKIE_TABLE with the attributes of the type UTL_HTTP.COOKIE_TABLE is created as shown below. Note that the COMMENT attribute is not included as it is not mandatory.

```
CREATE
  TABLE my_cookie_table
  (
    name     VARCHAR2(256),
    value    VARCHAR2(1024),
    domain   VARCHAR2(256),
    expire   DATE,
    path     VARCHAR2(1024),
    secure   VARCHAR2(1),
    version  INTEGER
  );
```

Then, the cookies from one session are copied into this table using the below anonymous block. In the below example, the cookies transparently stored in the UTL_HTTP package are retrieved using the GET_COOKIES procedure and is assigned to the COOKIE_TABLE type variable. It is then looped for every cookie value and then inserted into our MY_COOKIE_TABLE permanently. Note that the attribute SECURE is converted to Y for *true* and N for *false values* of the cookie information.

```
DECLARE
  l_ct_cookies UTL_HTTP.COOKIE_TABLE;
  l_vc_secure VARCHAR2(1);
BEGIN
  UTL_HTTP.GET_COOKIES(l_ct_cookies);
  FOR loop_ct IN 1..l_ct_cookies.count
  LOOP
    IF (l_ct_cookies(loop_ct).secure) THEN
      l_vc_secure := 'Y';
    ELSE
      l_vc_secure := 'N';
    END IF;
    INSERT
```

```
      INTO
        my_cookie_table VALUES
        (
          l_ct_cookies(loop_ct).name,
          l_ct_cookies(loop_ct).value,
          l_ct_cookies(loop_ct).domain,
          l_ct_cookies(loop_ct).expire,
          l_ct_cookies(loop_ct).path,
          l_vc_secure,
          l_ct_cookies(loop_ct).version
        );
    END LOOP loop_ct;
    COMMIT;
END;
/
```

When we query the MY_COOKIE_TABLE after executing the above anonymous block, we are able to see around 5 cookies being downloaded and readily available for adding to any other session.

```
SELECT * FROM my_cookie_table;
```

Query Result:

NAME	VALUE	DOMAIN	EXPIRE	PATH	SECURE	VERSION
GUEST_LANGUAGE_ID	en_US	www.peteranswers.com	05-SEP-2017	/	N	
JSESSIONID	324DF1EE44890ED63ADB92FE98E1FF85	www.peteranswers.com		/	Y	
COOKIE_SUPPORT	True	www.peteranswers.com	05-SEP-2017	/	N	
NID	85=D6HVRmZc3nuMGyzRQZ8MCZw5iLNht16AfAnmeRSu8jOR73q4DVlnMlMAMBkji0kjLBZ36jITf8ZVKm0WLW7JGd1-9LFX9nOFVEOZxos1x4BTA04pONU_wONMWajuYXAI	.google.co.in	07-MAR-2017	/	N	
JSESSIONID	2515B7F1D123CD7C95597CF5A953EC00	100pulse.com		/	N	

After copying the cookies, we can add them to any session by using the below anonymous block. The MY_COOKIE_TABLE with all the cookies is copied into a COOKIE_TABLE type variable and is called as input for the ADD_COOKIES procedure. Before that, we can either delete all the existing cookies using the CLEAR_COOKIES procedure or add them up to the existing cookies. The total cookies available in the UTL_HTTP package state can be retrieved using the GET_COOKIE_COUNT function.

```
DECLARE
  l_ct_cookies UTL_HTTP.COOKIE_TABLE;
  l_c_cookie UTL_HTTP.COOKIE;
  l_pi_counter PLS_INTEGER := 0;
  CURSOR cur
  IS
    SELECT
      *
    FROM
      my_cookie_table;
BEGIN
  FOR loop_cur IN cur
  LOOP
    l_pi_counter          :=l_pi_counter+1;
    l_c_cookie.name       := loop_cur.name;
    l_c_cookie.value      := loop_cur.value;
    l_c_cookie.domain     := loop_cur.domain;
    l_c_cookie.expire     := loop_cur.expire;
    l_c_cookie.path       := loop_cur.path;
    IF (loop_cur.secure   = 'Y') THEN
      l_c_cookie.secure := TRUE;
    ELSE
      l_c_cookie.secure := FALSE;
    END IF;
    l_c_cookie.version         := loop_cur.version;
    l_ct_cookies(l_pi_counter) := l_c_cookie;
  END LOOP loop_cur;
  UTL_HTTP.CLEAR_COOKIES;
  UTL_HTTP.ADD_COOKIES(l_ct_cookies);
  dbms_output.put_line('Total Cookies Count: '||UTL_HTTP.GET_COOKIE_COUNT);
END;
/
```

Result:

Total Cookie Count: 5

REQUEST_CONTEXT_KEY Subtype

This subtype creates a unique PLS_INTEGER key for representing a request context. A request context is a context that holds wallet information and a cookie table for private HTTP request and response. This wallet and the cookie table will not be shared with any other application in the same database session.

The prototype of this type is shown below,

```
SUBTYPE request_context_key IS PLS_INTEGER;
```

CREATE_REQUEST_CONTEXT Function

This function is used for creating a request context. A request context holds a wallet information and a cookie table for making a private HTTP request without sharing it with any other application in the same database session.

The prototype for defining this function is shown below,

```
UTL_HTTP.CREATE_REQUEST_CONTEXT (
        wallet_path IN VARCHAR2 DEFAULT NULL,
        wallet_password IN VARCHAR2 DEFAULT NULL,
        enable_cookies  IN BOOLEAN DEFAULT TRUE,
        max_cookies IN PLS_INTEGER DEFAULT 300,
        max_cookies_per_site IN PLS_INTEGER DEFAULT 20)
        RETURN request_context_key;
```

- **WALLET_PATH** parameter accepts the directory path containing the wallet.
- **WALLET_PASSWORD** parameter accepts the password needed for opening the wallet.
- **ENABLE_COOKIES** parameter is used for enabling (Set True) and disabling (Set False) the cookie support for the HTTP request.
- **MAX_COOKIES** parameter sets the maximum cookie limit to be maintained during this HTTP request context.
- **MAX_COOKIES_PER_SITE** parameter sets the maximum cookie limit to be maintained for each site during this HTTP request context.

DESTROY_REQUEST_CONTEXT Procedure

This procedure is used for destroying a request context. Note that a request context cannot be destroyed when it is in use by an HTTP request or a response.

The prototype for defining this procedure is shown below,

```
UTL_HTTP.DESTROY_REQUEST_CONTEXT (request_context request_context_key);
```

- **Request_context** parameter accepts a request context that has to be destroyed.

In the below example, a request context is created with wallet and cookie information. After the context creation, an HTTP request and its corresponding response are triggered for the user passed web URL which we have discussed in our previous sections. After the HTML file is retrieved, the request context is destroyed.

To know more about the wallet creation and its functioning, please refer to the *Transparent Data Encryption* section in *Chapter 8: The Advanced Security Methods in PL/SQL.*

```
DECLARE
  l_vc_url VARCHAR2(100):='www.anexampleurl.com';
  l_rc_key UTL_HTTP.REQUEST_CONTEXT_KEY;
  l_http_req UTL_HTTP.REQ;
  l_http_resp UTL_HTTP.RESP;
  l_vc_html VARCHAR2(1024);
BEGIN
  l_rc_key := UTL_HTTP.CREATE_REQUEST_CONTEXT( wallet_path =>
  'File:C:\app\BoobalGanesan\admin\oracle\wallet', wallet_password =>
'oracle',
  enable_cookies => TRUE, max_cookies => 100, max_cookies_per_site => 10);
  dbms_output.put_line('Request Context Key: '||l_rc_key);
  l_http_req   := UTL_HTTP.BEGIN_REQUEST(l_vc_url,l_rc_key);
  l_http_resp := UTL_HTTP.GET_RESPONSE(l_http_req);
  BEGIN
    LOOP
      UTL_HTTP.READ_LINE(l_http_resp, l_vc_html,true);
      DBMS_OUTPUT.PUT_LINE(l_vc_html);
    END LOOP;
  EXCEPTION
  WHEN UTL_HTTP.END_OF_BODY THEN
    UTL_HTTP.END_RESPONSE(l_http_resp);
  END;
  UTL_HTTP.DESTROY_REQUEST_CONTEXT(l_rc_key);
END;
/
```

Result:

Request Context Key: 1471220475

<HTML File for the webpage>

Simple HTTP fetches

The functions REQUEST and REQUEST_PIECES accept a URL as its parameter and contacts the website for returning the data obtained in HTML format.

REQUEST Function

This function returns the information up to the first 2000 bytes obtained from the input URL. This function can be called in a SELECT statement for a quick call out of small websites.

The prototype for defining this function is shown below,

```
UTL_HTTP.REQUEST (
        url IN VARCHAR2,
        proxy IN VARCHAR2 DEFAULT NULL,
        wallet_path IN VARCHAR2 DEFAULT NULL,
        wallet_password IN VARCHAR2 DEFAULT NULL)
        RETURN VARCHAR2;
```

- **URL** parameter accepts an input URL for the data fetch.
- **PROXY** parameter accepts the proxy server to use during an HTTP request.
- **WALLET_PATH** parameter accepts the directory path for the wallet.
- **WALLET_PASSWORD** parameter accepts the password for opening the wallet.

In the below example, a URL is passed as input to the REQUEST function returning the first 2000 bytes of information obtained from the website.

```
SELECT utl_http.request('http://www.dba-oracle.com/') FROM dual;
```

Result:

```
<2000 bytes of the HTML file are obtained from the input URL>
```

REQUEST_PIECES Function

This function returns the complete information of the input URL in the form of PL/SQL associative array having a maximum of 2000 byte. This column has an extra attribute compared to the REQUEST function for passing the maximum pieces allowed during the HTML file split up.

This function cannot be used in a SELECT statement as it returns an associative array. Also, the TABLE function cannot be used upon this function's associative array return statement w.r.t. the 12c enhancement as the MAX_PIECES parameter uses a non-SQL datatype.

The prototype of the HTML_PIECES type and the REQUEST_PIECES function is shown below,

```
TYPE html_pieces IS TABLE OF VARCHAR2(2000) INDEX BY BINARY_INTEGER;

UTL_HTTP.REQUEST_PIECES(
        url IN VARCHAR2,
        max_pieces IN NATURAL DEFAULT 32767,
        proxy IN VARCHAR2 DEFAULT NULL,
        wallet_path IN VARCHAR2 DEFAULT NULL,
        wallet_password IN VARCHAR2 DEFAULT NULL)
        RETURN html_pieces;
```

- **MAX_PIECES** parameter accepts a positive integer value for determining the maximum number of chunks the obtained HTML must be split into.

In the below example, the REQUEST_PIECES function requests for a maximum of 100 chunks of 2000-bytes information from the input URL. This function's return statement is then looped to print all the available chunks of 2000 bytes (The last chunk may contain <=2000 bytes).

```
DECLARE
  l_html_pieces utl_http.html_pieces;
  LEN PLS_INTEGER;
BEGIN
  l_html_pieces:=UTL_HTTP.REQUEST_PIECES('http://www.google.com', 100);
  dbms_output.put_line('Total chunks: '||l_html_pieces.count);
  FOR loop_chunks IN 1..l_html_pieces.count
  LOOP
    dbms_output.put_line('Chunk #'||loop_chunks||':
'||l_html_pieces(loop_chunks));
  END LOOP loop_chunks;
END;
/
```

Result:

```
Total chunks: 24
Chunk #1: <HTML file of 2000 bytes>
Chunk #2: <HTML file of 2000 bytes>
Chunk #3: <HTML file of 2000 bytes>
...
...
Chunk #24: <HTML file of <=2000 bytes>
```

UTL_FILE

This package was introduced in the Oracle version 7.3.4 for reading and writing any operating system flat file that is accessible in our database server. This new feature allowed us to write the flat file data into the database tables along with the flexibility of PL/SQL with an ease.

The different objects available in this package are described below.

Directory

Prior to the Oracle release 9i, the UTL_FILE_DIR initialization parameter was used for determining the directories which can be read or written by the UTL_FILE package. This became a security threat as the directories present inside this parameter are accessible by any other database user. To mitigate this security concern, Oracle has introduced the CREATE DIRECTORY syntax for creating directories with more security for working alongside the OS files. Either read or write access to the directories created using this syntax can be granted to individual users or roles.

The prototype for creating a directory is shown below,

```
CREATE DIRECTORY <Directory_name> AS '<Directory_path>';
```

The prototype for granting access to the directories to the database users is shown below,

```
GRANT [READ] | [WRITE] ON DIRECTORY <Directory_name> TO <Database_user>;
```

FILE_TYPE Record Type

This type is actually a PL/SQL record type which is used for holding all the information related to the file for processing by the UTL_FILE package. This type acts as a handle for the consecutive calls to the UTL_FILE package to manipulate the file content. We must not reference the individual attributes of this type or manipulate them as it is specifically to be handled by the UTL_FILE package.

The prototype of the FILE_TYPE record type is shown below,

```
TYPE file_type IS RECORD (
   id          BINARY_INTEGER,
   datatype    BINARY_INTEGER,
   byte_mode   BOOLEAN);
```

- **ID** parameter returns a numeric file handler number which is generated internally for processing.
- **DATATYPE** parameter indicates the data type of the file.
- **BYTE_MODE** parameter is to indicate whether the file is open as a text file or as a binary file.

FOPEN and FOPEN_NCHAR Functions

The FOPEN function opens the file in the database character set and returns the handle which can be then used for manipulating the file content.

The FOPEN_NCHAR function opens the file in the national character set and manipulates it in UNICODE instead of the database character set.

The file handles returned by these functions must be passed to the subsequent calls to the UTL_FILE subprograms, that it must not be referenced or changed by the database users.

The prototype of the FOPEN function is shown below,

```
UTL_FILE.FOPEN (
    location     IN VARCHAR2,
    filename     IN VARCHAR2,
    open_mode    IN VARCHAR2,
    max_linesize IN BINARY_INTEGER DEFAULT 1024)
RETURN FILE_TYPE;
```

The prototype of the FOPEN_NCHAR function is shown below,

```
UTL_FILE.FOPEN_NCHAR (
    location     IN VARCHAR2,
    filename     IN VARCHAR2,
    open_mode    IN VARCHAR2,
    max_linesize IN BINARY_INTEGER DEFAULT 1024)
RETURN FILE_TYPE;
```

- **LOCATION** parameter accepts the directory location of the file.
- **FILENAME** parameter accepts the name of the file in the directory.
- **OPEN_MODE** parameter accepts the mode in which the file is to be opened. Possible modes are shown below,
    → **R** opens the file in read mode. **RB** opens the file in read byte mode. If we want to open a file in read mode, the file must already exist.
    → **W** opens the file in read + write replace mode. When we open a file in replace mode, all the existing content of the file is replaced. **WB** opens a file in write byte mode. If we want to open a file in write mode, the file will either be created if not present or be emptied if already present.
    → **A** opens the file in read + write in append mode. When we open a file in append mode, all the existing lines of the file are kept in a place where the new lines are appended after the last line in the file. **AB** opens the file in append byte mode. If we want to open a file in append mode, the file must already exist.
- **MAX_LINESIZE** parameter accepts the maximum characters to be returned by a single line including the newline character. The minimum and the maximum values are 1 and 32,767 respectively.

IS_OPEN Function

This function returns a Boolean *true* if the file handle points to a file which is already open or if it is not null and a Boolean *false* if the file handle is *null*, meaning that the file is closed.

The prototype of the IS_OPEN function is shown below,

```
UTL_FILE.IS_OPEN (
    file IN FILE_TYPE)
  RETURN BOOLEAN;
```

- **FILE** parameter accepts the active file handle for validation.

FCOPY Procedure

This procedure is used for copying from one file to another. If the *start_line* and *end_line* parameters are omitted, the complete file is copied else, the portion specified by these two parameters from the file is copied. The source file is opened in the read mode and the destination file is opened in the write mode.

The prototype of the FCOPY procedure is shown below,

```
UTL_FILE.FCOPY (
    src_location     IN VARCHAR2,
    src_filename     IN VARCHAR2,
    dest_location    IN VARCHAR2,
    dest_filename    IN VARCHAR2,
    start_line       IN BINARY_INTEGER DEFAULT 1,
    end_line         IN BINARY_INTEGER DEFAULT NULL);
```

- **SRC_LOCATION** parameter accepts the directory name of the source file.
- **SRC_FILENAME** parameter accepts the name of the source file.
- **DEST_LOCATION** parameter accepts the destination file directory name.
- **DEST_FILENAME** parameter accepts the destination file name.
- **START_LINE** parameter accepts the line number from which the copying should begin.
- **END_LINE** parameter accepts the line number till which the copying should end.

FFLUSH Procedure

This procedure flushes the pending data identified by the file handle into the file. This procedure is useful when we want to read the file while it is still open. For example, the debugging and logging files can be read immediately once they are flushed with messages.

The prototype of the FFLUSH procedure is shown below,

```
UTL_FILE.FFLUSH (file IN FILE_TYPE);
```

- **FILE** parameter accepts the active file handle.

FGETATTR Procedure

This procedure returns the information about the attributes of the OS file.

The prototype of the FGETATTR procedure is shown below,

```
UTL_FILE.FGETATTR(
    location    IN VARCHAR2,
    filename    IN VARCHAR2,
    fexists     OUT BOOLEAN,
    file_length OUT NUMBER,
    block_size  OUT BINARY_INTEGER);
```

- **LOCATION** parameter accepts the directory name of the input file.
- **FILENAME** parameter accepts the name of the input file.
- **FEXISTS** parameter returns a Boolean *true* if the file exists and a *false* if not.
- **FILE_LENGTH** parameter returns the length of the file in bytes. Returns a Boolean *null* if the file does not exist.
- **BLOCK_SIZE** parameter returns the file's block size in bytes. Returns a Boolean *null* if the file does not exist.

FGETPOS Procedure

This procedure returns the current relative position of the file handle in an open file in bytes. It raises an exception if the file is not open. It returns a 0 if the file handle is at the beginning of the file.

The prototype of the FGETPOS procedure is shown below,

```
UTL_FILE.FGETPOS (
   file IN FILE_TYPE)
 RETURN PLS_INTEGER;
```

- **FILE** parameter accepts the active file handle.

FSEEK Procedure

This procedure adjusts the file pointer forward or backward within the file by the number of bytes specified as input. This procedure is used for reading backward without closing and re-opening the file.

The prototype of the FSEEK procedure is shown below,

```
UTL_FILE.FSEEK (
    file             IN OUT UTL_FILE.FILE_TYPE,
    absolute_offset  IN PL_INTEGER DEFAULT NULL,
    relative_offset  IN PLS_INTEGER DEFAULT NULL);
```

- **FILE** parameter accepts the active file handle.
- **ABSOLUTE_OFFSET** parameter accepts the bytes using which the procedure seeks to an absolute location. The default is *null*.
- **RELATIVE_OFFSET** parameter accepts the bytes which act as the number of bytes to seek forward or backward. The default is *null*.
  → **Positive Integer** seeks forward. If the file reaches the end of the file before the number of bytes specified, the pointer is placed at the end of the file.
  → **Negative Integer** seeks backward. If the file reaches the beginning of the file before the number of bytes specified, the pointer is placed at the start of the file.
  → **Zero** states the current position.

GET_LINE, GET_LINE_NCHAR, and GET_RAW Procedures

These procedures read the text from an open file identified by its handle and place them in the output buffer parameter. The text can read up to the end of the file or up to the *len* parameter but not more than the *max_linesize* parameter specified in the FOPEN function.

With the GET_LINE_NCHAR procedure, we can read a text file in UNICODE instead of database character set. The file used in this function must be opened in national charset with UTF8 encoded. If we intend to use any other variable than NVARCHAR2 type, PL/SQL will perform an implicit conversion from the *buffer* parameter to the resultant variable after reading the text.

With the GET_RAW procedure, we can read the RAW string value from the file and adjust the file pointer accordingly by the number of bytes read ignoring the terminators.

The prototype of the GET_LINE procedure is shown below,

```
UTL_FILE.GET_LINE (
   file        IN FILE_TYPE,
   buffer      OUT VARCHAR2,
   len         IN PLS_INTEGER DEFAULT NULL);
```

The prototype of the GET_LINE_NCHAR procedure is shown below,

```
UTL_FILE.GET_LINE_NCHAR (
   file        IN FILE_TYPE,
   buffer      OUT NVARCHAR2,
   len         IN PLS_INTEGER DEFAULT NULL);
```

The prototype of the GET_LINE_NCHAR procedure is shown below,

```
UTL_FILE.GET_RAW (
   file        IN UTL_FILE.FILE_TYPE,
   buffer      OUT NOCOPY RAW,
   len         IN PLS_INTEGER DEFAULT NULL);
```

- **FILE** parameter accepts the active file handle.
- **BUFFER** parameter receives the line read from the file.
- **LEN** parameter accepts the number of lines to be read from the file. If it is null, Oracle supplies the value of the *max_linesize* parameter specified in the FOPEN function.

NEW_LINE Procedure

This procedure adds one or more line terminators to the file identified by the file handler.

The prototype of the NEW_LINE procedure is shown below,

```
UTL_FILE.NEW_LINE (
   file    IN FILE_TYPE,
   lines   IN BINARY_INTEGER default 1);
```

- **FILE** parameter accepts the active file handle.
- **LINES** parameter accepts the number of line terminators to be written to the file. The default is 1.

PUT and PUT_NCHAR Procedures

These procedures write the text string passed as input to the buffer parameter to the file which is opened for the *write* operation that is identified by the file handler. No line terminator is appended by them. We must use NEW_LINE to terminate the line or use PUT_LINE to perform both the PUT and NEW_LINE operations.

With the PUT_NCHAR procedure, we can write the text string in UNICODE instead of the database charset.

The prototype of the PUT procedure is shown below,

```
UTL_FILE.PUT (
    file      IN FILE_TYPE,
    buffer    IN VARCHAR2);
```

The prototype of the PUT_NCHAR procedure is shown below,

```
UTL_FILE.PUT (
    file      IN FILE_TYPE,
    buffer    IN NVARCHAR2);
```

- **FILE** parameter accepts the active file handle.
- **BUFFER** parameter accepts lines to be written to the file.

PUT_LINE and PUT_LINE_NCHAR Procedures

These procedures write the text string from the buffer to the open file and terminate the line with the platform specific line terminating characters. This is the combination of PUT or PUT_NCHAR and NEW_LINE procedures.

The prototype of the PUT_LINE procedure is shown below,

```
UTL_FILE.PUT_LINE (
    file      IN FILE_TYPE,
    buffer    IN VARCHAR2,
    autoflush IN BOOLEAN DEFAULT FALSE);
```

The prototype of the PUT_LINE_NCHAR procedure is shown below,

```
UTL_FILE.PUT_LINE_NCHAR (
    file      IN FILE_TYPE,
    buffer    IN NVARCHAR2);
```

- **FILE** parameter accepts the active file handle.
- **BUFFER** parameter accepts lines to be written to the file.
- **AUTOFLUSH** parameter flushes the buffer to disk after the *write* operation.

PUTF and PUTF_NCHAR Procedures

These are the formatted versions of the PUT and the PUT_NCHAR procedures respectively. It accepts an input string with the formatting elements *%n* and *%s* and up to five arguments to be replaced by the consecutive instances of the *%s* format element from the input string.

The prototype of the PUTF procedure is shown below,

```
UTL_FILE.PUTF (
   file   IN FILE_TYPE,
   format IN VARCHAR2,
   [ arg1 IN VARCHAR2 DEFAULT NULL,
   . . .
   arg5   IN VARCHAR2 DEFAULT NULL]);
```

The prototype of the PUTF_NCHAR procedure is shown below,

```
UTL_FILE.PUTF_NCHAR (
   file   IN FILE_TYPE,
   format IN NVARCHAR2,
   [ arg1 IN NVARCHAR2 DEFAULT NULL,
   . . .
   arg5   IN NVARCHAR2 DEFAULT NULL]);
```

FCLOSE Procedure

The FCLOSE procedure closes an open file using the file handle. If there is a buffered data yet to be written before this procedure call, then we may encounter the WRITE_ERROR exception during this procedure call.

The prototype of the FCLOSE procedure is shown below,

```
UTL_FILE.FCLOSE (file IN OUT FILE_TYPE);
```

- **File** parameter accepts the active file handle and returns it as *null* after closing it.

Summary

457

FCLOSE_ALL Procedure

This procedure comes in handy when we want to close all the active file handlers during an abnormal termination of our program. Usually, this procedure is used in the exception sections.

The prototype of the FCLOSE_ALL procedure is shown below,

```
UTL_FILE.FCLOSE_ALL;
```

> Note: The FCLOSE_ALL procedure does not make the active file handle as *null* unlike the FCLOSE procedure, but no read or write operations are allowed on a file that was closed using the FCLOSE_ALL procedure. Also, the IS_OPEN function will return a Boolean *true* even though it was close using this procedure.

FRENAME Procedure

This procedure is used for renaming an existing file to a new user defined name.

The prototype of the FRENAME function is shown below,

```
UTL_FILE.FRENAME (
    src_location      IN    VARCHAR2,
    src_filename      IN    VARCHAR2,
    dest_location     IN    VARCHAR2,
    dest_filename     IN    VARCHAR2,
    overwrite         IN    BOOLEAN DEFAULT FALSE);
```

- **SRC_LOCATION** parameter accepts the source file's directory name.
- **SRC_FILENAME** parameter accepts the source file's name.
- **DEST_LOCATION** parameter accepts the destination directory name of the destination file.
- **DEST_FILENAME** parameter accepts the new name of the file.
- **OVERWRITE** parameter accepts a Boolean *true* for overwriting the destination file if it is already present. The default is *false*, which does not overwrite.

FREMOVE Procedure

This procedure is used for deleting a disk file.

The prototype of the FREMOVE function is shown below,

```
UTL_FILE.FREMOVE (
   location IN VARCHAR2,
   filename IN VARCHAR2);
```

- **LOCATION** parameter accepts the directory name.
- **FILENAME** parameter accepts the file name to be removed.

In the below example, a directory is created on the local disk granting read and write access to the user C##.

```
CREATE DIRECTORY dir AS 'C:\Users\Boobal Ganesan\Desktop\Folder';

GRANT READ, WRITE ON DIRECTORY dir TO C##;
```

In the below example, the file *input_file.txt* is opened in *read* mode. The file's current status is verified using the IS_OPEN function and then the process begins. Once, after confirming that this file is open, the first two lines of the input file are copied into a new file *copy_file.txt* using the FCOPY procedure, whose attributes are then retrieved using the FGETATTR procedure.

The file is read!

The GET_LINE procedure buffers the first line of the input file into the L_VC_BUFFER variable. Note that only the first 32,000 characters of the first line are read for every GET_LINE call. The buffer variable is then printed using the PUT_LINE procedure. After the first line is read, the position of the handle is checked using the FGETPOS function.

The above whole process is looped to print all the rows from the input file and once the file reaches its very end, the *no_data_found* exception is raised and the input file's handle is closed. Also, the copy file is removed as the last process in our below example.

```
DECLARE
   l_vc_buffer VARCHAR2(32767);
   l_file_handle utl_file.file_type;
   l_b_fexists      BOOLEAN;
   l_vc_fexists     VARCHAR2(100);
   l_n_file_length NUMBER;
   l_bi_block_size binary_integer;
   l_n_pos NUMBER;
BEGIN
   l_file_handle:=utl_file.fopen('DIR','input_file.txt','R');
   IF utl_file.is_open(l_file_handle) THEN
     utl_file.fcopy ( 'DIR', 'input_file.txt', 'DIR', 'copy_file.txt', 1, 2);
```

```
        utl_file.fgetattr( 'DIR', 'copy_file.txt', l_b_fexists, l_n_file_length,
l_bi_block_size);
        IF l_b_fexists THEN
            l_vc_fexists:='exists with the file length: '||l_n_file_length||' and
with the block size: '||l_bi_block_size;
        ELSE
            l_vc_fexists:='does not exist';
        END IF;
        dbms_output.put_line('The copy file copy_file.txt '||l_vc_fexists);
        dbms_output.put_line('-- File Read Starts --');
        LOOP
            utl_file.get_line(l_file_handle, l_vc_buffer, 32000);
            l_n_pos:=utl_file.fgetpos(l_file_handle);
            dbms_output.put_line('The position in bytes is: '||l_n_pos);
            dbms_output.put_line(l_vc_buffer);
        END LOOP;
    END IF;
EXCEPTION
WHEN no_data_found THEN
    utl_file.fclose(l_file_handle);
    dbms_output.put_line('-- File Read Ends --');
    utl_file.fremove('DIR','copy_file.txt');
END;
/
```

Result:

```
The copy file copy_file.txt exists with the file length: 141 and with the
block size: 0

-- File Read Starts --
The position in bytes is: 46
"What would you have me do?" he said at last.
The position in bytes is: 139
"You know I did all a father could for their education, and they have both
turned out fools.
The position in bytes is: 205
Hippolyte is at least a quiet fool, but Anatole is an active one.
The position in bytes is: 249
That is the only difference between them."
-- File Read Ends --
```

In the below example, a quote from *The Canterville Ghost* by the famous writer Mr. Oscar Wilde is written into a file from a VARCHAR2 variable. Firstly, the file to be written is opened in *write* format. Then the quote from the input variable is written into the file handle using the PUT procedure and the handle is moved to the next line using the NEXT_LINE procedure. After the writing process, a signature denoting the time at which the file is written is appended to the output file using the PUTF procedure and once again the handle is moved to the next line. After all necessary data are written into the output file, the file handler is flushed to complete the writing process using the FFLUSH procedure.

The output file is then renamed to *The Canterville Ghost.txt* using the FRENAME procedure after the file handle is closed.

```
DECLARE
  l_vc_input_text VARCHAR2(32767):='I know that in this country mortmain is
held to apply to trinkets as well as to land, and it is quite clear to me
that these jewels are, or should be, heirlooms in your family.';
  l_file_handle utl_file.file_type;
BEGIN
  l_file_handle:=utl_file.fopen('DIR','output_file.txt','W',32760);
  utl_file.put(l_file_handle,l_vc_input_text);
  utl_file.new_line(l_file_handle);
  utl_file.putf(l_file_handle,'This file was created at %s.',SYSTIMESTAMP);
  utl_file.new_line(l_file_handle);
  utl_file.fflush(l_file_handle);
  utl_file.fclose(l_file_handle);
  utl_file.frename ( 'DIR', 'output_file.txt', 'DIR', 'The Canterville
Ghost.txt');
END;
/
```

UTL_ENCODE

The UTL_ENCODE package was introduced in the Oracle release version 9i for encoding and decoding the raw data, primarily the body of an email message, while transmitting them between the hosts. This package also helps in converting the chunk files into more organized parts of the UTL_FILE package.

This package is not to be confused with the encryption technology as encoding is the process of converting a sequence of characters into a certain format, resulting in efficient transmission or storage and encryption is the process of scrambling the data and making it decipherable only by the intended recipients with a private key.

This package has five subprograms for encoding and decoding. They are,

BASE64_ENCODE and BASE64_DECODE Functions

The ENCODE function converts the binary RAW input to its BASE64 encoded form and the DECODE function accepts the BASE64 encoded form of the RAW data and converts back to its original format.

The prototypes of these functions are shown below,

```
UTL_ENCODE.BASE64_ENCODE (r IN RAW) RETURN RAW;

UTL_ENCODE.BASE64_DECODE (r IN RAW) RETURN RAW;
```

- **R** parameter contains the RAW string

In the below example, a VARCHAR2 string is converted to RAW using the UTL_RAW.CAST_RAW function. After this conversion, the RAW string is then encoded into its BASE64 form through the UTL_ENCODE.BASE64_ENCODE function. This encoded RAW data is to be used during transmission and at the receiving end this string is to be converted back to its original form using the UTL_ENCODE.BASE64_DECODE function. The original VARCHAR2 string can be then extracted from this RAW string using the UTL_RAW.CAST_TO_VARCHAR2 function similar to the below example.

```
DECLARE
  l_vc_var1 VARCHAR2(32767):='UTL_ENCODE';
  l_rw_var2 RAW(32767);
BEGIN
  dbms_output.put_line('Original string: '||l_vc_var1);
  l_rw_var2:= utl_raw.cast_to_raw(l_vc_var1);
  dbms_output.put_line('Original RAW string: '||l_rw_var2);
  l_rw_var2:= utl_encode.base64_encode(l_rw_var2);
  dbms_output.put_line('Encoded RAW string: '||l_rw_var2);
  l_rw_var2:= utl_encode.base64_decode(l_rw_var2);
  dbms_output.put_line('Decoded RAW string: '||l_rw_var2);
  l_vc_var1:=utl_raw.cast_to_varchar2(l_rw_var2);
  dbms_output.put_line('Decoded Original string: '||l_vc_var1);
END;
/
```

Result:

```
Original string: UTL_ENCODE
Original RAW string: 55544C5F454E434F4445
Encoded RAW string: 5656524D5830564F5130394552513D3D
Decoded RAW string: 55544C5F454E434F4445
Decoded Original string: UTL_ENCODE
```

MIMEHEADER_ENCODE and MIMEHEADER_DECODE Functions

The ENCODE function returns the encoded output in the form =?<charset>?<encoding>?<Original text>?= for the input string.

The DECODE function accepts the encoded string of the form =?<charset>?<encoding>?<Original text>?= and returns the original string.

- **CHARSET** value in the output format is supplied as input to this function. If it is *null*, the database character set is selected by default.
- **ENCODING** value in the output format is either Q or B for quoted-printable encode or BASE64 encode respectively.

- **ORIGINAL_TEXT** value in the output format is the original text used for encoding.

The prototypes of these functions are shown below,

```
UTL_ENCODE.MIMEHEADER_ENCODE (
   buf             IN   VARCHAR2 CHARACTER SET ANY_CS,
   encode_charset  IN   VARCHAR2 DEFAULT NULL,
   encoding        IN   PLS_INTEGER DEFAULT NULL)
 RETURN string VARCHAR2 CHARACTER SET buf%CHARSET;

UTL_ENCODE.MIMEHEADER_DECODE (
   buf     IN    VARCHAR2 CHARACTER SET ANY_CS)
  RETURN data VARCHAR2 CHARACTER SET buf%CHARSET;
```

- **BUF** parameter accepts the text data in case of the ENCODE and encoded text data in case of the DECODE functions.
- **ENCODE_CHARSET** parameter accepts the target character set. The default is *null*.
- **ENCODING** parameter accepts either UTL_ENCODE.BASE64, UTL_ENCODE.QUOTED_PRINTABLE or *null*. In the case of *null*, UTL_ENCODE.QUOTED_PRINTABLE value is considered by default.

In the below example, an input VARCHAR2 string is converted into the MIME heading format using the MIMEHEADER_ENCODE function and it is decoded back to its original value using the MIMEHEADER_DECODE function.

```
DECLARE
  l_vc_var1 VARCHAR2(32767):='UTL_ENCODE';
BEGIN
  l_vc_var1 := utl_encode.mimeheader_encode(l_vc_var1);
  dbms_output.put_line('Encoded String: '||l_vc_var1);
  l_vc_var1 := utl_encode.mimeheader_decode(l_vc_var1);
  dbms_output.put_line('Decoded String: '||l_vc_var1);
END;
/
```

Result:

```
Encoded String: =?WINDOWS-1252?Q?UTL=5FENCODE?=
Decoded String: UTL_ENCODE
```

QUOTED_PRINTABLE_ENCODE and QUOTED_PRINTABLE_DECODE Functions

The ENCODE function accepts a binary input and encodes it to its quoted printable format.

The DECODE function accepts a quoted printable format string and converts to its original binary input.

The prototypes of these functions are shown below,

```
UTL_ENCODE.QUOTED_PRINTABLE_ENCODE (r IN RAW) RETURN RAW;

UTL_ENCODE.QUOTED_PRINTABLE_DECODE (r IN RAW) RETURN RAW;
```

- **R** parameter accepts the RAW string and the RAW string containing the quoted-printable data string for the ENCODE and the DECODE functions respectively.

In the below example, a VARCHAR2 string is converted to RAW and is passed as input to the QUOTED_PRINTABLE_ENCODE function which returns the quoted-printable format of the input string. This RAW result is then decoded back to the original RAW string using the QUOTED_PRINTABLE_DECODE function.

```
DECLARE
  l_vc_var1 VARCHAR2(32767):=''''||chr(13)||'UTL_ENCODE'||'''';
  l_rw_var2 raw(32767);
BEGIN
  dbms_output.put_line('Original String: '||l_vc_var1);
  l_rw_var2 := utl_raw.cast_to_raw(l_vc_var1);
  dbms_output.put_line('Original RAW String: '||l_rw_var2);
  l_rw_var2 := utl_encode.quoted_printable_encode(l_rw_var2);
  dbms_output.put_line('Encoded RAW String: '||l_rw_var2);
  l_rw_var2 := utl_encode.quoted_printable_decode(l_rw_var2);
  dbms_output.put_line('Decoded RAW String: '||l_rw_var2);
  l_vc_var1:=utl_raw.cast_to_varchar2(l_rw_var2);
  dbms_output.put_line('Original String: '||l_vc_var1);
END;
/
```

Result:

```
Original String: '
UTL_ENCODE'
Original RAW String: 0D55544C5F454E434F4445
Encoded RAW String: 3D304455544C5F454E434F4445
Decoded RAW String: 0D55544C5F454E434F4445
Original String: '
UTL_ENCODE'
```

TEXT_ENCODE and TEXT_DECODE Functions

The ENCODE function encodes a text string using either BASE64 or QUOTED_PRINTABLE format.

The DECODE function decodes the text which was encoded using either BASE64 or QUOTED_PRINTABLE format. Note that the same format has to be used during both encoding and decoding process to avoid the *ORA-29296: invalid encoded string* exception.

The prototypes of these functions are shown below,

```
UTL_ENCODE.TEXT_ENCODE (
   buf            IN   VARCHAR2 CHARACTER SET ANY_CS,
   encode_charset IN   VARCHAR2 DEFAULT NULL,
   encoding       IN   PLS_INTEGER DEFAULT NULL)
 RETURN string VARCHAR2 CHARACTER SET buf%CHARSET;

UTL_ENCODE.TEXT_DECODE(
   buf            IN   VARCHAR2 CHARACTER SET ANY_CS,
   encode_charset IN   VARCHAR2 DEFAULT NULL,
   encoding       IN   PLS_INTEGER DEFAULT NULL)
 RETURN string VARCHAR2 CHARACTER SET buf%CHARSET;
```

- **BUF** parameter accepts the text data and the encoded text data for the ENCODE and the DECODE functions respectively.
- **ENCODE_CHARSET** parameter accepts the source and the target character set for the ENCODE and the DECODE functions respectively.
- **ENCODING** parameter accepts either BASE64, QUOTED_PRINTABLE, or *null* as the encoding format. In the case of *null*, the QUOTED_PRINTABLE format is considered by default.

In the below example, a VARCHAR2 string is encoded and decoded back using the BASE64 encoding format and the AL32UTF8 character set.

```
DECLARE
  l_vc_var1 VARCHAR2(32767):='UTL_ENCODE';
BEGIN
  dbms_output.put_line('Original String: '||l_vc_var1);
  l_vc_var1 :=
utl_encode.text_encode(l_vc_var1,'AL32UTF8',UTL_ENCODE.BASE64);
  dbms_output.put_line('Encoded String: '||l_vc_var1);
  l_vc_var1:=utl_encode.text_decode(l_vc_var1,'AL32UTF8',
UTL_ENCODE.BASE64);
  dbms_output.put_line('Decoded String: '||l_vc_var1);
END;
/
```

Result:

```
Original String: UTL_ENCODE
Encoded String: VVRMX0VOQ09ERQ==
Decoded String: UTL_ENCODE
```

UUENCODE and UUDECODE Functions

The ENCODE function reads the RAW input string and encodes it to the UUENCODE formatted string. The DECODE function reads the RAW string of UUENCODE format and decodes it back to its original RAW string format.

THE UUENCODE and UUDECODE are a popular utility for encoding and decoding files exchanged between systems, popularly between UNIX systems. Thus, it is called as a UU (UNIX to UNIX encoding/decoding).

The prototype of these functions is shown below,

```
UTL_ENCODE.UUENCODE (
    r          IN RAW,
    type       IN PLS_INTEGER DEFAULT 1,
    filename   IN VARCHAR2,
    permission IN VARCHAR2) RETURN RAW;

UTL_ENCODE.UUDECODE (r IN RAW) RETURN RAW;
```

- **R** parameter accepts the RAW and encoded RAW string for the ENCODE and the DECODE functions respectively.
- **TYPE** parameter accepts a number indicating the type of UUENCODED output. The available options are listed below. The default is 1.
    - ➜ 1 – Complete (Includes header, body, and footer).
    - ➜ 2 – Header_piece.
    - ➜ 3 – Middle_piece.
    - ➜ 4 – End_piece.
- **FILENAME** parameter accepts the filename for the encoded text. The default is uuencode.txt.
- **PERMISSION** parameter accepts the permission mode. Default is 0.

In the below example, the input string is encoded/ decoded using UUENCODE/ UUDECODE functions respectively.

```
DECLARE
  l_vc_var1 VARCHAR2(32767):='UTL_ENCODE';
  l_rw_var2 raw(32767);
BEGIN
  dbms_output.put_line('Original String: ' || l_vc_var1);
  l_rw_var2:=utl_raw.cast_to_raw(l_vc_var1);
  dbms_output.put_line('Original RAW String: ' || l_rw_var2);
  l_rw_var2:= utl_encode.uuencode(l_rw_var2);
  dbms_output.put_line('Encoded RAW String: ' || l_rw_var2);
  l_rw_var2:= utl_encode.uudecode(l_rw_var2);
  dbms_output.put_line('Decoded RAW String: ' || l_rw_var2);
  l_vc_var1:=utl_raw.cast_to_varchar2(l_rw_var2);
  dbms_output.put_line('Decoded Original String: ' || l_vc_var1);
END;
/
```

Results:

```
Original String: UTL_ENCODE
Original RAW String: 55544C5F454E434F4445
Encoded RAW String:
626567696E2030207575656E636F64652E7478740D0A2E3535312C3754352E30545D24313020
200D0A0A656E64
Decoded RAW String: 55544C5F454E434F4445
Decoded Original String: UTL_ENCODE
```

UTL_SMTP (Simple Mail Transfer Protocol)

This package was the first available email utility in Oracle which was introduced in the version 8i. This package requires that the programmer understands the details of the underlying SMTP protocol features. This package by default comes installed with the UTL_TCP package, with our database installation. If not, we can find the scripts in the below location and install them in the SYS schema and provide public grants for the other users in the database.

```
ORACLE_HOME/RDBMS/ADMIN/utlsmtp.sql
ORACLE_HOME/RDBMS/ADMIN/utltcp.sql
```

 Note: This package is capable of only sending emails and cannot receive any!

The UTL_SMTP package provides interfaces to the protocols consisting of certain commands for sending emails to an SMTP server. These protocols have both procedural and functional forms of interface. The functional form returns the reply from the SMTP server for each command sent in the form of success or failure. The procedural form raises an exception when the command sent is failed.

During the mail process, the body of the DATA command is transferred in 8-bits, whereas, the other SMTP commands are converted to US7ASCII (7-bit ASCII) and then transmitted.

Most of the APIs is overloaded as procedures and functions in the UTL_SMTP package because the procedural API fails with an exception if the reply from the server falls into an exception, but the function API returns the REPLY message for users to analyze during an exceptional scenery.

The objects and commands available in this package are described below,

CONNECTION Record Type

This record type is used for representing an SMTP connection.

The prototype of this record type is shown below,

```
TYPE connection IS RECORD (
    host            VARCHAR2(255),
    port            PLS_INTEGER,
    tx_timeout      PLS_INTEGER,
    private_tcp_con utl_tcp.connection,
    private_state   PLS_INTEGER
);
```

- **HOST** parameter holds the name of the target host when a connection is established. Holds *null* in case of no connection.
- **PORT** parameter holds the port of the connected target host. Holds *null* in case of no connection.
- **TX_TIMEOUT** parameter holds the time in seconds that this package waits before giving up on the read/write operation. 0 indicates no wait and *null* indicates to wait forever.
- **PRIVATE_TCP_CON** and **PRIVATE_STATE** parameters are for internal use and must not be modified.

> 🔔 Note: Modifying the parameters other than the internally used ones has no effect on the connection.

REPLY Record Type and REPLIES Index-by-table

These types are used to represent SMTP reply line(s). When an SMTP command responds with a single-line reply, the REPLY record type is used and when it responds with a multi-line reply, an associative array (REPLIES) of REPLY record type is used. In the case of the REPLY type, If the SMTP server returns more than one line of reply, the last line of the reply is only returned.

The prototypes of these types are shown below,

```
TYPE reply IS RECORD (
  code    PLS_INTEGER,
  text    VARCHAR2(508)
);

TYPE replies IS TABLE OF reply INDEX BY BINARY_INTEGER;
```

- **CODE** parameter holds a 3-digit reply code.
- **TEXT** parameter holds the text message for the corresponding reply code.

OPEN_CONNECTION Functions

There are two overloaded OPEN_CONNECTION functions to open up an SMTP server connection. The function with CONNECTION record type as its RETURN type raises an exception when there is an error in the connection. The function with REPLY record type as its RETURN type does not result in any exception as the error message is returned through its RETURN type for the user to analyze.

The prototypes of these functions are shown below,

```
UTL_SMTP.OPEN_CONNECTION (
    host        IN VARCHAR2,
    port        IN PLS_INTEGER DEFAULT 25,
    c           OUT connection,
    tx_timeout IN PLS_INTEGER DEFAULT NULL)
RETURN reply;

UTL_SMTP.OPEN_CONNECTION (
    host        IN VARCHAR2,
    port        IN PLS_INTEGER DEFAULT 25,
    tx_timeout IN PLS_INTEGER DEFAULT NULL)
RETURN connection;
```

- **C** parameter returns the SMTP connection.

COMMAND Function/ Procedure and COMMAND_REPLIES Function

These subprograms are used to invoke a generic SMTP command. The COMMAND subprograms are to be used only when a single line reply is expected. If the SMTP server returns more than one line of reply, the last line of the reply is only returned. The COMMAND_REPLIES function is to be used when multiple reply lines are expected.

The prototypes of these subprograms are shown below,

```
UTL_SMTP.COMMAND (
    c   IN OUT NOCOPY connection,
    cmd IN            VARCHAR2,
    arg IN            VARCHAR2 DEFAULT NULL)
RETURN reply;
```

```
UTL_SMTP.COMMAND (
   c   IN OUT NOCOPY connection,
   cmd IN            VARCHAR2,
   arg IN            VARCHAR2 DEFAULT NULL);

UTL_SMTP.COMMAND_REPLIES (
   c     IN OUT NOCOPY    connection,
   cmd   IN               VARCHAR2,
   arg   IN               VARCHAR2 DEFAULT NULL)
RETURN replies;
```

- **CMD** parameter accepts the SMTP command which is to be sent to the server.
- **ARG** parameter accepts an optional argument for the SMTP command. Space will be sent between the CMD and the ARG parameter values.

NOOP Function and Procedure

These APIs does not have any impact except for returning a successful reply from the SMTP mail server. This is often used to check if the server is still connected or not. This command will always reply with a single line message with the message code: 250.

The prototypes of these subprograms are shown below,

```
UTL_SMTP.NOOP (c IN OUT NOCOPY connection) RETURN reply;
```

```
UTL_SMTP.NOOP (c IN OUT NOCOPY connection);
```

HELO and EHLO Function/ Procedure

These subprograms perform the initial handshaking with the server after connecting with reference to the RFC 821 note, which states that the client must identify itself to the server after they get connected.

The HELO function returns the single-line reply from the SMTP server using the REPLY record type, whereas the EHLO function returns the multi-line extended information about its configuration using the REPLIES index-by-table type.

The prototypes of these subprograms are shown below,

```
UTL_SMTP.HELO (
   c       IN OUT NOCOPY connection,
   domain IN VARCHAR2)
RETURN reply;

UTL_SMTP.HELO (
   c       IN OUT NOCOPY connection,
   domain IN VARCHAR2);
```

```
UTL_SMTP.EHLO (
    c        IN OUT NOCOPY connection,
    domain IN VARCHAR2)
RETURN replies;

UTL_SMTP.EHLO (
    c        IN OUT NOCOPY connection,
    domain IN VARCHAR2);
```

- **DOMAIN** parameter accepts the domain name of the client host for identification.

VRFY Function

This function verifies the validity of the destination email address and if it is successful, the recipient's full name and mailbox path are returned back. This API call must be made after OPEN_CONNECTION, and HELO or EHLO calls.

The prototype of this function is shown below,

```
UTL_SMTP.VRFY (
    c          IN OUT NOCOPY connection
    recipient IN VARCHAR2)
RETURN reply;
```

HELP Function

This function sends the help command to the SMTP server. The return message from the server is in multi-line using the REPLIES index-by-table type.

The prototype of this function is shown below,

```
UTL_SMTP.HELP (
    c          IN OUT NOCOPY connection,
    command    IN VARCHAR2 DEFAULT NULL)
RETURN replies;
```

RCPT Function and Procedure

These subprograms specify the recipient of an email message. To send an email to multiple recipients, this API must be called multiple times, once for each recipient. This API must be called prior call to OPEN_CONNECTION, HELO or EHLO, and MAIL.

The prototypes of these subprograms are shown below,

```
UTL_SMTP.RCPT (
   c          IN OUT NOCOPY connection,
   recipient  IN VARCHAR2,
   parameters IN VARCHAR2 DEFAULT NULL)
RETURN reply;

UTL_SMTP.RCPT (
   c          IN OUT NOCOPY connection,
   recipient  IN VARCHAR2,
   parameters IN VARCHAR2 DEFAULT NULL);
```

- **RECIPIENT** parameter accepts the email address of the recipient user.
- **PARAMETERS** parameter accepts the additional parameter to the RCPT command.

MAIL Function and Procedure

These subprograms initiate the mail transaction with the destination mailbox. They do not send the email message, but only prepares them followed by RCPT and DATA to complete the transaction. The initial handshake must have been performed using HELO or EHLO APIs before this process.

The prototypes of these subprograms are shown below,

```
UTL_SMTP.MAIL (
   c          IN OUT NOCOPY connection,
   sender     IN VARCHAR2,
   parameters IN VARCHAR2 DEFAULT NULL)
RETURN reply;

UTL_SMTP.MAIL (
   c          IN OUT NOCOPY connection,
   sender     IN VARCHAR2,
   parameters IN VARCHAR2 DEFAULT NULL);
```

- **SENDER** parameter accepts the email address of the user sending the message.
- **PARAMETERS** parameter accepts the additional parameter to the MAIL command.

RSET Function and Procedure

This API terminates the current email transaction by abandoning the email that was being composed. This API must be called only after OPEN_CONNECTION and before DATA or OPEN_DATA is called. This call must be made before the email is sent, as it would be too late to terminate the transaction.

The prototypes of these subprograms are shown below,

```
UTL_SMTP.RSET (c IN OUT NOCOPY connection) RETURN reply;

UTL_SMTP.RSET (c IN OUT NOCOPY connection);
```

OPEN_DATA Function and Procedure

These subprograms send the DATA command to the SMTP server so that the server is ready to accept the actual email message using the WRITE_DATA or WRITE_RAW_DATA subprograms. After the email message is sent, the data transfer can be terminated using the CLOSE_DATA subprogram. Using any other API other than the above list after the DATA command will raise the INVALID_OPERATION exception.

The OPEN_DATA subprogram can be called only after OPEN_CONNECTION, HELO or EHLO, MAIL, and RCPT has been called.

The prototypes of these subprograms are shown below,

```
UTL_SMTP.OPEN_DATA (c IN OUT NOCOPY connection) RETURN reply;

UTL_SMTP.OPEN_DATA (c IN OUT NOCOPY connection);
```

WRITE_DATA and WRITE_RAW_DATA Procedures

These procedures are used to write the body of the email message. We must repeat calls to these procedures to append the text data to the email message. There is no function version of these APIs as the server does not respond back before the CLOSE_DATA call.

These procedures must be called only after OPEN_CONNECTION, HELO or EHLO, MAIL and RCPT have been called and must end with CLOSE_DATA call.

The single-byte VARCHAR2 data can be sent using the WRITE_DATA call where it is converted to 7-bit ASCII data before it is sent. The multi-byte VARCHAR2 data can be sent by first converting them to RAW type and then sending them using the WRITE_RAW_DATA call.

The prototypes of these procedures are shown below,

```
UTL_SMTP.WRITE_DATA (
    c       IN OUT NOCOPY connection,
    data IN VARCHAR2 CHARACTER SET ANY_CS);

UTL_SMTP.WRITE_RAW_DATA (
    c       IN OUT NOCOPY connection
    data IN RAW);
```

- **DATA** parameter accepts the body of the email message to be sent.

CLOSE_DATA Function and Procedure

These subprograms end the call to the email message by sending the <CR><LF>.<CR><LF> (Carriage Return and Line Feed). These subprograms must be called only after OPEN_CONNECTION, HELO or EHLO, MAIL, and RCPT has been called.

The prototypes of these subprograms are shown below,

```
UTL_SMTP.CLOSE_DATA (c IN OUT NOCOPY connection) RETURN reply;
```

```
UTL_SMTP.CLOSE_DATA (c IN OUT NOCOPY connection);
```

QUIT Function and Procedures

These APIs terminates the SMTP connection and disconnects it which was established in the first place using the OPEN_CONNECTION call. If there is an ongoing mail transaction, it is terminated similarly to the RSET API. After the SMTP connection is closed, the HOST and the PORT parameters of the CONNECTION record type are reset.

The prototypes of these subprograms are shown below,

```
UTL_SMTP.QUIT (c IN OUT NOCOPY connection) RETURN reply;
```

```
UTL_SMTP.QUIT (c IN OUT NOCOPY connection);
```

In the below example, an email message with CLOB attachment is sent using the UTL_SMTP package. Unlike its successor, the UTL_MAIL package, this package does not need to set up an initialization parameter to indicate the mail server as it is accepted as a parameter during the SMTP connection. After the initial handshake process using the HELO API, the sender, and the receiver information is accepted using the MAIL and RCPT APIs respectively. The mail subject and the body are written using the WRITE_DATA procedure along with the CLOB attachment. The CLOB variable is looped with an offset until the complete attachment is sent. After the email message is sent, the SMTP connection is terminated using the QUIT API.

```
DECLARE
  l_smtp_conn UTL_SMTP.CONNECTION;
  l_cl_var1 CLOB    :='Clob attachment';
  l_n_offset NUMBER:=15000;
BEGIN
  l_smtp_conn := UTL_SMTP.OPEN_CONNECTION('mail.daredevil.com','25');
  UTL_SMTP.HELO(l_smtp_conn, 'mail.daredevil.com');
  UTL_SMTP.MAIL(l_smtp_conn, '"Kick Buttowsky"
kick.buttowsky@daredevil.com');
  UTL_SMTP.RCPT(l_smtp_conn, '"Gunther Magnuson"
gunther.magnuson@daredevil.com');
  UTL_SMTP.OPEN_DATA(l_smtp_conn);
  UTL_SMTP.WRITE_DATA(l_smtp_conn, 'From : "Kick Buttowsky"
kick.buttowsky@daredevil.com'||UTL_TCP.CRLF);
  UTL_SMTP.WRITE_DATA(l_smtp_conn, 'To : "Gunther Magnuson"
gunther.magnuson@daredevil.com'||UTL_TCP.CRLF);
  UTL_SMTP.WRITE_DATA(l_smtp_conn, 'Subject : Its time to
kick!'||UTL_TCP.CRLF);
  UTL_SMTP.WRITE_DATA(l_smtp_conn, UTL_TCP.CRLF || 'Big Stunt - tomorrow
morning at the dead man''s drop!');
  FOR loop_att IN 1 .. TRUNC(DBMS_LOB.getlength(l_cl_var1)/l_n_offset)
  LOOP
    UTL_SMTP.write_data(l_smtp_conn, DBMS_LOB.substr(l_cl_var1, l_n_offset,
loop_att * l_n_offset + 1));
  END LOOP;
  UTL_SMTP.write_data(l_smtp_conn, UTL_TCP.crlf);
  UTL_SMTP.CLOSE_DATA(l_smtp_conn);
  UTL_SMTP.QUIT(l_smtp_conn);
EXCEPTION
WHEN OTHERS THEN
    UTL_SMTP.QUIT(l_smtp_conn);
END;
/
```

UTL_MAIL

This package is a simple utility for sending emails with features like attaching at a maximum of one file per email, carbon copy (CC), and blind carbon copy (BCC) and was introduced in the Oracle version 10g to be the replacement for its clumsy predecessor, the UTL_SMTP package.

> 🔔 Note: This package is capable of only sending emails and cannot receive any!

This package requires the SMTP_OUT_SERVER initialization parameter to be explicitly set to the UTL_MAIL's out-bound email's SMTP host and port in the *init.ora* file. We can set multiple SMTP servers in the SMTP_OUT_SERVER initialization parameter separated by commas. If the first server from the list is not available, the second one will be used and so on. If this parameter is not set, the host will default to the DB_DOMAIN value and the port will be defaulted to 25.

Due to the security concern in the SMTP_OUT_SERVER parameter setup, the UTL_MAIL package does not come installed with our database and we have to take care of that. The scripts required for installing the UTL_MAIL package are available in the below location in our Oracle home directory.

```
ORACLE_HOME/RDBMS/ADMIN/utlmail.sql
ORACLE_HOME/RDBMS/ADMIN/prvtmail.plb
```

The UTLMAIL.SQL script contains the package specification and the PRVTMAIL.PBL script contains the package body.

After executing the above scripts, the UTL_MAIL package will be available for general use after which the SMTP_OUT_SERVER parameter has to be configured. This can be done by performing an ALTER statement at the system level as shown below,

```
ALTER SYSTEM SET SMTP_OUTP_SERVER='mail.companyx.com, mail.companyy.com'
SCOPE=BOTH;
```

In the above example, if the COMPANYX server is unavailable, the COMPANYY server will pitch in.

The UTL_MAIL package internally uses the UTL_TCP and UTL_SMTP packages for sending out emails. It's just that the complexity has been reduced within the below described three simple procedures.

SEND Procedure

The SEND procedure is a one lined easy form of the UTL_SMTP package for packaging and delivering the email messages to the SMTP server for forwarding them to the appropriate receivers.

The prototype of the SEND procedure is shown below,

```
UTL_MAIL.SEND (
    sender     IN VARCHAR2 CHARACTER SET ANY_CS,
    recipients IN VARCHAR2 CHARACTER SET ANY_CS,
    cc         IN VARCHAR2 CHARACTER SET ANY_CS DEFAULT NULL,
    bcc        IN VARCHAR2 CHARACTER SET ANY_CS DEFAULT NULL,
    subject    IN VARCHAR2 CHARACTER SET ANY_CS DEFAULT NULL,
    message    IN VARCHAR2 CHARACTER SET ANY_CS,
    mime_type  IN VARCHAR2 DEFAULT 'text/plain; charset=us-ascii',
    priority   IN PLS_INTEGER DEFAULT 3,
    replyto    IN VARCHAR2 CHARACTER SET ANY_CS DEFAULT NULL);
```

- **SENDER** parameter accepts the email address of the sender.

- **RECIPIENTS** parameter accepts the comma separated recipient email addresses.
- **CC** parameter accepts the email addresses of the CC recipients in a comma separated manner.
- **BCC** parameter accepts the email addresses of the BCC recipients in a comma separated manner.
- **SUBJECT** parameter accepts the subject for the email message.
- **MESSAGE** parameter accepts the email's body text.
- **MIME_TYPE** parameter accepts the format of the message. It stands for Multipurpose Internet Mail Extensions.
- **PRIORITY** parameter accepts the priority to be set for the email message. 1 being the highest and 5 being the lowest on the priority. The default is 3.
- **REPLYTO** parameter accepts the email address to whom the sent mail should reply back.

In the below example, the SMTP_OUT_SERVER initialization parameter is set to the MYCOMPANY's corporate mail server and a job application mail has been sent to the HR team of Oracle Corporation for the Oracle PL/SQL developer position using the UTL_MAIL package with an ease.

```
ALTER system SET smtp_out_server='mail.mycompany.com' scope=both;
/

DECLARE
  l_vc_sender      VARCHAR2(100):='adamwalker1989@ mycompany.com';
  l_vc_recipients VARCHAR2(100):='hr@oracle.com';
  l_vc_cc          VARCHAR2(100);
  l_vc_bcc         VARCHAR2(100) :='adamwalker1989@ mycompany.com';
  l_vc_subject     VARCHAR2(100) :='Reg: Job application for PL/SQL
developer';
  l_vc_message     VARCHAR2(4000):='Dear HR,' ||chr(10) ||chr(10)
||'Greetings!' ||chr(10) ||'I am very interested in applying for the PL/SQL
developer job posted on the Oracle magazine recently. My qualifications and
experience match your specifications almost exactly...';
  l_vc_mime_type  VARCHAR2(4000):='text/plain; charset=us-ascii';
  l_pi_priority pls_integer     := 1;
  l_vc_replyto VARCHAR2(100)     :='adamwalker1989@ mycompany.com';
BEGIN
  utl_mail.send(l_vc_sender,
                l_vc_recipients,
                l_vc_cc,
                l_vc_bcc,
                l_vc_subject,
                l_vc_message,
                l_vc_mime_type,
                l_pi_priority,
                l_vc_replyto);
END;
/
```

SEND_ATTACH_VARCHAR2 Procedure

This package is used for sending VARCHAR2 typed attachments along with the email.

The prototype for the SEND_ATTACH_VARCHAR2 procedure is shown below,

```
UTL_MAIL.SEND_ATTACH_VARCHAR2 (
    sender        IN VARCHAR2 CHARACTER SET ANY_CS,
    recipients    IN VARCHAR2 CHARACTER SET ANY_CS,
    cc            IN VARCHAR2 CHARACTER SET ANY_CS DEFAULT NULL,
    bcc           IN VARCHAR2 CHARACTER SET ANY_CS DEFAULT NULL,
    subject        IN VARCHAR2 CHARACTER SET ANY_CS DEFAULT NULL,
    message       IN VARCHAR2 CHARACTER SET ANY_CS DEFAULT NULL,
    mime_type     IN VARCHAR2 CHARACTER SET ANY_CS DEFAULT 'text/plain;
charset=us-ascii',
    priority      IN PLS_INTEGER DEFAULT 3,
    attachment    IN VARCHAR2 CHARACTER SET ANY_CS,
    att_inline    IN BOOLEAN DEFAULT TRUE,
    att_mime_type IN VARCHAR2 CHARACTER SET ANY_CS DEFAULT 'text/plain;
charset=us-ascii',
    att_filename  IN VARCHAR2 CHARACTER SET ANY_CS DEFAULT NULL,
    replyto       IN VARCHAR2 CHARACTER SET ANY_CS DEFAULT NULL);
```

- **ATTACHMENT** parameter accepts the text file to be attached in the form of a variable.
- **ATT_INLINE** parameter accepts a Boolean *true* to make the attachment viewable inline or a Boolean *false* if not.
- **ATT_MIME_TYPE** parameter accepts the MIME type for the attachment.
- **ATT_FILENAME** parameter accepts the string filename of the attachment.

In the below example, the resume of the candidate has been attached to the job application email using the SEND_ATTACH_VARCHAR2 procedure. If the attachment is a file, then we must use the UTL_FILE package to read the file and send them as shown below.

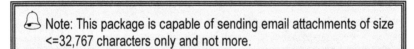

> Note: This package is capable of sending email attachments of size <=32,767 characters only and not more.

```
ALTER system SET smtp_out_server='mail.mycompany.com' scope=both;
/

DECLARE
    l_vc_sender     VARCHAR2(100):='adamwalker1989@mycompany.com';
    l_vc_recipients VARCHAR2(100):='hr@oracle.com';
    l_vc_cc         VARCHAR2(100);
    l_vc_bcc        VARCHAR2(100) :='adamwalker1989@mycompany.com';
```

```
    l_vc_subject    VARCHAR2(100) :='Reg: Job application for PL/SQL
developer';
    l_vc_message    VARCHAR2(4000):='Dear HR,' ||chr(10) ||chr(10)
||'Greetings!' ||chr(10) ||'I am very interested in applying for the PL/SQL
developer job posted on the Oracle magazine recently. My qualifications and
experience match your specifications almost exactly...';
    l_vc_mime_type  VARCHAR2(100):='text/plain; charset=us-ascii';
    l_pi_priority pls_integer      := 1;
    l_vc_attachment varchar2(32767):='My Resume . . . ';
    l_b_att_inline BOOLEAN:=false;
    l_vc_att_mime_type VARCHAR2(100):='text/plain; charset=us-ascii';
    l_vc_att_filename VARCHAR2(100):='Curriculum Vitae';
    l_vc_replyto VARCHAR2(100)       :='adamwalker1989@mycompany.com';
BEGIN
    utl_mail.send_attach_varchar2(l_vc_sender,
                    l_vc_recipients,
                    l_vc_cc,
                    l_vc_bcc,
                    l_vc_subject,
                    l_vc_message,
                    l_vc_mime_type,
                    l_pi_priority,
                    l_vc_attachment,
                    l_b_att_inline,
                    l_vc_att_mime_type,
                    l_vc_att_filename,
                    l_vc_replyto);
END;
/
```

SEND_ATTACH_RAW Procedure

This package is used for sending RAW typed attachments along with the email. This
procedure works similar to the SEND_ATTACH_VARCHAR2 procedure, but with a
RAW file for its attachment.

The prototype for the SEND_ATTACH_VARCHAR2 procedure is shown below,

```
UTL_MAIL.SEND_ATTACH_VARCHAR2 (
    sender        IN VARCHAR2 CHARACTER SET ANY_CS,
    recipients    IN VARCHAR2 CHARACTER SET ANY_CS,
    cc            IN VARCHAR2 CHARACTER SET ANY_CS DEFAULT NULL,
    bcc           IN VARCHAR2 CHARACTER SET ANY_CS DEFAULT NULL,
    subject       IN VARCHAR2 CHARACTER SET ANY_CS DEFAULT NULL,
    message       IN VARCHAR2 CHARACTER SET ANY_CS DEFAULT NULL,
    mime_type     IN VARCHAR2 CHARACTER SET ANY_CS DEFAULT 'text/plain;
charset=us-ascii',
    priority      IN PLS_INTEGER DEFAULT 3,
    attachment    IN RAW,
    att_inline    IN BOOLEAN DEFAULT TRUE,
    att_mime_type IN VARCHAR2 CHARACTER SET ANY_CS DEFAULT 'text/plain;
charset=us-ascii',
    att_filename  IN VARCHAR2 CHARACTER SET ANY_CS DEFAULT NULL,
    replyto       IN VARCHAR2 CHARACTER SET ANY_CS DEFAULT NULL);
```

Summary

We have learned and mastered the important utility packages which are commonly used in our day to day programming lives in this chapter with sufficient facts and examples.

In the next chapter, we will be learning about configuring and working with non-Oracle databases using the Heterogeneous Services.

Heterogeneous Services in Oracle

In this chapter, we are going to learn about the heterogeneous services concepts for configuring and manipulating the SQL Service database data in Oracle. This chapter consists of the below sections in brief.

1) Introduction to Heterogeneous Services concepts and Oracle's synchronous/asynchronous integration with the other databases.

2) Introduction to the Heterogeneous Services architecture, Agents, and Components.

3) Configuring the Oracle database gateway to access SQL Server database.

4) Features of the Oracle database gateways like SQL & PL/SQL support, MVIEW support, and SQL Server statement support.

5) Advantages and restrictions of the heterogeneous services.

6) Data dictionary views in Oracle for the heterogeneous services.

Introduction to Heterogeneous Services

Heterogeneous Services (HS) is available in Oracle starting with version 8i to provide generic technology for accessing data from non-Oracle databases in the Oracle database server.

Integrating the databases in an organization is one big challenge as they may have several different databases running on different applications. Consolidating all the data into a single database is often impossible as the application that they run against one database may not have an equivalent application running on the other. Until this merging happens, we can make use of the heterogeneous services to access data between the different database systems. Even before accessing data from non-Oracle databases, there are significant differences which are to be considered cautiously. The dialects, datatypes, and the features used in one database may or may not be available on the other. This problem is addressed by Oracle as explained in the below sections.

Oracle Synchronous and Asynchronous Integration

If the client application needs to modify or add data to multiple databases, it must open connections to each of them leading to some complex logic and data integrity issues between the databases when they are live. To resolve this synchronization issue, Oracle provides the concept of distributed processing, where the application connects to one database (local) and the local database transparently connects to the other database (remote). The SQL dialects and the data dictionary of the Oracle database are used for the non-Oracle database through the heterogeneous services.

Oracle also offers asynchronous integration between the databases using Oracle streams for data propagation, Messaging gateway for communication between the Oracle and the non-Oracle databases, and Open system interfaces offering open interfaces such as OCI, ODBC, and JDBC, enabling customers either to write their own applications or third party tools to access the Oracle database.

Heterogeneous Services Architecture

The heterogeneous services component in Oracle communicates with the heterogeneous services agent which in-turn communicates with the non-Oracle database system. This process flow can be divided into three parts as described below,

1) **Heterogeneous Services Component** which performs the process related to the heterogeneous service connectivity.

2) **Heterogeneous Services Agent** which is common to all heterogeneous service products. This agent communicates with the database and provides multithreading support.

3) **The Driver** is not specific to the Oracle systems as it is used for communicating with the non-Oracle system.

Heterogeneous Services Agents

The heterogeneous services agent and the non-Oracle system-specific driver components are collectively called as the agent process. This process mainly exists to isolate the Oracle database from the third-party library code which is linked from the non-Oracle database system client. If this agent process does not exist, the problem in the library code could cause the Oracle database to fail. Thus, with the help of this agent process, even if there is a fatal error in the library code, only the agent process will be terminated, leaving the Oracle database unharmed.

This agent process starts when a user access data from the non-Oracle database for the first time through the database link and ends until the database connection is closed or the database link is terminated explicitly.

Types of Heterogeneous Services Agents

The two types of heterogeneous services agents are,

1) **Oracle Database Gateways** is a gateway that is designed for accessing a specific non-Oracle system. With these gateways, we can access the data from a non-Oracle instance, without needing to know their location. When the data is returned, they are presented in a way such that they reside in a remote instance of the Oracle distributed server rather than in an external database.

2) **Oracle Database Gateway for ODBC Agent** contains only the generic code and the customer is required to provide their own drivers to access the non-Oracle systems that have an ODBC interface. However, if the non-Oracle database supports the ODBC protocols, we can use the Oracle Database Gateway for ODBC to connect to them.

Heterogeneous Services Components

The components of the heterogeneous services components are,

1) **Transaction Service** component enables the non-Oracle database to be integrated into the Oracle transaction and sessions. When we access the data from non-Oracle database using the DB link from an Oracle database, we implicitly set up an authenticated session in the non-Oracle database. Then this session is closed at the end of the Oracle user session.

2) **SQL Service** handles all the SQL-related operations performed in an Oracle database. The operations performed by this service include,

   → Mapping the Oracle's internal SQL-related calls to the heterogeneous services driver API, which is then mapped to the non-Oracle client API through the drivers.

   → Back and forth conversion of data from the Oracle database's datatype to the non-Oracle database's datatype.

→ Translating from the SQL dialect of the Oracle database to the SQL dialect of the non-Oracle database.

→ The missing functionalities in the non-Oracle database are compensated by implicitly issuing multiple queries and performing the post processing to get the desired results.

→ Translating the Oracle database data dictionaries to fetch the required data from the non-Oracle database data dictionaries.

Heterogeneous Services Configuration Information

The heterogeneous services gateway has the configuration information stored in the driver which is uploaded to the server once the connection is established to the gateway. The configuration information available in the gateway is,

Data Dictionary Translation Views

These help the heterogeneous services to translate the data dictionary tables and views in Oracle database into queries that can be used for fetching the relevant information from the non-Oracle database system.

Heterogeneous Services Initialization Parameters

These parameters help us to fine-tune the performance and memory utilization of the heterogeneous services component and the gateway. They also inform the gateway and the heterogeneous services about the configuration of the non-Oracle database system. For e.g., The language in which the non-Oracle system runs and their properties.

These initialization parameters can be set in the gateway initialization files and can be tested for a session by querying the V$HS_PARAMETER system view.

Capabilities

Capabilities tell the users about the limitations of the non-Oracle database system like their datatype and SQL equivalents. These are non-configurable and cannot be changed by the users.

Oracle Database Gateway Configuration: SQL Server

The tasks below are to be performed to configure the database gateway for the SQL Server 2014.

The Gateway Process Flow

The below steps explain the sequence of events when we query the non-Oracle database through the gateway.

1) The client application sends a query to the Oracle database using the Oracle Net services.

2) The heterogeneous services translate the SQL dialect from the Oracle database to the SQL statement that is understood by the non-Oracle database.

3) Now, the translated SQL statement is sent to the gateway from Oracle Net services.

4) During the first transaction, an authenticated session is created in the non-Oracle database system.

5) The gateway retrieves the data from non-Oracle database using the translated SQL statement.

6) The gateway converts the data retrieved from the non-Oracle database to the format that is compatible with the Oracle database. Mostly, datatype conversion takes place.

7) The gateway returns the data to the Oracle database using the Oracle Net services.

8) Finally, the Oracle database passes the query results to the client application using the Oracle Net services. The DB link remains open until the DB session is closed or the DB link is explicitly closed.

Gateway Initialization Parameter Configuration

The gateway system identifier (SID) is an alphanumeric string which is used for identifying a gateway instance. We need one gateway SID for every SQL Server database that we are planning to access.

We can define our gateway SID, which in-turn has to be the initialization parameter file name in the location,

```
$ORACLE_HOME\HS\ADMIN\initSQLEXPRESS.ora
```

Where *init* in the filename represents it as the initialization file and the remaining string *SQLEXPRESS* represents the gateway SID.

This ORA file needs the below parameters to be configured based on the user's interest in the SQL Server database characteristics.

```
HS_FDS_CONNECT_INFO = SQLEXPRESS
HS_FDS_TRACE_LEVEL = TRUE
HS_RPC_FETCH_REBLOCKING= OFF
HS_FDS_FETCH_ROWS = 1
HS_TRANSACTION_MODEL=SINGLE_SITE
HS_NLS_NCHAR=UCS2
HS_LANGUAGE=AMERICAN_AMERICA.UTF8
```

- **HS_FDS_CONNECT_INFO** parameter describes the connection to the SQL Server database. The system DSN name created in Windows for the SQL Server database is set to this parameter.

  The system DSN can be created by following the below steps on a Windows machine.

  1) Go to Control Panel -> System and Security -> Administrative Tools -> Double click on the ODBC Data Sources (Either 32 or 64 based on the SQL Server bit version).
  2) Go to the *System DSN* tab of the *ODBC Data Source Administrator* pop-up.
  3) Click on the *Add* option to select the SQL Server driver and click *Finish*.
  4) The Create a New Data Source wizard opens up requesting for the DSN name, description, and the SQL server's hostname respectively. Click *Next*.
  5) The next tab provides the authentication method. Choose the preferred one and click *Next* and select the default database for the DSN. Click *Next* to move on to the final tab.
  6) The next tab provides some checkboxes for language change, logging, translation of character data, and etc. Click *Finish* to create a system DSN.

- **HS_FDS_TRACE_LEVEL** parameter is set to *true* or *false* to enable or disable the error tracing respectively.
- **HS_RPC_FETCH_REBLOCKING** parameter controls whether the heterogeneous services should optimize the data transfer between the Oracle database and the HS agent connected to the SQL Server database.

- Setting this parameter to *ON* enables re-blocking, meaning that the data fetched from the SQL Server buffer are not sent to Oracle until the fetched amount of data is equal or higher than the value set for the HS_RPC_FETCH_SIZE parameter.
- Setting this parameter to *OFF*, disabling the re-blocking, thus the data is sent immediately from the agent to the server.

- **HS_FDS_FETCH_ROWS** parameter specifies the fetch array size. This is the number of rows that has to be fetched from the SQL Server database to the Oracle database at a one-time instance.

- **HS_TRANSACTION_MODEL** parameter specifies the type of transmission model to be used when the SQL Server database is updated by a transaction.
  - The value READ_ONLY allows the Oracle database only to read the SQL Server database.
  - The value SINGLE_SITE allows the Oracle database to both reads and write the SQL Server database.

- **HS_NLS_NCHAR** parameter specifies the character set that the gateway agent must use to retrieve the graphic data.

- **HS_LANGUAGE** parameter specifies the character set that the gateway agent must use to access the SQL Server data source. The format is *territory[.]character_set*.

Oracle Net Listener Configuration

The Oracle net listener listens to the incoming requests for an Oracle instance. For the Oracle gateway to listen to an instance, we must register an entry to the *listener.ora* file in the below location,

```
$ORACLE_HOME\NETWORK\ADMIN\listener.ora
```

The prototype of the *listener.ora* file entry is shown below,

```
LISTENER=
        (ADDRESS=
            (PROTOCOL=TCP)
            (HOST=host_name)
            (PORT=port_number)
        )
```

Where, the *ADDRESS* subparameter in the LISTENER parameter contains the hostname and the port number of the SQL Server database on which the Oracle Net listener listens.

In our case, the below entry is added to the existing LISTENER parameter,

```
(ADDRESS = (PROTOCOL = TCP)(HOST = localhost)(PORT = 1433)
```

To direct the listener to start the gateway in response to the incoming requests, an entry has to be made to the SID_LIST_LISTENER parameter in the *listener.ora* file.

The prototype of the SID_LIST_LISTENER parameter entry is shown below,

```
SID_LIST_LISTENER=
    (SID_LIST=
        (SID_DESC=
            (SID_NAME=<Gateway_sid>)
            (ORACLE_HOME=<Oracle_home>)
            (PROGRAM=dg4odbc)
        )
    )
```

Where *dg4odbc* is the value for the PROGRAM parameter, which is the executable name of the Oracle database gateway for ODBC (Open Database Connectivity).

In our case, the below entry is added to the existing SID_LIST_LISTENER parameter,

```
(SID_DESC=
        (SID_NAME = SQLEXPRESS)
        (ORACLE_HOME=C:\app\BoobalGanesan\product\12.1.0\dbhome_1)
        (PROGRAM = dg4odbc)
    )
```

After these entries are added to the *listener.ora*, the listener has to be reloaded to initiate the new settings to get into effect. Use the *lsnrctl stop* and *lsnrctl start* commands to reload the listener using the command prompt.

Oracle Database Gateway Access Configuration

The Oracle database configuration has to be performed before communicating with the gateway over Oracle Net. To configure, we must add the connection descriptors of the SQL Server database to the *tnsnames.ora* in the below default location,

```
$ORACLE_HOME\NETWORK\ADMIN\tnsnames.ora
```

The prototype of the connection descriptor for the SQL Server database for the gateway access is shown below,

```
<Connect_descriptor>=
```

```
(DESCRIPTION=
   (ADDRESS=
      (PROTOCOL=TCP)
      (HOST=host_name)
      (PORT=port_number)
   )
   (CONNECT_DATA=
      (SID=gateway_sid))
   (HS=OK))
```

In our case, the below entry is added to the existing *tnsnames.ora* file,

```
SQLEXPRESS =
  (DESCRIPTION=
    (ADDRESS=(PROTOCOL=tcp)(HOST=localhost)(PORT=1433))
      (CONNECT_DATA=(SID=SQLEXPRESS))
      (HS=OK)
    )
```

Creation of Database Links in Oracle

The connection between the Oracle database and the gateway is established through a database link, which stays until the Oracle session is explicitly terminated or the DB link is closed.

The prototype of the database link in Oracle database is shown below,

```
CREATE PUBLIC DATABASE LINK <DB_link_name> CONNECT TO "user" IDENTIFIED BY
"password" USING '<Connect_descriptor>';
```

In our case, the below script is used for creating the database link which is used for establishing the connection.

```
CREATE PUBLIC DATABASE LINK sqlexpress USING 'SQLEXPRESS';
```

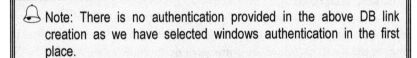 Note: There is no authentication provided in the above DB link creation as we have selected windows authentication in the first place.

After the DB link has been created, we can test the data fetch from the Oracle database from the SQL Server database by querying through any of the tables in the *master* database, as that is the DB which we have configured during the system DSN creation.

> 🔔 Note: We need to make sure the necessary privileges are placed
> upon the table that is being queried.

When the CUSTOMER table, which was already created in the SQL Server database is queried, it returns the complete data set as shown below,

```
SELECT * FROM customer@sqlexpress;
```

Script Output:

CUST_ID	CUST_NAME	CUST_DOB	CUST_ADD	CUST_EMAIL	CUST_PHONE
1001	Steven Markle	1975-03-08	10 Av – NY	steven@markle.com	6501241434
1002	James Marlow	1985-02-16	12 Av – NY	james@marlow.com	6501247234
1003	Jason Mallin	1984-06-14	15 Av – NY	jason@malin.com	6501241968
1004	Stephen Stiles	1979-10-26	17 Av – NY	stephen@stiles.com	6501242030
1005	John Russell	1968-10-01	21 Av – NY	john@russell.com	6501241322
1006	Peter Tucker	1973-01-30	25 Av – NY	peter@tucker.com	6501241011

Features of Oracle Database Gateways

The major features and limitations of accessing the SQL Server database to the Oracle database are described below.

SQL & PL/SQL Support

Even though the heterogeneous service can incorporate the SQL Server database into the Oracle distributed sessions, there are some generic limitations that are to be duly noted before working with them. They are,

Things to know before using the SQL Server objects in SQL,

1) Implicit date conversions are not supported and we must explicitly convert them using the *to_date* function.

2) The ROWID pseudo column is not supported.

3) SELECT.. FOR UPDATE.. OF functionality does not work in SQL as the locking mechanism is based on the ROWID pseudo column.

4) CONNECT BY clauses are not supported in SQL statements.

5) The INSERT, DELETE, or UPDATE statements having a subquery with bind variables and expressions as a part of the operands to a mathematical or a string function, they fail with an error.

6) The UPDATE statement SET clause does not allow VIEWs and DATA DICTIONARY TABLES within them.

7) EXPLAIN PLAN FOR statement returns no useful information about the underlying query as it does not return any column statistics and does not allow optimizer hints to force an operation.

8) When concatenating two numbers (Either using the pipe symbol or the CONCAT function) using the gateway, it returns their sum.

   For e.g., Select 1||1 from dual@SQLEXPRESS; statement returns **2**, whereas the similar statement in Oracle returns 11.

9) The SQL statements that do arithmetic operations between date and date, or the date and number will fail as it is not supported in SQL Server.

Things to know before using the SQL Server objects in PL/SQL,

1) By default, the remote procedures and functions do not return any values or result sets until we enable the HS_FDS_PROC_IS_FUNC and HS_FDS_RESULTSET_SUPPORT parameters to true respectively.

2) As the ROWID feature is not supported, SELECT.. FOR UPDATE.. OF and WHERE.. CURRENT.. OF functionalities are not supported by the cursors.

3) Multiple open statements or cursors within the same transaction are not advised as they might lock each other as they use different connections in SQL Server.

4) TCL statements in a cursor loop terminate the loop with a *fetch out of sequence* exception.

5) OUT parameters of remote procedures and functions must be initialized to an empty string.

6) The remote procedures and functions can have REF-Cursors only as their OUT parameters and not as IN or INOUT.

7) When negative numbers are used as the second parameter in the SUBSTR function, it results in some incorrect results due to the incompatibility in this function between Oracle and SQL Server database.

8) Remote packages are not supported.

Materialized View Support

Materialized views can be used for replicating data between Oracle and non-Oracle databases. These views act as a physical storage that refreshes at specific time intervals copying the data from the non-Oracle database to the Oracle database, thus, synching them both.

The limitation of using an MVIEW in a non-Oracle database table is listed down below,

1) MVIEWS can only be created in Oracle as other databases do not support them.

2) FAST REFRESH fails as it requires the underlying table to be present in Oracle database. In this case, we can use COMPLETE REFRESH method.

3) ROW ID and OBJECT ID based materialized views are not supported as the non-Oracle databases do not have any implementation of them.

Non-Oracle Database Statement Support

The pass-through SQL feature allows us to use non-Oracle SQL statements, when there is no equivalent functionality in Oracle, by bypassing the Oracle query parser directly to the non-Oracle database for processing.

This process is performed by the virtual DBMS_HS_PASSTHROUGH package which resides in the non-Oracle database. Any calls to this package are mapped to the appropriate APIs of the non-Oracle database through the heterogeneous services using a database link which is transparent to the user.

When we execute a DDL statement in the non-Oracle database, the particular transaction would be auto-committed, whereas, the linking transaction in the Oracle database still expects for a TCL operation. When we perform a rollback, there is an inconsistency between both the systems, resulting in *global data inconsistency*.

 Note: We can optionally choose to close the long idle gateway sessions automatically by setting the HS_IDLE_TIMEOUT (0 to 9999 minutes) parameter. When a gateway session is idle for more than the specified time limit, any pending gateway transaction will be rolled back and the session will be terminated.

Supported Subprograms

The subprograms of the DBMS_HS_PASSTHROUGH package are described below along with their prototypes.

OPEN_CURSOR Function

This function opens a cursor for executing an SQL statement in the non-Oracle database. This function returns a cursor which must be used in the subsequent statements to process the SQL. This function allocates memory during its call, which is then de-allocated during the CLOSE_CURSOR function call.

The prototype of this function is shown below,

```
DBMS_HS_PASSTHROUGH.OPEN_CURSOR RETURN BINARY_INTEGER;
```

PARSE Procedure

This procedure parses an SQL statement at the non-Oracle database system.

The prototype of this procedure is shown below,

```
DBMS_HS_PASSTHROUGH.PARSE (
    c    IN BINARY_INTEGER NOT NULL,
    stmt IN VARCHAR2 NOT NULL);
```

- **C** parameter accepts the cursor variable that is associated with the current pass-through process which was returned by the OPEN_CURSOR function.

- **STMT** parameter accepts the SQL statement, which is to be parsed.

BIND_VARIABLE, BIND_OUT_VARIABLE, and BIND_INOUT_VARIABLE Procedures

The BIND_VARIABLE, BIND_OUT_VARIABLE, and BIND_INOUT_VARIABLE procedures bind IN, OUT, and IN OUT type variables in a positional manner with the PL/SQL program variables respectively.

The prototypes of these procedures are shown below,

```
DBMS_HS_PASSTHROUGH.BIND_VARIABLE (
  c IN BINARY_INTEGER NOT NULL,
  p IN BINARY_INTEGER NOT NULL,
  v IN [DATE | NUMBER | VARCHAR2],
  n IN VARCHAR2);

DBMS_HS_PASSTHROUGH.BIND_OUT_VARIABLE (
  c IN BINARY_INTEGER NOT NULL,
  p IN BINARY_INTEGER NULL,
  v OUT [DATE | NUMBER | VARCHAR2],
  n IN VARCHAR2);

DBMS_HS_PASSTHROUGH.BIND_INOUT_VARIABLE (
  c IN BINARY_INTEGER NOT NULL,
  p IN BINARY_INTEGER NOT NULL,
  v IN OUT [DATE | NUMBER | VARCHAR2],
  n IN VARCHAR2);
```

- **P** parameter accepts the position of the bind variable in the SQL statement. Starts with 1.
- **V** parameter accepts/ returns the value or the variable to be passed to/ retrieved from the bind variable. Allowed datatypes are DATE, NUMBER, and VARCHAR2.
- **N** parameter accepts the optional name for the bind variable.

EXECUTE_IMMEDIATE and EXECUTE_NON_QUERY Functions

The EXECUTE_IMMEDIATE and the EXECUTE_NON_QUERY functions execute a non-query statement without and with BIND variables respectively in the non-Oracle database through the passthrough SQL protocol. These functions return the number of rows affected by the SQL statement which is executed by them.

Note: Non queries include DML and DDL statements.

The prototypes of these functions are shown below,

```
DBMS_HS_PASSTHROUGH.EXECUTE_IMMEDIATE (
   s IN VARCHAR2 NOT NULL)
RETURN BINARY_INTEGER;

DBMS_HS_PASSTHROUGH.EXECUTE_NON_QUERY (
   s IN VARCHAR2 NOT NULL)
 RETURN BINARY_INTEGER;
```

- **S** parameter accepts the VARCHAR2 statement that is to be executed immediately.

FETCH_ROW Function

This function fetches result sets from the query executed. When we execute this function when all the rows are fetched, we may face the *no_data_found* exception.

The prototype of this function is shown below,

```
DBMS_HS_PASSTHROUGH.FETCH_ROW (
   c IN BINARY_INTEGER NOT NULL,
   f IN BOOLEAN)
RETURN BINARY_INTEGER;
```

- **F** parameter is an optional parameter to either re-execute the statement (when *true*) or to fetch the next row (when *false*).

GET_VALUE Procedure

This procedure retrieves column values from a SELECT statement or from an OUT bind parameter.

The prototype of this procedure is shown below,

```
DBMS_HS_PASSTHROUGH.GET_VALUE (
   c IN BINARY_INTEGER NOT NULL,
   p IN BINARY_INTEGER NOT NULL,
   v OUT [DATE | VARCHAR2 | NUMBER]);
```

- **V** parameter accepts the variable that is to be used for storing the column value retrieved.

CLOSE_CURSOR Procedure

This procedure closes the cursor and releases the memory allocated during the OPEN_CURSOR call after the non-query statement has been executed at the non-Oracle system. When the input cursor number is not open during this procedure call, the call is considered to be NO-OP (No Operation).

The prototype of this procedure is shown below,

```
DBMS_HS_PASSTHROUGH.CLOSE_CURSOR (c IN BINARY_INTEGER NOT NULL);
```

In the below example, an ALTER statement for decreasing the length for the column CUST_NAME from 200 to 50 in the SQL Server database is executed using the passthrough package. As this is a DDL operation, the number of affected rows returned by this statement is 0.

```
DECLARE
  l_n_var1 NUMBER;
BEGIN
  l_n_var1:=dbms_hs_passthrough.execute_immediate@sqlexpress('ALTER TABLE
customer ALTER COLUMN cust_name varchar(50)');
  dbms_output.put_line('Number of rows affected: '||l_n_var1);
END;
/
```

Result:

```
Number of rows affected: 0
```

In the below example, an update statement for updating the CUST_ADD field of the CUSTOMER table for an input customer ID which is passed as a bind variable is executed using the EXECUTE_NON_QUERY function. The function call returns the number of rows affected by the update statement.

```
DECLARE
  l_i_cur_id INTEGER;
  l_n_var1      NUMBER;
  l_n_cust_id   NUMBER:=1004;
BEGIN
  l_i_cur_id:=dbms_hs_passthrough.open_cursor@sqlexpress;
  dbms_hs_passthrough.parse@sqlexpress(l_i_cur_id, 'update customer set
"cust_add"=''99 Av - NY'' where "cust_id"=?');
  dbms_hs_passthrough.bind_variable@sqlexpress(l_i_cur_id, 1, l_n_cust_id);
  l_n_var1:=dbms_hs_passthrough.execute_non_query@sqlexpress(l_i_cur_id);
  dbms_hs_passthrough.close_cursor@sqlexpress(l_i_cur_id);
  dbms_output.put_line('Number of rows affected: '||l_n_var1);
END;
/
```

Result:

```
Number of rows affected: 1
```

In the below example, an SQL Server SELECT statement (not supported by Oracle) is parsed and then looped to fetch all the rows fetched one by one using the FETCH_ROW function. After a row is fetched, the columns from the fetched row are mapped to a variable based on its position using the GET_VALUE procedure and then printed.

```
DECLARE
  l_n_cust_id     NUMBER;
  l_vc_cust_name  VARCHAR2(50);
  l_i_cur_id      INTEGER;
  l_i_row         INTEGER;
BEGIN
  l_i_cur_id := dbms_hs_passthrough.open_cursor@sqlexpress;
  dbms_hs_passthrough.parse@sqlexpress(l_i_cur_id, 'select top 5 cust_id,
cust_name from customer');
  LOOP
    l_i_row := dbms_hs_passthrough.fetch_row@sqlexpress(l_i_cur_id);
    EXIT
  WHEN l_i_row = 0;
    dbms_hs_passthrough.get_value@sqlexpress(l_i_cur_id, 1, l_n_cust_id);
    dbms_hs_passthrough.get_value@sqlexpress(l_i_cur_id, 2, l_vc_cust_name);
    dbms_output.put_line(l_n_cust_id||' - '||l_vc_cust_name);
  END LOOP;
  dbms_hs_passthrough.close_cursor@sqlexpress(l_i_cur_id);
END;
/
```

Result:
```
1001 - Steven Markle
1002 - James Marlow
1003 - Jason Mallin
1004 - Stephen Stiles
1005 - John Russell
```

Restrictions in SQL Remote Mapping

1) A DDL statement cannot be remotely mapped. To make this happen, we must use the passthrough feature.

2) The non-Oracle database cannot retrieve data from the originating Oracle database while executing a DML statement.

For example, the below statement will fail with *all tables in the SQL statement must be at the remote database* exception.

```
INSERT INTO customer@sqlexpress SELECT * FROM customer_arc;
```

The workaround for this limitation is by looping through the CUSTOMER_ARC table data and inserting it into the CUSTOMER table in the non-Oracle database.

3) As the functions, USER, USERENV, and SYSDATE perform a callback to the Oracle database, the below statements may fail with *all tables in the SQL statement must be at the remote database* exception.

```
DELETE FROM customer@sqlexpress WHERE "cust_dob">sysdate;
```

The workaround for this limitation is to pass the function's return value in a variable and use it for performing the above DML statement.

4) The tables with TYPE columns and reference columns cannot be remotely mapped.

5) The statement with duplicate bind variables cannot be remotely mapped.

6) The statement with user defined operators, LONG column and sequences must be mapped to the node where they are defined.

7) The statement containing a table expression cannot be remotely mapped.

Advantages of Heterogeneous Services in Oracle

When other databases are connected to Oracle, they enjoy the full potential of the Oracle database like SQL parsing, and query optimization. The other main advantages of the heterogeneous services are,

Transparent Data Access

We can create synonyms over the objects from the non-Oracle database so that their physical location is avoided in their call resulting in complete transparent data access. This transparency eliminates the application developers to customize their applications to access data from a non-Oracle database system, thus increasing in the portability of the application.

Avoiding Data Duplication and Inconsistency

The Oracle database gateway allows applications to access data from non-Oracle databases directly by eliminating the data movement from one location to another. This contributes to a reduction in disk storage space and data duplication at multiple locations.

As the data movement is avoided, we don't have to compromise on the data inconsistency or un-synchronization.

Common SQL Statements

The heterogeneous services in Oracle accept SQL statements belonging to the Oracle database and pass the appropriate SQL statement of the non-Oracle database to fetch data from them through the gateways.

Common Oracle Tools

Both Oracle and non-Oracle database data can be fetched using a single set of Oracle tools rather developing or learning new tools.

Sophistication of using Other Database Languages

Oracle enables us to fetch data from non-Oracle databases using the Oracle SQLs. But when we want to use the SQL of the non-Oracle database to be used for fetching the data, the passthrough feature of the heterogeneous service helps in this matter. This feature bypasses the Oracle query processor and transmits the query to the non-Oracle database for processing in its own language.

Data Dictionary Views

We can use the heterogeneous services data dictionary views to access information about the heterogeneous services. The different views available are,

S. No.	View Name	Description
1	HS_BASE_CAPS	Displays all the capabilities supported by heterogeneous services.
2	HS_CLASS_CAPS	Displays all the capabilities supported by each class.
3	HS_CLASS_INIT	Displays all the initialization parameters for each class.
4	HS_FDS_CLASS	Displays all the classes accessible by the Oracle server.
5	HS_FDS_INST	Displays all the instances accessible by the Oracle server.
6	HS_INST_CAPS	Displays all the capabilities supported by each instance.
7	HS_INST_INIT	Displays all the initialization parameters for each instance.
8	V$HS_SESSION	Displays all the sessions for each agent along with its database link.
9	V$HS_PARAMETER	Displays all the HS parameters and their registered values in the Oracle database.

Summary

We started this chapter by learning about the heterogeneous services and their integration types. The later section explained us about the heterogeneous services architecture, their agents, components and their configuration setup. The final section described us about the various features of the heterogeneous services like their support for Oracle, restrictions, advantages, along with the data dictionary views.

In the next chapter, we will be learning about the Advanced Interfaced Methods for using Java and C programs in Oracle PL/SQL.

Advanced Interface Methods in Oracle

This chapter will tour us through the Advanced Interface Methods in Oracle by establishing the communication between Oracle and the programs written in other languages through PL/SQL. This chapter covers the below sections in detail.

7) Introduction to External Procedures and their architectural structure.

8) The configuration of the Oracle Net Services.

9) Executing External Procedures written in Java language using PL/SQL.

10) Executing External Procedures written in C language using PL/SQL.

11) Advantages and Limitations of using External Procedures in PL/SQL.

Introduction to External Procedures

External procedures are introduced in the Oracle version 8 (as External Routines) to bridge the gap between Oracle database and non-PL/SQL programs. These provide the ability to establish the communication between the Oracle database and the external programs written in languages such as C, C++, COBOL, DOT NET, Java, and Visual Basic. Each of these languages has their advantage and the choice can be made by considering the programmer's expertise, the point of view, and portability.

Generally, C language is preferred to execute most computation-intensive tasks efficiently and Java is preferred when portability and security are our major criteria. From the performance point of view, Java methods run within the address space of the server but C programs are dispatched as external procedures and run on the server side outside the address space of it.

Thus, considering all these factors, there could be scenarios in our application development requiring us to code not in one but in more than one programming language.

> 🔔 Note: The external procedure can be written in any language as long as it is callable by C.

The External Procedures are stored as Dynamic Link Library (DLL) files on the server and then it has to be registered through a call specification. After it is successfully registered, it is ready to be used in PL/SQL.

In this chapter, we will be discussing the coupling of PL/SQL programs and the external programs written in Java and C languages.

Architecture of External Procedures

The languages used for creating the external procedures must be capable of transforming themselves into a shared library. Also, the OS which we use must support the existence of the shared libraries for Oracle to communicate. The Windows platforms use the Dynamic Link Library (.dll files) and the UNIX/ LINUX platforms use the Shared Object (.so files) as their implementation of the shared libraries. For Java, the shared libraries are called as *libunits*. These libraries are basically programs which are capable of sharing themselves either as a whole or as a part of multiple applications; thus reducing memory consumption in multisession environments.

When an application calls an external procedure for the first time, the Oracle listener starts a session-specific agent called as EXTPROC, which remains active throughout the session and gets terminated when the session ends. Thus, it is called only once for any number of external procedure requests to avoid the overhead. An external procedure must be converted to a shared library file for it to be accessed in PL/SQL. By the connection details specified in the listener file, a network connection is established between the Oracle database and the EXTPROC agent, through which the application shares the name of the DLL file, name of the external procedure, and the parameters of the external procedure with the agent. After receiving the necessary information, the EXTPROC agent loads the DLL file (if it is not already loaded), runs the external procedure and returns back the output values to the application.

> 🔔 Note: The listener must start the EXTPROC agent on same the machine where the application's Oracle server resides.

When a PL/SQL program invokes an external procedure, the process is called as a *callout*. When an external procedure calls a statement which in turn hits the Oracle database to perform an operation, the process is called as a *callback*.

The external procedures use the PL/SQL libraries for their communication between the DLL files and the PL/SQL engine. The PL/SQL libraries map the PL/SQL datatypes to the external language's equivalent during data exchange.

The below illustration depicts the complete flow of the External Procedures. A call to the PL/SQL program is made from the application is performed. When the PL/SQL program calls a procedure which is created using an external language, the network verification is performed. When the network is resolved using the details in the listener file, the listener goes on to start the EXTPROC agent which loads the shared library, sends arguments (if any), executes the program code in the library file, and returns them back to its parent process subsequently till the application receives it.

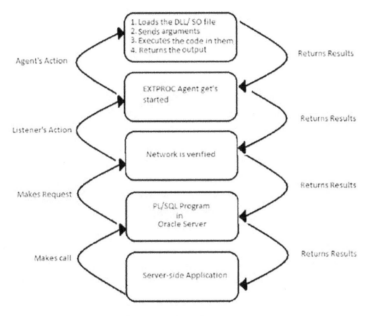

Fig. 11.1 Architectural illustration of External Procedures

When there is a failure in any of the level, the EXTPROC agent fails with an appropriate exception. As the agent process is performed away from the database, any failure of the agent process does not have any impact on the database, rather it returns an error to the PL/SQL engine which is reported back to the application.

Oracle Net Services Configuration

ORAcle Common Language Runtime (ORACLR) is a language-neutral environment that provides services that help in coordinating the non-PL/SQL programs in PL/SQL. When the PL/SQL runtime engine receives a request for executing a non-PL/SQL program, the call is transferred to the connection: ORACLR_CONNECTION_DATA, which is the default TNS service connection in the *tnsnames.ora* file for the external procedures to activate the EXTPROC agent. This is configured by the Oracle Net Configuration Assistant during the time of database installation. Once the connection and listener details in the *tnsnames.ora* and *listener.ora* files are configured and validated for the current active listener, the EXTPROC agent is started to load and execute the DLL files. However, this default configuration can be modified manually to ensure enhanced security standards.

The configuration of these two files is described in the below sections.

TNSNAMES.ORA

The *tnsnames.ora* file contains the service names which allows any request to connect to its appropriate active listener. The connection requests are taken care by first matching the ADDRESS parameter between the service names in the *tnsnames.ora* file to the ADDRESS parameter of the active listener process. Once they are matched, the connections are established by using the SERVICE_NAME and SERVER sub-parameters from the CONNECT_DATA parameter. We can add any number of database connection details to *tnsnames.ora* and *listener.ora* files by adding their appropriate ADDRESS and CONNECT_DATA parameters as a new connection with a unique connection descriptor name.

The *tnsnames.ora* file can be found in the below default location.

```
$ORACLE_HOME\NETWORK\ADMIN\tnsnames.ora
```

The standard *tnsnames.ora* file after the database installation provides the below two service names.

```
ORACLR_CONNECTION_DATA =
  (DESCRIPTION =
    (ADDRESS_LIST =
      (ADDRESS = (PROTOCOL = IPC) (KEY = EXTPROC1522))
    )
    (CONNECT_DATA =
      (SID = CLRExtProc)
      (PRESENTATION = RO)
    )
```

```
    )
ORCL =
  (DESCRIPTION =
    (ADDRESS = (PROTOCOL = TCP) (HOST = localhost) (PORT = 1522))
    (CONNECT_DATA =
      (SERVER = DEDICATED)
      (SERVICE_NAME = orcl)
    )
  )
```

The ORACLR_CONNECTION_DATA connection descriptor is used for activating the EXTPROC agent, where the KEY parameter has the format of EXTPROC<PORT_NUMBER> and the PROTOCOL parameter has a fixed value of IPC for receiving Internet Procedure Calls. The PRESENTATION is an optimized parameter which is used for character set and datatype conversion between the server and the client only when required. The available options for this parameter are TTC, JavaTTC, HTTP, FTP, GIOP, IMAP (for EMAIL purpose), POP (for EMAIL purpose), IM APSSL (for EMAIL purpose), and RO. For the external procedures, this parameter will default to RO (Remote Operation). This parameter indicates the PRESENTATION layer that a Remote Procedure Call has to be made between the server and the client.

The ORCL connection descriptor is used for mapping the listeners of the standard databases using the port number, host address, and service name details. Note that the PROTOCOL parameter has the value of TCP as the connection is established using the Transfer Control Protocol.

LISTENER.ORA

The listener is a database process that waits in the server "listening" for connection requests. Once it finds one, it allocates the necessary process to get the connection up and running.

The *listener.ora* file can be found in the below default location.

```
$ORACLE_HOME\NETWORK\ADMIN\listener.ora
```

The standard *listener.ora* file after the database installation provides the below two entries.

```
LISTENER =
  (DESCRIPTION_LIST =
    (DESCRIPTION =
      (ADDRESS = (PROTOCOL = TCP) (HOST = localhost) (PORT = 1522))
      (ADDRESS = (PROTOCOL = IPC) (KEY = EXTPROC1522))
    )
```

```
  )
SID_LIST_LISTENER =
  (SID_LIST =
    (SID_DESC =
      (SID_NAME = CLRExtProc)
      (ORACLE_HOME = C:\app\BoobalGanesan\product\12.1.0\dbhome_1)
      (PROGRAM = extproc)
      (ENVS = "EXTPROC_DLLS=ONLY:
C:\app\BoobalGanesan\product\12.1.0\dbhome_1\bin\oraclr12.dll")
    )
  )
```

The first entry is the LISTENER, which is the name of the listener process. The LISTENER has a list of addresses consisting of either PROTOCOL, HOST, and a PORT for database connectivity or PROTOCOL and a KEY for external program access. We can see that this listener can listen to both IPC as well as TCP requests. Note that the address parameters in the ORACLR_CONNECTION_DATA entry in the *tnsnames.ora* file and the LISTENER entry in the *listener.ora* files match.

The second entry is the SID_LIST_LISTENER, which is of the format SID_LIST_<Listener name>. This entry defines the SIDs for which the listener listens to the incoming connection requests of the database.

1) The SID_DESC parameter contains the complete definition of the SIDs with SID_NAME (which matches with the SID value in the CONNECT_DATA sub-parameter of the ORACLR_CONNECTION_DATA parameter in the *tnsnames.ora* file) acting as the EXTPROC agent identifier.

2) ORACLE_HOME parameter defining the Oracle home directory.

3) PROGRAM parameter is for the program identification of the EXTPROC agent, which should be a valid ".exe" file in the *$ORACLE_HOME\bin* directory for the agent to access the libraries.

4) The ENVS parameter is to change the default directory for the accessing the library files.

 Note: The exception *ORA-28576: Lost RPC connection to external procedure agent* is raised when the listener is not able to establish a connection with the EXTPROC agent.

The possible values for the ENVS parameter are,

1) "EXTPROC_DLLS=ANY" allows the EXTPROC agent to load any DLL file from the server without any validation. The security risk in using this option is high and it is not recommended for production environments.

2) "EXTPROC_DLLS=<DLL File Location>:<DLL File Location>: …" allows the EXTPROC agent to load the mentioned DLLs (separated by a colon) from the default location ($ORACLE_HOME\bin). Note that the location of the DLLs cannot be other than the BIN directory if this option is selected. The security risk is   average.   E.g., "EXTPROC_DLLS=C:\sharedlibrary\test1.dll:C:\sharedlibrary\test2.dll".

3) "EXTPROC_DLLS=ONLY:<DLL File Location>:<DLL File Location>: …" allows the agent to load the mentioned DLLs (separated by a colon) from any directory on the server. The security risk is very minimal and it is highly recommended   for   secure   environments.   E.g., "EXTPROC_DLLS=ONLY:C:\sharedlibrary\test1.dll:D:\libraryfiles\test3.dll".

> 🔔 Note: The exception *ORA-28595: Extproc agent: Invalid DLL path* is raised when there is no DLL file present in the mentioned path in the ENVS parameter.

To ensure maximum security in the production environments, we must separate the database connectivity and external program access by creating additional entries. Before we do this, we must take the backup of the current *listener.ora* file and rename it (e.g., *listener_bk.ora*). Just in case we make any mistake or accidently remove any viable content during this change, we can always use the backup file to set everything straight back up.

After the split up of the standard listener.ora file, it looks like below,

```
LISTENER =
  (DESCRIPTION_LIST =
    (DESCRIPTION =
      (ADDRESS = (PROTOCOL = TCP) (HOST = localhost) (PORT = 1522))
      )
  )

SID_LIST_LISTENER =
  (SID_LIST =
    (SID_DESC =
      (SID_NAME = <database_name>)
      (ORACLE_HOME = C:\app\BoobalGanesan\product\12.1.0\dbhome_1)
    )
```

```
  )
LISTENER_EXTPROC =
  (DESCRIPTION_LIST =
    (DESCRIPTION =
      (ADDRESS = (PROTOCOL = IPC) (KEY = EXTPROC1522))
      )
  )

SID_LIST_LISTENER_EXTPROC =
  (SID_LIST =
    (SID_DESC =
      (SID_NAME = CLRExtProc)
      (ORACLE_HOME = C:\app\BoobalGanesan\product\12.1.0\dbhome_1)
      (PROGRAM = extproc)
      (ENVS = "EXTPROC_DLLS=ONLY:
C:\app\BoobalGanesan\product\12.1.0\dbhome_1\bin\oraclr12.dll")
    )
  )
```

After all the above processes are done, we must reboot the listener to get all the new changes get into effect. This can be performed by the utilities *lsnrctl stop <listener name>* and *lsnrctl start <listener name>* in the command line window.

Now, after both the database connectivity listener and the external programs listener are restarted, we can verify whether or not they are truly working by using the *tnsping* command line utility on the ORACLR_CONNECTION_DATA alias as below,

```
$ tnsping ORACLR_CONNECTION_DATA

TNS Ping Utility for 64-bit Windows: Version 12.1.0.2.0 - Production on 16-
OCT-2
016 20:25:31

Copyright (c) 1997, 2014, Oracle.  All rights reserved.

Used parameter files:
C:\app\BoobalGanesan\product\12.1.0\dbhome_1\network\admin\sqlnet.ora


Used TNSNAMES adapter to resolve the alias
Attempting to contact (DESCRIPTION = (ADDRESS_LIST = (ADDRESS = (PROTOCOL =
IPC)
(KEY = EXTPROC1522))) (CONNECT_DATA = (SID = CLRExtProc) (PRESENTATION =
RO)))
OK (20 msec)
```

If the above result is returned, it means that we have successfully configured a separate listener for the EXTPROC agent and it works fine.

```
TNS Ping Utility for 64-bit Windows: Version 12.1.0.2.0 - Production on 16-
OCT-2
016 20:35:16
```

```
Copyright (c) 1997, 2014, Oracle.  All rights reserved.

Used parameter files:
C:\app\BoobalGanesan\product\12.1.0\dbhome_1\network\admin\sqlnet.ora


Used TNSNAMES adapter to resolve the alias
Attempting to contact (DESCRIPTION = (ADDRESS_LIST = (ADDRESS = (PROTOCOL =
IPC)
(KEY = EXTPROC1522))) (CONNECT_DATA = (SID = CLRExtProc) (PRESENTATION =
RO)))
TNS-12541: TNS:no listener
```

If the above failure is returned, there could be some possible mismatch in the ADDRESS parameter of the *listener.ora* and *tnsnames.ora* files, which we should check and resolve before proceeding further.

If *TNS-03505: Failed to resolve name* error is received, it means that the service does not exist or is down.

Loading Java Class Methods in PL/SQL

The Java classes and source files are stored as schema objects in the database as Java is a natively part of the Oracle database. Thus, the EXTPROC agent, listener, or any environment parameters are not used as a means of communication between Java and Oracle, where it is taken care by the Java Virtual Machine (JVM). JVM interprets the Java compilation and executes the run-time object code. This need for JVM makes "Java in Oracle" a bit slower than other languages in Oracle.

As Oracle natively supports Java, there is no need for the shared library as a third wheel instead, there is a Java Shared Library called as LIBUNIT, which is automatically loaded by the EXTPROC agent.

Java understands Oracle easily so there are no big type conversions needed between the PL/SQL wrapper and the Java class/ source file. As Java uses the Java pool in the SGA part of the memory, there is a possibility for a Java program to use up the SGA memory resulting in memory issues.

The below steps are to be undertaken to implement Java class/ source files in PL/SQL.

Loading Java Class/ Source Files in Oracle

A Java class or a source file can be loaded into the Oracle database so that it is made immediately available for the PL/SQL program accessing it. Whenever a Java class or a source file is loaded in the form of OS files, the Oracle JVM library manager loads Java class files and resources from the OS location into the RDBMS libunits.

These two processes to load Java class or source file are explained below,

CREATE JAVA Syntax

We can either create a Java class object or a source file object which in-turn creates the appropriate classes by itself.

The prototype for creating a Java source file object is shown below,

```
CREATE OR REPLACE [AND COMPILE| RESOLVE] java
[source NAMED | class] <Primary_name> [AuthID [CURRENT_USER | DEFINER]]
[AS <Java_source_file>] | [USING BFILE (<Directory_name>, <File_name>)]
```

- **AND COMPILE | RESOLVE** clause compiles the Java class/ source file upon its creation. Compile and Resolve are synonymous keywords. If this clause is omitted, the Java object may be in INVALID state after its creation and we may need to execute an "Alter Java [class | source] <Primary_name> COMPILE;" to make it VALID.

- **SOURCE NAME** clause is used to specify that a Java source file is used for the load.

- **CLASS** clause is used to specify that a Java class is used for the load.

- **PRIMARY_NAME** clause is the name for the Java object that is to be created.

- **AS** clause lets us use the Java source file in character form.

- **USING** clause lets us use the Java source file stored in a location.

Using Java Source File

In this method, a Java source code can be used in the CREATE JAVA statement to create a schema object without needing us to convert them into a ".class" file externally. Upon successful creation of the Java source object, the classes available in the Java source code are automatically created as Java class objects in the database.

In the below example, a Java source with one class file for squaring the input number is created as a Java source object in the database.

```
CREATE OR REPLACE AND COMPILE JAVA SOURCE NAMED SQUARE
AS
    public class SQUARE {
        public static int SQUARE (int var1) {
            return var1*var1;}}
```

We can check the created Java source and class files in the USER_OBJECTS data dictionary as below,

```
SELECT object_id,
  object_name,
  object_type,
  created,
  status
FROM user_objects
WHERE object_name='SQUARE';
```

Script Output:

OBJECT_ID	OBJECT_NAME	OBJECT_TYPE	CREATED	STATUS
93493	SQUARE	JAVA SOURCE	20-OCT-16	VALID
93495	SQUARE	JAVA CLASS	20-OCT-16	VALID

Using Java Class File

By using this method, a single Java class file can be created as a database object.

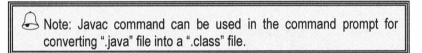
> Note: Javac command can be used in the command prompt for converting ".java" file into a ".class" file.

As a first step, a directory has to be created to store the class file as shown below,

```
CREATE DIRECTORY java_class_dir AS 'C:\Program Files\Java';
```

Upon placing the class file in the above directory, a Java class object can be created in the database by executing the below script.

```
CREATE AND COMPILE JAVA CLASS USING BFILE (java_class_dir, 'SQUARE.class');
```

We can check the created Java class file in the USER_OBJECTS data dictionary as below,

```
SELECT object_id,
  object_name,
  object_type,
```

```
  created,
  status
FROM user_objects
WHERE object_name='SQUARE';
```

Script Output:

OBJECT_ID	OBJECT_NAME	OBJECT_TYPE	CREATED	STATUS
93495	SQUARE	JAVA CLASS	20-OCT-16	VALID

LOADJAVA Utility

The loadjava utility can be used for uploading a Java class file into the database using the command prompt. The steps to be followed are,

1) Firstly, the location of the Java file has to be set as the current location in the command window as shown below,

```
C:\Users\Boobal Ganesan>cd C:\Users\Boobal Ganesan\Desktop\JavaPrograms

C:\Users\Boobal Ganesan\Desktop\JavaPrograms>
```

2) Next, the loadjava utility can be used for the Java file which has to be uploaded as shown below,

```
C:\Users\Boobal Ganesan\Desktop\JavaPrograms>loadjava -user c##/oracle
SQUARE.java
```

Upon completion, there will not be any message confirmation whether the load has been successful or not. The data dictionary USER_OBJECTS can be browsed through to find the loaded Java file.

```
SELECT object_id,
  object_name,
  object_type,
  created,
  status
FROM user_objects
WHERE object_name='SQUARE';
```

Script Output:

OBJECT_ID	OBJECT_NAME	OBJECT_TYPE	CREATED	STATUS
93493	SQUARE	JAVA SOURCE	20-OCT-16	INVALID
93495	SQUARE	JAVA CLASS	20-OCT-16	INVALID

Here, the loaded objects are invalidated during their upload. They can be made valid by executing the below statements.

```
ALTER java source square compile;
```

Creating and Validating PL/SQL Wrapper for the Java Class

The Java class and source objects created in the above steps are stored in the RDBMS libunits. These library objects can be published by creating a PL/SQL wrapper (Procedures and Functions) on them.

> Note: All the Java class methods accessed by the PL/SQL wrapper functions must be static. Thus, resulting them not thread safe.

The prototype for defining a PL/SQL wrapper function is shown below,

```
CREATE OR REPLACE FUNCTION <Function_name> (<Parameter list>) RETURN
<Datatype>
AS
  Language Java
  Name '<Java_method>';
```

- **LANGUAGE** clause defines the language used by the external procedure. In this case, Java. If we omit this clause, the default is C.

- The **NAME** clause string uniquely identifies the Java method.

> Note: We may encounter the *ORA-06521: PL/SQL: Error mapping function* exception when the NAME parameter is incorrectly configured.

We must also make sure that the parameters list matches between the Java program and the PL/SQL wrapper with appropriate datatypes.

> Note: We may encounter the *ORA-00932: inconsistent datatypes* exception if an inappropriate datatype is used in between the Java and the Oracle programs.

In the below example, a function with one input parameter and a return type, both of NUMBER datatype are created for the Java class created in the above sections.

```
CREATE OR REPLACE FUNCTION fn_square(ip_var1 number) RETURN number
AS
   Language Java Name 'SQUARE.SQUARE(int) return int';
```

This function can be verified by executing it in a simple SQL statement by passing a numeric input value as shown below,

```
SELECT fn_square(10) FROM dual;
```

Result:

100

Loading C Shared Library in PL/SQL

When an application makes a call to a C program, the Oracle database starts up the EXTPROC agent and passes down the name of the shared library (DLL file), the name of the external procedure, and the parameters of the external procedure. After getting this information, the EXTPROC agent loads the shared library (DLL file) and executes the external procedure by passing the appropriate parameter values, which is then returned back to the application.

Creating a C Program

We will create and compile the below C program which is very simple so that a person with any programming knowledge could easily understand it without having any deep knowledge of the C language.

Similar to the PL/SQL engine, which is responsible for the compilation of the PL/SQL program units, the C compiler validates the syntax and converts the ".C" file into object file ".O" or a shared library file ".DLL", which can be then linked into other ".C" files to work as a single entity.

> Note: We must not use external static variables or global variables as they are not thread safe.

The following *add.c* file consists of a simple program which receives two integer inputs and returns their sum. To note, there is no *main()* function in this program. The *main()* functions are required when we want the program to act as a standalone program and they must be avoided when we want it to be used as a shared library. The extension *__declspec(dllexport)* is specific to Microsoft for exporting the program into a DLL file.

```
__declspec(dllexport)
int add (int num1, int num2)
{
  return num1 + num2;
}
```

Compiling a C Program

This step is required to check the validity of the program. Any GNU GCC (Compiler Collection) compilers like MinGW (Minimalistic GNU for Windows) or CYGWIN (CYGnus for WINdows) can be used for compiling a C program. When the below command is executed in the command prompt, an object file ".O" will be created upon successful validation of the ".C" file.

```
C:\MinGW\bin>gcc -c add.c -o add.o
```

- **-c** parameter denotes the compilation of the *add.c* file.

- **-o** parameter denotes the output file, *add.o* generated from the *add.c* file.

Note that the *add.c* source file must be placed in the *C:\MinGW\bin* location and the object file ".O" will be created in the same location. If the ".C" file is in some other location than the said, the current directory of command prompt must be changed to the ".C" file location and *C:\MinGW\bin* must be added to the environment variables (if not added already).

Shared Library Creation from a C Program

The shared library file ".DLL" can be created by executing the below GCC command in the command prompt which is pointed at the current location of the ".C" file as shown below.

```
C:\MinGW\bin>gcc -c add.c -o add.dll
```

- **-c** parameter denotes the compilation of the *add.c* file.

- **-o** parameter denotes the output file of *add.dll* generation from the *add.c* file.

The generated DLL file is saved in the same directory as that of the *add.c* file. I.e., *C:\MinGW\bin*.

EXTPROC DLL Parameter Setup

When the default configuration of the *tnsnames.ora* and *listener.ora* files are used, the EXTPROC process is called directly by the Oracle database without needing to change them. But the DLL file to be used by the external procedure must be set in the environment variable EXTPROC_DLLS, which restricts the DLLs that EXTPROC process can load. This environment variable can be set in any of the below two locations.

The *extproc.ora* file in the below location,

```
$ORACLE_HOME\hs\admin\extproc.ora
```

Can be set as,

1) **SET EXTPROC_DLLS= ANY** to skip the DLL file checking.

2) **SET EXTPROC_DLLS= <DLL File Location>:<DLL File Location>: ...** to load the DLLs from the BIN location of the Oracle home directory.

3) **SET EXTPROC_DLLS= ONLY:<DLL File Location>:<DLL File Location>: ...** to load the DLLS from any location in the server.

Or

The *ENVS* parameter of the *listener.ora* file located in the below directory,

```
$ORACLE_HOME\NETWORK\ADMIN\listener.ora
```

Can be set as,

1) **ENVS ="EXTPROC_DLLS= ANY"** to skip the DLL file checking.

2) **ENVS ="EXTPROC_DLLS= <DLL File Location>:<DLL File Location>: ..."** to load the DLLs from the BIN location of the Oracle home directory.

3) **ENVS ="EXTPROC_DLLS= ONLY:<DLL File Location>:<DLL File Location>: ..."** to load the DLLS from any location in the server.

In our case, we are going to set the *ENVS* parameter in the *listener.ora* file as shown below,

```
ENVS ="EXTPROC_DLLS= $ORACLE_HOME\BIN\add.dll"
```

After the parameter is set, the listener has to be restarted to make the changes get into effect.

PL/SQL Library Creation

A library is a schema object that can be used for identifying a shared library file from the OS in the PL/SQL subprograms.

From the Oracle version 12c, we can configure the EXTPROC agent to run as a designated user credential instead of using the operating system privileges of the listener user. This supplied user credential is associated with the EXTPROC process, which then authenticates on behalf of the provided user credential before loading the shared library, thus enhancing the security of the EXTPROC agent. The user credential can be created with the help of the DBMS_CREDENTIAL API.

The prototype for defining the DBMS_CREDENTIAL API is shown below,

```
dbms_credential.create_credential(
credential_name IN VARCHAR2,
username        IN VARCHAR2,
password        IN VARCHAR2,
database_role   IN VARCHAR2 DEFAULT NULL,
windows_domain  IN VARCHAR2 DEFAULT NULL,
comments        IN VARCHAR2 DEFAULT NULL,
enabled         IN BOOLEAN  DEFAULT TRUE);
```

Also, from 12c onwards, a directory object can be used to specify the location of the shared library instead of a raw location.

The prototype for creating a library object with the above two enhancements in place is shown below,

```
CREATE OR REPLACE library <Library_name>
[IS | AS]
[<'DLL filename with location'> | <'DLL filename'> IN <Directory_name>]
CREDENTIAL <Credential_name>;
```

- **LIBRARY_NAME** parameter is a user-defined name for the DLL file, which is used for referencing the DLL file in the OS disk in the PL/SQL subprograms.

- **DLL FILENAME WITH LOCATION** clause holds the complete path of the DLL file within single quotes.

- **DLL FILENAME** clause holds the DLL filename within single quotes.

- **DIRECTORY_NAME** clause holds the name of the directory object created over the DLL file location.

- **CREDENTIAL_NAME** clause holds the credential name created for the user supplied credential which is used for authenticating the EXTPROC agent.

> 🔔 Note: The CREATE LIBRARY syntax does not throw any error in case the DLL file is not present at the mentioned location.

Firstly, a CREDENTIAL object is created for the user supplied credentials as shown below,

```
BEGIN
dbms_credential.create_credential(credential_name=>'my_credentials',
username=>'c##', password=>'oracle');
END;
/
```

The created credential can be verified by querying the below data dictionary view.

```
SELECT credential_name, username, enabled FROM user_credentials;
```

Script Result:

CREDENTIAL_NAME	USERNAME	ENABLED
MY_CREDENTIALS	c##	TRUE

Next, a directory object is created for the shared library location as shown below,

```
CREATE OR REPLACE directory dll_dir
AS
  '$ORACLE_HOME\BIN';
```

The created directory can be verified by querying the below data dictionary view.

```
SELECT owner, directory_name, directory_path FROM all_directories WHERE
directory_name='DLL_DIR';
```

Script Result:

OWNER	DIRECTORY_NAME	DIRECTORY_PATH
C##	DLL_DIR	$ORACLE_HOME\BIN

Now, the library object can be created with the credential and the directory objects in place as shown below,

```
CREATE OR REPLACE LIBRARY EXTPROC_DLL
AS
  'add.dll' IN dll_dir
credential my_credential;
```

PL/SQL Wrapper Creation

The Oracle database can only use the external procedures that have been published. The publishing can be accomplished by creating a PL/SQL wrapper as the call specification that acts as an interface to invoke the external procedure which is in its DLL form mapped to a PL/SQL library.

The PL/SQL wrapper maps the name, return types, parameter types for the C external procedures to their respective PL/SQL counterparts. This wrapper is created in the usual way of creating any procedures and functions but instead of the BEGIN...END block, we have to write the AS LANGUAGE, NAME, LIBRARY, AGENT IN, WITH CONTEXT, and the PARAMETERS clauses. These clauses record the attributes required for coupling the external procedure language and the PL/SQL.

The prototype for defining an external procedure in a PL/SQL function is shown below,

```
CREATE OR REPLACE FUNCTION <Function_name> <Parameter_list>
  RETURN <Data_type>
AS
  LANGUAGE C
  LIBRARY <Library_name>
  [NAME <External_procedure_name>]
  [AGENT IN <Parameter_list>]
  [WITH CONTEXT]
  [<Parameter_list>];
```

- **LANGUAGE** clause defines the language used by the external procedure. In this case, C. If we omit this clause, the default is C.

- **LIBRARY** clause defines the name of the library object created on the DLL file created from the ".C" source file. If use double quotation on the <Library_name> section, then it becomes case sensitive.

- **NAME** clause defines the name of the external procedure. If we use double quotation on the <External_procedure_name> section, then it becomes case sensitive. If we omit this clause, then the external procedure name defaults to the upper case of the PL/SQL subprogram name.

- **AGENT IN** clause specifies which parameter holds the name of the agent that runs this external procedure. This clause is used when the agent EXTPROC runs multiple agent processes so that if one agent fails, the next one completes the process.

- **WITH CONTEXT** clause passes context pointers to the external procedures.

- **<PARAMETER_LIST>** clause specifies the parameters and the datatypes that are to be passed to the external procedures in a way that their position and the datatype matches appropriately with the parameters of the external procedure. For every formal parameter, there must be an appropriate parameter with compatible datatype to the external procedure language in this clause.

 Note: The maximum number of parameters that can be passed to an external procedure is 128. If any of the parameters passed is either a float or a double type, then it is considered as 2 parameters. Thus, the total parameters that can be passed in this scenario are less than 128.

In our case, we have coded the below PL/SQL function to access the external C program,

```
CREATE OR REPLACE FUNCTION fn_add(
    ip_n_param1 pls_integer,
    ip_n_param2 pls_integer)
  RETURN NUMBER
AS
  LANGUAGE C
  LIBRARY EXTPROC_DLL
  NAME "add"
  PARAMETERS (ip_n_param1 INT, ip_n_param2 INT);
```

After creating the above function, we can verify the complete call specification using this function in a SELECT statement as shown below,

```
SELECT fn_add(1,2) FROM dual;
```

Result:
3

Advantages of External Programs in PL/SQL

Memory Consumption

The External Procedures are executed in a place outside the memory (in the case of C language) used by the Oracle server, thus heavy usage of the database memory is avoided.

Shared Library Files

As the External Procedures use shared library files for processing, these can be used among different applications in a multi-user environment instead of duplicating them.

Program Strength

As multiple languages are involved in a single task, the capability of the program gets a whole new level of flexibility and adaptation. The strengths of each language get added up and their weaknesses get reduced as a result. For example, the features that are not available or unsupported by PL/SQL can be used in PL/SQL from another language.

Performance Enhancement

As the complex computations are moved from client to server, the performance is very much increased as the client-server round trips are avoided.

Limitations of External Programs in PL/SQL

Deployment Complexity

Having more than one language in a program could make our code deployment complex.

Code Debug

Debugging the code for error or for change can be tiresome if not properly trained in all the languages used by the program.

Languages Compatibility

The support between the languages used must be taken into consideration before working with them. For example, Oracle 12c supports JDK 6 and 7. Using JDK versions other than these might give us some hard time.

Summary

This chapter started by covering the basic idea and the architecture of the external programs. We learned the Oracle Net Services configuration for making the Oracle environment suitable for communicating with the external routines in the next section. We demonstrated the execution of Java and C programs as external procedures in PL/SQL with real time examples in the later section. In the final section, we have discussed the advantages and the limitations while using external language procedures in Oracle PL/SQL.

In the next chapter, we will learn all about working with the Large Objects.

Working with Large Objects

For every application created, there is a craving need for efficient storage of large text and binary objects in the database used by it. The definition of the word "large" varies depending on the nature of the applications. In some applications, the maximum storage could be in the range of kilobytes whereas in another it could be in Megabytes or Gigabytes. Often, it means that the object size is beyond the maximum length of the character datatype in the database, i.e., greater than 32,767 bytes for the VARCHAR2 datatype (From 12c).

The main purpose of storing the large binary objects in the database rather maintaining it outside as a plain file system is to create a strong link between this non-relational data with the relational data that is stored in the database. Oracle has introduced the LOB datatypes in its 8th version, making them the better means of storage for the media files and fat character based files than the LONG datatypes. Prior to the Oracle version 8, the LONG and LONG RAW were the only datatypes available for storing large structured and unstructured data. With numerous restrictions placed upon them by Oracle back then, it was a lot easier to store the multimedia files in the operating system as flat files rather having them in the database. This need for a stable storage mechanism of the large object files led to the creation of the LOB datatypes making the use for the LONG and LONG RAW datatypes obsolete.

We will be understanding the LOB types and their advanced storage properties in detail through the below topics.

12) Introduction to Large Objects.

13) Introduction to SecureFile LOB.

14) DB_SECUREFILE initialization parameter.

15) New Features in SecureFile with Oracle 12c.

16) LOB Classification.

17) DBMS_LOB API for manipulating the LOB types.

18) Migrating columns from LONG to LOB.

19) Migrating Columns from BasicFile LOB to SecureFile LOB.

20) Restrictions on the LOB types.

Introduction to Large Objects

Large objects are a set of datatypes, that are designed to hold a large amount of structured, semi-structured and unstructured data in an efficient way.

The structured data are character-based documents that are easily interpreted by the database upon their storage. Large text documents are an example of the structured data. The semi-structured data are usually a character-based document that is made up of a logical structure which is not naturally interpreted by the database when they are stored. XML documents are an example of the semi-structured data and can be processed or interpreted with the help of the applications like Oracle XML DB, Oracle Spatial and Graph, and Oracle Multimedia DICOM. The Character Large Objects (CLOB) and National Character Large Objects (NCLOB) are ideally suitable for storing and manipulating both structured and semi-structured data. Binary File Objects (BFILE) datatype can be used for loading the read-only structured and semi-structured operating system files into CLOB/ NCLOB instances and process them in our application.

The unstructured data, on the other hand, is usually a binary format file which cannot be easily broken down into simple logical structures. Examples of unstructured data are image, audio, and video files. These types of data consist of a long stream of 0s and 1s that are responsible for switching the pixels ON and OFF so that we can enjoy a picture. However, these bits cannot be broken down anymore to be understood by the database. The Binary Large Objects (BLOB) datatype can be used for storing and processing a large amount of unstructured binary data. The Binary File Objects (BFILE) datatype can be used for loading the read-only unstructured operating system files into BLOB instance and process them in our application.

The four LOB datatypes available in the Oracle database can be summed as below,

- **CLOB** (Character Large Object) type is used for reading and writing character based large structured and semi-structured data like text and XML files in an efficient manner.

- **NCLOB** (National Character Large Object) type is used for reading and writing Unicode character based large structured and semi-structured data like text and XML files containing UNICODE characters.

- **BLOB** (Binary Large Object) type is used for reading and writing binary-based large unstructured data like image, audio, and video files.

- **BFILE** (Binary File) type is used for reading the character and binary files stored outside the database through their locators stored in the database.

The LONG and LONG RAW datatypes are still supported, but only for backward compatibility. Any new applications created must avoid the LONG types and make use of the LOB types. The limitations of LONG and LONG RAW types are mastered by the introduction of the LOB types. Thus, the legacy applications with LONG types must migrate their data to LOB types for optimum results.

Introduction to SecureFile LOB

Prior to 11g, the only storage property for the LOB columns was "BasicFile", as we initially thought that the LOBs would never grow beyond a limit and would not be loaded frequently. When these ideas were proven wrong due to the demanding application needs, a must sophisticated storage property called as "SecureFile" was introduced in the version 11g offers better storage options like intelligent compression technique, advanced security features, deduplication, better caching and secure data management. The SecureFile LOB is the default storage option for the LOBs starting from 12c, whereas in 11g, the BasicFile LOB was the default option.

The SecureFile LOB has a new architecture featuring new network protocol, disk format, space management, better redo and undo formats, buffer caching, and intelligent input and output subsystem. These features deliver better storage and optimum performance for the large binary data in the database.

> Note: The Optimized algorithms in SecureFile LOB make it up to 10x faster than the BasicFile LOB.

The advanced features of SecureFile LOB are described below,

Write Gather Cache

SecureFile uses a new cache called as *write gather cache*, that buffers data up to 4 MB during any *write* operation before flushing the data on a commit or automatically before it reaches its limit. This allows larger space allocation, large disk I/O, and improved write performance due to reduced disk space. It is allocated from the buffer cache per transaction basis, thus only one WGC is allocated for all SecureFile LOBs in a single transaction.

Intelligent Space Allocation

SecureFile LOBs only works on the tablespaces managed with Automatic Segment Space Management (ASSM), which is a self-adaptable space management system providing a fast allocation of contiguous blocks and automatic reclaiming of the freed space. By default, Oracle enables ASSM in all its tablespaces from its 11g version.

The segment space type of a tablespace can be verified by querying the below data dictionary view,

```
SELECT tablespace_name, segment_space_management FROM dba_tablespaces;
```

Script Result:

TABLESPACE_NAME	SEGMENT_SPACE_MANAGEMENT
SYSTEM	MANUAL
SYSAUX	AUTO
UNDOTBS1	MANUAL
TEMP	MANUAL
USERS	AUTO

Note that the SEGMENT_SPACE_MANAGEMENT value cannot be changed after the tablespace is created. To upgrade an existing tablespace to use ASSM, we must

1) Create a new tablespace with SEGMENT SPACE MANAGEMENT set to AUTO.
2) Use the ALTER ... MOVE syntax to move the objects in the old tablespace to the newly created tablespace.
3) Drop the old tablespace.
4) Rename the new tablespace with the old tablespace's name.

Dynamic Chunk Size

SecureFile LOB uses dynamic chunk size setting to reduce the fragmentation problem, whereas in BasicFile LOB that the chunk size is always static. A fixed chunk size setting leads to internal fragmentation if it is too large for the data or poor write performance if it is too small for the data. With dynamic chunk size, a large portion of the disk is internally allocated for the data depending on its size. Thus, this property of the SecureFile storage mechanism provides efficient storage and high performance on the unstructured data of all shapes and sizes.

Intelligent Prefetching

The performance of the READ operation is enhanced by prefetching the data from the disk before it is transmitted over the network by keeping the track of the access patterns. The read latency is reduced by the overlap of the network round-trip with the disk I/O for the pre-fetched data, thus increasing the throughput.

High Speed Network Layer

This new protocol does not need any temporary staging while reading or writing bulk data between the client and the server, resulting in high read/ write performance.

No LOB Index Contention

The BasicFile LOB uses Balanced tree indexes for access navigation and managing the deleted spaces, causing contention and performance degradation in super active environments. SecureFile LOB, on the other hand, does not use an index for managing such metadata. Instead, it uses private metadata blocks that are located in the data blocks in the LOB segment, thus greatly increasing the performance.

No High Water Mark Contention

The deleted space reclamation is performed by the SecureFile LOB in the background automatically. This property of SecureFile LOB avoids high water mark contention, unlike the BasicFile LOB.

Less User Tuned Parameters

The complex user tuned parameters which are difficult to tune for unpredictable changes in the workloads like FREEPOOLS, FREELISTS, FREELIST GROUPS and

PCTVERSION are not needed for SecureFile LOBs. They maintain the internal statistics to auto-tune the space management process, ensuring high performance.

Advanced Logging

A new type of logging called as FILESYSTEM_LIKE_LOGGING logs only the metadata for the SecureFile LOB and reduces the mean time to recover from database failures. This is similar to the loggings available with the popular file systems. To use this logging, the LOB must be in NOCACHE mode. Also, the LOBs set to NOLOGGING is internally converted to FILESYSTEM_LIKE_LOGGING. This logging type is not supported for the BasicFile LOBs.

Deduplication

The deduplication feature automatically enables the Oracle database to detect duplicate LOB data in a column or in a partition and saves space by storing only one copy of the data in the database. This is a part of the Oracle's Advanced Compress Options.

> 🔔 Note: Deduplication does not span across partitions or sub-partitions for partitioned SecureFile LOB columns.

The below image depicts the functioning of the Deduplication feature.

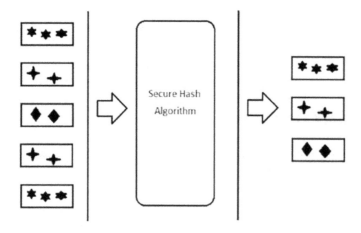

Fig.12.1. Pictorial representation of the Deduplication feature

The Oracle server intelligently maintains a unique secure hash key for all the LOBs stored in the database using a secure hash algorithm. A unique hash value for all the incoming LOB data are created and are compared against the maintained hash codes.

1. If they match, the column is updated with the existing data's LOB locator and the incoming duplicate LOB data is not stored in the database.

2. If they do not match, a fresh copy of the incoming LOB data is stored in the database.

> 🔔 Note: Oracle streams do not support SecureFile LOBs that are Deduplicated.

The Deduplication option not only simplifies the storage mechanism but also results in a significantly better copy and write operations. This feature can be enabled by including the DEDUPLICATE option and disabled by including the KEEP_DUPLICATES option in the LOB storage clause.

The prototype of enabling or disabling the Deduplication feature in an already existing table is shown below,

```
ALTER TABLE <Table_name> MODIFY LOB (<LOB_column_name>) (<DEDUPLICATE |
KEEP_DUPLICATES>);
```

Compression

This feature enables server-side compression for the unstructured data using industry standard compression algorithms, allowing random reads and writes to the SecureFile LOB data. This feature not only reduces the storage space, but also helps in improving the performance of the database by reducing the I/O on the disk, buffer cache usage, redo log generation, and encryption overhead. The Oracle server will automatically turn off this feature if it produces no save on the space during the compression or if the data is already compressed, thus saving the unnecessary compression process.

This feature is also a member of the Oracle's Advanced Compression Options. Note, that the table compression plays no role in the SecureFile LOB compression. The below image depicts the comparison between a compressed and a decompressed SecureFile LOB data.

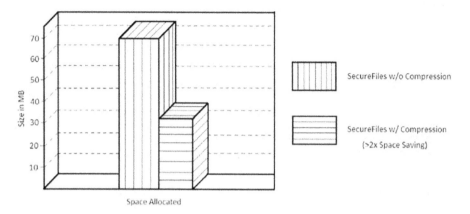

Fig.12.2. Comparison between a compressed and a decompressed SecureFile LOB

The Compression feature can be enabled by including the COMPRESS option and disabled by including the NOCOMPRESS option in the LOB storage clause.

The prototype of enabling or disabling the Compression feature in an already existing table is shown below,

```
ALTER TABLE <Table_name> MODIFY LOB (<LOB_column_name>) (<COMPRESS [LOW |
HIGH | MEDIUM] | NOCOMPRESS>);
```

Encryption

Oracle has introduced an advanced encryption facility for the LOBs by encrypting them using the Transparent Data Encryption (TDE) feature. The database automatically manages the key for the SecureFile LOB data within the table's metadata, transparently encrypts/ decrypts the data at the block level, backs them up, and generates the redo file on the disk. These keys are maintained independently of any application.

The encryption algorithms supported by the SecureFile LOB are,

1. 3DES168: Triple Data Encryption Standard with a 168-bit encryption key.

2. AES128: Advanced Encryption Standard with a 128-bit encryption key.

3. AES192: Advanced Encryption Standard with a 192-bit encryption key.

4. AES256: Advanced Encryption Standard with a 256-bit encryption key.

Advanced PL/SQL Programming

For more information on creating the keystore, setting the master encryption key, and then encrypting the data using the Transparent Data Encryption algorithm, please refer to the Chapter 8: *Advanced Security Methods in PL/SQL*.

This feature is also a member of the Oracle's Advanced Compression Options. The Encryption on a SecureFile LOB can be enabled by using the ENCRYPT option and disabled by using the DECRYPT option in the LOB storage clause.

The prototype of enabling or disabling the Encryption feature in an already existing table is shown below,

```
ALTER TABLE <Table_name> MODIFY LOB (<LOB_Column_name>)
(<ENCRYPT USING <Encryption_algorithm> | DECRYPT>);
```

Or,

```
ALTER TABLE <Table_name> MODIFY (<LOB_Column_name>
<ENCRYPT USING <Encryption_algorithm> | DECRYPT>);
```

DB_SECUREFILE Initialization Parameter

The DB_SECUREFILE initialization parameter in the *init.ora* file controls the default action of the database to specify the SecureFile usage policy.

The values accepted by this parameter are shown below,

1) **NEVER** – Any LOB that is specified as SecureFile are created as BasicFile. All SecureFile LOB specific options like Deduplication, Encryption, and Compression will cause an exception. The default storage options for the BasicFile will be used if not specified.

2) **PERMITTED** – Any LOB that is specified as SecureFile will be created as the same. This is the default value if the COMPATIBLE initialization parameter is set to 11.2.0.x.

3) **PREFERRED** – All LOBs are created as SecureFile by default unless BasicFile is explicitly mentioned in the LOB storage clause or if the tablespace is in Manual Segment Space Management (MSSM) mode. This is the default value if the COMPATIBLE initialization parameter is set to 12.0.0.0 or higher.

4) **ALWAYS** – All LOBs in ASSM mode are created as SecureFile and all LOBs in non-ASSM mode are created as BasicFile unless explicitly specified. All the

BasicFile storage options will be ignored and the default SecureFile LOB storage options will be used if they are unspecified.

5) **IGNORE** – All LOBs are created as BasicFile LOB by default. Any errors associated with the SecureFile storage option will be ignored.

> 🔔 Note: If the COMPATIBLE initialization parameter is less than 11.1.0, then all the LOBs are treated as BasicFile LOB.

If there is a LOB column with two partitions, one having its data in the ASSM tablespace and the other having its data in the non-ASSM tablespace. Then, the LOBs in the ASSM tablespace will be treated as SecureFile LOB and the LOBs in the non-ASSM tablespace will be treated as BasicFile LOB.

This parameter can be set either at the database level by using the ALTER SYSTEM syntax or the session level by using the ALTER SESSION syntax.

The prototype of setting this parameter is shown below,

```
ALTER <SESSION | SYSTEM> SET DB_SECUREFILE = < NEVER | PERMITTED | PREFERRED
| ALWAYS | IGNORE >;
```

And the parameter's current setting can be verified by executing the SHOW PARAMETER statement as shown below,

```
SHOW PARAMETER DB_SECUREFILE;
```

NAME	TYPE	VALUE
db_securefile	string	ALWAYS

New Features in SecureFile with Oracle 12c

1. Parallel DML support for SecureFile has been enhanced, providing improved performance.

2. SecureFile LOB is the default option for the LOBs, instead of BasicFile.

3. Data pump uses SecureFile as default LOB storage. Thus, we can convert all LOB columns as SecureFile from BasicFile during data pump import.

---

4. SecureFile supports components that enable HTTP, WebDAV, and FTP access to Database File System over the internet using various XML DB server protocols.

LOB Classification

The LOB types can be classified into Internal and External LOBs based on where they store their data.

A LOB instance has a unique locator and a value. The LOB value is the actual data to be stored in the database and the LOB locator acts as a pointer to the location of the LOB value, which is stored either in the database in case of internal LOBs or in an externally located operating system file in case of external LOBs.

> Note: The LOB value is always stored in the LOB segment in the same or different tablespace.

Internal LOBs

The Internal LOBs supports the storage and retrieval of their data from the database tablespace in an optimized and efficient way. The supported datatypes are CLOB, NCLOB, and BLOB. In SQL, the internal LOBs can be used to specify the datatype of table columns or attributes of a PL/SQL object type, where their data are stored in the permanent tablespace in the database. In PL/SQL, they can be used to specify the local and global LOB variables, which store their data in the temporary tablespace in the database.

Internal LOBs use copy semantics. With copy semantics, both the LOB value and its locator are copied into the table's cell logically during assignment or any DML operation, ensuring that the LOB column/ variable holds a unique LOB instance.

The Internal LOBs can be still classified into two types as Persistent and Temporary based on whether they store their data permanently in the table rows or temporarily in a PL/SQL session through instantiation and assignment.

Persistent LOBs

The persistent LOBs store their data permanently in the table columns and actively participate in the database transactions as it abides by the ACID properties (Atomicity, Consistency, Isolation, and Durability) like any other database object.

CLOB, NCLOB and BLOB Types

The CLOB and NCLOB datatypes are read-write character and UNICODE character large datatypes typically used for storing structured (Long text data) and semi-structured data (Long XML data or UNICODE characters) in the database respectively. The CLOB types use the database character set format for the stored data, whereas the NCLOB types use the national character set format for the same.

The BLOB datatypes are read-write binary large datatypes, that lets us store large binary files like video, audio, and PDF documents in the database.

> 🔔 Note: These datatypes can be read and written only in the session's scope.

The maximum size of these types can range from 8 TB to 128 TB based on the DB_BLOCK_SIZE initialization parameter, which is set during the database creation in the init.ora file. The formula for calculating the maximum size of the LOB type is *(4 GB - 1) * DB_BLOCK_SIZE value*. Once this parameter is set, there is no going back for any change except for re-creating the database. The maximum value that can be set for the DB_BLOCK_SIZE parameter is 16 KB for Linux X86 environments and 32 KB for other environments. However, setting this parameter's value to its maximum may affect the I/O operations.

The DB_BLOCK_SIZE parameter value can be verified by querying the V$PARAMETER table as shown below,

```
SELECT name,
  value,
  description
FROM v$parameter
WHERE name = LOWER('DB_BLOCK_SIZE');
```

Query Result

NAME	VALUE	DESCRIPTION
db_block_size	8192	Size of database block in bytes

Or can be verified by executing the below SHOW PARAMETER statement as shown,

```
SHOW PARAMETER DB_BLOCK_SIZE;
```

NAME   TYPE   VALUE
------------- ------- -----
db_block_size integer 8192

Here, the DB_BLOCK_SIZE parameter is set to 8 KB. Thus, the maximum value of the LOB types is limited to 8 TB. Note, that the NCLOB datatype uses 2 bytes for a single character in AL16UTF16 character set, thus limiting itself to a maximum of 4 TB and 3 bytes for a single character in UTF8 character set, thus limiting itself to a maximum 2 TB~ with this DB_BLOCK_SIZE setting.

The persistent LOB columns store only the locator in its cell, which points to the location where the actual data resides. The original data for the persistent LOB columns are usually stored separately from the rest of the row from the table in the LOB segment.

The CLOB and NCLOB support implicit (starting from 10g) and explicit conversions.

➔ When we assign a VARCHAR2/ NVARCHAR2 values directly to CLOB/ NCLOB columns, they are implicitly converted to their respective target datatypes. Prior to 12c, SQL supported implicit conversion of 4000 characters and PL/SQL supported implicit conversion of up to 32,767 characters for the VARCHAR2/ NVARCHAR2 columns. From 12c, both SQL and PL/SQL supports implicit conversion of 32,767 characters for the VARCHAR2/ NVARCHAR2 columns provided that we have upgraded our VARCHAR2/ NVARCHAR2 columns to support 32,767 characters in SQL.

➔ When we want to assign a CLOB/ NCLOB value to DATE, NUMBER, VARCHAR2/ NVARCHAR2 columns or variables, we must explicitly use the TO_DATE, TO_NUMBER, TO_CHAR functions for type casting. Note that the format string must be appropriate for the DATE type and the character limit must not exceed 32,767 for the VARCHAR2/ NVARCHAR2 columns.

➔ When we want to assign BLOB value to RAW columns/ variables or RAW value to BLOB columns/ variables, Oracle takes care of the conversion implicitly. Note that the byte limit for the BLOB column while assigning it to the RAW column must not exceed 32,767 bytes.

The internal LOBs are basically object types and are different from the scalar datatypes. The cell in a LOB column can be in any of the below described 3 states. The operations performed on the LOB columns differ based on their states.

- **Null** – This state can be reached by assigning/ inserting a *null* value to the CLOB/ NCLOB/ BLOB variable/ column respectively. This state has no locator or value and its length is *null*.

- **Empty** – This state can be reached by initializing a CLOB/ NCLOB variable or column with EMPTY_CLOB() constructor, which is available in the STANDARD package and a BLOB variable or column with EMPTY_BLOB() constructor, which is available in the STANDARD package. This state has an active locator but no value and its length are 0 (Zero) bytes.

- **Populated** – This state can be reached by assigning/ inserting a not null string value to the CLOB/ NCLOB variable/ column and a hexadecimal value to the BLOB variable/ column respectively. This state has both the locator and the value. The length of the variable/ column in this state is definite.

Creating CLOB, NCLOB, and BLOB Columns

Persistent LOB instances can be created using the CREATE TABLE statements.

The prototype of creating a LOB instance using the CREATE TABLE statement is shown below,

```
CREATE TABLE <Table_Name>
  (
    [<LOB_Col1> <LOB_Datatype> DEFAULT [EMPTY_CLOB() | EMPTY_BLOB() |
<Default_String_Value>]] [,...]
  )
  [LOB
  (
    [<LOB_Col1>] [,...]
  )
        STORE AS [SECUREFILE | BASICFILE | <LOB_Segment_Name>]
        (
          [TABLESPACE <Tablespace_Name>]
          [<ENABLE | DISABLE> STORAGE IN ROW]
          [CHUNK <Chunk_Size_in_Integer>]
          [PCTVERSION <PCTVERSION_in_Integer>]
          [FREEPOOLS <FREEPOOLS_Size_in_Integer>]
          [COMPRESS [HIGH | LOW] | NOCOMPRESS]
          [RETENTION <MAX | MIN <Integer_Value> | AUTO | NONE>]
          [KEEP_DUPLICATES | DEDUPLICATE]
          [ENCRYPT <Encryption_Specification> | DECRYPT]
          [CACHE | CACHE READS | NOCACHE] <LOGGING | NOLOGGING |
FILESYSTEM_LIKE_LOGGING>
```

```
            [STORAGE (<MINEXTENTS | MAXEXTENTS>)]
            [INDEX <LOB_Index_Name>
                    [PCTFREE <PCTFREE_Value_in_Integer> | PCTUSED
<PCTUSED_Value_in_Integer> | INITRANS <INITRANS_Value_in_Integer>]
                    [Index_Storage_Clause]
            ]
          )
    ];
```

- **EMPTY_CLOB() and EMPTY_BLOB()** functions are used for the empty initialization of the CLOB and BLOB columns respectively.
- **STORE AS** clause specifies the type of storage for the LOB columns.
  - ➔ **SECUREFILE** for storing the LOBs in high-performance mode. This is the default value from 12c.
  - ➔ **BASICFILE** for storing the LOBs in the traditional mode.
- **TABLESPACE** clause specifies the tablespace in which the LOB data are to be stored.
- **ENABLE | DISABLE STORAGE IN ROW** clause enables or disables the LOB value to be stored in the row (inline) along with the other columns if its length is less than 4kb minus system control information. The default value is ENABLE.
- **CHUNK** clause specifies the number of bytes to be allocated for the LOB manipulation. The default value is one Oracle database block size.
- **PCTVERSION** clause specifies the maximum percentage of the overall LOB storage space used for maintaining older versions of the LOB. The default value is 10.
- **FREEPOOLS** clause specifies the number of groups of free lists for the LOB segment. The default value is 1 for a single instance database or the number of instances in an RAC environment. This parameter is ignored if the LOB storage is SecureFile.
- **COMPRESS** clause specifies that the unstructured data is compressed at the server level. This clause is available only for the SecureFile LOB.
  - ➔ **HIGH** indicates that the table must be compressed with high compression ratio.
  - ➔ **LOW** indicates that the table must be compressed with low compression ratio.
  - ➔ **MEDIUM** indicates that the table must be compressed with medium compression ratio. This is the default value.
- **NOCOMPRESS** clause specifies that the unstructured data compression is disabled. This clause is available only for the SecureFile LOB.
- **RETENTION** clause specifies whether the LOB segment has to be retained for flashback and consistent read purposes. In auto undo mode, Retention is the default unless we mention PCTVERSION. We cannot specify both, though.

- ➔ **MAX** indicates that the undo should be retained until the LOB segment has reached the MAXSIZE.
- ➔ **MIN** indicates that the undo should limit the retention duration for the LOB segment to *n* seconds.
- ➔ **AUTO** indicates to retain undo that is sufficient for the Read-consistent purpose only.
- ➔ **NONE** indicates that there is no undo required for Flashback or Read-consistent purpose.
- **KEEP_DUPLICATES | DEDUPLICATE** clause is valid only for SecureFile LOB storage. This clause specifies whether to enable or disable the elimination of duplicate LOB data in a column or tablespace. The default value is KEEP_DUPLICATES.
- **ENCRYPT | DECRYPT** clause is valid only for SecureFile LOB storage. Specify ENCRYPT to encrypt all the LOBs in the column and specify DECRYPT to keep the LOB data in clear text. The default value is DECRYPT.
- **CACHE** clause is specified when the data is accessed frequently by placing the blocks received at the most recently used end of the Least Recently Used (LRU) list in the buffer cache during a full table scan.
- **NOCACHE** clause is specified when the data are not frequently accessed by placing the blocks received at the least recently used end of the LRU list.
- **CACHE READS** clause specifies that the LOB values are brought into the buffer cache only during the read operations and not during the write operations.
- **STORAGE** clause specifies the storage characteristics of the table and the LOB data segment.
- **INDEX** clause provides the LOB index specification.
    - ➔ **PCTFREE** specifies the percentage of space in each data block of the database object reserved for future updates. The value range is 0 to 99. The default value is 10.
    - ➔ **PCTUSED** specifies the minimum percentage of used space for each data block of the database. The value range is 0 to 99. The default value is 40.
    - ➔ **INITRANS** specifies the initial number of concurrent transaction entries allocated within each data block to the database object. The value range is 1 to 255. The default value is 1.

The below snippet creates the table TBL_INT_CLOB with three LOB columns consisting of CLOB, NCLOB, and BLOB types by defaulting them to the empty initialization as shown. We have created the CLOB type as SecureFile LOB and the NCLOB, BLOB types as BasicFile LOB as shown.

```
CREATE TABLE tbl_int_lob
  (
    col1_number NUMBER default null,
    col2_clob CLOB DEFAULT empty_clob(),
```

```
    col3_nclob NCLOB DEFAULT empty_clob(),
    col4_blob BLOB DEFAULT empty_blob()
)
lob(col2_clob)
store AS SECUREFILE
(
    tablespace users
    compress high
    deduplicate
    decrypt
    disable STORAGE IN row
    chunk 4096
    retention none
    cache reads
)
lob(col3_nclob)
store AS basicfile
(
    disable STORAGE IN row
    chunk 4096
    freepools 1
    retention none
    cache reads
    STORAGE (minextents 2)
)
    lob(col4_blob)
store AS basicfile
(
    disable STORAGE IN row
    chunk 4096
    freepools 1
    retention none
    cache reads
    STORAGE (minextents 2)
);
```

After the creating the above table, we can verify its LOB metadata by querying the USER_LOBS data dictionary view as shown below,

```
SELECT table_name,
    column_name,
    tablespace_name,
    securefile,
    encrypt,
    compression,
    deduplication
FROM user_lobs
WHERE table_name='TBL_INT_LOB';
```

Script Output:

TABLE_NAME	COLUMN_NAME	TABLESPACE_NAME	SECUREFILE	ENCRYPT	COMPRESSION	DEDUPLICATION
TBL_INT_LOB	COL2_CLOB	USERS	YES	NO	HIGH	LOB
TBL_INT_LOB	COL3_NCLOB	SYSTEM	NO	NONE	NONE	NONE
TBL_INT_LOB	COL4_BLOB	SYSTEM	NO	NONE	NONE	NONE

Inserting into CLOB, NCLOB, and BLOB Columns

In SQL, an INSERT statement initializes the CLOB, NCLOB, and BLOB columns with characters, national, and binary characters respectively as shown below,

```
INSERT
INTO tbl_int_lob
  (
    col1_number,
    col2_clob,
    col3_nclob,
    col4_blob
  )
  VALUES
  (
    1,
    rpad('A', 4000, 'A'),
    rpad(n'Â', 4000, n'Â'),
    rawtohex('BLOB test value')
  );
COMMIT;
```

In PL/SQL, an INSERT statement initializes and then returns its locator value through the RETURNING INTO clause into a local variable in OUT mode as "pass by reference". Thus, any changes made to the local variable affect the original data in the scope of this transaction.

```
DECLARE
  l_cl_var1 CLOB;
  l_ncl_var2 NCLOB;
  l_bl_var3 BLOB;
BEGIN
  INSERT
  INTO tbl_int_lob
    (
      col1_number,
      col2_clob,
      col3_nclob,
      col4_blob
    )
    VALUES
    (
      1,
      rpad('A', 4000, 'A'),
      rpad(n'Â', 4000, n'Â'),
      rawtohex('BLOB test value')
    )
  RETURNING col2_clob,
    col3_nclob,
    col4_blob
  INTO l_cl_var1,
    l_ncl_var2,
    l_bl_var3;
  COMMIT;
END;
/
```

Updating CLOB, NCLOB, and BLOB Columns

In SQL, an UPDATE statement can be used for setting the CLOB, NCLOB, and BLOB values if it is small as shown below. Note the literal *n* placed before the UNICODE character indicating that the string is a national character.

```
UPDATE tbl_int_lob
SET col2_clob    =rpad('B', 4000, 'B'),
  col3_nclob     =rpad(n'♥', 4000, n'♥'),
  col4_blob      =rawtohex('Updated BLOB test value')
WHERE col1_number=1;
```

In PL/SQL, a UPDATE statement can be used for setting the CLOB, NCLOB, and BLOB values and their locators can be returned to local variables through the RETURNING INTO clause as shown in the below example. The local variable is passed by reference and is in the OUT mode of operation. We can make changes to the original data by modifying the locator in the local variable in the scope of this session.

```
DECLARE
  l_cl_var1 CLOB;
  l_ncl_var2 NCLOB;
  l_bl_var3 BLOB;
BEGIN
  UPDATE tbl_int_lob
  SET col2_clob    =rpad('B', 4000, 'B'),
    col3_nclob     =rpad(n'♥', 4000, n'♥'),
    col4_blob      =rawtohex('Updated BLOB test value')
  WHERE col1_number=1 RETURNING col2_clob,
    col3_nclob,
    col4_blob
  INTO l_cl_var1,
    l_ncl_var2,
    l_bl_var3;
  COMMIT;
END;
/
```

Deleting CLOB, NCLOB, and BLOB Columns

The conventional DELETE statement can be used for removing the row containing the CLOB, NCLOB, and BLOB data as shown below,

```
DELETE FROM tbl_int_lob WHERE col1_number=1;
```

But when we want to remove only the scalar LOB data, we can update the CLOB/NCLOB column to empty by using the EMPTY_CLOB() function and the BLOB column to empty by using the EMPTY_BLOB() function as shown below. Note that the locators will be still present, whereas their corresponding data will be released from its memory.

```
UPDATE tbl_int_lob
SET col2_clob    =empty_clob(),
    col3_nclob   =empty_clob(),
    col4_blob    =empty_blob()
WHERE col1_number=1;
```

External LOBs

The External LOB type can be used instead of the internal LOBs when the volume of the data is large or if it is stored outside the database as an operating system file in the server. The External LOBs store only the locator in the table's column, but its actual value resides outside the database in hard disks, network-mounted filesystems, CD-ROMs, Photo CDs, and DVDs. External LOB uses reference semantics. With reference semantics, only the LOB locator is copied during INSERT and assignment operations while the data is stored outside the database.

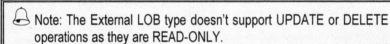 Note: The External LOB type doesn't support UPDATE or DELETE operations as they are READ-ONLY.

The only External LOB type available in the Oracle database is BFILE.

BFILE: Binary File

BFILE is a read-only datatype that the database uses to access external binary files with a maximum size limit of 4 GB. Even though the BFILE and the BLOB types intends to store binary data, they both work differently from each other. Both the BFILE and BLOB column stores only the locators which point to the actual data that resides outside the ROW, but the BLOB type stores its binary data inside the database whereas the BFILE type stores its data outside the database in the OS layer. The BFILE type is capable of storing external binary files which can be in PDF, GIF, JPEG, MPEG, MPEG2, text, or other formats.

 Note: BFILE data is not under transaction control and is not stored by database backups.

Additional to the other LOB types, the BFILE type requires an external directory upon which a DIRECTORY object has to be created in the database and a file containing data to be available in the server location with necessary grants provided to the appropriate user to access the file. If we wound up dropping the BFILE type, we only remove the reference to the file along with its locator information from the database where the original file resides safely in its physical directory outside the database.

While working with the BFILE type, we need to secure both the physical and the logical directories. The physical directory stores the actual file on the server, which has to be safeguarded against unauthorized access and manipulation at the OS level. The logical directory acting as the alias for the physical directory must be protected against unauthorized database users by granting privileges to the appropriate users and restricting the rest.

The session level initialization parameter, SESSION_MAX_OPEN_FILES defines the number of files to be opened for a session. This parameter resides in the *spfile[db_name].ora* file in the *$ORACLE_HOME\database* location with a default value of 10. This value can be altered by firing an ALTER statement at the session level as shown below,

```
ALTER SESSION SET session_max_open_files=15;
```

```
Session altered.
```

Creating Virtual Directory

A virtual directory is a non-schema object which points to a physical directory in the operating system. The virtual directory created will be owned by the SYS user and he/ she will be responsible for granting the appropriate READ/ WRITE privileges to the intended users to maintain the file integrity.

The prototype of creating a directory object in the database is shown below,

```
CREATE OR REPLACE directory <Directory_name>
AS
   '<Directory_location>';
```

In our example below, the SYS user creates a directory object for the Pictures folder in the *F:* drive as shown.

```
CREATE OR REPLACE directory extlob_dir
AS
   'F:\Pictures';
```

Once the directory is created, the READ privilege is provided to the desired user as shown below,

```
GRANT READ ON extlob_dir TO C##;
```

Creating BFILE Column

The CREATE TABLE statement with a BFILE datatype column can be used for accessing external binary files. The below script creates a table with one NUMBER and one BFILE column.

```
CREATE TABLE tbl_ext_lob
  (
    col1_number NUMBER,
    col2_bfile BFILE
  );
```

```
Table TBL_EXT_LOB created.
```

Inserting into BFILE Column

An INSERT statement can be used to insert a BFILE column. The column uses the BFILENAME built-in function which initializes the BFILE column and returns the BFILE locator that is associated with the physical binary file on the external file system.

The BFILENAME function accepts two input parameters.

1st Parameter: The name of the directory object where the actual file is located within single quotes.

2nd Parameter: The name of the file in the directory with extension within single quotes.

The below statement can be used to load the image file *Batman.jpg* from the *EXTLOB_DIR* directory location as shown below,

```
INSERT INTO tbl_ext_lob VALUES(1, bfilename('EXTLOB_DIR','Batman.jpg'));

Commit;
```

After the external file is inserted and committed, the image file can be looked up using any Oracle IDEs. In our case, we have looked upon the BFILE column using the SQL Developer versioned 4.1.3.20 as shown below.

Fig 12.3. BFILE Image Lookup through the SQL Developer 4.1.3.20

Updating BFILE Column

An UPDATE statement can be used for updating a BFILE column with an external file as shown below,

```
UPDATE tbl_ext_lob SET col2_bfile=bfilename('EXTLOB_DIR', 'Superman.jpg')
where col1_number=1;

Commit;
```

Deleting BFILE Column

A BFILE column along with its complete row can be removed from the table by issuing a DELETE statement as shown below,

```
DELETE tbl_ext_lob WHERE col1_number=1;

Commit;
```

Also, a BFILE column can be dereferenced from the external file it is associated with by updating it to *null* as shown below,

```
UPDATE tbl_ext_lob SET col2_bfile=null WHERE col1_number=1;

Commit;
```

DBMS_LOB

The DBMS_LOB is an Oracle built-in package which contains a set of procedures and functions that can be used for performing READ/ WRITE operations on internal/ temporary LOBs and READ only operations on external LOBs. This package is owned by SYS with EXECUTE privilege granted to public.

The subprograms provided by the DBMS_LOB package are described below,

OPEN Procedures

These procedures can be used for opening internal, external, or temporary LOBs in the requested mode.

The prototypes of these overloaded procedures are shown below,

```
DBMS_LOB.OPEN (
   lob_loc    IN OUT NOCOPY BLOB,
   open_mode IN            BINARY_INTEGER);

DBMS_LOB.OPEN (
   lob_loc    IN OUT NOCOPY CLOB CHARACTER SET ANY_CS,
   open_mode IN            BINARY_INTEGER);

DBMS_LOB.OPEN (
   file_loc  IN OUT NOCOPY BFILE,
   open_mode IN            BINARY_INTEGER:= dbms_lob.file_readonly);
```

- **LOB_LOC** parameter accepts the LOB locator for CLOB, NCLOB, and BLOB types.
- **FILE_LOC** parameter accepts the LOB locator for BFILE type.
- **OPEN_MODE** parameter defines the mode in which the LOB must open in. The available modes are,
    → **0 or DBMS_LOB.LOB_READONLY** constants can be used for internal and temporary LOB types when we want to open them in READ mode.

- → **1 or DBMS_LOB.LOB_READWRITE** constants can be used for internal and temporary LOB types when we want to open them in the READ/ WRITE mode.
- → **0 or DBMS_LOB.FILE_READONLY** constants can be used for external LOB type when we want to open it in READ mode. This is the default value for the OPEN_MODE parameter in case of BFILE type.

In the below snippet, the CLOB variable is not initialized with either EMPTY_CLOB() constructor or any NOT NULL value. Thus, it fails with an *ORA-22275: invalid LOB locator specified* exception when we try to open it using the OPEN procedure.

```
DECLARE
  l_cl_var1 CLOB;
BEGIN
  dbms_lob.open(l_cl_var1,dbms_lob.lob_readonly);
END;
/
```

Error report -
```
ORA-06502: PL/SQL: numeric or value error: invalid LOB locator specified:
ORA-22275
ORA-06512: at "SYS.DBMS_LOB", line 1007
ORA-06512: at line 4
```

ISOPEN Functions

These functions can be used to check whether the LOB is open or not using their locator by returning the integer 1 if it is open and the integer 0 if they are not.

For the external LOBs, the openness is associated with the locator. If there are two locators namely A and B for an external file. If the locator A is opened and the locator B is not, then, the ISOPEN function returns 1 or A and 0 for B.

For the internal LOBs, the openness is associated with the LOB. If there are two locators namely A and B for an internal LOB. If the locator A is opened and the locator B is not, then, the ISOPEN function returns 1 for both A and B locators. Here, as the LOB is opened by the locator A, it is internally opened by all the other associated locators.

The prototypes of these overloaded functions are shown below,

```
DBMS_LOB.ISOPEN (
   lob_loc IN BLOB)
  RETURN INTEGER;

DBMS_LOB.ISOPEN (
   lob_loc IN CLOB CHARACTER SET ANY_CS)
  RETURN INTEGER;
DBMS_LOB.ISOPEN (
   file_loc IN BFILE)
  RETURN INTEGER;
```

CLOSE Procedures

These procedures can be used for closing any previously opened internal, temporary, and external LOBs. When the file which is trying to be closed is not yet opened, the procedures fails with an *ORA-22289: cannot perform operation on an unopened file or LOB* exception. To avoid this exception, always perform a check on the LOBs on its openness using the ISOPEN functions before closing them.

We must always close an opened LOB so that we don't fill up the maximum number of open files limit and raise the *ORA-22290: operation would exceed the maximum number of opened files or LOBs.*

The prototypes of these overloaded procedures are shown below,

```
DBMS_LOB.CLOSE (
   lob_loc    IN OUT NOCOPY BLOB);

DBMS_LOB.CLOSE (
   lob_loc    IN OUT NOCOPY CLOB CHARACTER SET ANY_CS);

DBMS_LOB.CLOSE (
   file_loc   IN OUT NOCOPY BFILE);
```

APPEND Procedures

These procedures append the contents of one CLOB, NCLOB, or a BLOB to another CLOB, NCLOB, or a BLOB respectively. The procedure fails with an *ORA-06502: PL/SQL: numeric or value error* if either the source or the target LOB is null.

The OPEN and CLOSE procedures are not mandatory when using the APPEND procedures. If they are not used, the functional and domain indexes on the LOB column are updated for every WRITE operation performed. This could adversely affect the performance of the append operation. Therefore, it is recommended to use OPEN and CLOSE APIs while using the APPEND procedures, even though they are not mandatory.

The prototypes of these overloaded procedures are shown below,

```
DBMS_LOB.APPEND (
   dest_lob IN OUT NOCOPY BLOB,
   src_lob  IN            BLOB);

DBMS_LOB.APPEND (
   dest_lob IN OUT NOCOPY CLOB CHARACTER SET ANY_CS,
   src_lob  IN            CLOB CHARACTER SET dest_lob%CHARSET);
```

- **DEST_LOB** parameter accepts and returns the locator for the LOB to which the data has to be appended.
- **SRC_LOB** parameter accepts the locator for the LOB from which the data has to be read.

In the below snippet, an NCLOB variable is appended to another NCLOB variable using the APPEND procedure. Here, the source NCLOB variable is opened in READ-ONLY mode and the target NCLOB variable is opened in READ-WRITE mode as shown below.

```
DECLARE
  l_ncl_var1 NCLOB:= n'A young man of exceeding beauty is dragged before the
governor of Basra, Khâlid ibn 'Abdallâh al-Qasrî. ';
  l_ncl_var2 NCLOB:= n'The boy confesses that he had entered a certain house
as a thief.';
BEGIN
  dbms_lob.open(l_ncl_var1,dbms_lob.lob_readwrite);
  dbms_lob.open(l_ncl_var2,dbms_lob.lob_readonly);
  dbms_lob.append(l_ncl_var1,l_ncl_var2);
  IF dbms_lob.isopen(l_ncl_var1)=1 THEN
    dbms_lob.close(l_ncl_var1);
  END IF;
  IF dbms_lob.isopen(l_ncl_var2)=1 THEN
    dbms_lob.close(l_ncl_var2);
  END IF;
  dbms_output.put_line(l_ncl_var1);
END;
/
```

Result:

```
A young man of exceeding beauty is dragged before the governor of Basra,
Khâlid ibn 'Abdallâh al-Qasrî. The boy confesses that he had entered a
certain house as a thief.
```

READ Procedures

These procedures read a portion of the LOB and return them through the BUFFER parameter. The OFFSET parameter defines the start position and the AMOUNT parameter defines the number of bytes or characters that are to be read. If the AMOUNT parameter is set past the total bytes or characters available in the LOB, then the OFFSET is set to 0 and an NO_DATA_FOUND exception is raised.

The prototypes of these overloaded procedures are shown below,

```
DBMS_LOB.READ (
  lob_loc IN              BLOB,
  amount  IN OUT NOCOPY INTEGER,
```

```
    offset  IN              INTEGER,
    buffer  OUT             RAW);

DBMS_LOB.READ (
    lob_loc IN              CLOB CHARACTER SET ANY_CS,
    amount  IN OUT NOCOPY   INTEGER,
    offset  IN              INTEGER,
    buffer  OUT             VARCHAR2 CHARACTER SET lob_loc%CHARSET);

DBMS_LOB.READ (
    file_loc IN             BFILE,
    amount   IN OUT NOCOPY  INTEGER,
    offset   IN             INTEGER,
    buffer   OUT            RAW);
```

- **AMOUNT** parameter accepts and returns the number of bytes (in the case of BLOB type) or characters (in the case of CLOB and NCLOB types) to write from the BUFFER value.
- **OFFSET** parameter accepts the offset value in bytes (in the case of BLOB type) or characters (in the case of CLOB and NCLOB types) from the start of the LOB, where the starting offset value is 1.
- **BUFFER** parameter returns the output buffer that was read.

A directory object for the path of the novel from the famous writer, Charles Dickens, is created as shown below,

```
CREATE OR REPLACE directory dir_read
AS
    'E:\Books\Novels\Classics\Charles Dickens';
```

During the FILE READ operation,

- If the directory object is unavailable, we may encounter the *ORA-22285 The directory leading to the file does not exist* exception.
- If we do not have necessary privilege on the directory object, we may encounter the *ORA-22286   User does not have the necessary access privileges on the directory alias and/ or file* exception.
- If the directory object has been invalidated, we may encounter the *ORA-22287 Directory alias is not valid* exception.

In the below code snippet, Charles Dicken's one of the famous plays, Oliver Twist, in the text file format is opened and read with an OFFSET value of 1, that is the file is read from the very first character, and with an AMOUNT value of 222, that is the first 222 characters are read. The read RAW data are type cast to VARCHAR2 and then printed using the PUT_LINE procedure as shown below.

If the file is unavailable during the FILE READ operation, we may encounter the *ORA-22288: file or LOB operation FILEOPEN failed* exception.

```
DECLARE
  l_bf_var1 bfile:=bfilename('DIR_READ','Oliver Twist.txt');
  l_raw_buffer raw(1000);
  l_i_amount INTEGER:=222;
BEGIN
  dbms_lob.open(l_bf_var1);
  dbms_lob.read(l_bf_var1,l_i_amount,1,l_raw_buffer);
  dbms_lob.close(l_bf_var1);
  dbms_output.put_line(utl_raw.cast_to_varchar2(l_raw_buffer));
END;
/
```

Result:

```
CHAPTER-I
TREATS OF THE PLACE WHERE OLIVER TWIST WAS BORN AND OF THE CIRCUMSTANCES
ATTENDING HIS BIRTH Among other public buildings in a certain town, which
for many reasons it will be prudent to refrain from mentioning
```

WRITE and WRITEAPPEND Procedures

The WRITE procedures write data into the CLOB, NCLOB, and BLOB types for the specified offset, starting from the beginning of the LOB from the buffer. They replace any existing data in the LOB at the offset for the specified length.

The WRITEAPPEND procedures append the specified amount of data to the end of the CLOB, NCLOB, and BLOB types. The difference between WRITE and WRITEAPPEND procedures is that in the WRITEAPPEND procedure, there will be no offset value for the LOB to replace the existing data.

The prototypes of the overloaded WRITE procedures are shown below,

```
DBMS_LOB.WRITE (
   lob_loc IN OUT NOCOPY BLOB,
   amount  IN            INTEGER,
   offset  IN            INTEGER,
   buffer  IN            RAW);

DBMS_LOB.WRITE (
   lob_loc IN OUT NOCOPY CLOB CHARACTER SET ANY_CS,
   amount  IN            INTEGER,
   offset  IN            INTEGER,
   buffer  IN            VARCHAR2 CHARACTER SET lob_loc%CHARSET);
```

The prototypes of the overloaded WRITEAPPEND procedures are shown below,

```
DBMS_LOB.WRITEAPPEND (
    lob_loc IN OUT NOCOPY BLOB,
    amount   IN            INTEGER,
    buffer   IN            RAW);

DBMS_LOB.WRITEAPPEND (
    lob_loc IN OUT NOCOPY CLOB CHARACTER SET ANY_CS,
    amount   IN            INTEGER,
    buffer   IN            VARCHAR2 CHARACTER SET lob_loc%CHARSET);
```

- **LOB_LOC** parameter accepts the LOB locator for CLOB, NCLOB, and BLOB types.
- **AMOUNT** parameter accepts the number of bytes (in the case of BLOB type) or characters (in the case of CLOB and NCLOB types) to write from the BUFFER value.
- **OFFSET** parameter accepts the offset value in bytes (in the case of BLOB type) or characters (in the case of CLOB and NCLOB types) from the start of the LOB, where the starting offset value is 1.
- **BUFFER** parameter accepts the input buffer to write.

For the WRITE and WRITEAPPEND procedures, when the AMOUNT value is less than 1 or greater than the buffer length, we may encounter the *ORA-21560: argument is null, invalid, or out of range* exception.

For the WRITE procedures, when the OFFSET value is less than 1 or greater than the maximum LOB size, we may encounter the *ORA-21560: argument is null, invalid, or out of range* exception.

In the below example, a buffer value of 67890 is written into a CLOB variable having 12345 as its original value using the WRITE procedure.

- The AMOUNT value is 4, thus only the first four characters of the buffer value are written into the CLOB variable. That is 6789.
- The OFFSET value is 3, thus the starting position for the write operation is from the third position of the CLOB variable.

When the WRITE procedure executes, it writes the value 126789 into the CLOB variable as shown below,

```
DECLARE
  l_cl_var1 CLOB:='12345';
BEGIN
  dbms_lob.open(l_cl_var1,dbms_lob.lob_readwrite);
  dbms_lob.write(l_cl_var1,4,3,'67890');
  dbms_output.put_line(l_cl_var1);
  dbms_lob.close(l_cl_var1);
END;
/
```

Result:

126789

In the below example, a table with one CLOB column is created and inserted with a bunch of statements as shown.

```
CREATE TABLE tbl_writeappend
  (col1 CLOB DEFAULT empty_clob()
  );

INSERT
INTO tbl_writeappend
  (
    col1
  )
  VALUES
  (
    'It has long been a grave question whether any government not too strong
for the liberties of its people can be strong enough to maintain its
existence in great emergencies. On this point, the present rebellion brought
our republic to a severe test, and the Presidential election, occurring in
regular course during the rebellion, added not a little to the strain…'
  );

Commit;
```

In the below block, the locator of the CLOB column from the above-created table is passed into the local CLOB variable. The WRITEAPPEND procedure appends the buffer text to the local CLOB variable for the corresponding AMOUNT value.

Note that the SELECT INTO statement requires a FOR UPDATE clause to lock the row and to avoid the *ORA-22920: row containing the LOB value is not locked* exception.

```
DECLARE
  l_cl_var1 CLOB;
  l_r_buffer VARCHAR2(100):= ' -- The Writings of Abraham Lincoln.';
BEGIN
  SELECT col1 INTO l_cl_var1 FROM tbl_writeappend FOR UPDATE;
```

```
   dbms_lob.writeappend(l_cl_var1, LENGTH(l_r_buffer), l_r_buffer);
   COMMIT;
END;
/
```

ERASE Procedures

These procedures can be used for deleting a portion of the internal LOBs or in whole. When the data is erased from the middle portion of the LOBs, zero-byte fillers and spaces are written for BLOBs and CLOBs/ NCLOBs respectively. The actual number of bytes/ characters to be erased may differ from the value specified in the AMOUNT parameter when the end of the LOB is reached before the AMOUNT value.

The prototypes of these overloaded procedures are shown below,

```
DBMS_LOB.ERASE (
   lob_loc IN OUT NOCOPY BLOB,
   amount  IN OUT NOCOPY INTEGER,
   offset  IN            INTEGER := 1);

DBMS_LOB.ERASE (
   lob_loc IN OUT NOCOPY CLOB CHARACTER SET ANY_CS,
   amount  IN OUT NOCOPY INTEGER,
   offset  IN            INTEGER := 1);
```

- **LOB_LOC** parameter accepts and returns the LOB locator for CLOB, NCLOB, and BLOB types.
- **AMOUNT** parameter accepts and returns the number of bytes (in the case of BLOB type) or characters (in the case of CLOB and NCLOB types) to write from the BUFFER value.
- **OFFSET** parameter accepts the offset value in bytes (in the case of BLOB type) or characters (in the case of CLOB and NCLOB types) from the start of the LOB, where the starting offset value is 1.

When the OFFSET or the AMOUNT value is less than 1 or greater than the maximum LOB size, we may encounter the *ORA-21560: argument is null, invalid, or out of range* exception.

In the below listing, the ERASE procedure is executed upon the English alphabets stored in a local CLOB variable with an offset of 10 by 10 characters as shown below.

```
DECLARE
   l_cl_var1 CLOB    :='ABCDEFGHIJKLMNOPQRSTUVWXYZ';
   l_i_amount INTEGER:=10;
BEGIN
   dbms_lob.open(l_cl_var1,1);
   dbms_lob.erase(l_cl_var1,l_i_amount,10);
```

```
   dbms_output.put_line(l_cl_var1);
   dbms_lob.close(l_cl_var1);
END;
/
```

Results:

ABCDEFGHI   TUVWXYZ

TRIM Procedures

These procedures trim the value of the internal LOB to the length specified in the NEWLEN parameter from left to right. The length for CLOB/ NCLOB and BLOB is specified in characters and bytes respectively.

When you try to trim a LOB with the NEWLEN parameter having its length more than the length of the LOB, we may encounter the *ORA-22926: specified trim length is greater than current LOB value's length* exception.

> Note: No exception is generated when we try to trim an empty LOB.

The prototypes of these overloaded procedures are shown below,

```
DBMS_LOB.TRIM (
   lob_loc IN OUT NOCOPY BLOB,
   newlen  IN            INTEGER);

DBMS_LOB.TRIM (
   lob_loc IN OUT NOCOPY CLOB CHARACTER SET ANY_CS,
   newlen  IN            INTEGER);
```

- **NEWLEN** parameter accepts the length to be trimmed from the internal LOB in characters and bytes for CLOBS/ NCLOBs and BLOBs respectively.

In the below code snippet, the first 5 characters of the CLOB variable are trimmed and returned as output.

```
DECLARE
   l_cl_var1  CLOB    :='ABCDEFGHIJKLMNOPQRSTUVWXYZ';
   l_i_newlen INTEGER :=5;
BEGIN
   dbms_lob.open(l_cl_var1,1);
   dbms_lob.trim(l_cl_var1,l_i_newlen);
   dbms_output.put_line(l_cl_var1);
   dbms_lob.close(l_cl_var1);
END;
/
```

Results:
ABCDE

DBMS_LOB

COPY Procedures

These procedures copy a part or whole of a source internal LOB to a target internal LOB with an offset and with the number of bytes/ characters for BLOBs/ CLOBs to copy.

If the destination LOB offset is beyond the length of the LOB, then zero-byte fillers (for BLOBs) or spaces (For CLOBs and NCLOBs) are inserted to the destination LOB.

The prototypes of these overloaded procedures are shown below,

```
DBMS_LOB.COPY (
   dest_lob    IN OUT NOCOPY BLOB,
   src_lob     IN           BLOB,
   amount      IN           INTEGER,
   dest_offset IN           INTEGER := 1,
   src_offset  IN           INTEGER := 1);

DBMS_LOB.COPY (
   dest_lob    IN OUT NOCOPY CLOB  CHARACTER SET ANY_CS,
   src_lob     IN            CLOB  CHARACTER SET dest_lob%CHARSET,
   amount      IN            INTEGER,
   dest_offset IN            INTEGER := 1,
   src_offset  IN            INTEGER := 1);
```

- **DEST_LOB** parameter accepts and returns the LOB locator of the copy target.
- **SRC_LOB** parameter accepts the LOB locator of the copy source.
- **AMOUNT** parameter accepts the number of bytes (in the case of BLOB type) or characters (in the case of CLOB and NCLOB types) to write from the BUFFER value.
- **DEST_OFFSET** parameter accepts the offset in bytes or characters for BLOBs and CLOBs/ NCLOBs respectively in the destination LOB for the start of the copy. The default value is 1.
- **SRC_OFFSET** parameter accepts the offset in bytes or characters for BLOBs and CLOBs/ NCLOBs in the source LOB for the start of the copy. The default value is 1.

In the below listing, the first 3 characters from the source CLOB is copied to the first three positions of the destination CLOB replacing the existing values as shown below.

```
DECLARE
  l_cl_dest CLOB:='ABCDEF';
  l_cl_src CLOB :='123456';
BEGIN
  dbms_lob.open(l_cl_dest,1);
  dbms_lob.open(l_cl_src,0);
  dbms_lob.copy(l_cl_dest,l_cl_src,3);
```

```
  dbms_lob.close(l_cl_dest);
  dbms_lob.close(l_cl_src);
  dbms_output.put_line(l_cl_dest);
END;
/
```

Results:

123DEF

INSTR and SUBSTR Functions

The INSTR functions return the matching position for the nth pattern in the LOB for the specified offset.

The prototypes of the overloaded INSTR functions are shown below,

```
DBMS_LOB.INSTR (
   lob_loc IN BLOB,
   pattern IN RAW,
   offset  IN INTEGER := 1,
   nth     IN INTEGER := 1)
  RETURN INTEGER;

DBMS_LOB.INSTR (
   lob_loc IN CLOB      CHARACTER SET ANY_CS,
   pattern IN VARCHAR2 CHARACTER SET lob_loc%CHARSET,
   offset  IN INTEGER := 1,
   nth     IN INTEGER := 1)
  RETURN INTEGER;

DBMS_LOB.INSTR (
   file_loc IN BFILE,
   pattern  IN RAW,
   offset   IN INTEGER := 1,
   nth      IN INTEGER := 1)
  RETURN INTEGER;
```

- **LOB_LOC** parameter accepts and returns the LOB locator for CLOB, NCLOB, and BLOB types.
- **FILE_LOC** parameter accepts the file locator of the external LOB file.
- **PATTERN** parameter accepts a set of bytes and characters for BLOBs and CLOBs/ NCLOBs respectively as a pattern.
- **OFFSET** parameter accepts the offset value in bytes (in the case of BLOB type) or characters (in the case of CLOB and NCLOB types) from the start of the LOB, where the starting offset value is 1. The default value is 1.
- **NTH** parameter accepts the occurrence. The default value is 1.

The SUBSTR functions return a bunch of characters or bytes from CLOBs/ NCLOBs or BLOBs that is specified in the AMOUNT parameter, starting from the specified offset. The default value for the AMOUNT and OFFSET parameters are 32,767 and 1 respectively. Even though the default AMOUNT parameter value is 32,767, it returns only 4kb in the SQL environments if the maximum string size for VARCHAR2 is not upgraded to support 32kb.

The prototypes of the overloaded SUBSTR functions are shown below,

```
DBMS_LOB.SUBSTR (
   lob_loc IN BLOB,
   amount  IN INTEGER := 32767,
   offset  IN INTEGER := 1)
 RETURN RAW;

DBMS_LOB.SUBSTR (
   lob_loc IN CLOB CHARACTER SET ANY_CS,
   amount  IN INTEGER := 32767,
   offset  IN INTEGER := 1)
 RETURN VARCHAR2 CHARACTER SET lob_loc%CHARSET;

DBMS_LOB.SUBSTR (
   file_loc IN BFILE,
   amount  IN INTEGER := 32767,
   offset  IN INTEGER := 1)
 RETURN RAW;
```

In the below anonymous block, a BLOB variable is searched for the string "dreamy thought" using the INSTR function and the first 13 bytes are extracted from it using the SUBSTR function.

```
DECLARE
   l_bl_var1 BLOB     := utl_raw.cast_to_raw('One afternoon I got lost in the
woods about a mile from the hotel, and presently fell into a train of dreamy
thought about animals which talk, and kobolds, and enchanted folk, and the
rest of the pleasant legendary stuff');
   l_rw_var2 raw(100):=utl_raw.cast_to_raw('dreamy thought');
BEGIN
   dbms_output.put_line('The location of the text "dreamy thought" in the LOB
=> '||dbms_lob.instr(l_bl_var1,l_rw_var2)||' Bytes');

   dbms_output.put_line('The first 13 bytes in the LOB =>
'||utl_raw.cast_to_varchar2(dbms_lob.substr(l_bl_var1,13,1)));
END;
/
```

Results:

```
The location of the text "dreamy thought" in the LOB => 103 Bytes
The first 13 bytes in the LOB => One afternoon
```

COMPARE Functions

These functions compare either a portion or the complete data of two LOB types belonging to the same type. Here,

- If the LOB_1=LOB_2, then the function returns the 0.
- If the LOB_1<LOB_2, then the function returns -1.
- If the LOB_1>LOB_2, then the function returns 1.

The prototypes of these overloaded functions are shown below,

```
DBMS_LOB.COMPARE (
   lob_1    IN BLOB,
   lob_2    IN BLOB,
   amount   IN INTEGER := DBMS_LOB.LOBMAXSIZE,
   offset_1 IN INTEGER := 1,
   offset_2 IN INTEGER := 1)
 RETURN INTEGER;

DBMS_LOB.COMPARE (
   lob_1    IN CLOB  CHARACTER SET ANY_CS,
   lob_2    IN CLOB  CHARACTER SET lob_1%CHARSET,
   amount   IN INTEGER := DBMS_LOB.LOBMAXSIZE,
   offset_1 IN INTEGER := 1,
   offset_2 IN INTEGER := 1)
 RETURN INTEGER;

DBMS_LOB.COMPARE (
   lob_1    IN BFILE,
   lob_2    IN BFILE,
   amount   IN INTEGER,
   offset_1 IN INTEGER := 1,
   offset_2 IN INTEGER := 1)
 RETURN INTEGER;
```

- **LOB_1** parameter accepts the locator of the first LOB type.
- **LOB_2** parameter accepts the locator of the second LOB type.
- **AMOUNT** parameter accepts the number of bytes or characters to compare in BLOBs or CLOBs/ NCLOBs. This parameter is mandatory for the external LOBs and it defaults to DBMS_LOB.LOBMAXSIZE constant.
- **OFFSET_1** parameter accepts the offset in bytes or characters for the first LOB type. The default value is 1.
- **OFFSET_2** parameter accepts the offset in bytes or characters for the second LOB type. The default value is 1.

A directory object is created for the IMAGES folder in the *F:* drive as shown below,

---

```
CREATE OR REPLACE directory dir_images
AS
  'F:\Images';
```

The two image files, *Iron Man.JPG* and *Green Lantern.JPG*, are compared with each other using the COMPARE function having the AMOUNT parameter as DBMS_LOB.LOBMAXSIZE, that is all the bytes between the two files are compared and their result is returned as shown in the below example.

```
DECLARE
  l_bf_var1 bfile :=bfilename('DIR_IMAGES','Iron Man.JPG');
  l_bf_var2 bfile :=bfilename('DIR_IMAGES','Green Lantern.JPG');
BEGIN
  dbms_lob.open(l_bf_var1,dbms_lob.file_readonly);
  dbms_lob.open(l_bf_var2,dbms_lob.file_readonly);

  dbms_output.put_line('The two images are '||
  CASE dbms_lob.compare(l_bf_var1, l_bf_var2, dbms_lob.lobmaxsize)
  WHEN 0 THEN
    'equal'
  ELSE
    'not equal'
  END);

  dbms_lob.close(l_bf_var1);
  dbms_lob.close(l_bf_var2);
END;
/
```

Results:

```
The two images are not equal
```

FRAGMENT_DELETE Procedures

These procedures can be used for deleting a fragment of data at the specified offset for the specified length without having the LOB data completely rewritten. These procedures can be used only on SecureFile LOBs.

The prototypes of these overloaded procedures are shown below,

```
DBMS_LOB.FRAGMENT_DELETE (
   lob_loc IN OUT NOCOPY BLOB,
   amount  IN            INTEGER,
   offset  IN            INTEGER);

DBMS_LOB.FRAGMENT_DELETE (
   lob_loc IN OUT NOCOPY CLOB CHARACTER SET ANY_CS,
   amount  IN            INTEGER,
   offset  IN            INTEGER);
```

- **LOB_LOC** parameter accepts and returns the LOB locator.
- **AMOUNT** parameter accepts the number of bytes or characters to be removed from the BLOB or CLOB/ NCLOB lob types respectively.
- **OFFSET** parameter accepts the bytes or characters to begin the deletion with from the BLOB or CLOB/ NCLOB lob types respectively.

The below table is created as SecureFile LOB and is inserted with the English alphabets as shown. Note that this table is used as an example for all the FRAGMENT_* procedures explained in the further sections.

```
CREATE TABLE tbl_fragment
  (col1 CLOB)
  lob(col1)
  store AS securefile
  TABLESPACE users;
/

INSERT INTO tbl_fragment (col1) VALUES ('ABCDEFGHIJKLMNOPQRSTUVWXYZ');

COMMIT;
```

In the below example, 5 characters starting from the 10th position are deleted using the FRAGMENT_DELETE procedure as shown.

```
DECLARE
  l_cl_var1 CLOB;
BEGIN
  SELECT col1 INTO l_cl_var1 FROM tbl_fragment FOR UPDATE;
  dbms_lob.fragment_delete(l_cl_var1,5,10);
  dbms_output.put_line(l_cl_var1);
  ROLLBACK;
END;
/
```

Results:

ABCDEFGHIOPQRSTUVWXYZ

FRAGMENT_INSERT Procedures

These procedures can be used for inserting a fragment of data at the specified offset that is passed through the BUFFER parameter. The limit for the data insertion is 32,767 characters or bytes. These procedures can only be used on SecureFile LOBs.

The prototypes of these overloaded procedures are shown below,

```
DBMS_LOB.FRAGMENT_INSERT (
    lob_loc       IN OUT NOCOPY BLOB,
    amount        IN            INTEGER,
    offset        IN            INTEGER,
    buffer        IN            RAW );

DBMS_LOB.FRAGMENT_INSERT (
    lob_loc       IN OUT NOCOPY CLOB CHARACTER SET ANY_CS,
    amount        IN            INTEGER,
    offset        IN            INTEGER,
    buffer        IN            VARCHAR2 CHARACTER SET lob_loc%CHARSET );
```

- **BUFFER** parameter accepts the data to be inserted into the LOB.

In the below code snippet, the buffer value of 12345 is inserted into the CLOB value starting from the 10th position as shown.

```
DECLARE
  l_cl_var1 CLOB;
BEGIN
  SELECT col1 INTO l_cl_var1 FROM tbl_fragment FOR UPDATE;
  dbms_lob.fragment_insert(l_cl_var1,5,10,'12345');
  dbms_output.put_line(l_cl_var1);
END;
/
```

Results:

ABCDEFGHI12345JKLMNOPQRSTUVWXYZ

FRAGMENT_MOVE Procedures

These procedures can be used for moving a fragment of data from one offset to the new specified offset location in the LOB. These procedures can only be used on SecureFile LOBs.

The prototypes of these overloaded procedures are shown below,

```
DBMS_LOB.FRAGMENT_MOVE (
    lob_loc       IN OUT NOCOPY BLOB,
    amount        IN            INTEGER,
    src_offset    IN            INTEGER,
    dest_offset   IN            INTEGER );
DBMS_LOB.FRAGMENT_MOVE (
    lob_loc       IN OUT NOCOPY CLOB CHARACTER SET ANY_CS,
    amount        IN            INTEGER,
    src_offset    IN            INTEGER,
    dest_offset   IN            INTEGER );
```

- **SRC_OFFSET** parameter accepts the offset for the cut operation on the data in bytes or characters from BLOB or CLOB/ NCLOB types respectively.
- **DEST_OFFSET** parameter accepts the offset for the paste operation on the data in bytes or characters from BLOB or CLOB/ NCLOB types respectively.

In the below anonymous block, the first 5 characters starting from the position 2 are moved to the position 20 in the CLOB data as shown.

```
DECLARE
  l_cl_var1 CLOB;
BEGIN
  SELECT col1 INTO l_cl_var1 FROM tbl_fragment FOR UPDATE;
  dbms_lob.fragment_move(l_cl_var1,5,2,20);
  dbms_output.put_line(l_cl_var1);
END;
/
```

Results:

AGHIJKLMNOPQRSBCDEFTUVWXYZ

FRAGMENT_REPLACE Procedures

These procedures can be used for replacing the data at the specified offset with the input data. The input data for the replacement cannot be more than 32,767 bytes or characters in case of the BLOB or CLOB types respectively. These procedures can only be used on SecureFile LOBs.

The prototypes of these overloaded procedures are shown below,

```
DBMS_LOB.FRAGMENT_REPLACE (
   lob_loc     IN OUT NOCOPY BLOB,
   old_amount IN            INTEGER,
   new_amount IN            INTEGER,
   offset     IN            INTEGER,
   buffer     IN            RAW);

DBMS_LOB.FRAGMENT_REPLACE (
   lob_loc     IN OUT NOCOPY CLOB CHARACTER SET ANY_CS,
   old_amount IN            INTEGER,
   new_amount IN            INTEGER,
   offset     IN            INTEGER,
   buffer     IN            VARCHAR2 CHARACTER SET lob_loc%CHARSET);
```

- **OLD_AMOUNT** parameter accepts the number of bytes or characters to be replaced in the BLOB or CLOB/ NCLOB types respectively.

- **NEW_AMOUNT** parameter accepts the number of bytes or characters to be replaced in the BLOB or CLOB/ NCLOB types respectively.

In the below example, the first 7 characters starting from the 2nd position are replaced with the first 5 characters of the input BUFFER value '1234567' as shown.

```
DECLARE
  l_cl_var1 CLOB;
BEGIN
  SELECT col1 INTO l_cl_var1 FROM tbl_fragment FOR UPDATE;
  dbms_lob.fragment_replace(l_cl_var1,7,5,2,'1234567');
  dbms_output.put_line(l_cl_var1);
END;
/
```

Results:

A12345IJKLMNOPQRSTUVWXYZ

ISSECUREFILE Functions

These functions can be used for verifying whether the input LOB locator is a SecureFile LOB or not. It returns a Boolean True if so, else a False.

The prototypes of these overloaded functions are shown below,

```
DBMS_LOB.ISSECUREFILE (lob_loc IN BLOB) RETURN BOOLEAN;

DBMS_LOB.ISSECUREFILE (lob_loc IN CLOB CHARACTER SET ANY_CS) RETURN BOOLEAN;
```

In the below code listing, a SecureFile LOB locator is passed to the ISSECUREFILE function, which returns the Boolean True value as shown.

```
DECLARE
  l_cl_var1 CLOB;
BEGIN
  SELECT col1 INTO l_cl_var1 FROM tbl_fragment;
  dbms_output.put_line
  (
    CASE
    WHEN dbms_lob.issecurefile(l_cl_var1) THEN
      'The locator is SecureFile LOB'
    ELSE
      'The locator is BasicFile LOB'
    END);
END;
/
```

Results:
The locator is SecureFile LOB

GETCHUNKSIZE Functions

These functions can be used for retrieving the amount of space used by the LOB chunk to save the LOB data. This value can be specified during the table creation as multiples of tablespace blocks in bytes. This chunk size will be used for accessing or modifying the LOB data by the data layer.

The default chunk size is equal to the DB_BLOCK_SIZE initialization parameter, which is 8,192 bytes minus the default system information, which could be less than 100 bytes.

The prototypes of these overloaded functions are shown below,

```
DBMS_LOB.GETCHUNKSIZE (lob_loc IN BLOB) RETURN INTEGER;

DBMS_LOB.GETCHUNKSIZE (lob_loc IN CLOB CHARACTER SET ANY_CS) RETURN INTEGER;
```

In the below example, the GETCHUNKSIZE function returns the total number of bytes allocated for the LOB data storage for the not null CLOB and BLOB variables as shown. Here, the function returns the chunk size as 8132 bytes for both the LOB types, thus the rest 60 bytes (8192 - 8132) is used for storing the default system information.

```
DECLARE
  l_cl_var1 CLOB:= 'Pneumonoultramicroscopicsilicovolcanoconiosis';
  l_bl_var2 BLOB:= utl_raw.cast_to_raw('Honorificabilitudinitatibus');
BEGIN
  dbms_output.put_line('The chunk size of the CLOB variable is
'||dbms_lob.getchunksize(l_cl_var1)||' Bytes');

  dbms_output.put_line('The chunk size of the BLOB variable is
'||dbms_lob.getchunksize(l_bl_var2)||' Bytes');
END;
/
```

Results:

```
The chunk size of the CLOB variable is 8132 Bytes
The chunk size of the BLOB variable is 8132 Bytes
```

GETLENGTH Functions

These functions can be used for returning the length of the specified internal or external LOB. They return the length in bytes (in the case of BLOB and BFILE types) and characters (in the case of CLOB and NCLOB types).

The prototypes of these overloaded functions are shown below,

```
DBMS_LOB.GETLENGTH (lob_loc IN BLOB) RETURN INTEGER;

DBMS_LOB.GETLENGTH (lob_loc IN CLOB CHARACTER SET ANY_CS) RETURN INTEGER;

DBMS_LOB.GETLENGTH (file_loc IN BFILE) RETURN INTEGER;
```

In the below code snippet, the GETLENGTH functions are executed for a Null, Empty, and a Not-null CLOBs as shown.

```
DECLARE
   l_cl_var1 CLOB;
   l_cl_var2 CLOB:= empty_clob();
   l_cl_var3 CLOB:= 'It is simply this. That Space, as our mathematicians
have it, is spoken of as having three dimensions, which one may call Length,
Breadth, and Thickness, and is always definable by reference to three
planes, each at right angles to the others. But some philosophical people
have been asking why three dimensions particularly—why not another direction
at right angles to the other three?—and have even tried to construct a Four-
Dimension geometry';
BEGIN
   dbms_output.put_line('Length of the Null CLOB is:
'||NVL(to_char(dbms_lob.getlength(l_cl_var1)),'Null'));

   dbms_output.put_line('Length of the Empty CLOB is:
'||dbms_lob.getlength(l_cl_var2));

   dbms_output.put_line('Length of the Not-null CLOB is:
'||dbms_lob.getlength(l_cl_var3));
END;
/
```

Results:

```
Length of the Null CLOB is: Null
Length of the Empty CLOB is: 0
Length of the Not-null CLOB is: 445
```

SETOPTIONS and GETOPTIONS Subprograms

The SETOPTIONS procedures can be used for enabling/ disabling the Compression, Encryption, and Deduplication options by overriding the default settings for the input internal LOB.

The GETOPTIONS functions can be used for retrieving the information on whether the Compression, Encryption and Deduplication options are enabled or not for the input internal LOB.

Note: The SETOPTIONS and GETOPTIONS subprograms can be used only upon the SecureFile LOB types.

The prototypes of the overloaded SETOPTIONS procedures are shown below,

```
DBMS_LOB.SETOPTIONS (
   lob_loc       IN BLOB,
   option_types IN PLS_INTEGER,
   options       IN PLS_INTEGER);

DBMS_LOB.SETOPTIONS (
   lob_loc       IN CLOB CHARACTER SET ANY_CS,
   option_types IN PLS_INTEGER,
   options       IN PLS_INTEGER);
```

The prototypes of the overloaded GETOPTIONS functions are shown below,

```
DBMS_LOB.GETOPTIONS (
   lob_loc       IN BLOB,
   option_types IN PLS_INTEGER)
 RETURN PLS_INTEGER;

DBMS_LOB.GETOPTIONS (
   lob_loc       IN CLOB CHARACTER SET ANY_CS,
   option_types IN PLS_INTEGER)
RETURN PLS_INTEGER;
```

- **LOB_LOC** parameter accepts an internal LOB locator.
- **OPTION_TYPES** parameter accepts the below options.
  - → **DBMS_LOB.OPT_COMPRESS** or **1** can be used for checking whether the input LOB is compressed or not.
  - → **DBMS_LOB.OPT_ENCRYPT** or **2** can be used for checking whether the input LOB is encrypted or not.
  - → **DBMS_LOB.OPT_DEDUPLICATE** or **4** can be used for checking whether the input LOB is Deduplicated or not.
- **OPTIONS** parameter accepts the below values.
  - → **COMPRESS_OFF** or 0 and **COMPRESS_ON** or 1 can be used for turning OFF or ON the compression settings.
  - → **ENCRYPT_OFF** or 0 and **ENCRYPT_ON** or 2 can be used for turning OFF or ON the encryption settings.
  - → **DEDUPLICATION_OFF** or 0 and **DEDUPLICATION_ON** or 4 can be used for turning OFF or ON the deduplication settings.

1) When the option DBMS_LOB.OPT_COMPRESS or 1 is passed as the second argument to the GETOPTIONS function, it returns 1 if the Compression is enabled or 0 if not.

2) When the option DBMS_LOB.OPT_ENCRYPT or 2 is passed as the second argument to the GETOPTIONS function, it returns 2 if the Encryption is enabled or 0 if not.

3) When the option DBMS_LOB.OPT_COMPRESS or 4 is passed as the second argument to the GETOPTIONS function, it returns 4 if the Deduplication is enabled or 0 if not.

A SecureFile LOB table with one CLOB column is created with Deduplication, Compression, and Encryption options enabled as shown below. The CLOB column is then inserted with a single row and is then committed.

```
CREATE TABLE tbl_options
  (col1 CLOB)
  lob
  (col1)
  store AS securefile
  (
     TABLESPACE users
     DEDUPLICATE
     COMPRESS HIGH
     ENCRYPT USING 'AES256'
  );
/

INSERT INTO tbl_options (col1) VALUES ('1234567890');

COMMIT;
```

In this example, the above-inserted LOB locator is passed as input to the GETOPTIONS function to check for the current status of the Compression, Deduplication, and Encryption options. Then, the Compression option is turned ON, the Deduplication and the Encryption options are turned OFF using the SETOPTIONS procedure. After altering the default option settings, their current status is retrieved again using the GETOPTIONS function as shown below,

```
DECLARE
   l_cl_var1 CLOB;
BEGIN
   SELECT col1 INTO l_cl_var1 FROM tbl_options FOR UPDATE;
   dbms_output.put_line ('Before setting the options: The LOB is '||
   CASE dbms_lob.getoptions(l_cl_var1, dbms_lob.opt_compress)
   WHEN 1 THEN
      'Compressed'
   WHEN 0 THEN
      'not Compressed'
   END||', '||
   CASE dbms_lob.getoptions(l_cl_var1, dbms_lob.opt_deduplicate)
   WHEN 4 THEN
      'Deduplicated'
   WHEN 0 THEN
      'not Deduplicated'
```

```
  END||', and '||
  CASE dbms_lob.getoptions(l_cl_var1, dbms_lob.opt_encrypt)
  WHEN 2 THEN
    'Encrypted'
  WHEN 0 THEN
    'not Encrypted'
  END);
  dbms_lob.setoptions(l_cl_var1, dbms_lob.OPT_COMPRESS,
dbms_lob.compress_on);
  dbms_lob.setoptions(l_cl_var1, dbms_lob.OPT_DEDUPLICATE,
dbms_lob.deduplicate_off);
  dbms_lob.setoptions(l_cl_var1, dbms_lob.OPT_ENCRYPT,
dbms_lob.encrypt_off);

  dbms_output.put_line ('After setting the options: The LOB is '||
  CASE dbms_lob.getoptions(l_cl_var1, dbms_lob.opt_compress)
  WHEN 1 THEN
    'Compressed'
  WHEN 0 THEN
    'not Compressed'
  END||', '||
  CASE dbms_lob.getoptions(l_cl_var1, dbms_lob.opt_deduplicate)
  WHEN 4 THEN
    'Deduplicated'
  WHEN 0 THEN
    'not Deduplicated'
  END||', and '||
  CASE dbms_lob.getoptions(l_cl_var1, dbms_lob.opt_encrypt)
  WHEN 2 THEN
    'Encrypted'
  WHEN 0 THEN
    'not Encrypted'
  END);
END;
/
```

Results:

```
Before setting the options: The LOB is Compressed, Deduplicated, and
Encrypted
After setting the options: The LOB is Compressed, not Deduplicated, and not
Encrypted
```

SETCONTENTTYPE and GETCONTENTTYPE Subprograms

The SETCONTENTTYPE procedures can be used for setting the content type string for the LOB data and the GETCONTENTTYPE functions can be used for retrieving the content type string set previously by the SETCONTENTTYPE procedures.

The prototypes of the overloaded SETCONTENTTYPE procedures are shown below,

```
DBMS_LOB.SETCONTENTTYPE (lob_loc IN OUT NOCOPY BLOB, contenttype IN
VARCHAR2);

DBMS_LOB.SETCONTENTTYPE (lob_loc IN OUT NOCOPY CLOB CHARACTER SET ANY_CS,
contenttype IN VARCHAR2);
```

The prototypes of the overloaded GETCONTENTTYPE functions are shown below,

```
DBMS_LOB.GETCONTENTTYPE (lob_loc IN BLOB) RETURN VARCHAR2;

DBMS_LOB.GETCONTENTTYPE (lob_loc IN CLOB CHARACTER SET ANY_CS) RETURN
VARCHAR2;
```

- **LOB_LOC** parameter accepts and returns the LOB locator whose content type has to be set or get.
- **CONTENTTYPE** parameter accepts the content string to be assigned.

A SecureFile LOB table is created and inserted with the English alphabets as shown below,

```
CREATE TABLE tbl_content (col1 CLOB)
  LOB (col1)
  store AS SecureFile
  TABLESPACE users;

INSERT INTO tbl_content VALUES ('ABCDEFGHIJKLMNOPQRSTUVWXYZ');

COMMIT;
```

The content type string 'Alphabets' is set to the LOB using the SETCONTENTTYPE procedure and it is retrieved back using the GETCONTENTTYPE function as shown below,

```
DECLARE
  l_cl_var1 CLOB;
BEGIN
  SELECT col1 INTO l_cl_var1 FROM tbl_content FOR UPDATE;
  dbms_lob.setcontenttype(l_cl_var1, 'Alphabets');
  dbms_output.put_line(l_cl_var1||'-' || dbms_lob.getContentType(l_cl_var1)
|| '-');
END;
/
```

```
Results:
```

```
ABCDEFGHIJKLMNOPQRSTUVWXYZ-Alphabets-
```

GET_STORAGE_LIMIT Functions

These functions can be used for retrieving the storage limit for the specified internal LOB. For the external LOBs, it is 4GB.

The prototypes of these overloaded functions are shown below,

```
DBMS_LOB.GET_STORAGE_LIMIT (lob_loc IN CLOB CHARACTER SET ANY_CS)
RETURN INTEGER;

DBMS_LOB.GET_STORAGE_LIMIT (lob_loc IN BLOB) RETURN INTEGER;
```

In the below example, the maximum storage limit for a not null CLOB, NCLOB, and BLOB types are retrieved using the GET_STORAGE_LIMIT function as shown. The result for the NCLOB column displays that it occupies half the space of CLOB and BLOB types because a single character in NCLOB occupies 2 bytes as the database's national character set is AL16UTF16.

```
DECLARE
  l_cl_var1 CLOB   :='A';
  l_ncl_var2 NCLOB:=n'♠ ♦ ♣ ♥';
  l_bl_var3 BLOB   :=utl_raw.cast_to_raw('B');
BEGIN
  dbms_output.put_line('The maximum storage limit for the CLOB type is
'||dbms_lob.get_storage_limit(l_cl_var1)||' Bytes');

  dbms_output.put_line('The maximum storage limit for the NCLOB type is
'||dbms_lob.get_storage_limit(l_ncl_var2)||' Bytes');

  dbms_output.put_line('The maximum storage limit for the BLOB type is
'||dbms_lob.get_storage_limit(l_bl_var3)||' Bytes');
END;
/
```

```
Results:
```

```
The maximum storage limit for the CLOB type is 34926674042940 Bytes
The maximum storage limit for the NCLOB type is 17463337021470 Bytes
The maximum storage limit for the BLOB type is 34926674042940 Bytes
```

CONVERTTOCLOB Procedure

This procedure can be used for converting any BLOB data into CLOB/ NCLOB type for the specified character set and the offsets. This procedure can be used upon the persistent and temporary LOBs as both source and target instances.

While the source BLOB instance is persistent and from a table, the corresponding row must be locked using the FOR UPDATE clause prior to the conversion.

Note that the target CLOB/ NCLOB instance cannot have both its locator and data empty. In other words, the target instance must have a data in it prior to this procedure's execution.

The prototype of this procedure is shown below,

```
DBMS_LOB.CONVERTTOCLOB(
    dest_lob      IN OUT NOCOPY CLOB CHARACTER SET ANY_CS,
    src_blob      IN            BLOB,
    amount        IN            INTEGER,
    dest_offset   IN OUT        INTEGER,
    src_offset    IN OUT        INTEGER,
    blob_csid     IN            NUMBER,
    lang_context  IN OUT        INTEGER,
    warning       OUT           INTEGER);
```

- **DEST_LOB** parameter accepts and returns the destination CLOB/ NCLOB instance.
- **SRC_BLOB** parameter accepts the source BLOB instance.
- **AMOUNT** parameter accepts the number of bytes to be converted from the source to target. To copy the complete source content, the constant DBMS_LOB.LOBMAXSIZE has to be passed.
- **DEST_OFFSET** parameter accepts and returns the offset in characters for the destination CLOB instance, before and after the conversion respectively. Specify the integer 1, to paste the converted data from the beginning of the CLOB.
- **SRC_OFFSET** parameter accepts and returns the offset in bytes for the source BLOB instance, before and after the conversion respectively.
- **BFILE_CSID** parameter accepts the character set ID of the external source file.
    - → **0** indicates that the default database character set is used for CLOB and national character set is used for NCLOB types.
    - → **871** indicates that UTF8 character set is used.
    - → **872** indicates that UTFE character set is used.
    - → **873** indicates that AL32UTF8 character set encoding is used.
    - → **1000** indicates that UTF16 character set encoding is used.
    - → **2000** indicates that AL16UTF16 character set encoding is used.

- ➔ **2002** indicates that AL16UTF16LE character set encoding is used.
- **LANG_CONTEXT** parameter accepts and returns the shift load status for the current load. This parameter is used only when we want to perform the next load as a continuing load from the same source. The default value is 0.
- **WARNING** parameter returns any abnormal loading messages while performing the load.

In the below code snippet, a BLOB instance with the database default character set and both its source and destination offsets as 1, is converted to CLOB type using the CONVERTOCLOB procedure as shown.

```
DECLARE
  l_bl_src BLOB :=utl_raw.cast_to_raw('This procedure converts BLOB data
into CLOB type');
  l_cl_dest CLOB          :='1';
  l_i_src_offset    INTEGER:=1;
  l_i_dest_offset   INTEGER:=1;
  l_i_lang_context INTEGER:=0;
  l_i_warning       INTEGER;
BEGIN
  dbms_lob.converttoclob(l_cl_dest, l_bl_src, dbms_lob.lobmaxsize,
l_i_dest_offset, l_i_src_offset, 0, l_i_lang_context, l_i_warning);

  dbms_output.put_line('The converted CLOB text is: '||l_cl_dest);

  dbms_output.put_line('Source and destination offsets after the conversion
are '||l_i_src_offset||', '||l_i_dest_offset||' respectively.');

END;
/
```

Result:

```
The converted CLOB text is: This procedure converts BLOB data into CLOB type
Source and destination offsets after the conversion are 49, 49 respectively.
```

CONVERTTOBLOB Procedure

This procedure can be used for converting the CLOB/ NCLOB data into BLOB type in binary format, for the specified character set and the offsets. This procedure can be used upon the persistent and temporary LOBs as both source and target instances.

While the source CLOB instance is persistent and from a table, the corresponding row must be locked using the FOR UPDATE clause prior to the conversion.

Note that the target BLOB instance cannot have both its locator and data empty. In other words, the target instance must have a data in it prior to this procedure's execution.

The prototype of this procedure is shown below,

```
DBMS_LOB.CONVERTTOBLOB(
    dest_lob      IN OUT NOCOPY BLOB,
    src_clob      IN     CLOB CHARACTER SET ANY_CS,
    amount        IN     INTEGER,
    dest_offset   IN OUT INTEGER,
    src_offset    IN OUT INTEGER,
    blob_csid     IN     NUMBER,
    lang_context  IN OUT INTEGER,
    warning       OUT    INTEGER);
```

- **DEST_LOB** parameter accepts and returns the destination BLOB instance.
- **SRC_CLOB** parameter accepts the source CLOB/ NCLOB instance.

In the below code listing, a CLOB instance with the default database character set and both its source and destination offsets as 1, is converted to BLOB type using the CONVERTOBLOB procedure as shown.

```
DECLARE
    l_cl_src CLOB :='This procedure converts CLOB data into BLOB type';
    l_bl_dest BLOB :=utl_raw.cast_to_raw('A');
    l_i_src_offset    INTEGER:=1;
    l_i_dest_offset   INTEGER:=1;
    l_i_lang_context INTEGER:=0;
    l_i_warning       INTEGER;
BEGIN
    dbms_lob.converttoblob(l_bl_dest, l_cl_src, dbms_lob.lobmaxsize,
l_i_dest_offset, l_i_src_offset, 0, l_i_lang_context, l_i_warning);

    dbms_output.put_line('The converted BLOB text is:
'||utl_raw.cast_to_varchar2(l_bl_dest));

    dbms_output.put_line('Source and destination offsets after the conversion
are '||l_i_src_offset||', '||l_i_dest_offset||' respectively.');

END;
/
```

Result:

```
The converted CLOB text is: This procedure converts CLOB data into BLOB type
Source and destination offsets after the conversion are 49, 49 respectively.
```

Temporary LOBs

The temporary LOBs are a part of the internal LOBs, thus only CLOB and BLOB can be temporary LOBs. A PL/SQL internal LOB variable, which is created and destroyed in a single session is called as a temporary LOB instance. For the temporary LOBs, their locator points to the location where its data reside in the temporary tablespace. Once the session expires, the temporary LOB's data are freed and its pointer becomes invalidated. If the process dies unexpectedly or if the database crashes in the middle of a LOB operation, the temporary LOBs are removed along with their data and their memory is freed up.

If the temporary LOB is inserted into a table row, its data moves from the temporary tablespace to the permanent tablespace and turns itself into a permanent LOB. To make a temporary LOB into permanent, we can make use of the DBMS_LOB.COPY API. The only difference between a permanent LOB and a temporary LOB is that the permanent LOB stores its data in a table row in the permanent tablespace and the temporary LOB stores its data in the session in the temporary tablespace.

There are two ways in creating a temporary LOB. They are

1) By creating a PL/SQL BLOB or CLOB/ NCLOB variable.
2) By using the DBMS_LOB.CREATETEMPORARY Procedures.

CREATETEMPORARY Procedures

When we use this method for creating the temporary LOBs, we don't need to initialize the temporary LOBs either using EMPTY_CLOB() or EMPTY_BLOB() constructors as they are by default initialized during their creation.

There is no support for consistent read, undo, backup, parallel processing, and transaction management for the temporary LOBs. Because of this, we must empty the temporary LOBs when we encounter an error and must not assign multiple locators to the same LOB instance to avoid performance degradation due to stagnant memory space.

The prototypes of these overloaded procedures are shown below,

```
DBMS_LOB.CREATETEMPORARY (
   lob_loc IN OUT NOCOPY BLOB,
   cache   IN            BOOLEAN,
   dur     IN            PLS_INTEGER:= DBMS_LOB.SESSION);

DBMS_LOB.CREATETEMPORARY (
   lob_loc IN OUT NOCOPY CLOB CHARACTER SET ANY_CS,
   cache   IN            BOOLEAN,
   dur     IN            PLS_INTEGER:= DBMS_LOB.SESSION);
```

*   **LOB_LOC** parameter accepts the temporary CLOB/ BLOB instance for its creation.

- **CACHE** parameter accepts a Boolean True if the LOB should be read into the buffer cache or a Boolean False if not.
- **DUR** parameter specifies whether the LOB must be freed up at the end of the session or the call.
  - → To free the LOB at the end of the session, we must specify either the constant DBMS_LOB.SESSION or the integer 10.
  - → To free the LOB at the end of the call, we must specify either the constant DBMS_LOB.CALL or the integer 12.

ISTEMPORARY Functions

These functions can be used for verifying whether a LOB instance is temporary by returning the integer 1 and the integer 0 when it is not. If the input locator is *null*, this function returns a *null*.

When a temporary LOB is freed up, its locator will be set to *null*. Even though its locator is freed up, this function will return a 0 unless it is explicitly assigned to *null*.

The prototypes of these overloaded functions are shown below,

```
DBMS_LOB.ISTEMPORARY (lob_loc IN BLOB) RETURN INTEGER;

DBMS_LOB.ISTEMPORARY (lob_loc IN CLOB CHARACTER SET ANY_CS) RETURN INTEGER;
```

- **LOB_LOC** parameter accepts the LOB locator that has to be verified for the temporary LOB check.

FREETEMPORARY Procedures

These procedures can be used for freeing up the temporary LOB memory from its default temporary tablespace location.

A temporary LOB instance can only be destroyed by using this API.

The prototypes of these overloaded procedures are shown below,

```
DBMS_LOB.FREETEMPORARY (lob_loc IN OUT NOCOPY BLOB);

DBMS_LOB.FREETEMPORARY (lob_loc IN OUT NOCOPY CLOB CHARACTER SET ANY_CS);
```

- **LOB_LOC** parameter accepts the LOB locator that has to be freed up.

In the below listing, a PL/SQL CLOB variable is created as temporary using the CREATETEMPORARY procedure, gets its state verified using the ISTEMPORARY function, and frees itself using the FREETEMPORARY procedure as shown below.

```
DECLARE
  l_cl_var1 CLOB;
BEGIN
  dbms_lob.createtemporary(l_cl_var1,true,dbms_lob.session);
  dbms_output.put_line
  (
    CASE dbms_lob.istemporary(l_cl_var1)
    WHEN 1 THEN
      'The LOB is temporary'
    WHEN 0 THEN
      'The LOB is not temporary'
    ELSE
      'The LOB has null locator'
    END);
  dbms_lob.freetemporary(l_cl_var1);
END;
/
```

Results:

The LOB is temporary

LOADBLOBFROMFILE Procedure

We can call this procedure to load an external LOB directly into a BLOB type. We can specify the both the source's and the target's offset in bytes for the load.

- If the offset specified for the target is beyond the end of the characters in the LOB, then the extra spaces are filled up with zero-byte fillers or spaces.
- If the offset specified for the target is less than the end of the characters in the LOB, then the existing data are overwritten.

The load process does not mandatorily expect explicit OPEN/ CLOSE APIs as the Functional and the Domain indexes are updated during each call instead. However, not using the OPEN/ CLOSE APIs updates the functional and the domain indexes for each call resulting in performance degradation.

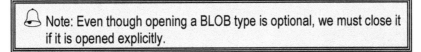

> 🔔 Note: Even though opening a BLOB type is optional, we must close it if it is opened explicitly.

The prototype of this procedure is shown below,

```
DBMS_LOB.LOADBLOBFROMFILE (
   dest_lob    IN OUT NOCOPY BLOB,
   src_bfile   IN            BFILE,
   amount      IN            INTEGER,
   dest_offset IN OUT        INTEGER,
   src_offset  IN OUT        INTEGER);
```

- **DEST_LOB** parameter accepts and returns the BLOB type as the target load.
- **SRC_BFILE** parameter accepts the input BFILE locator as the source load.
- **AMOUNT** parameter accepts the number of bytes that is to be loaded from the external file. To load the complete file, we must use the DBMS_LOB.LOBMAXSIZE constant or the integer 18446744073709551615.
- **DEST_OFFSET** parameter accepts and returns the destination offset in bytes for the target BLOB type.
- **SRC_OFFSET** parameter accepts and returns the source offset in bytes of the source BFILE type.

A directory object for the *Movies\English* folder from the *F:* drive is created as shown below,

```
CREATE OR REPLACE directory dir_movies
AS
   'F:\Movies\English';
```

In the below anonymous block, a temporary BLOB is created and is opened in Read/ Write mode, and an external file is opened for the movie file *Pearl Harbor.MKV* in Read mode. The complete movie file is then copied into the temporary BLOB variable using the LOADBLOBFROMFILE procedure with both the source and destination offsets as 1. After the load is completed, the size of the video file is retrieved using the GETLENGTH function as shown. Finally, the temporary LOB and the binary file are closed.

```
DECLARE
   l_bf_src bfile        :=bfilename('DIR_MOVIES', 'Pearl Harbor.MKV');
   l_bl_dest BLOB        :=empty_blob();
   l_i_src_offset  INTEGER:=1;
   l_i_dest_offset INTEGER:=1;
BEGIN
   dbms_lob.createtemporary(l_bl_dest, true, dbms_lob.session);

   dbms_lob.open(l_bf_src, dbms_lob.file_readonly);

   dbms_lob.open(l_bl_dest, dbms_lob.lob_readwrite);

   dbms_lob.loadblobfromfile(l_bl_dest, l_bf_src, dbms_lob.lobmaxsize,
l_i_dest_offset, l_i_src_offset);
```

```
    dbms_output.put_line('Total size of the movie file is
'||dbms_lob.getlength(l_bl_dest)||' Bytes');

    dbms_lob.close(l_bf_src);

    dbms_lob.close(l_bl_dest);
END;
/
```

Result:

```
Total size of the movie file is 1326711745 Bytes
```

LOADCLOBFROMFILE Procedure

This procedure loads the external file data into an internal CLOB/ NCLOB type with appropriate datatype conversion along with offset definitions and the number of characters to be copied from both the source and the target.

The destination character set is the always the same as the database character set in case of CLOB and national character set in case of NCLOB. Note that the source file can also contain Unicode character set.

The load process does not mandatorily expect explicit OPEN/ CLOSE APIs as the Functional and the Domain indexes are updated during each call instead. However, not using the OPEN/ CLOSE APIs updates the functional and the domain indexes for each call resulting in performance degradation.

The prototype of this procedure is shown below,

```
DBMS_LOB.LOADCLOBFROMFILE (
   dest_lob      IN OUT NOCOPY CLOB CHARACTER SET ANY_CS,
   src_bfile     IN            BFILE,
   amount        IN            INTEGER,
   dest_offset   IN OUT        INTEGER,
   src_offset    IN OUT        INTEGER,
   bfile_csid    IN            NUMBER,
   lang_context  IN OUT        INTEGER,
   warning          OUT        INTEGER);
```

- **DEST_LOB** parameter accepts and returns the CLOB type as the target load.
- **SRC_BFILE** parameter accepts the input BFILE locator as the source load.

- **AMOUNT** parameter accepts the number of bytes that is to be loaded from the external file. To load the complete file, we must use the DBMS_LOB.LOBMAXSIZE constant or the integer 18446744073709551615.
- **DEST_OFFSET** parameter accepts and returns the destination offset in bytes for the target BLOB type.
- **SRC_OFFSET** parameter accepts and returns the source offset in bytes of the source BFILE type.
- **BFILE_CSID** parameter accepts the character set ID of the external source file.
    - ➔ **0** indicates that the default database character set is used for CLOB and national character set is used for NCLOB types.
    - ➔ **871** indicates that UTF8 character set is used.
    - ➔ **872** indicates that UTFE character set is used.
    - ➔ **873** indicates that AL32UTF8 character set encoding is used.
    - ➔ **1000** indicates that UTF16 character set encoding is used.
    - ➔ **2000** indicates that AL16UTF16 character set encoding is used.
    - ➔ **2002** indicates that AL16UTF16LE character set encoding is used.
- **LANG_CONTEXT** parameter accepts and returns the shift load status for the current load. This parameter is used only when we want to perform the next load as a continuing load from the same source. The default value is 0.
- **WARNING** parameter returns any abnormal loading messages while performing the load.

A directory object for the *Books\Novels* folder from the *E:* drive is created as shown below,

```
CREATE OR REPLACE directory dir_novels
AS
   'E:\Books\Novels';
/
```

In the below anonymous block, a temporary CLOB is created and is opened in Read/Write mode, and an external file is opened for the novel *The Time Travelers Wife.PDF* in Read mode. The complete PDF file is then copied into the temporary CLOB variable using the LOADCLOBFROMFILE procedure with both the source and destination offsets as 1. After the load is completed, the temporary CLOB is converted into permanent by inserting its instance into a table as a row. Then, the total size of the novel is retrieved using the GETLENGTH function as shown below.

```
DECLARE
   l_cl_dest CLOB :=empty_clob();
   l_bf_src bfile :=bfilename('DIR_NOVELS', 'The Time Travelers Wife.PDF');
   l_i_dest_offset  INTEGER:=1;
   l_i_src_offset   INTEGER:=1;
   l_i_lang_context INTEGER:=0;
```

```
   l_i_warning        INTEGER;
BEGIN

   dbms_lob.createtemporary(l_cl_dest, true, dbms_lob.session);

   dbms_lob.open(l_bf_src, dbms_lob.file_readonly);

   dbms_lob.loadclobfromfile(l_cl_dest, l_bf_src, dbms_lob.lobmaxsize,
l_i_dest_offset, l_i_src_offset, 0 , l_i_lang_context, l_i_warning);

   dbms_lob.close(l_bf_src);

   INSERT INTO tbl_int_lob (col1_number, col2_clob) VALUES (2, l_cl_dest);

   COMMIT;

   dbms_output.put_line('The total size of the PDF file is
'||dbms_lob.getlength(l_cl_dest)||' Bytes');
END;
/
```

Result:

The total size of the PDF file is 1311171 Bytes

LOADFROMFILE Procedures

These procedures can be used when we want to load external files into BLOB, CLOB, and NCLOB types along with offset definition and the number of bytes to be copied from both the source and the target.

The load process does not mandatorily expect explicit OPEN/ CLOSE APIs as the Functional and the Domain indexes are updated during each call instead. However, not using the OPEN/ CLOSE APIs updates the functional and the domain indexes for each call resulting in performance degradation.

These procedures work similar to both LOADCLOBFROMFILE and LOADBLOBFROMFILE procedures, but it does not provide language context for the CLOB/ NCLOB columns.

The prototypes of these overloaded procedures are shown below,

```
DBMS_LOB.LOADFROMFILE (
    dest_lob    IN OUT NOCOPY BLOB,
    src_file    IN            BFILE,
    amount      IN            INTEGER,
    dest_offset IN            INTEGER  := 1,
    src_offset  IN            INTEGER  := 1);

DBMS_LOB.LOADFROMFILE (
    dest_lob     IN OUT NOCOPY CLOB CHARACTER SET ANY_CS,
```

```
   src_file     IN               BFILE,
   amount       IN               INTEGER,
   dest_offset  IN               INTEGER   := 1,
   src_offset   IN               INTEGER   := 1);
```

A directory object for the *Music\One Direction* folder from the *F*: drive is created as shown below,

```
CREATE OR REPLACE directory dir_songs
AS
  'F:\Music\One Direction';
```

In the below anonymous block, a temporary BLOB is created and is opened in Read/ Write mode, and an external file is opened for the number, *What Makes You Beautiful.MP3* in Read mode. The complete MP3 file is then copied into the temporary CLOB variable using the LOADFROMFILE procedure with both the source and destination offsets as 1. After the load is completed, the size of the number is retrieved using the GETLENGTH function as shown below.

```
DECLARE
   l_bf_src bfile         :=bfilename('DIR_SONGS', 'What Makes You
Beautiful.MP3');
   l_bl_dest BLOB         :=empty_blob();
   l_i_src_offset  INTEGER:=1;
   l_i_dest_offset INTEGER:=1;
BEGIN
  dbms_lob.createtemporary(l_bl_dest, true, dbms_lob.session);

  dbms_lob.open(l_bf_src, dbms_lob.file_readonly);

  dbms_lob.open(l_bl_dest, dbms_lob.lob_readwrite);

  dbms_lob.loadfromfile(l_bl_dest, l_bf_src, dbms_lob.lobmaxsize);

  dbms_output.put_line('Total size of the audio file is
'||dbms_lob.getlength(l_bl_dest)||' Bytes');

  dbms_lob.close(l_bf_src);

  dbms_lob.close(l_bl_dest);
END;
/
```

Results:

```
Total size of the audio file is 10539475 Bytes
```

FILEOPEN Procedure

This procedure can be used for opening a BFILE in Read-only mode. To open an external file successfully, the directory object for the full path of the file, and the filename with the appropriate extension has to be passed as the first and second parameters of the BFILENAME function respectively. Note that the filename is case insensitive. This procedure is synonymous to the OPEN procedure.

The prototype of this procedure is shown below,

```
DBMS_LOB.FILEOPEN (
    file_loc    IN OUT NOCOPY   BFILE,
    open_mode   IN              BINARY_INTEGER := file_readonly);
```

- **FILE_LOC** parameter accepts the BFILE locator.
- **OPEN_MODE** parameter accepts the mode in which the external file has to be opened up. The only mode available for opening a BFILE is DBMS_LOB.FILE_READONLY, which is the default mode.

FILEEXISTS Function

This function can be used for verifying whether or not the specified external file is present in the mentioned directory location. This function must be used before opening a BFILE to avoid the *ORA-22288: file or LOB operation FILEOPEN failed*
The system cannot find the file specified exception.

This function returns 1 if the file exists and 0 if not.

The prototype of this function is shown below,

```
DBMS_LOB.FILEEXISTS (file_loc IN BFILE) RETURN INTEGER;
```

- **FILE_LOC** parameter accepts the BFILE locator.

FILEISOPEN Function

This function can be used for verifying whether or not an external binary file is opened. This function must be used before performing any operations on the binary file to avoid

---

the *ORA-22289: cannot perform FILEISOPEN operation on an unopened file or LOB* exception.

This function returns 1 if the file is open and 0 if not.

The prototype of this function is shown below,

```
DBMS_LOB.FILEISOPEN (file_loc IN BFILE) RETURN INTEGER;
```

- **FILE_LOC** parameter accepts the BFILE locator.

FILEGETNAME Procedure

This procedure can be used for retrieving the directory object name and the filename of the external file that is associated with the input LOB locator. This procedure does not confirm whether the physical file or the directory actually exists or not.

The prototype of this procedure is shown below,

```
DBMS_LOB.FILEGETNAME (
    file_loc  IN  BFILE,
    dir_alias OUT VARCHAR2,
    filename  OUT VARCHAR2);
```

- **FILE_LOC** parameter accepts the input BFILE locator.
- **DIR_ALIAS** parameter returns the directory object name.
- **FILENAME** parameter returns the name of the BFILE.

FILECLOSE Procedure

This procedure can be used for closing a BFILE type that has been already opened through the FILEOPEN or OPEN procedures. If we try to close a BFILE that has been already closed or not opened, we may encounter the *ORA-22289: cannot perform FILECLOSE operation on an unopened file or LOB* exception.

The prototype of this procedure is shown below,

```
DBMS_LOB.FILECLOSE (file_loc IN OUT NOCOPY BFILE);
```

- **FILE_LOC** parameter accepts the BFILE locator.

FILECLOSEALL Procedure

This procedure can be used for performing a close operation on all the opened BFILEs in the current session. When we try to execute this procedure in a session where no external file is opened, we may encounter the *ORA-22289: cannot perform FILECLOSEALL operation on an unopened file or LOB* exception.

The prototype of this procedure is shown below,

```
DBMS_LOB.FILECLOSEALL;
```

A directory object is created for the *Games* folder from the *G:* drive as shown below,

```
CREATE OR REPLACE directory dir_games
AS
  'G:\Games';
```

In the below code snippet, a BFILE locator for the game file *The Elder Scrolls V Skyrim.zip* from the DIR_GAMES directory object is assigned to a BFILE variable and its size is retrieved using the GETLENGTH function. Meanwhile, the file's existence is verified using the FILEEXISTS function and the file's open status is verified using the FILEISOPEN function as shown below.

```
DECLARE
  l_bf_var1 bfile :=bfilename('DIR_GAMES', 'The Elder Scrolls V
Skyrim.ZIP');
  l_vc_dir_name VARCHAR2(30);
  l_vc_filename VARCHAR2(30);
BEGIN
  IF dbms_lob.fileexists(l_bf_var1)=1 THEN
    dbms_lob.fileopen(l_bf_var1);
    IF dbms_lob.fileisopen(l_bf_var1)=1 THEN
      dbms_lob.filegetname(l_bf_var1, l_vc_dir_name, l_vc_filename);

      dbms_output.put_line(l_vc_filename||' file consists of
'||dbms_lob.getlength(l_bf_var1)||' Bytes');
      dbms_lob.fileclose(l_bf_var1);
    ELSIF dbms_lob.fileisopen(l_bf_var1)=0 THEN
      dbms_output.put_line('The BFILE is not open!');
    END IF;
  ELSIF dbms_lob.fileexists(l_bf_var1)=0 THEN
    dbms_output.put_line('The BFILE does not exist!');
  END IF;
END;
/
```

Results:

```
The Elder Scrolls V Skyrim.ZIP game file consists of 4273517357 Bytes
```

Migrating Columns from LONG to LOB

Any existing applications with LONG/ LONG RAW columns must be migrated to their appropriate LOB types to enjoy the flexibility, robustness, and support of the LOB types.

Few advantages of the LOB types over the LONG types are listed below,

1) A table can have only one LONG column, but the limit for the number of LOB columns in a table is limited only by the maximum number of columns. I.e., 1000.

2) Object types cannot have LONG columns as their attributes, whereas they can have LOB columns as their attributes.

3) Both LONG and LOB columns cannot be indexed. However, we can specify a LOB column in the indextype specification of a domain index. In addition, Oracle text allows us to define an index on the CLOB column.

4) LOB columns support random access to data, whereas LONG columns support only to sequential access.

5) The RETURN type of a stored function cannot be LONG but can be of LOB type.

6) Predefined functions, expressions or conditions cannot be used in the columns with LONG type but can be used on the LOB types.

7) The maximum size limit of a LONG column is only 2 GB whereas in the case of LOB columns it is 8 TB – 128 TB, which is based on the database initialization parameter.

8) Both LONG and LOB columns cannot be used in the DISTINCT, ORDER BY and GROUP BY clauses of a query. However, LOB columns can be used in the above clauses if they are type cast or if they are an attribute of an object type.

9) LONG columns cannot be used in the WHERE condition for comparison, whereas LOB columns can be used by casting them to an appropriate datatype through explicit conversion. Both LONG and LOB columns can be used in the WHERE condition of a query for IS NULL or IS NOT NULL checks.

10) CREATE TABLE AS SELECT (CTAS) cannot be used in the SELECT statement having LONG columns, whereas it is possible in case the SELECT statement has LOB columns.

11) INSERT INTO SELECT cannot be used when the SELECT statement has a LONG column, whereas it is possible when the statement has LOB columns.

12) LONG column dumps data in the same segment. In the case of LOB columns, only the LOB locator is stored in the table column, whereas the CLOB and BLOB data can be stored in a different tablespace or in a separate segment called as LOBSEGMENT. BFILE data is stored outside the database in the form of an external file.

13) LONG columns do not support national character set, whereas the NCLOB type provides national character set support.

14) LOB columns have a special API, DBMS_LOB for performing LOB operations precisely, which is not available for the LONG columns.

Prerequisites for Migration LONG Columns to LOB Columns

1. Any domain indexes on the LONG columns must be dropped before converting/migrating them to LOB columns.

2. Prevent generation of redo logs during the LONG to LOB migration process to avoid performance problems. This can be done through the below steps.

   2.1. Set the table with LONG columns to NOLOGGING prior to its migration by using the below ALTER statement.

   ```
   ALTER TABLE <Table_name> NOLOGGING;
   ```

   2.2. Migrate the LONG columns to LOB columns with NOCACHE in the STORE AS clause as we must specify NOCACHE when the table is in NOLOGGING mode as shown below,

   ```
   ALTER TABLE <Table_name> MODIFY (<Column_name> CLOB [DEFAULT
   <default_value>]) LOB (<Column_name>) STORE
   AS
     (NOCACHE NOLOGGING);
   ```

2.3. Change the table from NOCACHE to CACHE by issuing the below ALTER statement,

```
ALTER TABLE <Table_name> MODIFY LOB (<Column_name>) (CACHE);
```

2.4. Change the table from NOLOGGING to LOGGING by issuing the below ALTER statement,

```
ALTER TABLE <Table_name> LOGGING;
```

Converting Tables from LONG to LOB Datatypes

There are three methods to convert LONG columns to CLOB or NCLOB columns and LONG RAW columns to BLOB columns as described below.

Note that the implicit conversion of NUMBER, DATE, ROW_ID, BINARY_INTEGER, and PLS_INTEGER types are permitted by PL/SQL to LONG columns, but the implicit conversion of these types to a LOB column is not allowed. If there are any implicit conversions in our existing application, for LONG columns, they must be converted to VARCHAR2 or RAW using the TO_CHAR or TO_RAW functions respectively, to avoid the error scenario in the applications after the migration process is completed.

Method 1: Using ALTER Statement to Convert LONG Columns to LOB Columns

We can use the ALTER statement to convert a LONG column to a LOB column.

The prototype of converting a LONG column to a LOB column is shown below,

```
ALTER TABLE <Table_name> MODIFY (<Column_name> <CLOB | NCLOB | BLOB>
[DEFAULT <Default_value>])
[LOB_storage_clause];
```

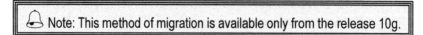

Note: This method of migration is available only from the release 10g.

Points to remember during this migration process,

- If we don't specify a default value during the migration, the default value for the LONG column becomes the default value for the LOB column.

- The only constraints supported by the LONG columns are NULL and NOT NULL, which will be maintained for the new LOB columns. To alter these constraints, we must issue another ALTER statement after the migration is completed.

- Any existing UPDATE OF triggers will fail as they are not supported by the LOB columns.

- The system requires twice the size of the table data to be reserved for migration as the ALTER statement copies the content of the table into a new location, and frees the old space only at the end of the operation.

Method 2: Copying a LONG column to a LOB column Using the TO_LOB Operator

We can use the TO_LOB operator on the LONG column to copy its data to a LOB column either by using the CREATE TABLE AS SELECT statement or by using the INSERT INTO SELECT statement.

The prototype of using the CTAS statement is shown below,

```
CREATE TABLE <Table_name1>
AS
SELECT to_lob(<Long_column_name>),
            <Other_column1>,
            <Other_column2>,
            . . .
FROM <Table_name2>;
```

The prototype of using the INSERT INTO SELECT statement is shown below,

```
INSERT
INTO TABLE <Table_name1>
  (
    <CLOB_column_nam>,
    <Other_column1>,
    <Other_column2>,
    . . .
  )
SELECT to_lob(<Long_column_name>),
            <Other_column1>,
            <Other_column2>,
            . . .
FROM <Table_name2>;
```

Points to remember during this migration process,

- The TO_LOB operator cannot be used for a LOB attribute of an object type.

- The TO_LOB operator cannot be used upon remote tables.

- The TO_LOB operator cannot be used in CREATE TABLE AS SELECT statement while creating an Index Organized table. To work around this limitation, we must create the IOT first, followed by moving the data into it by using the INSERT INTO SELECT statement.

- The TO_LOB operator cannot be used in a PL/SQL block. However, this is possible if the TO_LOB operator is inside an EXECUTE IMMEDIATE statement.

Method 3: Online Redefinition of Tables with LONG Columns

This method is suitable when we want the table to be highly available during the migration process. Using this process, we can convert a LONG column to CLOB or NCLOB column and a LONG RAW column to BLOB column. This conversion can be performed by using the TO_LOB operator on the LONG column in the column mapping of the DBMS_REDEFINITION.START_REDEF_TABLE() procedure.

This migration can be performed through the below process.

1. Create an intermediate table defining a CLOB/ NCLOB and BLOB column for each LONG and LONG RAW column respectively in the original table to be migrated.

2. Start the redefinition process by calling the DBMS_REDEFINITION.START_REDEF_TABLE procedure with the TO_LOB operator on the LONG column in the column mapping parameter.

```
DBMS_REDEFINITION.START_REDEF_TABLE (
    'Schema_name',
    'Original_table_name',
    'Intermediate_table_name',
    'TO_LOB(Long_column_name) LOB_COLUMN',
    'Options_flag',
    'Orderby_columns');
```

3. The dependent objects of the table being redefined is cloned onto the intermediate table and registers the dependent objects using the DBMS_REDEFINITION.COPY_TABLE_DEPENDENTS procedure.

4. The redefinition process is completed by executing the DBMS_REDEFINITION.FINISH_REDEF_TABLE procedure.

Migrating Columns from BasicFile LOB to SecureFile LOB

The SecureFile LOB provides File system-like performance for its data, which was not possible by the BasicFile LOB. The BasicFile LOB storage mechanism is still available, but are less effective than the SecureFile LOBs. By migrating the LOBs from BasicFile to SecureFile, the performance of the LOB data processing can improve from 3x to 6x with enhanced security. As the SecureFile LOB follows a completely new storage architecture, it was impossible to keep on-disk compatibility with the BasicFile LOB implementation, making it unsuitable for an "in-place" migration from BasicFile to SecureFile. Performing this migration does not require any code change to the applications and the SecureFile are 100% backward compatible.

Note that the generation of REDO data during the BasicFile to SecureFile migration must be prevented as they could lead to performance implications. This can be done by creating the SecureFile LOB storage property as NOLOGGING during its creation and can be modified to LOGGING when the migration is completed.

There are two techniques by which the BasicFile can be migrated to SecureFile. They are explained below,

Method 1: Online Redefinition of Tables with BasicFile LOB

This is the recommended method for migrating LOBs from BasicFile to SecureFile. It can be done at the table level or at the partition level without taking them offline. We can also redefine the migration in parallel if the system has sufficient resources for parallel execution, but it requires additional space equal to or greater than the space used by the table or the partition temporarily during the migration.

Note: If the table to be redefined does not sport a primary key or a unique key with all the columns having NOT NULL constraints when using the option DBMS_REDEFINITION.CONS_USE_PK or the integer 1 during the redefinition, we may encounter the *ORA-12089: cannot online redefine table %S with no primary key* exception.

During this process, we must create an empty interim table with the same structure as that of the original table that has to be redefined, with its storage property as SecureFile along with the required advanced options like Deduplication, Encryption, and Compression.

The table TBL_SRC that has to be migrated from BasicFile to SecureFile is created below with sample data as shown.

```
CREATE TABLE tbl_src
  (
    p_id NUMBER PRIMARY KEY,
    c_lob CLOB
  )
  LOB (c_lob)
  STORE AS Basicfile;

INSERT INTO tbl_src VALUES (1,'A');
INSERT INTO tbl_src VALUES (2,'B');

COMMIT;
```

Note that the above table Create statement has its storage property as BasicFile explicitly specified, as the default storage type for the tables during their creation starting from 12c is SecureFile.

Now, an intermediate table with its storage property as SecureFile and with a structure similar to that of the source table is created as shown below,

```
CREATE TABLE tbl_int
  (
    p_id    NUMBER,
    c_lob CLOB
  )
  LOB (c_lob)
  STORE AS SECUREFILE
  (NOCACHE FILESYSTEM_LIKE_LOGGING);
```

START_REDEF_TABLE Procedure

This procedure can be used for initiating the redefinition process. The prototype of this procedure is shown below,

```
DBMS_REDEFINITION.START_REDEF_TABLE (
    uname                   IN   VARCHAR2,
    orig_table              IN   VARCHAR2,
    int_table               IN   VARCHAR2,
    col_mapping             IN   VARCHAR2 := NULL,
    options_flag            IN   BINARY_INTEGER := 1,
    orderby_cols            IN   VARCHAR2 := NULL,
    part_name               IN   VARCHAR2 := NULL,
    continue_after_errors   IN   BOOLEAN := FALSE
    copy_vpd_opt            IN   BINARY_INTEGER := CONS_VPD_NONE);
```

- **UNAME** parameter accepts the schema name of both the source and the intermediate tables.
- **ORIG_TABLE** parameter accepts the name of the source table that has to be redefined.
- **INT_TABLE** parameter accepts the name of the intermediate table for the redefinition. This parameter can accept a comma-delimited list of intermediate tables.
- **COL_MAPPING** parameter accepts the columns from the source table that has to be mapped to the intermediate table in a comma separated manner.
- **OPTIONS_FLAG** indicates the type of redefinition method to be used. The possible values are,
    - → **DBMS_REDEFINITION.CONS_USE_PK** or the integer **1** value performs the redefinition using the primary key or the unique key with all the columns having NOT NULL constraints upon it.
    - → **DBMS_REDEFINITION.CONS_USE_ROWID** or the integer **2** value performs the redefinition using the table's ROWID.
- **ORDERBY_COLS** parameter accepts the list of columns either in ascending or descending manner with which to sort the rows during the initial instantiation of the intermediate table. The default is null.
- **PART_NAME** parameter accepts the name of the partition being redefined. If multiple partitions are to be redefined, specify them in a comma-separated manner. Null implies that the entire table must be redefined. The default is null.
- **CONTINUE_AFTER_ERRORS** parameter accepts a Boolean True or False to allow the redefinition on the next partition if the current partition fails. This applies only to batched partition redefinition.
- **COPY_VPD_OPT** parameter specifies how the VPD policies are handled during the online redefinition.

➜ **CONS_VPD_AUTO** or the integer **2** value indicates to copy the VPD policies automatically.

➜ **CONS_VPD_MANUAL** or the integer **4** value indicates to copy the VPD policy manually.

➜ **CONS_VPD_NONE** or the integer **1** value indicates that there are no VPD policies in the source table. This is the default value.

In the below code snippet, the redefinition is kick-started using the START_REDEF_TABLE procedure for the source table TBL_SRC and the intermediate table TBL_INT as shown below.

```
EXEC DBMS_REDEFINITION.START_REDEF_TABLE(uname=>'C##',
orig_table=>'TBL_SRC', int_table=>'TBL_INT', col_mapping=>'P_ID,C_LOB');
```

After starting the redefinition, a materialized view is created and associated with the intermediate table. If you try to drop the intermediate table, you may encounter the *ORA-12083: must use DROP MATERIALIZED VIEW to drop %S.%S* exception. Also, the data from the table TBL_SRC is copied into the TBL_INT table.

If we face the *ORA-23539: table "C##"."TBL_SRC"* *currently being redefined* exception during the redefinition process, we can abort it using the DBMS_REDEFINITION.ABORT_REDEF_TABLE procedure and re-start the redefinition process again.

COPY_TABLE_DEPENDENTS Procedure

This procedure clones the dependent objects of the source table like GRANTS, TRIGGERS, CONSTRAINTS, and PRIVILEGES on to the intermediate table and registers them. This procedure does not re-register objects.

The prototype of this procedure is shown below,

```
DBMS_REDEFINITION.COPY_TABLE_DEPENDENTS(
    uname             IN VARCHAR2,
    orig_table        IN VARCHAR2,
    int_table         IN VARCHAR2,
    copy_indexes      IN PLS_INTEGER := 1,
    copy_triggers     IN BOOLEAN := TRUE,
    copy_constraints  IN BOOLEAN := TRUE,
    copy_privileges   IN BOOLEAN := TRUE,
    ignore_errors     IN BOOLEAN := FALSE,
    num_errors        OUT PLS_INTEGER,
    copy_statistics   IN BOOLEAN := FALSE,
    copy_mvlog        IN BOOLEAN := FALSE);
```

• **COPY_INDEXES** parameter accepts flags whether or not to copy the indexes.

- → The integer **0** indicates not to copy the indexes.
- → The constant **DBMS_REDEFINITION.CONS_ORIG_PARAMS** or the integer **1** indicates to copy the indexes using the physical parameters of the source indexes. This is the default value.
- **COPY_TRIGGERS** parameter accepts a Boolean value whether or not to copy the triggers.
  - → **True** value indicates that the triggers must be copied. This is the default value.
  - → **False** value indicates that the triggers must not be copied.
- **COPY_CONSTRAINTS** parameter accepts a Boolean value whether or not to copy the constraints.
  - → **True** value indicates that the constraints must be copied. This is the default value.
  - → **False** value indicates that the constraints must not be copied.
- **COPY_PRIVILEGES** parameter accepts a Boolean value whether or not to copy the privileges.
  - → **True** value indicates that the privileges must be copied. This is the default value.
  - → **False** value indicates that the privileges must not be copied.
- **IGNORE_ERRORS** parameter indicates whether or not to continue the copy process in the event of an error.
  - → **True** value indicates that the copy process must continue to the next object if the current object results in error.
  - → **False** value indicates that the copy process must terminate if any object results in error. This is the default value.
- **NUM_ERRORS** parameter returns the number of errors occurred during the object copy process.
- **COPY_STATISTICS** parameter indicates whether or not to copy the statistics.
  - → **True** value indicates that the statistics must be copied.
  - → **False** value indicates that the statistics must not be copied. This is the default value.
- **COPY_MVLOG** parameter indicates whether or not to copy the MVIEW logs.
  - → **True** value indicates that the MVIEW logs must be copied.
  - → **False** value indicates that the MVIEW logs must not be copied. This is the default value.

In the below code listing, the object dependencies of the table TBL_SRC are cloned to the table TBL_INT with the default values to the COPY_TABLE_DEPENDENTS procedure as shown below,

```
DECLARE
  l_pi_error_count pls_integer := 0;
BEGIN
  DBMS_REDEFINITION.COPY_TABLE_DEPENDENTS(uname=>'C##',
orig_table=>'TBL_SRC', int_table=>'TBL_INT', num_errors=>l_pi_error_count);
  DBMS_OUTPUT.PUT_LINE('Errors:= ' || l_pi_error_count);
END;
/
```

Results:

```
Errors:= 0
```

Here, we have not encountered any errors during the dependent object cloning process and the primary key constraint is copied from the source table to the intermediate table.

FINISH_REDEF_TABLE Procedure

This procedure completes the redefinition process by redefining the source table with the intermediate table's data and attributes. Until this process is completed, the source table will be locked.

The prototype of this procedure is shown below,

```
DBMS_REDEFINITION.FINISH_REDEF_TABLE (
   uname                 IN    VARCHAR2,
   orig_table            IN    VARCHAR2,
   int_table             IN    VARCHAR2,
   part_name             IN    VARCHAR2 := NULL,
   dml_lock_timeout      IN    PLS_INTEGER := NULL,
   continue_after_errors IN    BOOLEAN := FALSE);
```

- **DML_LOCK_TIMEOUT** parameter accepts the value for the timeout in seconds between 0 and 1,000,000 for waiting at the locks before failing. The default value is null.

In the below code listing, the FINISH_REDEF_TABLE procedure is used for completing the redefinition process, as shown.

```
EXEC DBMS_REDEFINITION.FINISH_REDEF_TABLE(uname=>'C##',
orig_table=>'TBL_SRC', int_table=>'TBL_INT');
```

After the redefinition is completed the trigger on the intermediate table will be dropped, the lock on the source table will be released, and the storage properties will be swapped between the source table and the intermediate table. That is, the source table will have its LOB as SecureFile and the intermediate table will have its LOB as BasicFile. This can be verified by querying the USER_LOBS data dictionary view as shown below,

---

```
SELECT table_name,
  securefile
FROM user_lobs
WHERE table_name IN ('TBL_SRC','TBL_INT');
```

Script Result:

TABLE_NAME	SECUREFILE
TBL_INT	NO
TBL_SRC	YES

The intermediate table can be dropped after the migration is completed or can be kept as a backup for future purpose.

Method 2: Partitioning

This is a non-migration process and requires downtime, thus this method must be used only for non-production like environments where the data availability is trivial. In this method, new partitions are created with the SecureFile feature enabled so that the incoming new LOB data are stored in the newly created partition enjoying the advanced features of the SecureFile, whereas the old data remains in the BasicFile storage, which can be migrated at a later date using the Online Redefinition process.

Restrictions in LOBs

1) LOB columns cannot be a part of the primary or unique key but can have only the NOT NULL constraint imposed upon them.

2) Clusters cannot contain LOB columns either as a keyed or non-keyed column.

3) In an AFTER UPDATE DML trigger, a LOB column cannot be specified in the UPDATE OF clause.

4) When performing an INSERT INTO SELECT operation, we can bind up to 4000 bytes of data to LOB columns and attributes. Without the bind variables, there is no restriction on the length restriction.

5) If a table has both LONG and LOB columns, we cannot bind more than 4000 characters to both LONG and LOB columns in the same SQL statement.

6) SQL functions and DBMS_LOB APIs are not supported for use with remote LOB columns.

Summary

We have toured through the basic introduction to the Large objects followed by their classification. In the next section, we have understood about the SecureFile, its initialization parameter, along with its 12c enhancements. We have also learned about the DBMS_LOB API and its subprograms individually with adequate examples of manipulating the large object types in the next section. We have compared the LONG and the LOB types in the next section. The later section explained us about the different migration techniques available for moving the data from LONG columns to LOB columns and for moving the LOBs from BasicFile to SecureFile. The final section listed out the limitations in the LOB types.

In the next chapter, we will be learning about the various performance tuning techniques.

Tuning PL/SQL for Performance

The Oracle RDBMS is like a big complex machine, where having a screw loose at any part of it could diversely affect the performance of the complete database. One of the biggest responsibilities of every programmer is to ensure that the database they work in is tuned properly for better performance. This can be done only if we have a better understanding of the architecture and the design of the database. This chapter guides us to the core sensitive areas which are responsible for the performance of the application in the database.

The areas that have to be keenly monitored in the database for tuning are Design, Application, Memory, Disk throughput, Database Contention, Operating system, and the Network. We will be understanding the different tuning strategies in detail through the below topics.

21) Introduction to the Database memory caches/ structures and their management methods.

22) Introduction to Compilation methods.

23) Understanding the PLSQL_CODE_TYPE initialization parameter.

24) Understanding the PLSQL_OPTIMIZE_LEVEL initialization parameter.

25) Enabling Intra-Unit inlining using the INLINE pragma.

26) Learning about the PL/SQL tuning best practices.

Tuning Memory for Performance

In this section, we are going to see about the memory allocation in the Oracle database and the various methods for managing them.

Database Memory Caches and Structures

Oracle database stores and retrieves data using memory caches and disks. The memory cache read is much faster than the disk access as the disk access takes a significant amount of time and process to compensate the physical IO operation. This is why we must store the frequently accessed objects in the memory and use them to avoid frequent disk access. This can be effectively done by the proper use of the Oracle database memory cache and increase the database performance.

The Oracle database memory caches that greatly influences the performance are,

Database Buffer Cache

The buffer cache is the memory area that stores the copy of the data blocks read from the data files. A buffer is a memory address where the recently accessed data blocks are temporarily cached. The database buffer cache is sized using the DB_CACHE_SIZE initialization parameter. The buffer cache mainly performs the below tasks,

1) Optimizes the physical IO process, by updating the data blocks in the cache and stores the metadata about the changes in the redo log buffer. Once a COMMIT is issued by the database user, the database writes the logs to the online redo log and instructs the *database writer* (DBW) to write the data blocks to the data files in the background.

2) Keeping the frequently accessed blocks in the buffer cache and stores the infrequently accessed blocks in the magnetic disk. When the Database Smart Flash Cache (DSFC) is enabled, a part of the buffer cache can reside in the flash cache, which can improve the performance of the access rather than from the disk.

> Note: DB_FLASH_CACHE_FILE and DB_FLASH_CACHE_SIZE initialization parameters can be used for configuring multiple flash devices. These devices are tracked and distributed by the buffer cache.

Buffer States

The Oracle database uses internal algorithms for maintaining the buffers in the cache, which can be in any of the states below.

• **Unused** – This is when the buffer is available for usage because it is never used or currently not being used. This is the primary choice for usage of the database.

- **Clean** – This is the state when the buffer is previously used and currently contains a read consistent version of a block in its time. The data held by the buffer are clean, thus the database can pin and use it. When the buffer is "pinned" in the cache, it is made available for the user accessing it without aging it out and by stopping the other sessions from accessing it.

- **Dirty** – This is the state when the buffer contains the modified data that has not been written into the disk. The database must checkpoint the block before using it.

Buffer Modes

When a user requests for the data from the buffer cache, the Oracle database retrieves them in any of the below modes,

- **Current Mode** – This mode retrieves the data from the buffer cache as it currently appears in the buffer cache.

- **Consistent Mode** – This mode retrieves the *read consistent version* of the block by using the *undo data* if needed.

Buffer I/O

This refers to the reads and writes of buffers in the buffer cache. When the requested buffer is not available, the Oracle database performs a physical IO and retrieves the buffer either from the flash cache or from the magnetic disk and loads it into the buffer cache. Then, a logical IO is performed to read the requested buffer from the buffer cache.

Buffer Writes

The *Database writer* (DBW) regularly writes cold and dirty buffers to the disk when,

1) A server process is unable to find clean buffers for writing new blocks into the buffer cache.

2) The database must advance the checkpoint, which is the SCN in the redo thread where the instance recovery must begin.

3) The tablespaces are in Read-only state or offline.

Buffer Reads

When the number of unused buffer limit is low, the database must erase buffers from the buffer cache using the below algorithms,

- When the **Flash cache is disabled**, the database overwrites the existing clean buffers and reuses them. If the overwritten buffers are requested later, the database fetches them from the disk.

- When the **Flash cache is enabled**, the database writes the buffers into the flash cache and overwrites them in the buffer cache. If the overwritten buffers are requested later, the database fetches them from the flash cache instead of the disk.

Buffer Pools

The database buffer cache is divided into a collection of buffers for managing the blocks. We can manually configure the buffer pools in the below possible ways,

- **Default Pool** – This is where the blocks are normally cached unless we manually configure the pools separately.

- **Keep Pool** – This is dedicated to storing the frequently accessed blocks which are aged out due to lack of space in the buffer cache. This pool is mainly used for avoiding the physical IO operations from the disk by retaining the objects in the memory.

- **Recycle Pool** – This pool is used for avoiding the infrequently accessed blocks from occupying space in the buffer cache by storing them in here.

Redo Log Buffer

The *Redo log buffer* in the SGA is used for storing the redo logs that holds the changes made to the database so that we can reconstruct these changes if required in the future. The database processes regularly copy the redo entry from the user memory space into the SGA and takes up space in the buffer.

The background processes, LGWR (Log Writer Process) writes the redo log sequentially into the disk and the DBW (Database Writer Process) writes the data blocks into the disk in a scattered manner. As users don't have to wait for the DBW to complete its write operation, the performance of the database is better.

Note: The LOG_BUFFER initialization parameter specifies the amount of memory to be used for buffering the redo entries.

Shared Pool Buffer

The *Shared pool* cache available in the SGA is involved in almost every action performed in the database and contains various types of program data like Parsed SQL, PL/SQL code, System parameters, Data dictionary information, Parallel execution messages, and the Control structures. The Shared pool buffer allocates memory in LRU fashion, that is, the portions of memory in the buffer can age out if not used frequently. The Shared pool buffer is sized using the SHARED_POOL_SIZE initialization parameter.

The different components pertaining to the shared pool are,

Library Cache

This memory structure stores executable SQL and PL/SQL code that are shared by the database sessions. This includes both the soft and hard parsed representation of the SQL statement.

Data Dictionary Cache

This is the collection of database tables and views that contain information about the database, its structures, its health, and its users. This cache is accessed frequently during the SQL statement parsing.

Server Result Cache

Unlike the buffer cache, the Server result cache holds the result sets and not the data blocks. The Server result cache contains both the SQL query result cache and the PL/SQL function result cache.

Reserved Pool

This is the memory area that can be used for allocating large contiguous chunks of memory. Generally, the database allocates the memory from the shared pool in small chunks and loads large objects in them without requiring a single contiguous area, thus reducing the risk of running out of contiguous memory due to fragmentation. This pool allows the database to allocate large contiguous chunks infrequently for operations like SQL cursors, Java, or PL/SQL in a most efficient manner.

Large Pool

This memory area is intended for the memory allocations that are larger than what the shared pool can allocate. The large pool generally allocates memory for interaction with multiple databases, Message buffers used in the parallel execution of statements, and Buffers for RMAN IO process slaves. The Large pool is sized using the LARGE_POOL_SIZE initialization parameter.

Memory allocation in Large pool avoids memory fragmentation that could arise when the Shared pool allocates memory to the database. This is because, when the memory is allocated to a session by the Large pool, it will be held up until the session releases it.

Java Pool

This is the memory area where all the session-specific Java code and data within the JVM are stored, including the Java objects that are migrated to the Java session at the end of the call. The Java pool is sized using the JAVA_POOL_SIZE initialization parameter.

The statistics provided by the Java Pool Advisor provides information about the library cache memory used for Java and predict the changes in the size of the Java pool that affect the parse rate. These statistics reset when the advisor is turned OFF.

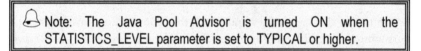

Note: The Java Pool Advisor is turned ON when the STATISTICS_LEVEL parameter is set to TYPICAL or higher.

Streams Pool

The *Streams pool* is exclusively used by Oracle streams for storing buffered queue messages and providing memory for capturing and applying processes. The Streams pool size starts with a zero until we configure it. The Streams pool is sized using the STREAMS_POOL_SIZE initialization parameter.

Process-private Memory

This memory is used for allocating memory for the operations such as sorting and hash joins.

In-Memory Column Store

This is an optional pool that can be used for storing the copies of tables and partitions in a columnar format for optimized rapid scans, aggregations, and joins. This memory structure does not replace the buffer cache but additionally stores the same data in a different format. By default, the objects that are defined INMEMORY will be populated in the IM column store. The In-Memory column store is sized using the INMEMORY_SIZE initialization parameter.

> 🔔 Note: This Pool is available only in the database version R12.1 and higher.

Database Memory Management Methods

The main motto of the database memory management is to reduce the physical IO overhead by either placing the required data in the memory or by efficiently retrieving the required data from the disk. To achieve this, the database memory caches must be properly set and effectively utilized. This can be done by properly managing the SGA and instance PGA memory structures.

- **SGA** stands for System Global Area. This consists of a group of shared memory structures, called as SGA components, that contains data and control information for one Oracle database instance shared by all server and background processes.

- **PGA** stands for Program Global Area. This is a non-shared memory containing the data and control information for every server and background processes. The collection of all PGAs is referred to as an *Instance PGA*.

Oracle provides the below methods to manage these memory structures, which are chosen by the initialization parameters.

Automatic Memory Management (AMM)

This is the recommended, automated and the simplest way to manage the instance memory by setting the two initialization parameters described below,

- **MEMORY_TARGET** – This dynamic parameter specifies the target memory size for which the database is tuned and redistributes the memory as needed between

---

the SGA and the instance PGA. As this is a dynamic parameter, there is no database restart required for changing it. With this set, the SGA_TARGET setting becomes the minimum size for the SGA and the PGA_AGGREGATE_TARGET setting becomes the minimum size of the instance PGA.

- **MEMORY_MAX_TARGET** – This static parameter specifies the maximum memory size, which defines the maximum limit for the MEMORY_TARGET parameter. As this parameter is static, it cannot be modified after the instance is started.

The total memory that the instance uses is solely based on the MEMORY_TARGET parameter and the instance automatically distributes the memory between the SGA and the instance PGA. Once the memory requirements change, the instance dynamically redistributes the memory again. Not enabling the Automatic Memory Management (AMM) leads us to manually set the size of the SGA and the instance PGA by using any of the below four methods.

> 🔔 Note: For tuning advice on the MEMORY_TARGET parameter, we must use the V$MEMORY_TARGET_ADVICE view.

Automatic Shared Memory Management (ASMM)

If Automatic Memory Management (AMM) is disabled, Oracle uses Automatic Shared Memory Management (ASMM) for managing the SGA memory. In this setting, Oracle automatically distributes the memory to individual SGA components based on the target size that we set for the total SGA memory using the SGA_TARGET initialization parameter. Changes in the value of this parameter resize the memory pools. If these pools are set to non-zero values, ASMM considers these values to be minimum levels. It is recommended to set these minimum values based on the minimum amount of memory an application component requires to function properly.

To enable Automatic Shared Memory Management,

1) We must set the STATISTICS_LEVEL to TYPICAL or ALL.

2) We must set the SGA_TARGET parameter to a non-zero value. This value must be less than or equal to the value of the SGA_MAX_SIZE initialization parameter (This parameter specifies the maximum size of the SGA for the lifetime of the

instance). This parameter can be set by querying the V$SGA_TARGET_ADVICE view and using the ALTER SYSTEM command.

To disable Automatic Shared Memory Management, we must set the value of the SGA_TARGET parameter to zero at instance startup.

When this mode is enabled, the sizes of the different SGA components adapts itself to the needs of the workload without any additional configuration. If we are using a Service Parameter file (SPFILE), the Oracle database remembers the sizes of the automatically tuned SGA components during the shutdown. Thus, the database instance does not need to recalculate the workload characteristics when the instance is started. Instead, it uses the previous instance information and continues to evaluate the workload before the shutdown.

The memory size of the Database Buffer cache, Shared Pool, Large Pool, Java Pool, and Streams Pool are automatically distributed by ASMM.

The below memory caches are not controlled by ASMM and are to be sized manually,

- Redo log buffer (Set by using the LOG_BUFFER initialization parameter).

- Other buffer caches like Keep (Set by using the DB_KEEP_CACHE_SIZE initialization parameter), Recycle (Set by using the DB_RECYCLE_CACHE_SIZE initialization parameter), and non-default block size.

- Fixed SGA and other internal allocations (Set by using the DB_nK_CACHE_SIZE initialization parameter).

> Note: The memory allocated to these parameters will be deducted from the value of the SGA_TARGET parameter when ASMM computes the values of the automatically tuned memory pools mentioned above.

Manual Shared Memory Management (MSMM)

If both the Automatic Memory Management (AMM) and the Automatic Shared Memory Management (ASMM) are disabled, then we must manually configure the SGA portion by setting the individual memory pools in the SGA. There is no separate initialization parameter for enabling this setting. To enable this setting, we just need to disable the Automatic Memory Management and the Automatic Shared Memory Management by setting the MEMORY_TARGET and the SGA_TARGET initialization parameters to 0 and then manually setting the various SGA components mentioned below.

The SGA components that have to be manually tuned for this setting are the Buffer cache, Shared pool, Large pool, Java pool, Streams pool, Result cache maximum size and other additional SGA initialization parameters.

Even though this method allows us to have more control over the SGA memory structure, more effort is required in maintaining the SGA components by manually configuring, monitoring and tuning them in a regular fashion as the database workload changes.

Automatic PGA Memory Management (APMM)

If Automatic Memory Management (AMM) is disabled, then the Oracle database uses Automatic PGA Memory Management (APMM) to manage its PGA memory. In this setting, Oracle database automatically distributes memory to work areas in the instance PGA based on the target size that we set for the total PGA memory using the PGA_AGGREGATE_TARGET initialization parameter. Oracle database tries to limit the PGA memory to this parameter value, but the system can exceed this limit sometimes. This overriding behavior in the memory limit can be controlled by setting the PGA_AGGREGATE_LIMIT initialization parameter, which poses a hard limit on the maximum PGA memory size limit. If this parameter is not set, Oracle database uses an appropriate default limit.

In this mode, all the configurations of the SQL work areas are automated and the various *_AREA_SIZE initialization parameters are ignored. During this mode, the WORKAREA_SIZE_POLICY must be set to AUTO. The total amount of PGA memory allocated to the active work areas is PGA_AGGREGATE_TARGET value minus the PGA memory allocated to the other components of the system. This memory is then allocated to the individual work areas based on their memory requirements.

Manual PGA Memory Management (MPMM)

If both the Automatic Memory Management (AMM) and the Automatic PGA Memory Management (APMM) are disabled, we must use this mode to manage the usage of the PGA memory manually by setting the SORT_AREA_SIZE, HASH_AREA_SIZE, BITMAP_MERGE_AREA_SIZE, and the CREATE_BITMAP_AREA_SIZE parameters to decide on the PGA memory to be allocated to the individual work areas.

In this mode, the WORKAREA_SIZE_POLICY must be set to MANUAL. This mode is not recommended as adjusting these parameters for the varying workload is a difficult task. Thus, Oracle database recommends us to use either AMM or APMM instead.

Introduction to the PL/SQL Virtual Machine

The PL/SQL Virtual Machine or the PVM is a database component that converts the user understandable program code into the machine code or the M code, makes calls to the database server, and returns the results to the calling environment. This PVM is actually written as a set of subroutines in C and placed as the Oracle executable.

Native and Interpreted Compilation Techniques

In versions prior to 9i, all the PL/SQL program units were compiled only in the Interpreted mode. In this mode, the PL/SQL units are compiled into a pseudocode, stored in the database, and interpreted at the run time. Even though this results in a very portable solution, it often has some performance issues compared to the natively compiled programs. To sort out this problem, Oracle has introduced the Native mode of compilation in its 9i release. This mode provides the capability to natively compile the PL/SQL program units into its appropriate C source code. Then, the Oracle executable writes this file out as an Operating System file and links it into shared libraries using the C compiler and linker commands located at the $ORACLE_HOME\plsql\spnc_commands file. This shared library is then loaded and executed during the corresponding PL/SQL unit's invocation at the runtime without any interpretation. To make this native compilation transparent to the users who are compiling the program and invoking it, we must configure it properly prior to its use.

This is the approach used in both the Oracle 9i and 10g releases, but the only difference was in the library file's storage location. In 9i, the shared library was stored in the file system, causing trouble with the RAC system and with the backup. This limitation was liberated in the 10g version by moving the shared libraries from the file system to the database dictionaries. Even though the shared library was moved into the data dictionary, they must be materialized in the file system during the runtime and compile time for OS related operations by setting the PLSQL_NATIVE_LIBRARY_DIR and the PLSQL_NATIVE_LIBRARY_SUBDIR_COUNT initialization parameters from the init.ora file. The materialization of these shared libraries in the file system is done automatically during the database startup. Starting from 10g, Oracle stores the result of the native compilation in the dictionary table, NCOMP_DLL$.

- **PLSQL_NATIVE_LIBRARY_DIR** initialization parameter is used by the PL/SQL compiler to specify the name of the directory where the shared libraries produced by the native compiler are stored.

- **PLSQL_NATIVE_LIBRARY_SUBDIR_COUNT** initialization parameter is used by the PL/SQL compiler to specify the number of subdirectories created in the directory specified by the *PLSQL_NATIVE_LIBRARY_DIR* parameter.

The performance improvement in the Native mode of compilation pitches in by reducing the runtime and the resources which taken by the Interpreted mode while scanning its M-Code. Both the Native mode and the Interpreted mode calls exactly the same PVM subroutine with the same set of arguments, but the difference is that the target machine code scanning effort for the Interpreted mode is during the runtime and for the Native mode it is moved from the runtime to the compile time, thus improving its runtime performance.

Even though the Native mode is a dream come true to the developers, it is a scary nightmare to the DBAs. This is because, the process is completely transparent to the developers, but makes the DBAs to do a whole lot of configuration setup by installing the C compiler, checking the *SPNC_COMMANDS* file from the *PLSQL* folder in the *Oracle home* directory, and setting up the *PLSQL_NATIVE_LIBRARY_DIR* and the *PLSQL_NATIVE_LIBRARY_SUBDIR_COUNT* initialization parameters. Also, there were customers who were not convinced installing the C compiler in their production systems and some were hesitant to pay to license the C compiler. These annoyances made the PL/SQL native mode of compilation underused in the Oracle 9i and 10g releases.

Real Native Compilation Technique

Oracle in its 11g release introduced the Real Native mode of compilation to remove the dependency on the C compiler, linker commands, and the initialization parameters by programming the Oracle executables to transform the machine code directly into the platform specific machine code and store it in the database without compromising on the compilation and the runtime.

As most of the dependencies are removed, the linker file (*SPNC_COMMANDS* file) and the initialization parameters (*PLSQL_NATIVE_LIBRARY_DIR* and *PLSQL_NATIVE_LIBRARY_SUBDIR_COUNT*) are made obsolete starting from the Oracle version 11g, thus reducing the responsibilities of the DBA on the configuration setup. The Real native mode of compilation also does not require the shared libraries to be materialized in the file system for any OS related operations.

The Real native mode of compilation is now controlled by the initialization parameter PLSQL_CODE_TYPE which can be set either in the SESSION level, SYSTEM level, or at the OBJECT_TYPE level as either NATIVE or INTERPRETED.

PLSQL_CODE_TYPE

This initialization parameter specifies the compilation mode for the PL/SQL units either at the database, session, or object level.

The prototype of the PLSQL_CODE_TYPE parameter is shown below,

```
PLSQL_CODE_TYPE=<INTERPRETED | NATIVE>;
```

> 🔔 Note: INTERPRETED is the mode with which the database is set during its creation.

- In the INTERPRETED mode, the PL/SQL program will be compiled into PL/SQL bytecode format, which is then executed by the PL/SQL engine.

- In the NATIVE mode, the PL/SQL program is compiled into the M-Code, which is executed natively by the database server during its runtime without incurring any interpreter overhead.

When this parameter is changed, it has no impact on the PL/SQL units that are already compiled as the PL/SQL units take the current compilation mode of the database only during their compilation.

The INTERPRETED mode of compilation tends to increase the performance of the PL/SQL program if it is frequently recompiled or if it spends most of its time executing SQLs. Thus, INTERPRETED mode generally opts the environment where the PL/SQL programs are still in their debugging phase of the development.

The NATIVE mode of compilation tends to increase the performance of the PL/SQL program if it has any computation intensive procedural operations, if it is called frequently with the same parameters by multiple sessions, or if it is recompiled rarely. Thus, NATIVE mode is generally suggested in an environment where the PL/SQL programs are in their production phase.

Altering the Compilation Mode of the Database

The compilation mode of the database can be set or altered using the PLSQL_CODE_TYPE initialization parameter at the SYSTEM level or at the SESSION level.

The prototype for setting the compilation mode either in the SYSTEM level or in the SESSION level is shown below,

```
ALTER <SYSTEM | SESSION> SET PLSQL_CODE_TYPE=<INTERPRETED | NATIVE>;
```

To alter the database for setting the compilation mode to NATIVE in the SYSTEM level is shown below,

```
ALTER SYSTEM SET PLSQL_CODE_TYPE=NATIVE;
```

```
System SET altered.
```

The current compilation mode of the database can be retrieved by,

1) Querying the V$PARAMETER table as shown below,

```
SELECT name, value FROM v$parameter WHERE name='plsql_code_type';
```

Script Result:

NAME	VALUE
plsql_code_type	NATIVE

Or by,

2) Executing the SHOW PARAMETER command as shown below,

```
SHOW PARAMETER PLSQL_CODE_TYPE;
```

```
NAME            TYPE    VALUE
--------------- ------- ------
plsql_code_type string  NATIVE
```

Altering the Compilation Mode of the Database Objects

The compilation modes can also be set at the object level using the ALTER statements.

The prototype for setting the compilation mode in the object level is shown below,

```
ALTER <OBJECT_TYPE> <OBJECT_NAME> COMPILE PLSQL_CODE_TYPE = <INTERPRETED |
NATIVE>;
```

If the object is recompiled without the *REUSE SETTINGS* clause, it takes the database's current compilation mode as its own. With this clause included in the compilation script, the object retains the mode it was last compiled in, instead of the database's current mode.

The prototype for compiling an object is shown below,

```
ALTER <OBJECT_TYPE> <OBJECT_NAME> COMPILE [BODY] [REUSE SETTINGS];
```

This scenario can be explained with the below examples,

Firstly, the compilation mode of the database is displayed as shown below,

```
SELECT name, value FROM v$parameter WHERE name='plsql_code_type';
```

Script Result:

NAME	VALUE
plsql_code_type	INTERPRETED

Then, a test procedure is created as shown below,

```
CREATE OR REPLACE PROCEDURE proc_test
IS
BEGIN
  dbms_output.put_line('This is a test procedure');
END;
/
```

```
Procedure PROC_TEST compiled
```

After the procedure is created, its compilation mode can be verified by querying the USER_PLSQL_OBJECT_SETTINGS data dictionary table as shown below,

```
SELECT name,
  type,
  plsql_code_type
FROM user_plsql_object_settings
WHERE name='PROC_TEST';
```

Script Result:

NAME	TYPE	PLSQL_CODE_TYPE
PROC_TEST	PROCEDURE	INTERPRETED

> ⚐ Note: The default compilation mode for the procedure will be the database's current mode.

Now, we can alter the current compilation mode of the above procedure to NATIVE by issuing the below ALTER statement,

```
ALTER PROCEDURE PROC_TEST COMPILE PLSQL_CODE_TYPE=NATIVE;
```

```
Procedure PROC_TEST altered.
```

Once the compilation mode is altered, we can verify it by querying the USER_PLSQL_OBJECT_SETTINGS data dictionary table again as shown below,

```
SELECT name,
  type,
  plsql_code_type
FROM user_plsql_object_settings
WHERE name='PROC_TEST';
```

Script Result:

NAME	TYPE	PLSQL_CODE_TYPE
PROC_TEST	PROCEDURE	NATIVE

The shared library file generated for the objects, which are in the NATIVE compilation mode are stored in the NCOMP_DLL$ table. For the procedure PROC_TEST, the generated shared library can be verified by executing the below query,

```
SELECT uo.object_name,
  uo.object_type,
  nd.dll,
  nd.dllname
FROM ncomp_dll$ nd,
  user_objects uo
WHERE nd.obj#  =uo.object_id
AND object_name='PROC_TEST';
```

Query Result:

OBJECT_NAME	OBJECT_TYPE	DLL	DLLNAME
PROC_TEST	PROCEDURE	(BLOB)	50524F435F544553545F5F5359535F5F 505F5F3938333437

The DLL is stored in the form of BLOB data as shown in the above query result.

When we try to recompile the procedure PROC_TEST with the *REUSE SETTINGS* clause, the mode in which the procedure is previously compiled is reused. In this case, the NATIVE mode is reused for the procedure instead of the database's current mode (INTERPRETED).

```
ALTER PROCEDURE PROC_TEST COMPILE REUSE SETTINGS;
```

```
Procedure PROC_TEST altered.
```

```
SELECT name,
   type,
   plsql_code_type
FROM user_plsql_object_settings
WHERE name='PROC_TEST';
```

Script Result:

NAME	TYPE	PLSQL_CODE_TYPE
PROC_TEST	PROCEDURE	NATIVE

When we recompile the procedure PROC_TEST without the *REUSE SETTINGS* clause, the procedure uses the database's current mode as its own. In this case, the database's current mode (INTERPRETED) is used.

```
ALTER PROCEDURE PROC_TEST COMPILE;
```

```
Procedure PROC_TEST altered.
```

```
SELECT name,
   type,
   plsql_code_type
FROM user_plsql_object_settings
WHERE name='PROC_TEST';
```

Script Result:

NAME	TYPE	PLSQL_CODE_TYPE
PROC_TEST	PROCEDURE	INTERPRETED

Altering the Compilation Mode of All the Objects in the Database

We can alter all the objects in the database to either NATIVE or INTERPRETED using the *dbmsupgnv.sql* or *dbmsupgin.sql* scripts respectively. These scripts are available in the $ORACLE_HOME/rdbms/admin/ directory.

> 🔔 Note: As the TYPE specifications and LIBRARY objects do not contain any SQL or PL/SQL code in them, they are not recompiled by the *dbmsupgnv.sql* script to NATIVE mode by default.

Compiling the entire database objects to NATIVE mode could diversely affect the performance of the database, if not done cautiously. We must consider the below pointers before determining whether to use either INTERPRETED or NATIVE mode of compilation for all the database objects.

We must choose to compile all the database objects to INTERPRETED mode,

1) When we have our database objects in their development stage and have them frequently debugged and recompiled.

2) When we have our PL/SQL units spend most of their time running SQLs rather PL/SQLs.

3) When we want the largest number (typically over 15,000) of PL/SQL units to be simultaneously active. Native mode uses shared memory for its PL/SQL units and having these many programs active could affect the system performance.

We must choose to compile all the database objects to NATIVE mode,

1) When we have our database objects in their production stage and have them rarely compiled or debugged.

2) When we have our PL/SQL units spend most of their time running computation-intensive PL/SQLs rather SQLs.

3) When we have many sessions invoking a PL/SQL unit that is compiled NATIVE, it is fetched from the SYSTEM tablespace into shared memory only once irrespective of the number of sessions invoking it. Once it is not used by any session, its space in the shared memory will be freed, thus reducing the memory load.

The following example describes how all the PL/SQL units in the database can be recompiled to NATIVE mode of compilation.

Step 1: Shut down all the Application services, and the TNS listeners either in *normal* or *immediate* mode using the SYS login as shown,

```
C:\Windows\system32>sqlplus /nolog

SQL*Plus: Release 12.1.0.2.0 Production on Sun Dec 11 01:56:10 2016

Copyright (c) 1982, 2014, Oracle.  All rights reserved.

SQL> CONN SYS AS SYSDBA
Enter password:
Connected.
SQL> shutdown immediate
```

```
Database closed.
Database dismounted.
ORACLE instance shut down.
```

Step 2: Start up the database in the *upgrade* mode to start the upgrade process.

```
SQL> startup upgrade
```

```
ORACLE instance started.

Total System Global Area 1694498816 bytes
Fixed Size                   3046416 bytes
Variable Size             1006633968 bytes
Database Buffers           671088640 bytes
Redo Buffers                13729792 bytes
Database mounted.
Database opened.
```

Step 3: Run the *$ORACLE_HOME/rdbms/admin/dbmsupgnv.sql* script as the SYS user. This script will update the compilation modes of all the database objects to NATIVE in their corresponding entry in the data dictionary tables. Note that this script will either complete successfully or rollback all the changes.

Note 1: The Package specifications rarely contain any executable code. Thus, to exclude the package specifications from recompilation by the *dbmsupgnv.sql* script to NATIVE mode, we must pass the command line parameter *True* along with the script. *False* is the default value, and it accepts the package specifications for recompilation.

Note 2: The *dbmsupgin.sql* script does not accept any command line parameters and does not skip any PL/SQL units.

```
SQL> @
C:\app\BoobalGanesan\product\12.1.0\dbhome_1\RDBMS\ADMIN\dbmsupgnv.sql True
```

PLSQL_CODE_TYPE   **617**

This script compiles all the PL/SQL units in the database in NATIVE mode but also invalidates them. Also, we have excluded the PACKAGE specifications for the compilation mode update by passing the command-line parameter value as *True*.

Step 4: Shutdown and Restart the database in *normal* mode.

```
SQL> shutdown normal

Database closed.
Database dismounted.
ORACLE instance shut down.
```

```
SQL> startup

ORACLE instance started.

Total System Global Area 1694498816 bytes
Fixed Size                  3046416 bytes
Variable Size            1006633968 bytes
Database Buffers          671088640 bytes
Redo Buffers               13729792 bytes
Database mounted.
Database opened.
```

Step 5: Set the PLSQL_CODE_TYPE initialization parameter to NATIVE at the SYSTEM level. This parameter will retain all the subsequently compiled PL/SQL units to NATIVE mode.

Step 6: Even though the invalidated PL/SQL units are recompiled automatically during their subsequent invocations, it is recommended that we validate them manually by using the *$ORACLE_HOME/rdbms/admin/utlrp.sql* script to avoid the on-demand recompilation latencies. If this script fails, we should re-run it to validate any remaining PL/SQL units that are still invalidated.

> Note: Before executing the *utlrp.sql* script, there should be no other session executing any DDL scripts as it could cause a possible deadlock. Thus, the database should be enabled in the RESTRICTED SESSION mode prior to the script execution.

```
SQL> ALTER SYSTEM ENABLE RESTRICTED SESSION;

System altered.
```

```
SQL> @C:\app\BoobalGanesan\product\12.1.0\dbhome_1\RDBMS\ADMIN\utlrp.sql
```

Step 7: After the execution of the *utlrp.sql* script is completed successfully, the database can disable the RESTRICTED SESSION mode that was previously enabled.

```
SQL> ALTER SYSTEM DISABLE RESTRICTED SESSION;
```

```
System altered.
```

We can now see that all the database objects except TYPE, LIBRARY (as they are not included in the *dbmsupgnv.sql* script for the compilation mode change), and PACKAGE specification (as we have excluded them during the update process by passing the command-line parameter value as *True*) by issuing the below query,

```
SELECT DISTINCT plsql_code_type
FROM all_plsql_object_settings
WHERE type NOT IN ('PACKAGE','TYPE','LIBRARY');
```

Script Result:

PLSQL_CODE_TYPE
NATIVE

To upgrade the database objects to INTERPRETED mode, we must replace the script *dbmsupgnv.sql* in Step 3 with the script *dbmsupgin.sql* and exclude the command-line parameter.

PLSQL_OPTIMIZE_LEVEL

Prior to the Oracle version 10gR1, the PL/SQL compiler does not apply any changes to the PL/SQL unit to improve their performance while translating them to the system code. In the release 10gR1, Oracle has introduced the initialization parameter PLSQL_OPTIMIZE_LEVEL to instruct the PL/SQL optimizer automatically to rearrange the source code, remove redundant and unreachable code, transform the FOR loops to Bulk Collect, and inline the subroutines for better performance. The PL/SQL optimizer performs the optimization techniques based on the level value that is set for the PLSQL_OPTIMIZE_LEVEL parameter. The possible values allowed for this parameter are 0, 1, 2 (Default), 3 (11g and higher only). The higher the value set for this parameter, the more the effort the PL/SQL optimizer makes to optimize the PL/SQL units.

Note: We must make sure that the SQL within the PL/SQL is tuned
properly before getting into the PL/SQL code optimization.

The prototype of the PLSQL_OPTIMIZE_LEVEL initialization parameter is shown below,

```
PLSQL_OPTIMIZE_LEVEL=<0|1|2|3>;
```

Where 2 is the default.

Altering the Optimization Level of the Database

The PL/SQL optimization level of the database can be set or altered using the PLSQL_OPTIMIZE_LEVEL initialization parameter at the SYSTEM level or at the SESSION level.

The prototype for setting the optimization level either at the SYSTEM or SESSION level is shown below,

```
ALTER <SYSTEM | SESSION> SET PLSQL_OPTIMIZE_LEVEL=<0|1|2|3>;
```

To alter the database for setting the optimization level to 3 in the SYSTEM level is shown below,

```
ALTER SYSTEM SET PLSQL_OPTIMIZE_LEVEL=3;
```

```
System SET altered.
```

The current optimization level of the database can be retrieved by,

1) Querying the V$PARAMETER table as shown below,

```
SELECT name, value FROM v$parameter WHERE name='plsql_optimize_level';
```

Script Result:

NAME	VALUE
plsql_optimize_level	3

Or by,

2) Executing the SHOW PARAMETER command as shown below,

Advanced PL/SQL Programming

```
SHOW PARAMETER PLSQL_OPTIMIZE_LEVEL;

NAME                  TYPE     VALUE
-------------------- -------- -----
plsql_optimize_level integer  3
```

Altering the Optimization Level of the Database Objects

The optimization level can also be set at the object level by using the ALTER statement.

The prototype for setting the optimization at the object level is shown below,

```
ALTER <OBJECT_TYPE> <OBJECT_NAME> COMPILE PLSQL_OPTIMIZE_LEVEL = <0|1|2|3>;
```

If the object is recompiled without the *REUSE SETTINGS* clause, it takes the database's current optimization level as its own. With this clause included in the compilation script, the object retains the optimization level it was last compiled, instead of the database's current optimization level.

The prototype for compiling an object is shown below,

```
ALTER <OBJECT_TYPE> <OBJECT_NAME> COMPILE [BODY] [REUSE SETTINGS];
```

This scenario can be explained with the below examples,

Firstly, the optimization level of the database is displayed as shown below,

```
SELECT name, value FROM v$parameter WHERE name='plsql_code_type';
```

Script Result:

NAME	VALUE
plsql_optimize_level	3

Then, a test procedure is created for the further demonstration of the PLSQL_OPTIMIZE_LEVEL parameter.

```
1.  CREATE OR REPLACE PROCEDURE proc_test authid current_user
2.  IS
3.  l_pi_start_time pls_integer;
4.  l_pi_end_time pls_integer;
5.  l_pi_cpu_start_time pls_integer;
6.  l_pi_cpu_end_time pls_integer;
7.  l_pi_var1 pls_integer;
8.  l_pi_var2 pls_integer;
```

```
 9.  FUNCTION func_test(ip_pi_var1 pls_integer)
10.  RETURN pls_integer
11.  IS
12.  BEGIN
13.  RETURN ip_pi_var1+ip_pi_var1;
14.  END;
15.  BEGIN
16.  l_pi_start_time      :=NULL;
17.  l_pi_cpu_start_time  :=NULL;
18.  l_pi_start_time      :=dbms_utility.get_time;
19.  l_pi_cpu_start_time  :=dbms_utility.get_cpu_time;
20.  FOR i IN
21.  (SELECT object_name FROM dba_objects
22.  )
23.  LOOP
24.  NULL;
25.  END LOOP i;
26.  FOR j IN
27.  (SELECT table_name,column_name FROM dba_tab_cols
28.  )
29.  LOOP
30.  l_pi_var2    :=0;
31.  l_pi_var2    :=1;
32.  END LOOP j;
33.  l_pi_var2    :=func_test(10);
34.  IF 1         =1 THEN
35.  l_pi_var2 :=100;
36.  ELSE
37.  l_pi_var2:=1000;
38.  END IF;
39.  Null;
40.  l_pi_end_time      :=dbms_utility.get_time;
41.  l_pi_cpu_end_time :=dbms_utility.get_cpu_time;
42.  dbms_output.put_line( 'Program run time: '||(l_pi_end_time -
     l_pi_start_time)/100||' Seconds');
43.  dbms_output.put_line( 'CPU run time: '||(l_pi_cpu_end_time -
     l_pi_cpu_start_time)/100||' Seconds');
44.  END;
45.  /
```

```
Procedure PROC_TEST compiled
```

After the procedure is created, its compilation mode can be verified by querying the USER_PLSQL_OBJECT_SETTINGS data dictionary table as shown below,

```
SELECT name,
  type,
  plsql_optimize_level
FROM user_plsql_object_settings
WHERE name='PROC_TEST';
```

Script Result:

NAME	TYPE	PLSQL_OPTIMIZE_LEVEL
PROC_TEST	PROCEDURE	3

Now, we can alter the current optimization level of the above procedure to 2 by issuing the below ALTER statement,

```
ALTER PROCEDURE PROC_TEST COMPILE PLSQL_OPTIMIZE_LEVEL=2;
```

```
Procedure PROC_TEST altered.
```

Once the optimization level is altered, we can verify it by querying the USER_PLSQL_OBJECT_SETTINGS data dictionary table again as shown below,

```
SELECT name,
   type,
   plsql_optimize_level
FROM user_plsql_object_settings
WHERE name='PROC_TEST';
```

Script Result:

NAME	TYPE	PLSQL_OPTIMIZE_LEVEL
PROC_TEST	PROCEDURE	2

When we try to recompile the procedure PROC_TEST with the *REUSE SETTINGS* clause, the Optimize level in which the procedure is previously compiled is reused. In this case, the level 2 is reused for the procedure instead of the database's current level (3).

```
ALTER PROCEDURE PROC_TEST COMPILE REUSE SETTINGS;
```

```
Procedure PROC_TEST altered.
```

```
SELECT name,
   type,
   plsql_optimize_level
FROM user_plsql_object_settings
WHERE name='PROC_TEST';
```

Script Result:

NAME	TYPE	PLSQL_OPTIMIZE_LEVEL
PROC_TEST	PROCEDURE	2

When we recompile the procedure PROC_TEST without the *REUSE SETTINGS* clause, the procedure uses the database's current optimization level as its own. In this case, the database's current optimization level (3) is used.

```
ALTER PROCEDURE PROC_TEST COMPILE;
```

```
Procedure PROC_TEST altered.
```

```
SELECT name,
  type,
  plsql_optimize_level
FROM user_plsql_object_settings
WHERE name='PROC_TEST';
```

Script Result:

NAME	TYPE	PLSQL_OPTIMIZE_LEVEL
PROC_TEST	PROCEDURE	3

Setting the PLSQL_OPTIMIZE_LEVEL parameter to "0"

In this setting, the PL/SQL optimizer does not optimize the program, but only maintains its evaluation order. It is not recommended to use this setting as it will forfeit most of the performance gains of the Oracle 12c compiler.

Also, with this setting, the PLSQL_CODE_TYPE parameter works only with the INTERPRETED mode of compilation and if we try to set it to NATIVE, we might encounter the PL/SQL warning, *PLW-06014: PLSQL_OPTIMIZE_LEVEL <= 1 turns off native code generation* stating that the NATIVE mode of compilation is turned OFF for the optimizer level <=1.

To demonstrate the functioning of this setting, we must first enable the session level PL/SQL warnings using the below ALTER statement,

```
ALTER SESSION SET PLSQL_WARNINGS='ENABLE:ALL';
```

To know more about PL/SQL warnings, please refer to the chapter 2, *Errors and Warnings in PL/SQL.*

Also, enable the NATIVE mode of compilation for the session by executing the below ALTER statement,

```
ALTER SESSION SET PLSQL_CODE_TYPE=NATIVE;
```

Now, we must recompile the procedure PROC_TEST with the PLSQL_OPTIMIZE_LEVEL parameter as "0" as shown below,

```
ALTER PROCEDURE PROC_TEST COMPILE PLSQL_OPTIMIZE_LEVEL=0;
```

After the procedure's optimizer level setting is lowered, we can check the warnings raised by querying the USER_ERRORS data dictionary table as shown below,

```
SELECT name,
  type,
  line,
  text,
  attribute
FROM user_errors
WHERE name='PROC_TEST';
```

Script Result:

NAME	TYPE	LINE	TEXT	ATTRIBUTE
PROC_TEST	PROCEDURE	0	PLW-06014: PLSQL_OPTIMIZE_LEVEL <= 1 turns off native code generation	WARNING
PROC_TEST	PROCEDURE	30	PLW-07206: analysis suggests that the assignment to 'L_PI_VAR2' may be unnecessary	WARNING

- The warning PLW-06014 in the above result set states that the NATIVE mode of compilation is disabled for the PLSQL_OPTIMIZE_LEVEL<=1.

- The warning PLW-07206 in the above result set states that the duplicate assigned to the variable L_PI_VAR2 is unnecessary. Even though the PL/SQL compiler recognizes it, it does not perform any action to improvise the code.

Finally, when we execute the PROC_TEST procedure with these settings, we get the below program and CPU run timings.

```
EXEC proc_test;
```

```
Results:

Program run time: 11.7 Seconds
CPU run time: 7.88 Seconds
```

Setting the PLSQL_OPTIMIZE_LEVEL parameter to "1"

In this setting, the PL/SQL compiler pitches in to perform a wide range of basic optimization techniques like skipping redundant and unnecessary code from the program without changing its original execution order.

The initialization parameter PLSQL_DEBUG, which was used for compiling PL/SQLs for debugging is now deprecated starting from the release R12.1. To enable debugging, we must set the PLSQL_OPTIMIZE_LEVEL parameter of the procedure to 1. So, having the deprecated parameter PLSQL_DEBUG set to True might issue the *PLW-06015: parameter PLSQL_DEBUG is deprecated; use PLSQL_OPTIMIZE_LEVEL = 1* warning.

To demonstrate the functioning of this setting, we must first enable the session level PL/SQL warnings using the below ALTER statement,

```
ALTER SESSION SET PLSQL_WARNINGS='ENABLE:ALL';
```

Also, enable the NATIVE mode of compilation and set the debug mode parameter to True for the session by executing the below ALTER statement,

```
ALTER SESSION SET PLSQL_CODE_TYPE=NATIVE;
ALTER SESSION SET PLSQL_DEBUG=TRUE;
```

Now, we must recompile the procedure PROC_TEST with the PLSQL_OPTIMIZE_LEVEL parameter as "1" as shown below,

```
ALTER PROCEDURE PROC_TEST COMPILE PLSQL_OPTIMIZE_LEVEL=1;
```

After the procedure's optimizer level is increased to 1, we can check the warnings raised by querying the USER_ERRORS data dictionary table as shown below,

```
SELECT name,
  type,
  line,
  text,
  attribute
FROM user_errors
WHERE name='PROC_TEST';
```

Script Result:

NAME	TYPE	LINE	TEXT	ATTRIBUTE
PROC_TEST	PROCEDURE	0	PLW-06015: parameter PLSQL_DEBUG is deprecated;	WARNING

			use PLSQL_OPTIMIZE_LEVEL = 1	
PROC_TEST	PROCEDURE	0	PLW-06014: PLSQL_OPTIMIZE_LEVEL <= 1 turns off native code generation	WARNING
PROC_TEST	PROCEDURE	30	PLW-07206: analysis suggests that the assignment to 'L_PI_VAR2' may be unnecessary	WARNING

- The warning PLW-06015 in the above result set indicates that the parameter PLSQL_DEBUG is deprecated and suggests us to use the PLSQL_OPTIMIZE_LEVEL=1 setting instead.

- The warning PLW-06014 in the above result set states that the NATIVE mode of compilation is disabled with the PLSQL_OPTIMIZE_LEVEL<=1 setting. Thus, the PLSQL_OPTIMIZE_LEVEL parameter value in either 0 or 1 is suitable only for INTERPRETED mode of compilation.

- Warning PLW-07206 in the above result set indicates that the redundant assignment to the variable L_PI_VAR2 is unnecessary and skips them during the program execution.

Finally, when we execute the PROC_TEST procedure with these settings, we get the below program and CPU run timings.

```
EXEC proc_test;
```

Results:

```
Program run time: 8.67 Seconds
CPU run time: 6.06 Seconds
```

Here, we can see a gain of ~30% in both the program run time and in the CPU run time from the previous optimizer setting, as the below described redundant codes are skipped from the program source code during its execution.

Redundant Codes in the Source Code are:

1) The *null* assignment to the variables, L_PI_START_TIME and L_PI_CPU_START_TIME in the line numbers 16 and 17 respectively, are already

null during their creation in the declaration section, thus making these two statements redundant.

2) The statements L_PI_VAR2=0 and L_PI_VAR2=1 are redundant as it assigns a literal integer for every iteration inside the loop. Also, the assignment of the first statement is overridden by the second statement. The PL/SQL compiler finds these properties, takes the first statement (L_PI_VAR2=0) out of the loop structure and skips the second statement (L_PI_VAR2=1) during the program execution.

Setting the PLSQL_OPTIMIZE_LEVEL parameter to "2"

This is the default optimization level, which engages in applying a wide range of sophisticated optimization techniques for the program by removing the dead code, removing unreachable code, explicitly inlining the subprograms, implicitly converting the FOR LOOPS into ARRAYs of bulk fetches, and refracting the source code as much as possible for better throughput.

To demonstrate the functioning of this setting, we must first enable the session level PL/SQL warnings using the below ALTER statement,

```
ALTER SESSION SET PLSQL_WARNINGS='ENABLE:ALL';
```

Also, enable the NATIVE mode of compilation for the session by executing the below ALTER statement,

```
ALTER SESSION SET PLSQL_CODE_TYPE=NATIVE;
```

Now, we must recompile the procedure PROC_TEST with the PLSQL_OPTIMIZE_LEVEL parameter as "2" as shown below,

```
ALTER PROCEDURE PROC_TEST COMPILE PLSQL_OPTIMIZE_LEVEL=2;
```

After the procedure's optimizer level is increased to 2, we can check the warnings raised by querying the USER_ERRORS data dictionary table as shown below,

```
SELECT name,
   type,
   line,
   text,
   attribute
FROM user_errors
WHERE name='PROC_TEST';
```

Script Result:

NAME	TYPE	LINE	TEXT	ATTRIBUTE
PROC_TEST	PROCEDURE	31	PLW-07206: analysis suggests that the assignment to 'L_PI_VAR2' may be unnecessary	WARNING
PROC_TEST	PROCEDURE	30	PLW-07206: analysis suggests that the assignment to 'L_PI_VAR2' may be unnecessary	WARNING
PROC_TEST	PROCEDURE	37	PLW-06002: Unreachable code	WARNING

- The warning PLW-07206 in the above result set indicates that the L_PI_VAR2 variable assignments inside the loop are unnecessary and the PL/SQL compiler removes them from the execution.

- The warning PLW-06002 in the above result set indicates that there is an unreachable code present in the program source code and the PL/SQL compiler removes it from the execution.

Finally, when we execute the PROC_TEST procedure with these settings, we get the below program and CPU run timings.

```
EXEC proc_test;
```

Results:

```
Program run time: 3.38 Seconds
CPU run time: 3.46 Seconds
```

Here, we can see a gain of ~90% in both the program run time and in the CPU run time from the previous optimizer setting. The reason for the performance improvement are described below,

1) Alongside with the dead code removal, this setting also works with the unreachable code, fixes them, and engages in a performance centric code restructuring.

2) This setting along with NCOMP mode converts all the FOR loops into ARRAY fetches with a limit of 100. This is shown by the result of the trace file output displayed below for the PLSQL_OPTIMIZE_LEVEL>=2 and PLSQL_OPTIMIZE_LEVEL<=1 settings.

Trace File Output for all recursive statements for PLSQL_OPTIMIZE_LEVEL<=1

CALL	COUNT	CPU	ELAPSED	DISK	QUERY	CURRENT	ROWS
Parse	2	0.00	0.00	0	0	0	0
Execute	2	0.00	0.22	0	0	0	0
Fetch	224210	4.15	4.36	0	119963	0	224208
----------	----------	--------	-------------	--------	----------	-------------	----------
		-		-			
Total	**224214**	4.15	4.36	0	119963	0	**224208**

The above trace file output is scripted out when the procedure code was executed with the PLSQL_OPTIMIZE_LEVEL parameter value set to <=1. The total number of rows processed is 2,24,208 and the total fetch operations performed is 2,24,214. This indicates that approximately 1 row is fetched for each fetch operation, resulting in CPU overhead and context switching.

Trace File Output for all recursive statements for PLSQL_OPTIMIZE_LEVEL>=2

CALL	COUNT	CPU	ELAPSED	DISK	QUERY	CURRENT	ROWS
Parse	2	0.00	0.00	0	0	0	0
Execute	2	0.00	0.22	0	0	0	0
Fetch	2243	1.92	2.01	0	19138	0	224208
----------	----------	--------	-------------	--------	----------	-------------	----------
		-		-			
Total	**2247**	1.92	2.25	0	19138	0	**224208**

The above trace file output is scripted out when the procedure code was executed with the PLSQL_OPTIMIZE_LEVEL parameter value set to >=2 in the NCOMP mode. The total number of rows processed is 2,24,208 and the total fetches performed is 2,247. This shows that the recursive statements are implicitly converted into ARRAY fetches with a limit of 100.

We can also explicitly inline the local subprograms used by the source code by issuing the PRAGMA INLINE compiler directive, which is explained in the later section.

Setting the PLSQL_OPTIMIZE_LEVEL parameter to "3"

This setting is introduced in the Oracle version 11g. This setting engages in the implicit inlining of suitable local subprograms along with all the optimization techniques performed by the PLSQL_OPTIMIZE_LEVEL=2 setting, i.e., dead code removal, converting recursive statements into ARRAY fetches with a limit of 100, unreachable code removal, and immense code restructuring.

> 🔔 Note: We cannot see the modified code after the optimization as the source code is compiled and then optimized. Not optimized and then compiled.

To demonstrate the functioning of this setting, we must first enable the session level PL/SQL warnings using the below ALTER statement,

```
ALTER SESSION SET PLSQL_WARNINGS='ENABLE:ALL';
```

Also, enable the NATIVE mode of compilation for the session by executing the below ALTER statement,

```
ALTER SESSION SET PLSQL_CODE_TYPE=NATIVE;
```

Now, we must recompile the procedure PROC_TEST with the PLSQL_OPTIMIZE_LEVEL parameter as "3" as shown below,

```
ALTER PROCEDURE PROC_TEST COMPILE PLSQL_OPTIMIZE_LEVEL=3;
```

After the procedure's optimizer level is increased to 3, we can check the warnings raised by querying the USER_ERRORS data dictionary table as shown below,

```
SELECT name,
  type,
  line,
  text,
  attribute
FROM user_errors
WHERE name='PROC_TEST';
```

Script Result:

NAME	TYPE	LINE	TEXT	ATTRIBUTE
PROC_TEST	PROCEDURE	33	PLW-06005: inlining of call of procedure 'FUNC_TEST' was done	WARNING
PROC_TEST	PROCEDURE	9	PLW-06006: uncalled procedure "FUNC_TEST" is removed.	WARNING
PROC_TEST	PROCEDURE	37	PLW-06002: Unreachable code	WARNING

- The warning PLW-06005 in the above result set indicates that the local subprogram is inlined implicitly. I.e., the local subprogram call is replaced with its source code to improve the performance of its execution.

- The warning <u>PLW-06002</u> in the above result set indicates that there is an unreachable code present in the program source code and the PL/SQL compiler removes it from the execution.

Finally, when we execute the PROC_TEST procedure with these settings, we get the below program and CPU run timings.

```
EXEC proc_test;
```

Results:

```
Program run time: 1.44 Seconds
CPU run time: 1.40 Seconds
```

Here, we can see a gain of ~50% in both the program run time and in the CPU run time from the previous optimizer setting by automatically inlining the local subprograms along with a wide range of other optimization techniques.

PRAGMA INLINE

A Pragma is a compiler directive, that instructs the compiler at the program compile time and not at runtime. The INLINE pragma is introduced in the Oracle version 11g for inlining the local subprograms on demand. Intra-unit in-lining or subprogram inlining refers to the replacement of the local subprogram calls with its body for better performance and optimization of the program execution.

The prototype for defining the INLINE pragma is shown below,

```
PRAGMA INLINE ('<Subprogram_name>', <'YES' | 'NO'>);
```

 Note 1: The parameters used by this pragma accepts only actual parameters and not formal parameters. That is, the parameter values to this pragma must be available during the compile time and not during the run time.

 Note 2: The single quotes used for all the three parameters are optional.

Any error in this pragma call will not result in any compilation error but just skips the pragma call.

- When we pass an inappropriate subprogram name as the first parameter in this pragma call, we might encounter the *PLW-05011: pragma INLINE for procedure 'PROC1' does not apply to any calls* warning.

- When we pass an inappropriate value as the second parameter in this pragma call, we might encounter the *PLW-05013: second parameter to pragma INLINE %S is not 'YES' or 'NO'* warning.

When a subprogram is not inlined during a program's execution, the calling program browses for the subprogram to be called, verifies its validity, executes the body content and returns the result to the calling program. The performance of this process is acceptable only if the called subprogram has large body content, called infrequently, and references many database objects.

When a subprogram is inlined during a program's execution, the program just replaces the subprogram call with its actual body content and executes as its own code. This process is recommended only if the subprogram has less code to perform, called frequently, and refers to less number of database objects.

The INLINE pragma can be used only when the PLSQL_OPTIMIZE_LEVEL parameter is set to 2 or 3. When the PLSQL_OPTIMIZE_LEVEL parameter is <=1, the inlining is turned off.

1) With the PLSQL_OPTIMIZE_LEVEL=2 setting, the INLINE pragma can be used for either turning ON or OFF the inlining option explicitly.

2) With the PLSQL_OPTIMIZE_LEVEL=3 setting, the INLINE pragma can be used only for turning OFF the inlining option as this setting automatically turns ON the inlining implicitly if the subprogram qualifies.

To demonstrate the functioning of the INLINE pragma, we must first enable the session level PL/SQL warnings using the below ALTER statement,

```
ALTER SESSION SET PLSQL_WARNINGS='ENABLE:ALL';
```

Also, enable the NATIVE mode of compilation for the session by executing the below ALTER statement,

```
ALTER SESSION SET PLSQL_CODE_TYPE=NATIVE;
```

To understand the subprogram inlining with the PLSQL_OPTIMIZE_LEVEL=2 setting, we must execute the below ALTER statement at the session level,

```
ALTER SESSION SET PLSQL_OPTIMIZE_LEVEL=2;
```

The below procedure with a local subprogram call is created for testing as shown,

```
1.   CREATE OR REPLACE PROCEDURE proc_inline
2.   IS
3.   PROCEDURE PROC
4.   IS
5.   BEGIN
6.   dbms_output.put_line('This is a local subprogram');
7.   END;
8.   BEGIN
9.   proc;
10.  END;
11.  /
```

When we execute this procedure, the local subprogram will not be implicitly inlined as it is not shown in the below USER_ERRORS data dictionary view,

```
EXEC proc_inline;
```

```
SELECT name,
  type,
  line,
  text,
  attribute
FROM user_errors
WHERE name='PROC_INLINE';
```

Script Result:

NAME	TYPE	LINE	TEXT	ATTRIBUTE
PROC_INLINE	PROCEDURE	1	PLW-05018: unit PROC_INLINE omitted optional AUTHID clause; default value DEFINER used	WARNING

When we modify the procedure by adding the PRAGMA INLINE compiler directive for inlining the subprogram as below,

```
1.   CREATE OR REPLACE PROCEDURE proc_inline
2.   IS
3.   PROCEDURE PROC
4.   IS
5.   BEGIN
6.   dbms_output.put_line('This is a local subprogram');
7.   END;
8.   BEGIN
9.   PRAGMA INLINE (PROC, YES);
10.  proc;
11.  END;
12.  /
```

We can see that the INLINE pragma statement in the above procedure has explicitly inlined the subprogram PROC as shown in the below USER_ERRORS view,

```
SELECT name,
  type,
  line,
  text,
  attribute
FROM user_errors
WHERE name='PROC_INLINE';
```

Script Result:

NAME	TYPE	LINE	TEXT	ATTRIBUTE
PROC_INLINE	PROCEDURE	1	PLW-05018: unit PROC_INLINE omitted optional AUTHID clause; default value DEFINER used	WARNING
PROC_INLINE	PROCEDURE	10	PLW-06004: inlining of call of procedure 'PROC' requested	WARNING
PROC_INLINE	PROCEDURE	10	PLW-06005: inlining of call of procedure 'PROC' was done	WARNING
PROC_INLINE	PROCEDURE	3	PLW-06006: uncalled procedure "PROC" is removed.	WARNING

The line numbers in the above script result-set displays the line at which inlining is requested and performed.

To understand the subprogram inlining with the PLSQL_OPTIMIZE_LEVEL=3 setting, we must execute the below ALTER statement,

```
ALTER SESSION SET PLSQL_OPTIMIZE_LEVEL=3;
```

The test procedure with a local subprogram call is created as shown,

```
1.   CREATE OR REPLACE PROCEDURE proc_inline
2.   IS
3.   PROCEDURE PROC
4.   IS
5.   BEGIN
6.   dbms_output.put_line('This is a local subprogram');
7.   END;
8.   BEGIN
9.   PROC;
10.  END;
11.  /
```

We can see that the local subprogram PROC is implicitly inlined with the program source code as shown in the below USER_ERRORS view,

---

```
SELECT name,
  type,
  line,
  text,
  attribute
FROM user_errors
WHERE name='PROC_INLINE';
```

Script Result:

NAME	TYPE	LINE	TEXT	ATTRIBUTE
PROC_INLINE	PROCEDURE	1	PLW-05018: unit PROC_INLINE omitted optional AUTHID clause; default value DEFINER used	WARNING
PROC_INLINE	PROCEDURE	9	PLW-06005: inlining of call of procedure 'PROC' was done	WARNING
PROC_INLINE	PROCEDURE	3	PLW-06006: uncalled procedure "PROC" is removed.	WARNING

When we update the procedure with the INLINE pragma call with its second parameter as NO for the subprogram, the automatic inlining is skipped as shown in the USER_ERRORS data dictionary view below,

```
1.  CREATE OR REPLACE PROCEDURE proc_inline
2.  IS
3.  PROCEDURE PROC
4.  IS
5.  BEGIN
6.  dbms_output.put_line('This is a local subprogram');
7.  END;
8.  BEGIN
9.  PRAGMA INLINE (PROC, NO);
10. PROC;
11. END;
12. /
```

```
SELECT name,
  type,
  line,
  text,
  attribute
FROM user_errors
WHERE name='PROC_INLINE';
```

Script Result:

NAME	TYPE	LINE	TEXT	ATTRIBUTE
PROC_INLINE	PROCEDURE	1	PLW-05018: unit PROC_INLINE omitted optional AUTHID clause; default value DEFINER used	WARNING
PROC_INLINE	PROCEDURE	10	PLW-06008: call of procedure 'PROC' will not be inlined	WARNING

When we add another INLINE pragma call (With its second parameter as YES) after the existing INLINE pragma call (Having its second parameter as NO) for the local subprogram, the automatic inlining is still skipped as the INLINE pragma with an NO overrides all further INLINE pragmas of the procedure.

```
1.   CREATE OR REPLACE PROCEDURE proc_inline
2.   IS
3.   PROCEDURE PROC
4.   IS
5.   BEGIN
6.   dbms_output.put_line('This is a local subprogram');
7.   END;
8.   BEGIN
9.   PRAGMA INLINE (PROC, NO);
10. PRAGMA INLINE (PROC, YES);
11. PROC;
12. END;
13. /
```

```
SELECT name,
  type,
  line,
  text,
  attribute
FROM user_errors
WHERE name='PROC_INLINE';
```

Script Result:

NAME	TYPE	LINE	TEXT	ATTRIBUTE
PROC_INLINE	PROCEDURE	1	PLW-05018: unit PROC_INLINE omitted optional AUTHID clause; default value DEFINER used	WARNING
PROC_INLINE	PROCEDURE	10	PLW-05010: duplicate pragma INLINE on procedure 'PROC'	WARNING
PROC_INLINE	PROCEDURE	11	PLW-06008: call of procedure 'PROC' will not be inlined	WARNING

When there is more than one call to the subprogram PROC after the INLINE pragma having its second parameter as NO, the pragma affects only the immediate declaration or the statement as shown below,

```
1.   CREATE OR REPLACE PROCEDURE proc_inline
2.   IS
3.   PROCEDURE PROC
4.   IS
5.   BEGIN
6.   dbms_output.put_line('This is a local subprogram');
7.   END;
8.   BEGIN
9.   PRAGMA INLINE (PROC, NO);
10. proc;
11. proc;
12. END;
13. /
```

```
SELECT name,
  type,
  line,
  text,
  attribute
FROM user_errors
WHERE name='PROC_INLINE';
```

Script Result:

NAME	TYPE	LINE	TEXT	ATTRIBUTE
PROC_INLINE	PROCEDURE	1	PLW-05018: unit PROC_INLINE omitted optional AUTHID clause; default value DEFINER used	WARNING
PROC_INLINE	PROCEDURE	10	PLW-06008: call of procedure 'PROC' will not be inlined	WARNING
PROC_INLINE	PROCEDURE	11	PLW-06005: inlining of call of procedure 'PROC' was done	WARNING

Tuning PL/SQL

We always choose SQL rather than PL/SQL as the right candidate for tuning, as the primary data actions are performed by SQL. There are situations where we need to concentrate on tuning the PL/SQL code, which can consume a large amount of CPU and memory. We must not wait until the PL/SQL program is completed and then tune it for performance. The below sections help us in understanding how we can tune the PL/SQL code as we write them.

Tuning the Logical Operators

PL/SQL evaluates the logical operators from its left-hand side to its right-hand side. Thus, placing the appropriate conditions that can determine the final outcome of the Boolean expression from the left reduces the number of evaluations that must be done, thus increasing the performance of the program. This is called as short-circuiting evaluation.

Short-circuit Evaluation of OR Operator

Placing the most likely expressions from the left-hand side of the OR operator helps the PL/SQL compiler to avoid evaluating the rest of the right-hand side expressions.

In the below example, a local function returning a Boolean *False* with a 5 second execution time is used as an evaluation expression along with a Boolean *True* to short-circuit the evaluation of the AND operator.

- When the least likely condition (FUNC_FALSE function) is used on the left-hand side and the most likely condition (Boolean True condition) is used as the second expression, the IF condition takes 5 seconds to complete executing both the expressions.

- When the most likely condition (Boolean True condition) is used on the left-hand side and the least likely condition (FUNC_FALSE function) is used as the second expression, the IF condition takes no time to complete as the first condition satisfies and exits the evaluation.

```
DECLARE
   l_n_start_time NUMBER;
   l_n_end_time   NUMBER;

   FUNCTION func_false
      RETURN BOOLEAN
   IS
   BEGIN
      dbms_lock.sleep(5);
      RETURN false;
   END;
BEGIN
   l_n_start_time:=dbms_utility.get_time;

   IF func_false OR true THEN
      NULL;
   END IF;

   l_n_end_time :=dbms_utility.get_time;

   dbms_output.put_line('Most likely condition at the right-hand side took
'||(l_n_end_time-l_n_start_time)/100||' Seconds');
   l_n_start_time:=dbms_utility.get_time;

   IF true OR func_false THEN
      NULL;
   END IF;

   l_n_end_time:=dbms_utility.get_time;

   dbms_output.put_line('Most likely condition at the left-hand side took
'||(l_n_end_time-l_n_start_time)/100||' Seconds');
END;
/
```

Results:

```
Most likely condition at the right-hand side took 5 Seconds
Most likely condition at the left-hand side took 0 Seconds
```

Short-circuit Evaluation of AND operator

Placing the least likely expressions from the left-hand side of the AND operator helps the PL/SQL compiler to avoid evaluating the rest of the right-hand side expressions.

In the below example, a local function returning a Boolean *True* with a 5 second execution time is used as an evaluation expression along with a Boolean *False* to short-circuit the evaluation of the AND operator.

- When the least likely condition (Boolean False condition) is used on the left-hand side and the most likely condition (FUNC_TRUE function) is used as the second expression, the IF condition takes no time to complete as the first condition exits the evaluation without needing to evaluate the second condition.

- When the most likely condition (FUNC_TRUE function) is used on the left-hand side and the least likely condition (Boolean False condition) is used as the second expression, the IF condition takes 5 seconds to complete as both the first and the second conditions are evaluated.

```
DECLARE
  l_n_start_time pls_integer;
  l_n_end_time pls_integer;

  FUNCTION func_true
    RETURN BOOLEAN
  IS
  BEGIN
    dbms_lock.sleep(5);
    RETURN true;
  END;
BEGIN
  l_n_start_time:=dbms_utility.get_time;

  IF func_true AND false THEN
    NULL;
  END IF;
  l_n_end_time :=dbms_utility.get_time;
  dbms_output.put_line('Least likely condition at the right-hand side took
'||(l_n_end_time-l_n_start_time)/100||' Seconds');
  l_n_start_time:=dbms_utility.get_time;

  IF false AND func_true THEN
    NULL;
  END IF;
  l_n_end_time:=dbms_utility.get_time;

  dbms_output.put_line('Least likely condition at the left-hand side took
'||(l_n_end_time-l_n_start_time)/100||' Seconds');
END;
/
```

```
Result:

Least likely condition at the right-hand side took 5 Seconds
Least likely condition at the left-hand side took 0 Seconds
```

Tuning the Branching Statements

PL/SQL evaluates the branching statements from top to bottom. Placing the most likely conditions from the top reduces the number of evaluations that must be done, thus increasing the performance of the program. In this section, we will be discussing on how to tune the CASE and IF..THEN..ELSIF statements.

Tuning CASE statements

In the below example, a local function returning a Boolean *false* with a 5-second delay is used as an evaluation expression along with a Boolean *True* for the CASE statement evaluation.

- When the least likely condition (FUNC_FALSE function) is used as the topmost expression and the most likely condition (Boolean True) is used as the second topmost expression, the CASE condition takes 5 seconds to complete as it evaluates both the first and the second expressions.

- When the most likely condition (Boolean True) is used as the top most condition and the least likely condition (FUNC_FALSE function) is used as the second topmost expression, the CASE condition takes no time to complete as the statement terminates just after evaluating the first expression.

```
DECLARE
  l_n_start_time pls_integer;
  l_n_end_time pls_integer;

  FUNCTION func_false
    RETURN BOOLEAN
  IS
  BEGIN
    dbms_lock.sleep(5);
    RETURN false;
  END;
BEGIN
  l_n_start_time:=dbms_utility.get_time;

  CASE
  WHEN func_false THEN
    NULL;
  WHEN true THEN
    NULL;
```

```
  END CASE;

  l_n_end_time :=dbms_utility.get_time;

  dbms_output.put_line('Least likely condition at the top took
'||(l_n_end_time-l_n_start_time)/100||' Seconds');

  l_n_start_time:=dbms_utility.get_time;

  CASE
  WHEN true THEN
    NULL;
  WHEN func_false THEN
    NULL;
  END CASE;

  l_n_end_time:=dbms_utility.get_time;

  dbms_output.put_line('Most likely condition at the top took
'||(l_n_end_time-l_n_start_time)/100||' Seconds');
END;
/
```

Results:

```
Least likely condition at the top took 5 Seconds
Most likely condition at the top took 0 Seconds
```

Tuning IF..THEN..ELSIF statements

In the below example, a local function returning a Boolean *false* with a 5-second delay is used as an evaluation expression along with a Boolean *True* for the IF..THEN..ELSIF statement evaluation.

- When the least likely condition (FUNC_FALSE function) is used as the topmost expression and the most likely condition (Boolean True) is used as the second topmost expression, the IF..THEN..ELSIF condition takes 5 seconds to complete as both the first and the second expression are evaluated.

- When the most likely condition (Boolean True) is used as the topmost expression and the least likely condition (FUNC_FALSE function) is used as the second topmost expression, the IF..THEN..ELSIF condition takes no time to complete as the statement terminates just after evaluating the first statement.

```
DECLARE
  l_n_start_time pls_integer;
  l_n_end_time pls_integer;

  FUNCTION func_false
    RETURN BOOLEAN
  IS
```

```
   BEGIN
     dbms_lock.sleep(5);
     RETURN false;
   END;
BEGIN
   l_n_start_time:=dbms_utility.get_time;

   IF func_false THEN
     NULL;
   elsif true THEN
     NULL;
   END IF;

   l_n_end_time :=dbms_utility.get_time;

   dbms_output.put_line('Least likely condition at the top took
'||(l_n_end_time-l_n_start_time)/100||' Seconds');

   l_n_start_time:=dbms_utility.get_time;

   IF true THEN
     NULL;
   elsif func_false THEN
     NULL;
   END IF;

   l_n_end_time:=dbms_utility.get_time;

   dbms_output.put_line('Most likely condition at the top took
'||(l_n_end_time-l_n_start_time)/100||' Seconds');
END;
/
```

Results:
```
Least likely condition at the top took 5 Seconds
Most likely condition at the top took 0 Seconds
```

Programming SQLs with Bind Variables

The bind variables play a vital role in the memory management and the performance enhancement of the PL/SQL blocks which contains SQL statements. When an SQL statement inside the PL/SQL block is executed multiple time with a unique value in its WHERE condition, it parses every single time. This is called as hard parsing.

```
DECLARE
   l_n_empno1 NUMBER:=100;
   l_n_empno2 NUMBER:=101;
   l_n_empno3 NUMBER:=102;
BEGIN
   EXECUTE immediate 'DELETE FROM emp WHERE empno='||l_n_empno1;
   EXECUTE immediate 'DELETE FROM emp WHERE empno='||l_n_empno2;
   EXECUTE immediate 'DELETE FROM emp WHERE empno='||l_n_empno3;
   COMMIT;
END;
/
```

By executing the V$SQL view with the appropriate columns, the parsing information related to the above statements can be gathered as like below,

```
SELECT sql_id,
    sql_text,
    first_load_time,
    hash_value
FROM v$sql
WHERE sql_text LIKE 'DELETE FROM employees WHERE employee_id=%';
```

Script output:

SQL_ID	SQL_TEXT	FIRST_LOAD_TIME	HASH_VALUE
74h6tddh415by	DELETE FROM EMP WHERE EMPNO=101	2016-12-17/15:57:58	1614845310
a53bt9r5nxg92	DELETE FROM EMP WHERE EMPNO=102	2016-12-17/15:57:58	3410935074
748vf6w35fk2b	DELETE FROM EMP WHERE EMPNO=100	2016-12-17/15:57:58	106383435

In the above result set, all three queries are parsed with different hash values.

However, when the query statement uses a bind variable instead of a hard-coded value, the query doesn't parse for the unique values of the bind variable, but just once, irrespective of the number of executions as the SQL statement uses its already parsed hash value stored in the shared SQL area of the database memory. This is called as soft parsing.

```
DECLARE
    l_n_empno1 NUMBER:=100;
    l_n_empno2 NUMBER:=101;
    l_n_empno3 NUMBER:=102;
BEGIN
    EXECUTE immediate 'DELETE FROM emp WHERE empno=:empno' USING l_n_empno1;
    EXECUTE immediate 'DELETE FROM emp WHERE empno=:empno' USING l_n_empno2;
    EXECUTE immediate 'DELETE FROM emp WHERE empno=:empno' USING l_n_empno3;
    COMMIT;
END;
/
```

Now, when we check the V$SQL view, the parsing information related to the above statements can be gathered as shown,

```
SELECT sql_id,
    sql_text,
    first_load_time,
    hash_value
FROM v$sql
WHERE sql_text LIKE 'DELETE FROM employees WHERE employee_id=%';
```

Script output:

SQL_ID	SQL_TEXT	FIRST_LOAD_TIME	HASH_VALUE
agudhkg04uu1p	DELETE FROM emp WHERE empno=:empno	2016-12-17/22:50:16	3226298421

We can compare the performance between the time taken by the hard parsed and soft parsed statements by creating the below table and inserting it with 10,000 rows using CONNECT BY LEVEL clause as shown.

```
CREATE TABLE tbl_bind_test (col1 NUMBER);

INSERT INTO tbl_bind_test
SELECT level FROM dual CONNECT BY level<=10000;

COMMIT;
```

Once the table is ready, we can loop it 10,000 times both with hard parsed and soft parsed variables so that we can compare the time taken by them both.

```
DECLARE
  l_n_count      NUMBER;
  l_n_start_time NUMBER;
  l_n_end_time   NUMBER;
BEGIN
  l_n_start_time:=dbms_utility.get_time;

  FOR loop_value IN 1..10000
  LOOP
    EXECUTE immediate 'SELECT COUNT(*) FROM tbl_bind_test WHERE
col1='||loop_value INTO l_n_count;
  END LOOP loop_value;

  l_n_end_time:=dbms_utility.get_time;

  dbms_output.put_line('Total time taken for executing hard parsed statement
in a loop: '||(l_n_end_time-l_n_start_time)/100||' Seconds');

  l_n_start_time:=dbms_utility.get_time;

  FOR loop_value IN 1..10000
  LOOP
    EXECUTE immediate 'SELECT COUNT(*) FROM tbl_bind_test WHERE col1=:col1'
INTO l_n_count USING loop_value;
  END LOOP loop_value;

  l_n_end_time:=dbms_utility.get_time;

  dbms_output.put_line('Total time taken for executing soft parsed statement
in a loop: '||(l_n_end_time-l_n_start_time)/100||' Seconds');
END;
/
```

```
Result:

Total time taken for executing hard parsed statement in a loop: 96.68
Seconds
Total time taken for executing soft parsed statement in a loop: 7.27 Seconds
```

With the above result, the time taken by the statement with bind variable took very less time compared to the one without bind variable.

Programming Parameters with Pass by Reference

The parameters of the subprograms in PL/SQL can be passed either by value or by its reference. The parameters in the "IN" mode are by default "passed by reference" and this cannot be changed. The parameters in the OUT or IN OUT mode are by default "passed by value", but this can be changed to "pass by reference" by using the NOCOPY hint in their declaration.

When we pass a parameter "by value", a copy of this parameter is assigned to the formal parameter of the subprogram. Any changes made to the parameter inside the subprogram have no impact on the original value that is passed.

When we pass a parameter "by reference", only the pointer to the location of the value is copied to the formal parameter instead of its value's copy. Any changes made to the parameter inside the subprogram affects the actual data as the modifications on the parameters inside the subprogram is done on the same memory location where the actual parameter resides.

> Note: If the OUT or IN OUT parameter of the subprogram is "passed by reference" and if the subprogram terminates midway of the execution by any exception, the value possessed by the parameters may no longer be valid.

Now, when we pass a large collection in OUT or IN OUT mode to the subprograms, they are "Passed by value" resulting in increased consumption of the available PGA memory leading to slowness in our session as well as other sessions that want to allocate the PGA memory.

In the below example, a nested table type with ~10 million elements is passed as input to the "Pass by value" and "Pass by reference" procedures. The session PGA memory consumed by both the procedures is captured using the V$MYSTAT and V$STATNAME tables as shown.

```
DECLARE
  l_n_start_sess_mem NUMBER;
  l_n_end_sess_mem    NUMBER;

type type_ntt
IS
  TABLE OF NUMBER;

  l_ntt_var1 type_ntt:=type_ntt();

FUNCTION func_sess_mem
  RETURN NUMBER
IS
  l_n_value NUMBER;
BEGIN
  SELECT ms.value
  INTO l_n_value
  FROM v$mystat ms,
    v$statname sn
  WHERE ms.statistic# = sn.statistic#
  AND sn.name          = 'session pga memory';
  RETURN l_n_value;
END;

PROCEDURE proc_pass_by_val(
    ip_ntt_var1 IN OUT type_ntt)
IS
  l_n_count NUMBER;
BEGIN
  l_n_count:=ip_ntt_var1.count;
END;

PROCEDURE proc_pass_by_ref(
    ip_ntt_var1 IN OUT nocopy type_ntt)
IS
  l_n_count NUMBER;
BEGIN
  l_n_count:=ip_ntt_var1.count;
END;
BEGIN
  l_ntt_var1.extend;
  l_ntt_var1(1):=1234567890;
  l_ntt_var1.extend(9999999,1);

  l_n_start_sess_mem:=func_sess_mem;
  proc_pass_by_val(l_ntt_var1);
  l_n_end_sess_mem:=func_sess_mem;

  dbms_output.put_line('The session PGA memory used by the "Pass by value"
procedure is '||(L_N_END_SESS_MEM-L_N_START_SESS_MEM)||' bytes');

  l_n_start_sess_mem:=func_sess_mem;
  proc_pass_by_ref(l_ntt_var1);
  l_n_end_sess_mem:=func_sess_mem;

  dbms_output.put_line('The session PGA memory used by the "Pass by
reference" procedure is '||(L_N_END_SESS_MEM-L_N_START_SESS_MEM)||' bytes');
END;
```

Results:

```
The session PGA memory used by the "Pass by value" procedure is 262144 bytes
The session PGA memory used by the "Pass by reference" procedure is 0 bytes
```

The above result states that the procedure with "pass by value" parameter takes a huge memory from the shared memory, whereas the procedure with "pass by reference" doesn't take any.

Yet, the NOCOPY hint always doesn't guarantee that the parameter will be "passed by reference". The situations where the parameters will not be passed by reference with the NOCOPY hint are,

1) When the call is a remote procedure call.

2) When the parameter involves an implicit conversion.

3) When an expression is passed as input to the parameter.

Avoiding NOT NULL Constraints

The PL/SQL variables that are declared with NOT NULL constraints will always perform a NOT NULL check on them during their every assignment. This will cause a performance degradation on the PL/SQL block's execution due to this additional check. To avoid this, we must create a null variable and explicitly enforce the NOT NULL constraint programmatically using the IF condition.

In the below example, a NOT NULL constrained variable and a Null variable with an explicitly enforced NOT NULL constraint gets assigned to integer values in a loop repetitively to find their Program runtime and CPU runtime.

```
DECLARE
  l_n_start_time NUMBER;
  l_n_end_time    NUMBER;
  l_n_cpu_start_time NUMBER;
  l_n_cpu_end_time    NUMBER;
  l_n_var1        NUMBER NOT NULL:=0;
  l_n_var2        NUMBER          :=0;
BEGIN
  l_n_start_time:=dbms_utility.get_time;
  l_n_cpu_start_time:=dbms_utility.get_cpu_time;

  FOR i IN 1..99999999
  LOOP
    l_n_var1:=i;
  END LOOP i;
```

```
  l_n_end_time :=dbms_utility.get_time;
  l_n_cpu_end_time:=dbms_utility.get_cpu_time;

  dbms_output.put_line('Run time taken by the NOT NULL constrained variable
is '||(l_n_end_time-l_n_start_time)/100||' Seconds');

  dbms_output.put_line('CPU time taken by the NOT NULL constrained variable
is '||(l_n_cpu_end_time-l_n_cpu_start_time)/100||' Seconds');

  l_n_start_time:=dbms_utility.get_time;
  l_n_cpu_start_time:=dbms_utility.get_cpu_time;

  FOR j IN 1..99999999
  LOOP
    IF j       IS NOT NULL THEN
      l_n_var2:=j;
    END IF;
  END LOOP j;

  l_n_end_time :=dbms_utility.get_time;
  l_n_cpu_end_time:=dbms_utility.get_cpu_time;

  dbms_output.put_line('Run time taken by the Null variable with explicit
NULL check is '||(l_n_end_time-l_n_start_time)/100||' Seconds');

  dbms_output.put_line('CPU time taken by the Null variable with explicit
NULL check is '||(l_n_cpu_end_time-l_n_cpu_start_time)/100||' Seconds');
END;
/
```

Results:

```
Run time taken by the NOT NULL constrained variable is 31.19 Seconds
CPU time taken by the NOT NULL constrained variable is 31.17 Seconds
Run time taken by the Null variable with explicit NULL check is 27.95
Seconds
CPU time taken by the Null variable with explicit NULL check is 27.93
Seconds
```

The above results state that the Runtime and the CPU time, taken by the *Null* variable with the explicit *Null* check is better than the NOT NULL constrained variable.

Avoiding Implicit Datatype Conversions

Whenever a value is assigned to a variable or passed as input parameter to a subprogram, an implicit datatype conversion takes place if the target type conflicts with the source data type. For example, if we assign a number value to a VARCHAR2 datatype, PL/SQL will convert it into a character value and store it in the variable. If we try to assign a string value to a NUMBER type, PL/SQL will convert it into a number value and store it in the variable provided that the string expression can be converted into a valid number value. However, these types of assignments may cause

---

Tuning PL/SQL   **649** performance degradation and result in a slower code. To reduce the implicit datatype conversions, we must use appropriate datatypes for the data storage. For example, we must not use a VARCHAR2 typed variable to store number or date values. Instead, we must use an appropriate datatype or anchored variables whenever possible in the PL/SQL blocks.

In the below example, the time taken by a NUMBER variable while storing a number value and character value of valid number format are retrieved for repetitive assignments using the FOR loop. The implicitly converted assignment loop takes 4 times as much as time taken by the unconverted assignment loop.

```
DECLARE
   l_n_start_time NUMBER;
   l_n_end_time   NUMBER;
   l_n_var1       NUMBER;
BEGIN
   l_n_start_time:=dbms_utility.get_time;

   FOR i IN 1..9999999
   LOOP
      l_n_var1:=TO_CHAR(i);
   END LOOP i;

   l_n_end_time :=dbms_utility.get_time;

   dbms_output.put_line('Run time taken by the implicitly converted variable
is '||(l_n_end_time-l_n_start_time)/100||' Seconds');

   l_n_start_time:=dbms_utility.get_time;

   FOR j IN 1..9999999
   LOOP
      l_n_var1:=j;
   END LOOP j;

   l_n_end_time :=dbms_utility.get_time;

   dbms_output.put_line('Run time taken by the explicitly converted variable
is '||(l_n_end_time-l_n_start_time)/100||' Seconds');
END;
/
```

Results:

```
Run time taken by the implicitly converted variable is 11.29 Seconds
Run time taken by the unconverted variable is 3.09 Seconds
```

Choosing COALESCE over NVL

The NVL and the COALESCE functions are basically the same. They return the first NOT NULL argument and if there are no NOT NULL arguments, they return *null*.

The main difference is that the NVL function accepts only two arguments, but the COALESCE function accepts a minimum of 2 and a maximum of 65535 arguments.

Another important difference between the NVL and COALESCE functions is that the NVL function evaluates both the arguments, but the COALESCE function stops its evaluation at the first occurrence of the not null argument. Because of this, there is a performance loss in the NVL function if the first argument is not null and the second argument consumes more time in its evaluation. This scenario is handled perfectly by the COALESCE function with two arguments.

In the below example, both the NVL and the COALESCE functions are passed with the literal "1" as their first argument and a function returning the literal "2" after a 5 second time gap as their second argument. The NVL function returns the first argument (literal "1") as it is the first NOT NULL argument but takes 5 seconds to finish the task as it also evaluates the second argument. The COALESCE function, on the other hand, returns the first argument (literal "1") as it is the first NOT NULL argument in no time as it doesn't have to evaluate the second argument.

```
DECLARE
   l_n_start_time NUMBER;
   l_n_end_time    NUMBER;
   l_n_var1        NUMBER;

   FUNCTION func_sleep
     RETURN NUMBER
   IS
   BEGIN
     dbms_lock.sleep(5);
     RETURN 2;
   END;
BEGIN
   l_n_start_time:=dbms_utility.get_time;
   l_n_var1       :=COALESCE(1,func_sleep);
   l_n_end_time   :=dbms_utility.get_time;

   dbms_output.put_line('Run time taken by the COALESCE function is
'||(l_n_end_time-l_n_start_time)/100||' Seconds');

   l_n_start_time:=dbms_utility.get_time;
   l_n_var1       :=NVL(1,func_sleep);
   l_n_end_time   :=dbms_utility.get_time;

   dbms_output.put_line('Run time taken by the NVL function is
'||(l_n_end_time-l_n_start_time)/100||' Seconds');
END;
/
```

Results:

```
Run time taken by the COALESCE function is 0 Seconds
Run time taken by the NVL function is 5 Seconds
```

Choosing the Appropriate Numeric Datatype

Most of the numeric datatypes are internal types that use library arithmetic to support portability across various applications. For e.g., NUMBER, INTEGER, FLOAT, etc. Because of this, they are very slow in performing intensive computations. However, Oracle introduced PLS_INTEGER in its version 7 to speed up the processing. PLS_INTEGERs uses machine arithmetic and does not support portability.

 Note: If a floating value is assigned to a PLS_INTEGER variable, it will be rounded off to the nearest integer value.

In the below example, both the NUMBER and the PLS_INTEGER variables are assigned to integer values repetitively in a loop. The time taken by the PLS_INTEGER variable is by far the best than the time taken by NUMBER variable.

```
DECLARE
  l_n_start_time NUMBER;
  l_n_end_time   NUMBER;
  l_n_var1 pls_integer;
  l_n_var2 NUMBER;
BEGIN
  l_n_start_time:=dbms_utility.get_time;

  FOR j IN 1..99999999
  LOOP
    l_n_var2:=j;
  END LOOP j;

  l_n_end_time :=dbms_utility.get_time;

  dbms_output.put_line('Run time taken by the NUMBER variable is
'||(l_n_end_time-l_n_start_time)/100||' Seconds');

  l_n_start_time:=dbms_utility.get_time;

  FOR i IN 1..99999999
  LOOP
    l_n_var1:=i;
  END LOOP i;

  l_n_end_time :=dbms_utility.get_time;

  dbms_output.put_line('Run time taken by the PLS_INTEGER variable is
'||(l_n_end_time-l_n_start_time)/100||' Seconds');
END;
/
```

Results:

```
Run time taken by the NUMBER variable is 26.54 Seconds
Run time taken by the PLS_INTEGER variable is 1 Seconds
```

Using Bulk Collect and FORALL for Performance

The Bulk Collect operation can be used in SELECT INTO, FETCH INTO, and RETURNING INTO statements for processing multiple records in a single fetch provided that the target variable must be a collection type. This operation can be used for reducing the context switching between the SQL and the PL/SQL engine by processing more than one row at a time with an increase in the CPU usage. As this is a CPU intensive task, this statement cannot be parallelized.

Consider the below FOR loop, that runs for every single row from the TABLE_NAME table.

```
BEGIN
  FOR i IN
  (SELECT * FROM table_name
  )
  LOOP
    -- Executable statements;
  END LOOP i;
END;
/
```

Starting from 10g, if the PLSQL_OPTIMIZE_LEVEL parameter is set to 2 or higher, the above FOR loop will be implicitly converted into an ARRAY fetch with a limit of 100 rows similar to the code shown below.

```
DECLARE
  CURSOR cur
  IS
    SELECT * FROM table_name;
type type_ntt
IS
  TABLE OF table_name%rowtype;
  l_ntt_var1 type_ntt;
BEGIN
  OPEN cur;
  LOOP
    FETCH cur bulk collect INTO l_ntt_var1 limit 100;
    EXIT
  WHEN cur%notfound;
    -- Executable statements;
  END LOOP;
  CLOSE cur;
END;
/
```

We can also use the BULK COLLECT clause to fetch all the rows pertaining to a single table as shown in the below listing,

```
DECLARE
type type_ntt
IS
  TABLE OF table_name%rowtype;
  l_ntt_var1 type_ntt;
BEGIN
  SELECT * bulk collect INTO l_ntt_var1 FROM table_name;
  -- Executable statements;
END;
/
```

The above block will result in better performance only if the table consists of fewer data. If the data set is more, it applies to more load on the CPU resulting in poor performance and slowness. This block must be converted into cursor FETCH INTO statement with an appropriate LIMIT in the case of large data.

The FORALL statement is not to be misunderstood for a loop. It processes only one DML statement once by sending them in bulk to the SQL engine unlike the FOR loop, which executes one or more DML statements row by row.

In the below example, a table is bulk collected into a nested table type and is processed with some business manipulation. Then, the nested table type variable is used for updating the primary table in bulk using the FORALL statement as shown below,

```
DECLARE
type type_ntt
IS
  TABLE OF table_name%rowtype;
  l_ntt_var1 type_ntt;
BEGIN
  SELECT * bulk collect INTO l_ntt_var1 FROM table_name;
  -- Executable statements
  forall i IN 1..l_ntt_var1.count
  UPDATE table_name
  SET column_name2 =l_ntt_var1(i).column_name2
  WHERE column_name1=l_ntt_var1(i).column_name1;
  COMMIT;
END;
/
```

Note, we must always try to convert this kind of blocks into a single SQL statement if at all possible. If the business conversion does not allow us to do this, only then we must go for bulk binding.

If any of the rows fails with an exception during the update process, the complete process will be terminated and the processed transactions will be rolled back. To avoid this, Oracle provides us the SAVE EXCEPTIONS clause. This clause can be used for logging the faulty records using the SQL%BULK_EXCEPTIONS array type while the proper records will be transacted normally. The SQL%BULK_EXCEPTIONS array type consists of two attributes as described below,

1) ERROR_INDEX: This attribute stores the faulty record's error index.

2) ERROR_CODE: This attribute stores the faulty record's exception message.

In the below example, the FORALL statement is backed up the SAVE EXCEPTIONS clause, which redirects the error prone records into the EXCEPTION block and then logs them for further actions.

```
DECLARE
type type_ntt
IS
  TABLE OF table_name%rowtype;
  l_ntt_var1 type_ntt;
  bulk_errors EXCEPTION;
  pragma exception_init(bulk_errors, -24381);
BEGIN
  SELECT * bulk collect INTO l_ntt_var1 FROM table_name;
  -- Executable statements
  forall i IN 1..l_ntt_var1.count SAVE exceptions
  UPDATE table_name
  SET column_name2  =l_ntt_var1(i).column_name2
  WHERE column_name1=l_ntt_var1(i).column_name1;
  COMMIT;
EXCEPTION
WHEN bulk_errors THEN
  FOR i IN 1..sql%bulk_exceptions.count
  LOOP
    dbms_output.put_line('Error Index is:
'||sql%bulk_exceptions(i).error_index);
    dbms_output.put_line('Error Message is: '||sqlerrm('-
'||sql%bulk_exceptions(i).error_code));
  END LOOP i;
END;
/
```

More examples of bulk binding are explained in *Chapter 6: The PL/SQL Types*.

Reducing Context Switching in Functions and Procedures

When we mix SQL and PL/SQL together, we get context switches. That is, the control is switched from the SQL engine to the PL/SQL engine and vice versa. This impacts the database by increasing the number of CPU processes and the time of execution of the program code. Oracle 12c has introduced two new features to reduce the impact of context switching. They are,

1) Functional and Procedural WITH clauses, and

2) Pragma UDF compiler directive.

The Functional and Procedural WITH clauses allows us to use the PL/SQL functions and procedures in SQL. Of course, we cannot call the procedure in SQL using the WITH clause, but we can call the procedure inside the function and call that function in SQL. These objects cannot be created, but only selected similarly to an SQL query.

The prototype for the Functional and Procedural WITH clause is shown below,

```
WITH
  PROCEDURE <Procedure_name> IS
  BEGIN
    <Execution_block>;
  END;
  FUNCTION <Function_name> RETURN <Datatype> IS
  BEGIN
    <Execution_block>;
  END;
SELECT <Function_name> FROM <Table_name>;
```

The Pragma UDF (User Defined Functions) directs the compiler that the function has to be prepared for execution in a SELECT statement to avoid context switching. Calling a function that is defined as UDF from PL/SQL might not provide any performance gain.

For demonstration, two functions with and without the PRAGMA UDF clause in its declaration section respectively, are created for calculating the tax incurred on the employee's corresponding salary.

```
CREATE OR REPLACE FUNCTION func_without_pragma(
    ip_n_sal NUMBER)
  RETURN pls_integer
IS
BEGIN
  RETURN ip_n_sal*0.3;
END;
/

CREATE OR REPLACE FUNCTION func_with_pragma(
    ip_n_sal NUMBER)
  RETURN pls_integer
IS
  PRAGMA UDF;
BEGIN
  RETURN ip_n_sal*0.3;
END;
/
```

In the below anonymous block, the three functions (Functional WITH clause, Function with and without the PRAGMA UDF clause), calculating the tax incurred in a similar fashion are bulk fetched into a nested table as shown. The timings of these operations are calculated and found that,

The *Function with UDF Pragma* is better than the *Functional WITH clause* is better than the *Function without UDF pragma*.

```
DECLARE
type type_rec
IS
  record
  (
    empno          NUMBER,
    ename          VARCHAR2(10),
    sal NUMBER,
    tax_incurred NUMBER);
type type_ntt
IS
  TABLE OF type_rec;
  l_ntt_var1 type_ntt;
  l_n_start_time     NUMBER;
  l_n_start_cpu_time NUMBER;
  l_n_end_time       NUMBER;
  l_n_end_cpu_time   NUMBER;
  l_n_var1           NUMBER;
  l_rf_var1 sys_refcursor;
BEGIN
  l_n_start_time     :=dbms_utility.get_time;
  l_n_start_cpu_time:= dbms_utility.get_cpu_time;

  OPEN l_rf_var1 FOR 'SELECT empno,
ename,
sal sal_per_month,
func_without_pragma(sal) sal_per_annum
FROM emp';

  FETCH l_rf_var1 BULK COLLECT INTO l_ntt_var1;
  CLOSE l_rf_var1;

  l_n_end_time       :=dbms_utility.get_time;
  l_n_end_cpu_time := dbms_utility.get_cpu_time;

  dbms_output.put_line('Function Without Pragma UDF: Run time=>
'||(l_n_end_time-l_n_start_time)/100||' Seconds, CPU time=>
'||(l_n_end_cpu_time-l_n_start_cpu_time)/100||' Seconds.');

  l_n_start_time     :=dbms_utility.get_time;
  l_n_start_cpu_time:= dbms_utility.get_cpu_time;

  OPEN l_rf_var1 FOR 'WITH FUNCTION func_with_clause(
ip_n_sal NUMBER)
RETURN pls_integer
IS
```

```
BEGIN
RETURN ip_n_sal*12;
END;
SELECT empno,
ename,
sal sal_per_month,
func_with_clause(sal) sal_per_annum
FROM emp';

  FETCH l_rf_var1 BULK COLLECT INTO l_ntt_var1;
  CLOSE l_rf_var1;

  l_n_end_time     :=dbms_utility.get_time;
  l_n_end_cpu_time:= dbms_utility.get_cpu_time;

  dbms_output.put_line('Functional WITH clause: Run time=> '||(l_n_end_time-
l_n_start_time)/100||' Seconds, CPU time=> '||(l_n_end_cpu_time-
l_n_start_cpu_time)/100||' Seconds.');

  l_n_start_time     :=dbms_utility.get_time;
  l_n_start_cpu_time:= dbms_utility.get_cpu_time;

  OPEN l_rf_var1 FOR 'SELECT empno,
ename,
sal sal_per_month,
func_with_pragma(sal) sal_per_annum
FROM emp';

  FETCH l_rf_var1 BULK COLLECT INTO l_ntt_var1;
  CLOSE l_rf_var1;

  l_n_end_time     :=dbms_utility.get_time;
  l_n_end_cpu_time:= dbms_utility.get_cpu_time;

  dbms_output.put_line('Function With Pragma UDF: Run time=>
'||(l_n_end_time-l_n_start_time)/100||' Seconds, CPU time=>
'||(l_n_end_cpu_time-l_n_start_cpu_time)/100||' Seconds.');
END;
/
```

Results:

```
Function Without Pragma UDF: Run time=> 2.25 Seconds, CPU time=> 2.21
Seconds.
Functional WITH clause: Run time=> 1.13 Seconds, CPU time=> 1.15 Seconds.
Function With Pragma UDF: Run time=> .68 Seconds, CPU time=> .67 Seconds.
```

Using Pipelined Table Functions

The Table function returns the PL/SQL collection in the heap table structure using the TABLE function in the FROM clause of a SELECT statement. The input to this function can be either a Nested table or a Ref Cursor. This function holds the entire collection elements in the memory until they are completed gathered and then they are returned back to the requesting query. Since the collections are held in memory until the last element is collected, it leads to wastage of memory and the first row takes really long time to return in case of large collection.

The prototype for defining the Table functions is,

```
TABLE(<Nested_table_type>);
```

Pipelining a table function avoids the heavy memory wastage and the time taken for returning the first row as the rows are piped out of the function as they are created. This function uses the keyword PIPELINED in its declaration and uses the PIPE ROW call to push the rows out of the function as they are created, rather building up the complete collection.

> Note: The pipelined table function requires an empty RETURN statement since there is no collection to be returned by the function. This statement ensures that the next fetch gets an NO_DATA_FOUND exception by transferring the control back to the requestor.

Thus, the Pipelined table function delivers with the power of PL/SQL and the performance of SQL.

The prototype for defining the Pipelined table functions is,

```
FUNCTION <Function_name>(<Parameter_list>)
RETURN <Nested_table_type> [PIPELINED]
IS
BEGIN
  ...
  RETURN;
END;
```

In the below example, a package with two functions is created for comparing the PGA memory occupied by the function returning a collection with pipelining and the function returning a collection without pipelining.

```
CREATE OR REPLACE PACKAGE pkg_pipe_table_test
IS
  FUNCTION func_with_pipe
    RETURN sys.odcinumberlist pipelined;
  FUNCTION func_without_pipe
    RETURN sys.odcinumberlist;
END;
/
CREATE OR REPLACE PACKAGE body pkg_pipe_table_test
```

```
IS
  FUNCTION func_with_pipe
    RETURN sys.odcinumberlist pipelined
  IS
    l_vt_var1 sys.odcinumberlist;
  BEGIN
    FOR i IN 1..32767
    LOOP
      pipe row (i);
    END LOOP i;
    RETURN;
  END;
  FUNCTION func_without_pipe
    RETURN sys.odcinumberlist
  IS
    l_vt_var1 sys.odcinumberlist:=sys.odcinumberlist();
  BEGIN
    FOR i IN 1..32767
    LOOP
      l_vt_var1.extend;
      l_vt_var1(i):=i;
    END LOOP i;
    RETURN l_vt_var1;
  END;
END;
/
```

In the below anonymous block, the session PGA memory of the two functions returning a collection of 32,767 elements is compared and found that the table function using pipelining consumes 20+ times less session memory compared to the table function not using pipelining.

```
DECLARE
  l_n_start_sess_mem NUMBER;
  l_n_end_sess_mem   NUMBER;

  FUNCTION func_sess_mem
    RETURN NUMBER
  IS
    l_n_value NUMBER;
  BEGIN
    SELECT ms.value
    INTO l_n_value
    FROM v$mystat ms,
      v$statname sn
    WHERE ms.statistic# = sn.statistic#
    AND sn.name          = 'session pga memory';
    RETURN l_n_value;
  END;
BEGIN
  l_n_start_sess_mem:=func_sess_mem;

  FOR i IN
  (SELECT * FROM TABLE(pkg_pipe_table_test.func_without_pipe)
  )
  LOOP
```

```
    NULL;
  END LOOP i;

  l_n_end_sess_mem:=func_sess_mem;

  dbms_output.put_line('The session PGA memory occupied by the function
without pipelining is: '||(l_n_end_sess_mem-l_n_start_sess_mem)||' Bytes');

  l_n_start_sess_mem:=func_sess_mem;

  FOR j IN
  (SELECT * FROM TABLE(pkg_pipe_table_test.func_with_pipe)
  )
  LOOP
    NULL;
  END LOOP j;

  l_n_end_sess_mem:=func_sess_mem;

  dbms_output.put_line('The session PGA memory occupied by the function with
pipelining is: '||(l_n_end_sess_mem-l_n_start_sess_mem)||' Bytes');
END;
/
```

Results:

```
The session PGA memory occupied by the function without pipelining is:
1507328 Bytes
The session PGA memory occupied by the function with pipelining is: 65536
Bytes
```

When we limit the number of rows returned by the Pipelined function explicitly, the function automatically raises the NO_DATA_NEEDED exception to stop the further execution of the function. We don't have to explicitly handle it unless we have an OTHERS exception clause inside the function.

In the below example, a function is created for piping 5 rows out of it. When we query the function using the TABLE function, we could see the 5 rows are piped out without the control getting into the exception block as shown below,

```
CREATE OR REPLACE FUNCTION func_pipe
  RETURN sys.odcinumberlist PIPELINED
IS
  l_n_var1 NUMBER:=0;
BEGIN
  LOOP
    l_n_var1:=l_n_var1+1;
    PIPE ROW (l_n_var1);
    EXIT WHEN l_n_var1=5;
  END LOOP;
RETURN;
EXCEPTION
WHEN no_data_needed THEN
  DBMS_OUTPUT.put_line('NO_DATA_NEEDED Exception Block');
```

```
   RAISE;
WHEN OTHERS THEN
   DBMS_OUTPUT.put_line('Some Fatal Error');
END;
/
```

```
SET SERVEROUTPUT ON
SELECT * FROM TABLE(func_pipe);
```

Results:

```
COLUMN_VALUE
------------
       1
       2
       3
       4
       5
```

But when we limit the actual number of rows returned, we can see that the control passes through the NO_DATA_NEED exception block to stop the execution as shown below,

```
SET SERVEROUTPUT ON
SELECT * FROM TABLE(func_pipe) where rownum<=3;
```

Results:

```
COLUMN_VALUE
------------
       1
       2
       3
```

NO_DATA_NEEDED Exception Block

Using Pipelined Parallel Table Functions

Pipelined parallel table functions increase the performance of the Pipelined table functions by sharing the workload between multiple processes and executing them in parallel. Behind the scenes, Oracle decides how to distribute the work across the available slave processes through the type of partition method mentioned. To enable parallelism in the Pipelined table functions, we must have at least one Ref Cursor input to the function and partition it by either HASH, RANGE or ANY with an optional column list from the Ref Cursor for partitioning. Also, we must mandatorily include the PARALLEL_ENABLE clause in the function declaration as shown in the below prototype.

The prototype for defining the Pipelined parallel table functions is,

```
FUNCTION <Function_name>(<Input_parameter1> <Ref_cursor_type>)
RETURN <Nested_table_type> [PIPELINED]
         [[ORDER | CLUSTER] <Input_parameter1> BY <Column_list>]
         PARALLEL_ENABLE(<PARTITION <Input_parameter1> BY
            <ANY | [ <HASH | RANGE> <Column_list>]>)
IS
BEGIN
  ...
END;
```

 Note: Only one input Ref Cursor must be specified in the PARTITION BY clause.

The <Ref_cursor_type> datatype in the above prototype must be a strongly typed Ref Cursor to use the <Column_list> clause in the PARTITION BY clause and the ORDER BY or CLUSTER BY clauses. If it is a weakly typed Ref Cursor, we can use the PARTITION BY ANY clause and we cannot use both the ORDER BY or CLUSTER BY clauses. It is recommended that we must not use weakly typed Ref Cursors for the Pipelined table functions.

If ORDER BY or CLUSTER BY clauses are not specified for the strongly typed Ref Cursor, the input rows are in a random order. Here, the ORDER BY clause sorts the respective rows of each instance pertaining to the Table function running on the slave process and the CLUSTER BY clause groups data with the same values together but does not sort the data between the values.

A table with 1,00,000 records is created for demonstration purpose as shown below.

```
CREATE TABLE tbl_parallel_test AS
SELECT level lvl FROM dual CONNECT BY level<=100000;
```

In the below code snippet, a package with two functions is created. One function uses Pipelining and the other one uses Pipelining in parallel with Hash partitioning on the LVL column of the TBL_PARALLEL_TEST table. During the record fetch in both the functions, the SID of the slave process is saved to the record type returned by the PIPE ROW statement.

```
CREATE OR REPLACE PACKAGE pkg_pipe_parallel_test
IS
TYPE type_rec
IS
  record
  (
    lvl NUMBER,
```

```
     sid NUMBER);
TYPE strong_ref_cur
IS
  REF
  CURSOR
    RETURN type_rec;
  TYPE type_ntt
IS
  TABLE OF type_rec;
  FUNCTION func_with_pipe(
     ip_rf_var1 strong_ref_cur)
    RETURN type_ntt pipelined;
  FUNCTION func_with_pipe_parallel(
     ip_rf_var1 strong_ref_cur)
    RETURN type_ntt pipelined parallel_enable(
     partition ip_rf_var1 BY hash(
       lvl));
END;
/

CREATE OR REPLACE PACKAGE body pkg_pipe_parallel_test
IS
  FUNCTION func_with_pipe(
     ip_rf_var1 strong_ref_cur)
    RETURN type_ntt pipelined
  IS
    l_rt_var1 type_rec;
  BEGIN
    LOOP
      FETCH ip_rf_var1 INTO l_rt_var1;
      EXIT
    WHEN ip_rf_var1%notfound;
      SELECT sid INTO l_rt_var1.sid FROM v$mystat WHERE rownum=1;
      pipe row (l_rt_var1);
    END LOOP;
    RETURN;
  END;
  FUNCTION func_with_pipe_parallel(
     ip_rf_var1 strong_ref_cur)
    RETURN type_ntt pipelined parallel_enable(
     partition ip_rf_var1 BY hash(
       lvl))
  IS
    l_rt_var1 type_rec;
  BEGIN
    LOOP
      FETCH ip_rf_var1 INTO l_rt_var1;
      EXIT
    WHEN ip_rf_var1%notfound;
      SELECT sid INTO l_rt_var1.sid FROM v$mystat WHERE rownum=1;
      pipe row (l_rt_var1);
    END LOOP;
    RETURN;
  END;
END;
/
```

In the below code listing, an anonymous block is used for comparing the program run time, the CPU run time, and the number of slave processes used for the execution of both the functions from the above package. From the result produced below, we can see that the function executed in parallel is ~3 times faster and uses 8 times less CPU time than the serially executed function as it uses 5 slave processes instead of one.

```
DECLARE
  l_n_count         NUMBER;
  l_n_start_time    NUMBER;
  l_n_end_time      NUMBER;
  l_n_start_cpu_time NUMBER;
  l_n_end_cpu_time  NUMBER;
BEGIN
  l_n_start_time    :=dbms_utility.get_time;
  l_n_start_cpu_time:=dbms_utility.get_cpu_time;

dbms_output.put_line('----- Start of Pipelined Table function -----');

  FOR loop_noparallel IN
  (SELECT sid,
    COUNT(*) cnt
  FROM TABLE(pkg_pipe_parallel_test.func_with_pipe(CURSOR
    (SELECT lvl,NULL sid FROM tbl_parallel_test t1
    )))
  GROUP BY sid
  )
  LOOP
    dbms_output.put_line('SID: '||loop_noparallel.sid||'; Total number of
rows handled: '||loop_noparallel.cnt);
  END LOOP loop_noparallel;

  l_n_end_time    :=dbms_utility.get_time;
  l_n_end_cpu_time:=dbms_utility.get_cpu_time;

  dbms_output.put_line('Pipe Function: Program run time=> '||(l_n_end_time-
l_n_start_time)/100||' Seconds, CPU run time=>'||(l_n_end_cpu_time-
l_n_start_cpu_time)/100||' Seconds');

  l_n_start_time    :=dbms_utility.get_time;
  l_n_start_cpu_time:=dbms_utility.get_cpu_time;

dbms_output.put_line('----- Start of Pipelined Parallel Table function -----
');

  FOR loop_parallel IN
  (SELECT sid,
    COUNT(*) cnt
  FROM TABLE(pkg_pipe_parallel_test.func_with_pipe_parallel(CURSOR
    (SELECT /*+parallel(t1,5)*/
```

```
        lvl,NULL sid FROM tbl_parallel_test t1
    )))
  GROUP BY sid
  )
  LOOP
   dbms_output.put_line('SID: '||loop_parallel.sid||'; Total number of rows
handled: '||loop_parallel.cnt);
  END LOOP loop_parallel;

   l_n_end_time    :=dbms_utility.get_time;
   l_n_end_cpu_time:=dbms_utility.get_cpu_time;

   dbms_output.put_line('Pipe Parallel Function: Program run time=>
'||(l_n_end_time-l_n_start_time)/100||' Seconds, CPU run
time=>'||(l_n_end_cpu_time-l_n_start_cpu_time)/100||' Seconds');
END;
/
```

Results:

```
----- Start of Pipelined Table function -----
SID: 19; Total number of rows handled: 100000
Pipe Function: Program run time=> 8.4 Seconds, CPU run time=>8.36 Seconds
----- Start of Pipelined Parallel Table function -----
SID: 54; Total number of rows handled: 19909
SID: 148; Total number of rows handled: 20035
SID: 375; Total number of rows handled: 20040
SID: 129; Total number of rows handled: 19886
SID: 278; Total number of rows handled: 20130
Pipe Parallel Function: Program run time=> 3.17 Seconds, CPU run time=>.03
Seconds
```

Summary

We started this chapter by understanding the database memory structure and their management methods following the different types of compilation techniques available in Oracle. In the later section, we discussed the PLSQL_CODE_TYPE and PLSQL_OPTIMIZE_LEVEL initialization parameters with necessary examples. The next section explained us about the subprogram inlining in Oracle using the INLINE pragma with adequate examples. The final section briefed us about the different PL/SQL tuning best practices with comparative examples.

In the next chapter, we will be learning about the Result caching and its different forms of usage. This technique is used for fantastic performance gains in the database code that are repeatedly executed.

Improving Performance using Caching Techniques

In the previous chapter, we learned the different types of memory components like Buffer cache, Redo Log buffer, Shared Pool, Reserved Pool, Large Pool, Java Pool, Streams Pool, and In-Memory column store, for faster data access. These memory pools are used for storing and retrieving the data that are frequently accessed by the Oracle database much faster than from disk by avoiding the physical IO.

The Result cache is a memory area, either in the SGA or in the Client application memory, that stores the result set of a SQL query or a PL/SQL function for repetitive use in a fast manner without hitting the disk. These result sets stored in the cache are spawned across multiple sessions until they become inconsistent. Whenever a SQL query or a PL/SQL function is executed more than once across same or different sessions, the result sets stored in the cache during the first time execution will be returned instead of performing the whole operation once again, thus boosting the performance of the database by avoiding the repetitive disk IO.

In this chapter, we will be understanding the Server Result Cache and Client Result Cache concepts, their different types, and configuration techniques in brief through the below topics.

27) Server Result Cache concepts and their configuration techniques.

28) SQL Query Result Cache and PL/SQL Function Result Cache concepts along with their configuration, characteristics, and restrictions.

29) Client Result Cache concepts.

30) Result Cache behavior in Oracle RAC environments.

31) Result Cache enhancement in R12.1, which allows us to create an Invoker Rights function with the RESULT_CACHE clause.

Summary   **667**

Server Result Cache Concepts

Prior to the introduction of the Result cache in the Oracle version 11g, Oracle used to cache the data blocks in the Buffer cache component of the database. When a query or a function is first executed in the database, the system searches for the data in the Buffer cache.

- If the data is not present (in case the query or the function is not executed earlier), the server performs a direct IO operation to retrieve the data from the disk, loads it into the Buffer cache as data blocks, and then from this data, the required result is returned to the user.

- If the data is already present (in case the query or the function is already executed), it is taken from the Buffer cache to build the result set requested and then returned to the user.

Successively when another session or user requests for the same data, the server uses the same data blocks from the buffer cache to build the result set and then returns them back to the user.

Now, why do we need the new Result cache functionality when the Buffer cache can store the data for reuse?

The reason is, the Buffer cache is capable of caching the data only in the form of data blocks, which is then needed to be built into the result sets format before sending it back to the user, but the Result cache stores the data in the result sets format itself. Thus, Result cache avoids the extra process of building or converting the data from data block format into the result set format. When the Result cache feature is enabled, the final result sets of a query or a function gets cached in the Shared pool. Subsequently, when a user executes the same query or function once again, the server just returns the result sets from the Server Result Cache section of the Shared pool, decreasing the response time.

> 🔔 Note: The Cached results become INVALID when the dependent objects are modified.

Another form of caching prior to the Result cache was the package level collection variables. The main drawback of this approach was that it was a session level caching technique and used the PGA memory. This leads to increased PGA memory, thus degrading the performance. The Result cache technique triumphs over this technique by storing its cached objects in the SGA memory instead of choking the PGA memory.

The Server Result Cache is a memory pool within the Shared Pool in the SGA, which contains the *SQL query result cache* (stores the result sets returned by the SQL queries) and the *PL/SQL function result cache* (stores the result sets returned by the PL/SQL functions).

The benefits of the Server result cache can be observed mostly in the OLAP applications. Preferably the queries which access more rows and return less number of them.

The following pictorial representation depicts the Oracle database's memory structure and the Result Cache's working mechanism through the three step process. Consider that the Result Cache technique has been enabled for the demonstration below.

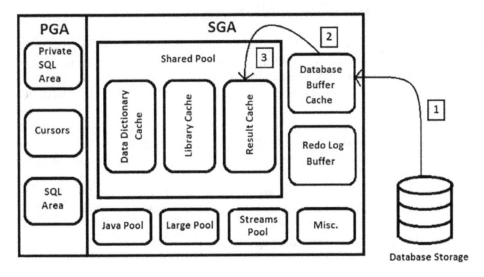

Fig. 14.1. Oracle Database Memory Structure

1) The data is read from the database and stored in the buffer cache in the form of data blocks when a query is executed for the first time.
2) Based on the WHERE condition of the query, the data is filtered in the Buffer cache.
3) The data is stored in the Result cache in its final result set format and is used when another user executes the same query from the same or different session.

Result Cache Latch (RC Latch)

The Result Cache Latch is a serialization device that can be used for controlling the access to the result cache. They tend to reduce the performance of the database due to undersized result cache or concurrent users accessing the result set to create fresh result cache entries. This is because there is only one RC latch on the result cache and only one user can effectively use it. Thus, setting the RESULT_CACHE_MODE initialization parameter to FORCE will result in a poor performance as every SQL statement will try to access the result cache in parallel. We must use the MANUAL option to manually invoke only the desired SQLs in result cache mode.

Thus, we should make sure that we use the result cache technique only for the functions that return less number of result sets and the SQL statements that do not run in parallel or on large static tables.

Server Result Cache Configuration

Oracle allocates the memory to the Server Result Cache module of the Shared pool during the database startup based on the total memory size of the Shared pool and its memory management method. The relationship between the memory allocated to the Server Result Cache and the memory management method used by the database is shown below,

1) **Automatic Memory Management:** In AMM method, 0.25% of the MEMORY_TARGET parameter value are pre-allocated to the Result Cache.

2) **Automatic Shared Memory Management:** In ASMM method, 0.5% of the SGA_TARGET parameter value are pre-allocated to the Result Cache.

3) **Manual Shared Memory Management:** In MSMM method, 1% of the SHARED_POOL_SIZE parameter value are pre-allocated to the Result Cache.

The size of the Server Result Cache grows upon usage until it reaches the maximum of 75% of the Shared Pool's size.

The query result will not be cached under the below circumstances,

1) When the maximum size limit is reached by the Result Cache pool, no more query results will be cached.

2) If the query result size is more than this maximum limit, it will not be cached.

The database deploys the LRU (Least Recently Used) mechanism for aging out the least likely used cache results to free the space out of the Server Result Cache.

Sizing Server Result Cache using the Initialization Parameters

Oracle has provided us with four initialization parameters for managing the Result Cache feature in the database. These parameters are described below,

1) **RESULT_CACHE_MODE** parameter determines the queries, which are capable of storing the result sets either in the Server or Client Result Caches and adds their result sets to the Result Cache. The result sets remain in the Result Cache unless they are invalidated or manually expelled using the FLUSH procedure from the DBMS_RESULT_CACHE package. The available modes for this parameter are,

   → **MANUAL** is the default value for this parameter. If this value is set, the queries with the /*+ RESULT_CACHE */ hint or table annotation can only be stored in the result cache.

   → **FORCE** option forces all the query result sets to be stored in the result cache. However, we can exclude any query result set from getting cached by using the hint /*+ NO_RESULT_CACHE */ during its execution. This option must be carefully used as it could result in database degradation due to Result Cache Latch, which is explained in the earlier section.

2) **RESULT_CACHE_MAX_SIZE** parameter specifies the maximum size allocated to the Server Result Cache, in bytes. If this parameter is set to 0, the Server Result Cache functionality will be disabled. Note that Oracle allows only 75% of Shared Pool memory to be used for Server Result Cache, thus we must restrict this allocation accordingly.

3) **RESULT_CACHE_MAX_RESULT** parameter specifies the maximum percentage of the RESULT_CACHE_MAX_SIZE parameter value allocated for a single result set. Valid values are between 1 and 100. The default value is 5.

4) **RESULT_CACHE_REMOTE_EXPIRATION** parameter specifies the expiration time for a result set in the Server Result Cache that depends on the remote database objects, in minutes. The default value is 0 and the maximum value is 2147483647. If this value is set to a non-zero value, the cache result set will not be invalidated even though its dependent remote object is modified.

We can query the V$PARAMETER table to check on these parameters and their attributes as shown below,

```
SELECT name,
  value,
  default_value,
  isses_modifiable,
  issys_modifiable,
  ispdb_modifiable,
  isinstance_modifiable
FROM v$parameter
WHERE name LIKE 'result_cache%';
```

Script Result:

NAME	VALUE	DEFAULT_V ALUE	ISSES...	ISSYS...	ISPDB...	ISINSTANC E...
result_cache_mode	MANUAL	NULL	TRUE	IMMEDIATE	TRUE	TRUE
result_cache_max_s ize	4259840	0	FALSE	IMMEDIATE	FALSE	TRUE
result_cache_max_r esult	5	1	FALSE	IMMEDIATE	FALSE	TRUE
result_cache_remot e_expiration	0	5	TRUE	IMMEDIATE	TRUE	TRUE

From the above table,

- The parameter RESULT_CACHE_MODE's current value is MANUAL, the default value is *null*, and it is modifiable in SESSION/ SYSTEM/ PDB/ INSTANCE level.

- The parameter RESULT_CACHE_MAX_SIZE's current value is 4259840, the default value is 0, it is modifiable in SYSTEM/ INSTANCE level, but not in SESSION/ PDB level as it is shared across all sessions/ PDBs.

- The parameter RESULT_CACHE_MAX_RESULT's current value is 5, the default value is 1, it is modifiable in SYSTEM/ INSTANCE level, but not in SESSION/ PDB level as it is shared across all sessions/ PDBs.

- The parameter RESULT_CACHE_REMOTE_EXPIRATION's current value is 0, default value is 5, and it is modifiable in SESSION/ SYSTEM/ PDB/ INSTANCE level.

Administering Server Result Cache using the DBMS_RESULT_CACHE package

The DBMS_RESULT_CACHE API can be used for controlling the Server Result Cache component of the Shared Pool. Both the SQL Result Cache and the PL/SQL Function Result Cache modules in the Server Result Cache component can be administered and regulated using this API. The different subprograms in this API are,

BYPASS Procedure

This procedure can be used for turning the Result Cache functionality ON or OFF.

→ If the bypass mode is set to *true*, the result set caching technique is bypassed for the current or all the sessions.

→ If the bypass mode is set to *false*, the caching functionality is resumed for operation.

This procedure is highly helpful when we need to apply a hot patch to a PL/SQL function whose results are cached earlier and these cached result sets cannot be flushed automatically unless the instance is rebooted. In this scenario, we must bypass the result cache feature by turning it ON, flushing the existing cached results, applying the patch, and then turning OFF the bypass feature.

> 🔔 Note: In RAC environments, we must execute the BYPASS procedure in all instances as they have their own Server Result Cache components.

The prototype of this procedure is shown below,

```
DBMS_RESULT_CACHE.BYPASS (bypass_mode IN BOOLEAN, session IN BOOLEAN);
```

- **BYPASS_MODE** accepts a Boolean *true* to bypass the Result Cache feature, or a *false* to turn the bypass mode OFF.
- **SESSION** accepts a Boolean *true* to apply the changes only to the current session or a *false* to apply it to all the sessions.

DELETE_DEPENDENCY Functions and Procedures

These are undocumented subprograms that can be used for deleting a specific database object from the Result Cache and invalidate all their dependent result sets.

The prototypes of these subprograms are shown below,

```
DBMS_RESULT_CACHE.DELETE_DEPENDENCY (
   owner IN VARCHAR2,
   name IN VARCHAR2)
RETURN NUMBER;

DBMS_RESULT_CACHE.DELETE_DEPENDENCY (
   owner IN VARCHAR2,
   name IN VARCHAR2);

DBMS_RESULT_CACHE.DELETE_DEPENDENCY (
   object_id IN NATURALN)
RETURN NUMBER;

DBMS_RESULT_CACHE.DELETE_DEPENDENCY (
   object_id IN NATURALN);
```

- **OWNER** parameter accepts the schema name of the input object.
- **NAME** parameter accepts the input object's name.
- **OBJECT_ID** parameter accepts the input object's ID from the data dictionary.

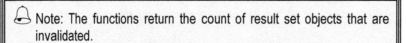 Note: The functions return the count of result set objects that are invalidated.

FLUSH Function and Procedure

These subprograms can be used for flushing the result sets from the Server Result Cache component of the Shared Pool. The memory held by the result sets could be either retained or released back to the system and the statistics gathered could be either retained or erased based on its input parameter values.

Note that the FLUSH function returns a Boolean *true* if all the result set objects are flushed from the memory cache or a *false* if not.

The prototypes of these subprograms are shown below,

```
DBMS_RESULT_CACHE.FLUSH (
   retainMem IN BOOLEAN DEFAULT FALSE,
   retainSta IN BOOLEAN DEFAULT FALSE)
  RETURN BOOLEAN;

DBMS_RESULT_CACHE.FLUSH (
   retainMem IN BOOLEAN DEFAULT FALSE,
   retainSta IN BOOLEAN DEFAULT FALSE);
```

- **RETAINMEM** parameter accepts a Boolean *true* if we want to retain the memory freed by the flush operation or a Boolean *false* if we want to release them back to the memory. The default value is *false*.
- **RETAINSTA** parameter accepts a Boolean *true* if we want to retain the existing cache statistics or a Boolean *false* if we want to clear them. The default value is *false*.

INVALIDATE Functions and Procedures

These subprograms can be used for invalidating all the result sets that are dependent on the input database object.

The prototypes of these subprograms are shown below,

```
DBMS_RESULT_CACHE.INVALIDATE (
   owner IN VARCHAR2,
   name IN VARCHAR2)
 RETURN NUMBER;

DBMS_RESULT_CACHE.INVALIDATE (
   owner IN VARCHAR2,
   name IN VARCHAR2);

DBMS_RESULT_CACHE.INVALIDATE (
  object_id IN BINARY_INTEGER)
 RETURN NUMBER;

DBMS_RESULT_CACHE.INVALIDATE (
   object_id IN BINARY_INTEGER);
```

- **OWNER** parameter accepts the schema name of the input object.
- **NAME** parameter accepts the input object's name.
- **OBJECT_ID** parameter accepts the input object's ID from the data dictionary.

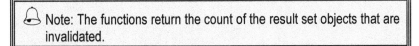 Note: The functions return the count of the result set objects that are invalidated.

INVALIDATE_OBJECT Functions and Procedures

These subprograms can be used for invalidating the specific result cache object from the Result Cache either using either the address ID or the cache ID.

The prototype for these subprograms are shown below,

```
DBMS_RESULT_CACHE.INVALIDATE_OBJECT (id IN BINARY_INTEGER) RETURN NUMBER;

DBMS_RESULT_CACHE.INVALIDATE_OBJECT (id IN BINARY_INTEGER);

DBMS_RESULT_CACHE.INVALIDATE_OBJECT (cache_id IN VARCHAR2) RETURN NUMBER;

DBMS_RESULT_CACHE.INVALIDATE_OBJECT (cache_id IN VARCHAR2);
```

- **ID** parameter accepts the address of the result set object that has to be invalidated in the Result Cache.
- **CACHE_ID** parameter accepts the cache ID of the result set object that has to be invalidated in the Result Cache.

> Note: The ID and the CACHE_ID values of a particular result set object can be obtained from the V$RESULT_CACHE_OBJECTS table.

MEMORY_REPORT Procedure

This procedure can be used for printing the report for the memory used by the Server Result Cache module.

The prototype of this procedure is shown below,

```
DBMS_RESULT_CACHE.MEMORY_REPORT (detailed IN BOOLEAN DEFAULT FALSE);
```

- **DETAILED** parameter accepts a Boolean *true* for a detailed report or a *false* for a standard report. The default value is *false*.

STATUS Function

This function can be used for checking on the status of the Result Cache functionality in the database.

The prototype of this function is shown below,

```
DBMS_RESULT_CACHE.STATUS RETURN VARCHAR2;
```

The possible values that can be returned by this function are,

- **BYPASS** – When the Cache functionality has been temporarily bypassed.
- **CORRUPT** – When the Cache is corrupted.
- **DISABLED** – When the Cache functionality has been disabled.
- **ENABLED** – When the Cache functionality has been enabled.
- **SYNC** – When the Cache is available, but synchronizing with the Oracle RAC nodes.

SQL Query Result Cache

The section below describes the ways in which we can specify the queries for result caching using the Result Cache hints and table annotations.

/*+RESULT_CACHE*/ Hint

Before starting our experiment, we must flush the Server Result Cache pool in the Shared Pool using the FLUSH API as shown below,

```
EXEC dbms_result_cache.flush;
```

The above statement will remove all the previously cached objects from the result cache. We can verify this by querying the V$RESULT_CACHE_OBJECTS view as shown below,

```
SELECT COUNT(*) CNT FROM v$result_cache_objects;
```

Script Results:

CNT
0

In this demonstration, we will be analyzing the SQL query result cache in the manual mode by setting the RESULT_CACHE_MODE parameter to MANUAL at the SYSTEM level as shown below,

```
ALTER SYSTEM SET RESULT_CACHE_MODE=MANUAL;
```

The current mode can be verified by issuing the below SHOW PARAMETER command as shown,

```
SHOW PARAMETER RESULT_CACHE_MODE;

NAME                TYPE    VALUE
----------------    ------  ------
result_cache_mode   string  MANUAL
```

After all the initial setup is done, the Oracle database will not cache any result set unless we explicitly use the /*+ *RESULT_CACHE* */ hint or annotate the table.

When we query the EMPLOYEES table having 2,29,376 rows for finding the number of employees in each department with the /*+ *RESULT_CACHE* */ hint for the first time, its query result set is added to the Result Cache for the future access.

```
SELECT
  /*+RESULT_CACHE GATHER_PLAN_STATISTICS*/
  deptno,
  COUNT(empno)
FROM employees e
GROUP BY deptno;
```

Elapsed: 00:00:11.539

The result set object in the Result Cache can be verified by querying the V$RESULT_CACHE_OBJECTS view with the object name as below,

```
SELECT id,
  type,
  status,
  name,
  scn,
  object_no
FROM v$result_cache_objects;
```

Script Result

ID	TYPE	STATUS	NAME	SCN	OBJECT_NO
0	Dependency	Published	C##.EMPLOYEES	5665956	99854
1	Result	Published	"SELECT /*+RESULT_CACHE GATHER_PLAN_STATISTICS*/ deptno, COUNT(empno) FROM employees e GROUP BY deptno"	1	Result

When we check the Plan table output for the above query, we can see that the result sets are cached and the A-ROWS column states that the actual number of rows fetched from the table is 229K, as it is the first time execution. Also, the STARTS column shows that all the operations are executed at least once during this execution.

Advanced PL/SQL Programming

Note that we have not used the EXPLAIN PLAN FOR syntax in the SELECT query for retrieving the Plan using the DISPLAY_CURSOR procedure.

```
SELECT * FROM TABLE(dbms_xplan.display_cursor(NULL, NULL, 'ALLSTATS LAST'));
```

Script Results

ID	OPERATION	NAME	STARTS	E-ROWS	A-ROWS	A-TIME	BUFFERS	0MEM	1MEM	USED-MEM
0	SELECT STATEMENT		1		3	11.53	1389			
1	RESULT CACHE	4538a7r4 sbdkf6nsk 2a9gjgy5 x	1		3	11.53	1389			
2	HASH GROUP BY		1	3	3	11.53	1389	1600K	1600K	1244K(0)
3	TABLE ACCESS FULL	EMPLOYEES	1	229K	229K	11.43	1389			

> 🔔 Note: To get the advanced Oracle plan as shown above, we must add the extra hint GATHER_PLAN_STATISTICS or set the STATISTICS_LEVEL parameter to ALL.

Now, when we re-execute the query, we can see that the elapsed time has reduced substantially,

```
SELECT
  /*+RESULT_CACHE GATHER_PLAN_STATISTICS*/
  deptno,
  COUNT(empno)
FROM employees e
GROUP BY deptno;
```

```
Elapsed: 00:00:00.001
```

When we check the Plan table output for the second time execution, we can see that the STARTS column shows that the HASH GROUP BY and TABLE ACCESS FULL operations are skipped for this execution. Also, the A-ROWS column shows that the actual number of rows returned is from the Result Cache and not from the physical table itself.

```
SELECT * FROM TABLE(dbms_xplan.display_cursor(NULL, NULL, 'ALLSTATS LAST'));
```

Script Results

ID	OPERATION	NAME	STARTS	E-ROWS	A-ROWS	A-TIME	0MEM	1MEM	USED-MEM
0	SELECT STATEMENT		1		3	0.01			
1	RESULT CACHE	4538a7r 4sbdkf6 nsk2a9gj gy5x	1		3	0.01			
2	HASH GROUP BY		0	3	0	0.01	1600K	1600K	1244K(0)
3	TABLE ACCESS FULL	EMPLO YEES	0	229K	0	0.01			

Now, we can check the memory report of the Result Cache module by executing the MEMORY_REPORT API as shown below,

```
EXEC dbms_result_cache.memory_report;
```

Results:

```
R e s u l t   C a c h e   M e m o r y   R e p o r t
[Parameters]
Block Size          = 1K bytes
Maximum Cache Size  = 4160K bytes (4160 blocks)
Maximum Result Size = 208K bytes (208 blocks)
[Memory]
Total Memory = 162312 bytes [0.023% of the Shared Pool]

... Fixed Memory = 5440 bytes [0.001% of the Shared Pool]
... Dynamic Memory = 156872 bytes [0.022% of the Shared Pool]
....... Overhead = 124104 bytes
....... Cache Memory = 32K bytes (32 blocks)
........... Unused Memory = 30 blocks
........... Used Memory = 2 blocks
............... Dependencies = 1 blocks (1 count)
............... Results = 1 blocks
................... SQL     = 1 blocks (1 count)
```

The above report shows the below information,

- Block size (1 KB) – Size of one block.
- Maximum cache size (4160 KB) – Maximum size of the Result Cache module sized by the RESULT_CACHE_MAX_SIZE parameter.
- Maximum result size (208 KB) – Maximum size of the result set sized by the RESULT_CACHE_MAX_RESULT parameter.
- Total memory allocated (162213 B) – Total memory allocated for the Result Cache module from the Shared Pool (0.023%).
  - ➔ The Fixed Memory (5440 B) – This is an Oracle predefined memory size for its internal use.
  - ➔ The Dynamic memory (156872 B) – The dynamic memory holds the cached result set objects.
    - o Unused cache memory (30 KB) – Total unused cache memory.
    - o Used cache memory (1 KB) – Total used cache memory, including its Dependencies, Results, SQL, and Invalidated objects.

/*+NO_RESULT_CACHE*/ Hint

This hint instructs the Oracle database not to cache the query results either in the Server or Client result caches. To demonstrate this scenario, we must set the RESULT_CACHE_MODE parameter to FORCE at the SYSTEM level as shown below,

```
ALTER SYSTEM SET RESULT_CACHE_MODE=FORCE;
```

The current mode can be verified by issuing the below SHOW PARAMETER command as shown,

```
SHOW PARAMETER RESULT_CACHE_MODE;

NAME                TYPE    VALUE
----------------    ------  ------
result_cache_mode   string  FORCE
```

Now, we will flush the Server Result Cache pool from the Shared Pool using the FLUSH API as shown below,

```
EXEC dbms_result_cache.flush;
```

The above statement will remove all the previously cached objects from the result cache and we can confirm this by querying the V$RESULT_CACHE_OBJECTS view as shown below,

```
SELECT COUNT(*) CNT FROM v$result_cache_objects;
```

Script Results:

CNT
0

After the setup is completed, when we execute the below query without using the /*+RESULT_CACHE*/ hint, we can see that the query is forcefully cached as shown below,

```
SELECT
  deptno,
  COUNT(empno)
FROM employees e
GROUP BY deptno;
```

The cached query result can be found from the below query,

```
SELECT id,
  type,
  status,
  name,
  scn,
  object_no
FROM v$result_cache_objects;
```

Script Result

ID	TYPE	STATUS	NAME	SCN	OBJECT_NO
0	Dependency	Published	C##.EMPLOYEES	5671808	99854
1	Result	Published	"SELECT deptno, COUNT(empno) FROM employees e GROUP BY deptno"	1	Result

When we flush the cache memory and try executing the query again using the /*+NO_RESULT_CACHE*/ hint, the result sets are not cached.

```
EXEC dbms_result_cache.flush;
```

```
SELECT
  /*+NO_RESULT_CACHE*/
  deptno,
  COUNT(empno)
FROM employees e
GROUP BY deptno;
```

The query result is not found in the Result cache memory, which is verified from the below query,

```
SELECT id,
  type,
  status,
  name,
  scn,
  object_no
FROM v$result_cache_objects;
```

```
no rows selected
```

Result Cache Table Annotation

We can also use the result cache table annotations to control the caching in the database. When we use the result cache table annotations, we don't have to add the hints to the SQLs anymore. We can also override the result cache table annotations by using the result cache hints as hints have more precedence than the table annotations.

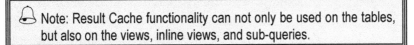

Note: Result Cache functionality can not only be used on the tables, but also on the views, inline views, and sub-queries.

Table Annotation Value as DEFAULT

If at least one table in the SQL query is set to DEFAULT, then the result caching technique is not enabled for this query, unless we specify the /*+RESULT_CACHE*/ hint or set the RESULT_CACHE_MODE parameter to FORCE. This is the default value when we create a table.

In the below code snippet, a table with its RESULT_CACHE mode as DEFAULT is created,

```
CREATE TABLE tbl_default RESULT_CACHE (MODE DEFAULT)
AS
SELECT level coll FROM dual CONNECT BY level<=1000;
```

When we query this table without any hints and with the RESULT_CACHE_MODE as MANUAL, the result sets returned will not be cached.

```
SELECT * FROM tbl_default;
```

The below query shows that the result sets pertaining to the TBL_DEFAULT table are not cached,

```
SELECT id,
  type,
  status,
  name,
  scn,
  object_no
FROM v$result_cache_objects
WHERE name='C##.TBL_DEFAULT';
```

```
no rows selected
```

Table Annotation Value as FORCE

When all the tables in a SQL query are marked as FORCE, then the query result will be cached irrespective of the RESULT_CACHE_MODE parameter value. Note that the /*+NO_RESULT_CACHE*/ hint can still stop this query from caching.

In the below code snippet, a table with its RESULT_CACHE mode as DEFAULT is created,

```
CREATE TABLE tbl_force RESULT_CACHE (MODE FORCE)
AS
SELECT level col1 FROM dual CONNECT BY level<=1000;
```

When we query this table without any hints irrespective of the RESULT_CACHE_MODE value, the result sets returned will be cached.

```
SELECT * FROM tbl_force;
```

The below query shows that the result sets pertaining to the TBL_FORCE table are cached,

```
SELECT id,
  type,
  status,
  name,
  scn,
  object_no
FROM v$result_cache_objects
WHERE name='C##.TBL_FORCE';
```

Script Result

ID	TYPE	STATUS	NAME	SCN	OBJECT_NO
238	Dependency	Published	C##.TBL_FORCE	5674060	99856
239	Result	Published	SELECT * FROM tbl_force	5765791	0

Monitoring the Result Cache

We can monitor the Server Result Cache using the below database views,

V$RESULT_CACHE_OBJECTS

This view lists all the result set objects in the Server Result Cache module along with their attributes. The important columns in this view are explained below,

- ID – Identifier of the cached object.
- TYPE – Type of the cache object.
  - RESULT
  - DEPENDENCY
- STATUS – Status of the cached object.
  - NEW – Result is under construction.
  - PUBLISHED – Result is available for use.
  - BYPASS – Result is bypassed for use.
  - EXPIRED – Result has exceeded the maximum expiration time.
  - INVALID – Result is no longer available for use.
- HASH – Hash value for the object.
- NAME – Name of the SQL or the PL/SQL function.
- NAMESPACE – Either SQL, or PL/SQL.
- DEPEND_COUNT – Number of dependencies or dependents.
- BLOCK_COUNT – Total number of blocks in the cached object.
- COLUMN_COUNT – Total number of columns in the result set object.
- ROW_COUNT – Total number of rows in the result set object.
- CACHE_ID – Cache ID for the result set object.
- CACHE_KEY – Cache key for the result set object.

V$RESULT_CACHE_STATISTICS

This view displays the various Result cache settings and their respective statistics. The columns in this view are explained below,

- ID – Identifier for the statistic name.
- NAME – Name of the statistic.
- Value – Value of the statistic.

The available statistics are described below,

- Block Size (in bytes) – Size of each memory block.
- Block Count Maximum – Maximum number of blocks allowed.
- Block Count Current – Number of block counts currently allocated.
- Result Size Maximum (in blocks) – Maximum number of blocks allowed for a single result set.
- Create Count Success – Number of cached result set objects successfully created.
- Create Count Failure – Total number of failed cached results.
- Find Count – Total number of cached result sets those were successfully found.
- Invalidation Count – Total number of invalidations.
- Delete Count Invalid – Total number of invalid cached result sets deleted.
- Delete Count Valid – Total number of valid cached result sets deleted.

V$RESULT_CACHE_MEMORY

The *Block Count Current* statistics from the V$RESULT_CACHE_STATISTICS represents the number of currently allocated blocks. The V$RESULT_CACHE_MEMORY view displays all the current memory blocks in the server result cache and its corresponding statistics like how many are free and how many are currently in use.

The total number of free blocks and in-use blocks can be found by executing the below query,

```
SELECT free, COUNT (*) cnt FROM v$result_cache_memory GROUP BY free;
```

Script Results

FREE	CNT
NO	2
YES	30

V$RESULT_CACHE_DEPENDENCY

This view displays the dependency details between the cached result set objects in the server result cache and the dependencies among them. The columns in this view are described below,

- RESULT_ID – Cached result's ID.
- DEPEND_ID – Dependent object's ID.
- OBJECT_NO – Dependent object's data dictionary number.

SQL Result Cache Invalidation

The cached result set gets invalidated either if the state of the table or the data is changed. There are two ways in which a SQL cached result set can be invalidated and they are,

Automatic Invalidation

If we alter the structure of the table or update the data in the table, then the previously cached result set object will be automatically invalidated and only in its next execution the query will be re-executed and the result generated will be cached in the Server Result Cache module.

In the below code snippet, the result sets of the EMPLOYEES table are cached in the Server Result Cache module as shown below,

```
SELECT /*+RESULT_CACHE*/ deptno, COUNT(empno) FROM employees e GROUP BY
deptno;
```

We can verify this by executing the below statement,

```
SELECT id,
   type,
   status,
   name,
   scn,
   object_no,
   cache_id
FROM v$result_cache_objects
WHERE name='SELECT /*+RESULT_CACHE*/ deptno, COUNT(empno) FROM employees e
GROUP BY deptno';
```

Script Result

ID	TYPE	STATUS	NAME	SCN	OBJECT_NO
1	Result	Published	SELECT /*+RESULT_CACHE*/ deptno, COUNT(empno) FROM employees e GROUP BY deptno	5687149	0

When to try to update and commit any row in the EMPLOYEES table as shown below, the cached result gets invalidated.

```
UPDATE employees SET sal=sal+1000 WHERE empno=105;
COMMIT;
```

We can verify the invalidated cache result by executing the below statement,

```
SELECT id,
  type,
  status,
  name,
  scn,
  object_no,
  cache_id
FROM v$result_cache_objects
WHERE name='SELECT /*+RESULT_CACHE*/ deptno, COUNT(empno) FROM employees e
GROUP BY deptno';
```

Script Result

ID	TYPE	STATUS	NAME	SCN	OBJECT_NO
1	Result	Invalid	SELECT /*+RESULT_CACHE*/ deptno, COUNT(empno) FROM employees e GROUP BY deptno	5687149	0

Now, we must re-execute the query to rebuild the result set in the cache area,

```
SELECT /*+RESULT_CACHE*/ deptno, COUNT(empno) FROM employees e GROUP BY
deptno;
```

When we query the V$RESULT_CACHE_OBJECTS table now, we can see both the newly rebuilt result set and the old invalidated result set as shown below,

```
SELECT id,
  type,
  status,
  name,
  scn,
  object_no,
  cache_id
FROM v$result_cache_objects
WHERE name='SELECT /*+RESULT_CACHE*/ deptno, COUNT(empno) FROM employees e
GROUP BY deptno';
```

Script Result

ID	TYPE	STATUS	NAME	SCN	OBJECT_NO
2	Result	Published	SELECT /*+RESULT_CACHE*/ deptno, COUNT(empno) FROM employees e GROUP BY deptno	5687332	0
1	Result	Invalid	SELECT /*+RESULT_CACHE*/ deptno, COUNT(empno) FROM employees e GROUP BY deptno	5687149	0

Note that the invalidated result set is held back in the cache memory until the instance is restarted, or manually deleted using the DELETE_DEPENDENCY API, or automatically aged out.

Manual Invalidation

We can also manually invalidate a result set if we are not sure about the cached result set's credibility. This can be done with the help of the INVALIDATE (to invalidate all the dependent cache objects of the input object) or the INVALIDATE_OBJECT (to invalidate a particular cache object) APIs.

The below code snippet invalidates a particular result set object using a cache ID,

```
EXEC
dbms_result_cache.invalidate_object(cache_id=>'4538a7r4sbdkf6nsk2a9gjgy5x');
```

The below code snippet invalidates all the dependent result set objects pertaining to an object ID.

```
EXEC dbms_result_cache.invalidate(object_id=>99854);
```

Result Cache Requirements

Enabling the result cache in a database does not ensure that the result sets will be cached in the Shared Pool. The following requirements must be met in order to cache the result sets.

Read Consistency Requirements

The following conditions must be met in order to cache a result set,

1) The SCN of the result set stored in the cache must retrieve the most current data in the database.
2) The query points to an explicit point in time using the Flashback query option.

Query Parameter Requirements

The Cached results of a parameterized query can be reused only when the queries are equivalent and the parameter values passed are the same. If the parameter values are different, the cached results may not be retrieved. The cached results are said to be parameterized if any of the below constructs are used in the query,

- Bind variables.
- DBTIMEZONE, SESSIONTIMEZONE, SYS_CONTEXT with constant variables, UID, and USER functions.
- NLS Parameters.

SQL Query Result Cache Restrictions

The result sets will not be cached if the objects below are used in the query,

- Temporary tables, and the tables belonging to SYS or SYSTEM users.
- Sequence pseudo columns like NEXTVAL and CURRVAL.
- SQL functions like CURRENT_DATE, CURRENT_TIMESTAMP, LOCAL_TIMESTAMP, SYS_CONTEXT with non-constant variables, SYS_GUID, SYSDATE, and SYSTIMESTAMP.

PL/SQL Function Result Cache

The PL/SQL function result cache works similar to the SQL query result cache. When a result-cached function is invoked, the database checks for the cache memory to find if there are any results from the previous invocation of this function with the same set of parameter values. If the cache does not contain any such result set pertaining to this function, the database executes the function and adds the return result set to the cache memory before returning the control to the invoker.

> Note: If the function results in an unhandled exception, the exception results are not stored in the cache memory.

We can cache a result-cached function once for every unique combination of the input parameter values. If the cache memory runs low, the cached results are aged out in an LRU fashion to accommodate more cache results.

Oracle database automatically identifies and stores all the objects that are referenced by the result-cached function. Thus, when any of these objects are altered, the cached results become invalid and must be recomputed. The best candidates for function result caching are the functions that are most often invoked, but references the objects that are less likely to be changed.

 Note: The database initialization parameter RESULT_CACHE_MODE does not make a PL/SQL function result cached. However, if the RESULT_CACHE_MODE is set to FORCE, all the SQL statements including the PL/SQL functions will be cached in the SQL query result cache.

To make a function result cached, we must include the RESULT_CACHE clause in the function's definition. In case if the function is wrapped in the packages, we must include this clause in the function's definition, both in the specification and the body of the package.

 Note: Prior to 12c, the database used the RELIES_ON clause to identify the objects whose state would affect the function's cached result. From 12c, Oracle database considers the state of all the objects that are referenced by the result-cached function to maintain the function's cached result and deprecated the RELIES_ON clause.

In the below listing, a result cache function returning the name of the employee for the input employee ID is created as shown,

```
CREATE OR REPLACE FUNCTION func_emp(
    ip_empno NUMBER)
  RETURN VARCHAR2 result_cache
IS
  l_vc_name employees.ename%type;
BEGIN
  SELECT ename INTO l_vc_name FROM employees WHERE empno=ip_empno;
  dbms_output.put_line(l_vc_name);
  RETURN l_vc_name;
END;
/
```

Note that the PUT_LINE procedure prints the employee name for every unique function call. If we lose the RESULT_CACHE clause in this function, the PUT_LINE procedure prints the employee name for every function call irrespective of the input parameter's uniqueness.

When we execute the below query to find the manager name for the first 5 employees, the result-cached function is called only thrice for the three unique manager names as shown below,

```
SELECT empno, ename, mgr, func_emp(mgr) FROM employees WHERE empno<=5;
```

Script Result:

EMPNO	ENAME	MGR	FUNC_EMP(MGR)
1	SMITH	7902	BLAKE
2	ALLEN	7698	JAMES
3	WARD	7698	JAMES
4	JONES	7839	FORD
5	MARTIN	7698	JAMES

```
DBMS OUTPUT:
BLAKE
JAMES
FORD
```

The below script result shows that the function has been called thrice (Create Count Success) and the function's result has been reused twice (Find Count).

```
SELECT *
FROM v$result_cache_statistics
WHERE NAME IN ('Create Count Success', 'Find Count');
```

Script Results

ID	NAME	VALUE	CON_ID
5	Create Count Success	3	0
7	Find Count	2	0

When we check the V$RESULT_CACHE_OBJECTS table, we can see that there are two dependency objects (FUNC_EMP function and EMPLOYEES table) and three result set objects (For three unique input calls) with their status as PUBLISHED. Also, note that the cache IDs of the result set objects are the same as they are produced from the same function.

```
SELECT id,
  type,
  status,
  name,
  scn,
  object_no,
  cache_id
FROM v$result_cache_objects;
```

Script Results

ID	TYPE	STATUS	NAME	SCN	OBJECT_NO	CACHE_ID
0	Dependency	Published	C##.FUNC_EMP	5694796	99985	C##.FUNC_EMP
1	Result	Published	"C##"."FUNC_EMP"::8."FUNC_EMP" #8287fb8db4848443 #1	5694796	0	3wf9mddjkq61m9h6 spkuf5agpr
2	Dependency	Published	C##.EMPLOYEES	5694796	99854	C##.EMPLOYEES
3	Result	Published	"C##"."FUNC_EMP"::8."FUNC_EMP" #8287fb8db4848443 #1	5694796	0	3wf9mddjkq61m9h6 spkuf5agpr
4	Result	Published	"C##"."FUNC_EMP"::8."FUNC_EMP" #8287fb8db4848443 #1	5694796	0	3wf9mddjkq61m9h6 spkuf5agpr

The function's result set object gets invalidated if the underlying data sources are altered/ updated if the function is recompiled, if we manually invalidate it by using the INVALIDATE or the INVALIDATE_OBJECT APIS.

In the below code listing, we recompile the result-cached function,

```
ALTER FUNCTION func_emp compile;
```

We can now see that all the result sets pertaining to the function FUNC_EMP are invalidated and will be republished only upon the function's next call.

```
SELECT id,
  type,
  status,
  name,
  scn,
  object_no,
  cache_id
FROM v$result_cache_objects;
```

Script Results

ID	TYPE	STATUS	NAME	SCN	OBJECT_NO	CACHE_ID
0	Dependency	Published	C##.FUNC_EMP	5696103	99985	C##.FUNC_EMP
1	Result	Invalid	"C##"."FUNC_EMP"::8."FUNC_EMP"#8287fb8db4848443 #1	5694796	0	3wf9mddjkq61m9h6sp kuf5agpr
2	Dependency	Published	C##.EMPLOYEES	5694796	99854	C##.EMPLOYEES
3	Result	Invalid	"C##"."FUNC_EMP"::8."FUNC_EMP"#8287fb8db4848443 #1	5694796	0	3wf9mddjkq61m9h6sp kuf5agpr
4	Result	Invalid	"C##"."FUNC_EMP"::8."FUNC_EMP"#8287fb8db4848443 #1	5694796	0	3wf9mddjkq61m9h6sp kuf5agpr

Function Result Cache Vs Deterministic Functions

A function is said to be deterministic only if it returns the same output for the same input at any point in time. The Deterministic function works pretty similar to the PL/SQL function result cache except for the fact that the Deterministic functions are session specific and the PL/SQL function result cache works across multiple sessions. Another difference between them would be that the Deterministic functions cannot be called in PL/SQL but the PL/SQL function result cache can be.

Thus, a function defined as Deterministic must run at least once for every unique session call, but the Function Result cache runs just once for the all the sessions.

Function Result Cache Restrictions

The PL/SQL function Result Cache must meet all the below conditions to be result cached,

1) It must not be defined inside an anonymous block.
2) It must not be a pipelined function.
3) It must not be inside a WITH clause.
4) It must not reference the data dictionary tables, temporary tables, sequences, or non-deterministic SQL functions.
5) It must not have any OUT or IN OUT parameters.
6) The IN parameters and the RETURN type of the function must not be of BLOB, CLOB, NCLOB, Ref Cursor, Collection, Object, and Record types.

Client Result Cache Concepts

The applications that use the Oracle database drivers and adapters built on OCI (Oracle Client Interface) libraries can get benefit out of the Client result cache by improving the performance and timings of the frequently executed queries. The Client Result Cache enables the client-side result caching of the SQL statement's result sets in the client memory rather than in the server memory. Also, the server scalability is greatly improved in Client Result Cache by reducing the server CPU time. Note that we must also enable OCI statement caching or cache statements at the application level while using the Client Result Cache.

The Client Result Cache is transparent, consistent, and is available for every process, so the multiple client sessions can simultaneously use matching cached results. The main advantage of the Client Result Cache is that the cache hit avoids the server round-trip as the Client Result Cache is situated in the client and not in the server. Thus, improving the performance of the database with a reduction in the number of the server resources. Also, the OCI client memory is cheaper than the Server memory.

For any application to keep its query result sets consistent across the database and session state changes is difficult, but the Client Result Cache transparently keeps its result sets consistently. When an object referenced to the cached result set object is modified, the invalidation of the cached result set is notified to the client on its next round trip to the server. If there is an open transaction, OCI ensures that the queries referencing the objects belonging to that transaction were sent to the server to rebuild the results rather than using their already cached version. This consistency mechanism ensures that the Client Result Cache is always intact with the database changes.

We can enable or disable the Client Result Cache at the Query level (by using the hints), Table level (by using annotations), or at the Session level (by using the session level parameters). Also, it is suggested that we enable Client Result Cache only for the queries and tables that seldom changes or for the session that query only read-only or seldom read tables.

> Note: When Client Result Cache is enabled, the result sets can be cached either on the Client, Server, or both. We can enable Client result cache even when the Server result cache is disabled.

The results of the following queries will not be cached in the Client result cache under any condition,

- Queries containing remote objects, complex type in the Select list, and PL/SQL function.
- Snapshot and Flashback queries.
- Queries containing the table for which a VPD policy is enabled.
- Queries which are executed in read-only and serializable transactions.

The initialization parameters required for setting up of the Client Result Cache are described below,

- **COMPATIBLE** – This parameter specifies the release version with which the database must maintain compatibility with. For example, to enable Client Result Cache, this parameter must be set at least to 11.0.0.0 and to enable Client Result Cache for views, this parameter must be set at least to 11.2.0.0.

- **CLIENT_RESULT_CACHE_SIZE** – This parameter specifies the maximum size of the Client Result Cache size for each OCI client process. The least and the default value is 0 (Disabled mode). The greatest value for this parameter can be either the available client memory or 2 GB. If we try to set it to more than 2 GB, it will be brought down to 2 GB. To enable Client Result Cache, we must at least set it to 32 KB.

- **CLIENT_RESULT_CACHE_LAG** – This parameter specifies the maximum time in milliseconds that Client Result Cache can lag behind changes in the database that impact its result sets. The default value is 3000.

> ⌂ Note: Both the CLIENT_RESULT_CACHE_SIZE and the CLIENT_RESULT_CACHE_LAG parameters are static. Thus, when we change their value using the ALTER SYSTEM command, we must the SCOPE=SPFILE clause and restart the database to make the changes get effect.

Result Caches in Oracle RAC Environments

In an Oracle RAC environment, each database instance maintains its own local result cache but spawns its cached result sets across the sessions which are attached to other instances. If a result set is not available in the local instance, instead of computing the result sets again, they are retrieved from the local cache results of other instances.

Even though the database instances have their own local result caches, the process of handling the cached object invalidation is wide across all the instances of the RAC database. If a cached result is invalidated in one RAC instance, they are invalidated in every other instance in the database to avoid inconsistency.

Result Cache Enhancement in Oracle R12c

Prior to the Oracle version 12c, an invoker rights function cannot be result cached. This is because, the PL/SQL engine uses the current user's privileges to resolve the function referenced database objects at the runtime, in the case of invoker rights function. Consider that an invoker rights function was allowed to be compiled with the RESULT_CACHE clause and an authorized user (say USER1) has already executed this function for a value (say 200) and stored his result in the cache memory. The Result cache functionality could be deliberately used by any unauthorized user (say USER2) to get the function's output for the same input value (200) without executing the function body and resolving the function referenced database objects. This could have caused some serious security violations.

This restriction has been lifted from the Oracle database version 12c, and now we can create a Result cached invoker rights function without any security breaches. From 12c, Oracle passes the name of the current user as an extra parameter along with the values of all the arguments passed to the function. Whenever this function is executed, Oracle checks to see if this function has been previously executed with the same set of parameters by the same user. This means that the result cache for an invoker rights function is logically partitioned by the current user.

Thus, we can see performance gains in the result cached invoker rights function only if it is called by the same user for the same set of arguments multiple times, similar to the Deterministic functions.

In the below example, an invoker rights function with the result cache feature is created as shown below,

```
CREATE OR REPLACE FUNCTION func_emp(
    ip_empno NUMBER)
  RETURN VARCHAR2 result_cache authid current_user
IS
  l_vc_name employees.ename%type;
BEGIN
  SELECT ename INTO l_vc_name FROM employees WHERE empno=ip_empno;
  dbms_output.put_line(l_vc_name);
  RETURN l_vc_name;
END;
/
```

If we try to create this function prior to 12c, we might encounter the *PLS-00999: implementation restriction (may be temporary) RESULT_CACHE is disallowed on subprograms in Invoker-Rights modules* exception.

Summary

We started this chapter by understanding the basic Result Caching concepts and learned the Server Result Cache techniques and their administration concepts for increasing the performance of the SQL statements and PL/SQL functions. The later section taught us the about the Client Result Cache concepts and their administration techniques. The next section explained the behavior of the Result Cache in the Oracle RAC environments. We ended this chapter by learning the R12.1 enhancement, which allows us to create an Invoker rights function with Result caching eliminating the security breach. In the next chapter, we will be understanding the PL/SQL analyzing and debugging techniques.

Analyzing & Debugging the PL/SQL

After the completion of the code development process followed by its performance tuning, we must analyze and debug the code in order to deploy it in the production for the long run. Analyzing the PL/SQL code helps us to identify the dependency of the program code, program references, unused parameters, monitor their metadata changes, and optimization settings for code maintenance, forecasting, and reporting purposes. Debugging the PL/SQL code helps us in understanding the presence of any programmatic or business exceptions and unused codes in our code and to fix them.

Oracle has provided us with a handful of data dictionary views, initialization parameters, and system packages for efficiently analyzing and debugging the PL/SQL code. Apart from the system packages, Oracle IDEs such as SQL Developer, PL/SQL Developer, etc. can also be used for controlled debugging.

We will be understanding the different analyzing and debugging techniques in this chapter in brief through the below topics.

32) Finding the code information using the data dictionary objects.

33) Finding the arguments and SQL statements in a PL/SQL unit using the PLSCOPE_SETTINGS parameter.

34) Describing a subprogram using the DBMS_DESCRIBE package.

35) Tracking the program and error propagation using the UTL_CALL_STACK package from and after R12.1.

36) PL/SQL expressions enhancement, Long identifiers, DEPRECATE and COVERAGE pragmas in R12.2.

37) Finding the metadata of a PL/SQL program using the DBMS_METADATA package.

38) Debugging the PL/SQL code using the SQL Developer IDE and DBMS_DEBUG package.

39) PL/SQL conditional compilation.

Finding Coding Information

The data dictionary tables and views are read-only objects which are created first during any database creation and are continuously updated while a database is open and in use. They consist of all the necessary information about every single database object accessible through the database for reporting, forecasting, and analysis purposes, thus reducing the unnecessary process and time in the clumsy line-by-line manual way of analysis. These objects are stored in the *Data Dictionary Cache* in the *Shared Pool* area.

The data dictionary objects are grouped in three sets which are distinguished from each other by their prefixes as shown in the below tabulation. By querying the appropriate view, we will be accessing the information that is relevant to us.

Data Dictionary View Sets

Prefix	User Access	Contents	Comments
DBA_	Database Administrators	All the objects in the database.	Some views may have additional columns containing useful information to the DBAs.
ALL_	All users	All the objects to which user has privilege.	Includes objects owned by all users. These views have a column named OWNER for identifying the owner of the object queried.
USER_	All users	All the objects owned by the user.	These views generally do not have the OWNER column as they only display the objects pertaining to the current user.

> Note: All the data dictionary objects and their comments can be queried from the DICT[IONARY] view and their column structure and comments can be queried from the DICT_COLUMNS view.

For our demonstration purpose, the below package is created with a function FUNC_ADD for adding two input numbers and a procedure PROC_SUB for subtracting two input numbers, for code analysis using the data dictionary views.

```
CREATE OR REPLACE PACKAGE pkg_test
IS
  FUNCTION func_add(
      ip_param1 NUMBER,
      ip_param2 NUMBER)
    RETURN NUMBER;
  PROCEDURE proc_sub(
      ip_param1 NUMBER,
      ip_param2 NUMBER,
      op_param3 OUT NUMBER);
END;
/
```

```
CREATE OR REPLACE PACKAGE body pkg_test
IS
  FUNCTION func_add(
      ip_param1 NUMBER,
      ip_param2 NUMBER)
    RETURN NUMBER
  IS
    l_n_var1 NUMBER;
  BEGIN
    l_n_var1:=ip_param1+ip_param2;
    RETURN l_n_var1;
  END;
  PROCEDURE proc_sub(
      ip_param1 NUMBER,
      ip_param2 NUMBER,
      op_param3 OUT NUMBER)
  IS
  BEGIN
    op_param3:=ip_param1-ip_param2;
    dbms_output.put_line('The Subtracted value is '||op_param3);
  END;
END;
/
```

There are several data dictionary objects available in the database that serve different purposes, out of which the below important ones are explained in brief,

USER_OBJECTS

This view displays the information about all the stored database objects in a row by row manner. It contains the necessary information about the database objects like its type, last modified time, validity, namespace, (EDITIONABLE) whether the object is editionable or not, and (ORACLE_MAINTAINED) whether the object is maintained by the Oracle database or by the user.

An object is said to be Editioned if there is more than one version of it is created in Editions enabled schema. This is mainly to facilitate the online application upgrades. If an object is Editioned, the EDITIONABLE column holds the character Y and if not, then the column holds the character N.

All the Oracle supplied objects are maintained internally by Oracle and the objects which are created by the users are not maintained by Oracle but by the user. Thus, the column ORACLE_MAINTAINED holds the character Y for all the objects that are maintained internally by the database and holds the character N for all the user created objects.

When we query the package PKG_TEST from the USER_OBJECTS view, we can see two rows pertaining to the PACKAGE and the PACKAGE BODY objects as shown below,

```
SELECT object_name,
  object_id,
  object_type,
  created,
  last_ddl_time,
  status,
  namespace,
  editionable,
  oracle_maintained
FROM user_objects
WHERE object_name='PKG_TEST';
```

Query Result

OBJECT_ NAME	OBJEC T_ID	OBJEC T_TYPE	CREA TED	LAST_D DL_TIM E	STATU S	NAMES PACE	EDITION ABLE	ORACLE_MAI NTAINED
PKG_TES T	100371	PACKA GE BODY	14-JAN-17	14-JAN-17	VALID	2	N	N
PKG_TES T	100370	PACKA GE	14-JAN-17	14-JAN-17	VALID	1	N	N

USER_OBJECT_SIZE

This view is mainly used by the compiler and the runtime engine. We can also query it to find the source, parsed, compiled, and error code sizes (in bytes) of our program. We can use this view to analyze the size of every program and break them down into multiple smaller subprograms or group multiple programs into a single program for better efficiency.

The below query lists down the source code, parsed code, compiled code, and error code sizes of the PKG_TEST package as shown,

```
SELECT * FROM user_object_size WHERE name='PKG_TEST';
```

Query Result

NAME	TYPE	SOURCE_ SIZE	PARSED_ SIZE	CODE_ SIZE	ERROR_ SIZE
PKG_TEST	PACKAGE BODY	367	106	364	0
PKG_TEST	PACKAGE	211	897	296	0

USER_SOURCE

This view contains the text source of all the database objects line by line, which can be used for searching a particular portion of the object code for analysis purpose or for exporting the source code with an ease.

The below query prints the source code of the PKG_TEST package using the USER_SOURCE view as shown,

```
SELECT * FROM user_source WHERE name='PKG_TEST';
```

Query Result

NAME	TYPE	LINE	TEXT	ORIGIN_CON_ID
PKG_TEST	PACKAGE	1	PACKAGE pkg_test	1
PKG_TEST	PACKAGE	2	IS	1
PKG_TEST	PACKAGE	3	FUNCTION func_add(	1
PKG_TEST	PACKAGE	4	ip_param1 NUMBER,	1
PKG_TEST	PACKAGE	5	ip_param2 NUMBER)	1
...	...	...	...	...
...	...	...	...	...

USER_PROCEDURES

Even though the name of the view talks only about the procedures, this view displays all the vital properties of the standalone procedures, standalone functions, and the subprograms in the packages.

The below query displays all the properties of the procedure and the function in the PKG_TEST package as shown,

```
SELECT object_name,
   object_type,
   procedure_name,
   subprogram_id,
   aggregate,
   pipelined,
   parallel,
   interface,
   deterministic
FROM user_procedures
WHERE object_name='PKG_TEST';
```

Query Result

OBJECT _NAME	OBJECT _TYPE	PROCEDU RE_NAME	SUBPROG RAM_ID	AGGRE GATE	PIPEL INED	PARA LLEL	INTER FACE	DETERM INISTIC	AUT HID
PKG_TE ST	PACKA GE		0	NO	NO	NO	NO	NO	DEFI NER
PKG_TE ST	PACKA GE	FUNC_ADD	1	NO	NO	NO	NO	NO	DEFI NER
PKG_TE ST	PACKA GE	PROC_SUB	2	NO	NO	NO	NO	NO	DEFI NER

USER_ARGUMENTS

This view displays all the arguments and its necessary information like position, datatype, default value, and the argument direction (IN, OUT, or IN OUT) of the standalone procedures/ functions and the subprograms in the packages.

The below query displays all the arguments and their properties of the procedure and the function in the PKG_TEST package as shown,

```
SELECT package_name,
  object_name,
  subprogram_id,
  argument_name,
  position,
  data_type,
  default_value,
  in_out,
  data_length
FROM user_arguments
WHERE package_name='PKG_TEST';
```

Query Result

PACKAGE _NAME	OBJECT_ NAME	SUBPROG RAM_ID	ARGUMENT _NAME	POSIT ION	DATA_ TYPE	DEFAULT_ VALUE	IN_ OUT	DATA_LE NGTH
PKG_TEST	FUNC_AD D	1		0	NUMBE R		OUT	22
PKG_TEST	FUNC_AD D	1	IP_PARAM1	1	NUMBE R		IN	22
PKG_TEST	FUNC_AD D	1	IP_PARAM2	2	NUMBE R		IN	22
PKG_TEST	PROC_S UB	2	IP_PARAM1	1	NUMBE R		IN	22
PKG_TEST	PROC_S UB	2	IP_PARAM2	2	NUMBE R		IN	22
PKG_TEST	PROC_S UB	2	OP_PARAM 3	3	NUMBE R		OUT	22

USER_DEPENDENCIES

This view provides the list of objects to and from which the given object is dependent. This view can be used for mass compiling or mass dropping the database objects in their dependency order during a database upgrade/ cleanup. If any of the dependent objects turns INVALID, this object also turns INVALID.

The DEPENDENCY_TYPE column shows whether the dependency is a referential (REF) dependency or a hard (HARD) dependency.

The below query displays all the dependencies of the PKG_TEST package as shown,

```
SELECT name,
  type,
  referenced_owner,
  referenced_name,
  referenced_type,
  dependency_type
FROM user_dependencies
WHERE name='PKG_TEST';
```

Query Result

NAME	TYPE	REFERENCED_O WNER	REFERENCED_N AME	REFERENCED_ TYPE	DEPENDENCY_ TYPE
PKG_TE ST	PACKA GE	SYS	STANDARD	PACKAGE	HARD
PKG_TE ST	PACKA GE BODY	SYS	STANDARD	PACKAGE	HARD
PKG_TE ST	PACKA GE BODY	SYS	DBMS_OUTPUT	PACKAGE	HARD
PKG_TE ST	PACKA GE BODY	SYS	PKG_TEST	PACKAGE	HARD

USER_PLSQL_OBJECT_SETTINGS & USER_STORED_SETTINGS

Both views are used to display the compilation parameter values of a PL/SQL object. The difference between them both is that the USER_PLSQL_OBJECT_SETTINGS view displays the parameters as columns and the USER_STORED_SETTINGS view displays them as rows in key-value pair format.

Also, the USER_STORED_SETTINGS view holds the deprecated PLSQL_COMPILER_FLAGS parameter, which holds the compilation mode (NATIVE or INTERPRETED) and the debug mode (DEBUG or NON_DEBUG).

From Oracle R12.1, the PLSQL_DEBUG parameter is also deprecated and the debug mode is internally turned ON when the PLSQL_OPTIMIZE_LEVEL is set to 0 or 1.

The below query displays the compilation parameters of the PKG_TEST package from the USER_PLSQL_OBJECT_SETTINGS view as shown,

```
SELECT name,
  type,
  plsql_optimize_level,
  plsql_code_type,
  plsql_debug,
  plsql_warnings,
  nls_length_semantics,
  plsql_ccflags,
  plscope_settings
FROM user_plsql_object_settings
WHERE name='PKG_TEST'
AND type='PACKAGE';
```

Query Result

NAME	TYPE	PLSQL_OP TIMIZE_LE VEL	PLSQL_C ODE_TYP E	PLSQL_D EBUG	PLSQL_ WARNIN G	NLS_LEN GTH_SE MANTICS	PLSQL _CCFL AGS	PLSCOPE_S ETTINGS
PKG_ TEST	PACKA GE	2	INTERPRE TED	FALSE	DISABLE: ALL	BYTE		IDENTIFIERS: ALL

The below query displays the compilation parameters of the PKG_TEST package from the USER_STORED_SETTINGS view as shown,

```
SELECT object_name,
  object_type,
  param_name,
  param_value
FROM user_stored_settings
where object_name='PKG_TEST'
and object_type='PACKAGE';
```

Query Result

OBJECT_NAME	OBJECT_TYPE	PARAM_NAME	PARAM_VALUE
PKG_TEST	PACKAGE	plsql_optimize_level	2
PKG_TEST	PACKAGE	plsql_code_type	INTERPRETED
PKG_TEST	PACKAGE	plsql_debug	FALSE
PKG_TEST	PACKAGE	nls_length_semantics	BYTE
PKG_TEST	PACKAGE	plsql_warnings	DISABLE:ALL
PKG_TEST	PACKAGE	plsql_ccflags	
PKG_TEST	PACKAGE	plscope_settings	IDENTIFIERS:ALL
PKG_TEST	PACKAGE	plsql_compiler_flags	INTERPRETED,NON_DEBUG

USER_ERRORS

This view displays all the current compilation errors and warnings of the PL/SQL objects stored in the database. We can also access this view by issuing the SHOW ERRORS command in the SQL*PLUS mode.

The below query displays the compilation errors in the PKG_TEST package displayed using the USER_ERRORS view when we accidently add the text "-" to the end of the package,

```
SELECT name,
  type,
  line,
  position,
  text,
  attribute,
  message_number
FROM user_errors
WHERE name='PKG_TEST';
```

Query Result

NAME	TYPE	LINE	POSITION	TEXT	ATTRIBUTE	MESSAGE_NUMBER
PKG_TEST	PACKAGE BODY	21	7	PLS-00103: Encountered the symbol "-" when expecting one of the following: begin end function pragma procedure The symbol "-" was ignored.	ERROR	103

PLSCOPE_SETTINGS

The PLSCOPE_SETTINGS is a compilation parameter which is introduced in the Oracle version 11g. This parameter can be used for gathering information about the identifiers in a stored PL/SQL database object during its compilation and makes it available in the USER_IDENTIFIERS data dictionary. This parameter provides information like the name of the identifier, which subprogram/ program they reside in, their usage (Whether they are declared, referenced, defined, or called), and a signature ID for uniquely identifying each identifier.

Note: This parameter does not gather identifier information for the wrapped code.

By default, this parameter is turned OFF, thus no identifier information will be collected unnecessarily. To gather all the identifier information, including the identifiers in the package body, we must set this parameter to 'IDENTIFIERS: ALL' in either SYSTEM, SESSION, or OBJECT level. Setting this parameter at the SYSTEM level will collect all the identifier information of all the database objects, thus resulting in slowness during the object compilation.

The prototype for setting this parameter at the SYSTEM or SESSION level is shown below,

```
ALTER <SYSTEM | SESSION> SET
PLSCOPE_SETTINGS='<IDENTIFIERS:ALL|NONE|PUBLIC|SQL|PLSQL> [,
STATEMENTS:ALL|NONE]';
```

The prototype for setting this parameter at the OBJECT level is shown below,

```
ALTER <OBJECT_TYPE> <OBJECT_NAME> COMPILE
PLSCOPE_SETTINGS='<IDENTIFIERS:ALL|NONE|PUBLIC|SQL|PLSQL> [,
STATEMENTS:ALL|NONE]' [REUSE SETTINGS];
```

- **IDENTIFIERS** value shows that identifiers from the PL/SQL code have to be gathered.
    - o **ALL** enables the collection of all source code identifier data.
    - o **NONE** disables the collection of all source code identifier data. This is the default value.
    - o **PUBLIC** enables the collection of all Public user identifier data except for DEFINITION.
    - o **SQL** enables the collection of all SQL identifier data.
    - o **PLSQL** enables the collection of all PLSQL identifier data.

- **STATEMENTS** value shows that SQL statements from the PL/SQL code have to be gathered.
    - o **ALL** enables the collection of all SQL statements used in the PL/SQL code.
    - o **NONE** disables the collection of SQL statements.

Note that the *STATEMENTS: ALL | NONE* option is available only from R12.2.

When we execute the below statement, all the identifiers in the current session are collected,

```
ALTER SESSION SET PLSCOPE_SETTINGS='IDENTIFIERS:ALL';
```

We can verify the current setting by querying the V$PARAMETER table as below,

```
SELECT name, value FROM v$parameter WHERE name='plscope_settings';
```

Script Result

NAME	VALUE
plscope_settings	IDENTIFIERS:ALL

Or by executing the SHOW PARAMETER command as shown below,

```
SHOW PARAMETER plscope_settings;
```

```
NAME              TYPE    VALUE
---------------- ------  ---------------
plscope_settings string  IDENTIFIERS:ALL
```

The collected data are stored in the SYSAUX tablespace. If the SYSAUX tablespace is unavailable and if we try to compile an object with *PLSCOPE_SETTINGS='IDENTIFIERS:ALL'* setting, the PL/SCOPE utility does not collect data for that object. The compiler will not issue a warning or an error but saves a warning in the *USER_ERRORS* view.

We can check the space occupied by the PL/SCOPE utility by checking the SYSAUX tablespace as shown below,

```
SELECT occupant_name,
  occupant_desc,
  schema_name,
  space_usage_kbytes
FROM v$sysaux_occupants
WHERE occupant_name='PL/SCOPE';
```

Script Result:

OCCUPANT_NA ME	OCCUPANT_DESC	SCHEMA_NAME	SPACE_USAGE_KBYTES
PL/SCOPE	PL/SQL Identifier Collection	SYS	2176

PLSCOPE_SETTINGS

The USER_IDENTIFIERS view was introduced in the Oracle version 11g and is populated by the PLSCOPE_SETTINGS compilation parameter value. This view can be used for describing the usage of identifiers in the stored objects that are owned by the current user.

> 🔔 Note: When the PLSCOPE_SETTINGS parameter value is set to IDENTIFIERS:NONE globally, this view turns empty.

In the below query, the identifiers and their usage in the PKG_TEST package are displayed.

```
SELECT name,
  type,
  object_type,
  listagg(usage, ', ')within GROUP(
ORDER BY usage) usage
FROM
  (SELECT DISTINCT name,
    type,
    usage,
    object_type
  FROM user_identifiers
  WHERE object_name='PKG_TEST'
  )
GROUP BY name,
  type,
  object_type
ORDER BY name,
  object_type;
```

Query Result

NAME	TYPE	OBJECT_TYPE	USAGE
FUNC_ADD	FUNCTION	PACKAGE	DECLARATION
FUNC_ADD	FUNCTION	PACKAGE BODY	DEFINITION
IP_PARAM1	FORMAL IN	PACKAGE	DECLARATION
IP_PARAM1	FORMAL IN	PACKAGE BODY	DECLARATION, REFERENCE
IP_PARAM2	FORMAL IN	PACKAGE	DECLARATION
IP_PARAM2	FORMAL IN	PACKAGE BODY	DECLARATION, REFERENCE
L_N_VAR1	VARIABLE	PACKAGE BODY	ASSIGNMENT, DECLARATION, REFERENCE
NUMBER	NUMBER DATATYPE	PACKAGE	REFERENCE
NUMBER	NUMBER DATATYPE	PACKAGE BODY	REFERENCE
OP_PARAM3	FORMAL OUT	PACKAGE	DECLARATION
OP_PARAM3	FORMAL OUT	PACKAGE BODY	ASSIGNMENT, DECLARATION, REFERENCE
PKG_TEST	PACKAGE	PACKAGE	DECLARATION
PKG_TEST	PACKAGE	PACKAGE BODY	DEFINITION
PROC_SUB	PROCEDURE	PACKAGE	DECLARATION
PROC_SUB	PROCEDURE	PACKAGE BODY	DEFINITION

From the above result, we can see that,

- The function FUNC_ADD and the procedure PROC_SUB are declared in the package specification and defined in the package body.
- The input parameters IP_PARAM1 and IP_PARAM2 are declared in the package specification and declared/ referenced in the package body.
- The output parameter OP_PARAM3 is declared in the package specification and declared/ referenced/ assigned in the package body.
- The local variable L_N_VAR1 is declared, referenced, and assigned in the package body.
- The datatype NUMBER is referenced in both the package specification and the body.

The USER_STATEMENTS view was introduced in the Oracle version R12.2 and is also populated by the PLSCOPE_SETTINGS compilation parameter value. This view can be used for reporting the occurrence of static and dynamic (EXECUTE IMMEDIATE and OPEN-FOR statements) SQLs in the PL/SQL units for the current user.

The below SQL displays all the PL/SQL objects owned by the current user, that have either EXECUTE IMMEDIATE or OPEN FOR statement along with either a Hint, a BULK COLLECT INTO statement, a RETURNING INTO statement, a into Record statement, a CURRENT OF statement, a FOR UPDATE statement, or a Bind variable.

```
SELECT object_name,
  line,
  full_text
FROM user_statements
WHERE type IN ('EXECUTE IMMEDIATE', 'OPEN')
AND 'YES' IN (has_hint, has_into_bulk, has_into_returning, has_into_record,
has_current_of, has_for_update, has_in_binds);
```

DBMS_DESCRIBE

The DBMS_DESCRIBE package can be used for describing the structure of a stored procedure or a function, but not a package as a whole. This package is created during the database installation through the *dbmsdesc.sql* script. The result of this package is synonymous to the USER_ARGUMENTS data dictionary view but can be used in the places where we want to return the structure of a program in the form of OUT parameters to the client environment. Thus, the USER_ARGUMENTS view can be used in the places where we want to manually verify the subprogram's description and the DBMS_DESCRIBE can be used effectively when we would like to return the subprogram's description to the client program.

Another difference would be like in USER_ARGUMENTS the datatype returned is in its descriptive format, whereas in the DBMS_DESCRIBE package, the datatype returned is in its integer code, which has to be decoded in order to retrieve its descriptive format.

This package contains only one procedure, namely DESCRIBE_PROCEDURE which accepts the name of the subprogram that has to be described and returns the required information using 13 index-by-table OUT parameters.

The prototype of this package is shown below,

```
DBMS_DESCRIBE.DESCRIBE_PROCEDURE(
    object_name             IN VARCHAR2,
    reserved1               IN VARCHAR2,
    reserved2               IN VARCHAR2,
    overload                OUT NUMBER_TABLE,
    position                OUT NUMBER_TABLE,
    level                   OUT NUMBER_TABLE,
    argument_name           OUT VARCHAR2_TABLE,
    datatype                OUT NUMBER_TABLE,
    default_value           OUT NUMBER_TABLE,
    in_out                  OUT NUMBER_TABLE,
    length                  OUT NUMBER_TABLE,
    precision               OUT NUMBER_TABLE,
    scale                   OUT NUMBER_TABLE,
    radix                   OUT NUMBER_TABLE,
    spare                   OUT NUMBER_TABLE
    include_string_constraints OUT BOOLEAN DEFAULT FALSE);
```

 Note: The INCLUDE_STRING_CONSTRAINTS is one mysterious OUT parameter with a DEFAULT value! We obviously cannot default any OUT parameters for the subprograms we create.

- The RESERVED1 and RESERVED2 parameters are reserved for future implementation and must be set to null during the procedure call.

The DBMS_DESCRIBE package declares the below two associative arrays, which are used for holding the data returned by it using its OUT parameters.

```
TYPE VARCHAR2_TABLE
IS
  TABLE OF VARCHAR2(30) INDEX BY BINARY_INTEGER;

TYPE NUMBER_TABLE
IS
  TABLE OF NUMBER INDEX BY BINARY_INTEGER;
```

In the below code listing, the function FUNC_ADD from the PKG_TEST package is described and its parameter values are looped and printed using the DBMS_DESCRIBE package as shown below,

```
DECLARE
  l_aa_overload dbms_describe.number_table;
  l_aa_position dbms_describe.number_table;
  l_aa_level dbms_describe.number_table;
  l_aa_arg_name dbms_describe.varchar2_table;
  l_aa_datatype dbms_describe.number_table;
  l_aa_default_value dbms_describe.number_table;
  l_aa_direction dbms_describe.number_table;
  l_aa_length dbms_describe.number_table;
  l_aa_precision dbms_describe.number_table;
  l_aa_scale dbms_describe.number_table;
  l_aa_radix dbms_describe.number_table;
  l_aa_spare dbms_describe.number_table;
BEGIN
  dbms_describe.describe_procedure('PKG_TEST.FUNC_ADD', NULL, NULL,
l_aa_overload, l_aa_position, l_aa_level, l_aa_arg_name, l_aa_datatype,
l_aa_default_value, l_aa_direction, l_aa_length ,l_aa_precision ,
l_aa_scale, l_aa_radix, l_aa_spare);
  FOR i IN 1..l_aa_position.count
  LOOP
    dbms_output.put_line('Parameter #: ' || l_aa_position(i));
    dbms_output.put_line('Argument Name: ' ||
NVL(l_aa_arg_name(i),'Function''s Return Type'));
    dbms_output.put_line( 'Datatype: '||
    CASE l_aa_datatype(i)
    WHEN 1 THEN 'VARCHAR2'
    WHEN 2 THEN 'NUMBER'
    WHEN 3 THEN 'BINARY_INTEGER or PLS_INTEGER or POSITIVE or NATURAL'
    WHEN 8 THEN 'LONG'
    WHEN 11 THEN 'ROWID'
    WHEN 12 THEN 'DATE'
    WHEN 23 THEN 'RAW'
    WHEN 24 THEN 'LONG RAW'
    WHEN 58 THEN 'OPAQUE TYPE'
    WHEN 96 THEN 'CHAR (ANSI FIXED CHAR) or CHARACTER'
    WHEN 106 THEN 'MLSLABEL'
    WHEN 121 THEN 'OBJECT'
    WHEN 122 THEN 'NESTED TABLE'
    WHEN 123 THEN 'VARRAY'
    WHEN 178 THEN 'TIME'
    WHEN 179 THEN 'TIME WITH TIME ZONE'
    WHEN 180 THEN 'TIMESTAMP'
    WHEN 181 THEN 'TIMESTAMP WITH TIME ZONE'
    WHEN 231 THEN 'TIMESTAMP WITH LOCAL TIME ZONE'
```

```
        WHEN 250 THEN 'PL/SQL RECORD'
        WHEN 251 THEN 'PL/SQL TABLE'
        WHEN 252 THEN 'PL/SQL BOOLEAN'
        END);
        dbms_output.put_line('Default Value: ' ||
        CASE l_aa_default_value(i)
        WHEN 0 THEN 'Not Defaulted'
        WHEN 1 THEN 'Defaulted'
        END);
        dbms_output.put_line('Argument Direction: ' ||
        CASE l_aa_direction(i)
        WHEN 0 THEN 'IN'
        WHEN 1 THEN 'OUT'
        WHEN 2 THEN 'IN OUT'
        END);
        dbms_output.put_line('Length: ' || l_aa_length(i));
        dbms_output.put_line(rpad('-',20,'-'));
    END LOOP;
END;
/
```

Result:

```
Parameter #: 0
Argument Name: Function's Return Type
Datatype: NUMBER
Default Value: Not Defaulted
Argument Direction: OUT
Length: 22
--------------------
Parameter #: 1
Argument Name: IP_PARAM1
Datatype: NUMBER
Default Value: Not Defaulted
Argument Direction: IN
Length: 22
--------------------
Parameter #: 2
Argument Name: IP_PARAM2
Datatype: NUMBER
Default Value: Not Defaulted
Argument Direction: IN
Length: 22
--------------------
```

UTL_CALL_STACK in R12.1

Oracle database has introduced the UTL_CALL_STACK package in its R12.1 version
to provide programmatic access and control to the call stack and error stack of a
program including the nested subprogram calls. Even though the
FORMAT_CALL_STACK and FORMAT_ERROR_STACK utilities, which were
available in the previous releases also does the subprogram and error stacking, it
provides an unstructured, uncontrolled, and an unreadable form of the output which
may not be useful during debugging.

Tracking the Program Propagation

For the comparison between both the call stack APIs, we have created the below anonymous block which nests the three procedures PROC1, PROC2, and PROC3. The procedures PROC3 calls PROC2, PROC2 calls PROC1, and PROC1 prints the call stack information using both the FORMAT_CALL_STACK and UTL_CALL_STACK APIs.

The below APIs from the UTL_CALL_STACK package are used in our program to print the call stack information in a more readable format.

- **DYNAMIC_DEPTH** function returns the total number of subprograms on the call stack from the current position of the call stack to its initial position.
- **LEXICAL_DEPTH** function returns the lexical nesting level of the subprogram at a particular dynamic depth.
- **UNIT_LINE** function returns the line number of the subprogram at a particular dynamic depth.
- **SUBPROGRAM** function returns the name of the subprogram at a particular dynamic depth.
- **CONCATENATE_SUBPRORAM** function returns the concatenated form of the calling and the called subprogram.

```
DECLARE
PROCEDURE proc3
IS
  PROCEDURE proc2
  IS
    PROCEDURE proc1
    IS
      l_pi_depth pls_integer := utl_call_stack.dynamic_depth();
    BEGIN
      dbms_output.put_line('***** FORMAT_CALL_STACK Start *****');
      dbms_output.put_line(dbms_utility.format_call_stack);
      dbms_output.put_line('***** FORMAT_CALL_STACK End *****');
      dbms_output.put_line('***** UTL_CALL_STACK Start *****');
      dbms_output.put_line( 'Lexical   Depth   Line    Name' );
      dbms_output.put_line( 'Depth                 Number      ' );
      dbms_output.put_line( '-------   -----   ----    ----' );
      FOR i IN reverse 1..l_pi_depth
      LOOP
        dbms_output.put_line(
        rpad( utl_call_stack.lexical_depth(i), 10 ) ||
        rpad( i, 7) ||
        rpad( TO_CHAR(utl_call_stack.unit_line(i), '99'), 9 ) ||
        utl_call_stack.concatenate_subprogram(
utl_call_stack.subprogram(i)));
      END LOOP i;
      dbms_output.put_line('***** UTL_CALL_STACK End *****');
    END;
```

```
  BEGIN
    proc1;
  END;
BEGIN
  proc2;
END;
BEGIN
  proc3;
END;
/
```

Results:

```
***** FORMAT_CALL_STACK Start *****
----- PL/SQL Call Stack -----
  object       line  object
  handle     number  name
00007FFDB0C26E90        11  anonymous block
00007FFDB0C26E90        24  anonymous block
00007FFDB0C26E90        27  anonymous block
00007FFDB0C26E90        30  anonymous block
***** FORMAT_CALL_STACK End *****

***** UTL_CALL_STACK Start *****
Lexical   Depth   Line    Name
Depth             Number
-------   -----   ----    ----
0         4       30      __anonymous_block
1         3       27      __anonymous_block.PROC3
2         2       24      __anonymous_block.PROC3.PROC2
3         1       19      __anonymous_block.PROC3.PROC2.PROC1
***** UTL_CALL_STACK End *****
```

From the above results, we can see that the FORMAT_CALL_STACK API was unable to drill down up to the initial call with no control over its output format. Even though it produces some useful information, we need to parse its result to use it, which is also a release dependent task as the format strings change over the releases. On the other hand, the result of the UTL_CALL_STACK package is structured and also provides the depth of the program call right from the initial call to its final call making it more helpful during the program debugging process.

Tracking the Error Propagation

When a call made to a nested procedure fails, the control traverses through the nested procedures in search of its calling procedure. The FORMAT_ERROR_STACK API was introduced as the traditional SQLERRM and SQLCODE functions were not able to track the exception propagation in modular programs. Still, the output generated by the FORMAT_ERROR_STACK API is unstructured and unformatted making them hard to parse to suit our need, which leads us to the creation of the UTL_CALL_STACK API.

In our below code listing, the procedure PROC3 has both the FORMAT_ERROR_STACK and UTL_CALL_STACK APIs in its exception section for tracking the error propagation. When we call the procedure PROC3, it in-turn calls PROC2, which in-turn calls PROC1, and PROC1 raises the NO_DATA_FOUND exception explicitly using the RAISE command. The raised exception is then propagated through PROC2 and returns the control back to PROC3 with the list of error's raised.

The below APIs from the UTL_CALL_STACK package are used in our program to print the error stack information in a more readable format.

- **ERROR_DEPTH** function returns the total number of errors in the stack.
- **ERROR_MSG** function returns the message of the error for the particular error depth.
- **ERROR_NUMBER** function returns the error code for the particular error depth.

```
DECLARE
PROCEDURE proc1
IS
BEGIN
  raise no_data_found;
EXCEPTION
WHEN OTHERS THEN
  raise zero_divide;
END;
PROCEDURE proc2
IS
BEGIN
  proc1;
EXCEPTION
WHEN OTHERS THEN
  raise too_many_rows;
END;
PROCEDURE proc3
IS
  l_pi_depth pls_integer;
BEGIN
  proc2;
EXCEPTION
WHEN OTHERS THEN
  l_pi_depth := utl_call_stack.error_depth();
  dbms_output.put_line('***** FORMAT_ERROR_STACK Start *****');
  dbms_output.put_line(dbms_utility.format_error_stack);
  dbms_output.put_line('***** FORMAT_ERROR_STACK End *****');
  dbms_output.put_line('***** UTL_CALL_STACK Start *****');
  DBMS_OUTPUT.put_line('Depth      Error      Error');
  DBMS_OUTPUT.put_line('.          Code       Message');
  DBMS_OUTPUT.put_line('--------- --------- --------------------');
  FOR i IN 1 .. l_pi_depth
  LOOP
```

```
    dbms_output.put_line(RPAD(i, 10) || RPAD('ORA-' ||
LPAD(UTL_CALL_STACK.error_number(i), 5, '0'), 10) ||
UTL_CALL_STACK.error_msg(i));
  END LOOP i;
  dbms_output.put_line('***** UTL_CALL_STACK End *****');
END;
BEGIN
  proc3;
END;
/
```

Result:

```
***** FORMAT_ERROR_STACK Start *****
ORA-01422: exact fetch returns more than requested number of rows
ORA-06512: at line 16
ORA-01476: divisor is equal to zero
ORA-06512: at line 8
ORA-01403: no data found
***** FORMAT_ERROR_STACK End *****

***** UTL_CALL_STACK Start *****
Depth     Error     Error
.         Code      Message
--------- --------- --------------------
1         ORA-01422 exact fetch returns more than requested number of rows

2         ORA-06512 at line 16

3         ORA-01476 divisor is equal to zero

4         ORA-06512 at line 8

5         ORA-01403 no data found
***** UTL_CALL_STACK End *****
```

From the above output, the FORMAT_ERROR_STACK API's result is clumsy and tough to parse, whereas the output of the UTL_CALL_STACK API is well formatted and easy for debugging.

PL/SQL Expressions Enhancement in R12.2

Starting from the Oracle database version R12.2, we may use static expressions in the variable declarations where previously only literal constants were allowed. Normally, whenever we declare a PL/SQL variable like VARCHAR2, we would just hard code its precision to its maximum length (i.e., 32767). But, what if the maximum size of the VARCHAR2 datatype increases in the future release? That would make us go into all our codes and change all our occurrences of 32767 to the new value.

Now, this latest enhancement has relieved us from hard coding the variables to their maximum datatype value by using static expressions in the subtype declarations.

This enhancement requires us to define a package that contains a constant value of our choice as shown below.

```
CREATE OR REPLACE PACKAGE pkg_exp
IS
    l_n_varchar2_max constant number:= 32767;
END;
/
```

Now, we can declare our variables in any PL/SQL units as like below. Note that we have also used expressions in the place of literals that can be determined at the compile time. Thus, any changes to the maximum size of a datatype require us to change them only in one place and not everywhere.

```
CREATE OR REPLACE PROCEDURE proc_exp
IS
   l_vc_desc1 VARCHAR2(pkg_exp.l_n_varchar2_max);
   l_vc_desc2 VARCHAR2(pkg_exp.l_n_varchar2_max/2);
   l_vc_desc3 VARCHAR2(to_number(TO_CHAR(sysdate,'yyyy')));
BEGIN
   ...
END;
/
```

This enhancement makes the variable declarations more compact, clear, flexible and adaptable to any change in the environment.

Long Identifiers in R12.2

Starting from the version R12.2, the maximum length of all the identifiers used and defined in the Oracle database is increased to 128 bytes from 30 bytes (Prior to R12.2). For this change to take place, the COMPATIBLE parameter has to be set to a value of 12.2.0 or higher.

This change was already hinted in the R12.1 data dictionary objects. The size of the OBJECT_NAME and SUBOJBECT_NAME column's datatype's precision was increased to 128 bytes as shown below. This value was 30 bytes prior to R12.1.

```
SELECT table_name,
  column_name,
  data_type,
  data_length
FROM user_tab_cols
WHERE table_name ='USER_OBJECTS'
AND column_name IN ('OBJECT_NAME', 'SUBOBJECT_NAME');
```

Script Result

TABLE_NAME	COLUMN_NAME	DATA_TYPE	DATA_LENGTH
USER_OBJECTS	OBJECT_NAME	VARCHAR2	128
USER_OBJECTS	SUBOBJECT_NAME	VARCHAR2	128

There is also a new function introduced in the R12.2 release to check this limit,

```
SELECT ORA_MAX_NAME_LEN_SUPPORTED FROM dual;
```

Script Result

ORA_MAX_NAME_LEN_SUPPORTED
128

Now, we can create any object with its name's maximum length falling under the limit of 128 bytes as shown below,

```
CREATE TABLE hi_i_am_a_table_with_more_than_30_characters_in_my_name (...);

CREATE VIEW hi_i_am_a_view_with_more_than_30_characters_in_my_name
AS SELECT ...;

CREATE PROCEDURE
   hi_i_am_a_procedure_with_more_than_30_characters_in_my_name
AS ...;
```

This helps us to define an object with its actual meaning rather than providing something harder to understand. This also helps us to easily migrate the objects from different databases which support more than 30 bytes in the object names without forcing us to change their name.

DEPRECATE Pragma in R12.2

This pragma marks a PL/SQL program as deprecated. When a PL/SQL unit is referencing a deprecated element, a warning is displayed provided that we have enabled our compile time warnings. This new pragma may only appear in the declaration section of a package specification, object specification, top-level procedure or function, along with an optional comment which is to be displayed along with the compiler warning message.

The prototype of this pragma is shown below,

```
PRAGMA deprecate(<PL/SQL_element>[, Optional_compile_time_warning_message]);
```

To demonstrate this pragma, we must first enable the PLSQL_WARNINGS parameter as shown below,

```
ALTER SESSION SET plsql_warnings = 'ENABLE:ALL';
```

In the below code snippet, the entire package is made deprecated. Note that the DEPRECATE pragma should appear first in the declaration section in this case.

```
CREATE PACKAGE pkg_deprecate AUTHID DEFINER
AS
  PRAGMA DEPRECATE(pkg_deprecate);
  PROCEDURE proc_old;
  FUNCTION func return number;
END;
/
```

In the below code listing, only the procedure PROC_OLD from the package is made deprecated. The optional comment states the procedure PROC_OLD is deprecated and the compiler advices us to use the PROC_NEW procedure instead. Note that the PRAGMA declaration is immediate to the procedure PROC_OLD's declaration.

```
CREATE PACKAGE pkg_deprecate AUTHID DEFINER
AS
  PROCEDURE proc_old;
  PRAGMA DEPRECATE (proc_old, 'PKG.PROC_OLD is deprecated. Use PKG.PROC_NEW
instead.');
  PROCEDURE proc_new;
END;
/
```

When we try to reference this deprecated procedure anywhere else, we might encounter an appropriate PL/SQL warning message along with our optional comment as shown below.

```
CREATE OR REPLACE PROCEDURE proc_test AUTHID DEFINER
IS
BEGIN
  pkg_deprecate.proc_old;
END;
/
```

```
PLW-06020: reference to a deprecated entity: PROC_OLD declared in
unit PKG_DEPRECATE[4,14]. PKG.PROC_OLD is deprecated. Use PKG.PROC_NEW
instead.
```

In the below example, an overloaded procedure with one input parameter is deprecated while its overloading partner remains untouched.

```
CREATE PACKAGE pkg_deprecate AUTHID DEFINER
AS
  PROCEDURE PROC(ip1 NUMBER);
  PRAGMA DEPRECATE (PROC, 'PKG.PROC with one input parameter is deprecated.
Use PKG.PROC with two input parameters instead.');
  PROCEDURE PROC(ip1 NUMBER, ip2 NUMBER);
END;
/
```

R12.2 has also introduced the below four compilation warnings for usage when the DEPRECATE pragma is used,

- **6019** - The entity was deprecated and could be removed in a future release. Do not use the deprecated entity.

- **6020** - The referenced entity was deprecated and could be removed in a future release. Do not use the deprecated entity. Follow the specific instructions in the warning if any are given.

- **6021** - Misplaced pragma. The pragma DEPRECATE should follow immediately after the declaration of the entity that is being deprecated. Place the pragma immediately after the declaration of the entity that is being deprecated.

- **6022** - This entity cannot be deprecated. Deprecation only applies to entities that may be declared in a package or type specification as well as to top-level procedure and function definitions. Remove the pragma.

COVERAGE Pragma in R12.2

This pragma marks a specific section of a PL/SQL code which is infeasible to be covered during a test run, thus helping us to improve the coverage accuracy.

The prototype of this pragma is shown below,

```
PRAGMA COVERAGE (<Coverage_parameter>);
```

The supported coverage parameters are,

- **NOT_FEASIBLE** – This value marks the entire block as infeasible that includes the beginning of the first declaration or statement that follows the pragma.
- **NOT_FEASIBLE_START** – This value starts the marking and may appear before any declaration or statement. If this parameter is used, it must be mandatorily followed by the COVERAGE pragma with an NOT_FEASIBLE_END parameter.
- **NOT_FEASIBLE_END** – This value ends the marking.

From R12.2, the new package DBMS_PLSQL_CODE_COVERAGE is introduced with supporting tables to collect the code coverage information even from a basic PL/SQL block.

A function with one input parameter which determines the execution flow of the function is created as shown below,

```
CREATE OR REPLACE FUNCTION func_test(
    ip_param1 IN NUMBER)
  RETURN NUMBER
IS
BEGIN
  IF ip_param1 BETWEEN 0 AND 5 THEN
    pragma coverage ('NOT_FEASIBLE');
    RETURN 0;
  ELSIF ip_param1 BETWEEN 6 AND 10 THEN
    RETURN 1;
  ELSE
    RETURN 2;
  END IF;
END func_test;
/
```

Now, to start the coverage test run, we must create the tables that hold the coverage test results by executing the CREATE_COVERAGE_TABLES procedure as shown below,

```
BEGIN
  dbms_plsql_code_coverage.create_coverage_tables;
END;
/
```

The CREATE_COVERAGE_TABLES API will accept a Boolean *true* to drop and re-create these tables if already present else a *false* to raise an error if the coverage tables already exist. The default value is *false*. This API will create the below three tables when executed,

- **DBMSPCC_RUNS** – This table includes a row for every coverage run.
- **DBMSPCC_UNITS** – This table includes all the program units for which the coverage data were gathered for a given run.
- **DBMSPCC_BLOCKS** – This table includes the code coverage information for each basic block.

After creating the necessary tables, we can very well start the coverage by executing the START_COVERAGE function with optional run comments returning the run ID, execute the FUNC_TEST function with an input value, and stop the coverage using the STOP_COVERAGE procedure as shown below.

```
DECLARE
  Run_ID pls_integer;
BEGIN
```

```
  Run_ID := DBMS_Plsql_Code_Coverage.Start_Coverage(Run_Comment=>'Code
Coverage for the function FUNC_TEST');
  DBMS_output.Put_Line(FUNC_TEST(7));
  DBMS_Plsql_Code_Coverage.Stop_Coverage();
END;
/
```

After the test run is completed, we can check the coverage information by executing the below query,

```
SELECT du.owner,
   du.name,
   du.type,
   db.covered,
   db.not_feasible
FROM dbmspcc_runs dr,
   dbmspcc_units du,
   dbmspcc_blocks db
WHERE dr.run_id    =du.run_id
AND du.object_id =db.object_id
AND dr.run_comment='Code Coverage for the function FUNC_TEST';
```

Here,

- The COVERED column is set to 1 if a basic block is covered or 0 if not.
- The NOT_FEASIBLE column is set to 1 if a basic block is marked as NOT_FEASIBLE using the COVERAGE pragma, or 0 if not.

DBMS_METADATA

This package was introduced in the Oracle version 9i to retrieve the DDL metadata of the database objects in either DDL format or XML format, which can be later used for recreating that object. This package is simple to use and can be used for extracting either a single database object or an entire Oracle database.

> 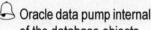 Oracle data pump internally uses this package to export the metadata of the database objects.

Prior to Oracle 9i version, we could retrieve the object metadata only using the user-defined SQL statements, Export utilities, and OCIDescribeAny interface, all of which have their own limitations,

- The user-defined SQL statements approach is limited to the specific Oracle version. So, when an Oracle version alters the database objects' storage properties, we must change the SQL statements to adapt to it.
- The export utilities produce the metadata in text format but lacks formatting. This approach always requires us to do extra formatting.
- The OCIDescribeAny interface approach does not support exporting all the database objects.

The various APIs provided by the DBMS_METADATA package can be used for setting the required format with the Pretty print feature, resulting in an output that requires no manual intervention.

 Note: The parameters can be passed only in positional notation and are case sensitive.

The different APIs provided by this package are described below,

GET_XXX Functions

The GET_XML, GET_DDL, GET_SXML, GET_DEPENDENT_XML, GET_DEPENDENT_DDL, GET_GRANTED_XML, GET_GRANTED_DDL functions let us fetch the metadata for the objects with a single call.

The below SQL is used for retrieving the metadata of the DUAL table in text format,

```
SELECT dbms_metadata.get_ddl('TABLE', 'DUAL') FROM dual;
```

Results:

```
CREATE TABLE "SYS"."DUAL"
   (
    "DUMMY" VARCHAR2(1)
   )
  PCTFREE 10 PCTUSED 40 INITRANS 1 MAXTRANS 255 NOCOMPRESS LOGGING STORAGE
   (
    INITIAL 16384 NEXT 1048576 MINEXTENTS 1 MAXEXTENTS 2147483645
PCTINCREASE 0 FREELISTS 1 FREELIST GROUPS 1 BUFFER_POOL DEFAULT FLASH_CACHE
DEFAULT CELL_FLASH_CACHE DEFAULT
   )
  TABLESPACE "SYSTEM";
```

The below SQL is used for retrieving the metadata of the IDX index in text format,

```
SELECT dbms_metadata.get_ddl('INDEX', 'IDX') FROM dual;
```

Results:

```
CREATE INDEX "SYS"."IDX" ON "SYS"."EMP"
  (
    "EMPNO"
  )
  PCTFREE 10 INITRANS 2 MAXTRANS 255 COMPUTE STATISTICS STORAGE
  (
    INITIAL 65536 NEXT 1048576 MINEXTENTS 1 MAXEXTENTS 2147483645
PCTINCREASE 0 FREELISTS 1 FREELIST GROUPS 1 BUFFER_POOL DEFAULT FLASH_CACHE
DEFAULT CELL_FLASH_CACHE DEFAULT
  )
  TABLESPACE "SYSTEM"
```

The below SQL is used for retrieving the metadata of the DUAL table in SXML format,

```
SELECT dbms_metadata.get_sxml('TABLE', 'DUAL') FROM dual;
```

Results:

```
<TABLE xmlns="http://xmlns.oracle.com/ku" version="1.0">
   <SCHEMA>SYS</SCHEMA>
   <NAME>DUAL</NAME>
   <RELATIONAL_TABLE>
      <COL_LIST>
         <COL_LIST_ITEM>
            <NAME>DUMMY</NAME>
            <DATATYPE>VARCHAR2</DATATYPE>
            <LENGTH>1</LENGTH>
         </COL_LIST_ITEM>
      </COL_LIST>
   ...
   ...
```

The below SQL is used for retrieving the DDLs granted to the user C## by the current user (SYS) in text format.

```
SELECT dbms_metadata.get_granted_ddl('SYSTEM_GRANT', 'C##') FROM dual;
```

Results:

```
GRANT CREATE ANY TRIGGER TO "C##"
GRANT CREATE ANY PROCEDURE TO "C##"
GRANT CREATE ANY TABLE TO "C##"
GRANT UNLIMITED TABLESPACE TO "C##"
```

The below SQL is used for retrieving the grants dependent on the DUAL table by the current user (SYS) in text format.

```
SELECT DBMS_METADATA.GET_DEPENDENT_DDL('OBJECT_GRANT', 'DUAL') FROM DUAL;
```

Results:

```
GRANT FLASHBACK ON "SYS"."DUAL" TO "APEX_050000"
GRANT SELECT ON "SYS"."DUAL" TO "APEX_050000"
GRANT FLASHBACK ON "SYS"."DUAL" TO "APEX_040200"
GRANT SELECT ON "SYS"."DUAL" TO PUBLIC WITH GRANT OPTION
```

OPEN and OPENW Functions

The OPEN function specifies the type of the object to be retrieved, its metadata version, and the object model.

This function returns the opaque handle to the class of objects that is used as input to the SET_FILTER, SET_COUNT, ADD_TRANSFORM, GET_QUERY, SET_PARSE_ITEM, FETCH_[XML | DDL | CLOB | XML_CLOB] and CLOSE APIs.

The OPENW function specifies the type of the object to be submitted, its metadata version, and the object model.

The prototypes of these functions are described below,

```
DBMS_METADATA.OPEN (
    object_type  IN VARCHAR2,
    version      IN VARCHAR2 DEFAULT 'COMPATIBLE',
    model        IN VARCHAR2 DEFAULT 'ORACLE',
    network_link IN VARCHAR2 DEFAULT NULL)
 RETURN NUMBER;

DBMS_METADATA.OPENW(
    object_type IN VARCHAR2,
    version      IN VARCHAR2 DEFAULT 'COMPATIBLE',
    model        IN VARCHAR2 DEFAULT 'ORACLE')
 RETURN NUMBER;
```

- **OBJECT_TYPE** accepts the type of the object to be retrieved.
- **VERSION** accepts the version of the metadata to be extracted.
    - **COMPATIBLE** is the default value. This value returns the metadata with a compatible format.
    - **LATEST** returns the metadata in the latest database format.
- **MODEL** accepts model to be used. Only supported model is ORACLE.
- **NETWORK_LINK** accepts the DB link of the object to be retrieved. *Null* indicates the current database.

ADD_TRANSFORM Function

This function is used for both the retrieval and the submission,

---

- During retrieval, this function specifies a transformation that FETCH_XXX API applies to the XML representation of the retrieved objects.
- During submission, this function specifies a transformation that CONVERT or PUT APIs applies to the XML representation of the submitted objects.

The prototype of this function is shown below,

```
DBMS_METADATA.ADD_TRANSFORM (
    handle      IN NUMBER,
    name        IN VARCHAR2,
    encoding    IN VARCHAR2 DEFAULT NULL,
    object_type IN VARCHAR2 DEFAULT NULL)
RETURN NUMBER;
```

- **HANDLE** accepts the handle returned by the OPEN/ OPENW functions during retrieval/ submission respectively.
- **NAME** accepts the transformation name. The possible transformation names are described in the *Transforms Available on ADD_TRANSFORM Function* table below.
- **ENCODING** accepts the global support character set name in which the stylesheet pointed by the name is encoded. The default value is *null*.
- **OBJECT_TYPE** accepts the object type of the object that is retrieved or submitted. The default value is *null*.

Transforms Available on ADD_TRANSFORM Function

OBJECT_TYPE	TRANSFORM_NAME	INPUT/ OUTPUT DOC TYPE	DESCRIPTION
ALL	DDL	XML/DDL	Convert XML to SQL for creating the object.
	MODIFY	XML/XML	Modifying the XML based on the transform.
SUBSET	SXML	XML/SXML	Convert XML to SXML.
	MODIFYSXML	SXML/SXML	Modifying the SXML based on the transform.
	SXMLDDL	SXML/DDL	Convert XML to SQL.
	ALTERXML	SXML Difference DOC/ ALTER_XML	Generate ALTER_XML from SXML difference document.
	ALTERDDL	ALTER_XML/ ALTER_DDL	Convert ALTER_XML to ALTER_DDL.

The opaque handle returned by this function is used as input to the SET_TRANSOFRM_PARAM and SET_REMAP_PARAM APIs. This handle refers to the transform, and not the set of objects to be retrieved or submitted (Like OPEN/ OPENW APIs).

SET_TRANSFORM_PARAM and SET_REMAP_PARAM Procedures

Both these procedures are used for retrieval and submission to specify the parameters to the XSLT stylesheet identified by the TRANSFORM_HANDLE for modifying the output of the transform.

The prototypes of these procedures are described below,

```
DBMS_METADATA.SET_TRANSFORM_PARAM (
    transform_handle   IN NUMBER,
    name               IN VARCHAR2,
    value              IN VARCHAR2 | BOOLEAN DEFAULT TRUE | NUMBER,
    object_type        IN VARCHAR2 DEFAULT NULL);

DBMS_METADATA.SET_REMAP_PARAM (
    transform_handle   IN NUMBER,
    name               IN VARCHAR2,
    old_value          IN VARCHAR2,
    new_value          IN VARCHAR2,
    object_type        IN VARCHAR2 DEFAULT NULL);
```

- **TRANSFORM_HANDLE** accepts the handle returned by the ADD_TRANSFORM or SESSION_TRANSFORM constant designating the DDL transform of the whole session. It does not accept the handle returned by the OPEN function.
- **NAME** accepts the name of the transform parameter. The available list is described in the below *DDL Transform List for Transform Parameters* table.
- **VALUE** accepts the value for the transform.
- **OLD_VALUE** accepts the old value for remapping.
- **NEW_VALUE** accepts the new value for remapping.
- **OBJECT_TYPE** accepts the object type to which the transform or remap parameter applies.

DDL Transform List for Transform Parameters

OBJECT_TYPE	NAME	DATATYPE	DESCRIPTION
ALL OBJECTS	PRETTY	BOOLEAN	• True – Indents output with proper line feeds (Default).
	SQLTERMINATOR		• True – Appends a SQL terminator (; or /) to each DDL statement. • Default value – False.

TABLE	CONSTRAINTS		• True – Includes all non-referential constraints in the DDL(Default).
	PARTITIONING		• True – Include partitioning clauses. • Default value – False.
	SEGMENT_ATTRIBUTES		• True – Includes segment attribute clauses in the DDL (Default).
	STORAGE		• True – Includes the storage clauses in the DDL (Default).
	TABLESPACE		• True – Includes the tablespace clause in the DDL (Default).
	REF_CONSTRAINTS		• True – Includes all referential constraints in the DDL. • Default value – False.
	CONSTRAINTS_AS_ALTER		• True – Includes table constraints as separate ALTER statements. • False – Includes table constraints as a part of CREATE TABLE statement (Default). • CONSTRAINTS transformation should be set to TRUE.
TABLE, TYPE	OID		• True – Includes OID clause in the DDL. • Default value – False.
Table	SIZE_BY_KEYWORD		• True – Includes the BYTE keyword in the CHAR and VARCHAR2 columns. • Default value – False.
TYPE, PACKAGE	SPECIFICATION		• True – Include the type or package spec in the DDL. • Default value – False.
TYPE, PACKAGE	BODY		• True – Include the type or package body in the DDL. • Default value – False.
VIEW	FORCE		• True – Include the FORCE keyword in the CREATE VIEW statement (Default).

FETCH_XXX Functions and Procedures

These subprograms return the metadata for the objects that is established by the OPEN function and its subsequent calls to the SET_FILTER, SET_COUNT, ADD_TRANSFORM APIs.

The different FETCH_XXX subprograms are,

- **FETCH_XML** function returns the metadata for an object in an XMLTYPE format.
- **FETCH_DDL** function returns the metadata for an object in DDL format in a nested table.
- **FETCH_CLOB** function returns the object as CLOB, either transformed or not.
- **FETCH_CLOB** procedure returns the objects by reference in an IN OUT parameter.
- **FETCH_XML_CLOB** procedure returns the XML metadata for the objects as a CLOB in an IN OUT parameter.

GET_QUERY Function

This function returns the queries that are used by the FETCH_XXX APIs for debugging purpose.

The prototype of this function is shown below,

```
DBMS_METADATA.GET_QUERY (handle IN NUMBER) RETURN VARCHAR2;
```

- **HANDLE** accepts the handle returned by the OPEN function.

SET_COUNT Procedure

This procedure defines the maximum number of objects to be retrieved in a single FETCH_XXX call. The default object returned by the FETCH_XXX APIs is 1 and it can be overridden using this procedure.

The prototype of this procedure is shown below,

```
DBMS_METADATA.SET_COUNT (
    handle           IN NUMBER,
    value            IN NUMBER,
    object_type_path IN VARCHAR2 DEFAULT NULL);
```

- **HANDLE** accepts the handle returned by the OPEN function.
- **VALUE** accepts the maximum number of objects to be retrieved.
- **OBJECT_TYPE_PATH** accepts the path name specific to the object types to which the count value applies. The default value is *Null*.
    - If not specified, the count is applied to all the objects.
    - If specified, the count is applied to only the specific node within the tree of the objects.

SET_FILTER Procedure

This procedure specifies the restrictions on the object to be retrieved.

The prototype of this procedure is described below,

```
DBMS_METADATA.SET_FILTER (
    handle          IN NUMBER,
    name            IN VARCHAR2,
    value           IN VARCHAR2 | BOOLEAN DEFAULT TRUE | NUMBER,
    object_type_path IN VARCHAR2 DEFAULT NULL);
```

- **HANDLE** accepts the handle returned by the OPEN function.
- **NAME** accepts the name of the filter. Few names are listed below,
    - For named objects - NAME, EXCLUDE_NAME_EXPR, NAME_EXPR.
    - For granted objects – GRANTEE, PRIVNAME, GRANTEE_EXPR, EXCLUDE_GRANTEE_EXPR.
    - For Package/ Type objects – BODY, and SPECIFICATION.
- **VALUE** accepts the value for the filter specified. For example,
    - NAME and SCHEMA filters accept the exact object name/ schema name.
    - BODY and SPECIFICATION filters accept either *True* or *False*.
- **OBJECT_TYPE_PATH** accepts the path name specific to the object types to which the count value applies. The default value is *Null*.
    - If not specified, the count is applied to all the objects.
    - If specified, the count is applied to only the specific node within the tree of the objects.

SET_PARSE_ITEM Procedure

This procedure can be used for enabling the output parsing and specifies an object attribute to be parsed and returned.

The prototype of this procedure used in object retrieval is described below,

```
DBMS_METADATA.SET_PARSE_ITEM (
   handle       IN NUMBER,
   name         IN VARCHAR2,
   object_type IN VARCHAR2 DEFAULT NULL);
```

The prototype of this procedure used in XML submission is described below,

```
DBMS_METADATA.SET_PARSE_ITEM (handle IN NUMBER, name IN VARCHAR2);
```

- **HANDLE** accepts the handle returned by the OPEN function.
- **NAME** accepts the name of the object to be parsed and returned. Few names are listed below,
  - For all objects – NAME, VERB, OBJECT_TYPE, and SCHEMA_NAME.
  - For triggers – ENABLE.
  - For dependent objects – BASE_OBJECT_NAME, BASE_OBJECT_SCHEMA, and BASE_OBJECT_TYPE.
- **OBJECT_TYPE** accepts the object type of the parsed item. If not specified, this parameter takes on the object type of the OPEN handle.

PUT Function

This function submits either an XML or a CLOB document, which contains the object metadata to the database to create the object.

The prototype of this function is described below,

```
DBMS_METADATA.PUT (
   handle     IN             NUMBER,
   document   IN             sys.XMLType | CLOB,
   flags      IN             NUMBER,
   results    IN OUT NOCOPY sys.ku$_SubmitResults)
 RETURN BOOLEAN;
```

- **HANDLE** accepts the handle returned by the OPENW function.
- **DOCUMENT** accepts either the XML or CLOB document containing the metadata for the type of the OPENW handle.
- **FLAGS** are reserved for future use. We can pass a 0 to avoid this parameter.
- **RESULTS** returns the detailed information on the errors occurred.

This function returns a Boolean *True* if the submission is successful or a *False* if the submission fails.

CLOSE Procedure

This procedure is used for invalidating the handle returned by the OPEN/ OPENW functions during both retrieval and submission.

The prototype of this procedure is described below,

```
DBMS_METADATA.CLOSE (handle IN NUMBER);
```

- **HANDLE** accepts the handle returned by the OPEN function.

In the below code snippet, the metadata of the table EMPLOYEES is copied from the schema HR and is executed in the EMP schema using the DBMS_METADATA APIs, excluding the data.

Firstly, the TABLE object type is retrieved using the OPEN (Retrieval) function with the handle L_PI_HANDLE1 for which the NAME and the SCHEMA filters are set using the SET_FILTER procedure. The submitted table is then fetched into the CLOB variable and its corresponding handle is closed.

During the retrieval, the TABLE object type is submitted using the OPENW (Submission) function with the handle L_PI_HANDLE2. Then, the original schema name is modified to the target schema name using the ADD_TRANSFORM and the SET_REMAP_PARAM APIs. Finally, the ADD_TRANSFORM API is used for converting the XML formatted output into the DDL format, which is then executed in the target schema using the PUT API.

The Boolean value returned by the PUT API determines whether or not errors have occurred during the DDL migration process. *True* indicates that there is no error and *False* indicates that errors have occurred. The errors occurred (if any) are looped and then finally printed sequentially.

```
DECLARE
   l_pi_handle1 pls_integer;
   l_pi_handle2 pls_integer;
   l_pi_modify pls_integer;
   l_pi_ddl pls_integer;
   l_vc_from_schema VARCHAR2(30):='HR';
   l_vc_to_schema   VARCHAR2(30):='EMP';
   l_vc_table_name  VARCHAR2(30):='EMPLOYEES';
   l_cl_var1 CLOB;
   l_ntt_errors sys.ku$_SubmitResults:=sys.ku$_SubmitResults();
   l_ntt_error sys.ku$_SubmitResult;
   l_b_result BOOLEAN;
BEGIN
   l_pi_handle1 :=dbms_metadata.open('TABLE');
```

```
  dbms_metadata.set_filter(l_pi_handle1, 'NAME', l_vc_table_name);

  dbms_metadata.set_filter(l_pi_handle1, 'SCHEMA', l_vc_from_schema);

  l_pi_modify :=DBMS_METADATA.ADD_TRANSFORM(l_pi_handle1, 'MODIFY');

  l_cl_var1    :=dbms_metadata.fetch_clob(l_pi_handle1);

  dbms_metadata.close(l_pi_handle1);

  l_pi_handle2:=dbms_metadata.openw('TABLE');

  l_pi_modify :=DBMS_METADATA.ADD_TRANSFORM(l_pi_handle2, 'MODIFY');

  DBMS_METADATA.SET_REMAP_PARAM(l_pi_modify, 'REMAP_SCHEMA',
l_vc_from_schema, l_vc_to_schema);

  l_pi_ddl    :=dbms_metadata.add_transform(l_pi_handle2, 'DDL');

  l_b_result := DBMS_METADATA.PUT(l_pi_handle2, l_cl_var1, 0, l_ntt_errors);

  dbms_metadata.close(l_pi_handle2);

  IF NOT l_b_result THEN
    FOR i IN l_ntt_errors.first..l_ntt_errors.last
    LOOP
      l_ntt_error:=l_ntt_errors(i);
      FOR j IN l_ntt_error.errorlines.first..l_ntt_error.errorlines.last
      LOOP
        dbms_output.put_line(l_ntt_error.errorlines(j).errortext);
      END LOOP j;
    END LOOP i;
  END IF;
END;
/
```

When we execute the above anonymous block, the EMPLOYEES table from the HR schema is created in the EMP schema.

Debugging PL/SQL Code

Traditionally, we would debug any PL/SQL code by placing the DBMS_OUTPUT.PUT_LINE procedure call at the required places in the program for debugging them. Now, we can debug our code using many IDEs like SQL Developer, PL/SQL Developer, etc. with an increased in the depth and accuracy while debugging large complex systems.

The tool debugging is better than the PUT_LINE procedure as the PUT_LINE procedure adds extra lines to the PL/SQL code, very less interactive, and extra removal effort before deploying the PL/SQL code into the production.

Before starting to debug an object in the database, we must enable the debugging by setting the PLSQL_CODE_TYPE parameter to INTERPRETED and the PLSQL_OPTIMIZE_LEVEL to 0 or 1. Note that the PLSQL_DEBUG parameter is deprecated from R12.1.

> Note: We need the EXECUTE on the object and the DEBUG CONNECT SESSION on the session privileges for debugging a PL/SQL object.

We must follow the below steps in order to debug a PL/SQL unit in the SQL Developer tool,

Step 1: After the debugging option is enabled, we must compile a PL/SQL unit with "Compile for Debug" option in the SQL Developer tool. We can confirm this by checking the green colored bug like symbol on the object in the object drop down viewer.

Step 2: Now, we must set a BREAKPOINT in the code so that the code execution halts at a specified point, by clicking on a line number.

Step 3: After the Step #2 is completed, we can start the debugging by clicking the RED bug icon (or CTRL + SHIFT + F10) near the RUN icon in the tool and then click OK for debugging, by specifying the input values (if any).

Step 4: Now, the control shifts to the next breakpoint and when we move our cursor towards the variables in the program, their current value will be displayed.

Step 5: We can now,

- Step into the next execution point by clicking the right pointed RED arrow or ALT + F3.
- Step into the next statement by clicking the "Step Over" button (Blue colored right down facing arrow) or F8.
- Step into the next block by clicking the "Step Into" button (Red colored right down facing arrow) or F7.
- Step out of the current block by clicking the "Step Out" button (Blue colored left down facing arrow) or Shift + F7.
- Step to the end of the method by clicking the "Step to the End of the Method" button (Blue colored right down facing arrow).

- Resume the rest of the program by clicking the "Resume" button (Blue colored play button) or F9.
- We can inspect the variables in the code to see their current execution values.
- We can deposit values into variables and change the flow of the execution.

We can also use the DBMS_DEBUG package, which is the PL/SQL interface to the PL/SQL debugging layer for debugging the server-side PL/SQL units. The SQL Developer tool by itself uses this package internally for debugging. For using this package, Oracle needs to create two sessions. One for debugging the PL/SQL code and the other one for the target session.

The target session becomes available for debugging by making initializing calls with the DBMS_DEBUG package. This marks the session so that the PL/SQL interpreter runs in debug mode and generates the debug events. Once the debug events are generated from the session, they are posted. In the cases where the debug events require a return notification, the interpreter pauses itself awaiting the reply.

Meanwhile, the debug session also initializes itself using the DBMS_DEBUG package telling it which target session must be supervised. The debug session, then calls the entry points in the DBMS_DEBUG package to read the events that were posted from the target session and to communicate with the target session.

PL/SQL Conditional Compilation

The conditional compilation allows us to produce different compilation results from the same PL/SQL code based on the flags set in the PLSQL_CCFLAGS parameter or the APIs in the DBMS_DB_VERSION package for checking the DB version, or user/ system defined package constants, or the initialization parameters available in the database.

The compiler flags are identified by a $$ prefix, while the conditional control is provided by the $IF..$THEN..$ELSIF..$ELSE..$END and $ERROR..$END syntax. Note that the IF block ends with an END clause and not with an END IF clause.

There are three types of PL/SQL conditional compilation constructs. They are,

Selection Directives

The *selection directives* are used for selecting between the alternative fragments of the source text at the compile time. This directive must test a Boolean condition for its selection. The rules for evaluating the static Boolean expression that the *selection directive* uses are similar to the rules that PL/SQL uses at run time.

For a demonstration of this directive, we have created a static Boolean variable in a package as shown below,

```
CREATE OR REPLACE PACKAGE pkg_selection
IS
  g_b_var1 CONSTANT BOOLEAN:=true;
END;
/
```

Then, a procedure PROC_SELECTION with the conditional control statements for the DBMS_DB_VERSION package, a Boolean literal, and a static Boolean variable is created and compiled.

```
CREATE OR REPLACE PROCEDURE proc_selection
IS
BEGIN
  $IF dbms_db_version.ver_le_12 or dbms_db_version.ver_le_12_1 $THEN
  dbms_output.put_line('The current database version is 12c');
  $ELSIF dbms_db_version.ver_le_11 or dbms_db_version.ver_le_11_1 or
dbms_db_version.ver_le_11_2 $THEN
  dbms_output.put_line('The current database version is 11g');
  $ELSIF dbms_db_version.ver_le_10 or dbms_db_version.ver_le_10_1 or
dbms_db_version.ver_le_10_2 $THEN
  dbms_output.put_line('The current database version is 10g');
  $END
  $IF FALSE $then
  dbms_output.put_line('Adhoc commenting');
  $END
  $IF pkg_selection.g_b_var1 $THEN
  dbms_output.put_line('The Boolean value is True');
  $ELSE
  dbms_output.put_line('The Boolean value is False');
  $END
END;
/
```

To view the post processed source code, we can execute the PRINT_POST_PROCESSED_SOURCE API as shown below,

```
EXEC dbms_preprocessor.print_post_processed_source('PROCEDURE', 'SYS',
'PROC_SELECTION');
```

Results:
```
PROCEDURE proc_selection
IS
BEGIN
 dbms_output.put_line('The current database version is 12c');
 dbms_output.put_line('The Boolean value is True');
END;
/
```

Inquiry Directives

The use of static package constants to determine the result of a *selection directive* is helpful only when all the *selection directive* in the source code uses the same static package constant. This is to make sure that the package constants bear the same meaning across all situations. Consider, if the static variables tend to change, the different units referring to it will pick up a new value before it can be next used. So, if our purpose is to select code based on the release of the database in which the testing is done, then testing the static package constant is definitely the best approach.

However, if our purpose is to conditionally compile a single program unit rather than all, then the above approach would be of no use. This is where the *inquiry directives* come into the picture. The inquiry directives are used for obtaining an independent value for itself from the compilation environment like,

- From a PL/SQL compilation parameter like,
    - **$$PLSQL_CODE_TYPE**.
    - **$$PLSQL_OPTIMIZE_LEVEL**.
    - **$$PLSQL_DEBUG** (Deprecated).
    - **$$PLSQL_WARNINGS**.
    - **$$PLSCOPE_SETTINGS**.

- User defined flags from the PLSQL_CCFLAGS parameter.

- Predefined flags like,
    - **$$PLSQL_LINE** – A PLS_INTEGER literal which returns the line number in the source code where the directive appears.
    - **$$PLSQL_UNIT** – A VARCHAR2 literal which returns the name of the current PL/SQL unit. If the PL/SQL unit is an anonymous block, this flag returns *null*.
    - **$$PLSQL_UNIT_OWNER** – A VARCHAR2 literal which returns the owner name of the current PL/SQL unit. If the PL/SQL unit is an anonymous block, this flag returns *null*.
    - **$$PLSQL_UNIT_TYPE** – A VARCHAR2 literal which returns the type of the current PL/SQL unit like – ANONYMOUS BLOCK, FUNCTION, PACKAGE, PACKAGE BODY, PROCEDURE, TRIGGER, TYPE, or TYPE BODY. Inside an anonymous block or non-DML trigger, this flag has the value ANONYMOUS BLOCK.

Now, let's set the PLSQL_CCFLAGS parameter for the *DEBUG_ON:TRUE* flag at the system level as shown below,

```
ALTER SYSTEM SET plsql_ccflags='debug_on:True';
```

The below procedure is created with all the inquiry directives assigned to its appropriate type variables and the PLSQL_CCFLAGS parameter flag *DEBUG_ON* used in a conditional control statement as shown below,

```
CREATE OR REPLACE PROCEDURE proc_inquiry
IS
  l_vc_plsql_code_type      VARCHAR2(30)  :=$$PLSQL_CODE_TYPE;
  l_n_plsql_optimize_level  NUMBER        :=$$PLSQL_OPTIMIZE_LEVEL;
  l_b_plsql_debug           BOOLEAN       :=$$PLSQL_DEBUG;
  l_vc_plsql_warnings       VARCHAR2(100):=$$PLSQL_WARNINGS;
  l_vc_plscope_settings     VARCHAR2(100):=$$PLSCOPE_SETTINGS;
  l_n_plsql_line            NUMBER        :=$$PLSQL_LINE;
  l_vc_plsql_unit           VARCHAR2(30)  :=$$PLSQL_UNIT;
  l_vc_plsql_unit_owner     VARCHAR2(30)  :=$$PLSQL_UNIT_OWNER;
  l_vc_plsql_unit_type      VARCHAR2(30)  :=$$PLSQL_UNIT_TYPE;
BEGIN
  $if $$debug_on $then
  dbms_output.put_line('Development code with debugging options like
DBMS_OUTPUT or Log tables insertion');
  $else
  dbms_output.put_line('Production code without debugging options');
  $end
END;
/
```

After the above procedure is created in the database, we can check its post-processed source code by executing the below script,

```
EXEC dbms_preprocessor.print_post_processed_source('PROCEDURE', 'SYS',
'PROC_INQUIRY');
```

Results:

```
PROCEDURE proc_inquiry
IS
  l_vc_plsql_code_type      VARCHAR2(30)  := 'INTERPRETED';
  l_n_plsql_optimize_level  NUMBER        := 2;
  l_b_plsql_debug           BOOLEAN       := FALSE;
  l_vc_plsql_warnings       VARCHAR2(100):= 'DISABLE:ALL';
  l_vc_plscope_settings     VARCHAR2(100):= 'IDENTIFIERS:ALL';
  l_n_plsql_line            NUMBER        := 8;
  l_vc_plsql_unit           VARCHAR2(30)  := 'PROC_INQUIRY';
  l_vc_plsql_unit_owner     VARCHAR2(30)  := 'SYS';
```

```
   l_vc_$$plsql_unit_type    VARCHAR2(30) := 'PROCEDURE';
BEGIN
   dbms_output.put_line('Development code with debugging options like
DBMS_OUTPUT or Log tables insertion');
END;
/
```

Error Directives

This directive can be used in places where we will fully want to cause a compilation error either due to compilation flags or due to some incomplete logic.

Now, we set few user-defined conditional compilation flags using the PLSQL_CCFLAGS parameter at the SYSTEM level as shown below,

```
ALTER SYSTEM SET plsql_ccflags='red:1, blue:2, green:3, random_color:4';
```

In the below code listing, a procedure is created where the RANDOM_COLOR compilation flag is compared to the RED, BLUE, and GREEN flags. In the ELSE part, the error directive is placed stating that the RANDOM_COLOR flag is unknown.

```
CREATE OR REPLACE PROCEDURE proc_error
 IS
BEGIN
$IF $$random_color=$$red $THEN
dbms_output.put_line('The color is red');
$ELSIF $$random_color=$$blue $THEN
dbms_output.put_line('The color is blue');
$ELSIF $$random_color=$$green $THEN
dbms_output.put_line('The color is green');
$ELSE
 $ERROR
  'Unknown color!!'
 $END
$END
END;
/
```

As the RANDOM_COLOR flag mismatches with the RED, BLUE, and GREEN flags, the code results in a compilation error with the message "Unknown Color!!". The error can be found in the USER_ERRORS data dictionary as shown below,

```
SELECT name,
  type,
  line,
  text,
  attribute
FROM user_errors
WHERE name='PROC_ERROR';
```

Script Result:

NAME	TYPE	LINE	TEXT	ATTRIBUTE
PROC_ERROR	PROCEDURE	11	PLS-00179: $ERROR: Unknown color!!	ERROR

Summary

We started this chapter by understanding the different data dictionary objects for finding the coding information, their arguments using the PLSCOPE_SETTINGS parameter, and their structure description using the DBMS_DESCRIBE package. In the next section, we learned the program and error propagation using the UTL_CALL_STACK package which is newly introduced in the release R12.1. The later sections taught us about the PL/SQL expression enhancement, long identifiers, DEPRECATE, and COVERAGE pragmas, which are newly introduced in the release R12.2. The next section described the DBMS_METADATA package for extracting the metadata information about the database objects. The later section made us clear on debugging the PL/SQL code using both the SQL Developer IDE and the DBMS_DEBUG package. The final section explained us about the various conditional compilation directives in detail.

In the next chapter, we will overview the profiling and tracing techniques in PL/SQL.

Tracing & Profiling the PL/SQL

The analyzing and debugging techniques that we have examined in the previous chapter might be useful in identifying specific bugs in our applications. However, they will not be sufficient to pinpoint all kinds of performance bottlenecks. To resolve this, Oracle has provided us with different kinds of tracing and profiling tools. Tracing an application provides us information like, which subprograms were called and which exceptions were raised. Profiling extends this information by including the timing information in an interactive HTML report format.

We will be understanding the different tracing and profiling techniques in this chapter in brief through the below topics.

40) Tracing PL/SQLs using the DBMS_TRACE package with the demonstration.

41) Profiling PL/SQLs using the DBMS_HPROF package by collecting, analyzing, and querying the profile output.

42) Using the plshprof utility to produce HTML reports for the raw profiler output data.

Tracing PL/SQLs using the DBMS_TRACE Package

As the complexity of our application grows, the harder it is to keep track of the program execution path. Yet, we must track our code to identify the potential performance bottlenecks. The DBMS_TRACE package serves this purpose by enabling and disabling tracing in our sessions.

Once we execute a PL/SQL program in a trace enabled session, the trace log containing information regarding the execution of the PL/SQL programs and the exceptions raised within those programs is created in the log tables. These log tables can be then debugged to understand the performance infiltrations and fix them accordingly.

> 🔔 Note: We cannot use PL/SQL tracing in a shared server environment.

Installing the Tracing Components

The DBMS_TRACE package by default gets installed during the Oracle 12c database installation. If we couldn't find this package in our database, we can very well install it manually by executing the below two scripts from the $ORACLE_HOME\RDBMS\ADMIN directory as SYS user, creating synonyms over them, and granting them to the public.

- **dbmspbt.SQL** script installs the DBMS_TRACE package's specification.
- **prvtpbt.plb** script installs the DBMS_TRACE package's body.

However, the trace log tables will not be installed by default during the Oracle 12c database installation and we have to do that manually by executing the **tracetab.SQL** script from the $ORACLE_HOME\RDBMS\ADMIN directory as SYS user, creating synonyms for them, and granting them to the public. This script creates the below two tables in the database.

- **PLSQL_TRACE_EVENTS** contains the accumulated data from all the trace runs.
- **PLSQL_TRACE_RUNS** contains the run specific information for the PL/SQL trace.

The interfaces available in the DBMS_TRACE package for tracing PL/SQL functions, procedures, and exceptions are described below,

SET_PLSQL_TRACE Procedure

This procedure can be used for enabling tracing for a PL/SQL unit in a session.

The prototype of this procedure is shown below,

```
DBMS_TRACE.SET_PLSQL_TRACE (trace_level INTEGER);
```

- **TRACE_LEVEL** parameter accepts one or more of the below-described Constants by summing them up for enabling tracing of multiple PL/SQL features simultaneously.
  - Two Constants for call tracing are,
    - **TRACE_ALL_CALLS** or **1** – Traces all calls.
    - **TRACE_ENABLED_CALLS** or **2** – Traces calls that are present in the tracing enabled programs. This Constant cannot

detect enabling in Remote Procedure Calls. Hence, RPCs are traced with the **TRACE_ALL_CALLS** or **1** Constant only.

o Two Constants for exception tracing are,

- **TRACE_ALL_EXCEPTIONS** or **4** – Traces all exceptions.
- **TRACE_ENABLED_EXCEPTIONS** or **8** – Traces exceptions that are present in the tracing enabled programs.

o Two Constants for SQL tracing are,

- **TRACE_ALL_SQL** or **32** – Traces all SQL statements.
- **TRACE_ENABLED_SQL** or **64** – Traces SQL statements that are present in the tracing enabled programs.

o Two Constants for line tracing are,

- **TRACE_ALL_LINES** or **128** – Traces each line.
- **TRACE_ENABLED_LINES** or **256** – Traces lines that are present in the tracing enabled programs.

o Six Constants for controlling the tracing are,

- **TRACE_LIMIT** or **16** – Traces only till the problematic area, thus saving lots of space by avoiding unwanted information. This Constant saves only the last 8192 records when tracing without filling up the database. This limit can be changed by setting the event 10940 to level n, which changes the record limit to $1024*n$.
- **TRACE_PAUSE** or **4096** – Pauses tracing. No information is traced until the trace is resumed using the **TRACE_RESUME** or **8192** Constants.
- **TRACE_RESUME** or **8192** – Resumes tracing.
- **TRACE_STOP** or **16384** – Stops tracing.
- **NO_TRACE_ADMINISTRATIVE** or **32768** – Prevents tracing of administrative events such as PL/SQL Trace Tool started, Trace flags changed, PL/SQL Virtual Machine started, PL/SQL Virtual Machine stopped.
- **NO_TRACE_HANDLED_EXCEPTIONS** or **65536** – Prevents tracing of exceptions that are handled.

🔔 Note: The control Constants TRACE_PAUSE, TRACE_RESUME, and TRACE_STOP should not be used in combination with other Constants.

PLSQL_TRACE_VERSION Procedure

This procedure gets the major and minor version number of the DBMS_TRACE package.

The prototype of this procedure is described below,

```
DBMS_TRACE.PLSQL_TRACE_VERSION (
    major OUT BINARY_INTEGER,
    minor OUT BINARY_INTEGER);
```

- **MAJOR** parameter returns the major version number of the DBMS_TRACE package.
- **MINOR** parameter returns the minor version number of the DBMS_TRACE package.

GET_PLSQL_TRACE_LEVEL Function

This function returns the current trace level as the sum of one or more event Constants.

The prototype of this function is described below,

```
DBMS_TRACE.GET_PLSQL_TRACE_LEVEL RETURN BINARY_INTEGER;
```

If tracing is not enabled, this function returns a zero.

CLEAR_PLSQL_TRACE Procedure

This procedure stops dumping the trace data for the current session.

The prototype of this procedure is described below,

```
DBMS_TRACE.CLEAR_PLSQL_TRACE;
```

PL/SQL Tracing Steps

The steps involved in PL/SQL code tracing are shown below,

1) Enable the tracing feature for the SYSTEM, SESSION, or a specific PROGRAM.

2) Start the tracing using the SET_PLSQL_TRACE procedure.

Advanced PL/SQL Programming

3) Execute the PL/SQL program that has to be traced.

4) Stop the tracing using the CLEAR_PLSQL_TRACE procedure.

To enable the tracing feature, we must make sure that the DBMS_TRACE package and the two tables, PLSQL_TRACE_RUNS and PLSQL_TRACE_EVENTS are present and available in the database. Then,

- If we are going to trace for all the programs, we must set the PLSQL_DEBUG parameter to *true* in either SYSTEM or SESSION level.

```
ALTER <SYSTEM | SESSION> SET PLSQL_DEBUG=TRUE;
```

- If we are going to trace for a specific program, we must compile the particular PL/SQL unit with DEBUG option as shown below,

```
ALTER <PROCEDURE | FUNCTION | PACKAGE BODY> <OBJECT_NAME> COMPILE DEBUG;
```

> 🔔 Note: The PLSQL_DEBUG initialization parameter has been deprecated in the Oracle database version 12c and forward. Instead, we must set the PLSQL_OPTIMIZE_LEVEL parameter to 0 or 1 in order to compile a PL/SQL unit for debugging.

PL/SQL Tracing - Demonstration

Let's create a simple procedure with exception handling as shown below for performing tracing.

```
CREATE OR REPLACE PROCEDURE proc_trace
IS
BEGIN
  dbms_output.put_line('Inside the PROC_TRACE procedure');
  raise no_data_found;
EXCEPTION
WHEN OTHERS THEN
  NULL;
END;
/
```

Once the above procedure is created, we must compile it in debugging mode by setting the PLSQL_OPTIMIZE_LEVEL parameter to 1 as shown below,

```
ALTER PROCEDURE proc_trace COMPILE PLSQL_OPTIMIZE_LEVEL=1;
```

Now, we must enable the tracing for this procedure by executing the SET_PLSQL_TRACE procedure with the necessary Constants. The list of Constants used must be separated using the "+" symbol. Here, we have used the TRACE_ALL_CALLS (for tracing all the calls), TRACE_ALL_EXCEPTIONS (for tracing all the exceptions), NO_TRACE_ADMINISTRATIVE (for avoiding the administrative trace lines in the output).

```
BEGIN
  dbms_trace.set_plsql_trace(dbms_trace.trace_all_calls +
dbms_trace.trace_all_exceptions + dbms_trace.no_trace_administrative);
END;
/
```

After enabling the tracing for the procedure, we must execute the program at least once as shown below,

```
BEGIN
  proc_trace;
END;
/
```

Once, the program execution is completed, we can disable the tracing using the CLEAR_PLSQL_TRACE procedure as shown below,

```
BEGIN
  dbms_trace.clear_plsql_trace;
END;
/
```

Now, we can verify the latest tracing information by querying the trace tables as shown below,

```
SELECT pe.event_seq,
  pe.event_comment,
  pe.event_unit,
  pe.event_unit_kind,
  pe.event_proc_name,
  pe.callstack,
  pe.errorstack
FROM plsql_trace_events pe
WHERE pe.runid=
  (SELECT MAX(pr.runid) FROM plsql_trace_runs pr
  )
ORDER BY pe.event_seq;
```

Script Result:

EVENT_SEQ	EVENT_COMMENT	EVENT_UNIT	EVENT_UNIT_KIND	EVENT_PROC_NAME	CALLSTACK	ERRORSTACK
1	Return from procedure call	DBMS_TRACE	PACKAGE BODY			
2	Return from procedure call	DBMS_TRACE	PACKAGE BODY			
3	Return from procedure call	DBMS_TRACE	PACKAGE BODY			
4	Procedure Call	<anonymous>	ANONYMOUS BLOCK			
5	Procedure Call	PROC_TRACE	PROCEDURE	PROC_TRACE		
6	Return from procedure call	DBMS_OUTPUT	PACKAGE BODY			
7	Exception raised	PROC_TRACE	PROCEDURE	PROC_TRACE	----- PL/SQL Call Stack -----	ORA-01403: no data found
8	Exception handled	PROC_TRACE	PROCEDURE	PROC_TRACE	----- PL/SQL Call Stack -----	ORA-01403: no data found
9	Return from procedure call	PROC_TRACE	PROCEDURE	PROC_TRACE		
10	Procedure Call	<anonymous>	ANONYMOUS BLOCK			
11	Procedure Call	DBMS_TRACE	PACKAGE BODY			
12	Procedure Call	DBMS_TRACE	PACKAGE BODY			
13	Procedure Call	DBMS_TRACE	PACKAGE BODY			
14	Return from procedure call	DBMS_TRACE	PACKAGE BODY			
15	Return from procedure call	DBMS_TRACE	PACKAGE BODY			
16	Procedure Call	DBMS_TRACE	PACKAGE BODY			

The above result set shows that every single event of the program control has been logged, which can be later used for analyzing and debugging the program unit completely.

Profiling PL/SQLs using the DBMS_HPROF Package

Even though the DBMS_TRACE package is capable of providing the program execution path, it doesn't provide the time taken by them for determining the performance of each unit. As profiling provides us the time taken at each step during the program execution, we can identify the potential bottlenecks in our program that can be fine-tuned for performance.

The DBMS_PROFILER package was introduced in the Oracle database version 8i to gather performance metrics at each level of the program as a flat file, but then the craving need for generating a dynamic execution program profile led us to the introduction of the DBMS_HPROF in 11g. The new package was hierarchical whereas the old package was non-hierarchical, meaning that the DBMS_PROFILER package was only able to record the time that a program spends in each of its subprograms, whereas the DBMS_HPROF package was capable of recording the time for each of its subprograms including its descendent subprograms.

The properties of a hierarchical profiler and its advantages over the non-hierarchical profiler are listed below,

1) Produces a dynamic HTML execution profile of a PL/SQL program organized by its descendant subprogram level information like,
    a. The number of calls to the subprogram.
    b. The time spent in the subprogram alone.
    c. The time spent both in the subprogram and its descendent subprograms.

2) Separate reports on SQL and PL/SQL time consumption.

3) Does not require any special preparation.

4) Stores the reports in the database hierarchical profile tables for custom report generation using IDEs like SQL Developer.

5) The successor for the DBMS_TRACE and DBMS_PROFILER packages due to its unappealing characteristics.

The hierarchical profiler mainly has the below two components,

1) The **Data Collector** component consists of the START_PROFILING and STOP_PROFILING APIs from the DBMS_HPROF package. These APIs are responsible for starting and stopping the hierarchical profiler and any subprogram

---

that is executed between these APIs will have their raw formatted profiler output written to a file.

2) The **Analyzer** component consists of the ANALYZE API from the DBMS_HPROF package. This component processes the raw formatted profiler output file and stores the result in the hierarchical profiler tables.

DBMS_HPROF Package

The DBMS_HPROF acts as a PL/SQL interface for profiling a PL/SQL unit's execution and returning a profile output with the time taken by individual subprogram call in a hierarchical manner.

The subprograms offered by this package are described below,

START_PROFILING Procedure

This procedure opens up a window in the user's session for collecting the raw profile output generated out during a PL/SQL unit's execution.

The prototype of this procedure is described below,

```
DBMS_HPROF.START_PROFILING (
    location  VARCHAR2 DEFAULT NULL,
    filename  VARCHAR2 DEFAULT NULL,
    max_depth PLS_INTEGER DEFAULT NULL);
```

- **LOCATION** parameter accepts a valid directory object for storing the raw profile output generated.
- **FILENAME** parameter accepts a user defined raw profile output file name that has to be created in the directory location.
- **MAX_DEPTH** parameter defines the maximum depth till which the profile information has to be gathered.
    - o When *null*, the profiler collects data of all the subprograms irrespective of their depths.
    - o When *not null*, the profiler collects data only for the subprograms up to the mentioned call depth.

After successful execution of this procedure, a "0-byte" file of the user defined name is created in the directory location.

STOP_PROFILING Procedure

This procedure stops collecting the profiler data in the user's session and dumps the collected data into the file created in the directory location.

The prototype of this procedure is described below,

```
DBMS_HPROF.STOP_PROFILING;
```

ANALYZE Function

This procedure analyzes the raw profile output generated in the directory location and stores the readable hierarchical output in the database profiler tables. This function is independent of the START_PROFILER/ STOP_PROFILER APIs and the *plshprof* utility.

The prototype of this function is described below,

```
DBMS_HPROF.ANALYZE (
    location      VARCHAR2,
    filename      VARCHAR2,
    summary_mode  BOOLEAN      DEFAULT FALSE,
    trace         VARCHAR2     DEFAULT NULL,
    skip          PLS_INTEGER  DEFAULT 0,
    collect       PLS_INTEGER  DEFAULT NULL,
    run_comment   VARCHAR2     DEFAULT NULL)
RETURN NUMBER;
```

- **LOCATION** parameter accepts the directory object of the raw output file.
- **FILENAME** parameter accepts the raw output filename from the directory location.
- **SUMMARY_MODE** parameter accepts a Boolean value for the summary generated.
  - When this parameter is set to *true*, only the top level summary information is generated into the tables.
  - When this parameter is set to *false*, the detailed analysis is done. This is the default value.
- **TRACE** parameter helps in analyzing only the subtrees rooted in the special quoted qualified formatted trace entry set for this parameter. If this parameter is set to *null*, the analysis is performed for the entire run. *Null* is the default value.
- **SKIP** parameter is used only when the TRACE parameter is set to a *not null* value. The parameter accepts a value for skipping the first skip number of invocations to the trace while analyzing the subtrees rooted at the trace specified by the TRACE parameter. The default value is 0.

- **COLLECT** parameter is used only when the TRACE parameter is set to a *not null* value. This parameter analyzes the number of invocations of traces passed as its input. By default, only 1 invocation is collected.
- **RUN_COMMENT** parameter accepts a user provided run comment.

This function returns a unique run identifier for any run of the analyzer for looking up at the results corresponding to this run at the database hierarchical tables.

 Note: Before executing this function, we must make sure that the database hierarchical tables are present in the schema to avoid *ORA-00942: table or view does not exist* exception.

Collecting Profile Output

To create a profile output, we must execute a PL/SQL unit between the execution of START_PROFILING and STOP_PROFILING APIs. For the profiling purpose, we have created the below procedure which takes a 5-second delay in its execution and calls a locally declared function which takes a 10-second delay in its execution as shown,

```
CREATE OR REPLACE PROCEDURE proc_profile
IS
  l_n_func_return NUMBER;
  FUNCTION func_profile
    RETURN NUMBER
  IS
  BEGIN
    dbms_lock.sleep(10);
    RETURN 1;
  END;
BEGIN
  dbms_output.put_line('Procedure Starts');
  dbms_lock.sleep(5);
  l_n_func_return:=func_profile;
  dbms_output.put_line('Procedure Ends');
END;
/
```

The complete step for the raw formatted profile output file generation is described below,

Firstly, we must create a directory object for storing the raw profile output file as shown below,

```
CREATE OR REPLACE directory dir_profile_output
AS
    'C:\Users\Boobal Ganesan\Desktop\Raw Profile Output';
```

Secondly, we must start the profiler window by executing the START_PROFILING API with the directory name and the user defined file name as shown below. Note that a "0-byte" file with the user specified name will be created in the directory location after the below script execution.

```
BEGIN
    DBMS_HPROF.START_PROFILING ('DIR_PROFILE_OUTPUT', 'hprof_output.log');
END;
/
```

After kick-starting the profiler window, we should execute the PROC_PROFILE procedure for gathering its profile output as a hierarchical raw output file as shown below,

```
EXEC proc_profile;
```

Finally, we must stop the profiler window by executing the STOP_PROFILING API as shown below,

```
BEGIN
    dbms_hprof.stop_profiling;
END;
/
```

Now, the "0-byte" file is loaded with hierarchical raw profile data as shown below.

 Note: The raw profile output changes in accordance with the Oracle database release version.

```
P#V PLSHPROF Internal Version 1.0
P#! PL/SQL Timer Started
P#C PLSQL."".""."__plsql_vm"
P#X 9
P#C PLSQL."".""."__anonymous_block"
P#X 101
P#C PLSQL."SYS"."PROC_PROFILE"::7."PROC_PROFILE"#980980e97e42f8ec #1
P#X 57
```

```
P#C PLSQL."SYS"."DBMS_OUTPUT"::11."PUT_LINE"#c5dd7e95abfe7e9f #109
P#X 3
P#R
...
...
...
P#C PLSQL."SYS"."DBMS_HPROF"::11."STOP_PROFILING"#980980e97e42f8ec #63
P#R
P#R
P#R
P#! PL/SQL Timer Stopped
```

Understanding the Raw Output File

The raw output file is intended to be understood by the analyzer for processing. However, even without the help of the analyzer, we can understand the basic function level trace of the program by using the below topics.

Each line of the profile output starts with an event indicator prefixed with the text **P#**. The different event indicators available in the raw profile data are described below,

- **P#V** denotes the PLSHPROF banner with the version number.
- **P#C** denotes the call event representing the call to the subprogram. Each call event entry includes the namespace, name, and type of the PL/SQL module, the name of the called subprogram, Hash signature of the called subprogram, and the line number at which the called subprogram is defined in the PL/SQL module.
- **P#R** denotes the return event representing the call returned from the subprogram.
- **P#X** represents the time elapsed between two events.
- **P#!** represents the internal comments.

The call event (**P#C**) and the return event (**P#R**) are properly nested that even if an exception causes the subprogram to exit, the profiler still reports a matching return event for the call made.

The special function names used by the hierarchical profiler to track certain operations are described below,

- **__plsql_vm** function tracks the calls made to the PL/SQL virtual machine.
- **__anonymous_block** function tracks the calls made to the anonymous block.
- **__pkg_init** function tracks the calls made to the package initialization block.
- **__static_sql_exec_lineline#** function tracks the calls made to the static SQL statement at the line **line#**.
- **__dyn_sql_exec_lineline#** function tracks the calls made to the dynamic SQL statement at the line **line#**.

- **__sql_fetch_lineline#** function tracks the calls made to the SQL FETCH statement at the line **line#**.

Analyzing Profile Output

The DBMS_HPROF.ANALYZE API processes the raw profile output and stores the results in the hierarchical database tables. Before starting to analyze the profile output file, we must create the hierarchical database tables as they are not installed by default.

The hierarchical tables can be created by executing the *dbmshptab.SQL* script from the *$ORACLE_HOME\RDBMS\ADMIN* location using the SYS user. After the tables are created, we must create a synonym over those tables with the same name and then grant them to the PUBLIC. After executing the table creation script, the below three tables will be created in the database.

1) **DBMSHP_RUNS** for holding the run specific information for the hierarchical profiler.
2) **DBMSHP_FUNCTION_INFO** for holding the information about each function in a run.
3) **DBMSHP_PARENT_CHILD_INFO** for holding the parent-child related information for each profiler run.

After the hierarchical tables are created, we must invoke the DBMS_HPROF.ANALYZE function as shown below.

```
DECLARE
  l_n_run_id NUMBER;
BEGIN
  l_n_run_id:=DBMS_HPROF.ANALYZE ('DIR_PROFILE_OUTPUT', 'hprof_output.log');
  dbms_output.put_line('The unique run ID for this run is '||l_n_run_id);
END;
/
```

Results:

```
The unique run ID for this run is 1
```

The above function call analyzes the raw profiler output file "*hprof_output.log*" and returns a unique identifier that can be used for querying a specific run in the hierarchical tables.

Querying the Profiler Tables

We can query the individual profiler tables as shown below,

The below query shows the total list of profiler runs available in the database,

```
SELECT * FROM dbmshp_runs;
```

Script Results:

RUNID	RUN_TIMESTAMP	TOTAL_ELAPSED_TIME	RUN_COMMENT
1	31-JAN-17 08.22.43.278000000 AM	9999571	

The below query shows the time elapsed (in milliseconds) for each program call along with the number of calls made and namespace of the called program. To identify overloaded subprograms uniquely, we can use the LINE# and the HASH columns in this table which are unique for every subprogram.

```
SELECT module,
  type,
  FUNCTION,
  line#,
  namespace,
  subtree_elapsed_time sub,
  function_elapsed_time func,
  calls
FROM dbmshp_function_info
WHERE runid=1;
```

Script Results:

MODULE	TYPE	SYM BOL	FUNCTION	LIN E#	NAMESP ACE	SUB	FUN C	CAL LS
		1	__anonymous_block	0	PLSQL	9999 552	190	2
		2	__plsql_vm	0	PLSQL	9999 571	19	2
DBMS_HP ROF	PACKAG E BODY	3	STOP_PROFILING	63	PLSQL	0	0	1
DBMS_LO CK	PACKAG E BODY	4	SLEEP	197	PLSQL	9999 245	9999 245	2
DBMS_OU TPUT	PACKAG E BODY	5	PUT_LINE	109	PLSQL	4	4	2
PROC_PR OFILE	PROCED URE	6	PROC_PROFILE	1	PLSQL	9999 362	102	1
PROC_PR OFILE	PROCED URE	7	PROC_PROFILE.FUN C_PROFILE	4	PLSQL	4999 986	11	1

The below query displays the parent-child information for each unique parent-child subprogram combination profiled for the run ID 1. The hierarchical tables can be joined together for generating custom reports.

```
SELECT parentsymid,
  childsymid,
  subtree_elapsed_time sub,
  function_elapsed_time func,
  calls
FROM dbmshp_parent_child_info
WHERE runid=1;
```

Script Results:

PARENTSYMID	CHILDSYMID	SUB	FUNC	CALLS
1	6	9999362	102	1
1	3	0	0	1
2	1	9999552	190	2
6	7	4999986	11	1
6	4	4999270	4999270	1
6	5	4	4	2
7	4	4999975	4999975	1

plshprof Utility

The *plshprof* is a command-line utility which can be used for generating HTML based reports from one or two raw profiler output files, or the difference between two raw profiler output files. The generated HTML report can be browsed through any browser with an ease, thus making it a powerful and improvised approach for analyzing the performance metrics of large applications.

The prototype of this utility is shown below,

```
plshprof [<option>...] <tracefile1> [<tracefile2>]
```

- **OPTION** parameter accepts any of the below options,
    o **–trace <symbol>** option specifies the function name of the tree root. There is no default value for this option.
    o **–skip <count>** option skips the first <count> number of calls. This option is used only with the trace <symbol> option. The default value is 0.
    o **–collect <count>** option collects information for the first <count> number of calls. This option is used only with the trace <symbol> option. The default value is 1.
    o **–output <filename>** option specifies the output filename. The default value is either *symbol.html* or *tracefile1.html*.

Advanced PL/SQL Programming

o **–summary** option prints the elapsed time. There is no default value for this option.

In the below code snippet, the *plshprof* utility is used with the *–summary* option to print the elapsed time of the profiled PL/SQL unit from its raw profiler output.

```
C:\Users\Boobal Ganesan\Desktop\New folder>plshprof -summary
hprof_output.log
```

Results:

```
PLSHPROF: Oracle Database 12c Enterprise Edition Release 12.1.0.2.0 - 64bit
Production
Total subtree time: 9999571 microsecs (elapsed time)
```

In the below code snippet, the *plshprof* utility is used with the *–output* option to generate a PL/SQL hierarchical profiler HTML difference report from two raw profiler output files.

```
C:\Users\Boobal Ganesan\Desktop\New folder>plshprof -output
hprof_diff_report hprof_output1.log hprof_output2.log
```

Results:

```
PLSHPROF: Oracle Database 12c Enterprise Edition Release 12.1.0.2.0 - 64bit
Production
[7 symbols processed]
```

In the below code listing, the *plshprof* utility is used with the *–output* option to produce HTML reports containing detailed reports displaying the performance metrics of the profiled PL/SQL unit using its raw profiler output file.

```
C:\Users\Boobal Ganesan\Desktop\New folder>plshprof -output hprof_reports
hprof_output.log
```

Results:

```
PLSHPROF: Oracle Database 12c Enterprise Edition Release 12.1.0.2.0 - 64bit
Production
[7 symbols processed]
[Report written to 'hprof_reports.html']
```

The HTML reports generated by the above step are shown below,

First Page of the Report

hprof_reports.html is the main report, which includes the summary information and hyperlinks to other pages of the report. This report's HTML view is shown below in text format,

```
PL/SQL Elapsed Time (microsecs) Analysis

9999571 microsecs (elapsed time) & 11 function calls

The PL/SQL Hierarchical Profiler produces a collection of reports that
present information derived from the profiler's output log in a variety
of formats. The following reports have been found to be the most
generally useful as starting points for browsing:

•   Function Elapsed Time (microsecs) Data sorted by Total Subtree
    Elapsed Time (microsecs)
•   Function Elapsed Time (microsecs) Data sorted by Total Function
    Elapsed Time (microsecs)

In addition, the following reports are also available:

•   Function Elapsed Time (microsecs) Data sorted by Function Name
•   Function Elapsed Time (microsecs) Data sorted by Total Descendants
    Elapsed Time (microsecs)
•   Function Elapsed Time (microsecs) Data sorted by Total Function
    Call Count
•   Function Elapsed Time (microsecs) Data sorted by Mean Subtree
    Elapsed Time (microsecs)
•   Function Elapsed Time (microsecs) Data sorted by Mean Function
    Elapsed Time (microsecs)
•   Function Elapsed Time (microsecs) Data sorted by Mean Descendants
    Elapsed Time (microsecs)
•   Module Elapsed Time (microsecs) Data sorted by Total Function
    Elapsed Time (microsecs)
•   Module Elapsed Time (microsecs) Data sorted by Module Name
•   Module Elapsed Time (microsecs) Data sorted by Total Function Call
    Count
•   Namespace Elapsed Time (microsecs) Data sorted by Total Function
    Elapsed Time (microsecs)
•   Namespace Elapsed Time (microsecs) Data sorted by Namespace
•   Namespace Elapsed Time (microsecs) Data sorted by Total Function
    Call Count
•   Parents and Children Elapsed Time (microsecs) Data
```

Function-Level Reports

The function-level reports produce a flat view of the profiler information sorted on a particular attribute like function time or subtree time. These reports include information like function time, descendant time, subtree time, the number of calls to the function, and the function name.

The *Function Elapsed Time (microsecs) Data sorted by Total Function Elapsed Time (microsecs)* report's HTML view is shown below in text format,

```
9999571 microsecs (elapsed time) & 11 function calls
```

Sub tree	Ind %	Fun ctio n	Ind %	Cu m %	Desce ndants	Ind %	Ca lls	Ind %	Function Name
999 924 5	100 %	9999 245	10 00%	100 %	0	0.0 0%	2	18. 20 %	SYS.DBMS_LOCK.SLEEP (Line 197)
999 955 2	100 %	190	0.0 0%	100 %	999936 2	100 %	2	18. 20 %	__anonymous_block
999 936 2	100 %	102	0.0 0%	100 %	999926 0	100 %	1	9.1 0%	SYS.PROC_PROFILE.PROC_ PROFILE (Line 1)
999 957 1	100 %	19	0.0 0%	100 %	999955 2	100 %	2	18. 20 %	__plsql_vm
499 998 6	50. 00 %	11	0.0 0%	100 %	499997 5	50. 00 %	1	9.1 0%	SYS.PROC_PROFILE.PROC_ PROFILE.FUNC_PROFILE (Line 4)
4	0.0 0%	4	0.0 0%	100 %	0	0.0 0%	2	18. 20 %	SYS.DBMS_OUTPUT.PUT_LI NE (Line 109)
0	0.0 0%	0	0.0 0%	100 %	0	0.0 0%	1	9.1 0%	SYS.DBMS_HPROF.STOP_P ROFILING (Line 63)

Module-Level Reports

Each module-level report consists of information like module time and the number of calls to functions in the module for each module like package or type sorted either by module time or module name.

The *Module Elapsed Time (microsecs) Data sorted by Module Name* report's HTML view is shown below in text format,

```
        9999571 microsecs (elapsed time) & 11 function calls
```

Module	Ind%	Calls	Ind%	Module Name
209	0.00%	4	36.40%	
0	0.00%	1	9.10%	SYS.DBMS_HPROF
9999245	100%	2	18.20%	SYS.DBMS_LOCK
4	0.00%	2	18.20%	SYS.DBMS_OUTPUT
113	0.00%	2	18.20%	SYS.PROC_PROFILE

Namespace-Level Reports

Each namespace-level report consists of namespace time and the number of calls to functions in the namespace for each namespace sorted either by time or number of calls.

The *Namespace Elapsed Time (microsecs) Data sorted by Namespace* report's HTML view is shown below in text format,

```
        9999571 microsecs (elapsed time) & 11 function calls
```

Function	Ind%	Calls	Ind%	Namespace
9999571	100%	11	100%	PLSQL

Parents and Children Reports for a Function

Every function tracked by the profiler has information about the caller (Parent) and the called (Child) function. For each parent function, the report provides information on the subtree time, function time, descendants time, and the number of calls. For each child function, the report provides information on the execution profile for the child when called by the parent function.

Summary

We have started this chapter by understanding Tracing using the DBMS_TRACE package with steps and examples. The next section explained us in detail about the profiling concept using the DBMS_HPROF package followed by the use of the plshprof utility for generating HTML performance metric reports.

In the next and the final chapter, we will be learning about the SQL injection attacks and the different ways to safeguard our database applications from them.

Securing PL/SQL from SQL Injections

We have learned to develop, fine tune, and identify performance related bottlenecks in our code and fix them in our earlier chapters. In this chapter, we will learn to fix any data breaches in our code due to SQL injection. Using this method, a hacker can pass a string input to an application with the hope of retrieving unauthorized data from the database. SQL injection is relatively a simple type of attack that can be avoided with strict coding practices.

We will understand the different SQL injection techniques and the various steps to overcome them in brief through the below topics.

43) Overview of the SQL injection technique and their different attacks.

44) Methods to avoid SQL injections.

45) Sanitizing and filtering the input data using the DBMS_ASSERT package.

46) Designing a SQL injection immune code.

47) Testing strategies for determining the SQL injection flaws.

SQL Injection Overview

SQL injection is a technique used by the hackers for manipulating the database by executing unintended commands using specially crafted string input, thereby gaining unauthorized access to the database in order to download or destroy the data that should be unavailable to them. The SQL injection techniques could differ, but the common process that is followed is by concatenating an incorrectly validated or non-validated string input into a dynamic SQL statement and executing it in the database.

The SQL injection attacks are divided into three categories are described below,

First Order Attack

In this method, the attacker passes a malicious string input to the program code and gets the code executed immediately. The degree of this attack is considered to be "One". An example of the first order attack is explained below.

The procedure PROC_EMP is created for displaying the name of the employees for the JOB that is passed as its input as shown below.

```
CREATE OR REPLACE PROCEDURE proc_emp(
    ip_vc_job IN VARCHAR2)
IS
  l_rc_var1 sys_refcursor;
  l_vt_var2 sys.odcivarchar2list;
BEGIN
  OPEN l_rc_var1 FOR 'select ename from emp where job='''||ip_vc_job||'''';
  FETCH l_rc_var1 bulk collect INTO l_vt_var2;
  FOR i IN l_vt_var2.first..l_vt_var2.last
  LOOP
    dbms_output.put_line(l_vt_var2(i));
  END LOOP i;
END;
/
```

When we pass a legitimate JOB description, we can retrieve the name of the employees belonging to that job category as shown below,

```
EXEC proc_emp('CLERK');
```

Results:

```
SMITH
ADAMS
JAMES
MILLER
```

The dynamic query inside the procedure looks like below when the legit input string is appended to it,

```
SELECT ename FROM emp WHERE job='CLERK'
```

Now, when we try to inject a malicious string as input, we can get all the employees' names as shown below,

```
EXEC proc_emp(''' or ''1''=''1');
```

Results:

```
SMITH
ALLEN
WARD
JONES
MARTIN
BLAKE
...
...
```

The dynamic query inside the procedure looks like below when the malicious input string is appended to it,

```
SELECT ename FROM emp WHERE job='' OR '1'='1'
```

In the above SQL, a *null* value is passed to the WHERE condition and an extra OR condition which always returns true is appended to the script using the crafted input string. This OR condition neglects the WHERE condition and returns all the rows from the EMP table.

We can safeguard the above procedure from SQL injection by binding the input string to the dynamic SQL instead of appending it as shown below,

```
CREATE OR REPLACE PROCEDURE proc_emp(
    ip_vc_job IN VARCHAR2)
IS
  l_rc_var1 sys_refcursor;
  l_vt_var2 sys.odcivarchar2list;
BEGIN
  OPEN l_rc_var1 FOR 'select ename from emp where job=:1' USING ip_vc_job;
  FETCH l_rc_var1 bulk collect INTO l_vt_var2;
  FOR i IN l_vt_var2.first..l_vt_var2.last
  LOOP
    dbms_output.put_line(l_vt_var2(i));
  END LOOP i;
END;
/
```

Now, when we try to inject the same malicious string as input, we can see that the procedure fails as the input passed is invalid.

```
EXEC proc_emp(''' or ''1''=''1');
```

Error report

```
ORA-06502: PL/SQL: numeric or value error
```

Second Order Attack

In this method, the attacker injects the malicious string input into a persistent storage, such as a data dictionary table, which is considered to be a trusted source in the Oracle universe. The actual attack takes place subsequently by another activity. The degree of this attack is considered to be "Two". An example of the second order attack is explained below.

For demonstration, we have created the table TEST for holding the table names of the tables from the data dictionary table.

```
CREATE TABLE test (col1 VARCHAR2(4000));
```

Now, a table with a cheeky name containing a DELETE statement over the EMPLOYEES table is created as below.

```
CREATE TABLE "TEST'); Delete Employees;--" (col1 NUMBER);
```

When we try to execute the below anonymous block for copying the table names from the data dictionary table into the TEST table, the EMPLOYEES table gets deleted along with it.

```
BEGIN
  FOR loop_table IN
  (SELECT table_name FROM user_tables
  )
  LOOP
    EXECUTE immediate 'BEGIN
INSERT INTO test VALUES
('''||loop_table.table_name||''' );
END;';
  END LOOP loop_table;
COMMIT;
END;
/
```

When a normal table input is passed to the EXECUTE IMMEDIATE clause, the block inside works as expected and looks as shown below,

```
BEGIN
INSERT INTO test VALUES
('EMPLOYEES' );
END;
```

But when the table with the tricky name is passed as input to the EXECUTE IMMEDIATE clause, the block inside it looks really scary as shown below,

```
BEGIN
INSERT INTO test VALUES
('T'); Delete employees;--' );
END;
```

This scenario can be avoided by binding the table name from the data dictionary to the dynamic query, instead of appending it directly. The modified anonymous block is shown below,

```
BEGIN
  FOR loop_table IN
  (SELECT table_name FROM user_tables
  )
  LOOP
    EXECUTE immediate 'BEGIN
INSERT INTO test VALUES
(:1);
END;' USING loop_table.table_name;
  END LOOP loop_table;
  COMMIT;
END;
/
```

Else, as a single SQL statement using the traditional INSERT INTO SELECT syntax as like below,

```
INSERT INTO test SELECT * FROM user_tables;

Commit;
```

Lateral Injection

In this method, the attacker manipulates the implicit function TO_CHAR by changing the environment variables like NLS_DATE_FORMAT or NLS_NUMERIC_CHARACTERS to implicitly accept user inputs. The lateral injection is demonstrated in the below section.

When we check the number of employees from the EMPLOYEES table, who are hired after *09-Dec-82* can be found by querying the below SQL statement. The result is 1.

```
SELECT COUNT(*) "Total count" FROM employees WHERE hiredate>'09-Dec-82';
```

Script Result

Total count
1

In the below script, we alter the NLS_DATE_FORMAT at the session level with a user defined text *"or 1=1"* appended to the date format as shown,

```
ALTER session SET nls_date_format='''DD-MON-RR''" or 1=1"';
```

Now, when we try to query the SYSDATE function, we can see that the string *"or 1=1"* is appended to the date retrieved as below,

```
SELECT sysdate FROM dual;
```

Script Result

SYSDATE
'20-FEB-17' or 1=1

In the below anonymous block, the count of employees who were hired after *09-Dec-82* is retrieved dynamically. As the date format has been modified, the WHERE condition of the SELECT statement is modified as,

```
WHERE hiredate>'09-Dec-82' OR 1=1;
```

Thus, returning the complete count of employees in the table rather than returning just the employee count who joined after *09-Dec-82* as demonstrated below,

```
DECLARE
   l_d_var1  DATE:='09-DEC-82';
   l_n_count NUMBER;
BEGIN
   EXECUTE immediate 'SELECT COUNT(*) FROM employees WHERE
hiredate>'||l_d_var1 INTO l_n_count;
   dbms_output.put_line('Total count: '||l_n_count);
END;
/
```

Results:

Total count: 14

This can be fixed by binding the variable in the WHERE condition rather than appending it similar to the below example.

```
DECLARE
   l_d_var1 DATE:='09-DEC-82';
   l_n_count NUMBER;
BEGIN
   EXECUTE immediate 'SELECT COUNT(*) FROM employees WHERE hiredate>:1' INTO
l_n_count USING l_d_var1;
   dbms_output.put_line('Total count: '||l_n_count);
END;
/
```

Results:

Total count: 1

Avoiding SQL Injection

There are several strategies that can be deployed to safeguard our code against the SQL injection attacks. They are,

Reducing the Attack Surface

The thumb rule to be followed while safeguarding our code is, *"If an interface is not available to the user, it is clearly unavailable to be abused".* Thus, we can reduce the attack surface by revoking the unnecessary database privileges on the objects to the users and expose necessary privileges only to the ones who requires it.

Avoiding Dynamic SQL with Concatenated Input

Dynamic SQLs with concatenated input presents the easiest entry point for SQL injections. We must replace them with static SQLs if at all possible. The static SQLs are compile-time fixed and they do not incur any runtime surprises.

Dynamic SQLs may be unavoidable if we are not sure of the full text of the SQL statements that must be executed or when we want to execute DDL statements in PL/SQL. Even if we must use dynamic SQLs, we must try not to construct it through a series of concatenated input values and use bind arguments instead. If we cannot avoid concatenating the input values, then we must consider validating the input values before concatenating them.

Use Bind Arguments

Bind arguments are definitely a safe replacement for the concatenated inputs. They eliminate the possibility of SQL injection and enhance the performance of the code. The bind arguments can be used in the WHERE clause, VALUES clause, or the SET clause of any SQL statement unless it is not used as Oracle identifiers (Table names or column names) or keywords.

Even though we must strive to use bind arguments with all dynamic SQL and PL/SQL statements, we cannot use them in DDL statements or as Oracle identifiers. In those places, we must sanitize the inputs before concatenating them.

Filter and Sanitize Input

The DBMS_ASSERT package contains a number of functions to validate the properties of the input values before concatenating them to the dynamic SQL and

PL/SQL code. If the condition which determines the property asserted in the function is not met, then a value error is raised. Else, the input value is returned through the return value.

> Note: We cannot validate the TNS string, String length, object privileges, or validity of the SQL objects using the DBMS_ASSERT package.

The various APIs supported by the DBMS_ASSERT package is described below,

ENQUOTE_LITERAL Function

This function enquotes a string literal by adding a leading and trailing single quotes to it. However, if the input string is already quoted, there will be no additional quotes added by this function.

The prototype of this function is described below,

```
DBMS_ASSERT.ENQUOTE_LITERAL (str VARCHAR2) RETURN VARCHAR2;
```

• **STR** accepts the string that is to be quoted.

In the below SQL, the RESULT1 returns the input string quoted with single quotes and the RESULT2 returns the input string as such as it is already quoted.

```
SELECT DBMS_ASSERT.ENQUOTE_LITERAL('ENQUOTE_LITERAL') result1,
  DBMS_ASSERT.ENQUOTE_LITERAL(q'('ENQUOTE_LITERAL')') result2
FROM dual;
```

Script Result

RESULT1	RESULT2
'ENQUOTE_LITERAL'	'ENQUOTE_LITERAL'

ENQUOTE_NAME Function

This function enquotes the input string within double quotation marks. However, if the input string is already quoted, there will be no additional quotes added by this function.

The prototype of this function is described below,

```
DBMS_ASSERT.ENQUOTE_NAME (
   str             VARCHAR2,
   capitalize      BOOLEAN DEFAULT TRUE)
RETURN VARCHAR2;
```

- **STR** accepts the input that is to be quoted.
- **CAPITALIZE** accepts a Boolean *True* to capitalize the input string (if it is not already bounded by any quotes) or a Boolean *False* to not to change the case of the input string.

In the below example, the Result #1 returns the capitalized and quoted input string, the Result #2 returns the quoted form of the input string, and the Result #3 returns the input string without any change as it is already quoted.

```
DECLARE
  l_vc_var1 VARCHAR2(100);
BEGIN
  l_vc_var1:=DBMS_ASSERT.ENQUOTE_NAME ('enquote_name',true);
  dbms_output.put_line('Result #1 =>'||l_vc_var1);
  l_vc_var1:=DBMS_ASSERT.ENQUOTE_NAME ('ENQUOTE_NAME',false);
  dbms_output.put_line('Result #2 =>'||l_vc_var1);
  l_vc_var1:=DBMS_ASSERT.ENQUOTE_NAME ('"ENQUOTE_NAME"');
  dbms_output.put_line('Result #3 =>'||l_vc_var1);
END;
/
```

Results:

```
Result #1 =>"ENQUOTE_NAME"
Result #2 =>"ENQUOTE_NAME"
Result #3 =>"ENQUOTE_NAME"
```

NOOP Function

This function returns the input string as such without any validation. This function can be used in the places where we want to mark a piece of code that is not to be tested for SQL injection.

The prototype of this function is shown below,

```
DBMS_ASSERT.NOOP (
  str        VARCHAR2 | CLOB CHARACTER SET ANY_CS)
  RETURN     VARCHAR2 | CLOB CHARACTER SET str%CHARSET;
```

In the below SQL, the input string is returned without any error or validation checking performed.

```
SELECT dbms_assert.noop('NOOP') FROM dual;
```

Result:

NOOP

SCHEMA_NAME Function

This function returns the input string if it represents an existing schema name in the current database. If the input schema name does not exist, the function fails with an *ORA-44001: invalid schema* exception.

The prototype of this function is shown below,

```
DBMS_ASSERT.SCHEMA_NAME (
  str         VARCHAR2 CHARACTER SET ANY_CS)
  RETURN      VARCHAR2 CHARACTER SET str%CHARSET;
```

- **STR** accepts a case sensitive and quoted schema names.

The below SQL verifies that the input string, *SYS*, is an existing schema name and returns it as its result.

```
SELECT DBMS_ASSERT.SCHEMA_NAME ('SYS') FROM dual;
```

Result:

SYS

The below SQL fails to verify the input string to be an existing schema by terminating the execution with an error as shown below,

```
SELECT DBMS_ASSERT.SCHEMA_NAME ('EMPLOYEE') FROM dual;
```

ORA-44001: invalid schema

SIMPLE_SQL_NAME Function

This function can be used for verifying whether or not the input is a simple SQL name. If the input string fails to qualify, the function fails with an *ORA-44003: invalid SQL name* exception.

Advanced PL/SQL Programming

The input string must meet the following validations,

1) The input string must start with an alphabet and may contain alphanumeric characters along with "_", "$", and "#" characters.
2) The input string can be enclosed in double quotes provided that the quotes are closed properly. When the input string is quoted, there is no restriction on the characters used in it and it can also start with a number.
3) The input string can have leading or trailing white spaces.

However, the length of the input string is not validated by this function.

The prototype of this function is shown below,

```
DBMS_ASSERT.SIMPLE_SQL_NAME (
  str        VARCHAR2 CHARACTER SET ANY_CS)
  RETURN     VARCHAR2 CHARACTER SET str%CHARSET;
```

- **STR** accepts the input string.

In the below SQL, the input string *Table_name* is validated to be a simple SQL name and is returned as output.

```
SELECT dbms_assert.simple_sql_name('Table_name') FROM dual;
```

Result:

Table_name

In the below SQL, the input string *Table name* fails to validate itself as a simple SQL name due to the existence of space character in the middle of the string.

```
SELECT dbms_assert.simple_sql_name('Table name') FROM dual;
```

ORA-44003: invalid SQL name

In the below SQL, the input string contains a trailing space, yet it qualifies to be a simple SQL name. Note that the returned result also contains the same trailing space in it.

```
SELECT dbms_assert.simple_sql_name('Table_name ') FROM dual;
```

Result:

Table_name

In the below SQL, the input string *"1Table name+"* qualifies to be a simple SQL name even though it has a space in it, starts with a number, and has a plus sign since it is enclosed by double quotes.

```
SELECT dbms_assert.simple_sql_name('"1Table name+"') FROM dual;
```

Result:

```
"1Table name+"
```

QUALIFIED_SQL_NAME Function

This function can be used for validating whether or not an input string is a qualified SQL name. A qualified SQL name is constructed using schema name, object name, and the database link name. If the input string fails to qualify as a qualified SQL name, then the function fails with an *ORA-44004: invalid qualified SQL name* exception.

A qualified SQL name supports the following syntax,

```
<local qualified name> = <simple name> {'.' <simple name>}
<database link name> = <local qualified name> ['@' <connection string>]
<connection string> = <simple name>
<qualified name> = <local qualified name> ['@' <database link name>]
```

The prototype of this function is shown below,

```
DBMS_ASSERT.QUALIFIED_SQL_NAME (
  str         VARCHAR2 CHARACTER SET ANY_CS)
  RETURN      VARCHAR2 CHARACTER SET str%CHARSET;
```

- **STR** accepts the input string.

In the below SQL, the input string is returned as it is validated to be a qualified SQL name as shown,

```
SELECT dbms_assert.qualified_sql_name ('HR.DEPT@Prod_db') FROM dual;
```

Results:
```
HR.DEPT@Prod_db
```

The below SQL fails with an exception as the input string does not qualify to be a qualified SQL name as shown,

```
SELECT dbms_assert.qualified_sql_name ('HR.DEPT@Prod_db D') FROM dual;
```

```
ORA-44004: invalid qualified SQL name
```

SQL_OBJECT_NAME Function

This function can be used for validating whether or not the input string is a qualified SQL identifier of an existing database object. The input object name is case insensitive unless it is enclosed in quotation marks. If a database link is specified, only the syntax of the Qualifier SQL name is verified, not the existence of the object or the DB link. If the input object is a synonym, the base object must exist to qualify.

If the input object name fails to qualify, the function fails with an *ORA-44002: invalid object name* exception.

The prototype of this function is shown below,

```
DBMS_ASSERT.SQL_OBJECT_NAME (
 str    VARCHAR2 CHARACTER SET ANY_CS)
 RETURN VARCHAR2 CHARACTER SET str%CHARSET;
```

- **STR** accepts the input string.

The below SQL validates and returns the object name as its input as shown,

```
SELECT dbms_assert.sql_object_name('EMPLOYEES') FROM dual;
```

Result:

EMPLOYEES

Even though the object EEE in the HH schema at the DDD database link does not exist, the function qualifies it by just verifying its syntax as the remote objects cannot be validated using this function.

```
SELECT dbms_assert.sql_object_name('HH.EEE@DDDD') FROM dual;
```

Result:

HH.EEE@DDDD

The below SQL fails with an exception as the input object does not exist in the database,

```
SELECT dbms_assert.sql_object_name('EMPLOYEE') FROM dual;
```

ORA-44002: invalid object name

Designing SQL Injection Immune Code

Even though there are no coding problems and if the design is poor, we might encounter SQL injections in our application. The below points are to be considered while designing our code to secure ourselves from SQL injection.

1) Using bind arguments.

2) Handling the Oracle identifiers carefully by,
   a. Filtering and sanitizing the input using DBMS_ASSERT package.
   b. Explicitly validating and enforcing limits for the identifiers.
   c. Filtering out the control characters such as CHR(10) from the identifiers.
   d. Pulling the database objects from the data dictionaries using their respective object ID rather than building them up by concatenating the supplied identifier.

3) Avoiding privilege escalations.

4) Being cautious of the "Filter" parameters and design them to prevent SQL injection.

5) Handling the exceptions carefully in such a way that we do not leak any metadata in the error messages that could help the SQL injectors to reverse engineer the original SQL query to prepare for an attack.

Testing the Code for SQL Injection Flaws

There is no particular method for testing our code, but there are a number of strategies that we can employ to find that our code is immune to SQL injection or not. Following the below strategies will gain us some minimum level of confidence in freedom from the SQL injection.

1) By thorough code review and by deploying a better testing strategy.

2) During a code review, we must find out all the dynamic SQL and PL/SQL statements and verify whether they all use bind variables instead of concatenated string inputs. In the places where bind variables cannot be used, we must make sure the inputs are sanitized and filtered.

3) Static code analysis must be used only for the initial code testing process because SQL injection arises from dynamically generated code.

4) Fuzz testing can be performed on the program by providing random input data to the program code for finding any bugs rather than assuring the quality of the code.

5) Generating test cases to test the input parameters in the program code individually for determining whether or not SQL injection is possible.

Summary

We started this chapter by learning the basics of SQL injection and their various attacks. The latter section explained us the different methodologies in which we can avoid SQL injections. The next section taught us to filter and sanitize our input values using the DBMS_ASSERT package. The next section helped us in understanding the different code design strategies to secure our code against SQL injection. The final section taught us about the test case preparation to determine the SQL injection flaws in our application code.

INDEX

D

E

O

P

Q

R

S

Z

About the Author

Boobal Ganesan is a young, talented, tech savvy and vivid writer. For almost six years he has worked as a technical architect focusing on the Oracle database, Application Express, and ACTIMIZE tool. As an Oracle Certified Advanced PL/SQL Professional, Boobal has worked on large and challenging projects. He has held responsibility for developing core Banking and Telecom Applications.

After receiving a Bachelor's degree, he started working with a Telecom company as a PL/SQL Developer. Boobal is currently working for a firm specializing in the banking and financial domain. He has given many presentations. He developed many ideas for fine-tuning the performance of various business critical systems.

He is a member of the All India Oracle User Group (AIOUG), a regular contributor to the PL/SQL society, a blogger and he has also been a major part of technical discussions in forums.

On the personal side, Boobal lives in Chennai, India with his family. A hardcore gamer for most of his life, he became a total movie buff. In his spare time, he likes adventurous trekking. He can be reached through boobalganesan1989@gmail.com for any comments, suggestions, or feedback regarding this book.